THE UNITED STATES
CONGRESSIONAL DIRECTORIES

THE
UNITED STATES
Congressional Directories
1789–1840

EDITED BY
Perry M. Goldman
&
James S. Young

1973
Columbia University Press
New York and London

Library of Congress Cataloging in Publication Data

United States. Congress.
    The United States Congressional Directories, 1789–
1840.

    Includes bibliographical references.
    1. United States. Congress—Registers.
I. Goldman, Perry M., ed.   II. Young, James
Sterling, ed.   III. Title.
JK1011.U53   328.73'0025   73-15907
ISBN 0-231-03365-6

THE UNITED STATES
CONGRESSIONAL DIRECTORIES

INTRODUCTION

How did American politics get to be the way it is, and where is it headed? The last decade has seen a surge of interest in the question of American political development. This interest reflects in part a national mood of restiveness and self-examination, and represents a search for a different America—in the past, or in the future. Shared by political scientists, sociologists, and historians, this interest also reflects a coming of age in the social sciences, and promises to make the study of the American political past an occasion for reunion among disciplines.

Masses, elites, and the linkages between them have tended to provide the three foci of interest in historically oriented scholarship on American political development. The emphasis has been clearly on the first of these three. Represented in the work of such scholars as Richard P. McCormick, Walter Dean Burnham, and Lee Benson,[1] knowledge about political movements and about the changing composition and behavior of electorates over time is now approaching the point of yielding major theories about American political development.

The study of linkages between masses and governing elites has been less systematic and comprehensive. It has focused on the institution of the political party, particularly upon its constituency and ideology, thus complementing the emphasis on electoral behavior. While Chambers and Burnham's *The American Party Systems*[2] seems certain to stimulate

[1] Richard P. McCormick, *The Second American Party System: Party Formation in the Jacksonian Era* (Chapel Hill: University of North Carolina Press, 1966).

Walter Dean Burnham, "The Changing Shape of the American Political Universe," *American Political Science Review*, 59 (1965): 7–28; and his "Party Systems and the Political Process," in *The American Party Systems: Stages of Political Development*, eds. William Nisbet Chambers and Walter Dean Burnham (New York: Oxford University Press, 1967), pp. 277–307. Lee Benson, *The Concept of Jacksonian Democracy: New York as a Test Case* (Princeton, New Jersey: Princeton University Press, 1961).

[2] Chambers and Burnham, eds., *The American Party*   *Stages of Political Development* (New York: Oxford University Press, 1967).

new work on the organizational and functional dimensions of party development, these aspects have thus far received comparatively little attention. The same is true of the development of nonparty linkages—that which Elmer Schattschneider has called the "pressure system."[3] The empirical base is thus still lacking to theorize persuasively about the institutionalization of democracy in America, and the development of what is perhaps the most elaborate apparatus for influencing both elites and electorates that has developed in any political system.

The least attention, however, has been given to the behavior of governing elites as a component in American political development. The systematic study of elites has tended to be confined to the era of the administrative state—the age of Franklin Roosevelt, of World War and and cold war, of the United States as superpower in the international arena. It has tended moreover to be dominated by a concern with the processes of public policy making. These emphases on the modern era and process are not merely coincidental, for the generation of scholars that established the study of governing elites as a behavior inquiry was a generation of scholars that Depression, war, and internationalism brought to Washington in massive numbers, as administrators, aides, and advisors. They wrote about the world they discovered—the world of a bureaucratizing state—and how it differed from the "formal" system of the Constitution and the textbooks. They wrote from the perspective in which they knew that world, as participants in a process of policy making. And they wrote in an intellectual environment conducive to a focus on process in the sense of political action at a time when decisions made in Washington had a dramatically enlarging social impact and when there was pervasive concern about the adequacy of democratic government to perform under the stress of successive emergencies of Depression, war, and global politics.

This generation produced a body of new knowledge about behavior and process at the national summit that is unparalleled for any other nation. But it is a body of knowledge oriented to the main objective of explaining how and why government does what it does. The question of how and why government, and the system of decision making locked into it, got to be the way it is was not on the agenda of social science during the time of the behaviorial revolution. In consequence, modern political science has produced not only remarkably few insights about elite behavior as a factor in American political development, but also remarkably few methods and tools for exploring that question or any other aspect of elite behavior except policy making. Indeed, the approaches associated with modern scholarship tend to be predicated

---

[3] Elmer E. Schattschneider, *The Semisovereign People: A Realist's View of Democracy in America* (New York: Holt, Rinehart and Winston, 1960), p. 29.

on conditions that cannot be met in the investigation of noncontemporary elites. They are predicated on the scholar's accessibility to the elite for the purposes of interview or participant observation, and on data about interactions involved in particular policy outcomes that are far more specific and inclusive than are typically recorded of the past. Of the kinds of tools and frameworks conventionally used in the study of contemporary governing elites, only two appear to have empirical requirements that are readily met in the historical record of the premodern state: those utilized in analyzing social backgrounds of governing groups, and those applied to the analysis to record votes in Congress or the Supreme Court.

Those who would study elites in relation to American political development thus tend to find small help from either traditional or modern approaches: traditional approaches scarcely serve the purposes of behavioral inquiry because they do not allow for the presence of informal structures and networks among the ruling groups; modern approaches are largely foreclosed to historical research because they posit insider vantage points or kinds of data that are not accessible. Thus the study of elites in American political development can move ahead only by creating its own conceptual tools and analytic frameworks, in which the limited data available in the historical record are made to answer the purposes of modern inquiry. This effort necessarily involves a departure from the process-orientation of contemporary elite studies.

A few steps in this direction have already been essayed. In *The Washington Community, 1800-1828*,[4] certain analytic frameworks and data requirements used by social anthropologists studying human communities were adopted in order to elicit from the historical record the structure, patterns and styles of interaction, and attitudes of the governing group in Jeffersonian Washington. Certain of the conceptual tools used by David B. Truman in the study of interest groups[5] were borrowed to analyze cohesion and leadership within the governing community. Some of the findings were examined in detail and applied to the Jacksonian era in portions of "The Republic of Virtue and Other Essays on the Politics of the Early National Period," a recent Columbia University doctoral dissertation.[6] Another example of ways in which

---

[4] James Sterling Young, *The Washington Community 1800-1828* (New York: Columbia University Press, 1966).

[5] David B. Truman, *The Congressional Party* (New York and London: John Wiley and Sons, 1959); *The Governmental Process* (New York: Alfred A. Knopf, 1960); "The Presidency and Congressional Leadership: Some Notes on Our Changing Constitution," *Proceedings of the American Philosophical Society*, 103 (October 1959): 687-92.

[6] Perry M. Goldman, "The Republic of Virtue and Other Essays on the Politics of Early National Period)" (Ph.D. diss., Columbia University, 1970).

elite behavior may be analyzed in the absence of detailed data about decision processes—and one that is specifically intended to elicit development aspects—is Nelson W. Polsby's analysis of the institutionalization of the House of Representatives.[7]

But these works only scratch the surface of opportunities for new knowledge about the role and function of governing elites in American political development, and for creating the new conceptual tools and methods necessary to gain it.

At least four different patterns of elite behavior—that is, different types of regime—are suggested in the historical record of the United States since 1787. Each of them appears to have been reinforced by supportive attitudes and structures in sufficient degree to have achieved some level of institutionalization.

One type may be called a constitutional regime. It implies attitudes and structures supportive of a segmented elite that behaves consistently, as a group, with the principles of separation of powers and checks and balances. In this regime leadership roles tend to be transitory and unpatterned, power and veto capability are dispersed among the segmented groups within the elite, and public-policy decisions made by the elite tend to be limited to courses of action that do not engender conflict or that are negotiated among these groups. Despite efforts to impose a party regime, constitutional regime appears to have been the prevailing pattern of elite behavior in the early years of the nation. It may be a recurrent pattern in American political development, and may persist as the dominant pattern for certain governing purposes today.

Party regime is a second type. It implies attitudes and structures supportive of a cohesive elite, in which leadership roles are recognized and sanctioned—sometimes inside, sometimes outside the formal governmental structure. In this regime power is based on success in controlling access to the elite and is developed upon an organization that places its personnel in the strategic elective and appointive positions in government. Public-policy decisions made in such a regime tend to cohere around courses of action that produce levels of support by the constituency and resources needed for the survival of the regime. Ideology may, however, become an independent and controlling factor in elite behavior. Party regime seems to have reached the apex of institutionalization in one-party states and also in localities in the era of machine politics and the urban bosses. On the national level the party may never have been the main basis for elite organization and behavior except, perhaps, in the microsystem of Congress.

Legislative regime and presidential regime imply attitudes and structures that support dominance by one of the constituent—and constitu-

[7] Nelson W. Polsby, "The Institutionalization of the U.S. House of Representatives," *American Political Science Review* 62 (March 1968): 144–68.

tionally legitimated—units in a segmented elite. The institutional dominance of that unit tends to be defined by its power to institute or prevent changes in public policy, and by its capacity to prescribe, preempt, intervene in, or otherwise influence action by other elite subgroups to that end. A conspicuous feature of these regimes appears to be the internal transformation of the dominant unit. A system of interfacing with other elite subgroups develops within the dominant unit to give sustained capacity for overseeing or intervening in the action of other elite subgroups. An advisory system develops within the unit, paralleling the expertise of other elite subgroups, which supports the capacity for independent and preemptive action. And a leadership structure develops within the dominant group for directing and defining the purposes of prescriptive, interventionist, or preemptive action. In the era of Congressional dominance, the development of the committee system tended to serve both the functions of oversight and expertise, and oligarchy seems to have been the leadership structure. In the era of Presidential dominance, the institutionalization of the Presidency in the past thirty years has seen the same functions served by the development of White House staff and staff agencies, and of the inner circle dominated by the President.

This development prompts a number of questions: What accounts for these and other possible variations in the way American governing elites have organized themselves? To what extent is the breakdown of one pattern and the rise of a new pattern generated by forces within, or forces without, the governing elite? Do these structural changes in elite behavior over time reflect changes in the role and function of government? Do they reflect different patterns of linkage between elites and masses? Do they reflect stages of political or economic development, and if so what can be anticipated as the next stage beyond Presidential dominance?

As long as the study of elite behavior is defined as the study of processes of policy, such questions as these rarely obtain a place on the agenda of social science. But elite behavior says much more about American political culture than about how public policies are made. The strategies and patterns around which elites organize themselves, and the values induced in support of those patterns, are central to the systematic rationalization of power in America. The men who wrote the Constitution were not the last, and theorists are not the only, Americans who have attempted to reconcile American antipower values with the necessity for governance. Every governing elite in American national history has had to do the same, and in the course of that process significantly different solutions have emerged in the patterns of their behavior, and therefore in the operative constitution of the Washington community. Not to know the inner dynamics of these patterns, or the process by which they emerge, is to be ignorant of a fundamental component of political change in America, and quite possibly to overlook the key to the nonrevolutionary history of American political change.

The study of Congress affords a prime opportunity, on both historical and scientific grounds, to study the role and function of elite behavior in American politics. The recently discovered and collated series of extant *Congressional Directories* which follows provides data about two of the three primary units of the Congressional community: the boardinghouse groups (or the Congressional messes, as the members called their fraternities) and the committee system.[8] Material on the third unit—the state delegations—is readily accessible in the pages of the *Biographical Directory of the American Congress 1774-1961*.[9] Forty-six *Congressional Directories*, covering the First Session of the First Congress through the Second Session of the Twenty-Sixth Congress (1789-1840-41), have been assembled thanks to the fortunate discovery of a number of dust-covered early *Directories* in the Senate Library in the Capitol building and to the gracious assistance and cooperation of archivists and librarians across the nation.[10] Since most

[8] The Congressional messes have been established as the basic social and political units of the Capitol Hill community during the Jeffersonian period. The rise of the committee system and its effects and its relationship to the boardinghouses is analyzed in Young, *Washington Community*, pp. 87-153, 198-205, 244, and Goldman, "Republic of Virtue," pp. 40-48, 67-104, 111-14, 122-36, 214-41. Information of the Congressional Committees is found scattered throughout successive issues of *The Debates and Proceedings in the Congress of the United States* (more popularly known as the *Annals*), 1st through 18th Congresses, 1789-1824, 42 vols. (Washington, D.C.: Gales and Seaton, 1832-61); the *Register of Debates in Congress*, 18th through 25th Congresses, 1825-37 (Washington, D.C.: Gales and Seaton, 1835-37); the *Congressional Globe*, 23d through 35th Congresses, 1833-59, 28 vols (Washington, D.C.: Blair and Rives or John C. Rives, 1837-60); and the successive editions of the *Journal of the House of Representatives* and the *Journal of the Senate of the United States*.

[9] *Biographical Directory of the American Congress 1774-1961* (Washington, D.C.: U.S. Government Printing Officer, 1961).

[10] Twelve *Directories* could not be found despite extensive efforts; they are probably not extant. They are those for the Second Session of the First Congress (1790), the Third Session of the First Congress (1790-91), the First Session of the Second Congress (1791-92), the First Session of the Third Congress (1793-94), the Second Session of the Fourth Congress (1796-97), the Second Session of the Fifth Congress (1797-98), the Second Session of the Sixth Congress (1800-1801), the Second Session of the Eighth Congress (1804-5), the Second Session of the Ninth Congress (1806-7), the Second Session of the Tenth Congress (1808-9), the Second Session of the Eleventh Congress (1809-10), and the Third Session of the Eleventh Congress (1810-11). Two *Directories* were of little use for our purposes. Those for the First Session of the Eighth and Ninth Congresses (1803-4, 1805-6) provide only a list of the members of the two Houses of Congress, according to states, and furnish no information on boardinghouse groups.

We wish to thank particularly James E. Mooney of the American Antiquarian Society, Jack Jackson of the Boston Athenaeum, R. J. McCarthy of the Columbia Historical Society, Joyce Bank of the William C. Clements Library, John D. Kilbourne of the Historical Society of Pennsylvania, Samuel J. Hough of the John

of our finest libraries possess a complete series of the *Congressional Directories* from 1840 on, and also in the interest of conserving space, we have chosen the fourth decade of the nineteenth century as our terminal date.   The earlier directories are rare items, which provide valuable data for the study of the Congressional community and which possess an interesting history in their own right.

Very little information is known about the embryonic predecessor of the contemporary *Congressional Directory*.[11]   The earliest *Directories* were compiled and printed, apparently in very small numbers, under contracts by private firms.   Designed chiefly for Congressional use, they were regarded as ephemera to be disposed of as soon as a particular Congress was over or a new issue was printed.   There was at least one Directory published for each Congress; and from the Twelfth Congress (1811) on, when the formal title "Congressional Directory" was first used, there was one for each session of Congress. The first *Directory*, although largely incomplete, was printed in the form of a broadside for use of the First Session of the First Congress in 1789.   Eight *Directories* have been located that were printed prior to 1800, when Washington, D.C., became the national capital (including one based on the *Philadelphia Directory* for 1798); all appeared as broadsides and listed legislators in alphabetical order by state delegations.   The first listing of "Members of the Senate and House of Representatives" published in Washington, D.C., was a seven-page pamphlet issued in 1801 for the First Session of the Seventh Congress. This *Directory* and its successors[12] were published in pamphlet form and in recognition of the importance of the boardinghouse groups the Congressmen were listed by boardinghouses rather than in alphabetical order or by state.[13]   Each group roster was headed by the name

---

Carter Brown Library, Lillian Tonkin of The Library Company of Philadelphia, Fredrick Goff of the Library of Congress, James J. Heslin of the New York Historical Society, Harold Merklen of the New York Public Library, Margery S. Blake and Ann D. Selvin of the Princeton University Library, Weymouth T. Jordan, Jr. of the Alderman Library, University of Virginia, and the staff of the Yale University Library and the United States Senate Library, Capitol Building, Washington, D.C.

[11] For detailed information on the publication of the *Congressional Directories* to 1820 see Meredith B. Colket, Jr. "The Early Congressional Directories," Columbia Historical Society Records 53-56 (Washington, D.C. 1959): 70-80.   We are indebted to Mr. Colket for much of what follows.   A brief history of the *Directories* is also provided in the Foreword in the *Biographical Directory of the American Congress*, pp. 9-10.

[12] The *Directory* for the Ninth Congress (1805) was printed as a broadside.

[13] From the Third Session of the Thirteenth Congress through the Second Session of the Fifteenth Congress (1814-19), the *Directories* changed format, listing Congressmen only by state delegation.   Beginning with the First Session of the Sixteenth Congress in 1820, legislators were listed by both state delegation and boardinghouse groups.   Occasionally, alphabetical lists of Senators and Representatives were also included; this became a standard feature in the *Directory* for the Second Session of the Twenty-Third Congress in 1834-35.

of the boardinghouse's proprietor and the groups were usually listed in order of the proximity of their lodgings to the Capitol. One may surmise, therefore, that mess membership was regarded as a permanent affiliation for the duration of a Congressional session, and that there was little shifting of individuals from one fraternity to another. The *Directories* are therefore probably the only comprehensive source of information about the residences of members of Congress during the early national period, for Washington directories were not published until 1822.

Congressional Directories periodically included additional information, which was to become a standard part of their format. The *Directory* for the Second Session of the Thirteenth Congress (1813–1814) provides the county and post office address of each legislator, while the following issue furnishes a list of the principal officers of the government and their residence. The *Directory* for the First Session of the Fourteenth Congress (1815–1816) enumerates the American ministers serving abroad and the foreign ministers stationed in the United States.[14] The *Directory* for the Second Session of the Fourteenth Congress (1816–1817) specifies the Standing Committees of the House and the Senate, while the issue for the Second Session of the Fifteenth Congress (1818–1819) enumerates certain of their Select Committees as well.[15] The *Congressional Directory* for the First Session of the Twenty-Second Congress (1831–1832) provides the Congressional district for each legislator. From 1801 to 1840 the *Directories* varied in size from seven to sixty-nine pages, the average being forty-five pages.

The *Congressional Directory* for the Second Session of the Twentieth Congress (1828–1829) was the most interesting and informative of all those which appeared during the period under consideration. In addition to the standard material, this issue features the Fourth Annual Message of President John Quincy Adams, a brief description of the Capitol, lists of the principal officers of the government (and their salaries), and the officers of Washington's municipal government. Included was such practical information as a list of the local banks (with their officers and business hours), and timetables on mail postings, deliveries, and stagecoach runs. A synoptical calendar was also furnished.

[14]Ministerial lists were not included in the *Directory* for the First Session of the Nineteenth Congress (1825–26).
[15]The *Directory* for the First Session of the Twenty-First Congress (1829–30) gives the meeting place of the Standing Committees of the House and the following issue does so for the Standing Committees of the House and Senate. Subsequent *Directories* continued to list the meeting place of the Standing Committees until this practice was terminated in the *Directory* for the First Session of the Twenty-Fourth Congress (1835–36).

The *Directory* for the First Session of the Thirtieth Congress bore on the title page the words "Complied and published for the use of Congress by the Postmaster of the House of Representatives." It was issued in 1848 by J. & G. S. Gideon and is generally considered to be the first official one, because it was the first edition ordered and paid for by Congress.[16] The *Congressional Directory* assumed its contemporary appearance shortly after the Civil War. At the start of the Second Session of the Thirty-Eighth Congress (1864–1865) the compilation and publication of the *Congressional Directory* was authorized under the supervision of the Joint Committee on Public Printing. When, in 1867, biographical sketches of Senators and Representatives appeared in the first edition of the *Congressional Directory* for the Second Session of the Fortieth Congress, the *Directory* had essentially attained its modern format.

The publication of *United States Congressional Directories, 1789–1840* makes it possible for scholars to pursue the systematic investigation of American political culture in new dimensions of historical depth and breadth. The residential patterns of the Congressional community and the role of the boardinghouse fraternities as building blocks out of which the more conventionally partisan Congressional politics eventually emerged may be more accurately determined.[17] Extensive exploration of the voting behavior of the boardinghouse groups and of the dynamics of group agreement can be undertaken, including the relationship to such variables as size of the group, composition of the group, and the nature of the policy issue involved. Comparisons of the voting cohesion on roll calls by boardinghouse groups and state delegations during the early national period may be made. An elaborate analysis of roll call votes might help to establish the fact that in its internal dynamics on policy issues the party "behaved" like a coalition of boardinghouse blocs. (To prove that a party behaved like a coalition one would have to supply evidence of negotiations between boardinghouse cliques, because the existence of a coalition cannot be proved from structure.) The evidence is suggestive on this point, especially if the boardinghouse groups were one-party in composition, as preliminary findings seem to indicate.

At any rate, during the Jeffersonian period "the scattering of the party membership into boardinghouse fraternities gave the party the sociological, if not necessarily the political, characteristics of a coali-

---

[16] The *Directory* for the Second Session of the Twenty-Second Congress (1832–33) contained the words "compiled and printed for the use of Congress" on its title-page.
[17] This paragraph and the next are based on suggestions in Young, *Washington Community, passim* and the quotations are from p. 275 n. 34 and p. 274 n. 31. See also Goldman, "Republic of Virtue," p. 99.

tion of blocs." We are better able to ascertain "whether there is a connection between the decline of the boardinghouse pattern and the decline of organized party dissidence. . . . For the erosion of the primary-group organizational base of the Congressional community, especially to the extent that it had served as a source of political cues for the members, may have created an environment more permissive and more heedful of parties." We can determine precisely when state delegations became an arithmetically more viable organizational base for majority formation than the fraternity system and document too how state delegations and boardinghouse fraternities became increasingly disparate structural elements in the Congressional community, and how, consequently, legislators tended to become ever more subject to two potentially conflicting fields of influence within their own community. Perhaps, too, analysis of the role and function of boardinghouse groups may prove to be applicable to the study of state politics and to the political culture of foreign nations at certain stages of their development.

The regular appearance of rosters of the Standing Committees of Congress in the *Congressional Directories* after 1816 testifies to the contemporary recognition of the rise of the committee system and the growth of the internal complexity in the structure and functions of the Senate and House of Representatives.[18] By 1814 the committee system had become the dominant force in the House of Representatives and in 1816 the Senate also resolved that most of its business be conducted by permanent standing committees.[19] The reorganization of Congress was intended to streamline governmental operations—to insure economy and efficiency in administration. By this means the increased burden of legislative work and responsibility after the War of 1812 could be more easily accommodated and more clearly delegated. Then too, the new system may well have been partly a response to the executive weakness of Madison and Monroe and partly "a functional adaptation to the early Congress' incapacity to organize itself for effective policy-making by majorities."[20] In any case, the

[18] Poslby, "Institutionalization of the U.S. House," especially pp. 155–56 wherein it is noted that during and after the War of 1812 Henry Clay won a new measure of independence for the Speakership in the American political system. "Under Clay five House Committees were constituted to oversee expenditures in executive departments, the first major institutionalization of the Congressional function of oversight."
[19] William Nisbet Chambers, *Political Parties in a New Nation: The American Experience, 1776–1809* (New York: Oxford University Press, 1963), p. 194 notes by 1814 "effective power was exercised not by the President, as had been the case with Jefferson, but by factional Congressional leaders working through the speakership, the caucus, and the committees. . . . A distinct Congressional as opposed to the presidential wing of the Republican party had emerged, and it intended to have its own way."
[20] Young, *Washington Community*, p. 151.

rise of the committee system, however much it might increase efficiency, would also contribute to the collapse of Presidential leadership, because by creating a new arena for policy making and offering the legislators a new means of exercising power, it introduced new, divisive forces into the Congressional community. "By 1825 the committee system had taken on most of its modern features—seniority rule and the House Rules Committee excepted—and had absorbed broad powers of initiative, amendment, and quasi-veto in legislation, as well as supervision of executive administration" and thereby helped seal the doom of Presidential leadership.[21] A thoroughgoing analysis of the Congressional committee system remains to be written[22] and we hope this publication may facilitate the effort.

If *United States Congressional Directories, 1789–1840*, becomes a standard reference work and stimulates new studies of the role and function of elite behavior in American political culture, we shall feel generously rewarded.

Spelling has been standardized in accordance with the *Biographical Directory of the American Congress 1774–1961* and annotations have been collated with that volume and with the *Journal of the Senate* and the *Journal of the House of Representatives*. Only those standing and select committees of the legislature specified in the *Directories* have been reprinted; these were the permanent and more important ones, and were usually formed during the first few days of each Congressional session. The editors have provided the first names of the Congressmen (the *Directories* list only the surnames in the boarding-house rosters), their home states, and appendicies listing those members who were not included in the *Directories* because of their failure to attend the session or to arrive and assume a lodging known to the printer before the *Directory* went to press.

An Appendix listing the members of the Standing Committees of the House of Representatives from the First Session of the First Congress through the First Session of the Fourteenth Congress is included for convenience. Lists of the Standing Committees of both houses of the legislature became a regular feature of the Directories beginning with the Second Session of the Fourteenth Congress in December 1816. We realize that at first glance it might be more useful to the reader if we had placed the names of Congressmen in alphabetical order within the boardinghouse groups, as was occasionally done by the contemporary printer. We have chosen, however, to reproduce the Directories as they were, for undoubtedly, the composition of a boardinghouse

[21] *Ibid.*, pp. 202–10; the quotation is from p. 202.
[22] See Goldman, "Republic of Virtue," pp. 122–36, 226–41.

influenced latecomers in their selection of an abode. "As their pre-
dominantly sectional composition suggests, few messes were chance
groups of men who happened to find themselves at the same lodging-
house."[23]   By listing the legislators as they registered and constituted
themselves, we preserve a true picture of the historic development of
their congressional fraternities.

[23] Young, *Washington Community*, p. 100.

CONGRESSIONAL DIRECTORY

FIRST CONGRESS, FIRST SESSION
(March 4, 1789–September 29, 1789)

New Hampshire
John Langdon, 37 Broad Street
Paine Wingate, 47 Broad Street

Massachusetts
Caleb Strong, 15 Great Dock Street
Tristram Dalton, 37 Broad Street

Connecticut
William S. Johnson, College
Oliver Ellsworth, 59 Water Street

New York
[Not yet chosen] [1]

New Jersey
William Paterson, 51 Wall Street
Jonathan Elmer, 47 Little Dock Street

Pennsylvania
William Maclay, Mr. Vandolsom's, near
  the Bear Market
Robert Morris, 39 Great Dock Street

Delaware
George Read, 15 Wall Street
Richard Bassett, 15 Wall Street

Maryland
Charles Carroll, 52 South Street
John Henry, City Tavern

Virginia
Richard Henry Lee, Greenwich
William Grayson

South Carolina
Pierce Butler
Ralph Izard, Broadway, near the Jays

Georgia
William Few, 91 William Street
James Gunn, 84 Broadway

SOURCE: Broadsheets at the Library of Congress and the John Carter Brown Library, which list only the New York City street addresses of eighteen Senators. Representatives are listed but their addresses are not given.
[1] Rufus King took his seat on July 25, 1789, and Philip John Schuyler took his seat on July 27, 1789.

CONGRESSIONAL DIRECTORY

FIRST CONGRESS, FIRST SESSION
(March 4, 1789–September 29, 1789)

President
George Washington, 3 Cherry Street

Vice President
John Adams, Greenwich Road

SENATORS OF THE UNITED STATES

New Hampshire
John Langdon, 37 Broad Street
Paine Wingate, 47 Broad Street

Massachusetts
Tristram Dalton, 37 Broad Street
Caleb Strong, 15 Great Dock Street

Connecticut
William S. Johnson, College
Oliver Ellsworth, 193 Water Street

New York
[Not yet chosen] [1]

New Jersey
Jonathan Elmer, 48 Great Dock Street
William Paterson, 51 Great Dock Street

Pennsylvania
William Maclay, Mr. Vandolsom's, near
the Bear Market
Robert Morris, 39 Great Dock Street

Delaware
Richard Bassett, 15 Wall Street
George Read, 15 Wall Street

Maryland
Charles Carroll, 52 Smith Street
John Henry, 27 Queen Street

Virginia
William Grayson, 57 Maiden Lane
Richard Henry Lee, Greenwich

South Carolina
Pierce Butler, 37 Great Dock Street
Ralph Izard, Broadway, opposite the
French Ambassador's

Georgia
William Few, 90 William Street
James Gunn, 34 Broadway

REPRESENTATIVES OF THE UNITED STATES

New Hampshire
Nicholas Gilman, Corner of Smith and
Wall Streets

Samuel Livermore, 37 Broad Street
Benjamin West [2]

SOURCE: *The New York Directory And Register For the Year 1789* whose entries are more complete than, and in some instances contradictory to, those in the *Congressional Directory*.

[1] See note 1, p. 13.

[2] Abiel Foster should be correctly listed in place of West.

Massachusetts
Fisher Ames, 15 Great Dock Street
George Leonard, 15 Great Dock Street
George Partridge, 15 Great Dock Street
Theodore Sedgwick, 15 Great Dock Street
Elbridge Gerry, Corner of Broadway and Thomas Streets
Benjamin Goodhue, 47 Broad Street
Jonathan Grout, 47 Broad Street
George Thacher, 47 Broad Street

Connecticut
Benjamin Huntington, 59 Water Street
Roger Sherman, 59 Water Street
Jonathan Sturges, 47 Broad Street
Jonathan Trumbull, 195 Water Street
Jeremiah Wadsworth, 195 Water Street

New York
Egbert Benson, Corner of King and Nassau Streets
William Floyd, 27 Queen Street
John Hathorn,[3] Mr. Strong's, near the Albany Pier
Jeremiah Van Rensselaer,[4] Mr. Strong's, near the Albany Pier
John Laurance, 14 Wall Street
Peter Silvester,[5] 45 Maiden Lane

New Jersey
Elias Boudinot, 12 Wall Street
Lambert Cadwalader, 15 Wall Street
James Schureman, 47 Little Dock Street
Thomas Sinnickson, 47 Little Dock Street

Pennsylvania
George Clymer, Mr. Anderson's, Pearl Street
Thomas Fitzsimons, Mr. Anderson's, Pearl Street
Thomas Hartley, 19 Maiden Lane
Daniel Hiester, 19 Maiden Lane

Frederick A. C. Muhlenberg, Rev. Dr. Kunzie's, 24 Chatham Row
Peter G. Muhlenberg, Rev. Dr. Kunzie's, 24 Chatham Row
Thomas Scott, Mr. Huck's, Corner of Smith and Wall Streets
Henry Wynkoop, Mr. Vandolsom's, near the Bear Market

Delaware
John Vining, 19 Wall Street

Maryland
Daniel Carroll, 52 Smith Street
William Smith, 52 Smith Street
George Gale, 52 Smith Street
Benjamin Contee, 15 Wall Street
Joshua Seney, 15 Wall Street
Michael Jenifer Stone, 15 Wall Street

Virginia
Theodoric Bland, 57 Maiden Lane
Josiah Parker, 57 Maiden Lane
Isaac Coles, 57 Maiden Lane
John Brown, 19 Maiden Lane
Alexander White, 19 Maiden Lane
John Page, 19 Maiden Lane
James Madison, 19 Maiden Lane
Samuel Griffin, White Conduit House, near the Hospital
Richard Bland Lee, 15 Wall Street
Andrew Moore, 15 Wall Street

South Carolina
Aedanus Burke, Mr. Huck's, Wall Street
Daniel Huger, Mr. Huck's, Wall Street
Thomas Tudor Tucker, Mr. Huck's, Wall Street
William L. Smith,[6] Broadway, next to the Spanish Minister's
Thomas Sumter, 40 Wall Street

Georgia
Abraham Baldwin, 193 Water Street
James Jackson, 63 Broadway
George Matthews, 63 Broadway

[3] Took his seat Apr. 23, 1789.
[4] Took his seat May 9, 1789.
[5] Took his seat Apr. 22, 1789.
[6] Took his seat Apr. 13, 1789.

CONGRESSIONAL DIRECTORY

SECOND CONGRESS, SECOND SESSION
(November 5, 1792–March 2, 1793)

SENATORS OF THE UNITED STATES

New Hampshire
John Langdon, 222 Market Street
Paine Wingate, 155 North Second Street

Massachusetts
George Cabot, 36 Union Street
Caleb Strong, 58 North Third Street

Rhode Island
Theodore Foster, 29 Callow Hill Road
Joseph Stanton, Jr., 125 South Second
Street

Connecticut
Oliver Ellsworth, 121 South Third
Street
Roger Sherman, 155 North Second
Street

Vermont
Stephen R. Bradley, 153 Market Street
Moses Robinson, 20 North Third Street

New York
Aaron Burr, 147 North Second Street
Rufus King, 104 Spruce Street

New Jersey
Philemon Dickinson, Chestnut Street,
Upper End

John Rutherfurd, 56 North Fourth
Street

Pennsylvania
Robert Morris, Corner of Market and
Sixth Street
Vacant[1]

Delaware
Richard Bassett
George Read, 33 Dock Street

Maryland
Charles Carroll of Carrollton[2]
John Henry, 170 Market Street

Virginia
James Monroe, 123 Arch Street
John Taylor[3]

Kentucky
John Brown, Corner of Third and Vine
Street
John Edwards, 28 Arch Street

North Carolina
Benjamin Hawkins, 170 Market Street
Samuel Johnston, 189 South Third
Street

SOURCE: A broadside at the Library of Congress which concludes that "The gentlemen to whose names no place of abode is annexed, have not arrived."
[1] The credentials of Albert Gallatin were presented Feb. 28, 1793, and ordered placed in the files; no further action taken during the Congress.
[2] Resigned Nov. 30, 1792.
[3] Took his seat Dec. 12, 1792.

South Carolina
Pierce Butler, Market between Seventh and Eighth Street
Ralph Izard, 165 Chestnut Street

Georgia
William Few, 14 Cherry Alley
James Gunn

REPRESENTATIVES OF THE UNITED STATES

New Hampshire
Nicholas Gilman, 9 North Fourth Street
Samuel Livermore, 235 Market Street
Jeremiah Smith, 9 North Fourth Street

Massachusetts[4]
Fisher Ames, 235 Market Street
Shearjashub Bourne, 65 Walnut Street
Elbridge Gerry, 105 North Front Street
Benjamin Goodhue, 72 North Third Street
Theodore Sedgwick, 104 Spruce Street
George Thacher, 235 Market Street
Artemas Ward, 155 North Second Street

Rhode Island
Benjamin Bourn, 235 Market Street

Connecticut
James Hillhouse, 72 North Third Street
Amasa Learned, 67 Pine Street
Jonathan Sturges, 72 North Third Street
Jonathan Trumbull, 67 Pine Street
Jeremiah Wadsworth

Vermont
Nathaniel Niles, 155 North Second Street
Israel Smith, 20 North Third Street

New York
Egbert Benson, 104 Spruce Street
James Gordon, 184 South Front Street
John Laurance, 155 Chestnut Street
Cornelius C. Schoonmaker, 38 North Third Street
Peter Silvester, 188 Spruce Street
Thomas Tredwell, 38 North Third Street

New Jersey
Elias Boudinot, 229 Market Street
Abraham Clark, 68 Market Street
Jonathan Dayton, 47 North Third Street
Aaron Kitchell, 68 Market Street

Pennsylvania
William Findley, 67 Vine Street
Thomas Fitzsimons, Corner of Spruce and Fourth Street
Andrew Gregg
Thomas Hartley, 105 North Front Street
Daniel Hiester, 67 Vine Street
Israel Jacobs, 42 South Second Street
John W. Kittera, 32 Market Street
Frederick A. C. Muhlenberg, 82 North Second Street

Delaware
John Vining

Maryland
Philip Key, 214 Market Street
John Francis Mercer, City Tavern
William Vans Murray, 81 South Third Street
William Hindman[5]
Upton Sheridine
Samuel Sterett

Virginia
William B. Giles, 170 Market Street
Samuel Griffin, 43 Spruce Street
Richard Bland Lee, 53 Race Street
James Madison, 170 Market Street
Andrew Moore, 184 South Front Street
John Page, 124 Market Street
Josiah Parker, 56 North Fourth Street

[4] The state listing incorrectly includes George Leonard, who was not a Representative in the Second Congress.
[5] Took his seat Jan. 30, 1793.

Abraham B. Venable, 170 Market Street
Alexander White, 18 Chestnut Street

Kentucky
Christopher Greenup,[6] 28 Arch Street
Alexander D. Orr,[7] Corner Vine and
  Third Street

North Carolina
John Baptista Ashe, 132 Vine Street
William Barry Grove, Corner Vine and
  Third Street
Nathaniel Macon, Corner Vine and
  Third Street
John Steele, 96 North Third Street

Hugh Williamson, Corner Vine and
  Third Street

South Carolina
Robert Barnwell, 104 Spruce Street
Daniel Huger, 9 North Fourth Street
William L. Smith, 165 Chestnut Street
Thomas Sumter, 110 North Second
  Street
Thomas Tudor Tucker, 9 North Fourth
  Street

Georgia
Abraham Baldwin, 67 Vine Street
John Milledge,[8] 67 Vine Street
Francis Willis, 63 North Sixth Street

[6] Took his seat Nov. 9, 1792.
[7] Took his seat Nov. 8, 1792.
[8] Took his seat Nov. 22, 1792.

CONGRESSIONAL DIRECTORY

THIRD CONGRESS, SECOND SESSION
(November 3, 1794–March 3, 1795)

SENATORS OF THE UNITED STATES

New Hampshire
John Langdon, 222 High Street
Samuel Livermore, 27 North Second
  Street

Massachusetts
George Cabot, 36 Union Street
Caleb Strong

Rhode Island
William Bradford, 18 Chestnut Street
Theodore Foster, 2 North Eighth Street

Connecticut
Oliver Ellsworth, 91 Spruce Street
[Stephen M. Mitchell]

Vermont
Stephen R. Bradley
Moses Robinson, 20 North Third Street

New York
Aaron Burr
Rufus King, 104 Spruce Street

New Jersey
Frederick Frelinghuysen
John Rutherfurd

Pennsylvania
Robert Morris, 1 South Sixth Street
James Ross

Delaware
John Vining
[Henry Latimer][1]

Maryland
John Henry
Richard Potts

Virginia
[Stevens T. Mason][2]
[Henrt Tazewell][3]

Kentucky
John Brown, 13 South Fourth Street
John Edwards, 27 North Second Street

North Carolina
Benjamin Hawkins, Mulberry Court
Alexander Martin, 90 Race Street

South Carolina
Pierce Butler
Ralph Izard, 51 South Fourth Street

Georgia
James Gunn
James Jackson, 67 Vine Street

SOURCE: Broadsides at the John Carter Brown Library and the New York Historical Society.
[1] Took his seat Feb. 28, 1795.
[2] Took his seat June 8, 1795, in the succeeding Congress.
[3] Took his seat Dec. 29, 1794.

REPRESENTATIVES OF THE UNITED STATES

New Hampshire
Nicholas Gilman, 81 North Sixth Street
John S. Sherburne, Mulberry Court
Jeremiah Smith, 12 South Third Street
Paine Wingate, 183 North Second Street

Massachusetts
Fisher Ames, 12 South Third Street
Shearjashub Bourne, 35 Walnut Street
David Cobb, 2 North Eighth Street
Peleg Coffin, Jr., 2 North Eighth Street
Henry Dearborn, 81 North Sixth Street
Samuel Dexter, 2 North Eighth Street
Dwight Foster, 2 North Eighth Street
Benjamin Goodhue, 53 Race Street
Samuel Holten, 128 North Second Street
William Lyman, 68 North Eighth Street
Theodore Sedgwick, 67 Pine Street
George Thacher, 72 Arch Street
Peleg Wadsworth, 72 Arch Street
Artemas Ward, 128 North Second Street

Rhode Island
Benjamin Bourn, 18 Chestnut Street
Francis Malbone, 18 Chestnut Street

Connecticut
Joshua Coit, 128 North Second Street
James Hillhouse, 53 Race Street
Amasa Learned, 67 Pine Street
Zephaniah Swift, 128 North Second Street
Uriah Tracy, 119 Chestnut Street
Jonathan Trumbull, 67 Pine Street
Jeremiah Wadsworth

Vermont
Nathaniel Niles, 128 North Third Street
Israel Smith, 27 North Second Street

New York
Theodorus Bailey, 170 Market Street
Ezekiel Gilbert, 21 South Fourth Street
Henry Glen, 81 North Sixth Street
James Gordon, 83 North Third Street
Thomas Tredwell, 29 Callowhill

John E. Van Allen, 83 North Third Street
Philip Van Cortlandt, 170 High Street
Peter Van Gaasbeck, 21 South Fourth Street
John Watts, 41 Spruce Street
[Silas Talbot]

New Jersey
John Beatty, 72 North Third Street
Elias Boudinot, 227 Arch Street
Lambert Cadwallader, 165 South Second Street
Jonathan Dayton, 72 North Third Street
[Aaron Kitchell][4]

Pennsylvania
James Armstrong, 153 North Third Street
William Findley, 67 Vine Street
Thomas Fitzsimons, Chestnut between Seventh and Eighth Street
Andrew Gregg, 67 Vine Street
Thomas Hartley, 153 North Third Street
Daniel Hiester, 67 Vine Street
William Irvine
John Wilkes Kittera, 32 High Street
William Montgomery, 201 Race Street
Frederick A. C. Muhlenberg, 82 North Second Street
John Peter G. Muhlenberg, 82 North Second Street
Thomas Scott, Indian Queen
John Smilie, 201 Race Street

Delaware
Henry Latimer,[5] 153 North Third Street

Maryland
Gabriel Christie, 273 South Front Street
George Dent, 273 South Front Street
Gabriel Duvall,[6] 41 Spruce Street
William Hindman, 104 Spruce Street

[4] Took his seat Jan. 29, 1795.
[5] Resigned Feb. 7, 1795, having been elected Senator.
[6] Took his seat Nov. 11, 1794.

William Vans Murray, 74 Union Street
Samuel Smith
Thomas Sprigg
Uriah Forrest[7]

Virginia
Thomas Claiborne, 73 North Third Street
Isaac Coles, 26 Spruce Street
William B. Giles, 170 High Street
Samuel Griffin, 43 Spruce Street
George Hancock, 170 High Street
Carter B. Harrison, 96 North Third Street
John Heath, 13 South Fourth Street
Richard Bland Lee, 29 North Second Street
James Madison, 4 North Eighth Street
Andrew Moore, 59 South Fifth Street
Joseph Neville, Conestoga Waggon
Anthony New, 73 North Third Street
John Nicholas, 96 North Third Street
John Page
Josiah Parker, 170 High Street
Francis Preston, 59 South Fifth Street
Robert Rutherford, 239 High Street
Abraham B. Venable, Mulberry Court
Francis Walker, 170 High Street

Kentucky
Christopher Greenup, 68 North Eighth Street
Alexander D. Orr, Southwest Corner of Fifth and Spruce Street

North Carolina
Thomas Blount, Southwest Corner of Fifth and Spruce Street
William Johnston Dawson, O'Ellers' Hotel
James Gillespie
William Barry Grove, 13 South Fourth Street
Nathaniel Macon, Southwest Corner of Fifth and Spruce Street
Joseph McDowell (P. G.), 68 North Eighth Street
Alexander Mebane, 72 North Third Street
Benjamin Williams
Joseph Winston, 72 North Third Street
Matthew Locke, 72 North Third Street

South Carolina
Lemuel Benton
John Hunter, 147 North Second Street
William L. Smith, 11 South Sixth Street
Andrew Pickens, 147 North Second Street
Richard Winn, 147 North Second Street
Robert Goodloe Harper[8]

Georgia
Abraham Baldwin, 67 Vine Street
Thomas P. Carnes, 273 South Front Street

Territory South of the River Ohio
James White,[9] O'Ellers' Hotel

[7] Resigned Nov. 8, 1794, and was succeeded by Benjamin Edwards, who took his seat Jan. 2, 1795.
[8] Took his seat Feb. 9, 1795.
[9] Took his seat Nov. 18, 1794.

CONGRESSIONAL DIRECTORY

FOURTH CONGRESS, FIRST SESSION
(December 7, 1795–June 1, 1796)

SENATORS OF THE UNITED STATES

New Hampshire
John Langdon, 192 High Street
Samuel Livermore, 18 North Third Street

Massachusetts
George Cabot, 67 Pine Street
Caleb Strong, 81 North Sixth Street

Rhode Island
William Bradford, 18 Chestnut Street
Theodore Foster, 45 Vine Street

Connecticut
Oliver Ellsworth,[1] 128 North Second Street
Jonathan Trumbull, 67 Pine Street

Vermont
Moses Robinson, 77 North Third Street
Elijah Paine, 18 North Third Street

New York
Aaron Burr, 270 High Street
Rufus King,[2] 104 Spruce Street

New Jersey
Frederick Frelinghuysen, 46 Walnut Street

John Rutherfurd, 13 South Fourth Street

Pennsylvania
William Bingham, [Near 146] South Third Street
James Ross, 94 South Third Street

Delaware
Henry Latimer, 67 Pine Street
John Vining, 100 North Third Street

Maryland
John Henry
Richard Potts

Virginia
Stevens T. Mason, 29 North Third Street
Henry Tazewell, 90 South Eighth Street

Kentucky
John Brown, 13 South Fourth Street
Humphrey Marshall, 112 South Second Street

North Carolina
Timothy Bloodworth, 206 Sassafras Street
Alexander Martin, 100 North Third Street

SOURCE: Broadsides at the American Antiquarian Society, the Boston Athenaeum, and the John Carter Brown Library (and confirmed by Stephen's *Philadelphia Directory for 1796*).
[1] Resigned Mar. 8, 1796.
[2] Resigned May 23, 1796, having been appointed minister to England.

South Carolina
Pierce Butler, 315 High Street
Jacob Read, 372 Chestnut Street

Georgia
James Gunn
George Walton[3]

REPRESENTATIVES OF THE UNITED STATES

New Hampshire
Abiel Foster, 2 North Eighth Street
Nicholas Gilman, 13 South Fourth Street
John S. Sherburne, Mulberry Court
Jeremiah Smith, 77 North Third Street

Massachusetts
Fisher Ames
Theophilus Bradbury, 2 North Eighth Street
Henry Dearborn, 13 South Fourth Street
Dwight Foster, 2 North Eighth Street
Nathaniel Freeman, Jr., 21 South Fourth Street
Benjamin Goodhue, 81 North Sixth Street
George Leonard, 35 Walnut Street
Samuel Lyman, 2 North Eighth Street
William Lyman, Mulberry Court
John Reed, 30 Walnut Street
Theodore Sedgwick, 104 Spruce Street
George Thacher, 77 North Third Street
Joseph B. Varnum, 13 South Fourth Street
Peleg Wadsworth, 77 North Third Street

Rhode Island
Benjamin Bourn, 18 Chestnut Street
Francis Malbone, 18 Chestnut Street

Connecticut
Joshua Coit, 128 North Second Street
Chauncey Goodrich, Corner Fourth and Spruce Street
Roger Griswold, 128 North Second Street
James Hillhouse, 81 North Sixth Street
Nathaniel Smith
Zephaniah Swift, 128 North Second Street
Uriah Tracy, 128 North Second Street

Vermont
Daniel Buck, 128 North Second Street
Israel Smith, 77 North Third Street

New York
Theodorus Bailey, 32 Callowhill
William Cooper, 127 Mulberry Street
Ezekiel Gilbert, 127 Mulberry Street
Henry Glen, 81 North Sixth
John Hathorn
Jonathan N. Havens, 163 North Third Street
Edward Livingston, 192 High Street
John E. Van Allen, 32 Callowhill
Philip Van Cortlandt, 32 Callowhill
John Williams, 32 Callowhill

New Jersey
Jonathan Dayton, 170 High Street
Thomas Henderson, 205 Mulberry Street
Aaron Kitchell, 205 Mulberry Street
Isaac Smith, 63 Cherry Street
Mark Thomson, 13 South Fourth Street

Pennsylvania
David Bard, 67 Vine Street
William Findley, 67 Vine Street
Albert Gallatin, 153 North Third Street
Andrew Gregg
Thomas Hartley, 153 High Street
Daniel Hiester, 67 Vine Street
John Wilkes Kittera, 170 High Street
Samuel Maclay, 163 North Third Street
Frederick A. C. Muhlenberg, 82 North Street
Samuel Sitgreaves, 104 Spruce Street
John Swanwick, Front Street opposite Lombard
Richard Thomas, 32 Mulberry Street
[John Richards][4]

Delaware
John Patten, 8 South Third Street

[3] Took his seat Dec. 18, 1795.
[4] Took his seat Jan. 18, 1796.

Maryland
Gabriel Christie, 12 Chancery Lane
Jeremiah Crabb
George Dent, 12 Chancery Lane
Gabriel Duvall,[5] 41 Spruce Street
William Hindman, 104 Spruce Street
William Vans Murray, 112 Spruce Street
Samuel Smith, 39 North Sixth Street
Thomas Sprigg

Virginia
Richard Brent, 39 North Sixth Street
Samuel J. Cabell, 68 North Eighth
    Street
Thomas Claiborne, 100 North Third
    Street
John Clopton, 100 North Third Street
Isaac Coles, 120 South Fifth Street
William B. Giles, 170 High Street
George Hancock, 287 South Front
    Street
Carter B. Harrison, 41 Spruce Street
George Jackson, 65 North Second
    Street
John Heath, 28 Mulberry Street
James Madison, 115 Spruce Street
Andrew Moore, 287 South Front Street
Anthony New, 100 North Third Street
John Nicholas, 29 North Third Street
John Page
Josiah Parker, 73 South Second Street
Francis Preston, 10 Pear Street
Robert Rutherford, 239 High Street
Abraham B. Venable, Mulberry Court

Kentucky
Christopher Greenup
Alexander D. Orr

North Carolina
Thomas Blount, Southwest Corner Fifth
    and Spruce Street
Nathan Bryan, 206 Sassafras
Dempsey Burges, 206 Sassafras
Jesse Franklin, 68 North Eighth Street
James Gillespie, 100 North Third Street
William Barry Grove, 204 Mulberry
    Street
James Holland, 68 North Eighth Street
Matthew Locke, 205 Mulberry Street
Nathaniel Macon, Southwest Corner
    Fifth and Spruce Streets
Absalom Tatom, 204 Mulberry Street

South Carolina
Lemuel Benton
Samuel Earle, 68 North Eighth Street
Wade Hampton, 75 Walnut Street
Robert Goodloe Harper, 61 Walnut
    Street
William L. Smith, 104 Spruce Street
Richard Winn

Georgia
Abraham Baldwin, 163 North Third
    Street
John Milledge, 67 Vine Street

Territory South of the River Ohio
James White[6]

---

[5] Resigned Mar. 28, 1796, having been elected judge of the Supreme Court of Maryland. He was succeeded by Richard Sprigg, Jr., who took his seat May 5, 1796.

[6] Served until June 1, 1796, when this territory was granted statehood as the state of Tennessee.

CONGRESSIONAL DIRECTORY

FIFTH CONGRESS, FIRST SESSION
(May 15, 1797–July 10, 1797)

SENATORS OF THE UNITED STATES

New Hampshire
John Langdon, 53 North Fourth Street
Samuel Livermore, 9 North Sixth Street

Massachusetts
Benjamin Goodhue, 81 North Sixth Street
Theodore Sedgwick, 9 North Eighth

Rhode Island
William Bradford, 73 South Second
Theodore Foster, 9 Powell Street

Connecticut
James Hillhouse, 81 North Sixth Street
Uriah Tracy, 228 North Second

Vermont
Elijah Paine, 35 Walnut Street
Isaac Tichenor, 39 Corner North Alley, in Sixth Street

New York
Philip Schuyler
John Laurence, 39 Corner North Alley, in Sixth Street

New Jersey
John Rutherfurd
Richard Stockton, 39 Corner North Alley, in Sixth Street

Pennsylvania
William Bingham, South Third near Spruce Street
James Ross

Delaware
John Vining, 39 Corner North Alley, in Sixth Street
Henry Latimer, 39 Corner North Alley, in Sixth Street

Maryland
John Henry, Francis' Hotel
John E. Howard, 110 South Third Street

Virginia
Stevens T. Mason, Corner of Market, in Fifth Street
Henry Tazewell, Mr. Beckley's, South Eighth Street

Kentucky
John Brown, Francis' Hotel
Humphrey Marshall

Tennessee
William Blount,[1] 68 North Eighth Street
William Cocke, 110 North Third Street

North Carolina
Alexander Martin, 100 North Third Street
Timothy Bloodworth, 148 Market Street

SOURCE: Broadside at the American Antiquarian Society.
[1] Expelled for "high misdemeanor" July 8, 1797.

South Carolina
Jacob Read, Corner Eleventh and Chestnut Street
John Hunter, 87 Vine Street

Georgia
James Gunn
Josiah Tattnall, 67 Vine Street

REPRESENTATIVES OF THE UNITED STATES

New Hampshire
Abiel Foster, 113 North Fifth Street
Jonathan Freeman, 113 North Fifth Street
William Gordon, Dr. Ruston's, Corner Eighth and Chestnut Street
Jeremiah Smith, Dr. Ruston's, Corner Eighth and Chestnut Street

Massachusetts
Theophilus Bradbury, 39 North Sixth Street
Dwight Foster, 28 South Second Street
Nathaniel Freeman, Jr., Francis' Hotel
Samuel Lyman, 113 North Fifth Street
Harrison Gray Otis, 9 North Eighth Street
John Reed, 30 Walnut Street
Samuel Sewall, 35 Walnut Street
William Shepard, 35 Walnut Street
Thomson J. Skinner, Francis' Hotel
George Thacher, 77 North Third Street
Joseph Bradley Varnum, Francis' Hotel
Peleg Wadsworth, 77 North Third Street
[Stephen Bullock]
[Isaac Parker]

Rhode Island
Christopher G. Champlin, 73 South Second Street
Elisha R. Potter, 73 South Second Street

Connecticut
Joshua Coit, 128 North Second Street
Samuel W. Dana, 128 North Second Street
James Davenport, 81 North Sixth
Chauncey Goodrich, Northwest Corner of Spruce and Fourth Streets
Roger Griswold, 128 North Second Street
Nathaniel Smith, 128 North Second Street
John Allen

Vermont
Matthew Lyon, 77 North Third Street
Lewis R. Morris

New York
David Brooks, 9 North Sixth Street
James Cochran, 9 North Sixth Street
Lucas C. Elmendorf, 53 North Fourth Street
Henry Glen, 81 North Sixth Street
Jonathan N. Havens, 53 North Fourth Street
Hezekiah L. Hasmer, 128 North Second Street
Edward Livingston, 53 North Fourth Street
John E. Van Alen, O'Ellers' Hotel
Philip Van Cortlandt, 53 North Fourth Street
John Williams, O'Ellers' Hotel

New Jersey
Jonathan Dayton, 41 Arch Street
James H. Imlay, Northwest Corner Eighth and Chestnut Street
James Schureman, Northwest Corner Eighth and Chestnut Street
Thomas Sinnickson, Northwest Corner Eighth and Chestnut Street
Mark Thompson, Northwest Corner Eighth and Chestnut Street

Pennsylvania
David Bard, 52 North Third Street
John Chapman, North Side Cherry, Fifth Door above Fifth Street
George Ege, 140 Market Street
William Findley
Albert Gallatin, 53 North Fourth Street
Andrew Gregg, 67 Vine Street
John A. Hanna, Sign of the Swan, Race Street
Thomas Hartley, 170 Market Street
John Wilkes Kittera, 41 Arch Street
Blair McClenachan, 96 South Fourth Street

Samuel Sitgreaves, Northwest Corner Chestnut and Eighth Street
John Swanwick, 237 South Front Street
Richard Thomas, 140 Market Street

Delaware
James A. Bayard, 39 North Sixth Street

Maryland
George Baer, Jr., 29 North Third Street
William Craik, 9 North Eighth Street
John Dennis, Corner of Dock and Walnut Street
George Dent, 12 North Eighth Street
William Hindman, 104 Spruce Street
William Matthews, 96 South Third Street
Samuel Smith
Richard Sprigg, Jr., 12 North Eighth Street

Virginia
Richard Brent
Samuel J. Cabell, 100 North Third Street
Thomas Claiborne, 100 North Third Street
Matthew Clay, Francis' Hotel
John Clopton, 100 North Third Street
John Dawson, 7 South Fourth Street
Thomas Evans, Mrs. Wilson's, Corner of Dock and Walnut Street
William B. Giles, O'Ellers' Hotel
Carter B. Harrison, Mr. Knap's, Spruce near Sixth Street
David Holmes, 170 Market Street
Walter Jones, Francis' Hotel
James Machir, 170 Market Street
Daniel Morgan, 170 Market Street
Anthony New, 100 North Third Street

John Nicholas, 53 North Fourth Street
Josiah Parker
Abram Trigg, 100 North Third Street
John Trigg, 100 North Third Street
Abraham B. Venable, O'Ellers' Hotel

Kentucky
Thomas T. Davis
John Fowler

North Carolina
Thomas Blount, 68 North Eighth Street
Nathan Bryan, 205 Mulberry Street
Dempsey Burges
James Gillespie, 96 North Third Street
William Barry Grove, Francis' Hotel
Matthew Locke, 205 Arch Street
Nathaniel Macon, 68 North Eighth Street
Joseph McDowell
Richard Stanford, 205 Mulberry Street
Robert Williams, 68 North Eighth Street

Tennessee[2]

South Carolina
Lemuel Benton
Robert Goodloe Harper, 127 South Third Street
John Rutledge, Jr., Northwest Corner of Vine and Third Streets
William L. Smith (Charleston district), 104 Spruce Street
William Smith (Spartan district)
Thomas Sumter

Georgia
Abraham Baldwin, Francis' Hotel
John Milledge, 67 Vine Street

[2] Lacked a representative until the following session of Congress.

CONGRESSIONAL
DIRECTORY

FIFTH CONGRESS, SECOND SESSION
(November 13, 1797–July 16, 1798)

SENATORS OF THE UNITED STATES

New Hampshire
John Langdon, 53 North Fourth Street
Samuel Livermore, 9 North Sixth Street

Massachusetts
Benjamin Goodhue, 28 South Second Street
Theodore Sedgwick

Rhode Island
Ray Greene,[1] 18 Chestnut Street
Theodore Foster, Francis' Hotel

Connecticut
James Hillhouse
Uriah Tracy, 128 North Second Street

Vermont
Elijah Paine, 141 South Second Street
Nathaniel Chipman,[2] 39 North Sixth Street

New York
Philip Schuyler[3]
John Laurance

New Jersey
John Rutherfurd
Richard Stockton, 39 North Sixth Street

Pennsylvania
William Bingham, South Third near Spruce Street
James Ross, Corner of Pine and Second Street

Delaware
John Vining[4]
Henry Latimer, 39 North Sixth Street

Maryland
John Henry[5]
John E. Howard

Virginia
Stevens T. Mason
Henry Tazewell, Mr. Beckley's, South Eighth Street

Kentucky
John Brown, 11 North Sixth Street
Humphrey Marshall

SOURCE: *Philadelphia Directory for 1798.*
[1] Took his seat Nov. 22, 1797.
[2] Took his seat Nov. 22, 1797.
[3] Resigned Jan. 3, 1798. He was succeeded by John Sloss Hobart, who took his seat Feb. 2, 1798; resigned Apr. 16, 1798, having been appointed judge of the United States district court of New York. William North was appointed to fill the vacancy, and took his seat May 21, 1798.
[4] Resigned Jan. 19, 1798. He was succeeded by Joshua Clayton, who took his seat Feb. 19, 1798.
[5] Resigned Dec. 10, 1797, having been elected governor. The *Directory* lists James Lloyd, who took his seat Jan. 11, 1798.

Tennessee
Joseph Anderson,[6] 100 North Third Street
Andrew Jackson[7]

North Carolina
Alexander Martin, 100 North Third Street
Timothy Bloodworth, Northwest Corner of Ninth and Filbert Street

South Carolina
Jacob Read, Corner of Eleventh and Chestnut Street
John Hunter

Georgia
James Gunn, 87 Vine Street
Josiah Tattnall

REPRESENTATIVES OF THE UNITED STATES

New Hampshire
Abiel Foster, 113 North Fifth Street
Jonathan Freeman, 113 North Fifth Street
William Gordon, 18 Chestnut Street
Peleg Sprague[8]

Massachusetts
Bailey Bartlett,[9] 128 North Second Street
Stephen Bullock, 30 Walnut Street
Dwight Foster, 28 South Second Street
Nathaniel Freeman, Jr.
Samuel Lyman, 113 North Fifth Street
Harrison Gray Otis, 323 High Street
Isaac Parker, 128 North Second Street
John Reed, 30 Walnut Street
Samuel Sewall, 128 North Second Street
William Shepard, 77 North Third Street
Thomson J. Skinner
George Thacher, 77 North Third Street
Joseph Bradley Varnum, Francis' Hotel
Peleg Wadsworth, 77 North Third Street

Rhode Island
Christopher G. Champlin, 18 Chestnut Street
Thomas Tillinghast, 113 North Fifth Street

Connecticut
John Allen, 86 Crown Street
Joshua Coit, 128 North Second Street
Samuel W. Dana, 128 North Second Street
William Edmond, 128 North Second Street
Chauncey Goodrich, Northwest Corner of Fourth and Spruce Street
Roger Griswold, 128 North Second Street
Nathaniel Smith, 86 Crown Street

Vermont
Matthew Lyon, 205 Arch Street
Lewis R. Morris, 39 North Sixth Street

New York
David Brooks
James Cochran, 39 North Sixth Street
Lucas C. Elmendorf, 53 North Fourth Street
Henry Glen, 28 South Second Street
Jonathan N. Havens, 53 North Fourth Street
Hezekiah L. Hosmer, 39 North Sixth Street
Edward Livingston, O'Ellers' Hotel
John E. Van Alen, 200 Arch Street
Philip Van Cortlandt, Francis' Hotel
John Williams, 200 Arch Street

New Jersey
Jonathan Dayton, 141 South Second Street
James H. Imlay, Northwest Corner of Pine and Second Street

---

[6] Took his seat Nov. 22, 1797.
[7] Took his seat Nov. 22, 1797; resigned in April 1798.
[8] Took his seat Dec. 15, 1797.
[9] Took his seat Nov. 27, 1797.

James Schureman, 11 North Sixth Street
Thomas Sinnickson, Northwest Corner of Pine and Second Street
Mark Thompson, Northwest Corner of Pine and Second Street

Pennsylvania
David Bard, 77 North Third Street
John Chapman, 9 North Second Street
William Findley, 67 Vine Street
Albert Gallatin, 53 North Fourth Street
Andrew Gregg
John A. Hanna, 105 North Front Street
Thomas Hartley, 132 Arch Street
Joseph Hiester[10]
John Wilkes Kittera
Blair McClenachan, 96 South Fourth Street
Samuel Sitgreaves, 104 Spruce Street
John Swanwick, Sixth, near Spruce Street
Richard Thomas, 32 Arch Street
[Robert Brown][11]
[Robert Waln][12]

Delaware
James A. Bayard, 39 North Sixth Street

Maryland
George Baer, Jr., 24 North Eighth Street
William Craik, 9 North Eighth Street
John Dennis, 127 South Third Street
George Dent, 24 North Eighth Street
William Hindman, 104 Spruce Street
William Matthews, 96 South Third Street
Richard Sprigg, Jr., 24 North Eighth Street
Samuel Smith

Virginia
Richard Brent, O'Ellers' Hotel
Samuel J. Cabell

Thomas Claiborne, 108 North Fourth Street
Matthew Clay, O'Ellers' Hotel
John Clopton, 100 North Third Street
John Dawson, 7 South Fourth Street
Thomas Evans, 127 South Third Street
William B. Giles
Carter B. Harrison, Mr. Knap's, Spruce near Sixth Street
David Holmes, 170 High Street
Walter Jones, Northwest Corner of Powell and Fifth Street
James Machir, 170 High Street
Daniel Morgan, Conestoga Waggon, High Street
Anthony New, 100 North Third Street
John Nicholas, 53 North Fourth Street
Josiah Parker
Abram Trigg, 100 North Third Street
John Trigg, 100 North Third Street
Abraham B. Venable, Mr. Knap's, Spruce near Sixth Street

Kentucky
Thomas T. Davis, Mr. Beckley's, South Eighth Street
John Fowler

North Carolina
Thomas Blount, Mr. Beckley's, South Eighth Street
Nathan Bryan[13]
Dempsey Burges
James Gillespie
William Barry Grove, 127 South Third Street
Matthew Locke, 205 Arch Street
Nathaniel Macon, 108 North Fourth Street
Joseph McDowell
Richard Stanford, 205 Arch Street
Robert Williams, 108 North Fourth Street

Tennessee
William C. C. Claiborne, 100 North Third Street

[10] Took his seat Dec. 1, 1797.
[11] Took his seat Dec. 4, 1798.
[12] Took his seat Dec. 3, 1798.
[13] Died June 4, 1798.

South Carolina
Lemuel Benton
Robert Goodloe Harper, 127 South
    Third Street
Thomas Pinckney,[14] Northwest Corner
    of Vine and Third Street
John Rutledge, Jr., Northwest Corner
    of Vine and Third Streets

William Smith (Spartan District), 24
    North Eighth Street
Thomas Sumter

Georgia
Abraham Baldwin, Francis' Hotel
John Milledge

[14] Took his seat Nov. 23, 1797.

CONGRESSIONAL DIRECTORY

FIFTH CONGRESS, THIRD SESSION
(December 3, 1798–March 3, 1799)

SENATORS OF THE UNITED STATES

New Hampshire
John Langdon, 53 North Fourth Street
Samuel Livermore, 71 South Fifth Street

Massachusetts
Benjamin Goodhue, 109 South Fifth Street
Theodore Sedgwick

Rhode Island
Ray Greene, 18 Chestnut Street
Theodore Foster, 79 North Third Street

Connecticut
James Hillhouse, 109 South Fifth Street
Uriah Tracy, 128 South Second Street

Vermont
Elijah Paine, 141 South Second Street
Nathaniel Chipman, 39 North Sixth Street

New York
James Watson,[1] 141 South Second Street
John Laurance, 155 Chestnut Street

New Jersey
Franklin Davenport[2]
Richard Stockton, 39 North Sixth Street

Pennsylvania
William Bingham, South Third near Spruce Street
James Ross, 80 South Third Street

Delaware
Henry Latimer, 39 North Sixth Street
William H. Wells[3]

Maryland
James Lloyd
John E. Howard, 110 South Third Street

Virginia
Stevens T. Mason
Henry Tazewell[4]

Kentucky
John Brown
Humphrey Marshall, 103 Arch Street

Tennessee
Joseph Anderson, 107 Arch Street
Daniel Smith,[5] 107 Arch Street

SOURCE: Broadsides at the American Antiquarian Society, the New York Public Library, and Yale University Library.
[1] Took his seat Dec. 11, 1798.
[2] Took his seat Dec. 19, 1798.
[3] Took his seat Feb. 4, 1799. The Directory erroneously lists Joshua Clayton, who died on Aug. 11, 1798.
[4] Died Jan. 24, 1799.
[5] Took his seat Dec. 6, 1798.

North Carolina
Alexander Martin, 74 North Third Street
Timothy Bloodworth, 135 Pine Street

South Carolina
Jacob Read, Corner Eleventh and Chestnut Street
Charles Pinckney[6]

Georgia
James Gunn, 67 North Second Street
Josiah Tattnall

REPRESENTATIVES OF THE UNITED STATES

New Hampshire
Abiel Foster, 161 Arch Street
Jonathan Freeman, 161 Arch Street
William Gordon, 18 Chestnut Street
Peleg Sprague, 71 South Fifth Street

Massachusetts
Bailey Bartlett, 128 North Second Street
Stephen Bullock, 30 Walnut Street
Dwight Foster, 109 South Fifth Street
Nathaniel Freeman, Jr.
Samuel Lyman, 161 Arch Street
Harrison Gray Otis, 9 North Eighth Street
Isaac Parker, 128 North Second Street
John Reed, 30 Walnut Street
Samuel Sewall, 71 South Fifth Street
William Shepard, 30 Walnut Street
Thomson J. Skinner
George Thacher, 77 North Third Street
Joseph Bradley Varnum, 13 South Fourth Street
Peleg Wadsworth, 77 North Third Street

Rhode Island
Christopher G. Champlin, 18 Chestnut Street
Thomas Tillinghast, 161 Arch Street

Connecticut
John Allen
Jonathan Brace, 128 North Second Street
Samuel W. Dana, 128 North Second Street
William Edmond, 128 North Second Street
Chauncey Goodrich, 91 Spruce Street
Roger Griswold, 128 North Second Street
Nathaniel Smith, 128 North Second Street

Vermont
Matthew Lyon
Lewis R. Morris, 39 North Sixth Street

New York
David Brooks, 71 South Fifth Street
James Cochran, 80 South Third Street
Lucas C. Elmendorf, 53 North Fourth Street
Henry Glen, 109 South Fifth Street
Jonathan N. Havens, 53 North Fourth Street
Hezekiah L. Hosmer, 141 South Second Street
Edward Livingston
John E. Van Alen, 2 North Fifth Street
Philip Van Cortlandt, 13 South Fourth Street
John Williams, 202 Arch Street

New Jersey
Jonathan Dayton, 141 South Second Street
James H. Imlay, 108 South Second Street
James Schureman,[7] Southwest Corner Fourth and Spruce Street

[6] Took his seat Feb. 16, 1799. The Directory erroneously lists John Hunter, who resigned on Nov. 26, 1798.
[7] Elected on Feb. 14, 1799, to fill the vacancy in the Senate caused by the resignation of John Rutherfurd, but did not take his seat until the following Congress, finishing out his term in the House.

Thomas Sinnickson, Southwest Corner Fourth and Spruce Street

Mark Thompson

Pennsylvania
David Bard, 211 Arch Street
John Chapman, 9 North Second Street
William Findley, 148 South Fourth Street
Albert Gallatin, 53 North Fourth Street
Andrew Gregg, 13 South Fourth Street
John A. Hanna, White Horse, Market Street
Thomas Hartley, 170 Market Street
Joseph Hiester, 102 Race Street
John Wilkes Kittera, 141 South Second Street
Blair McClenachan, 96 South Fourth Street
Robert Brown,[8] White Swan, Race Street
Robert Waln, Second between Walnut and Spruce Street
Richard Thomas, Conestoga Waggon, Market Street

Delaware
James A. Bayard

Maryland
George Baer, Jr., 66 North Eighth Street
William Craik, 9 North Eighth Street
John Dennis, 161 Arch Street
George Dent, 66 North Eighth Street
William Hindman, City Tavern
William Matthews, 66 North Eighth Street
Richard Sprigg, Jr., 66 North Eighth Street
Samuel Smith, 192 Market Street

Virginia
Richard Brent
Samuel Cabell
Thomas Claiborne
Matthew Clay
John Clopton, 205 Arch Street
John Dawson, 271 Market Street
Thomas Evans, 161 Arch Street
Joseph Eggleston, 72 South Fifth Street

Carter B. Harrison, 53 North Fourth Street
David Holmes, 13 South Fourth Street
Walter Jones, 20 North Ninth Street
James Machir, Conestoga Waggon, Market Street
Daniel Morgan, Conestoga Waggon, Market Street
Anthony New, 205 Arch Street
John Nicholas, 53 North Fourth Street
Josiah Parker, 22 North Ninth Street
Abram Trigg, 68 North Eighth Street
John Trigg, 68 North Eighth Street
Abraham B. Venable, 72 South Fifth Street

Kentucky
Thomas T. Davis
John Fowler

North Carolina
Thomas Blount, 107 Arch Street
Richard Dobbs Spaight,[9] 74 North Third Street
Dempsey Burges
James Gillespie
William Barry Grove
Matthew Locke, 205 Arch Street
Nathaniel Macon, 72 South Fifth Street
Joseph McDowell
Richard Stanford, 205 Arch Street
Robert Williams

Tennessee
William C. C. Claiborne, 107 Arch Street

South Carolina
Lemuel Benton
Robert Goodloe Harper, 127 South Third Street
Thomas Pinckney, City Tavern
John Rutledge, Jr., City Tavern
William Smith (Spartan District), 66 North Eighth Street
Thomas Sumter

Georgia
Abraham Baldwin, 13 South Fourth Street
John Milledge

[8] Took his seat Dec. 4, 1798.
[9] Took his seat Dec. 10, 1798.

CONGRESSIONAL DIRECTORY

SIXTH CONGRESS, FIRST SESSION
(December 2, 1799–May 14, 1800)

SENATORS OF THE UNITED STATES

New Hampshire
John Langdon, 53 North Fourth Street
Samuel Livermore, 7 North Sixth Street

Massachusetts
Samuel Dexter, 107 Arch Street
Benjamin Goodhue, 109 South Fifth
Street

Connecticut
James Hillhouse, 109 South Fifth Street
Uriah Tracy, 128 North Second Street

Rhode Island
Theodore Foster, 13 South Fourth
Street
Ray Greene, 18 Chestnut Street

Vermont
Nathaniel Chipman, 39 North Sixth
Street
Elijah Paine, 37 North Fourth Street

New York
John Laurance, 155 Chestnut Street
James Weston,[1] 141 South Second
Street

New Jersey
Jonathan Dayton, 141 South Second
Street

James Schureman,[2] 141 South Second
Street

Pennsylvania
William Bingham, South Third Street
James Ross, 37 Dock Street

Delaware
William H. Wells, 39 North Sixth Street
Henry Latimer, 39 North Sixth Street

Maryland
John E. Howard
James Lloyd

Virginia
Stevens T. Mason
Wilson C. Nicholas[3]

Kentucky
John Brown, 90 South Eighth Street
Humphrey Marshall, 31 North Eighth
Street

Tennessee
Joseph Anderson, 31 North Eighth
Street
William Cocke, 74 North Third Street

North Carolina
Timothy Bloodworth
Jesse Franklin

SOURCE: Broadsides at the American Antiquarian Society, the John Carter
Brown Library, and the Historical Society of Pennsylvania (and confirmed by the
Philadelphia Directory for 1800).
[1] Resigned Mar. 19, 1800.
[2] Took his seat Dec. 3, 1799.
[3] Took his seat Jan. 3, 1800.

South Carolina
Charles Pinckney
Jacob Read, Corner of South Fourth
    and Union Street

Georgia
Abraham Baldwin, 13 South Fourth
    Street
James Gunn, 143 Chestnut Street

REPRESENTATIVES OF THE UNITED STATES

New Hampshire
Abiel Foster, 161 Arch Street
Jonathan Freeman, 161 Arch Street
William Gordon, 107 Arch Street
James Sheafe

Massachusetts
Bailey Bartlett, 128 North Second
    Street
Phanuel Bishop, Francis' Hotel
Dwight Foster, 109 South Fifth Street
Harrison Gray Otis, 323 Market Street
Silas Lee, 7 North Sixth Street
Samuel Lyman, 161 Arch Street
John Reed, 30 Walnut Street
Samuel Sewall,[4] 107 Arch Street
Theodore Sedgwick, 39 North Sixth
    Street
William Shepard, 30 Walnut Street
George Thacher, 77 North Third Street
Joseph B. Varnum, Francis' Hotel
Peleg Wadsworth, 77 North Third Street
Lemuel Williams, 61 Arch Street[5]

Connecticut
Jonathan Brace, 178 Spruce Street
Samuel W. Dana, 128 North Second
    Street
John Davenport, 109 South Fifth Street
William Edmond, 128 North Second
    Street
Chauncey Goodrich, 178 Spruce Street
Elizur Goodrich, 178 Spruce Street
Roger Griswold, 128 North Second
    Street

Rhode Island
John Brown, 9 North Eighth Street
Christopher G. Champlin, 9 North
    Eighth Street

Vermont
Matthew Lyon, 68 North Eighth Street
Lewis R. Morris, 39 North Sixth Street

New York
Theodorus Bailey, Francis' Hotel
John Bird, 141 South Second Street
William Cooper, 7 North Sixth Street
Lucas C. Elmendorf, 198 Arch Street
Henry Glen, 109 South Fifth Street
Edward Livingston, O'Ellers' Hotel
Jonas Platt, 128 North Second Street
John Thompson, St. Mery's, Market
    Street between Tenth and Eleventh
    Street
Philip Van Cortlandt, Francis' Hotel
John Smith[6]

New Jersey
John Condit, St. Mery's, Market Street
    between Tenth and Eleventh Street
Franklin Davenport, 39 North Sixth
    Street
James H. Imlay, 107 Arch Street
Aaron Kitchell, St. Mery's, Market
    Street between Tenth and Eleventh
    Street
James Linn, St. Mery's, Market Street
    between Tenth and Eleventh Street

Pennsylvania
Robert Brown, 118 North Third Street
Andrew Gregg, 118 Market Street
Albert Gallatin, 20 North Ninth Street
John A. Hanna, 118 Market Street
Joseph Hiester, 118 North Third Street
Thomas Hartley
John Wilkes Kittera, 141 South Second
    Street
Michael Leib, 253 North Second Street

[4] Resigned Jan. 10, 1800.
[5] The *Philadelphia Directory* lists the address as 161 Arch Street.
[6] Took his seat Feb. 27, 1800.

John Peter G. Muhlenberg, 118 North Third Street
John Smilie, 113 Callowhill Street
Richard Thomas, North Fourth Street, First Door South of the University
Robert Waln
Henry Woods, 37 Dock Street

Delaware
James A. Bayard, 39 North Sixth Street

Maryland
George Baer
William Craik, 130 Spruce Street
Gabriel Christie, Southeast Corner of Filbert and Ninth Street
George Dent, 101 South Fifth Street
John Dennis
Joseph H. Nicholson, 53 North Fourth Street
Samuel Smith, City Tavern
John C. Thomas, 7 South Fourth Street

Virginia
Samuel J. Cabell, Franklin Court
Matthew Clay, Franklin Court
John Dawson, O'Ellers' Hotel
Joseph Eggleston
Thomas Evans, 18 Chestnut Street
Edwin Grey, 74 North Third Street
Samuel Goode
David Holmes, Francis' Hotel
George Jackson, 67 North Second Street
Henry Lee, Franklin Court
John Marshall, 17 Filbert Street
John Nicholas, 53 North Fourth Street
Anthony New, 31 North Eighth Street
Levin Powell, 18 Chestnut Street
Robert Page, Francis' Hotel
Josiah Parker, Franklin Court
John Randolph, 53 North Fourth Street

Abraham Trigg, 68 North Eighth Street
John Trigg, 68 North Eighth Street

North Carolina
Willis Alston, 53 North Fourth Street
Joseph Dickson, 74 North Third Street
William Barry Grove, 101 South Fifth Street
Archibald Henderson, 74 North Third Street
William H. Hill, 101 South Fifth Street
Nathaniel Macon, 53 North Fourth Street
Richard Stanford, 205 Arch Street
Richard Dobbs Spaight
David Stone, 53 North Fourth Street
Robert Williams

South Carolina
Robert Goodloe Harper, O'Ellers' Hotel
Benjamin Huger
Abraham Nott, 74 North Third Street
Thomas Pinckney
John Rutledge, Jr., City Tavern
Thomas Sumter

Georgia
James Jones, 67 Vine Street
Benjamin Taliaferro, 67 Vine Street

Tennessee
William C. C. Claiborne, 31 North Eighth Street

Kentucky
Thomas T. Davis
John Fowler

Territory Northwest of the River Ohio
William Henry Harrison,[7] 341 Market Street

[7] Resigned in Mar. 1800.

CONGRESSIONAL DIRECTORY

SEVENTH CONGRESS, FIRST SESSION
(December 7, 1801–May 3, 1802)

Mrs. Cannon, North of the Capitol
Anthony New, Va.
Thomas T. Davis, Ky.
Isaac Van Horne, Penn.
John Clopton, Va.
Thomas Claiborne, Va.
John Stewart, Penn.

Miss Finigan, North of the Capitol
Aaron Ogden (S), N.J.
Gouverneur Morris (S), N.Y.
Aaron Dayton (S), N.J.
John E. Howard (S), Md.
William H. Wells (S), Del.
Samuel White (S), Del.
Benjamin Walker, N.Y.
Killian K. Van Rensselaer, N.Y.
Thomas Morris, N.Y.
Lewis R. Morris, Vt.
John Campbell, Md.

Mrs. Wilson, North of the Capitol
Abraham Baldwin (S), Ga.
Theodore Foster (S), R.I.
George Logan (S), Penn.
Nathaniel Macon, N.C.
William B. Giles, Va.
Joseph H. Nicholson, Md.
Willis Alston, N.C.
Charles Johnson, N.C.
Edwin Gray, Va.
John Randolph, Va.

Tunicleff's Hotel
Christopher Ellery (S), R.I.

John Bacon, Mass.
William Helms, N.J.
Josiah Smith, Mass.
James Mott, N.J.
Ebenezer Elmer, N.J.
Joseph Stanton, Jr., R.I.

Stell's Hotel, East of the Capitol
Jonathan Mason (S), Mass.
James Sheafe (S), N.H.
Henry Woods, Penn.
James A. Bayard, Del.
William H. Hill, N.C.

Mr. Birch, East of the Capitol
John A. Hanna, Penn.
Joseph Hiester, Penn.
Andrew Gregg, Penn.
John Condit, N.J.
Robert Brown, Penn.
Henry Southard, N.J.

Mr. King, East of the Capitol
Dwight Foster (S), Mass.
James Hillhouse (S), Conn.
Elias Perkins, Conn.
John Davenport, Conn.
John C. Smith, Conn.
Manasseh Cutler, Mass
Ebenezer Mattoon, Mass.
Nathan Read, Mass.

Mrs. Finch
John Breckinridge (S), Ky.
Phanuel Bishop, Mass.

NOTE: Copies are located at the Columbia Historical Society, the Library of Congress, the William L. Clements Library, and the Western Reserve Historical Society.

38

John Trigg, Va.
Abram Trigg, Va.
Samuel J. Cabell, Va.
Thomas Moore, S.C.
Richard Sprigg, Jr.,[1] Md.
John Taliaferro, Va.
Philip R. Thompson, Va.
William Butler, S.C.
Lucas C. Elmendorf, N.Y.
Nasworthy Hunter,[2] Deleg., Miss. Terr.

Mr. Frost, Jersey Ave.
Uriah Tracy (S), Conn.
Simeon Olcott (S), N.H.
Thomas Boude, Penn.
Joseph Hemphill, Penn.
Benjamin Tallmadge, Conn.
Abiel Foster, N.H.
Roger Griswold, Conn.
Samuel Tenney, N.H.
John Stanly, N.C.
Lemuel Williams, Mass.
Calvin Goddard, Conn.
Archibald Henderson, N.C.

Stelle's, Jersey House
Stephen R. Bradley (S), Vt.
James Jackson (S), Ga.
Robert Wright (S), Md.
Joseph B. Varnum, Mass.
Philip Van Cortlandt, N.Y.
John Milledge, Ga.
William Eustis, Mass.
Richard Cutts, Mass.

Mr. Lund Washington, Jersey Ave.[3]
Jesse Franklin (S), N.C.
Theodorus Bailey, N.Y.
John Smith, N.Y.
John P. Van Ness, N.Y.
Samuel L. Mitchill, N.Y.
David Thomas, N.Y.
David Holmes, Va.
Richard Stanford, N.C.

Captain Coil's, Six Buildings
William Cocke (S), Tenn.

Mr. Rogers, Pennsylvania Ave. near the Treasury Dept.
George Jackson, Va.
Paul Fearing, Deleg., Terr. Northwest of the River Ohio
Samuel W. Dana, Conn.

Dr. Harrison, near Rhodes City Tavern
Nathaniel Chipman (S), Vt.

Mr. Frost, near the Seven Buildings
William Shepard, Mass.
Thomas Tillinghast, R.I.
Peleg Wadsworth, Mass.

Mrs. Turner, Six Buildings, Pennsylvania Ave.
Michael Leib, Penn.
William Hoge, Penn.

Major Cushing, Six Buildings, Pennsylvania Ave.
William Jones, Penn.

Mr. Barney's Inn, Georgetown
Joseph Anderson (S), Tenn.
John Archer, Md.
William Dickson, Tenn.
Thomas Newton, Jr., Va.

Mr. George Plater, Georgetown
Thomas Plater, Md.

Georgetown
John Dennis, Md.

Mr. J. Nourse, Georgetown
John Smith, Va.

Secretary of the Navy, Jersey Ave.
Wilson C. Nicholas (S), Va.
Samuel Smith, Md.

[1] Resigned Feb. 11, 1802. He was succeeded by Walter Bowie, who took his seat Mar. 24, 1802.
[2] Died Mar. 11, 1802.
[3] A Mr. "J. Smith" is also listed; however all of the J. Smith's in this Congress have been accounted for.

Mr. O'Neal, near the Six Buildings
Thomas Sumter (S),[4] S.C.

Ten Buildings, Jersey Ave.
Stevens T. Mason (S), Va.

APPENDIX

Benjamin Taliaferro, Ga.
John Brown (S), Ky.
John Fowler, Ky.
Daniel Hiester, Md.
Seth Hastings,[5] Mass.
Joseph Pierce, N.H.
George B. Upham, N.H.
John Armstrong (S),[6] N.Y.
David Stone (S), N.C.
William Barry Grove, N.C.
James Holland, N.C.
Robert Williams, N.C.

James Ross (S), Penn.
John Smilie, Penn.
John Ewing Colhoun (S), S.C.
Benjamin Huger, S.C.
Thomas Lowndes, S.C.
John Rutledge, S.C.
Israel Smith, Vt.
Richard Brent, Va.
Matthew Clay, Va.
John Dawson, Va.
John Stratton, Va.

[4] Took his seat Dec. 19, 1801.
[5] Took his seat Jan. 11, 1802.
[6] Resigned Feb. 5, 1802. He was succeeded by De Witt Clinton, who took his seat Feb. 23, 1802.

CONGRESSIONAL DIRECTORY

SEVENTH CONGRESS, SECOND SESSION
(December 6, 1802–March 3, 1803)

Miss Finigan
Jonathan Mason (S), Mass.
Gouverneur Morris (S), N.Y.
Aaron Ogden (S), N.J.
Jonathan Dayton (S), N.J.
John E. Howard (S), Md.
Samuel White (S), Del.
Killian K. Van Rensselaer, N.Y.
Samuel Hunt, N.H.
John Campbell, Md.
Lewis R. Morris, Vt.

Mr. Burch
John Breckinridge (S), Ky.
Nathaniel Macon, N.C.
Joseph H. Nicholson, Md.
Willis Alston, N.C.
Thomas Wynns,[1] N.C.
John Taliaferro, Va.

Mr. Gregory
John Clopton, Va.
Thomas Claiborne, Va.

Mr. Tunicliff
Christopher Ellery (S), R.I.
Joseph B. Varnum, Mass.
David Thomas, N.Y.
John Condit, N.J.
Henry Southard, N.J.
Ebenezer Elmer, N.J.
Joseph Stanton, Jr., R.I.
John Bacon, Mass.
Josiah Smith, Mass.
Richard Cutts, Mass.

John A. Hanna, Penn.
Edwin Gray, Va.

Mr. Stelle
Stephen R. Bradley (S), Vt.
James Jackson (S), Ga.
Henry Woods, Penn.
John Dennis, Md.
James Mott, N.J.
Thomas Morris, N.Y.
Thomas Lowndes, S.C.
John Rutledge, S.C.
Benjamin Huger, S.C.
Matthew Clay, Va.
William Helms, N.J.
Israel Smith, Vt.
William H. Hill, N.C.

Mr. Frost
William Plumer (S),[2] N.H.
Uriah Tracy (S), Conn.
Benjamin Tallmadge, Conn.
Samuel Tenney, N.H.
Samuel Thatcher, Mass.
Nathan Read, Mass.
Lemuel Williams, Mass.

Mrs. Finch
John Trigg, Va.
Thomas M. Greene, Deleg., Miss. Terr.
Abram Trigg, Va.

Mr. Coyle
Simeon Olcott (S), N.H.
Roger Griswold, Conn.

NOTE: Copies are located at the American Antiquarian Society, the Boston Athenaeum, and the William L. Clements Library.

[1] Took his seat Dec. 7, 1802.
[2] Took his seat Dec. 14, 1802.

Abiel Foster, N.H.
Samuel W. Dana, Conn.
Thomas Boude, Penn.
Calvin Goddard, Conn.
John Stanly, N.C.
Seth Hastings, Mass.
Paul Fearing,[3] Deleg., Terr. Northwest
  of the River Ohio
Joseph Hemphill, Penn.
Archibald Henderson, N.C.
Ebenezer Mattoon, Mass.

Mrs. Williams
De Witt Clinton (S), N.Y.
Robert Wright (S), Md.
Samuel Smith, Md.
Walter Bowie, Md.
John Randolph, Va.

Mr. Washington
Theodore Foster (S), R.I.
Jesse Franklin (S), N.C.
Thomas Sumter (S), S.C.
Abraham Baldwin (S), Ga.
John Smith, N.Y.
Samuel L. Mitchill, N.Y.
David Meriwether, Ga.
Richard Stanford, N.C.
David Holmes, Va.
Theodorus Bailey, N.Y.
Lucas C. Elmendorf, N.Y.

Mr. Blagden
Dwight Foster (S),[4] Mass.
John Davenport, Conn.
Elias Perkins, Conn.
John C. Smith, Conn.

Mrs. Fownes
Anthony New, Va.
John Smilie, Penn.
John Stewart, Penn.
Issac Van Horne, Penn.

Mr. Speak
William Shepard, Mass.

George B. Upham, N.H.
Peleg Wadsworth, Mass.
Thomas Tillinghast, R.I.
Manasseh Cutler, Mass.

Mrs. Sweeney
Phanuel Bishop, Mass.
George Jackson, Va.

Mr. Lovell
Andrew Gregg, Penn.
Joseph Hiester, Penn.
Robert Brown, Penn.
Michael Lieb, Penn.
William Dickson, Tenn.
Thomas Moore, S.C.
William Hoge, Penn.
Philip R. Thompson, Va.
William Butler, S.C.
Daniel Hiester, Md.

Mr. McLaughlin
Thomas Newton, Jr., N.J.

Mr. Barney
John Dawson, Va.
John Archer, Md.

Mr. O'Neal
James Holland, N.C.

Mr. D. C. Brent
Stevens T. Mason (S), Va.
Richard Brent, Va.

Mr. Beckley
William Eustis, Mass.

Georgetown
Thomas Plater, Md.

Mr. Nourse
John Smith, Va.

[3] A question was raised as to his right to retain his seat after Nov. 29, 1802, when the territory was granted statehood as the State of Ohio; as no other representative appeared, he was permitted to retain his seat.
[4] Resigned Mar. 2, 1803.

Pennsylvania Ave.
John P. Van Ness,[5] N.Y.

Mrs. Osborne
George Logan (S), Penn.

APPENDIX

James Hillhouse (S), Conn.
William H. Wells (S), Del.
James A. Bayard, Del.
Peter Early,[6] Ga.
John Brown (S), Ky.
Thomas T. Davis, Ky.
John Fowler, Ky.
Philip Van Cortlandt, N.Y.
Benjamin Walker, N.Y.
David Stone (S), N.C.
William Barry Grove, N.C.
Robert Williams, N.C.

James Ross (S), Penn.
William Jones, Penn.
Pierce Butler (S),[7] S.C.
Richard Winn,[8] S.C.
Joseph Anderson (S), Tenn.
William Cocke (S), Tenn.
Nathaniel Chipman (S), Vt.
Wilson C. Nicholas (S), Va.
Samuel J. Cabell, Va.
William B. Giles, Va.
John Stratton, Va.

[5] Seat declared forfeited Jan. 17, 1803, because he had accepted and exercised the office of major of militia, under authority of the United States, within the Territory of Columbia.

NOTE: Ohio was admitted as a State into the Union, Nov. 29, 1802, from territory known as the "Northwest Territory," which was originally ceded to the United States by Virginia. Ohio had no representation during this session of Congress.

[6] Took his seat Jan. 10, 1803.

[7] Elected on Nov. 4, 1802, to fill the vacancy caused by death of John E. Colhoun.

[8] Took his seat Jan. 24, 1803.

CONGRESSIONAL DIRECTORY

TENTH CONGRESS, FIRST SESSION
(October 26, 1807–April 25, 1808)

Mr. Coyle
James Hillhouse (S), Conn.
Timothy Pickering (S), Mass.
Benjamin Tallmadge, Conn.
Josiah Quincy, Mass.
Martin Chittenden, Vt.
John Davenport, Conn.
Lewis B. Sturges, Conn.
Jonathan O. Moseley, Conn.
Epaphroditus Champion, Conn.
Samuel W. Dana, Conn.
Timothy Pitkin, Conn.
William Stedman, Mass.
Jabez Upham, Mass.

Mrs. Dowson
John Gaillard (S), S.C.
Samuel Smith (S), Md.
Wilson C. Nicholas, Va.

Mr. Claxton
Buckner Thruston (S), Ky.
Dennis Smelt, Ga.
Willis Alston, N.C.
Lemuel J. Alston, S.C.
Jacob Richards, Penn.
William A. Burwell, Va.
Thomas Kenan, N.C.
David Holmes, Va.
George Poindexter, Deleg., Miss. Terr.
John Claiborne, Va.
John Rea, Penn.
John Boyle, Ky.

Mr. Tim
Samuel Maclay (S), Penn.
Jesse Franklin (S), N.C.
Andrew Moore (S), Va.
Daniel Smith (S), Tenn.
Edwin Gray, Va.
William Hoge, Penn.
Jesse Wharton, Tenn.
Peterson Goodwyn, Va.
Samuel Smith, Penn.
Richard Stanford, N.C.
William Blackledge, N.C.
Meshack Franklin, N.C.
Daniel Montgomery, Jr., Penn.
John Harris, N.Y.
George W. Campbell, Tenn.
Marmaduke Williams, N.C.

Mr. Kean
Thomas Blount, N.C.
Burwell Bassett, Va.
Benjamin Parke,[1] Deleg., Ind. Terr.

Mr. Washington
Orchard Cook, Mass.
Clement Storer, N.H.
William Milnor, Penn.
Joseph Calhoun, S.C.
John Culpepper,[2] N.C.
Daniel M. Durell, N.H.

Mr. Lindsay
John Pope (S), Ky.

NOTE: Copies are located at the Library of Congress and the Yale University Library.

[1] Resigned Mar. 1, 1808.

[2] Election contested by Duncan McFarland; the House on Jan. 2, 1808, declared his seat vacant on account of irregularities; subsequently elected, and took his seat Feb. 23, 1808.

Richard M. Johnson, Ky.
Joseph Desha, Ky.
John Rowan, Ky.

Mr. Burch
Evan S. Alexander, N.C.
James Elliott, Vt.

Mrs. Sweney
Thomas Moore, S.C.
Alexander Wilson, Va.
Richard Winn, S.C.

Mr. Stelle
Daniel C. Verplanck, N.Y.
Philip Van Cortlandt, N.Y.
William W. Bibb, Ga.
George M. Troup, Ga.
Howell Cobb, Ga.
William Kirkpatrick, N.Y.

Mr. Frost
Stephen R. Bradley (S), Vt.
Samuel L. Mitchill (S), N.Y.
Philip Reed (S), Md.
John Montgomery, Md.
William McCreery, Md.
Nicholas R. Moore, Md.
Samuel Taggart, Mass.
Walter Jones, Va.
Samuel Riker, N.Y.
Francis Gardner, N.H.

Mrs. Beckley
George Clinton, N.Y.
Nicholas Gilman (S), N.H.

Mr. Matchin
Nahum Parker (S), N.H.
Jonathan Robinson (S), Vt.
Joseph B. Varnum, Mass.
James Fisk, Vt.
William Findley, Penn.
Peter Carleton, N.H.
Jedediah K. Smith, N.H.
James Witherell, Vt.
Ezekiel Bacon,[3] Mass.
Jacob Crowninshield,[4] Mass.

Mrs. Hamilton
James Turner (S), N.C.
David R. Williams, S.C.
Robert Marion, S.C.
John Taylor, S.C.
John Morrow, Va.
Nathaniel Macon, N.C.

Mr. Doyne
John Smith (S), N.Y.
Joseph Anderson (S), Tenn.
David Thomas, N.Y.
William Helms, N.J.
James I. Van Alen, N.Y.
John Russell, N.Y.
John Thompson, N.Y.
Josiah Masters, N.Y.
John Rhea, Tenn.
Peter Swart, N.Y.
Gordon S. Mumford, N.Y.
Benjamin Howard, Ky.
Reuben Humphrey, N.Y.
Thomas Newton, Jr., Va.
John Blake, Jr., N.Y.

Miss Finigan
Samuel White (S), Del.
James A. Bayard (S), Del.
Barent Gardenier, N.Y.
Joseph Lewis, Jr., Va.
Killian K. Van Rensselaer, N.Y.
Daniel Clark, Deleg., Terr. of Orleans
Nicholas Van Dyke,[5] Del.
Charles Goldsborough, Md.
James Kelly, Penn.

Mr. Myer
John Condit (S), N.J.
Aaron Kitchell (S), N.J.
Andrew Gregg (S), Penn.
Edward Tifflin (S), Ohio
Abram Trigg, Va.
Jeremiah Morrow, Ohio
Robert Jenkins, Penn.
William Butler, S.C.
James Holland, N.C.
Matthias Richards, Penn.
David Bard, Penn.

[3] Took his seat Nov. 2, 1807.
[4] Died Apr. 15, 1808.
[5] Took his seat Dec. 2, 1807.

John Hiester, Penn.
John Lambert, N.J.
Thomas Newbold, N.J.

Mr. Huddleston
Robert Brown, Penn.
Robert Whitehill, Penn.
John Clopton, Va.
John Pugh, Penn.
John Porter, Penn.
Ezra Darby,[6] N.J.
Henry Southard, N.J.
James Sloan, N.J.

Mrs. Suter
John Chandler, Mass.
Richard Cutts, Mass.

Mr. Speake
Benjamin Howard (S), R.I.
Ebenezer Seaver, Mass.
Isaiah L. Green, Mass.
John Smilie, Penn.
Josiah Dean, Mass.
Daniel Ilsley, Mass.
Isaac Wilbour, R.I.
Joseph Barker, Mass.
Nehemiah Knight, R.I.

President's House
John W. Eppes, Va.

Mr. O'Neal
John Milledge (S), Ga.
George Jones (S),[7] Ga.
Matthew Lyon, Ky.

Mr. Crawford
Thomas Sumter (S), S.C.
John Randolph, Va.
James M. Garnett, Va.
Edward Lloyd, Md.
Lemuel Sawyer, N.C.
Joseph Clay, Penn.

Mr. Rind
John Campbell, Md.

Mr. Semme
Philip B. Key, Md.

Mr. Florest
John Dawson, Va.
Roger Nelson, Md.

Mr. Love
John Love, Va.

Mr. Hellen
John Quincy Adams (S), Mass.

APPENDIX

Chauncey Goodrich (S),[8] Conn.
Archibald Van Horne, Md.
William Ely, Mass.
Edward St. Loe Livermore, Mass.
George Clinton, Jr., N.Y.
John Smith (S), Ohio

Elisha Mathewson (S),[9] R.I.
William B. Giles (S), Va.
Matthew Clay, Va.
John B. Jackson, Va.
John Smith, Va.

[6] Died Jan. 28, 1808. He was succeeded by Adam Boyd, who took his seat Apr. 1, 1808.
[7] Served until Nov. 7, 1807. He was succeeded by William H. Crawford, who took his seat Dec. 9, 1807.
[8] Took his seat Nov. 27, 1807.
[9] Took his seat Nov. 20, 1807.

CONGRESSIONAL DIRECTORY

ELEVENTH CONGRESS, FIRST SESSION
(May 22, 1809–June 28, 1809)

Mrs. Hamilton, Capitol Hill
James Turner (S), N.C.
William W. Bibb, Ga.
James Cochran, N.C.
William Kennedy, N.C.
Nathaniel Macon, N.C.
Robert Marion, S.C.
John Taylor, S.C.

Mr. Matchin, Capitol Hill
Elisha Mathewson (S), R.I.
Nahum Parker (S), N.H.
Jonathan Robinson (S), Vt.
William Findley, Penn.
Barzillai Gannett, Mass.
Gideon Gardner, Mass.
Samuel Shaw, Vt.
Joseph B. Varnum, Mass.

Mrs. Frost, Capitol Hill
Epaphroditus Champion, Conn.
Martin Chittenden, Vt.
John Davenport, Conn.
William Ely, Mass.
Timothy Pitkin, Conn.
Jonathan O. Moseley, Conn.
Richard Jackson, Jr., R.I.
William Stedman, Mass.
Lewis B. Sturges, Conn.
Benjamin Tallmadge, Conn.
Jabez Upham, Mass.

Mr. Long's Hotel, Capitol Hill
Howell Cobb, Ga.
John Dawson, Va.
Edwin Gray, Va.

Nicholas R. Moore, Md.
Roger Nelson, Md.

Mr. Stelle's Hotel, Capitol Hill
Dennis Smelt, Ga.
Archibald Van Horne, Md.

Mrs. Wilson, Capitol Hill
    House No. 1
Nicholas Gilman (S), N.H.
    House No. 2
The Washington Mess
James A. Bayard (S), Del.
Samuel White (S), Del.
James Breckinridge, Va.
John Campbell, Md.
James Emott, N.Y.
Charles Goldsborough, Md.
Thomas R. Gold, N.Y.
Herman Knickerbacker, N.Y.
Joseph Lewis, Jr., Va.
Robert Le Roy Livingston, N.Y.
Archibald McBryde, N.C.
Joseph Pearson, N.C.
John Stanly, N.C.
James Stephenson, Va.
Jacob Swoope, Va.
Nicholas Van Dyke, Del.
Killian K. Van Rensselaer, N.Y.

Miss Regan, Capitol Hill
Thomas Moore, S.C.
Robert Witherspoon, S.C.

Mr. Washington, Capitol Hill
Daniel Blaisdell, N.H.

NOTE: Copies are located at the Columbia Historical Society and the Library of Congress.

William Chamberlain, Vt.
Robert Jenkins, Penn.
William Milnor, Penn.
Vincent Mathews, N.Y.
Samuel Taggart, Mass.

Mr. Timm, Capitol Hill
Joseph Anderson (S), Tenn.
Jesse Franklin (S), N.C.
Andrew Gregg (S), Penn.
Michael Leib (S), Penn.
Jenkin Whiteside (S),[1] Tenn.
William Anderson, Penn.
Meshack Franklin, N.C.
Peterson Goodwyn, Va.
William Helms, N.J.
Robert Weakley, Tenn.

Mr. Claxton, Capitol Hill
Buckner Thruston (S), Ky.
Orchard Cook, Mass.
Thomas Kenan, N.C.
George Poindexter, Deleg., Miss. Terr.
John Rea, Penn.
Benjamin Say, Penn.
Lemuel Sawyer, N.C.

Mr. Coyle, Capitol Hill
Chauncey Goodrich (S), Conn.
Samuel W. Dana (S), Conn.

Mrs. Lane, Capitol Hill
Pleasant M. Miller, Tenn.
John Roane, Va.
Daniel Sheffey, Va.

Mrs. Meyer, Capitol Hill
John Condit (S),[2] N.J.
John Lambert (S), N.J.
Matthew Clay, Va.
James Cox, N.J.
Daniel Hiester, Penn.
Aaron Lyle, Penn.
Matthias Richards, Penn.
John Ross, Penn.
George Smith, Penn.

Mrs. Dawson, Capitol Hill
House in which she resides
John Gaillard (S), S.C.
William B. Giles (S), Va.
Samuel Smith (S), Md.
Jonathan Fisk, N.Y.
John Love, Va.
Alexander McKim, Md.
Peter B. Porter, N.Y.
George M. Troup, Ga.
House next door
John C. Chamberlain, N.H.
William Hale, N.H.
Nathaniel A. Haven, N.H.
Jonathan H. Hubbard, Vt.
Edward St. Loe Livermore, Mass.
James Wilson, N.H.
House opposite side of the way
John Lloyd (S), Mass.
Benjamin Pickman, Jr., Mass.
Josiah Quincy, Mass.

Mr. Doyne, Penn. Ave.
Obadiah German (S), N.Y.
Gurdon S. Mumford, N.Y.
John Nicholson, N.Y.
Thomas Sammons, N.Y.
John Thompson, N.Y.
Uri Tracy, N.Y.

Mr. Richard, Penn. Ave.
Francis Malbone (S),[3] R.I.
William Baylies,[4] Mass.
Elisha R. Potter, R.I.
Laban Wheaton, Mass.

Mr. Huddleston, Penn. Ave.
Adam Boyd, N.J.
Robert Brown, Penn.
William Crawford, Penn.
Jacob Hufty, N.J.
Thomas Newbold, N.J.
John Porter, Penn.
Ebenezer Sage, N.Y.
Henry Southard, N.J.
Robert Whitehill, Penn.

[1] Elected to fill the vacancy caused by the resignation of Daniel Smith, and took his seat May 26, 1809.
[2] Took his seat May 24, 1809.
[3] Died June 4, 1809.
[4] Served until June 28, 1809. He was succeeded by Charles Turner, Jr., who contested his election and took his seat June 28, 1809.

Finigan, Penn. Ave.
Richard Brent (S), Va.
Burwell Bassett, Va.
William A. Burwell, Va.
Thomas Newton, Jr., Va.

Mr. Lindsay, Penn. Ave.
William Butler, S.C.
Henry Crist, Ky.
Joseph Desha, Ky.
James Holland, N.C.
Richard M. Johnson, Ky.
Samuel McKee, Ky.
Jeremiah Morrow, Ohio
Samuel Smith, Penn.

Mr. Speak, Penn. Ave.
Return J. Meigs, Jr. (S), Ohio
Joseph Calhoun, S.C.
John Rhea, Tenn.
Ebenezer Seaver, Mass.
John Smilie, Penn.

Mrs. Suter, F. St.
Willis Alston, N.C.
Lemuel J. Alston, S.C.
John G. Jackson, Va.

President's House
Richard Cutts, Mass.

Mr. Woodside, Penn. Ave.
John Brown, Md.

Mr. O'Neal, Penn Ave.
John Pope (S), Ky.
Ezekiel Bacon, Mass.
John W. Eppes, Va.
Thomas Gholson, Jr., Va.
Benjamin Howard, Ky.
Matthew Lyon, Ky.

Mr. Nourse, Georgetown
John Smith, Va.

Mrs. Thompson, Penn. Ave.
James Hillhouse (S), Conn.
Timothy Pickering (S), Mass.

Mr. Crawford, Georgetown
Philip B. Key, Md.
Julien de L. Poydras, Deleg., Terr. of
    Orleans
John Randolph, Va.
Richard Stanford, N.C.

Mr. Florist, Georgetown
Barent Gardenier, N.Y.

APPENDIX

John Milledge (S), Ga.
William H. Crawford (S), Ga.
Philip Reed (S), Md.
John Montgomery, Md.
Ezekiel Whitman, Mass.
John Smith (S), N.Y.
N.Y.[5]
Erastus Root, N.Y.

Stanley Griswold (S),[6] Ohio
David Bard, Penn.
Thomas Sumter (S), S.C.
Richard Winn, S.C.
Stephen R. Bradley (S), Vt.
John Clopton, Va.
Walter Jones, Va.
Wilson C. Nicholas, Va.

[5] William Denning resigned before qualifying. Samuel Mitchill was elected to fill the vacancy, and took his seat in the third session of this Congress.
[6] Took his seat June 2, 1809.

CONGRESSIONAL DIRECTORY

TWELFTH CONGRESS, FIRST SESSION
(November 4, 1811 – July 6, 1812)

Mrs. Hamilton, Capitol Hill
Josiah Bartlett, Jr., N.H.
Samuel Dinsmoor, N.H.
John A. Harper, N.H.
George Sullivan, N.H.

Mrs. Digg, Capitol Hill
Robert Le Roy Livingston,[1] N.Y.

Mr. Matchin, Capitol Hill
Jonathan Robinson (S), Vt.
Lewis Condict, N.J.
James Fisk, Vt.
George C. Maxwell, N.J.
Thomas Newbold, N.J.
Benjamin Pond, N.Y.
John Roane, Va.
Samuel Shaw, Vt.
Charles Turner, Jr., Mass.
William Widgery, Mass.

Miss Finigan, Capitol Hill
James A. Bayard (S), Del.
Outerbridge Horsey (S), Del.
Harmanus Bleecker, N.Y.
Thomas R. Gold, N.Y.
Henry M. Ridgely, Del.

Mr. Claxton, Capitol Hill
Stevenson Archer, Md.
Ezekiel Bacon, Mass.
Burwell Bassett, Va.
William Blackledge, N.C.
Edwin Gray, Va.
Felix Grundy, Tenn.

William R. King, N.C.
Samuel L. Mitchill, N.Y.
Anthony New, Ky.
Stephen Ormsby, Ky.
Israel Pickens, N.C.
William Rodman, Penn.
Adam Seybert, Penn.
Peleg Tallman, Mass.

Mr. Smith, Capitol Hill
Elias Earle, S.C.
Abner Lacock, Penn.
Jonathan Roberts, Penn.

Mr. Bailey, Capitol Hill
Philip Reed (S), Md.
Thomas Gholson, Jr., Va.
Peterson Goodwyn, Va.
George Poindexter, Deleg., Miss. Terr.
John Taliaferro,[2] Va.

Mr. Coyle, Capitol Hill
Samuel W. Dana (S), Conn.
Chauncey Goodrich (S), Conn.
James Milnor, Penn.
Timothy Pitkin, Conn.
Josiah Quincy, Mass.

Mr. Burch, Capitol Hill
Abijah Bigelow, Mass.
Elijah Brigham, Mass.
Epaphroditus Champion, Conn.
Martin Chittenden, Vt.
William Ely, Mass.
Asa Fitch, N.Y.

NOTE: A copy is located at the Columbia Historical Society.
[1] Resigned May 6, 1812.
[2] Took his seat Dec. 2, 1811, after successfully contesting the election of John P. Hungerford, who served until Nov. 29, 1811.

Lyman Law, Conn.
Jonathan O. Moseley, Conn.
Lewis B. Sturges, Conn.

Mrs. Dowson, No. 1, Capitol Hill
John Gaillard (S), S.C.
William A. Burwell, Va.
Joseph Kent, Md.
Alexander McKim, Md.
Peter B. Porter, N.Y.
Silas Stow, N.Y.
George M. Troup, Ga.
Robert Wright, Md.

Mrs. Dowson, No. 2, Capitol Hill
William H. Crawford (S), Ga.
Charles Tait (S), Ga.
John Taylor (S), S.C.
James Turner (S), N.C.
William W. Bibb, Ga.
Howell Cobb, Ga.
Bolling Hall, Ga.
Nathaniel Macon, N.C.
David R. Williams, S.C.

Mrs. Dowson, No. 3, Capitol Hill
George M. Bibb (S), Ky.
Henry Clay, Ky.
Langdon Cheves, S.C.
John C. Calhoun, S.C.
William Lowndes, S.C.
Matthew Clay, Va.

Mrs. Wilson
Aylett Hawes, Va.
Thomas Newton, Jr., Va.
James Pleasants, Va.
Thomas Wilson,[3] Va.

Miss Heyer, Capitol Hill
John Davenport, Conn.
James Emott, N.Y.
Richard Jackson, Jr., R.I.
Elisha R. Potter, R.I.
Benjamin Tallmadge, Conn.

Mrs. Wadsworth, Capitol Hill
William Reed, Mass.
Samuel Taggart, Mass.

Mrs. Lane, N.J. Ave.
William Butler, S.C.
Richard Winn, S.C.

Mr. Ball, N.J. Ave.
Willis Alston, N.C.
Roger Davis, Penn.
Bolling Hall, Ga.
John Hyneman, Penn.

Davis' Hotel, Penn. Ave.
John Condit (S), N.J.
John Dawson, Va.
William Findley, Penn.
Aaron Lyle, Penn.
Samuel McKee, Ky.
Jeremiah Morrow, Ohio
William Piper, Penn.
George Smith, Penn.

Mr. Huddleston, Penn. Ave.
John Lambert (S), N.J.
Robert Brown, Penn.
Adam Boyd, N.J.
David Bard, Penn.
William Crawford, Penn.
Jacob Hufty, N.J.
James Morgan, N. J.
Evenezer Sage, N. Y.
Robert Whitehill, Penn.

Mr. Boyd, Penn. Ave.
John Pope (S), Ky.

Mr. Stelle, Penn. Ave.
Joseph Anderson (S), Tenn.
George W. Campbell (S), Tenn.
Jesse Franklin (S), N.C.
Jeremiah B. Howell (S), Penn.
Michael Leib (S), Penn.
William Anderson, Penn.
Meshack Franklin, N.C.

Mrs. Doyne, Penn. Ave.
Obadiah German (S), N.Y.
John Smith (S), N.Y.
Danial Avery, N.Y.
Thomas B. Cooke, N.Y.
William Paulding, Jr., N.Y.

[3] Also listed at Crawford's Hotel.

Lemuel Sawyer, N.C.
Thomas Sammons, N.Y.
Uri Tracy, N.Y.

Mr. Varnum, Penn. Ave.
Joseph B. Varnum (S), Mass.

Mr. Speake, Penn. Ave.
Isaiah L. Green, Mass.
Obed Hall, N.H.
Jonathan Jennings, Deleg., Ind. Terr.
Arunah Metcalf, N.Y.
Ebenezer Seaver, Mass.
John Smilie, Penn.
William Strong, Vt.

Dr. Catlet, E St.
Joseph Desha, Ky.
Richard M. Johnson, Ky.

Rhode's Hotel, Penn. Ave.
Andrew Gregg (S), Penn.
John Rhea, Tenn.
John Sevier, Tenn.

Mrs. Suter, F St.
Stephen R. Bradley (S), Vt.
Charles Cutts (S), N.H.
Alexander Campbell (S), Ohio
Thomas Worthington (S), Ohio
Peter Little, Md.

Mr. O'Neale, Penn. Ave.
Nicholas Gilman (S), N.H.
Samuel Smith (S), Md.
Thomas Blount,[4] N.C.
Pierre Van Cortlandt, Jr., N.Y.

Robert Brent, Penn. Ave.
Joseph Pearson, N.C.

Mr. Woodside, Seven Buildings
James Lloyd (S), Mass.
Samuel Ringgold, Md.

Mrs. Thompson, Seven Buildings
Richard Brent (S), Va.
James Breckinridge, Va.

Crawford's Hotel, Georgetown
John Baker, Va.
Charles Goldsborough, Md.
Philip B. Key, Md.
Joseph Lewis, Jr., Va.
Hugh Nelson, Va.
John Randolph, Va.
Richard Stanford, N.C.
Thomas Wilson,[5] Va.

Mr. Turner, Georgetown
William B. Giles (S), Va.

Mr. Nourse, Georgetown
John Smith, Va.

APPENDIX

Philip Stuart, Md.
Francis Carr,[6] Mass.
Richard Cutts, Mass.
William M. Richardson, Mass.
Leban Wheaton, Mass.
Leonard White, Mass.
James Cochran, N.C.

Archibald McBryde, N.C.
Joseph Lefever, Penn.
William Hunter (S)[7], R.I.
Thomas Moore, S.C.
John Clopton, Va.
William McCoy, Va.
Daniel Sheffey, Va.

[4] Died Feb. 7, 1812.
[5] Also listed at Mrs. Wilson's.
[6] Elected to fill the vacancy caused by the failure of Barzillai Gannet to qualify, and took his seat June 3, 1812. Gannet had resigned in 1812.
[7] Took his seat Nov. 25, 1811.

CONGRESSIONAL DIRECTORY

TWELFTH CONGRESS, SECOND SESSION
(November 2, 1812 – March 3, 1813)

Mrs. Hamilton, Capitol Hill
Joseph Anderson (S), Tenn.
Jesse Franklin (S), N.C.
William Anderson, Penn.
William Butler, S.C.
James Cochran, N.C.
Elias Earle, S.C.
Meshack Franklin, N.C.
Jonathan Roberts, Penn.
Thomas Wilson, Va.

Mr. Burch, Capitol Hill
Jonathan Robinson (S), Vt.
Benjamin Pond, N.Y.
Francis Carr, Mass.
Joseph Desha, Ky.
John A. Harper, N.H.
Thomas Moore, S.C.
John Roane, Va.
William Widgery, Mass.

Mr. Rhode, Capitol Hill
Epaphroditus Champion, Conn.
Martin Chittenden, Vt.
Elijah Brigham, Mass.
Abijah Bigelow, Mass.
William Ely, Mass.
Asa Fitch, N.Y.
Lyman Law, Conn.
Jonathan O. Moseley, Conn.

Tomlinson's Hotel, Capitol Hill
Matthew Clay, Va.
Lemuel Sawyer, N.C.

Mr. Ball, Capitol Hill
James Fisk, Vt.
John M. Hyneman, Penn.

Mrs. Hamilton, Jr.
John Davenport, Conn.
Lewis B. Sturges, Conn.
Samuel Taggart, Mass.
Laban Wheaton, Mass.

Mr. Claxton, Capitol Hill
Stevenson Archer, Md.
Burwell Basset, Va.
William Blackledge, N.C.
Ezekiel Bacon, Mass.
Felix Grundy, Tenn.
William R. King, N.C.
Samuel L. Mitchill, N.Y.
Anthony New, Ky.
Stephen Ormsby, Ky.
Israel Pickens, N.C.
William Rodman, Penn.
Adam Seybert, Penn.

Mrs. Bailey, Capitol Hill
John Dawson, Va.
Peterson Goodwyn, Va.
George Poindexter, Deleg., Miss Terr.
John Taliaferro, Va.

Mr. Coyl
Samuel W. Dana (S), Conn.
Chauncey Goodrich (S), Conn.
James Milnor, Penn.
Timothy Pitkin, Conn.

Miss Hyer
James Emott, N.Y.
Richard Jackson, Jr., R.I.
Elisha R. Potter, R.I.
William Reed, Mass.
Benjamin Tallmadge, Conn.

NOTE: A copy is located at the American Antiquarian Society.

Mrs. Wadsworth, Capitol Hill
William Hunter (S), R.I.
Harmanus Bleecker, N.Y.
John Baker, Va.
Archibald McBryde, N.C.
Henry M. Ridgely, Del.

Mrs. Bushby, Capitol Hill
Philip Reed (S), Md.
Willis Alston, N.C.
John C. Calhoun, S.C.
Lewis Condict, N. J.
Thomas Gholson, Jr., Va.
Bolling Hall, Ga.
James Pleasants, Va.

Mrs. Dowson, No. 1, Capitol Hill
John Gaillard (S), S.C.
William B. Giles (S), Va.
Joseph Kent, Md.
Alexander McKim, Md.
Silas Stow, N.Y.
Robert Wright, Md.

Mrs. Dowson, No. 2, Capitol Hill
William H. Crawford (S), Ga.
Charles Tait (S), Ga.
John Taylor (S), S.C.
Jesse Turner (S), N.C.
William W. Bibb, Ga.
Nathaniel Macon, N.C.
David R. Williams, S.C.

Mrs. Dowson, No. 3, Capitol Hill
Henry Clay, Ky.
Samuel Ringgold, Md.

Mr. Lindsey, N.J. Ave.
Abner Lacock, Penn.

Mrs. Lane
Richard Winn, S.C.

Mr. Dalton, Navy Yard
Leonard White, Mass.

Alexander's Buildings (Near the Marine Barracks)
Philip Stuart, Md.

Mrs. Doyn, Penn. Ave.
Stephen R. Bradley (S), Vt.
Alexander Campbell (S), Ohio
Obadiah German (S), N.Y.
Jeremiah B. Howell (S), R.I.
Michael Leib (S), Penn.
John Smith (S), N.Y.
Daniel Avery, N.Y.
Thomas B. Cooke, N.Y.
Aylett Hawes, Va.
Thomas Sammons, N.Y.
Uri Tracy, N.Y.

Davis' Hotel, Penn. Ave.
No. 1
John Condit (S), N.J.
Allan B. Magruder (S),[1] La.
William Findley, Penn.
Aaron Lyle, Penn.
Samuel McKee, Ky.
Jeremiah Morrow, Ohio
Thomas Newbold, N.J.
George Smith, Penn.
No. 2
James Lloyd (S), Mass.
Josiah Quincy, Mass.

Mr. Huddleston, Penn. Ave.
John Lambert (S), N.J.
Robert Brown, Penn.
Adam Boyd, N.J.
David Bard, Penn.
William Crawford, Penn.
Jacob Hufty, N.J.
George C. Maxwell, N.J.
James Morgan, N.J.
Ebenezer Sage, N.Y.
Robert Whitehill, Penn.

Mr. Varnum, opposite the Centre Market
Joseph B. Varnum (S), Mass.
Charles Turner, Jr., Mass.
William M. Richardson, Mass.

Rev. Brown, opposite the Centre Market
John Clopton, Va.

Mrs. Dinmore, Penn. Ave.
Roger Davis, Penn.
Isaiah L. Green, Mass.

[1] Took his seat Nov. 18, 1812.

Arunah Metcalf, N.Y.
Samuel Shaw, Vt.
Ebenezer Seaver, Mass.
John Smilie,[2] Penn.

Mr. Van Zandt, Penn. Ave.
Charles Cutts (S), N.H.

Mr. Hoyt, Corner of E and Eleventh St.
Samuel Dinsmoor, N.H.
Obed Hall, N.H.
Jonathan Jennings, Deleg., Ind. Terr.
William Strong, Vt.

Mrs. Carter, F St.
George M. Troup, Ga.

Mrs. Suter, F St.
Andrew Gregg (S), Penn.
William McCoy, Va.
John Rhea, Tenn.
Peter Little, Md.
John Sevier, Tenn.

Mr. Wheaton
Thomas Newton, Jr., Va.

President's House
Richard Cutts, Mass.

Mr. O'Neale, Penn. Ave.
Nicholas Gilman (S), N.H.
Samuel Smith (S), Md.
Thomas R. Gold, N.Y.
Charles Goldsborough, Md.
Pierre Van Cortlandt, Jr., N.Y.

Mrs. Thompson, Penn. Ave.
Outerbridge Horsey (S), Del.
James Breckinridge, Va.
Hugh Nelson, Va.

Crawford's Hotel, Georgetown
John Randolph, Va.
Philip B. Key, Md.
Joseph Lewis, Jr., Va.
Richard Stanford, N.C.

Mr. Catlet, Bridge St., Georgetown
Richard M. Johnson, Ky.

Mrs. Coolidge, Bridge St., Georgetown
Langdon Cheves, S.C.
William Lowndes, S.C.

Mr. Nourse, above Georgetown
John Smith, Va.

APPENDIX

James A. Bayard (S), Del.
William Barnett,[3] Ga.
George M. Bibb (S), Ga.
John Pope (S), Ky.
Thomas Posey (S),[4] La.
James Brown (S),[5] La.
Thomas B. Robertson,[6] La.
Isaiah L. Green, Mass.
Peleg Tallman, Mass.
Josiah Bartlett, Jr., N.H.

George Sullivan, N.H.
Thomas P. Grosvenor,[7] N.Y.
William Paulding, Jr., N.Y.
Peter B. Porer, N.Y.
William Kennedy,[8] N.C.
Joseph Pearson, N.C.
Thomas Worthington (S), Ohio
Joseph Lefever, Penn.
William Piper, Penn.
George W. Campbell (S), Tenn.

[2] Died Dec. 30, 1812.
[3] Took his seat Nov. 17, 1812.
[4] Appointed to fill the vacancy caused by resignation of John N. Destrehan, and took his seat Dec. 7, 1812.
[5] Elected to fill the vacancy caused by resignation of John N. Destrehan, and took his seat Feb. 5, 1813.
[6] Took his seat Dec. 23, 1812.
[7] Took his seat Jan. 30, 1813.
[8] Took his seat Jan. 30, 1813.

Richard Brent (S), Va.
William A. Burwell, Va.
Edwin Gray, Va.
Daniel Sheffey, Va.

Shadrack Bond,[9] Deleg., Ill. Terr.[10]
Edward Hempstead,[11] Deleg., Terr. of Mo.[12]

[9] Took his seat Dec. 3, 1812.

[10] Formed by an act approved Feb. 3, 1809, from a portion of Indiana Territory and from lands originally ceded to the United States by the state of Virginia, and granted a delegate in Congress.

[11] Took his seat Jan. 4, 1813.

[12] Formed by an act approved June 4, 1812, from lands ceded by France to the United States by the Treaty of Paris of Apr. 30, 1803, theretofore known as the "District of Louisiana," and granted a delegate in Congress.

CONGRESSIONAL DIRECTORY

THIRTEENTH CONGRESS, FIRST SESSION
(May 24, 1813–August 2, 1813)

Capitol Hill, near Tomlinson's Hotel
Henry Clay, Ky.

Mrs. Hamilton, Senior, Capitol Hill
Joseph Anderson (S), Tenn.
William Anderson, Penn.
Elias Earle, S.C.
Samuel Farrow, S.C.
Thomas K. Harris, Tenn.
James Kilbourne, Ohio
Thomas Montgomery, Ky.

Mr. Rhode, Capitol Hill
Abijah Bigelow, Mass.
Elijah Brigham, Mass.
Epaphroditus Champion, Conn.
William Ely, Mass.
Lyman Law, Conn.
Jonathan O. Moseley, Conn.
Timothy Pitkin, Conn.
Lewis B. Sturges, Conn.

Mr. Burch, Capitol Hill
Jesse Bledsoe (S), Ky.
James Caldwell, Ohio
John Desha, Ky.
John M. Hyneman, Penn.
John Roane, Va.

Tomlinson's Hotel, Capitol Hill
John P. Hungerford, Va.
William S. Smith, N.Y.
Abiel Wood, Mass.

Long's Hotel, Capitol Hill
Dudley Chase (S), Vt.

Jonathan Robinson (S), Vt.
Ezra Butler, Vt.
Charles Rich, Vt.
Richard Skinner, Vt.

Mr. Ball, Capitol Hill
John Lambert (S), N.J.
James Fisk, Vt.
Jacob Hufty, N.J.

Mrs. Queen, Capitol Hill
Alexander Boyd, N.Y.
George Bradbury, Mass.
Bradbury Cilley, N.H.
Daniel Dewey, Mass.
William Hale, N.H.
Samuel M. Hopkins, N.Y.
Jacob Markell, N.Y.
Hosea Moffitt, N.Y.
Samuel Taggart, Mass.
Joel Thompson, N.Y.
Roger Vose, N.H.

Mrs. Mather, Capitol Hill
Samuel W. Dana (S), Conn.
Nathaniel Ruggles, Mass.

Mr. Elliott, Capitol Hill
Robert Whitehill, Penn.

Mrs. Hamilton, Junior, Capitol Hill
William Baylies, Mass.
John Reed, Mass.
Samuel Smith, N.H.
Laban Wheaton, Mass.

NOTE: Copies are located at the American Antiquarian Society and the Philadelphia Public Library.

Jeduthun Wilcox, N.H.
John Wilson, Mass.

Mr. Claxton, Capitol Hill
Stevenson Archer, Md.
John H. Bowen, Tenn.
Peter Forney, N.C.
Felix Grundy, Tenn.
Parry W. Humphreys, Tenn.
John Kershaw, S.C.
William R. King, N.C.
Stephen Ormsby,[1] Ky.
Israel Pickens, N.C.
John Rea,[2] Penn.
Adam Seybert, Penn.
Solomon P. Sharp, Ky.

Dr. J. Ewell, Capitol Hill
Lewis Condict, N.J.
John Dawson, Va.

Mrs. Hyer, Capitol Hill
Egbert Benson, N.Y.
John Davenport, Conn.
Richard Jackson, Jr., R.I.
Thomas J. Oakley, N.Y.
Jotham Post, Jr., N.Y.
Elisha R. Potter, R.I.
William Reed, Mass.
Samuel Sherwood, N.Y.
Zebulon R. Shipherd, N.Y.
Benjamin Tallmadge, Conn.
Elisha J. Winter, N.Y.

Mrs. Wadsworth, Capitol Hill
William Hunter (S), R.I.
Timothy Pickering, Mass.
Thomas Cooper, Del.
Moss Kent, N.Y.
Cyrus King, Mass.
Nathaniel W. Howell, N.Y.
James Geddes, N.Y.
Henry M. Ridgely, Del.

Mr. Coyle, Capitol Hill
David Daggett (S), Conn.
William Coxe, N.J.
James Schureman, N.J.
Richard Stockton, N.J.

Artemas Ward, Jr., Mass.
Daniel Webster, N.H.

Mrs. Dowson, No. 1, Capitol Hill
John Gaillard (S), S.C.
William A. Burwell, Va.
John J. Chappell, S.C.
David R. Evans, S.C.
Theodore Gourdin, S.C.
Joseph Kent, Md.
Alexander McKim, Md.
Nicholas R. Moore, Md.
Robert Wright, Md.

Mrs. Dowson, No. 2, Capitol Hill
William B. Bulloch (S), Ga.
Charles Tait (S), Ga.
John Taylor (S), S.C.
James Turner (S), N.C.
William W. Bibb, Ga.
John Forsyth, Ga.
Nathaniel Macon, N.C.
Thomas Telfair, Ga.

Mrs. Dowson, No. 3, Capitol Hill
James Brown (S), La.
Eligius Fromentin (S), La.
Langdon Cheves, S.C.
William Lowndes, S.C.
Thomas B. Robertson, La.

Mrs. Bushby, Capitol Hill
Richard Brent (S), Va.
Willis Alston, S.C.
William Barnett, Ga.
John C. Calhoun, S.C.
Meshack Franklin, N.C.
Bolling Hall, Ga.
Joseph Kerr, Va.
William H. Murfree, N.C.
James Pleasants, Va.
Jonathan Roberts, Penn.
Bartlett Yancey, N.C.

Mr. Lindsay, N.J. Ave.
Abner Lacock (S), Penn.
Isaac Griffin, Penn.
Isaac Smith, Penn.
Thomas Wilson,[3] Penn.

[1] Took his seat May 28, 1813.
[2] Took his seat May 28, 1813.
[3] Took his seat May 28, 1813.

Mrs. Lane, N.J. Ave.
Francis White, Va.

Mr. Dunn, Eastern Branch
Jared Irwin, Penn.

Near The Marine Barrack
Philip Stuart, Md.

Mr. Brush, Penn. Ave.
Daniel Avery, N.Y.
Oliver C. Comstock, N.Y.
John Culpepper, N.C.
Peter Denoyelles, N.Y.
Aylett Hawes, Va.
Daniel Sheffey, Va.

Davis' Hotel, Penn. Ave.
John Condit (S), N.J.
Jeremiah Morrow (S), Ohio
Shadrack Bond, Deleg., Ill. Terr.
James Clark, Ky.
William P. Duvall, Ky.
William Findley, Penn.
Jonathan Fisk, N.Y.
John Gloninger, Penn.
Jonathan Jennings, Deleg., Ind. Terr.
John Lovett, N.Y.
Aaron Lyle, Penn.
Samuel McKee, Ky.
John McLean, Ohio
Adamson Tannehill, Penn.
Thomas Ward, N.J.

Mr. Huddleston, Penn. Ave.
Davis Bard, Penn.
Robert Brown, Penn.
John Clopton, Va.
John Conrad, Penn.
William Crawford, Penn.
Samuel D. Ingham, Penn.
John Lefferts, N.Y.
Ebenezer Sage, N.Y.

Mr. Varnum, near the Centre Market
Joseph B. Varnum (S), Mass.

Levi Hubbard, Mass.
James Parker, Mass.

Mr. Brent, near the Potomac Bridge
Joseph Pearson, N.C.

Mrs. Odlin, Penn. Ave.
Obadiah German (S), N.Y.
Michael Lieb (S), Penn.
John Alexander, Ohio
William C. Bradley, Vt.
John W. Taylor, N.Y.

Mr. Hoyt, Eleventh St., West
William Strong, Vt.

Mrs. Dinmore, Penn. Ave.
Roger Davis, Penn.

Mrs. Suter, F St.
John G. Jackson, Va.
William McCoy, Va.
John Rhea Tenn.
John Sevier, Tenn.

Mrs. Carter, F St.
George M. Troup, Ga.

Mrs. Clark, F St.
Thomas Gholson, Jr., Va.
Thomas Newton, Jr., Va.

Mr. Woodside, Penn. Ave.
Christopher Gore (S),[4] Mass.
Rufus King (S), N.Y.

Mr. O'Neale, Penn. Ave.
Nicholas Gilman (S), N.H.
Robert H. Goldsborough (S),[5] Md.
Samuel Smith (S), Md.
John W. Eppes, Va.
Charles Goldsborough, Md.
Samuel Ringgold, Md.

Mrs. Wilson, Penn. Ave.
George W. Campbell (S), Tenn.
Charles Cutts (S),[6] N.H.

[4] Took his seat May 28, 1813.
[5] Took his seat May 27, 1813.
[6] Appointed to fill vacancy in term commencing Mar. 4, 1813, there having been no election, and took his seat May 24, 1813. Jeremiah Mason was elected to fill the vacancy, and took his seat June 21, 1813.

Jeremiah B. Howell (S), R.I.
David Stone (S), N.C.

Mr. Rush, Penn. Ave.
Charles J. Ingersoll, Penn.

Mr. Nourse, I St., near Georgetown
John Smith, Va.

Crawford's Hotel, Georgetown
Thomas Worthington (S), Ohio
Thomas M. Bayly, Va.
James Breckinridge, Va.

Hugh Caperton, Va.
Samuel Davis, Mass.
William Gaston, N.C.
Thomas P. Grosevenor, N.Y.
Alexander C. Hanson, Md.
William Kennedy, N.C.
Joseph Lewis, Jr., Va.
Morris S. Miller, N.Y.
Hugh Nelson, Va.
Richard Stanford, N.C.

Mrs. Coolidge, Georgetown
Outerbridge Horsey (S), Del.

APPENDIX

William H. Wells (S),[7] Del.
George M. Bibb (S), Ky.
Samuel Hopkins, Ky.
Richard M. Johnson, Ky.
William M. Richardson, Mass.
John M. Bowers,[8] N.Y.
Abraham J. Hasbrouck, N.Y.
Reasin Beall,[9] Ohio

William Creighton, Jr.,[10] Ohio
Hugh Glasgow, Penn.
William Piper, Penn.
Peterson Goodwyn, Va.
James Johnson, Va.
William Lattimore, Deleg., Miss. Terr.
Edward Hempstead, Deleg., Terr. of Mo.

[7] Took his seat June 10, 1813.
[8] Took his seat June 21, 1813.
[9] Took his seat June 8, 1813.
[10] Took his seat June 15, 1813.

CONGRESSIONAL DIRECTORY

THIRTEENTH CONGRESS, SECOND SESSION
(December 6, 1813–April 18, 1814)

North of the Capitol, near Mr. Brent's
Henry Clay,[1] Ky.

Mr. Ball, East Capitol St., near the Market House, Capitol Hill
James Fisk, Vt.
Charles Rich,[2] Vt.
Richard Skinner,[3] Vt.

Mr. Bayly, Carroll's Row, Capitol Hill
James Clark, Ky.
Theodore Gourdin, S.C.
Peterson Goodwyn, Va.
Thomas Montgomery, Ky.

Mr. Brush, Penn. Ave.
John Culpepper, N.C.
Aylett Hawes, Va.
James Johnson, Va.
Thomas Newton, Jr., Va.

Mr. Burch, North B St., near Tomlinson's Hotel, Capitol Hill
Bradbury Cilley, N.H.
Daniel Dewey,[4] Mass.
James Geddes, N.Y.
Samuel M. Hopkins, N.Y.
Nathaniel W. Howell, N.Y.
Moss Kent, N.Y.
Timothy Pickering, Mass.
Zebulon R. Shipherd, N.Y.

Mr. Beall, Navy Yard
William Anderson,[5] Penn.

Mrs. Bushby, Law's Houses, N.J. Ave., near the Bank, Capitol Hill
Thomas M. Bayly, Va.
Ezra Butler, Vt.
Hugh Caperton, Va.
Oliver C. Comstock, N.Y.
Peter Denoyelles, N.Y.
William Kennedy, N.C.
William Lattimore, Deleg., Miss. Terr.
Hugh Nelson, Va.
William Strong, Vt.

Mr. Brown, near General Post Office
John Clopton, Va.

Mr. Claxton, South B St., Capitol Hill
Willis Alston, N.C.
Stevenson Archer, Md.
John H. Bowen, Tenn.
John C. Calhoun, S.C.
Edward Crouch, Penn.
Peter Forney, N.C.
Felix Grundy, Tenn.
Parry W. Humphreys, Tenn.
William R. King, N.C.
Stephen B. Ormsby, Ky.
Israel Pickens, N.C.
John Rea, Penn.

NOTE: A copy is located at the American Antiquarian Society.
[1] Resigned Jan. 19, 1814, to accept a "special and important diplomatic mission."
[2] Also listed at Mrs. Oldin's.
[3] Also listed at Mrs. Oldin's.
[4] Resigned Feb. 24, 1814, having been appointed justice of the supreme judicial court of Mass.
[5] Also listed at Mrs. Hamilton's (the Elder).

Adam Seybert, Penn.
Solomon P. Sharp, Ky.

Mr. Coyle, South B St., Capitol Hill
David Daggett (S), Conn.
William Coxe, N.J.
John Davenport, Conn.
Cyrus King, Mass.
Timothy Pitkin, Conn.
James Schureman, N.J.
Richard Stockton, N.J.
Daniel Webster, N.H.

Mrs. Carter, F St.
George M. Troup, Ga.

Crawford's Hotel, Georgetown
Christopher Gore (S), Mass.
Rufus King (S), N.Y.
Thomas Worthington (S), Ohio
William Gaston, N.C.
Joseph Lewis, Jr., Va.
Richard Stockton, N.C.
Samuel Davis, N.Y.

Davis' Hotel, Penn. Ave.
Jeremiah Morrow (S), Ohio
John Alexander, Ohio
William Creighton, Jr., Ohio
John Dawson,[6] Va.
William P. Duvall, Ky.
William Findley, Penn.
Abraham J. Hasbrouck, N.Y.
Edward Hempstead, Deleg., Mo. Terr.
John Lovett, N.Y.
Aaron Lyle, Penn.
Samuel McKee, Ky.
John McLean, Ohio
William Piper, Penn.
Adamson Tannehill, Penn.
Thomas Ward, N.J.

Mrs. Dinmore, Penn. Ave.
Jonathan Robinson (S), Vt.
Roger Davis, Penn.

Mr. Dunn, near the Eastern Branch
Jared Irwin, Penn.

Mrs. Dowson, No. 1, Law's Houses, N.J.
Ave., near Bank, Capitol Hill
John Gaillard (S), S.C.
William B. Giles (S), Va.
William A. Burwell, Va.
Joseph Kent, Md.
Alexander McKim, Md.
Nicholas R. Moore, Md.
Robert Wright, Md.

Mrs. Dowson, No. 2, Law's Houses, N.J.
Ave., near Bank, Capitol Hill
William W. Bibb (S), Ga.
Richard Brent (S), Va.
Charles Tait (S), Ga.
John Taylor (S), S.C.
James Turner (S), N.C.
John Forsyth, Ga.
Nathaniel Macon, N.C.
Thomas Telfair, Ga.
Bartlett Yancy, N.C.

Mrs. Dowson, No. 3, Law's Houses, N.J.
Ave., near Bank, Capitol Hill
George M. Bibb (S), Ky.
Jesse Bledsoe (S), Ky.
James Brown (S), La.
Thomas B. Robertson, La.

Dr. J. Ewell's, N.J. Ave., opposite Rap-
ine's Bookstore, Capitol Hill
John W. Eppes, Va.
William H. Murfree, N.C.
James Pleasants, Va.

Mrs. Hamilton (the Elder), Washington's
Houses, North of the Capitol
Joseph Anderson (S), Tenn.
Eligius Fromentin (S), La.
William Anderson,[7] Penn.
Thomas Gholson, Jr., Va.
Thomas K. Harris, Tenn.
James Kilbourne, Ohio

Mrs. Hamilton (the Younger), Penn.
Ave., opposite the Bank, Capitol Hill
William Baylies, Mass.
John Reed, Mass.
Roger Vose, N.H.

[6] Died Mar. 31, 1814.
[7] Also listed at Mr. Beall's.

Laban Wheaton, Mass.
Jeduthun Wilcox, N.H.
John Wilson, Mass.

Mr. Hanson, Georgetown
Thomas P. Grosvenor, N.Y.
Alexander C. Hanson, Md.

Miss Heyer, near the Bank, Capitol Hill
Richard Jackson, Jr., R.I.
Thomas J. Oakley, N.Y.
Jotham Post, Jr., N.Y.
Elisha R. Potter, R.I.
Samuel Sherwood, N.Y.
Benjamin Tallmadge, Conn.

Mr. Huddleston, Penn. Ave., near Davis's Hotel
Daniel Avery, N.Y.
David Bard, Penn.
Robert Brown, Penn.
John Conrad, Penn.
William Crawford, Penn.
Hugh Glasgow, Penn.
Samuel D. Ingham, Penn.
John Lefferts, N.Y.
Ebenezer Sage, N.Y.
Daniel Udree, Penn.
James Whitehill, Penn.

Mrs. Lane, Law's Ten Buildings, N.J. Ave.
Francis White, Va.

Mr. Lindsay, Law's Ten Buildings, N.J. Ave.
Abner Lacock (S), Penn.
Reasin Beall, Ohio
Isaac Griffin, Penn.
Jonathan Jennings, Deleg., Ind. Terr.
Isaac Smith, Penn.
Thomas Wilson, Penn.

Mr. Machen, North B St., near Tomlinson's, Capitol Hill
Langdon Cheves, S.C.

Mrs. McCardle, Carroll's Row, Capitol Hill
Alexander Boyd, N.Y.
Samuel Taggart, Mass.
Joel Thompson, N.Y.

Mrs. Meyer, South B St., Capitol Hill
John Lambert (S), N.J.
Jacob Hufty, N.J.
Jacob Markell, N.Y.
Hosea Moffitt, N.Y.
Nathaniel Ruggles, Mass.
Lewis B. Sturges, Conn.
Artemas Ward, Jr., Mass.
Elisha J. Winter, N.Y.
William Hale, N.H.

Mr. Nourse, near Georgetown
John Smith, Va.

Mrs. Odlin, Penn. Ave.
Dudley Chase (S), Vt.
Obadiah German (S), N.Y.
Jeremiah B. Howell (S), R.I.
Michael Leib (S),[8] Penn.
William C. Bradley, Vt.
Jonathan Fisk, N.Y.
Charles Rich,[9] Vt.
Richard Skinner,[10] Vt.
John W. Taylor, N.Y.

Mr. O'Neal, Franklin House, near West Market
Nicholas Gilman (S), N.H.
Robert H. Goldsborough (S), Md.
Jeremiah Mason (S), N.H.
Samuel Smith (S), Md.

Mrs. Queen, Carroll's Row, Capitol Hill
William Barnett, Ga.
Shadrack Bond, Deleg., Ill. Terr.
James Caldwell, Ohio
John J. Chappell, S.C.
Joseph Desha, Ky.
John Kerr, Va.
John Kershaw, S.C.

---

[8] Resigned Feb. 28, 1814 to become postmaster of Philadelphia. He was succeeded by Jonathan Roberts, who took his seat Feb. 28, 1814.
[9] Also listed at Mr. Ball's.
[10] Also listed at Mr. Ball's.

Mr. Rhode, South B St., near Tom-
linson's, Capitol Hill
Samuel W. Dana (S), Conn.
Abijah Bigelow, Mass.
George Bradbury, Mass.
Elijah Brigham, Mass.
Epaphroditus Champion, Conn.
William Ely, Mass.
Lyman Law, Conn.
Jonathan O. Moseley, Conn.

Pennsylvania Ave.
Samuel Ringgold,[11] Md.

Mr. Rush, near West Market
Charles J. Ingersoll, Penn.

Mrs. Suter, F St., near Treasury Dept.
William McCoy, Va.
John Rhea, Tenn.
John Sevier, Tenn.
John G. Jackson, Va.

Mrs. Thompson, near West Market
James Breckinridge, Va.
Daniel Sheffey, Va.

Tomlinson's Hotel, Capitol Hill
John P. Hungerford, Va.
William S. Smith, N.Y.
Abiel Wood, Mass.

Mr. Varnum, near Centre Market
Joseph B. Varnum (S), Mass.
Levi Hubbard, Mass.
James Parker, Mass.

Mrs. Wadsworth, N.J. Ave., near Bank,
Capitol Hill
Outerbridge Horsey (S), Del.
William Hunter (S), R.I.
William H. Wells (S), Del.
Thomas Cooper, Del.
William Reed, Mass.
Henry M. Ridgely, Del.

Mr. Wheaton, F St., near Treasury Dept.
Lewis Condict (S), N.J.
Elias Earle, S.C.
Meshack Franklin, N.C.
Bolling Hall, Ga.
Jonathan Roberts,[12] Penn.

Mrs. Wilson, Seven Buildings, Penn. Ave.
George W. Campbell (S),[13] Tenn.
David Stone (S), N.C.

Mr. Woodside, Six Buildings
Morris S. Miller, N.Y.

Mrs. Young, near the Washington Bridge
Joseph Pearson, N.C.

Georgetown, near the Market
David R. Evans, S.C.
Samuel Farrow, S.C.

Georgetown
William Lowndes, S.C.

New Jersey Ave., opposite Rapine's
Bookstore
Samuel Ringgold,[14] Md.

Near the Marine Barracks
Philip Stuart, Md.

APPENDIX

Alfred Cuthbert,[15] Ga.
Samuel Hopkins, Ky.
Richard M. Johnson, Ky.

Charles Goldsborough, Md.
William M. Richardson, Mass.
Samuel Smith, N.H.

[11] Also listed at N.J. Ave.
[12] Resigned Feb. 24, 1814, having been elected Senator.
[13] Resigned Feb. 11, 1814. He was succeeded by Jesse Wheaton, who took his seat Apr. 9, 1814.
[14] Also listed at Penn. Ave.
[15] Took his seat Feb. 7, 1814.

John Condit (S), N.J.   John Gloninger, Penn.
William Irving,[16] N.Y.   John Roane, Va.
John M. Bowers,[17] N.Y.

[16] Took his seat Jan. 22, 1814.
[17] Served until Dec. 20, 1813.   He was succeeded by Isaac Williams, Jr. who successfully contested the election, and took his seat Jan. 24, 1814.

CONGRESSIONAL DIRECTORY

THIRTEENTH CONGRESS, THIRD SESSION
(September 19, 1814–March 3, 1815)

SENATORS OF THE UNITED STATES

New Hampshire
Jeremiah Mason, Crawford's Hotel, Georgetown
Thomas W. Thompson, Mr. Coyle, Capitol Hill

Massachusetts
Christopher Gore, Crawford's Hotel, Georgetown
Joseph B. Varnum, Mr. Varnum, near Centre Market

Rhode Island
Jeremiah B. Howell, Mrs. Hamilton (Elder), Centre Market
William Hunter, Mrs. Wadsworth, Capitol Hill

Connecticut
David Daggett, Mr. Coyle, Capitol Hill
Samuel W. Dana, Crawford's Hotel, Georgetown

Vermont
Dudley Chase, Mr. Brush, near Centre Market
Jonathan Robinson, Mrs. Dinsmore, Penn. Ave.

New York
Obadiah German, Mrs. Odlin, Penn. Ave.

Rufus King, Crawford's Hotel, Georgetown

New Jersey
John Condit, McKeowin's Hotel, Penn. Ave.
John Lambert, Mrs. Dinsmore, Penn. Ave.

Pennsylvania
Abner Lacock, Mrs. Lindsay, Capitol Hill
Jonathan Roberts, Mrs. Lindsay, Capitol Hill

Delaware
Outerbridge Horsey, Mrs. Wadsworth, Capitol Hill
William H. Wells, Mrs. Wadsworth, Capitol Hill

Maryland
Robert H. Goldsborough, Crawford's Hotel, Georgetown
Samuel Smith, O'Neale's Hotel, West Market

Virginia
Richard Brent,[1] O'Neale's Hotel, West Market
William B. Giles, Mrs. Dowson, Capitol Hill

NOTE: Copies are located at the American Antiquarian Society, the Columbia Historical Society, and the Library of Congress. A broadside is located at the Boston Athenaeum.

[1] Died Dec. 30, 1814. He was succeeded by James Barbour, who took his seat Jan. 11, 1815.

North Carolina
David Stone,[2] Mrs. Wilson, Seven Buildings
James Turner, O'Neale's Hotel, West Market

South Carolina
John Gaillard, Mrs. Dowson, Capitol Hill
John Taylor, Mr. McLean, Penn. Ave.

Georgia
William W. Bibb, Mr. McLean, Penn. Ave.
Charles Tait, Mrs. Dowson, Capitol Hill

Kentucky
George Walker,[3] McKeowin's Hotel, Penn. Ave.

Jesse Bledsoe,[4] Mrs. Lindsay, Capitol Hill

Tennessee
Joseph Anderson, Mrs. Hamilton (Elder), Centre Market
Jesse Wharton, McKeowin's Hotel, Penn. Ave.

Ohio
Jeremiah Morrow
Thomas Worthington[5]

Louisiana
James Brown, Mrs. Dowson, Capitol Hill
Eligius Fromentin, Mr. Shoemaker, North F St.

REPRESENTATIVES OF THE UNITED STATES

New Hampshire
Bradbury Cilley, Mr. Heath, East of General Post Office
William Hale, Mr. Peltz, Penn. Ave.
Roger Vose, Mr. Peltz, Penn. Ave.
Daniel Webster, Crawford's Hotel, Georgetown
Jeduthun Wilcox, Mrs. Odlin, Penn. Ave.
Samuel Smith

Massachusetts
William Baylies, Mrs. Odlin, Penn. Ave.
Abijah Bigelow, Mr. Peltz, near Centre Market
George Bradbury, Mrs. Odlin, Penn. Ave.

Elijah Brigham, Mr. Peltz, near Centre Market
Samuel Dana,[6] McKeowin's Hotel, Penn. Ave.
Samuel Davis, Crawford's Hotel, Georgetown
William Ely, Mr. Peltz, near Centre Market
Levi Hubbard, Mr. Varnum, near Centre Market
John W. Hulbert,[7] Mr. Kearney, North F St.
Cyrus King, Mr. Coyle, Capitol Hill
James Parker, Mr. Varnum, near Centre Market
Timothy Pickering, Mrs. Thompson, Six Buildings

[2] Resigned Dec. 24, 1814. Francis Locke was chosen to fill the vacancy, but did not qualify.
[3] Appointed to fill the vacancy caused by resignation of George M. Bibb, and took his seat Oct. 10, 1814. He was succeeded by William T. Barry, who took his seat Feb. 2, 1815.
[4] Resigned Dec. 24, 1814. He was succeeded by Isham Talbot, who took his seat Feb. 2, 1815.
[5] Resigned Dec. 1, 1814. He was succeeded by Joseph Kerr, who took his seat Dec. 30, 1814.
[6] Took his seat Sept. 22, 1814.
[7] Took his seat Sept. 26, 1814.

John Reed, Mrs. Odlin, Penn. Ave.

William Reed, Mrs. Wadsworth, Capitol Hill

Nathaniel Ruggles, Mrs. Odlin, Penn. Ave.

Samuel Taggart, Mr. Heath, East of General Post Office

Artemas Ward, Jr., Mr. Peltz, near Centre Market

Laban Wheaton, Mrs. Odlin, Penn. Ave.

John Wilson, Mrs. Hamilton (Younger)

Abiel Wood

Connecticut

Epaphroditus Champion, Mr. Peltz, near Centre Market

John Davenport, Mr. Coyle, Capitol Hill

Lyman Law, Mr. Peltz, near Centre Market

Jonathan O. Moseley, Mr. Peltz, near Centre Market

Timothy Pitkin, Mr. Coyle, Capitol Hill

Lewis B. Sturges, Mr. Gillis, Penn. Ave.

Benjamin Tallmadge, Miss Heyer, N.J. Ave.

Rhode Island

Richard Jackson, Jr., Miss Heyer, N.J. Ave.

Elisha R. Potter, Miss Heyer, N.J. Ave.

Vermont

William C. Bradley, Mr. Brush, near Centre Market

Ezra Butler, Mrs. Dinmore, Penn. Ave.

James Fisk, Mr. Brush, near Centre Market

Richard Skinner, Mrs. Hamilton (Elder)

William Strong, Mr. Huddleston, near Centre Market

Charles Rich, Mrs. Hamilton (Elder)

New York

Daniel Avery, Mr. Huddleston, near Centre Market

Alexander Boyd, Mr. Heath, East of General Post Office

Oliver C. Comstock, Mr. Huddleston, near Centre Market

Peter Denoyelles, Mr. Huddleston, near Centre Market

Jonathan Fisk, Mr. Stephenson

James Geddes, Mrs. Thompson, Six Buildings

Thomas P. Grosvenor, Mr. Kearney, F St.

Abraham Hasbrouck, McKeowin's Hotel

Samuel M. Hopkins

Nathaniel W. Howell

William Irving, Mrs. Dowson, Capitol Hill

Moss Kent, O'Neale's Hotel, West Market

John Lefferts, Mr. Huddleston, near Centre Market

John Lovett, McKeowin's Hotel

Jacob Markell, Mr. Heath, East of General Post Office

Morris S. Miller, Crawford's Hotel, Georgetown

Hosea Moffitt, Mr. Heath, East of General Post Office

Thomas J. Oakley, Miss Heyer, Capitol Hill

Jotham Post, Jr., Miss Heyer, Capitol Hill

Ebenezer Sage, Mr. Huddleston, near Centre Market

Samuel Sherwood, Mrs. Odlin, Penn. Ave.

Zebulon R. Shipherd, Mr. Heath, East of General Post Office

William S. Smith, Mrs. Mathers, Capitol Hill

John W. Taylor, Mr. Brush, near Centre Market

Joel Thompson, Mr. Heath, East of General Post Office

Isaac Williams, Jr., Mr. Huddleston, near Centre Market

Elisha J. Winter, Mrs. Mathers, Capitol Hill

New Jersey

Thomas Bines,[8] Mr. Hyatt, near Centre Market

Lewis Condict, Mr. Wheaton, F St.

William Coxe, Mr. Coyle, Capitol Hill

[8] Took his seat Nov. 2, 1814.

James Schureman, Mr. Coyle, Capitol Hill

Richard Stockton, Mr. Coyle, Capitol Hill

Thomas Ward, McKeowin's Hotel, Penn. Ave.

Pennsylvania

William Anderson, Mrs. Hamilton (Elder), Capitol Hill

David Bard, Mr. Huddleston, near Centre Market

Robert Brown, Mr. Huddleston, near Centre Market

John Conrad, Mr. Huddleston, near Centre Market

William Crawford, Mr. Huddleston, near Centre Market

Edward Crouch, Mrs. Myer, near Centre Market

Roger Davis, Mrs. Dinmore, Penn. Ave.

William Findley, Mrs. Myer, near Centre Market

Hugh Glasgow, Mr. Huddleston, near Centre Market

Isaac Griffin, Mrs. Lindsay, Capitol Hill

Samuel Henderson[9]

Charles J. Ingersoll, O'Neale's, Franklin House

Samuel D. Ingham, Mr. Huddleston, near Centre Market

Jared Irwin, Mr. Dunn, Eastern Branch

Aaron Lyle, Mrs. Myer, near Centre Market

William Piper, Mrs. Myer, near Centre Market

John Rea, Mrs. Myer, near Centre Market

Adam Seybert, Mrs. Dowson, Capitol Hill

Amos Slaymaker[10]

Isaac Smith, Mrs. Lindsay, Capitol Hill

Adamson Tannehill, Mrs. Myer, near Centre Market

Daniel Udree, Mr. Huddleston, near Centre Market

Thomas Wilson, Mrs. Lindsay, Capitol Hill

Delaware

Thomas Cooper, Mrs. Wadsworth, Capitol Hill

Henry M. Ridgely, Mrs. Wadsworth, Capitol Hill

Maryland

Stevenson Archer, Mr. Burch, Penn. Ave.

Charles Goldsborough, Crawford's Hotel, Georgetown

Alexander C. Hanson, Georgetown

Joseph Kent, McKeowin's Hotel, Penn. Ave.

Alexander McKim, Mrs. Dowson, Capitol Hill

Nicholas R. Moore, Mrs. Dowson, Capitol Hill

Samuel Ringgold, O'Neale's, Franklin House

Philip Stuart, Near Marine Barracks

Robert Wright, Mrs. Lindsay, Capitol Hill

Virginia

Philip P. Barbour, Mr. Brush, near Centre Market

Thomas M. Bayly, O'Neale's, Franklin House

James Breckinridge, Mrs. Thompson, Six Buildings

William A. Burwell, Mr. Shoemaker, F St.

Hugh Caperton, Crawford's Hotel, Georgetown

John Clopton, Mr. Brown, West of General Post Office

John W. Eppes, Mrs. Suter, Penn. Ave.

Thomas Gholson, Jr., Mrs. Wilson, Seven Buildings

Peterson Goodwyn, Mr. Magruder

Aylett Hawes, Mr. Brush, near Centre Market

John P. Hungerford, McKeowin's Hotel, Penn. Ave.

John G. Jackson, Mrs. Suter, Penn. Ave.

James Johnson, Miss Finigan, F St.

John Kerr, Mrs. Queen, West of General Post Office

---

[9] Took his seat Nov. 29, 1814.
[10] Took his seat Dec. 12, 1814.

Joseph Lewis, Jr., Crawford's Hotel, Georgetown

William McCoy, Mrs. Suter, Penn. Ave.

Hugh Nelson, Mrs. Hamilton (Younger)

Thomas Newton, Jr., Mrs. Wilson, Seven Buildings

James Pleasants, Mr. Brush, near Centre Market

John Roane, Mrs. Clark, F St.

Daniel Sheffey, Mr. Clephan, F St.

John Smith, Mr. Nourse

Franics White, Miss Finigan, F St.

North Carolina

Willis Alston, Mrs. McCardell, Penn. Ave.

John Culpepper, Mr. Bestor, Penn. Ave.

Peter Forney, Mrs. Queen, West of General Post Office

Meshack Franklin, Mrs. Clark, F St.

William Gaston, Crawford's Hotel, Georgetown

William Kennedy, Mrs. Hamilton (Younger)

William R. King, Mrs. Wilson, Seven Buildings

Nathaniel Macon, Mrs. Clark, F St.

William H. Murfree, O'Neale's Hotel, West Market

Joseph Pearson, Mrs. Young, near Washington Bridge

Israel Pickens, Mrs. Wilson, Seven Buildings

Richard Stanford, Crawford's Hotel, Georgetown

Bartlett Yancy, Mr. Burch, Penn. Ave.

South Carolina

John C. Calhoun, Mr. Burch, Penn. Ave.

John J. Chappell, Mrs. Queen, West of General Post Office

Langdon Cheves, Capitol Hill

Elias Earle, Mrs. Lindsay, Capitol Hill

David R. Evans, Mrs. Coolidge, Georgetown

Samuel Farrow, Mrs. Wheaton, F St.

Theodore Gourdin, Mrs. Wheaton, F St.

John Kershaw, Mrs. Queen, West of General Post Office

William Lowndes, Mrs. Dowson, Capitol Hill

Georgia

William Barnett, Mrs. Myer, near Centre Market

Alfred Cuthbert, McKeowin's Hotel, Penn. Ave.

John Forsyth, Mr. Norwell, Penn. Ave.

Bolling Hall, Mrs. Clark, F St.

Thomas Telfair, Mr. McLean, Penn. Ave.

George M. Troup, F St.

Kentucky

James Clark, Mr. Burch, Penn. Ave.

Joseph H. Hawkins, McKeowin's Hotel, Penn. Ave.

Joseph Desha, Mrs. Myer, near Centre Market

William P. Duvall, McKeowin's Hotel, Penn. Ave.

Samuel Hopkins, McKeowin's Hotel, Penn. Ave.

Richard M. Johnson, Mr. Brown, North E St.

Samuel McKee, McKeowin's Hotel, Penn. Ave.

Thomas Montgomery, McKeowin's Hotel, Penn. Ave.

Stephen Ormsby, Mr. Brush, Penn. Ave.

Solomon P. Sharp, Mr. Burch, Penn. Ave.

Tennessee

John H. Bowen, Mr. Burch, Penn. Ave.

Newton Cannon,[11] Miss Finigan, F St.

Thomas K. Harris, Mrs. Queen, West of General Post Office

Parry W. Humphreys, Mrs. Suter, Penn. Ave.

John Rhea, Mrs. Suter, Penn. Ave.

John Sevier, Mrs. Suter, Penn. Ave.

Ohio

John Alexander, Mr. Brush, Penn. Ave.

David Clendenin[12]

James Caldwell, Mrs. Myer, near Centre Market

[11] Took his seat Oct. 15, 1814.
[12] Took his seat Dec. 22, 1814.

William Creighton, Jr., Mr. Burch, Penn. Ave.

James Kilbourne, Mrs. Myer, near Centre Market

John McLean, Mrs. Myer, near Centre Market

Louisiana
Thomas B. Robertson, Mrs. Dowson, Capitol Hill

Mississippi Territory
William Lattimore (Deleg.), Mrs. Queen, West of General Post Office

Indiana Territory
Jonathan Jennings (Deleg.), Mrs. Dinmore, Penn. Ave.

Illinois Territory
Benjamin Stephenson (Deleg.),[13] Mrs. Suter, Penn. Ave.

Territory Of Missouri
Rufus Easton (Deleg.),[14] Mrs. Suter, Penn. Ave.

[13] Took his seat Nov. 14, 1814.
[14] Took his seat Nov. 16, 1814.

CONGRESSIONAL DIRECTORY

FOURTEENTH CONGRESS, FIRST SESSION
(December 4, 1815–April 30, 1816)

Mr. Burch, Capitol Hill
Stevenson Archer, Md.
Philip P. Barbour, Va.
Joseph H. Bryan, N.C.
James W. Clark, N.C.
Thomas Gholson, Jr., Va.
Aylett Hawes, Va.
William H. Murfree, N.C.
William Mayrant, S.C.
Ballard Smith, Va.
Bartlett Yancy, N.C.

Mr. Bestor, near Centre Market
John Culpepper, N.C.

Mr. Brown, near City Post Office
Richard M. Johnson, Ky.

Mr. Brush, Penn. Ave.
John Alexander, Ohio
William T. Barry (S), Ky.
Dudley Chase (S), Vt.
James Clark, Ky.
William Creighton, Jr., Ohio
Rufus Easton, Deleg., Terr. of Mo.
Alney McLean, Ky.
John Hahn, Penn.
Thomas Newton, Jr., Va.
Stephen Ormsby, Ky.
James Pleasants, Va.
William H. Roane, Va.
John Savage, N.Y.
John W. Taylor, N.Y.

Mr. Coyle, Capitol Hill
Daniel Chipman, Vt.

David Daggett (S), Conn.
Samuel W. Dana (S), Conn.
John Davenport, Conn.
Thomas R. Gold, N.Y.
Cyrus King, Mass.
Charles Marsh, Vt.
Thomas W. Thompson (S), N.H.

Mr. Claxton, Capitol Hill
Samuel R. Betts, N.Y.
Burwell Bassett, Va.
Samuel S. Conner, Mass.
Newton Cannon, Tenn.
Benjamin Hardin, Ky.
Bennett H. Henderson, Tenn.
William Lattimore, Deleg., Miss. Terr.
Albion K. Parris, Mass.
Samuel Powell, Tenn.
James B. Reynolds, Tenn.
Isaac Thomas, Tenn.
Micah Taul, Ky.
John Williams (S), Tenn.
Jonathan Ward, N.Y.

Mrs. Clarke, F St.
William A. Burwell, Va.
Bolling Hall, Ga.
Wilson Lumpkin, Ga.
Lewis Williams, N.C.
Richard Henry Wilde, Ga.

Crawford's Hotel, Georgetown
Christopher Gore (S), Mass.
Robert H. Goldsborough (S), Md.
William Gaston, N.C.
John W. Hulbert, Mass.

NOTE: Copies are located at the American Antiquarian Society and the Boston Athenaeum.

John C. Herbert, Md.
Rufus King (S), N.Y.
Joseph Lewis, Jr., Va.
Elijah H. Mills, Mass.
Hugh Nelson, Va.
Richard Stanford,[1] N.C.

Mr. Campbell, Penn. Ave.
John G. Jackson, Va.
Benjamin Stephenson, Deleg., Ill. Terr.

Mr. Carnahan, Georgetown
Jonathan Jennings, Deleg., Ind. Terr.

Mr. Dunn, near the Eastern Branch
Jared Irwin, Penn.

Mrs. Dowson, Capitol Hill
James Barbour (S), Va.
William W. Bibb (S), Ga.
James Brown (S), La.
John C. Calhoun, S.C.
Henry Clay, Ky.
John Gaillard (S), S.C.
Nathaniel Macon (S),[2] N.C.
Henry Middleton, S.C.
Peter B. Porter,[3] N.Y.
Thomas B. Robertson, La.
Nathan Sanford (S), N.Y.
James Turner (S), N.C.
John Taylor (S), S.C.
Charles Tait (S), Ga.
Henry St. George Tucker, Va.
John Taylor, S.C.
Thomas Telfair, Ga.

Mr. Frost, Capitol Hill
William Baylies, Mass.
John L. Boss, Jr., R.I.
George Bradbury, Mass.
Nathaniel Ruggles, Mass.
Abraham H. Schenck, N.Y.
Samuel Taggart, Mass.
James W. Wilkin, N.Y.

Mrs. Hamilton, Capitol Hill
Eligius Fromentin (S), La.
Daniel M. Forney, N.C.
Jeremiah B. Howell (S), R.I.
William C. Love, N.C.
Enos T. Throop, N.Y.
John B. Yates, N.Y.

Miss Heyer, Capitol Hill
Daniel Cady, N.Y.
Joseph Hopkinson, Penn.
Moss Kent, N.Y.
James B. Mason, R.I.
William Milnor, Penn.
John Sergeant,[4] Penn.
Thomas Smith, Penn.

Mr. Huddleston, Penn. Ave.
Asa Adgate,[5] N.Y.
James Birdsall, N.Y.
Micah Brooks, N.Y.
Ephraim Bateman, N.J.
Oliver C. Comstock, N.Y.
Henry Crocheron, N.Y.
Lewis Condict, N.J.
William Crawford, Penn.
Hugh Glasgow, Penn.
Jabez D. Hammond, N.Y.
Henry Southard, N.J.
George Townsend, N.Y.
Westel Willoughby, Jr.,[6] N.Y.

Mr. Hanson, Georgetown
Thomas P. Grosvenor, N.Y.

Mrs. Lindsay, Capitol Hill
David Clendenin, Ohio
Isaac Griffin, Penn.
Samuel D. Ingham, Penn.
Abner Lacock (S), Penn.
William Maclay, Penn.
William Piper, Penn.
Thomas Wilson, Penn.

[1] Died Apr. 9, 1816.
[2] Elected to fill the vacancy caused by resignation of Francis Locke, and took his seat Dec. 13, 1815, the day he resigned from the House.
[3] Resigned Jan. 23, 1816.
[4] Seated Dec. 6, 1815.
[5] Seated Dec. 7, 1815.
[6] Successfully contested the election of William S. Smith, and took his seat Dec. 13, 1815.

William Wilson, Penn.
William Woodward, S.C.

Mrs. Meyers, Penn. Ave.
Ezra Baker, N.J.
James Caldwell, Ohio
William Darlington, Penn.
Joseph Desha, Ky.
Joseph Hiester, Penn.
Aaron Lyle, Penn.
John McLean, Ohio
Jeremiah Morrow (S), Ohio
Benjamin Ruggles (S), Ohio
James J. Wilson (S), N.J.
James M. Wallace, Penn.
John Whiteside, Penn.

Mr. Magruder, Thirteenth St.
Peterson Goodwyn, Va.

Mr. Meigs, F St.
John Forsyth, Ga.

Mrs. McCardell, Capitol Hill
Charles H. Atherton, N.H.
Bradbury Cilley, N.H.
Luther Jewett, Vt.
Asa Lyon, Vt.
Jeremiah Nelson, Mass.
Hosea Moffitt, N.Y.
Timothy Pickering, Mass.
Isaac Tichenor (S), Vt.

McKeowin's Hotel, Penn. Ave.
John Condict (S), N.J.
Alfred Cuthbert, Ga.
Outerbridge Horsey (S), Del.
John Lovett, N.Y.
Samuel McKee, Ky.
Solomon P. Sharp, Ky.
Thomas Clayton, Del.

Mr. McLeod, Capitol Hill
John P. Hungerford, Va.
Thomas Moore, S.C.
Erastus Root,[7] N.Y.
John Ross, Penn.
Robert Wright, Md.

Mrs. Odlin, Penn. Ave.
Benjamin Brown, Mass.
Chauncey Langdon, Vt.
John Noyes, Vt.
Thomas Rice, Mass.
Solomon Strong, Mass.
Lewis B. Sturges, Conn.
Laban Wheaton, Mass.

Mr. Peltz, Penn. Ave.
Elijah Brigham,[8] Mass.
Epaphroditus Champion, Conn.
Lyman Law, Conn.
Jonathan O. Moseley, Conn.
John Reed, Mass.
Roger Vose, N.H.
Jeduthun Wilcox, N.H.

Queen's Hotel, Capitol Hill
Benjamin Tallmadge, Conn.
Thomas Cooper, Del.

Mr. Scott, Capitol Hill
Victory Birdseye, N.Y.
John Clopton, Va.
Peter H. Wendover, N.Y.

Mrs. Stannard, Georgetown
James Breckenridge, Va.
Benjamin Huger, S.C.

Mrs. Suter, near the President's House
George W. Campbell (S), Tenn.
James Johnson, Va.
John Kerr, Va.
William McCoy, Va.

Mrs. Wadsworth, Capitol Hill
George Baer, Md.
William Hunter (S), R.I.
Daniel Sheffey, Va.
Magnus Tate, Va.

Mr. Waterson, Capitol Hill
Thomas Burnside,[9] Penn.
Jonathan Roberts (S), Penn.

[7] Successfully contested the election of John Adams, and took his seat Dec. 26, 1815.
[8] Died Feb. 22, 1816.
[9] Seated Dec. 11, 1815.

Mrs. Wilson, Seven Buildings
John J. Chappell, S.C.
William R. King, N.C.
Israel Pickens, N.C.

Mr. Young, Capitol Hill
Charles Goldsborough, Md.

Mr. Varnum, near Centre Market
Joseph B. Varnum (S), Mass.

Capitol Hill, opposite Bank
William Lowndes, S.C.

Georgetown, Dist. of Col.
Alexander C. Hanson,[10] Md.

Near the Navy Yard
Philip Stuart, Md.

APPENDIX

Timothy Pitkin, Conn.
William H. Wells (S), Del.
Isham Talbot (S), Ky.
Vacant Senate seat, Md. (Mar. 4, 1815–
Jan. 28, 1816)
Samuel Smith,[11] Md.
William Pinkney,[12] Md.
James Carr, Mass.
Asahel Stearns, Mass.
Artemas Ward, Jr., Mass.
William Hale, N.H.

Jeremiah Mason (S), N.H.
Daniel Webster, N.H.
Benjamin Bennet, N.J.
Thomas Ward, N.J.
William Irving, N.Y.
James Kilbourne, Ohio
William Findley, Penn.
John Woods,[13] Penn.
William G. Blount,[14] Tenn.
Armistead T. Mason (S),[15] Va.
John Randolph, Va.

[10] Resigned in 1816.
[11] Seated Feb. 4, 1816.
[12] Resigned Apr. 18, 1816, having been appointed minister to Russia.
[13] Never qualified, owing to illness.
[14] Seated Jan. 8, 1816.
[15] Seated Jan. 22, 1816.

CONGRESSIONAL DIRECTORY

FOURTEENTH CONGRESS, SECOND SESSION
(December 2, 1816–March 3, 1817)

Mr. Burch, Capitol Hill
Stevenson Archer, Md.
Philip P. Barbour, Va.
Joseph H. Bryan, N.C.
James Caldwell, Ohio
James W. Clark, N.C.
Aylett Hawes, Va.
Charles Hooks, N.C.
Israel Pickens, N.C.
Ballard Smith, Va.
Bartlett Yancy, N.C.

Bailey's Hotel, Capitol Hill
Eli P. Ashmun (S), Mass.
George M. Troup (S), Ga.
Robert Wright, Md.
Magnus Tate, Va.

Mr. Bailey, Capitol Hill
Samuel R. Betts, N.Y.
Nathaniel Ruggles, Mass.
Asahel Stearns, Mass.
Lewis B. Sturges, Conn.
Benjamin Tallmadge, Conn.
Artemas Ward, Jr., Mass.

Mr. Brush, Penn. Ave.
Asa Adgate, N.Y.
John Alexander, Ohio
Benjamin Bennet, N.J.
Micah Brooks, N.Y.
William Crawford, Penn.
Archibald S. Clarke, N.Y.
Hugh Glasgow, Penn.

Waller Taylor (S),[1] Ind.
James W. Wilkin,[2] N.Y.

Mr. Bestor, near the Theatre
John Culpepper, N.C.
William Woodward, S.C.

Mr. Brown, near General Post Office
Oliver C. Comstock, N.Y.
Thomas Fletcher, Ky.
Richard M. Johnson, Ky.

Mr. Claxton, Capitol Hill
Burwell Bassett, Va.
James Carr, Mass.
Samuel S. Conner, Mass.
William Lattimore, Deleg., Miss. Terr.
Albion K. Parris, Mass.
Abraham H. Schenck, N.Y.
Micah Taul, Ky.
John Tyler,[3] Va.
Jonathan Ward, N.Y.

Mr. Coyle, Capitol Hill
David Daggett (S), Conn.
John Davenport, Conn.
Cyrus King, Mass.
Charles Marsh, Vt.
Timothy Pitkin, Conn.
Thomas W. Thompson (S), N.H.

Mrs. Clarke, F St.
William A. Burwell, Va.
William Henry Harrison, Ohio

NOTE: Copies are located at the Boston Athenaeum, the Library of Congress, and the New York Public Library.
[1] Seated Dec. 12, 1816 and also listed at Mrs. Clarke's.
[2] Also listed at Mr. McLeod's.
[3] Seated Dec. 17, 1816.

James Noble (S),[4] Ind.
Stephen Ormsby, Ky.

Crawford's Hotel, Georgetown
Thomas P. Grosvenor, N.Y.
John C. Herbert, Md.
Joseph Lewis, Jr., Va.

Mr. Dowson, No. 1, Capitol Hill
James Brown (S), La.
John Gaillard (S), S.C.
Armistead T. Mason (S), Va.
Thomas B. Robertson, La.
Nathan Sanford (S), N.Y.
Samuel Smith, Md.
Henry St. George Tucker, Va.

Mr. Dowson, No. 2, Capitol Hill
James Barbour (S), Va.
John C. Calhoun, S.C.
Weldon N. Edwards, N.C.
Daniel M. Forney, N.C.
William C. Love, N.C.
Nathaniel Macon (S), N.C.
Charles Tait (S), Ga.
John Taylor, S.C.
Thomas Telfair, Ga.

Davis' Hotel, Penn. Ave.
John Condit (S), N.J.
Peterson Goodwyn, Va.
William Hendricks,[5] Ind.
John Lovett, N.Y.
Aaron Lyle, Penn.
Jeremiah Morrow (S), Ohio
Samuel McKee, Ky.
William Piper, Penn.
Nathaniel Pope, Deleg., Ill. Terr.
James B. Reynolds, Tenn.
Erastus Root, N.Y.
Benjamin Ruggles (S), Ohio
John Scott,[6] Deleg., Terr. of Mo.
Solomon P. Sharp, Ky.
Isham Talbot (S), Ky.

Mrs. Doyne, Penn. Ave.
Thomas Rice, Mass.
Solomon Strong, Mass.

Mr. Frost, Capitol Hill
Jeremiah Mason (S), N.H.
Daniel Webster, N.H.

Mrs. Fitzgerald, N.J. Ave.
Jonathan Roberts (S), Penn.

Mr. Gaither, Penn. Ave.
Thomas Newton, Jr., Va.
James Pleasants, Va.
William H. Roane, Va.

Miss Heyer, Capitol Hill
William Baylies, Mass.
John L. Boss, Jr. R.I.
George Bradbury, Mass.
Daniel Cody, N.Y.
Thomas Clayton, Del.
Outerbridge Horsey (S), Del.
Joseph Hopkinson, Penn.
James B. Mason, R.I.
William Milnor, Penn.
Thomas Smith, Penn.

Herronimus' Hotel, Penn. Ave.
William G. Blount, Tenn.
George W. Campbell (S), Tenn.
Newton Cannon, Tenn.
Bennett H. Henderson, Tenn.
Jared Irwin, Penn.
Hugh Nelson, Va.
Samuel Powell, Tenn.
Montfort Stokes (S),[7] N.C.
Isaac Thomas, Tenn.
Lewis Williams, N.C.
John Williams (S), Tenn.

Mr. Hyatt, Penn. Ave.
Benjamin Adams, Mass.
Epaphroditus Champion, Conn.
William Hale, N.H.
Lyman Law, Conn.
Jonathan O. Moseley, Conn.
John Noyes, Vt.
John Reed, Mass.
Roger Vose, N.H.
Jeduthun Wilcox, N.H.

[4] Seated Dec. 12, 1816 and also listed at Mr. Brush's.
[5] Seated Dec. 11, 1816.
[6] Rufus Easton contested Scott's election, and on Jan. 13, 1817, the election was declared illegal and the seat vacant.
[7] Seated Dec. 16, 1816.

Mr. Huddleston, near General
Post Office
Daniel Avery,[8] N.Y.
Ephraim Bateman, N.J.
Henry Crocheron, N.Y.
Henry Southard, N.J.
George W. Townsend, N.Y.

Mr. Hamilton, near Treasury Office
Jeremiah B. Howell (S), R.I.
John W. Taylor, N.Y.

Mrs. Lindsay, Penn. Ave.
David Clendenin, Ohio
Isaac Griffin, Penn.
John Hahn, Penn.
Samuel D. Ingham, Penn.
Abner Lacock (S), Penn.
William Maclay, Penn.
Thomas Wilson, Penn.
William Wilson, Penn.
William P. Maclay,[9] Penn.

Mrs. McCardell, Capitol Hill
Charles H. Atherton, N.H.
Samuel Dickens, N.C.
Luther Jewett, Vt.
Chauncey Langdon, Vt.
Asa Lyon, Vt.
Hosea Moffitt, N.Y.
Jeremiah Nelson, Mass.
Timothy Pickering, Mass.
Isaac Tichenor (S), Vt.

Mr. McLeod, Capitol Hill
James Birdsall, N.Y.
Lewis Condict, N.J.
William Findley, Penn.
Jabez D. Hammond, N.Y.
John P. Hungerford, Va.
John Ross, Penn.
John Savage, N.Y.
Westel Willoughby, Jr.,[10] N.Y.

Mrs. Mathers, Capitol Hill
Ezra Baker, N.J.
Victory Birdseye, N.Y.
Peter H. Wendover, N.Y.

Mrs. Meyer, Penn. Ave.
Dudley Chase (S), Vt.
William Darlington, Penn.
Joseph Desha, Ky.
Joseph Hiester, Penn.
Thomas Moore, S.C.
James M. Wallace, Penn.
John Whiteside, Penn,
James J. Wilson (S), N.J.

Mr. O'Neale, near Six Buildings
Robert H. Goldsborough (S), Md.
Charles Goldsborough, Md.
Benjamin Hardin, Ky.
Alney McLean, Ky.

Mrs. Odlin, Penn. Ave.
Daniel Sheffey, Va.

Queen's Hotel, Capitol Hill
George Baer, Md.
Thomas Cooper, Del.
William Hunter (S), R.I.
John W. Hulbert, Mass.
Elijah H. Mills, Mass.
William H. Wells (S), Del.

Mrs. Queen, F St.
John Forsyth, Ga.
Richard H. Wilde, Ga.

Mr. Scott, Capitol Hill
Benjamin Brown, Mass.
Samuel Taggart, Mass.
Laban Wheaton, Mass.

Mrs. Suter, Penn. Ave.
James Johnson, Va.
John Kerr, Va.
Peter Little, Md.
William McCoy, Va.

Mrs. Stannard, Georgetown
Benjamin Huger, S.C.
Thomas M. Nelson,[11] Va.

Semmes' Hotel, Georgetown
John Randolph, Va.

[8] Seated Dec. 3, 1816.
[9] Seated Dec. 3, 1816.
[10] Also listed at Mr. Brush's.
[11] Seated Dec. 4, 1816.

Mrs. Thompson, Six Buildings
James Breckenridge, Va.

Mr. Varnum, near Centre Market
Joseph B. Varnum (S), Mass.

Mrs. Wilson, Seven Buildings
John J. Chappell, S.C.
William Creighton, Jr., Ohio
Martin D. Hardin (S),[12] Ky.
William Irving, N.Y.

Dr. Worthington, Georgetown
William Gaston, N.C.

Pennsylvania Ave.
Henry Clay, Ky.

Capitol Hill, N.J. Ave.
William Lowndes, S.C.

Georgetown
George Peter, Md.
Henry Middleton, S.C.

Near the Navy Yard
Philip Stuart, Md.

APPENDIX

Samuel W. Dana (S), Conn.
Zadock Cook,[13] Ga.
Bolling Hall, Ga.
Wilson Lumpkin, Ga.
Jonathan Jennings,[14] Dele., Ind. Terr.
Eligius Fromentin (S), La.
Alexander C. Hanson[15] Md.
Bradburry Cilley, N.H.
Thomas R. Gold, N.Y.
Moss Kent, N.Y.

Rufus King (S), N.Y.
John B. Yates, N.Y.
William H. Murfree, N.C.
James Kilbourne, Ohio
John Sergeant, Penn.
John Woods,[16] Penn.
Stephen D. Miller,[17] S.C.
William Smith (S),[18] S.C.
John G. Jackson, Va.
Daniel Chipman,[19] Vt.

STANDING COMMITTEES OF THE HOUSE OF REPRESENTATIVES

WAYS AND MEANS

Chairman: William Lowndes, S.C.

Samuel Smith, Md.
Jonathan O. Moseley, Conn.
William A. Burwell, Va.

James W. Wilkin, N.Y.
William Gaston, N.C.
Bennett H. Henderson, Tenn.

[12] Seated Dec. 5, 1816.
[13] Took his seat Jan. 23, 1817.
[14] Served until Dec. 11, 1816 when Ind. Terr. was granted statehood.
[15] Seated Jan. 2, 1817.
[16] Never qualified, owing to illness.
[17] Seated Jan. 2, 1817.
[18] Seated Jan. 10, 1817.
[19] Resigned May 5, 1816.

ELECTIONS

Chairman: John W. Taylor, N.Y.

Timothy Pickering, Mass.
John Hahn, Penn.
Roger Vose, N.H.

Lyman Law, Conn.
Isaac Thomas, Tenn.
John Kerr, Va.

COMMERCE AND MANUFACTURES

Chairman: Thomas Newton, Jr., Va.

John Savage, N.Y.
John W. Hulbert, Mass.
Albion K. Parris, Mass.

William Milnor, Penn.
James B. Mason, R.I.
Daniel M. Forney, N.C.

CLAIMS

Chairman: Bartlett Yancy, N.C.

John Alexander, Ohio
Peterson Goodwyn, Va.
John Davenport, Conn.

Aaron Lyle, Penn.
Benjamin Hardin, Ky.
Asa Lyon, Vt.

DISTRICT OF COLUMBIA

Chairman: Henry St. George Tucker, Va.

Joseph Lewis, Jr., Va.
Jared Irwin, Penn.
Peter H. Wendover, N.Y.

John C. Herbert, Md.
John Taylor, S.C.
George Peter, Md.

PUBLIC LANDS

Chairman: Thomas B. Robertson, La.

Alney McLean, Ky.
Cyrus King, Mass.
Lewis B. Sturges, Conn.

William Henry Harrison, Ohio
Lewis Williams, N.C.
William Hendricks, Ind.

POST OFFICE AND POST ROADS

Chairman: Samuel D. Ingham, Penn.

Newton Cannon, Tenn.
James Breckenridge, Va.
Daniel Avery, N.Y.

James Carr, Mass.
James Caldwell, Ohio
John Noyes, Vt.

PENSIONS AND REVOLUTIONARY CLAIMS

Chairman: John J. Chappell, S.C.

James B. Reynolds, Tenn.
Philip Stuart, Md.
Henry Southard, N.J.

Jeduthun Wilcox, N.H.
Laban Wheaton, Mass.
Henry Crocheron, N.Y.

PUBLIC EXPENDITURES
Chairman: Israel Pickens, N.C.

Philip P. Barbour, Va.	Abraham H. Schenck, N.Y.
Jabez D. Hammond, N.Y.	Thomas Wilson, Penn.
Epaphroditus Champion, Conn.	Jeremiah Nelson, Mass.

JUDICIARY
Chairman: Hugh Nelson, Va.

Richard Henry Wilde, Ga.	Stephen Ormsby, Ky.
Joseph Hopkinson, Penn.	Daniel Webster, N.H.
Robert Wright, Md.	William C. Love, N.C.

PRIVATE LAND CLAIMS
Chairman: Solomon P. Sharp, Ky.

James W. Clark, N.C.	Charles H. Atherton, N.H.
Thomas Telfair, Ga.	Benjamin Huger, S.C.

ACCOUNTS
Chairman: Peter Little, Md.

John Reed, Mass.	Weldon N. Edwards, N.C.

REVISAL AND UNFINISHED BUSINESS
Chairman: Lewis Condict, N.J.

George Bradbury, Mass.	William Maclay, Penn.

*On so much of the Public Accounts and Expenditures
as relate to the Department of State*

Chairman: John B. Yates, N.Y.

James B. Mason, R.I.	Weldon N. Edwards, N.C.

*On so much of the Public Accounts and Expenditures
as relate to the Treasury Department*

Chairman: Samuel Smith, Md.

John W. Hulbert, Mass.	John Hahn, Penn.

*On so much of the Public Accounts and Expenditures
as relate to the Department of War*

Chairman: Erastus Root, N.Y.

Daniel M. Forney, N.C.	Daniel Sheffey, Va.

*On so much of the Public Accounts and Expenditures
as relate to the Navy Department*

Chairman: Stevenson Archer, Md.

Wilson Lumpkin, Ga.	Benjamin Huger, S.C.

*On so much of the Public Accounts and Expenditures
as relate to the Post Office*

Chairman: Newton Cannon, Tenn.

Albion K. Parris, Mass.   William Milnor, Penn.

*On so much of the Public Accounts and Expenditures
as relate to the Public Buildings*

Chairman: Lewis Condict, N.J.

William Darlington, Penn.   John Reed, Mass.

SELECT COMMITTEES APPOINTED ON VARIOUS PARTS OF THE PRESIDENT'S MESSAGE

On so much as relates to Foreign Affairs

Chairman: John Forsyth, Ga.

Samuel Smith, Md.   Ezra Baker, N.J.
Thomas P. Grosvenor, N.Y.   Artemas Ward, Jr., Mass.
Cyrus King, Mass.   William Darlington, Penn.

On so much as relates to Military Affairs

Chairman: Richard M. Johnson, Ky.

Samuel S. Conner, Mass.   George Peter, Md.
Joseph Desha, Ky.   Thomas M. Nelson, Va.
Thomas Ward, N.J.   Samuel Dickens, N.C.

On so much as relates to the Reorganization of the Militia

Chairman: William Henry Harrison, Ohio

Benjamin Tallmadge, Conn.   Michah Taul, Ky.
William G. Blount, Tenn.   John P. Hungerford, Va.
William H. Roane, Va.   Charles Marsh, Vt.

On so much as relates to Naval Affairs

Chairman: James Pleasants, Va.

Samuel R. Betts, N.Y.   Thomas B. Robertson, La.
John Culpepper, N.C.   Asahel Stearns, Mass.
John Lovett, N.Y.   David Clendenin, Ohio

On so much as relates to the Indian Tribes

Chairman: Isaac Thomas, Tenn.

Isaac Griffin, Penn.   William Woodward, S.C.
Asa Adgate, N.Y.   William McCoy, Va.
George Baer, Md.   Thomas Fletcher, Ky.

On so much as relates to a uniformity of Weights and Measures

Chairman: Timothy Pitkin, Conn.

John C. Calhoun, S.C.   William Hale, N.H.
Joseph Hopkinson, Penn.   William Crawford, Penn.
Samuel McKee, Ky.   Archibald S. Clarke, N.Y.

On so much as relates to a National University

Chairman: Richard Henry Wilde, Ga.

Robert Wright, Md.   Samuel Powell, Tenn.
James Breckenridge, Va.   James Birdsall, N.Y.
John C. Herbert, Md.   Joseph Hiester, Penn.

On so much as relates to Roads and Canals

Chairman: Thomas Wilson, Penn.

Micah Brooks, N.Y.   Bartlett Yancy, N.C.
Thomas Clayton, Del.   Benjamin Adams, Mass.
Ephraim Bateman, N.J.   Aylett Hawes, Va.

On so much as relates to the African Slave Trade

Chairman: Timothy Pickering, Mass.

Oliver C. Comstock, N.Y.   Samuel Taggart, Mass.
Lewis Condict, N.J.   Bradbury Cilley, N.H.
Henry St. George Tucker, Va.   Charles Hooks, N.C.

*On so much as relates to the Office of
Attorney General, and an Additional Office*

Chairman: William Lowndes, S.C.

Burwell Bassett. Va.   John Forsyth, Ga.
William Wilson, Penn.   Benjamin Bennet, N.J.
Nathaniel Ruggles, Mass.   Magnus Tate, Va.

On so much as relates to a Uniform National Currency

Chairman: John C. Calhoun, S.C.

Daniel Webster, N.H.   Benjamin Hardin, Ky.
John W. Hulbert, Mass.   George Townsend, N.Y.
John Whiteside, Penn.   Hugh Glasgow, Penn.

STANDING COMMITTEES OF THE SENATE
OF THE UNITED STATES

FOREIGN RELATIONS

Chairman: James Barbour, Va.

Nathaniel Macon, N.C.   Samuel W. Dana, Conn.
Rufus King, N.Y.   Abner Lacock, Penn.

FINANCE

Chairman: George W. Campbell, Tenn.

Jeremiah Mason, N.H.   Rufus King, N.Y.
Thomas W. Thompson, N.H.   George M. Troup, Ga.

COMMERCE AND MANUFACTURES
Chairman: William Hunter, R.I.

Nathan Sanford, N.Y.   George W. Campbell, Tenn.
Jonathan Roberts, Penn.   Jeremiah Mason, N.H.

MILITARY AFFAIRS
Chairman: John Williams, Tenn.

Armistead T. Mason, Tenn.   John Condit, N.J.
George M. Troup, Ga.   Martin D. Hardin, Ky.

MILITIA
Chairman: Joseph B. Varnum, Mass.

Isaac Tichenor, Vt.   Armistead T. Mason, Va.
Abner Lacock, Penn.   John Williams, Tenn.

NAVAL AFFAIRS
Chairman: Charles Tait, Ga.

Jeremiah B. Howell, R.I.   Eligius Fromentin, La.
Nathan Sanford, N.Y.   David Daggett, Conn.

PUBLIC LANDS
Chairman: Jeremiah Morrow, Ohio

James Brown, La.   James Noble, Ind.
Waller Taylor, Ind.   Robert H. Goldsborough, Md.

CLAIMS
Chairman: Jonathan Roberts, Penn.

James J. Wilson, N.J.   Isaac Tichenor, Vt.
Robert H. Goldsborough, Md.   Armistead T. Mason, Va.

JUDICIARY
Chairman: Dudley Chase, Vt.

Isham Talbot, Ky.   William Hunter, R.I.
David Daggett, Conn.   Waller Taylor,[20] Ind.

POST OFFICE AND POST ROADS
Chairman: James J. Wilson, N.J.

Eli P. Ashmun, Mass.   Isham Talbot, Ky.
Thomas W. Thompson, N.H.   Dudley Chase, Vt.

---

[20] The *Senate Journal* lists Charles Tait (Ga.).

PENSIONS
Chairman: Jeremiah B. Howell, R.I.

Joseph B. Varnum, Mass.   William H. Wells, Del.
John Condit, N.J.   Jonathan Roberts, Penn.

DISTRICT OF COLUMBIA
Chairman: Armistead T. Mason, Va.

Robert H. Goldsborough, Md.   David Daggett, Conn.
Nathaniel Macon, N.C.   Montfort Stokes, N.C.

SELECT COMMITTEES ON THE PRESIDENT'S MESSAGE

On so much as relates to a uniformity of Weights and Measures

Chairman: Samuel W. Dana, Conn.

Martin D. Hardin, Ky.   Rufus King, N.Y.
Jeremiah Morrow, Ohio   Benjamin Ruggles, Ohio

On so much as relates to a National University

Chairman: James Brown, La.

David Daggett, Conn.   John Condit, N.J.
Jeremiah Mason, N.H.   Robert H. Goldsborough, Md.

On so much as relates to Roads and Canals

Chairman: Outerbridge Horsey, Del.

Jeremiah Morrow, Ohio   Eli P. Ashmun, Mass.
Abner Lacock, Penn.   Eligius Fromentin, La.

On so much as relates to the African Slave Trade

Chairman: Outerbridge Horsey, Del.

Benjamin Ruggles, Ohio   Martin D. Hardin, Ky
Charles Tait, Ga.   David Daggett, Conn.

On so much as relates to the Office of Attorney General, and an Additional Department

Chairman: Nathan Sanford, N.Y.

Nathaniel Macon, N.C.   David Daggett, Conn.
John Williams, Tenn.   Jeremiah Mason, N.H.

CONGRESSIONAL DIRECTORY

FIFTEENTH CONGRESS, FIRST SESSION
(December 1, 1817–April 20, 1818)

Mr. Burch, Capitol Hill
Samuel C. Crafts, Vt.
Zadock Cook, Ga.
James Fisk (S), Vt.
Salma Hale, N.H.
Samuel D. Ingham, Penn.
William P. Maclay, Penn.
John Murray, Penn.
William Maclay, Penn.
Mark Richards, Vt.
Starling Tucker, S.C.
Nathaniel Upham, N.H.
William Wilson, Penn.
Lewis Williams, Penn.

Bailey's Hotel, Capitol Hill
Robert H. Goldsborough (S), Md.
Walter Leake (S),[1] Miss.
Philip J. Schuyler, N.Y.
Nathaniel Terry, Conn.
Rensselaer Westerle, N.Y.

Mr. Bailey, No. 1, Capitol Hill
William Lee Ball, Va.
Philip P. Barbour, Va.
Joseph H. Bryan, N.C.
George F. Strother, Va.
Thomas Settle, N.C.
James S. Smith, N.C.

Mr. Bailey, No. 2, Capitol Hill
Lemuel Sawyer, N.C.

Mr. Bailey, No. 3, Capitol Hill
Daniel Cruger, N.Y.
Harrison Gray Otis (S), Mass.
John F. Parrott, N.H.
Nathaniel Ruggles, Mass.
Jonathan Mason,[2] Mass.

Mr. Brown, near General Post Office
Oliver C. Comstock, N.Y.
Richard M. Johnson, Ky.

Mr. Claxton, Capitol Hill
William G. Blount, Tenn.
Burwell Bassett, Va.
John Holmes, Mass.
Francis Jones, Tenn.
Marcus Morton, Mass.
Anthony New, Ky.
Albion K. Parris,[3] Mass.
Zabdiel Sampson, Mass.
Henry Shaw, Mass.
John Savage, N.Y.
John Tyler, Va.
David Walker, Ky.

Mr. Coyle, Capitol Hill
James Burrill, Jr. (S), R.I.
John L. Boss, Jr., R.I.
John P. Cushman, N.Y.
David Daggett (S), Conn.
Uriel Holmes, Conn.
Timothy Pitkin, Conn.
Thomas S. Williams, Conn.

NOTE: Copies are located at the Boston Athenaeum and the Library of Congress.
[1] Took his seat Dec. 11, 1817.
[2] Also listed at Herronimus' Hotel.
[3] Resigned Feb. 3, 1818.

Mr. Dowson, No. 1, Capitol Hill
Joseph Bloomfield, N.J.
John Gaillard (S), S.C.
William Irving, N.Y.
Thomas M. Nelson, Va.
Thomas B. Robertson, La.
Nathan Sanford (S), N.Y.
Adam Seybert, Penn.
Samuel Smith, Md.
Henry St. George Tucker, Va.
George M. Troup (S), Ga.

Mr. Dowson, No. 2, Capitol Hill
Joel Abbot, Ga.
Richard C. Anderson, Jr., Ky.
James Barbour (S), Va.
John J. Crittenden (S), Ky.
Thomas W. Cobb, Ga.
Joel Crawford, Ga.
Weldon N. Edwards, N.C.
Daniel M. Forney, N.C.
Thomas H. Hall, N.C.
Nathaniel Macon (S), N.C.
Stephen D. Miller, S.C.
James Owen, N.C.
William Smith (S), S.C.
Charles Tait (S), Ga.
William Terrell, Ga.

Mrs. Clarke, F St.
John W. Eppes (S), Va.
Robert S. Garnett, Va.
William Henry Harrison, Ohio
James Johnson, Va.

Crawford's Hotel, Georgetown
Thomas Bayly, Md.
Edward Colston, Va.
John C. Herbert, Md.
Rufus King (S), N.Y.
Charles F. Mercer, Va.
James Pindall, Va.

Davis' Hotel, Penn. Ave.
William A. Burwell, Va.
Peterson Goodwyn,[4] Va.

Jeremiah Morrow (S), Ohio
Wilson Nesbitt, S.C.
Nathaniel Pope, Deleg., Ill. Terr.
Tunstall Quarles, Ky.
George Robertson, Ky.
John Scott,[5] Deleg., Mo. Terr.
David Trimble, Ky.

Miss Finegan, Penn. Ave.
Charles Kinsey, N.J.
Isaac Williams, Jr., N.Y.

Mr. Gaither, Penn. Ave.
William McCoy, Va.
James Pleasants, Va.
Thomas Speed, Ky.

Miss Heyer, Capitol Hill
Isaac Darlington, Penn.
Joseph Hopkinson, Penn.
William J. Lewis, Va.
Lewis McLane, Del.
Levi Pawling, Penn.
John Sergeant, Penn.
Jesse Slocumb, N.C.

Herronimus' Hotel, near Penn. Ave.
Archibald Austin, Va.
John Floyd, Va.
James Noble (S), Ind.
George Poindexter,[6] Miss.
Alexander Smyth, Va.
Montfort Stokes (S), N.C.
Waller Taylor (S), Ind.

Mr. Hyatt, Penn. Ave.
Benjamin Adams, Mass.
Samuel C. Allen, Mass.
Josiah Butler, N.H.
William Hendricks, Ind.
Jonathan O. Moseley, Conn.
John Ross,[7] Penn.
Solomon Strong, Mass.

Mrs. Hamilton, near the Bank of the Metropolis
Isham Talbot (S), Ky.

[4] Died Feb. 21, 1818.
[5] Took his seat Dec. 8, 1817.
[6] Took his seat Dec. 15, 1817.
[7] Resigned Feb. 24, 1818. He was succeeded by Thomas J. Rogers, who took his seat Mar. 24, 1818.

Mr. Huddleston, near General Post
  Office
Ephraim Bateman, N.J.
Benjamin Bennet, N.J.
Tredwell Scudder, N.Y.
Henry Southard, N.J.
George Townsend, N.Y.

Mrs. Lindsay, Penn. Ave.
John W. Campbell, Ohio
Elias Earle, S.C.
Samuel Herrick, Ohio
Abner Lacock (S), Penn.
John Linn, N.J.
David Marchand, Penn.
Robert Moore, Penn.
Christian Tarr, Penn.

Mr. McLeod, Capitol Hill
Mahlon Dickerson (S), N.J.
Ebenezer Huntington, Conn.
Jeremiah Nelson, Mass.
Benjamin Orr, Mass.
Samuel B. Sherwood, Conn.
Isaac Tichenor (S), Vt.
Ezekiel Whitman, Mass.
James W. Wilkin, N.Y.

Mrs. McCardle, Capitol Hill
Herman Allen, Vt.
Levi Barber, Ohio
Philemon Beecher, Ohio
Peter Hitchcock, Ohio
Benjamin Ruggles (S), Ohio
Charles Rich, Vt.
Ballard Smith, Va.
John W. Taylor, N.Y.
Peter H. Wendover, N.Y.

Mrs. Meyer, Penn. Ave.
Andrew Boden, Penn.
Joseph Desha, Ky.
Benjamin Ellicott, N.Y.
Joseph Hiester, Penn.
Thomas Patterson, Penn.
Jacob Spangler, Penn.
James M. Wallace, Penn.
John Whiteside, Penn.
James J. Wilson (S), N.J.

Mrs. Mathers, Capitol Hill
Thomas Culbreth, Md.
Philip Reed, Md.

O'Neal's Hotel, Penn. Ave.
Joseph Bellinger, S.C.
Thomas Claiborne, Tenn.
Samuel Hogg, Tenn.
George W. L. Marr, Tenn.
Samuel Ringgold, Md.
John Rhea, Tenn.
John Williams (S), Tenn.
Thomas H. Williams (S),[8] Miss.

Mrs. Odlin, Penn. Ave.
John Herkimer, N.Y.
Thomas Lawyer, N.Y.

Queen's Hotel, Capitol Hill
Eli P. Ashmun (S), Mass.
Clifton Clagett, N.H.
John R. Drake, N.Y.
Walter Folger, Jr., Mass.
Joshua Gage, Mass.
Outerbridge Horsey (S), Del.
William Hunter, Vt.
Josiah Hasbrouck, N.Y.
Thomas H. Hubbard, N.Y.
Dorrance Kirtland, N.Y.
Arthur Livermore, N.H.
David L. Morril (S), N.H.
Orsamus C. Merrill, Vt.
John Palmer, N.Y.
Henry R. Storrs, N.Y.
James Tallmadge, Jr., N.Y.
Caleb Tompkins, N.Y.

Tennison's Hotel, Penn. Ave.
Hugh Nelson, Va.

Mrs. Thompson, Six Buildings
Nathaniel Silsbee, Mass.

Mr. Washington, Capitol Hill
George Mumford, N.C.
Thomas Newton, Jr., Va.
James Porter, N.Y.
Jonathan Roberts (S), Penn.
John C. Spencer, N.Y.
Clement Storer (S), N.H.

[8] Took his seat Dec. 11, 1817.

Mrs. Wilson, Seven Buildings
George W. Campbell (S), Tenn.

Mr. Westerfield, Eleventh St. West
Felix Walker, N.C.

Commodore Porter, North of President's
House
William Anderson, Penn.

Colonel Bumford, opposite and near the
President's House
Henry Baldwin, Penn.

F St.
John Forsyth, Ga.

Georgetown
George Peter, Md.

Georgetown
Henry Middleton, S.C.

Near Centre Market
William Lowndes, S.C.

Near the Navy Yard
Peter Little, Md.

Near the Navy Yard
Philip Stuart, Md.

Penn. Ave.
Henry Clay, Ky.

APPENDIX

John Crowell,[9] Deleg., Ala. Terr.
Samuel W. Dana (S), Conn.
Willard Hall, Del.
Nicholas Van Dyke (S), Del.
Eligius Fromentin (S), La.
Henry Johnson,[10] La.
Alexander C. Hanson (S), Md.
Timothy Fuller, Mass.
Elijah H. Mills, Mass.

Thomas Rice, Mass.
John Wilson, Mass.
David A. Ogden, N.Y.
James Stewart,[11] N.C.
Alexander Ogle, Penn.
William Hunter (S), R.I.
James B. Mason, R.I.
James Ervin, S.C.
Eldred Simkins,[12] S.C.

STANDING COMMITTEES OF THE
HOUSE OF REPRESENTATIVES

WAYS AND MEANS

Chairman: William Lowndes, S.C.

Samuel Smith, Md.
William A. Burwell, Va.
Timothy Pitkin, Conn.

Joel Abbot, Ga.
John Sergeant, Penn.
David Trimble, Ky.

[9] Took his seat Mar. 9, 1818.
[10] William C. C. Claiborne died Nov. 23, 1817, never having qualified. Henry Johnson was elected to fill the vacancy, and took his seat Feb. 26, 1818.
[11] Took his seat Jan. 26, 1818.
[12] Took his seat Feb. 9, 1818.

ELECTIONS

Chairman: John W. Taylor, N.Y.

John Tyler, Va.
Orsamus C. Merrill, Vt.
Henry Shaw, Mass.

John L. Boss, Jr., R.I.
Ezekiel Whitman, Mass.
Solomon Strong, Mass.

COMMERCE AND MANUFACTURES

Chairman: Thomas Newton, Jr., Va.

Adam Seybert, Penn.
Jonathan O. Moseley, Conn.
William Irving, N.Y.

Louis McLane, Del.
Joel Crawford, Ga.
Charles Kinsey, N.J.

CLAIMS

Chairman: Lewis Williams, N.C.

Charles Rich, Vt.
Ephraim Bateman, N.J.
William McCoy, Va.

Ebenezer Huntington, Conn.
Philip J. Schuyler, N.Y.
David Walker, Ky.

DISTRICT OF COLUMBIA

Chairman: John C. Herbert, Md.

Stephen D. Miller, S.C.
George Peter, Md.
Andrew Boden, Penn.

George F. Strother, Va.
Thomas Claiborne, Tenn.
Thomas W. Cobb, Ga.

PUBLIC LANDS

Chairman: Thomas B. Robertson, La.

Richard C. Anderson, Jr., Ky.
Charles F. Mercer, Va.
John W. Campbell, Ohio

William Hendricks, Ind.
Nathaniel Terry, Conn.
George W. L. Marr, Tenn.

POST OFFICE AND POST ROADS

Chairman: Samuel D. Ingham, Penn.

William G. Blount, Tenn.
Levi Barber, Ohio
George Townsend, N.Y.

Jeremiah Nelson, Mass.
Edward Colston, Va.
William Terrell, Ga.

PENSIONS AND REVOLUTIONARY CLAIMS

Chairman: John Rhea, Tenn.

James W. Wilkin, N.Y.
Nathaniel Ruggles, Mass.
William P. Maclay, Penn.

Samuel B. Sherwood, Conn.
Benjamin Ellicott, N.Y.
James Owen, N.C.

PUBLIC EXPENDITURE

Chairman: Joseph Desha, Ky.

William Anderson, Penn.
Robert S. Garnett, Va.
John P. Cushman, N.Y.

Thomas Culbreth, Md.
William Hunter, Vt.
Uriel Holmes, Conn.

JUDICIARY

Chairman: Thomas M. Nelson, Va.

Joseph Hopkinson, Penn.
John C. Spencer, N.Y.
Weldon N. Edwards, N.C.

Philemon Beecher, Ohio
Arthur Livermore, N.H.
Salma Hale, N.H.

ACCOUNTS

Chairman: Peter Little, Md.

Benjamin Bennet, N.J.

Samuel C. Allen, Mass.

PRIVATE LAND CLAIMS

Chairman: Samuel Herrick, Ohio

Joseph Hiester, Penn.
James Pindall, Va.

Samuel Hogg, Tenn.
Caleb Tompkins, N.Y.

REVISAL AND UNFINISHED BUSINESS

Chairman: John Savage, N.Y.

John Whiteside, Penn.

Rensselaer Westerlo, N.Y.

EXPENDITURES IN THE DEPARTMENT OF STATE

Chairman: John Forsyth, Ga.

Josiah Hasbrouck, N.Y.

Tredwell Scudder, N.Y.

EXPENDITURES IN THE TREASURY DEPARTMENT

Chairman: William Lowndes, S.C.

Heman Allen, Vt.

David Marchand, Penn.

EXPENDITURES IN THE DEPARTMENT OF WAR

Chairman: Richard M. Johnson, Ky.

Starling Tucker, S.C.

John Herkimer, N.Y.

EXPENDITURES IN THE DEPARTMENT OF THE NAVY

Chairman: James Pleasants, Va.

Henry R. Storrs, N.Y.

Zabdiel Sampson, Mass.

EXPENDITURES IN THE POST OFFICE

Chairman: Samuel D. Ingham, Penn.

Thomas H. Hubbard, N.Y.   Ebenezer Huntington, Conn.

EXPENDITURES ON THE PUBLIC BUILDINGS

Chairman: Henry St. George Tucker, Va.

John R. Drake, N.Y.   Benjamin Orr, Mass.

SELECT COMMITTEES OF THE HOUSE OF REPRESENTATIVES APPOINTED ON VARIOUS PARTS OF THE PRESIDENT'S MESSAGE

On so much as relates to Foreign Affairs

Chairman: John Forsyth, Ga.

John Holmes, Mass	James Porter, N.Y.
Philip P. Barbour, Va.	Benjamin Orr, Mass.
Thomas B. Robertson, La.	Peterson Goodwyn, Va.

On so much as relates to Military Affairs

Chairman: Richard M. Johnson, Ky.

Joseph Bloomfield, N.J.	Wilson Nesbitt, S.C.
Philip Reed, Md.	Daniel M. Forney, N.C.
Thomas M. Nelson, Va.	Joshua Gage, Mass.

On so much as relates to the Militia

Chairman: William Henry Harrison, Ohio

Ballard Smith, Va.	Francis Jones, Tenn.
Tunstall Quarles, Ky.	John Linn, N.J.
Thomas S. Williams, Conn.	Marcus Morton, Mass.

On so much as relates to Naval Affairs

Chairman: James Pleasants, Va.

Nathaniel Silsbee, Mass.	Samuel Ringgold, Va.
Peter H. Wendover, N.Y.	Lemuel Sawyer, N.C.
John F. Parrott, N.H.	Philip J. Schuyler, N.Y.

On so much as relates to Indian Affairs

Chairman: Henry Southard, N.J.

Isaac Williams, Jr., N.Y.	Josiah Butler, N.H.
John Murray, Penn.	Mark Richards, Vt.
Jesse Slocumb, N.C.	Christian Tarr, Penn.

On so much as relates to Roads, Canals, and Seminaries of Learning

Chairman: Henry St. George Tucker, Va.

James Tallmadge, Jr., N.Y.	Clifton Clagett, N.H.
Samuel D. Ingham, Penn.	George Robertson, Ky.
Henry R. Storrs, N.Y.	William Lewis, Va.

On so much as relates to the Introduction of Slaves from Amelia Island

Chairman: Henry Middleton, S.C.

James S. Smith, N.C.   William Lee Ball, Va.
Nathaniel Upham, N.H.   George Mumford, N.C.
Thomas Lawyer,[13] N.Y.   Zadock Cook, Ga.

On so much as relates to Public Buildings and Additional Edifices

Chairman: Albion K. Parris, Mass.

Burwell Basset, Va.   John Forsyth, Ga.
Joseph Bellinger, S.C.   Samuel C. Crafts, Vt.
John W. Taylor, N.Y.   Walter Folger, Jr., Mass.

*On so much as relates to the Surviving Officers and Soldiers
of the Revolutionary Army*

Chairman: Joseph Bloomfield, N.J.

Philip Reed, Md.   Samuel Smith, Md.
Philip Stuart, Md.   James M. Wallace, Penn.
John Rhea, Tenn.   Thomas H. Hall, N.C.

STANDING COMMITTEES OF THE SENATE

FOREIGN RELATIONS

Chairman: James Barbour, Va.

Nathaniel Macon, N.C.   Rufus King, N.Y.
Abner Lacock, Penn.   George M. Troup, Ga.

FINANCE

Chairman: George W. Campbell, Tenn.

Rufus King, N.Y.   John W. Eppes, Va.
Isham Talbot, Ky.   Nathaniel Macon, N.C.

COMMERCE AND MANUFACTURES

Chairman: Nathan Sanford, N.Y.

Outerbridge Horsey, Del.   David L. Morril, N. H.
James Burrill, Jr., R.I.   Mahlon Dickerson, N.J.

MILITARY AFFAIRS

Chairman: George M. Troup, Ga.

John Williams, Tenn.   Isaac Tichenor, Vt.
Abner Lacock, Penn.   Waller Taylor, Ind.

MILITIA

Chairman: Clement Storer, N.H.

James Noble, Ind.   Jonathan Roberts, Penn.
Nathaniel Macon, N.C.   Benjamin Ruggles, Ohio

[13] The *Annals of Congress* lists Lemuel Sawyer (N.C.)

NAVAL AFFAIRS

Chairman: Charles Tait, Ga.

Nathan Sanford, N.Y.   John J. Crittenden, Ky.
David Daggett, Conn.   Thomas H. Williams, Miss.

PUBLIC LANDS

Chairman: Jeremiah Morrow, Ohio

James Fisk, Vt.   Waller Taylor, Ind.
Thomas H. Williams, Miss.   William Hunter, R.I.

CLAIMS

Chairman: Jonathan Roberts, Penn.

David L. Morril, N.H.   Benjamin Ruggles, Ohio
Robert H. Goldborough, Md.   James J. Wilson, N.J.

JUDICIARY

Chairman: John J. Crittenden, Ky.

James Burrill, Jr., R.I.   Harrison Gray Otis, Mass.
William Smith, S.C.   Walter Leake, Miss.

POST OFFICES AND POST ROADS

Chairman: James J. Wilson, N.J.

Eli P. Ashmun, Mass.   James Fisk, Vt.
Benjamin Ruggles, Ohio   Montfort Stokes, N.C.

PENSIONS

Chairman: James Noble, Ind.

Clement Storer, N.H.   Abner Lacock, Penn.
Nicholas Van Dyke, Del.   Isham Talbot, Ky.

DISTRICT OF COLUMBIA

Chairman: Robert H. Goldsborough, Md.

James Barbour, Va.   David Daggett, Conn.
John W. Eppes, Va.   Montfort Stokes, N.C.

LIBRARY

Chairman: Mahlon Dickerson, N.J.

Rufus King, N.Y.   Charles Tait, Ga.

*On so much of the President's Message as relates to Roads, Inland Navigation,
and Seminaries of Learning*

Chairman: Abner Lacock, Penn.

Rufus King, N.Y.   James Barbour, Va.
Harrison Gray Otis, Mass.   Jeremiah Morrow, Ohio

CONGRESSIONAL DIRECTORY

FIFTEENTH CONGRESS, SECOND SESSION
(November 16, 1818–March 3, 1819)

Mr. Bayly, Capitol Hill
Abner Lacock (S), Penn.

Mr. Bestor, Tenth St.
Isaac Williams, Jr., N.Y.
John Linn, N.J.
David Marchand, Penn.
Robert Moore, Penn.
Christian Tarr, Penn.
William Hendricks, Ind.

Mr. Brown, near City Post Office
Oliver C. Comstock, N.Y.
Richard M. Johnson, Ky.

Colonel Bumford, North of President's House
Henry Baldwin, Penn.

Mr. Burch, Capitol Hill
John Williams (S), Tenn.
Samuel C. Crafts, Vt.
Mark Richards, Vt.
William Maclay, Penn.
William P. Maclay, Penn.
John Murray, Penn.
William Wilson, Penn.
Jesse Slocumb, N.C.
James S. Smith, N.C.
Lewis Williams, N.C.
Starling Tucker, S.C.
Zadock Cook, Ga.

Mr. Coyle, Capitol Hill
Prentiss Mellen (S), Mass.
James Burrill, Jr. (S), R.I.
David Daggett (S), Conn.
John L. Boss, Jr., R.I.
James B. Mason, R.I.
Timothy Pitkin, Conn.
Nathaniel Terry, Conn.
Thomas S. Williams, Conn.

Crawford's Hotel, Georgetown
Rufus King (S), N.Y.
Outerbridge Horsey (S), Del.
Robert H. Goldsborough (S), Md.
Alexander C. Hanson (S), Md.
Jesse B. Thomas (S),[1] Ill.
Thomas Bayly, Md.
John C. Herbert, Md.
Edward Colston, Va.
Charles F. Mercer, Va.
James Pindall, Va.

Davis' Hotel, Penn. Ave.
William A. Palmer (S), Vt.
Jeremiah Morrow (S), Ohio
Benjamin Ruggles (S), Ohio
Timothy Fuller, Mass.
Heman Allen,[2] Vt.
William Irving, N.Y.
William A. Burwell, Va.
Thomas M. Nelson, Va.
Henry St. George Tucker, Va.
Joel Crawford, Ga.

NOTE: Copies are located at the Boston Athenaeum, the New York Public Library and the Yale University Library. The original lists the Congressmen according to states; it has been rearranged according to boardinghouses.
[1] Took his seat Dec. 4, 1818.
[2] Resigned Apr. 20, 1818.

William Terrell, Ga.
Henry Clay, Ky.
George Robertson, Ky.
David Trimble, Ky.
Levi Barber, Ohio
Philemon Beecher, Ohio
John W. Campbell, Ohio
John Scott, Deleg., Terr. of Mo.

Mr. Dowson, No. 1, Capitol Hill
Nathan Sanford (S), N.Y.
Mahlon Dickerson (S), N.J.
Henry Johnson (S), La.
Thomas H. Williams (S),[3] Miss.
John Gaillard, S.C.
William Smith, S.C.
Joseph Bloomfield, N.J.
Adam Seybert, Penn.
Samuel Smith, Md.
James Stewart,[4] N.Y.
Eldred Simkins, S.C.
Thomas Butler, La.

Mr. Dowson, No. 2, Capitol Hill
James Barbour (S), Va.
Nathaniel Macon (S), N.C.
John J. Crittenden (S), Ky.
William J. Lewis, Va.
William Davidson,[5] N.C.
Weldon N. Edwards, N.C.
Thomas H. Hall, N.C.
Stephen D. Miller, S.C.
Joel Abbot, Ga.
Thomas W. Cobb, Ga.
Richard C. Anderson, Jr., Ky.
John McLean,[6] Ill.
John Crowell, Deleg., Ala. Terr.

Mr. Fitzgerald, N.J. Ave.
Jonathan Roberts (S), Penn.

Mr. Fletcher, near City Post Office
Enoch Lincoln, Mass.
Marcus Morton, Mass.
Orsamus C. Merrill, Vt.
Josiah Hasbrouck, N.Y.
Thomas H. Hubbard, N.Y.

John Palmer, N.Y.
James W. Wilkin, N.Y.

Mr. Frost, Capitol Hill
Isaac Tichenor (S), Vt.
Jeremiah Nelson, Mass.
Ebenezer Huntington, Conn.
Samuel B. Sherwood, Conn.
Lemuel Sawyer, N.C.

Mr. Gaither, Penn. Ave.
John W. Eppes (S), Va.
William McCoy, Va.
James Pleasants, Va.
Thomas Speed, Ky.

Georgetown
George Peter, Md.

Herronimus' Hotel, Georgetown
Eligius Fromentin (S), La.
Philip J. Schuyler, N.Y.
Rensselaer Westerlo, N.Y.
John Floyd, Va.
George Poindexter, Miss.

Miss Heyer, Capitol Hill
Henry R. Storrs, N.Y.
Isaac Darlington, Penn.
Joseph Hopkinson, Penn.
Levi Pawling, Penn.
John Sergeant, Penn.
Louis McLane, Del.

Mrs. Hickey, Capitol Hill
Henry Shaw, Mass.
James Porter, N.Y.
Thomas Culbreth, Md.
Anthony New, Ky.
David Walker, Ky.

Mrs. Huddleston, near Post Office
Tredwell Scudder, N.Y.
George Townsend, N.Y.
Ephraim Bateman, N.J.
Benjamin Bennet, N.J.
Henry Southard, N.J.

[3] Took his seat Dec. 11, 1817.
[4] Took his seat Jan. 26, 1818.
[5] Took his seat Dec. 2, 1818.
[6] Took his seat Dec. 4, 1818.

Mr. Hyatt, Penn. Ave.
James Noble (S), Ind.
Nathaniel Upham, N.H.
Benjamin Adams, Mass.
Samuel C. Allen, Mass.
Thomas Rice, Mass.
John Wilson, Mass.
Jonathan R. Moseley, Conn.
George Mumford,[7] N.C.

Mr. Little, near the Navy Yard
Peter Little, Md.

Mrs. McCardle, Capitol Hill
Walter Leake (S), Miss.
Arthur Livermore, N.H.
John Holmes, Mass.
Zabdiel Sampson, Mass.
Sylvester Gilbert, Conn.
John W. Taylor, N.Y.
Peter H. Wendover, N.Y.
Ballard Smith, Vir.
Francis Jones, Tenn.
Peter Hitchcock, Ohio

McGowan's Hotel, Penn. Ave.
Waller Taylor (S), Ind.
Archibald Austin, Va.
William Lee Ball, Va.
James Johnson, Va.
John Pegram, Va.
John Tyler, Va.
Thomas Settle, N.C.
William Henry Harrison, Ohio

Mr. McLeod, Penn. Ave.
Jonathan Mason, Mass.
Ezekiel Whitman, Mass.
Daniel Cruger, N.Y.
Alexander Smyth, Va.
Tunstall Quarles, Ky.

Mr. Maddox, near City Post Office
John R. Drake, N.Y.
Dorrance Kirtland, N.Y.
Caleb Tompkins, N.Y.
Charles Kinsey, N.J.

Mrs. Meyer, near Centre Market
James J. Wilson (S), N.J.
Benjamin Ellicott, N.Y.
Andrew Boden, Penn.
Joseph Hiester, Penn.
Jacob Hostetter, Penn.
Samuel Moore, Penn.
Alexander Ogle, Penn.
Thomas Patterson, Penn.
Thomas J. Rogers, Penn.
James M. Wallace, Penn.
John Whiteside, Penn.

Near City Post Office
John Forsyth (S),[8] Ga.

Near Georgetown
Henry Middleton, S.C.

Near the Navy Yard
Philip Stuart, Md.

Near the Navy Yard
Joseph Desha, Ky.

Ninth St.
William Lowndes, S.C.

Mrs. Odlin, Penn. Ave.
Isham Talbot (S), Ky.
John Herkimer, N.Y.
Samuel Herrick, Ohio

O'Neal's Hotel, Penn. Ave.
John H. Eaton (S), Tenn.
Samuel Ringgold, Md.
Joseph Bellinger, S.C.
Thomas Claiborne, Tenn.
Samuel Hogg, Tenn.
John Rhea, Tenn.

Commodore Porter, North of President's House
William Anderson, Penn.

Miss Queen, Capitol Hill
John F. Parrott, N.H.

[7] Died Dec. 31, 1818. He was succeeded by Charles Fisher, who took his seat Feb. 11, 1819.
[8] Resigned his House seat, and took his Senate seat on Nov. 23, 1818.

Thomas Lawyer, N.Y.
Philip Reed, Md.

Mr. Queen, Capitol Hill
Walter Folger, Jr., Mass.
Benjamin Orr, Mass.
Nathaniel Ruggles, Mass.
John P. Cushman, N.Y.
James Tallmadge, Jr., N.Y.

Mrs. Rosseau, Penn. Ave.
Burwell Bassett, Va.

Strother's Hotel, Penn. Ave.
Harrison Gary Otis (S), Mass.
Ninian Edwards (S),[9] Ill.
David A. Ogden, N.Y.
Philip P. Barbour, Va.
Robert S. Garnett, Va.
Hugh Nelson, Va.
Thomas Nelson, Jr., Va.
George F. Strother, Va.
Joseph H. Bryan, N.C.
James Owen, N.C.
William G. Blount, Tenn.

Mrs. Thompson, Six Buildings
Salma Hale, N.H.
Nathaniel Silsbee, Mass.

Mrs. Thornton, Capitol Hill
David L. Morril (S), N.H.
Josiah Butler, N.H.
Clifton Clagett, N.H.
Joshua Gage, Mass.
William Hunter, Vt.
Charles Rich, Vt.

Mr. Washington, Capitol Hill
Clement Storer (S), N.H.
Nicholas Van Dyke (S), Del.
John Savage, N.Y.
John C. Spencer, N.Y.
Elias Earle, S.C.
James Ervin, S.C.

Mr. Williams, near Branch Bank
Felix Walker, N.C.

APPENDIX

Samuel W. Dana (S), Conn.
Willard Hall, Del.
Robert R. Reid,[10] Ga.
Charles Tait (S), Ga.
Elijah H. Mills, Mass.

Solomon Strong, Mass.
Montfort Stokes (S),[11] N.C.
William Hunter (S), R.I.
Wilson Nesbitt, S.C.
George W. L. Marr, Tenn.

STANDING COMMITTEES OF THE
HOUSE OF REPRESENTATIVES

WAYS AND MEANS

Chairman: Samuel Smith, Md.

William A. Burwell, Va.
Timothy Pitkin, Conn.
John Sergeant, Penn.

David Trimble, Ky.
Joel Crawford, Ga.
James Tallmadge, Jr., N.Y.

[9] Took his seat Dec. 4, 1818.
[10] Took his seat Feb. 18, 1819.
[11] Listed at Mr. Dowson's without No. 1 or No. 2 being specified.

ELECTIONS

Chairman: John W. Taylor, N.Y.

Alexander Smyth, Va.
Orsamus C. Merrill, Vt.
Henry Shaw, Mass.

John L. Boss, Jr., R.I.
Ezekiel Whitman, Mass.
Christian Tarr, Penn.

COMMERCE AND MANUFACTURES

Chairman: Thomas Newton, Jr., Va.

Adam Seybert, Penn.
Louis McLane, Del.
Jonathan Mason, Mass.

William Irving, N.Y.
Henry Baldwin, Penn.
Charles Kinsey, N.J.

CLAIMS

Chairman: Lewis Williams, N.C.

Charles Rich, Vt.
William McCoy, Va.
Samuel Moore, Penn.

David Walker, Ky.
Thomas Culbreth, Md.
Sylvester Gilbert, Conn.

DISTRICT OF COLUMBIA

Chairman: John C. Herbert, Md.

George Peter, Md.
Andrew Boden, Penn.
Thomas W. Cobb, Ga.

Thomas Claiborne, Tenn.
Edward Colston, Va.
Philip Stewart, Md.

PUBLIC LANDS

Chairman: George Poindexter, Miss.

Charles F. Mercer, Va.
John W. Campbell, Ohio
William Hendricks, Ind.

Nathaniel Terry, Conn.
Francis Jones, Tenn.
Thomas Butler, La.

POST OFFICE AND POST ROADS

Chairman: Arthur Livermore, N.H.

William G. Blount, Tenn.
Levi Barber, Ohio
George Townsend, N.Y.

Zabdiel Sampson, Mass.
William Terrell, Ga.
Thomas Settle, N.C.

PENSIONS AND REVOLUTIONARY CLAIMS

Chairman: John Rhea, Tenn.

James W. Wilkin, N.Y.
Nathaniel Ruggles, Mass.
William P. Maclay, Penn.

Benjamin Ellicott, N.Y.
James Owen, N.C.
Benjamin Orr, Mass.

PUBLIC EXPENDITURE

Chairman: Joseph Desha, Ky.

William Anderson, Penn.
Robert S. Garnett, Va.
John P. Cushman, N.Y.

James S. Smith, N.C.
William Hunter, Vt.
Thomas S. Williams, Conn.

JUDICIARY

Chairman: Hugh Nelson, Va.

Joseph Hopkinson, Penn.
Weldon N. Edwards, N.C.
Philemon Beecher, Ohio

Henry R. Storrs, N.Y.
Tunstall Quarles, Ky.
Jonathan O. Moseley, Conn.

PRIVATE LAND CLAIMS

Chairman: George Robertson, Ky.

James Pindall, Va.
Samuel Hogg, Tenn.
Thomas H. Hubbard, N.Y.

Thomas Bayly, Md.
Robert Moore, Penn.
Ballard Smith, Va.

ENROLLED BILLS

House
William Wilson, Penn.
Thomas Speed, Ky.

Senate
James Noble, Ind.

REVISAL AND UNFINISHED BUSINESS

Chairman: John W. Taylor, N.Y.

Salma Hale, N.H.

John Whiteside, Penn.

ACCOUNTS

Chairman: Peter Little, Md.

Benjamin Bennet, N.J.

Isaac Darlington, Penn.

LIBRARY

House
Adam Seybert, Penn.
Jonathan Mason, Mass.
William Irving, N.Y.

Senate
Mahlon Dickerson, N.J.
Rufus King, N.Y.
Eligius Fromentin, La.

On Expenditures in the Department of State

Chairman: Josiah Hasbrouck, N.Y.

Tredwell Scudder, N.Y.

(one vacant)

On Expenditures in the Treasury Department

Chairman: William Lowndes, S.C.

Samuel C. Allen, Mass.

David Marchand, Penn.

On Expenditures in the Department of War

Chairman: Richard M. Johnson, Ky.
Starling Tucker, S.C.   John Herkimer, N.Y.

On Expenditures in the Department of the Navy

Chairman: James Pleasants, Va.
Henry R. Storrs, N.Y.   Zabdiel Sampson, Mass.

On Expenditures in the Post Office

Chairman: Thomas H. Hubbard, N.Y.
Ebenezer Huntington, Conn.   (one vacant)

On Expenditures on the Public Buildings

Chairman: Henry St. George Tucker, Va.
John R. Drake, N.Y.   Benjamin Orr, Mass.

SELECT COMMITTEES APPOINTED ON VARIOUS PARTS
OF THE PRESIDENT'S MESSAGE

On so much as relates to Foreign Affairs

Chairman: John Holmes, Mass.
Philip P. Barbour, Va.   Henman Allen, Vt.
John C. Spencer, N.Y.   Joseph Hopkinson, Penn.
Henry Baldwin, Penn.   (one vacant)

On so much as relates to Military Affairs

Chairman: Richard M. Johnson, Ky.
Philip Reed, Md.   Joshua Gage, Mass.
Thomas M. Nelson, Va.   James Stewart, N.C.
Ebenezer Huntington, Conn.   George Peter, Md.

On so much as relates to the Navy and Naval Depots

Chairman: James Pleasants, Va.
Nathaniel Silsbee, Mass.   Philip Schuyler, N.Y.
John F. Parrott, N.H.   Thomas Rogers, Penn.
Lemuel Sawyer, N.C.   Ephraim Bateman, N.J.

On so much as relates to the Civilization of the Indian Tribes

Chairman: Henry Southard, N.J.
Isaac Williams, Jr., N.Y.   Mark Richards, Vt.
John Murray, Penn.   Josiah Butler, N.H.
Felix Walker, N.C.   John Pegram, Va.

*On so much as relates to the Unlawful Introduction of Slaves into the
United States*

Chairman: Henry Middleton, S.C.

Nathaniel Upham, N.H.	George Mumford, N.C.
Thomas Lawyer, N.Y.	Enoch Lincoln, Mass.
John Floyd, Va.	John Linn, N.J.

SELECT COMMITTEES APPOINTED ON THE
FOLLOWING SUBJECTS

MILITIA

Chairman: William Henry Harrison, Ohio

Alexander Smyth, Va.	Francis Jones, Tenn.
Tunstall Quarles, Ky.	John Savage, N.Y.
Marcus Morton, Mass.	James Owen, N.C.

ROADS AND CANALS

Chairman: Henry St. George Tucker, Va.

Henry R. Storrs, N.Y.	James Porter, N.Y.
William J. Lewis, Va.	Samuel C. Crafts, Vt.
John Sergeant, Penn.	David Marchand, Penn.

PUBLIC BUILDINGS

Chairman: Joseph Bellinger, S.C.

Benjamin Adams, Mass.	Thomas Bayly, Md.
Clifton Clagett, N.H.	Thomas Rice, Mass.
Walter Folger, Jr., Mass.	(one vacant)

REVOLUTIONARY PENSIONS

Chairman: Joseph Bloomfield, N.J.

William A. Burwell, Va.	John R. Drake, N.Y.
Alexander Ogle, Penn.	John Herkimer, N.Y.
James M. Wallace, Penn.	John Wilson, Mass.

STANDING COMMITTEES OF THE SENATE OF THE
UNITED STATES

FOREIGN RELATIONS

Chairman: Nathaniel Macon, N.C.

James Barbour, Va.	Abner Lacock, Penn.
Rufus King, N.Y.	David Daggett, Conn.

FINANCE

Chairman: John W. Eppes, Va.

Isham Talbot, Ky.   Nathaniel Macon, N.C.
Rufus King, N.Y.   John H. Eaton, Tenn.

COMMERCE AND MANUFACTURES

Chairman: Nathan Sanford, N.Y.

Mahlon Dickerson, N.J.   Outerbridge Horsey, Del.
James Burrill, Jr., R.I.   David L. Morril, N.H.

MILITARY AFFAIRS

Chairman: John Williams, Tenn.

Abner Lacock, Penn.   Waller Taylor, Ind.
Isaac Tichenor, Vt.   Clement Storer, N.H.

NAVAL AFFAIRS

Chairman: Nathan Sanford, N.Y.

Charles Tait, Ga.   David Daggett, Conn.
Thomas H. Williams, Mass.   John J. Crittenden, Ky.

PUBLIC LANDS

Chairman: Jeremiah Morrow, Ohio

Thomas H. Williams, Miss.   William Hunter, R.I.
Waller Taylor, Ind.   Henry Johnson, La.

MILITIA

Chairman: Benjamin Ruggles, Ohio

James Noble, Ind.   Nathaniel Macon, N.C.
Jonathan Roberts, Penn.   Clement Storer, N.H.

CLAIMS

Chairman: Robert H. Goldsborough, Md.

James J. Wilson, N.J.   Benjamin Ruggles, Ohio
Jonathan Roberts, Penn.   David L. Morril, N.H.

JUDICIARY

Chairman: James Burrill, Jr., R.I.

John J. Crittenden, Ky.   William Smith, S.C.
Harrison Gray Otis, Mass.   Walter Leake, Miss.

POST OFFICE AND POST ROADS

Chairman: Montfort Stokes, N.C.

James J. Wilson, N.J.   Prentiss Mellen, Mass.
William A. Palmer, Vt.   Benjamin Ruggles, Ohio

PENSIONS

Chairman: Abner Lacock, Penn.

James Noble, Ind.   Isham Talbot, Ky.
Nicholas Van Dyke, Del.   Clement Storer, N.H.

DISTRICT OF COLUMBIA

Chairman: Robert H. Goldsborough, Md.

David Daggett, Conn.   John W. Eppes, Va.
James Barbour, Va.   Alexander C. Hanson, Md.

CONGRESSIONAL DIRECTORY

SIXTEENTH CONGRESS, FIRST SESSION
(December 6, 1819–May 15, 1820)

Mr. Burch, Capitol Hill
Josiah Butler, N.H.
Samuel C. Crafts, Vt.
John Fay, N.Y.
John McCreary, N.C.
James Overstreet, N.C.
Harmanus Peck, N.Y.
Mark Richards, Vt.
Starling Tucker, N.C.
Nathaniel Upham, N.H.

Mrs. Blake, Thirteenth St.
William Davidson, Va.
Montfort Stokes (S), N.C.
Bernard Smith, N.J.

Mr. Bestor, Penn. Ave.
John Culpepper, Va.
Jeremiah Nelson, Mass.

Mr. Ball, Capitol Hill
William Strong, Vt.

Mr. Claxton, Capitol Hill
Henry H. Bryan, Tenn.
Clifton Clagett, N.H.
Josiah Cushman, Mass.
John Cocke, Tenn.
Henry W. Edwards, Conn.
Nathaniel Hazard, R.I.
Francis Jones, Tenn.
Martin Kinsley, Mass.
Walter Leake (S), Miss.
Enoch Lincoln, Mass.
David L. Morril (S), N.H.

Marcus Morton, Mass.
James Parker, Mass.
John Russ, Conn.

Mr. Coyle, Capitol Hill
James Burrill, Jr. (S), R.I.
Samuel W. Dana (S), Conn.
William Hunter (S), R.I.
John F. Parrott (S), N.H.
Prentiss Mellen (S), Mass.

Congress Hotel, Capitol Hill
Samuel C. Allen, Mass.
Joseph Buffum, Jr., N.H.
Samuel Edwards, Penn.
Arthur Livermore, N.H.
Samuel Lathrop, Mass.
Ezra Meech, Vt.
William Plumer, Jr., N.H.
William A. Palmer (S), Vt.
Elisha Phelps, Conn.
Charles Rich, Vt.
James Stevens, Conn.

Mrs. Clark, F St.
Robert S. Garnett, Va.
Hugh Nelson, Va.
Thomas Newton, Jr., Va.
George F. Strother,[1] Va.

Crawford's Hotel, Georgetown
Thomas Bayly, Md.
Louis McLane, Del.
Charles F. Mercer, Va.

NOTE: Copies are located at the Boston Athenaeum, the New York Public Library and the Alderman Library of the University of Virginia.
[1] Resigned Feb. 10, 1820.

Raphael Neale, Md.
Harrison Gray Otis (S), Mass.
James Pindall, Va.
Charles Pinckney, S.C.
Thomas Van Swearingen, Va.
Henry R. Warfield, Md.

Mr. Dowson, No. 1, Capitol Hill
Joseph Bloomfield, N.J.
Joseph Brevard, S.C.
Thomas Butler, La.
Joseph Kent, Md.
Jonathan Mason, N.H.
William Smith (S), S.C.
Samuel Smith, Md.
Eldred Simkins, S.C.
John W. Walker (S),[2] Ala.
Henry Johnson (S),[3] La.

Mr. Dowson, No. 2, Capitol Hill
Joel Abbot, Ga.
James Barbour (S), Va.
Hutchins G. Burton, N.C.
Thomas W. Cobb, Ga.
John Elliot (S), Ga.
John Randolph, Va.
Weldon N. Edwards, Va.
Thomas H. Hall, N.C.
Nathaniel Macon (S), N.C.
William Terrell, Ga.

Davis' Hotel, Penn. Ave.
Robert Allen, Tenn.
William A. Burwell, Va.
Tunstall Quarles, Ky.
Benjamin Ruggles (S), Ohio
George Robertson, Ky.
John Sloane, Ohio
John Scott, Deleg., Mo. Terr.
David Trimble, Ky.
William Pinkney (S),[4] Md.

Mr. Fletcher, near General Post Office
Philemon Beecher, Ohio

John W. Campbell, Ohio
Daniel P. Cook, Ill.
Timothy Fuller, Mass.
Thomas R. Ross, Ohio
William W. Woodbridge,[5] Deleg., Mich. Terr.

Mrs. Gaither, Penn. Ave.
Ephraim Bateman, N.J.
William McCoy, Va.
James Pleasants (S),[6] Va.
Henry Southard, N.J.
Jared Williams, Va.

Miss Heyer, Capitol Hill
Thomas Forrest, Penn.
Joseph Hemphill, Penn.
James Jones, Va.
Henry R. Storrs, N.Y.
Randall S. Street, N.Y.
James Strong, N.Y.
John Sergeant, Penn.

Mr. Hyatt, Penn. Ave.
Benjamin Adams, Mass.
William Hendricks, Ind.
Jonas Kendall, Mass.
James Noble (S), Ind.
Jonathan O. Moseley, Conn.

Mrs. Hickey, Capitol Hill
Thomas Culbreth, Md.
John W. Taylor, N.Y.
Henry Shaw, Mass.
David Walker,[7] Ky.

Mrs. Hamilton, near General Post Office
Elias Earle, S.C.
Walter Lowrie (S), Penn.
Samuel Gross, Penn.
Samuel Moore, Penn.

Mrs. Harrison, Georgetown
Outerbridge Horsey (S), Del.

---

[2] Took his seat Dec. 14, 1819.
[3] Boarded either at Dowson's No. 1 or Dowson's No. 2.
[4] Took his seat Jan. 4, 1820.
[5] Took his seat Mar. 2, 1820.
[6] Took his Senate seat after resigning his House seat on Dec. 14, 1819. He was succeeded in the House by William S. Archer, who took his seat Jan. 18, 1820.
[7] Died Mar. 1, 1820.

Mrs. McCardle, Capitol Hill
Walter Case, N.Y.
Samuel Eddy, R.I.
John Holmes, Mass.
Mark L. Hill, Mass.
Zabdiel Sampson, Mass.
Ballard Smith, Va.
Caleb Tompkins, N.Y.
Solomon Van Rensselaer, N.Y.
Peter H. Wendover, N.Y.
Silas Wood, N.Y.

Mr. McLeod, Penn. Ave.
Edward Dowse, Mass.
Nathaniel Silsbee, Mass.
Alexander Smyth, Va.
Ezekiel Whitman, Mass.

Mrs. Meyer, near Centre Market
Andrew Boden, Penn.
William Darlington, Penn.
George Denison, Penn.
David Fullerton, Penn.
Ezra C. Gross, N.Y.
Joseph Hiester, Penn.
Jacob Hibshman, Penn.
Jacob Hostetter, Penn.
Thomas Patterson, Penn.
Nathaniel Pitcher, N.Y.
Thomas J. Rogers, Penn.
James M. Wallace, Penn.
James J. Wilson (S), N.J.

Mrs. Odlin, Penn. Ave.
Samuel Herrick, Ohio
John Linn, N.J.
William P. Maclay, Penn.
David Marchand, Penn.
Robert Moore, Penn.
John Murray, Penn.
Christian Tarr, Penn.

O'Neale's Hotel, Penn. Ave.
Stevenson Archer, Md.
John H. Eaton (S), Tenn.
Benjamin Hardin, Ky.

John Rhea, Tenn.
Christopher Rankin, Miss.
Thomas H. Williams (S), Miss.

Mrs. Peyton, C St., North
William Brown, Ky.
Henry Brush, Ohio
John Crowell,[8] Ala.
Henry Clay, Ky.
Joel Crawford, Ga.
Ninian Edwards (S), Ill
John Floyd, Va.
Alney McLean, Ky.
Thomas Metcalfe, Ky.
Robert R. Reid, Ga.
William A. Trimble (S), Ohio
Freeman Walker (S),[9] Ga.
John Williams (S), Tenn.

Miss Polk, Penn. Ave.
John A. Cuthbert, Ga.

Mr. Queen, Capitol Hill
Richard C. Anderson, Jr., Ky.
Walter Folger, Jr., Mass
Samuel A. Foote, Conn.
Charles Hooks, N.C.
James Lanman (S), Conn.
William Logan (S), Ky.
Orsamus C. Merrill,[10] Vt.
James S. Smith, N.C.
Jesse Slocumb, N.C.
Isaac Tichenor (S), Vt.
Gideon Tomlinson, Conn.

Mrs. Queen, Penn. Ave.
Nathaniel Allen, N.Y.
Robert Clark, N.Y.
Jacob H. De Witt, N.Y.
William D. Ford, N.Y.
Aaron Hackley, Jr., N.Y.
George Hall, N.Y.
Jonathan Richmond, N.Y.

Strother's Hotel, Penn. Ave.
James Brown (S),[11] La.

[8] Took his seat Dec. 14, 1819.
[9] Took his seat Dec. 15, 1819.
[10] Served until Jan. 12, 1820. Succeeded by Rollin C. Mallory, who successfully contested the election and took his seat Jan. 13, 1820.
[11] Lived either at Strother's Hotel or near it.

Philip P. Barbour, Va.
John D. Dickinson, N.Y.
Samuel Ringgold, Md.
Edward Lloyd (S),[12] Md.

Mr. Sawyer, Penn. Ave.
Caleb Baker, N.Y.

Mr. Tims, Capitol Hill
Newton Cannon, Tenn.
Charles Fisher, N.C.
Thomas Settle, N.C.
Jesse B. Thomas (S), Ill.
Lewis Williams, N.C.

Tennison's Hotel, Penn. Ave.
Mark Alexander, Va.
William Lee Ball, Va.
James Johnson,[13] Va.
Severn E. Parker, Va.
Nathan Sanford (S), N.Y.
Waller Taylor (S), Ind.
John Tyler, Va.

Mr. Washington, Capitol Hill
Mahlon Dickerson (S), N.J.
James Ervin, S.C.
John Gaillard (S), S.C.

Wallard Hall, Del.
Joseph S. Lyman, N.Y.
Robert Monell, N.Y.
Albert H. Tracy, N.Y.
Nicholas Van Dyke (S), Del.
Robert Philson, Penn.

Mrs. Wilson, F St.
George Tucker, Va.

Mr. Williams, Thirteenth St.
Felix Walker, N.C.

Private Residences:
Mr. Fitsgerald, N.J. Ave.
Jonathan Roberts (S), Penn.
Mr. Meigs, F. St.
Henry Meigs, N.Y.
Colonel Bumford, North of the President's House
Henry Baldwin, Penn.
Mr. Little, near the Navy Yard
Peter Little, Md.
Ninth St.
William Lowndes, S.C.
Mr. Brown
Richard M. Johnson (S), Ky.

APPENDIX

William R. King (S),[14] Ala.
Charles Kinsey,[15] N.J.
Rufus King (S), N.Y.

Ebenezer Sage,[16] N.Y.
Lemuel Sawyer, N.C.

STANDING COMMITTEES OF THE HOUSE OF REPRESENTATIVES

WAYS AND MEANS

Chairman: Samuel Smith, Md.

William A. Burwell, Va.
David Trimble, Ky.
Joel Crawford, Ga.

Jonathan O. Moseley, Conn.
Henry Shaw, Mass.
John Tyler, Va.

[12] Took his seat Dec. 27, 1819.
[13] Resigned Feb. 1, 1820.
[14] Took his seat Dec. 22, 1819.
[15] Took his seat Feb. 16, 1820.
[16] Never appeared to claim his seat. Succeeded by James Guyon, Jr., who successfully contested the election and took his seat Jan. 14, 1820.

ELECTIONS

Chairman: John W. Taylor, N.Y.

Ezekiel Whitman, Penn.   William Brown, Ky.
Orsamus C. Merrill, Vt.   Starling Tucker, S.C.
Christian Tarr, Penn.   John Sloane, Ohio

COMMERCE

Chairman: Thomas Newton, Jr., Va.

Alney McLane, Del.   Robert Allen, Tenn.
Gideon Tomlinson, Conn.   Mark L. Hill, Mass.
Jonathan Mason, Mass.   Walter Folger, Jr., Mass.

MANUFACTURES

Chairman: Henry Baldwin, Penn.

Henry Meigs, N.Y.   Thomas Forrest, Penn.
Peter Little, Md.   James Parker, Mass.
Alney McLean, Ky.   Thomas R. Ross, Ohio

CLAIMS

Chairman: Lewis Williams, N.C.

Charles Rich, Vt.   John A. Culbreth, Ga.
William McCoy, Va.   Henry W. Edwards, Conn.
Samuel Moore, Penn.   Thomas Metcalfe, Ky.

DISTRICT OF COLUMBIA

Chairman: Joseph Kent, Md.

Thomas W. Cobb, Ga.   Thomas Van Swearingen, Va.
Charles F. Mercer, Va.   David Fullerton, Penn.
Raphael Neale, Md.   Bernard Smith, N.J.

PUBLIC LANDS

Chairman: Robert C. Anderson, Jr., Ky.

William Hendricks, Ind.   Daniel P. Cook, Ill.
Francis Jones, Tenn.   Ballard Smith, Va.
Jeremiah Nelson, Mass.   James Stevens, Conn.

PRIVATE LAND CLAIMS

Chairman: John W. Campbell, Ohio

James Pindall, Va.   Henry H. Bryan, Tenn.
Christopher Rankin, Miss.   Albert H. Tracy, N.Y.
Robert Moore, Penn.   Samuel Eddy, R.I.

POST OFFICE AND POST ROADS

Chairman: Arthur Livermore, N.H.

Zabdiel Sampson, Mass.   Caleb Tompkins, N.Y.
John Russ, Conn.   David Walker, Ky.
John Culpepper, N.C.   Hutchins G. Burton, N.C.

PENSIONS AND REVOLUTIONARY CLAIMS

Chairman: John Rhea, Tenn.

William P. Maclay, Penn.   John Linn, N.J.
Thomas Settle, N.C.   Randall S. Street, N.Y.
Samuel C. Allen, Mass.   James Jones, Va.

PUBLIC EXPENDITURES

Chairman: Eldred Simkins, S.C.

Jesse Slocumb, N.C.   Edward Dowse, Mass.
Joseph Hiester, Penn.   William Plumer, Jr., N.H.
Nathaniel Hazard, R.I.   William D. Ford, N.Y.

JUDICIARY

Chairman: John Sergeant, Penn.

Philemon Beecher, Ohio   Joseph Brevard, S.C.
George Robertson, Ky.   Enoch Lincoln, Mass.
Robert R. Reid, Ga.   George Tucker, Va.

ACCOUNTS

Chairman: James S. Smith, N.C.

Ephraim Bateman, N.J.   Nathaniel Upham, N.H.

REVISAL AND UNFINISHED BUSINESS

Chairman: Marcus Morton, Mass.

Josiah Butler, N.H.   William Lee Ball, Va.

On Expenditures in the Department of State

Chairman: John Holmes, Mass.

Hermanus Peek, N.Y.   Jacob Hibshman, Penn.

On Expenditures in the Department of the Treasury

Chairman: David Trimble, Ky.

George Hall, N.Y.   Samuel Gross, Penn.

On Expenditures in the Department of War

Chairman: Henry Brush, Ohio

James Overstreet, S.C.   Ezra C. Gross, N.Y.

On Expenditures in the Department of the Navy

Chairman: Stevenson Archer, Md.

John Fay, N.Y.   Joseph Buffum, Jr., N.H.

On Expenditures in the Post Office

Chairman: Arthur Livermore, N.H.

Aaron Hackley, Jr., N.Y.   Robert Monell, N.Y.

On Expenditures on the Public Buildings

Chairman: Henry Meigs, N.Y.

William Strong, Vt.   Jacob Hostetter, Penn.

On Enrolled Bills

House
William Darlington, Conn.
Samuel A. Foote, Conn.

Senate
James J. Wilson, N.J.

SELECT COMMITTEES APPOINTED ON VARIOUS PARTS OF THE PRESIDENT'S MESSAGE

On so much as relates to Foreign Affairs

Chairman: William Lowndes, S.C.

John Holmes, Mass.   John Randolph, Va.
Hugh Nelson, Va.   Philip P. Barbour, Va.
John P. Dickinson, N.Y.   Stevenson Archer, Md.

On so much as relates to Military Affairs

Chairman: Alexander Smyth, Va.

Solomon Van Rensselaer, N.Y.   Samuel Ringgold, Md.
Henry Brush, Ohio   Joshua Cushman, Mass.
John Cocke, Tenn.   Severn E. Parker, Va.

On so much as relates to the Navy and Naval Affairs[17]

Chairman: Nathaniel Silsbee, Mass.

James Johnson, Va.   Thomas H. Hall, N.C.
Peter H. Wendover, N.Y.   George Dennison, Penn.
Henry R. Warfield, Md.   Samuel Eddy, R.I.

On so much as relates to the Unlawful Introduction of Slaves into the United States

Chairman: Joseph Hemphill, Penn.

Charles F. Mercer, Va.   Thomas J. Rogers, Penn.
James Strong, N.Y.   Samuel Lathrop, Mass.
Samuel Edwards, Penn.   Joel Abbot, Ga.

[17]The *Journal of the House of Representatives* lists James Pleasants (Va.) as Chairman, Nathaniel Silsbee as a committee member, and does not list Samuel Eddy as a member of the committee.

SELECTED COMMITTEES APPOINTED
ON THE FOLLOWING SUBJECTS

MILITIA

Chairman: Newton Cannon, Tenn.

Tunstall Quarles, Ky.   George F. Strother, Va.
Samuel Herrick, Ohio   Jonathan Richmond, N.Y.
John Floyd, Va.   Jonas Kendall, Mass.

INDIAN AFFAIRS

Chairman: Henry Southard, N.J.

James M. Wallace, Penn.   Martin Kinsley, Mass.
Felix Walker, N.C.   Mark Richards, Vt.
Jared Williams, Va.   Caleb Baker, N.Y.

ROADS AND CANALS

Chairman: Henry R. Storrs, N.Y.

Samuel C. Crafts, Vt.   William Hendricks, Ind.
James Pindall, Va.   William Davidson, N.C.
David Marchand, Penn.   Randall J. Street, N.Y.

PUBLIC BUILDINGS

Chairman: Thomas W. Cobb, Ga.

Joseph S. Lyman, N.Y.   Charles Fisher, N.C.
Robert S. Garnett, Va.   Walter Case, N.Y.
John Murray, Va.   John McCreary, S.C.

REVOLUTIONARY PENSIONS

Chairman: Joseph Bloomfield, N.J.

Clifton Clagett, N.H.   Benjamin Adams, Mass.
Nathaniel Pitcher, N.Y.   Robert Clark, N.Y.
Mark Alexander, Va.   Thomas Patterson, Penn.

Payment for Horses and other Property lost in the Seminole War

Chairman: Newton Cannon, Tenn.

Francis Jones, Tenn.   William Davidson, N.C.
Alney McLean, Ky.   Albert H. Tracy, N.Y.
Robert R. Reid, Ga.   Solomon Van Rensselaer, N.Y.

JOINT COMMITTEE: LIBRARY OF CONGRESS

House   Senate
Charles Pinckney, S.C.   Mahlon Dickerson, N.J.
Silas Wood, N.Y.   William Hunter, R.I.
Henry Meigs, N.Y.   Samuel W. Dana, Conn.

STANDING COMMITTEES OF THE SENATE
OF THE UNITED STATES

FOREIGN AFFAIRS

Chairman: James Brown, La.

William Hunter, R.I.
James Barbour, Va.

Nathaniel Macon, N.C.
Freeman Walker, Ga.

FINANCE

Chairman: Nathan Sanford, N.Y.

Nathaniel Macon, N.C.
John H. Eaton, Tenn.

Samuel W. Dana, Conn.
William Logan, Ky.

COMMERCE AND MANUFACTURES

Chairman: Nathan Sanford, N.Y.

Mahlon Dickerson, N.J.
Benjamin Ruggles, Ohio

Outerbridge Horsey, Del.
James Burrill, Jr., R.I.

MILITARY AFFAIRS

Chairman: John J. Williams, Tenn.

William A. Trimble, Ohio
Isaac Tichenor, Vt.

Waller Taylor, Ind.
John Elliott, Ga.

MILITIA

Chairman: James Noble, Ind.

Isaac Tichenor, Vt.
James Lanman, Conn.

Montfort Stokes, N.C.
William R. Walker, Ala.

NAVAL AFFAIRS

Chairman: James Pleasants, Va.

John F. Parrott, N.H.
John W. Walker, Ala.

John Gaillard, S.C.
Thomas H. Williams, Miss.

PUBLIC LANDS

Chairman: Thomas H. Williams, Miss.

Waller J. Taylor, Ind.
Walter Lowrie, Penn.

Jesse B. Thomas, Ill.
William Hunter, R.I.

CLAIMS

Chairman: Jonathan Roberts, Penn.

James J. Wilson, N.J.
Benjamin Ruggles, Ohio

David L. Morril, N.H.
Nicholas Van Dyke, Del.

JUDICIARY

Chairman: William Smith, S.C.

Walter Leake, Miss.
William Logan, Ky.

James Burrill, Jr., R.I.
Harrison Gray Otis, Mass.

POST OFFICE AND POST ROADS

Chairman: Montfort Stokes, N.C.

James J. Wilson, N.J.
Ninian Edwards, Ill.

William A. Palmer, Vt.
Prentiss Mellen, Mass.

PENSIONS

Chairman: Nicholas Van Dyke, Del.

James Noble, Ind.
John H. Eaton, Tenn.

John Elliott, Ga.
James J. Wilson, N.J.

DISTRICT OF COLUMBIA

Chairman: Outerbridge Horsey, Del.

William Hunter, R.I.
James Lanman, Conn.

James Pleasants, Va.
Harrison Gray Otis, Mass.

PUBLIC BUILDINGS

Chairman: Jonathan Roberts, Penn.

John Gaillard, S.C.
James Burrill, Jr., R.I.

Prentiss Mellen, Mass.
James Lanman, Conn.

CONGRESSIONAL DIRECTORY

SIXTEENTH CONGRESS, SECOND SESSION
(November 13, 1820–March 3, 1821)

Mr. Burch, Capitol Hill
Robert Allen, Tenn.
Henry H. Bryan, Tenn.
Samuel C. Crafts, Vt.
John C. Gray, Va.
Arthur Livermore, N.H.
John McCreary, S.C.
Thomas Montgomery, Ky.
James Overstreet, S.C.
William A. Palmer (S), Vt.
Elisha Phelps, Conn.
Charles Rich, Vt.
Mark Richards, Vt.
James Stevens, Conn.
Starling Tucker, S.C.

Brown's Hotel, Penn. Ave.
William A. Burwell,[1] Va.
James W. Bates, Deleg. Ark. Terr.
John Floyd, Va.
David Holmes (S), Miss.
Edward B. Jackson, Va.
James Lanman (S), Conn.
Thomas Metcalfe, Ky.
George Robertson, Ky.
Henry R. Storrs, N.Y.
John Scott, Deleg., Terr. of Mo.
Thomas Van Swearingen, Va.
David Trimble, Ky.
John Williams (S), Tenn.
Lewis Williams, N.C.

Mr. Bestor, C St.
John Culpepper, N.C.
John Linn,[2] N.J.
William P. Maclay, Penn.
David Marchand, Penn.
Ballard Smith, Va.
Christian Tarr, Penn.

Mrs. Blake, Penn. Ave.
William Brown, Ky.
William Davidson, N.C.
William Hendricks, Ind.
Bernard Smith, N.J.

Mr. Brown, near General Post Office
James Barbour (S), Va.
Richard M. Johnson (S), Ky.

Mrs. Ball, near General Post Office
Charles Kinsey, N.J.

Mr. Claxton, Capitol Hill
Stevenson Archer, Md.
Joseph Buffum, Jr., N.H.
Thomas Culbreth, Md.
Clifton Clagett, N.H.
John Cocke, Tenn.
Nathaniel Hazard,[3] R.I.
Martin Kinsley, Mass.
Ezra Meech, Vt.
Rollin C. Mallory,[4] Vt.

NOTE: Copies are located at the American Antiquarian Society, the Boston Athenaeum, the Library of Congress, and the New York Public Library.
[1] Died Feb. 16, 1821.
[2] Died Jan. 5, 1821.
[3] Died Dec. 17, 1820.
[4] Successfully contested the election of Orsamus C. Merrill and took his seat Jan. 13, 1820.

David L. Morril (S), N.H.
James Parker, Mass.
William Plumer, Jr., N.H.
William Strong, Vt.

Crawford's Hotel, Georgetown
Samuel Edwards, Penn.
Benjamin Gorham,[5] Mass.
Outerbridge Horsey (S), Del.
Joseph Hemphill, Penn.
Rufus King (S), N.Y.
Louis McLane, Del.
Charles F. Mercer, Va.
Raphael Neale, Md.
Harrison Gray Otis (S), Mass.
Charles Pinckney, S.C.

Mr. Dowson, No. 1, Capitol Hill
Joseph Bloomfield, N.J.
Joseph Brevard, S.C.
William Eustis, Mass.
James Jones, Va.
William R. King (S), Ala.
Joseph Kent, Md.
Samuel Smith, Md.
John W. Walker (S), Ala.

Mr. Dowson, No. 2, Capitol Hill
William S. Archer,[6] Va.
Hutchins G. Burton, N.C.
Thomas W. Cobb, Ga.
Weldon N. Edwards, N.C.
John Elliott (S), Ga.
Thomas H. Hall, N.C.
Nathaniel Macon (S), N.C.
John Randolph, Va.
William Terrell, Ga.

Mr. Davis, near General Post Office
Francis Johnson, Ky.

Mr. Fletcher, near General Post Office
Samuel C. Allen, Mass.
Joshua Cushman, Mass.

John W. Campbell, Ohio
Daniel P. Cook, Ill.
Samuel Lathrop, Mass.
Thomas R. Ross, Ohio
Solomon Van Rensselaer, N.Y.
James Strong, N.Y.
Solomon Sibley,[7] Deleg., Mich. Terr.

Mrs. Gaither, Penn. Ave.
Ephraim Bateman, N.J.
William McCoy, Va.
James Pleasants, Va.
Henry Southard, N.J.
Jared Williams, Va.

Mrs. Hickey, Capitol Hill
Josiah Mutler, N.H.
Walter Folger, Jr., Mass.
Charles Hooks, N.C.
Marcus Morton, Mass.
Henry Shaw, Mass.
Jesse Slocumb,[8] N.C.
James S. Smith, N.C.
John W. Taylor, N.Y.

Mr. Hyatt, Penn. Ave.
Benjamin Adams, Mass.
Henry W. Edwards, Conn.
Jonas Kendall, Mass.
Jonathan O. Moseley, Conn.
Jeremiah Nelson, Mass.
John Russ, Conn.
Nathaniel Upham, N.H.

Mrs. Hamilton, near City Hall
Walter Case, N.Y.
Elias Earle, S.C.
Jacob H. De Witt, N.Y.
William D. Ford, N.Y.
Caleb Tompkins, N.Y.
Peter H. Wendover, N.Y.

Miss Heyer, Capitol Hill
Randall S. Street, N.Y.

[5] Elected to fill the vacancy caused by the resignation of Jonathan Mason, and took his seat Nov. 27, 1820.
[6] Elected to fill the vacancy caused by the resignation of James Pleasants, and took his seat Jan. 18, 1820.
[7] Elected to fill the vacancy caused by the resignation of William W. Woodridge, and took his seat Nov. 20, 1820.
[8] Died Dec. 20, 1820. He was succeeded by William S. Blackledge, who took his seat Feb. 7, 1821.

John Sergeant, Penn.
Nathaniel Silsbee, Mass.
Ezekiel Whitman, Mass.

Mr. McLeod, Capitol Hill
James Burrill, Jr. (S),[9] R.I.
John Chandler (S), Me.
Samuel W. Dana (S), Conn.
Samuel Eddy, R.I.
John Holmes (S), Me.
William Hunter (S), R.I.
John F. Parrott (S), N.H.
Alexander Smyth, Va.

Mrs. McCardle, Capitol Hill
Joel Abbot, Ga.
Philemon Beecher, Ohio
Joel Crawford, Ga.
James Guyon, Jr.,[10] N.Y.
Mark L. Hill, Mass.
William Smith (S), S.C.
Isaac Tichenor (S), Vt.
Silas Wood, N.Y.

Mr. McGowan, Penn. Ave.
Hugh Nelson, Va.
Thomas Newton, Jr., Va.

Mrs. Myer, near Centre Market
Robert Clark, N.Y.
William Darlington, Penn.
Timothy Fuller, Mass.
John Fay, N.Y.
Ezra C. Gross, N.Y.
Jacob Hibshman, Penn.
Jacob Hostetter, Penn.
Thomas Patterson, Penn.
Robert Philson, Penn.
Nathaniel Pitcher, N.Y.
Thomas J. Rogers, Penn.
James J. Wilson (S),[11] N.J.
James M. Wallace, Penn.

O'Neale's Hotel, Penn. Ave.
John H. Eaton (S), Tenn.
John Rhea, Tenn.
Thomas H. Williams (S), Miss.

Mrs. Peyton, C St.
Henry Brush, Ohio
John Crowell, Ala.
Ninian Edwards (S), Ill.
Charles Fisher, N.C.
Aaron Hackley, Jr., N.Y.
Alney McLean, Ky.
Robert R. Reid, Ga.
William A. Trimble (S), Ohio
Isham Talbot (S),[12] Tenn.
Freeman Walker (S), Ga.

Mr. Patterson, Capitol Hill
Thomas G. McCullough, Penn.
Gideon Tomlinson, Conn.
Samuel A. Foote, Conn.
Jesse B. Thomas (S), Ill.

Miss Polk, Penn. Ave.
Thomas Bayly, Md.
James Noble (S), Ind.
Benjamin Ruggles (S), Ohio
John Sloane, Ohio

Mrs. Queen, Penn. Ave.
Nathaniel Allen, N.Y.
Newton Cannon, Tenn.
George Hall, N.Y.
Jonathan Richmond, N.Y.

Mr. Sawyer, Penn. Ave.
Richard C. Anderson, Jr., Ky.
Caleb Baker, N.Y.
Samuel Gross, Penn.
Walter Lowrie (S), Penn.
Robert Moore, Penn.
Samuel Moore, Penn.
John Murray, Penn.

[9] Died Dec. 25, 1820. He was succeeded by Nehemiah R. Knight, who took his seat Jan. 20, 1821.
[10] Successfully contested the election of Ebenezer Sage, and took his seat Jan. 14, 1820.
[11] Resigned Jan. 8, 1821. He was succeeded by Samuel L. Southard, who took his seat Feb. 16, 1821.
[12] Elected to fill the vacancy caused by the resignation of William Logan, and took his seat Nov. 27, 1820.

Strother's Hotel, Penn. Ave.
Thomas Butler, La.
John D. Dickinson, N.Y.
Henry Johnson (S), La.
Edward Lloyd (S), Md.
Samuel Ringgold, Md.

Mr. Sears, near General Post Office
Lemuel Sawyer, N.C.
Felix Walker, N.C.

Tennison's Hotel, Penn. Ave.
Mark Alexander, Va.
William Lee Ball, Va.
Philip P. Barbour, Va.
Francis Jones, Tenn.
Thomas Lee Moore, Va.
Severn E. Parker, Va.
Nathan Sanford (S), N.Y.
Waller Taylor (S), Ind.
John Tyler, Va.

Mrs. Tucker, Penn. Ave.
George Denison, Penn.
Thomas Forrest, Penn.
Enoch Lincoln, Mass.
Robert Monell, N.Y.
Albert H. Tracy, N.Y.

Mr. Tims, Capitol Hill
Mahlon Dickerson (S), N. J.
John Gaillard (S), S.C.
William Lowndes, S.C.
Eldred Simkins, S.C.
Nicholas Van Dyke (S), Del.

Mr. Wilson, F St.
George Tucker, Va.

Mr. Ward, Penn. Ave.
Robert S. Garnett, Va.

Private Residences
Near Strother's Hotel, Penn. Ave.
James Brown (S), La.
Colonel Bumford, North of the President's House
Henry Baldwin, Penn.
Mr. Little, near Navy Yard
Peter Little, Md.
Penn. Ave.
Henry Meigs, N.Y.
Mr. Fitzgerald, N.J. Ave.
Jonathan Roberts (S), Penn.
Dr. Warfield, Georgetown
Henry R. Warfield, Md.
Mr. Williams, F St.
Felix Walker, N.C.

APPENDIX

Willard Hall,[13] Del.
John A. Cuthbert, Ga.
Henry Clay, Ky.

Benjamin Hardin, Ky.
Joseph Dane,[14] Me.
William Pinkney (S),[15] Md.

[13] Resigned Jan. 22, 1821.

[14] Elected to fill the vacancy caused by the resignation of John Holmes, a Representative from Massachusetts. He resided in the new state of Maine and took his seat Dec. 11, 1820. Maine was admitted as a State into the Union on Mar. 5, 1820. Previous to Mar. 3, 1820, Maine was a part of Massachusetts, and was called the "District of Maine"; its Representatives were numbered with those of Massachusetts. By compact between the two states, Maine became a separate and independent state, and by act of Congress of Mar. 3, 1820, was admitted into the Union as such—the admission to date from the 15th of the same month. An act of Congress, approved Apr. 7, 1820, provided "That in the election of Representatives in the Seventeenth Congress, the State of Massachusetts shall be entitled to choose 13 Representatives only; and the State of Maine shall be entitled to choose 7 Representatives. . . ." The Directory lists Joshua Cushman, Joseph Dane, Mark L. Hill, Martin Kinsley, Enoch Lincoln, James Parker, and Ezekiel Whitman as Representatives from Maine; however, only Joseph Dane was a Representative from Maine in the Sixteenth Congress. The other Congressmen represented Massachusetts.

[15] Elected to fill the vacancy caused by the death of Alexander C. Hanson, and took his seat Jan. 4, 1820.

Aaron Hobart,[16] Mass.
Elijah H. Mills (S),[17] Mass.
Christopher Rankin, Miss.
Joseph S. Lyman, N.Y.
Hermanus Peek, N.Y.
Thomas Settle, N.C.

Montfort Stokes (S), N.C.
Samuel Herrick, Ohio
Andrew Boden, Penn.
Joseph Hiester,[18] Penn.
James Ervin, S.C.

STANDING COMMITTEES OF THE
HOUSE OF REPRESENTATIVES

ELECTIONS
Chairman: David Trimble, Ky.

Christian Tarr, Ky.
Starling Tucker, S.C.
John Sloan, Ohio

Robert Clark, N.Y.
Charles Hooks, N.C.
Thomas L. Moore, Va.

PUBLIC LANDS
Chairman: Richard C. Anderson, Jr., Ky.

William Hendricks, Ind.
John Cooke, Tenn.
Ballard Smith, Va.

James Stevens, Conn.
Robert Monell, N.Y.
Henry Brush, Ohio

PENSIONS AND REVOLUTIONARY CLAIMS
Chairman: John Rhea, Tenn.

William P. Maclay, Penn.
William Brown, Ky.
Samuel C. Allen, Mass.

John Linn, N.J.
Randall S. Street, N.Y.
James Jones, Va.

AGRICULTURE
Chairman: Thomas Forrest, Penn.

Clifton Clagett, N.H.
Ezra Meech, Vt.
Jonathan Richmond, N.Y.

Samuel Ringgold, Md.
Robert S. Garnett, Va.
Elias Earle, S.C.

WAYS AND MEANS
Chairman: Samuel Smith, Md.

Louis McLane, Del.
William A. Burwell, Va.
Henry Shaw, Mass.

Albert H. Tracy, N.Y.
Thomas R. Ross, Ohio
Francis Jones, Tenn.

[16] Elected to fill the vacancy caused by the resignation of Zabdiel Sampson, and took his seat Dec. 18, 1820.
[17] Elected to fill the vacancy caused by the resignation of Prentiss Mellen, and took his seat Dec. 1, 1820.
[18] Resigned in Dec. 1820, having been elected Governor. Daniel Udree was elected to fill the vacancy, and took his seat Jan. 8, 1821.

POST OFFICE AND POST ROADS

Chairman: Arthur Livermore, N.H.

John Culpepper, N.C.
John Russ, Conn.
Caleb Tompkins, N.Y.

Martin Kinsley, Mass.
Richard M. Johnson, Ky.
John C. Gray, Va.

PUBLIC EXPENDITURES

Chairman: Eldred Simkins, S.C.

Jesse Slocumb, Penn.
Thomas J. Rogers, Penn.
Thomas W. Cobb, Ga.

Benjamin Adams, Mass.
William D. Ford, N.Y.
Thomas Montgomery, Ky.

REVISAL AND UNFINISHED BUSINESS

Chairman: Marcus Morton, Mass.

Josiah Butler, N.H.

William Lee Ball, Va.

CLAIMS

Chairman: Lewis Williams, N.C.

Charles Rich, Vt.
William McCoy, Va.
Samuel Moore, Penn.

Aaron Hackley, Jr., N.Y.
Henry W. Edwards, Conn.
Thomas Metcalfe, Ky.

DISTRICT OF COLUMBIA

Chairman: Joseph Kent, Md.

Charles F. Mercer, Va.
Raphael Neale, Md.
Thomas Van Swearingen, Va.

Bernard Smith, N.J.
Henry Meigs, N.Y.
Thomas G. McCullough, Penn.

PRIVATE LAND CLAIMS

Chairman: John W. Campbell, Ohio

Thomas Butler, La.
Robert Moore, Penn.
Samuel Eddy, R.I.

Nathaniel Pitcher, N.Y.
Edward B. Jackson, Va.
John Crowell, Ala.

ACCOUNTS

Chairman: James S. Smith, N.C.

Ephraim Bateman, N.J.

Nathaniel Upham, N.H.

COMMERCE

Chairman: Thomas Newton, Jr., Va.

Gideon Tomlinson, Conn.
Rollin C. Mallory, Vt.
Jeremiah Nelson, Mass.

Mark L. Hill, Mass.
Peter H. Wendover, N.Y.
Joel Abbot, Ga.

JUDICIARY

Chairman: John Sergeant, Penn.

Philemon Beecher, Ohio   Enoch Lincoln, Mass.
George Robertson, Ky.   George Tucker, Va.
Joseph Brevard, S.C.   William Plumer, Jr., N.H.

MANUFACTURES

Chairman: Henry Baldwin, Penn.

Nathaniel Allen, N.Y.   James Parker, Mass.
Peter Little, Md.   Charles Kinsey, N.J.
Alney McLean, Ky.   Charles Fisher, N.C.

On Expenditures in the Department of State

Chairman: Hermanus Peek, N.Y.

Henry H. Bryan, Tenn.   Jacob Hibshman, Penn.

On Expenditures in the Department of the Treasury

Chairman: David Trimble, Ky.

George Hall, N.Y.   Samuel Gross, Penn.

On Expenditures in the Department of War

Chairman: Henry Brush, Ohio

James Overstreet, S.C.   Ezra C. Gross, N.Y.

On Expenditures in the Department of the Navy

Chairman: William S. Archer, Va.

John Fay, N.Y.   Joseph Buffum, Jr., N.H.

On Expenditures in the Post Office

Chairman: Arthur Livermore, N.H.

Aaron Hackley, Jr., N.Y.   Robert Monell, N.Y.

On Expenditures on the Public Buildings

Chairman: Henry Meigs, N.Y.

William Strong, Vt.   Jacob Hostetter, Penn.

On Enrolled Bills

House   Senate
William Darlington, Penn.   James J. Wilson, N.J.
Samuel A. Foote, Conn.

SELECT COMMITTEES APPOINTED ON VARIOUS PARTS OF THE PRESIDENT'S MESSAGE

On so much as relates to Foreign Affairs

Chairman: William Lowndes, S.C.

John Randolph, Va.   John D. Dickinson, N.Y.
Jonathan O. Moseley, Conn.   Robert R. Reid, Ga.
Hugh Nelson, Va.   Stevenson Archer, Md.

On so much as relates to Military Affairs

Chairman: Alexander Smyth, Va.

Solomon Van Rensselaer, N.Y.
John Cocke, Tenn.
Joshua Cushman, Mass.

Hutchins G. Burton, N.C.
Robert Moore, Penn.
John Russ, Conn.

On so much as relates to Naval Affairs

Chairman: Philip P. Barbour, Va.

Timothy Fuller, Mass.
Henry R. Warfield, Md.
Walter Case, N.Y.

Thomas H. Hall, N.C.
George Denison, Penn.
Joel Crawford, Ga.

On so much as relates to the Slave Trade

Chairman: Joseph Hemphill, Penn.

Charles F. Mercer, Va.
James Strong, N.Y.
Samuel Edwards, Penn.

Thomas J. Rogers, Penn.
John McCreary, S.C.
Walter Folger, Jr., Mass.

On so much as relates to Indian Affairs

Chairman: Henry Southard, N.J.

Thomas Bayly, Md.
James M. Wallace, Penn.
Felix Walker, N.C.

Jared Williams, Va.
Caleb Baker, N.Y.
Samuel Gross, Penn.

SELECT COMMITTEES APPOINTED ON THE FOLLOWING SUBJECTS

On the subject of the Militia

Chairman: Newton Cannon, Tenn.

Ezra C. Gross, N.Y.
William Strong, Vt.
Thomas Patterson, Penn.

Lemuel Sawyer, N.C.
James Overstreet, S.C.
Jacob Hostetter, Penn.

On the subject of Roads and Canals

Chairman: Henry R. Storrs, N.Y.

Samuel C. Crafts, Vt.
David Marchand, Penn.
Weldon N. Edwards, N.C.

Randall S. Street, N.Y.
Thomas Montgomery, Ky.
William Hendricks, Ind.

On the subject of Public Buildings

Chairman: Silas Wood, N.Y.

Jonas Kendall, Mass.
Mark Alexander, Va.
Thomas H. Hall, N.C.

John Murray, Penn.
Samuel C. Crafts, Vt.
Joseph Buffum, Jr., N.H.

On the subject of Revolutionary Pensions

Chairman: Joseph Bloomfield, N.J.

Weldon N. Edwards, N.C.
Jacob H. De Witt, N.Y.
Jacob Hibshman, Penn.

Nathaniel Hazard, R.I.
John Fay, N.Y.
Mark Alexander, Va.

On the subject of the Constitution of Missouri

Chairman: William Lowndes, S.C.

John Sergeant, Penn.

Samuel Smith, Md.

JOINT COMMITTEE

LIBRARY OF CONGRESS

House	Senate
Rollin C. Mallary, Vt.	Mahlon Dickerson, N.J.
Severn E. Parker, Va.	Samuel W. Dana, Conn.
Robert Allen, Tenn.	William Hunter, R.I.

STANDING COMMITTEES OF THE SENATE OF THE UNITED STATES

FOREIGN RELATIONS

Chairman: James Barbour, Va.

James Brown, La.
Rufus King, N.Y.

Nathaniel Macon, N.C.
William Hunter, R.I.

FINANCE

Chairman: Nathan Sanford, N.Y.

Samuel W. Dana, Conn.
John Holmes, Me.

Nathaniel Macon, N.C.
John H. Eaton, Tenn.

COMMERCE AND MANUFACTURES

Chairman: Mahlon Dickerson, N.J.

James Burrill, Jr., R.I.
Nathan Sanford, N.Y.

Benjamin Ruggles, Ohio
Outerbridge Horsey, Del.

MILITARY AFFAIRS

Chairman: John Williams, Tenn.

Waller Taylor, Ind.
Richard M. Johnson, Ky.

William A. Trimble, Ohio
John Elliott, Ga.

MILITIA

Chairman: James Noble, Ind.

Montfort Stokes, N.C.   Isaac Tichenor, Vt.
John Chandler, Me.   James Lanman, Conn.

NAVAL AFFAIRS

Chairman: James Pleasants, Va.

Thomas H. Williams, Miss.   John F. Parrott, N.H.
John W. Walker, Ala.   Francis Walker, Ga.

PUBLIC LANDS

Chairman: Jesse B. Thomas, Ill

Walter Lowrie, Penn.   Waller Taylor, Ind.
Nicholas Van Dyke, Del.   John H. Eaton, Tenn.

INDIAN AFFAIRS

Chairman: David Holmes, Miss.

Henry Johnson, La.   Richard M. Johnson, Ky.
Walter Lowrie, Penn.   William R. King, Ala.

CLAIMS

Chairman: James J. Wilson, N.J.

David L. Morril, N.H.   Jonathan Roberts, Penn.
Nicholas Van Dyke, Del.   Benjamin Ruggles, Ohio

JUDICIARY

Chairman: William Smith, S.C.

William Pinckney, Md.   James Burrill, Jr., R.I.
John Holmes, Me.   Freeman Walker, Ga.

POST OFFICE AND POST ROADS

Chairman: Montfort Stokes, N.C.

William A. Palmer, Vt.   James J. Wilson, N.J.
John Chandler, Me.   Ninian Edwards, Ill.

PENSIONS

Chairman: James Noble, Ind.

James J. Wilson, N.J.   John Elliott, Ga.
Isaac Tichenor, Vt.   John H. Eaton, Tenn.

DISTRICT OF COLUMBIA

Chairman: Outerbridge Horsey, Del.

Edward Lloyd, Md.   James Lanman, Conn.
William Hunter, R.I.   James Barbour, Va.

ACCOUNTS

Chairman: Jonathan Roberts, Penn.
James Lanman, Conn.   James Burrill, Jr., R.I.

ROADS AND CANALS

Chairman: Rufus King, N.Y.
Walter Lowrie, Penn.   William A. Trimble, Ohio
Samuel W. Dana, Conn.   Nathaniel Macon, N.C.

CONGRESSIONAL DIRECTORY

SEVENTEENTH CONGRESS, FIRST SESSION
(December 3, 1821–May 8, 1822)

Mr. Burch, Capitol Hill
Joel Abbot, Ga.
Robert Allen, Tenn.
James Blair, S.C.
George R. Gilmer, Ga.
Benjamin Hardin, Ken.
James Overstreet, S.C.
William Smith, Va.
William Smith (S), S.C.
Wiley Thompson, Ga.

Brown's Hotel, Penn. Ave.
Philip P. Barbour, Va.
James Barbour (S), Va.
Thomas H. Benton (S),[1] Mo.
William L. Ball, Va.
Elisha Litchfield, N.Y.
Richard McCarty, N.Y.
Nathaniel Pitcher, N.Y.
John Scott, Mo.
Andrew Stewart, Penn.
Andrew Stevenson, Va.
Arthur Smith, Va.
David Trimble, Ky.
Thomas Van Swearingen, Va.
Reuben H. Walworth, N.Y.

Mrs. Blake, Tenth St., West
George Holcombe, N.J.
Joseph Kent, Md.
Raphael Neale, Md.
Caesar A. Rodney,[2] Del.
John S. Smith, Ky.
Montfort Stokes (S), N.C.

Samuel L. Southard (S), N.J.
Samuel H. Woodson, Ky.

Mrs. Ball, near General Post Office
James W. Bates, Deleg., Ark. Terr.
Daniel P. Cook, Ill.
Waller Taylor (S), Ind.
Isham Talbot (S), Ky.

Brady's Hotel, Georgetown
Jeremiah Cosden,[3] Md.
Benjamin Gorham, Mass.
Rufus King (S), N.Y.
Charles F. Mercer, Va.
Elijah H. Mills (S), Mass.
Harrison Gray Otis (S), Mass.

Mr. Brown E St., North
John T. Mason, Ky.
Richard M. Johnson (S), Ky.

Mrs. Claxton, Capitol Hill
David Barton (S), Mo.
Burwell Bassett, Va.
John Cocke, Tenn.
Aaron Hobart, Mass.
Matthew Harvey, N.H.
Jabez Leftwich, Va.
David L. Morril (S), N.H.
Aaron Matson, N.H.
Anthony New, Ky.
William Plumer, Jr., N.H.
Thomas Whipple, Jr., N.H.

[1] Took his seat Dec. 6, 1821.
[2] Resigned Jan. 24, 1822, having been elected Senator, and took his Senate seat the same day.
[3] Served until Mar. 19, 1822, when he was succeeded by Philip Reed who contested his election.

Mr. Coyle, Capitol Hill
John H. Eaton (S), Tenn.
David Holmes (S), Miss.
Joseph Hemphill, Penn.
James Lanman (S), Conn.
John F. Parrott (S), N.H.
Christopher Rankin, Miss.
Thomas H. Williams (S), Miss.

Mr. Dowson, No. 1, Capitol Hill
John Elliott (S),[4] Ga.
William Eustis, Mass.
Timothy Fuller, Mass.
William R. King (S), Ala.
Nathaniel Macon (S),[5] N.C.
Jonathan Russell,[6] Mass.
Samuel Smith, Md.
John W. Walker (S), Ala.

Mr. Dowson, No. 2, Capitol Hill
Mark Alexander, Va.
William S. Archer, Va.
Hutchins G. Burton, N.C.
Weldon N. Edwards, N.C.
Thomas H. Hall, N.C.
John Randolph, Va.
Romulus M. Saunders, N.C.
Edward F. Tattnall, Ga.

Mr. Davis, E St., North
Francis Johnson, Ky.
Thomas Metcalfe, Ky.

Mr. Dunn, Capitol Hill
Josiah Crudup, N.C.

Mr. Emack, Capitol Hill
Edward B. Jackson, Va.

Mr. Frost, Capitol Hill
Levi Barber, Ohio
David Chambers, Ohio
John Chandler (S), Me.

William Findlay (S),[7] Penn.
John Holmes (S), Me.
Walter Lowrie (S), Penn.
Benjamin Ruggles (S), Ohio
John Sloane, Ohio
Jesse B. Thomas (S), Ill.

Mr. Fletcher, near General Post Office
Samuel C. Allen, Mass.
Charles Borland, Jr., N.Y.
Lewis Bigelow, Mass.
Joshua Cushman, Me.
Samuel Lathrop, Mass.
Solomon Van Rensselaer,[8] N.Y.
Phineas White, Vt.
William D. Williamson, Me.

Mrs. Gaither, Penn. Ave.
Ephraim Bateman, N.J.
William McCoy, Va.
James Matlack, N.J.
Jared William, Va.
James Pleasants (S), Va.

Mrs. Gardiner, Twelfth St., West
Alexander Smyth, Va.

Miss Heyer, Capitol Hill
James Buchanan, Penn.
Gideon Barstow, Mass.
William Milnor, Penn.
James McSherry, Penn.
John Sergeant, Penn.
Henry R. Warfield, Md.

Mrs. Hickey, Capitol Hill
Josiah Butler, N.H.
Cadwallader D. Colden,[9] N.Y.
William Hendricks, Ind.
John W. Taylor, N.Y.

Mr. Hyatt, Penn. Ave.
Joseph Dane, Me.

---

[4] Also listed at Dowson's No. 2.
[5] Also listed at Dowson's No. 2.
[6] Also listed at McLeod's.
[7] Took his seat Dec. 17, 1821.
[8] Resigned Jan. 14, 1822. Stephen Van Rensselaer was elected to fill the vacancy, and took his seat Mar. 12, 1822.
[9] Successfully contested the election of Peter Sharpe, and took his seat Dec. 12, 1821.

Henry W. Edwards, Conn.
Jeremiah Nelson, Mass.
John Reed, Mass.
Nathaniel Upham, N.H.
John Russ, Conn.

Mrs. Hamilton, Capitol Hill
Samuel C. Crafts, Vt.
Elias Keyes,[10] Vt.
John Mattocks, Vt.
William A. Palmer, (S) Vt.
Charles Rich, Vt.
Horatio Seymour, (S) Vt.

Mrs. Myer, near Centre Market
John Brown, Penn.
William Darlington, Penn.
Patrick Farrelly, Penn.
John Findlay,[11] Penn.
James S. Mitchell, Penn.
Thomas Murray, Jr.,[12] Penn.
John Philips, Penn.
Thomas Patterson, Penn.
Thomas J. Rogers, Penn.
Ludwig Worman, Penn.

Mr. McLeod, Capitol Hill
Lewis Condict, N.J.
Job Durfee, R.I.
Samuel Eddy, R.I.
Nehemiah R. Knight (S), R.I.
Jonathan Russell,[13] Mass.
Ezekiel Whitman, Me.

Mr. Mecklin, near West Market
Churchill C. Cambreleng, N.Y.
Joel R. Poinsett, S.C.

Mrs. Peyton, C St., North
Francis Baylies, Mass.

John Floyd, Va.
John Gebhard, N.Y.
Thomas H. Hubbard, N.Y.
Joseph Kirkland, N.Y.
George McDuffie, S.C.
William B. Rochester, N.Y.
Robert R. Reid, Ga.
David Woodcock, N.Y.
John William (S), Tenn.
Nicholas Ware (S),[14] Ga.

Miss Polk, C St., North
Thomas Bayly, Md.
John W. Campbell, Ohio
James Noble (S), Ind.
George Plumer, Penn.
John Tod, Penn.
Joseph Vance,[15] Ohio

Queen's Hotel, Capitol Hill
Noyes Barber, Conn.
William S. Blackledge, N.C.
George Cassedy, N.J.
Henry W. Connor, N.C.
Charles Hooks, N.C.
Ebenezer Herrick, Me.
Mark L. Hill, Me.
Rollin C. Mallory, Vt.
Jeremiah H. Pierson, N.Y.
Thomas R. Ross, Ohio
Ebenezer Stoddard, Conn.
Ansel Sterling, Conn.
Samuel Swan, N.J.
Gideon Tomlinson, Conn.
William W. Van Wyck, N.Y.
Robert Wright, Md.
Lewis Williams, N.C.
Silas Wood, N.Y.
Elijah Boardman (S), Conn.
Elias Keyes,[16] Vt.

[10] Also listed at Queen's Hotel.
[11] Took his seat Dec. 12, 1821.
[12] Took his seat Dec. 12, 1821.
[13] Also listed at Dowson's No. 1.
[14] Took his seat Dec. 21, 1821.
[15] On previous pages this name appears as "John Vance." It is believed that this is an error that arose through a printer's error in the first issue of the *Congressional Directory* for the Seventeenth Congress, caused by the typesetter carrying the name of "John" of Sloane's down to that of "Vance." The House *Journal* does not show that a "John Vance" was ever a Representative from Ohio, but in the same directory, under "Alphabetical List of Boarding Houses with the Members in each," the list of boarders at Miss Polk's home included "Joseph Vance," but no "John."
[16] Also listed at Mrs. Hamilton's.

Mrs. Queen, the Elder, Penn. Ave.
Samuel Campbell, N.Y.
James Hawkes, N.Y.
Elijah Spencer, N.Y.
Micah Sterling, N.Y.

Mrs. Queen, the Younger, Penn. Ave.
Francis Jones, Tenn.
John Long, Va.
Gabriel Moore, Ala.
Archibald McNeill, Va.
Ninian Edwards (S), Ill.

Mr. Rapine, Capitol Hill
Joseph Gist, S.C.
Starling Tucker, S.C.
John Wilson, S.C.

Mr. Rockendorf, Penn. Ave.
Robert S. Garnett, Va.
Thomas Newton, Jr., Va.
Hugh Nelson, Va.

Strother's Hotel, Penn. Ave.
John D. Dickinson, N.Y.
Henry W. Dwight, Mass.
Lewis McLane, Del.
John J. Morgan, N.Y.
Walter Patterson, N.Y.
James De Wolf (S), R.I.
Martin Van Buren (S), N.Y.

Mrs. Stewart, Penn. Ave.
Thomas Montgomery, Ky.

Mr. Sawyer, Penn. Ave.
Newton Cannon, Tenn.
George Denison, Penn.
Samuel Gross, Penn.
Samuel Moore, Penn.

Mrs. Tucker, Penn. Ave.
Alfred Conkling, N.Y.

Enoch Lincoln, Me.
Charles H. Ruggles, N.Y.
Solomon Sibley, Deleg., Mich. Terr.
Albert H. Tracy, N.Y.

Mr. Tims, Capitol Hill
William Lowndes, S.C.
John Gaillard (S), S.C.
Nicholas Van Dyke (S), Del.
Mahlon Dickerson (S), N.J.

Mr. Ward, Penn. Ave.
Henry Johnson (S), La.

Mrs. Wilson, F St., North
Thomas R. Mitchell, S.C.
George Tucker, Va.

Private Residences
Near Strother's Hotel, Penn. Ave.
James Brown (S), La.
Mr. Friend, near the Navy Yard
Daniel Burrows, Conn.
Colonel Bumford
Henry Baldwin, Penn.
Commodore Porter
Samuel Edwards, Penn.
Corner Fifteenth St., West and Penn. Ave.
Josiah S. Johnston, La.
Mr. Little, near the Navy Yard
Peter Little, Md.
Colonel Henderson, Navy Yard
Thomas L. Moore, Va.
Colonel Thompson, near Georgetown
Joseph Nelson, Md.
Mr. Wurtz, near the Capitol
Lemuel Sawyer, Va.
Mr. Cochran, F St., North
John Rhea, Tenn.
Mr. Williams, Thirteenth St., West
Felix Walker, N.C.

APPENDIX

Vacant,[17] Del. (S)
Alfred Cuthbert, Ga.

James D. Breckinridge,[18] Ky.
Edward Lloyd (S), Md.

[17] This vacancy existed from Mar. 4, 1821 to Jan. 23, 1822.
[18] Elected to fill the vacancy caused by the death of Winfield Bullock, and took his seat Jan. 2, 1822.

William Pinkney,[19] Md.
William A. Trimble (S),[20] Ohio

Henry H. Bryan,[21] Tenn.
James Jones, Va.

STANDING COMMITTEES OF THE
HOUSE OF REPRESENTATIVES

ELECTIONS

Chairman: John Sloane, Ohio

Weldon N. Edwards, N.C.
Starling Tucker, S.C.
Thomas L. Moore, Va.

Reuben H. Walworth, N.Y.
Thomas J. Rogers, Penn.
Arthur or William Smith,[22] Va.

WAYS AND MEANS

Chairman: Samuel Smith, Md.

John Tod, Penn.
Nathaniel Pitcher, N.Y.
Thomas R. Mitchell, S.C.

Francis Jones, Tenn.
Wiley Thompson, Ga.
Andrew Stevenson, Va.

CLAIMS

Chairman: Lewis Williams, N.C.

Charles Rich, Vt.
William McCoy, Va.
Samuel Moore, Penn.

Henry W. Edwards, Conn.
Thomas Metcalfe, Ky.
Elisha Litchfield, N.Y.

COMMERCE

Chairman: Thomas Newton, Jr., Va.

Gideon Tomlinson, Conn.
Mark L. Hill, Me.
William Milnor, Penn.

Joseph Kirkland, N.Y.
Joel Abbot, Ga.
George McDuffie, S.C.

PUBLIC LANDS

Chairman: Christopher Rankin, Miss.

John Scott, Mo.
William Hendricks, Ind.
Daniel P. Cook, Ill.

Andrew Stewart, Penn.
Newton Cannon, Tenn.
Micah Sterling, N.Y.

[19] Died Feb. 25, 1822.
[20] Died Dec. 13, 1821. He was succeeded by Ethan Allen Brown, who was elected to fill the vacancy, and took his seat Jan. 15, 1821.
[21] The Committee on Elections reported on Feb. 17, 1823, that he had been duly elected, but he appears never to have taken his seat.
[22] The *Congressional Directory* lists Smith (Va.). This could refer either to Arthur or William Smith of that State. However, the *Journal of the House of Representatives* lists John S. Smith (Ky.).

POST OFFICE AND POST ROADS

Chairman: Francis Johnson, Ky.

Charles Hooks, N.C.
Samuel Gross, Penn.
Ebenezer Stoddard, Conn.

Samuel Campbell, N.Y.
Ephraim Bateman, N.J.
James Overstreet, S.C.

DISTRICT OF COLUMBIA

Chairman: Joseph Kent, Md.

Charles F. Mercer, Va.
Raphael Neale, Md.
James Matlack, N.J.

Thomas Patterson, Penn.
William B. Rochester, N.Y.
Rollin C. Mallary, Vt.

JUDICIARY

Chairman: John Sergeant, Penn.

William Plumer, Jr., N.H.
John D. Dickinson, N.Y.
Hugh Nelson, Va.

Hutchins G. Burton, N.C.
Romulus M. Saunders, N.C.
Josiah S. Johnston, La.

PENSIONS AND REVOLUTIONARY CLAIMS

Chairman: John Rhea, Tenn.

Peter Little, Md.
Samuel Eddy, R.I.
Anthony New, Ky.

Robert Allen, Tenn.
William Smith, Va.
Thomas H. Hubbard, N.Y.

PUBLIC EXPENDITURES

Chairman: Thomas Montgomery, Ky.

Henry W. Dwight, Mass.
Samuel C. Crafts, Vt.
John Gebhard, N.Y.

Joseph Gist, S.C.
Levi Barber, Ohio
Edward F. Tattnall, Ga.

PRIVATE LAND CLAIMS

Chairman: John W. Campbell, Ohio

Alfred Conkling, N.Y.
Gabriel Moore, Ala.
Ezekiel Whitman, Me.

Nathaniel Upham, N.H.
Ansel Sterling, Conn.
Josiah Crudup, N.C.

MANUFACTURES

Chairman: Henry Baldwin, Penn.

Samuel H. Woodson, Ky.
Job Durfee, R.I.
John Floyd, Va.

Henry W. Connor, N.C.
John Nelson, Md.
Lewis Condict, N.J.

AGRICULTURE

Chairman: Josiah Butler, N.H.

Francis Baylies, Mass.
Robert S. Garnett, Va.
James Buchanan, Penn.

Archibald McNeill, N.C.
Joseph Vance, Ohio
James Blair, S.C.

REVISAL AND UNFINISHED BUSINESS

Chairman: Samuel Lathrop, Mass.

Daniel Burrows, Conn.   Thomas R. Ross, Ohio

ACCOUNTS

Chairman: Samuel C. Allen, Mass.

Samuel Swan, N.J.   Benjamin Ruggles, Ohio

On Expenditures in the Department of State

Chairman: Silas Wood, N.Y.

Mark Alexander, Va.   Noyes Barber, Conn.

On Expenditures in the Treasury Department

Chairman: Albert H. Tracy, N.Y.

Elias Keyes, Vt.   George Holcombe, N.J.

On Expenditures in the War Department

Chairman: George Tucker, Va.

David Chambers, Ohio   Enoch Lincoln, Me.

On Expenditures in the Navy Department

Chairman: Samuel Edwards, Penn.

Walter Patterson, N.Y.   Phineas White, Vt.

On Expenditures in the Post Office

Chairman: George Denison, Penn.

David Woodcock, N.Y.   Lemuel Sawyer, N.C.

On Expenditures on the Public Buildings

Chairman: Jeremiah Nelson, Mass.

Jeremiah H. Pierson, N.Y.   Jabez Leftwich, Va.

SELECT COMMITTEES

REVOLUTIONARY PENSIONS

Chairman: John Cocke, Tenn.

John Reed, Mass.	John Long, N.C.
Thomas Whipple, Jr., N.H.	Edward B. Jackson, Va.
John Wilson, S.C.	Ebenezer Herrick, Me.

SLAVE TRADE

Chairman: Benjamin Gorham, Mass.

Joseph Hemphill, Penn.	John T. Johnson, Ky.
Joel R. Poinsett, S.C.	Charles Borland, Jr., N.Y.
John Phillips, Penn.	Thomas Van Swearingen, Va.

MILITARY AFFAIRS

Chairman: William Eustis, Mass.

Solomon Van Rensselaer, N.Y.   William Darlington, Penn.
John Cocke, Tenn.   John S. Smith, Ky.
Burwell Bassett, Va.   James Matlack, N.J.

FOREIGN AFFAIRS

Chairman: Jonathan Russell, Mass.

Caesar A. Rodney, Del.   John W. Taylor, N.Y.
Robert Wright, Md.   William S. Archer, Va.
William A. Trimble, Ohio   Patrick Farrelly, Penn.

NAVAL AFFAIRS

Chairman: Louis McLane, Del.

Timothy Fuller, Mass.   Churchill C. Cambreleng, N.Y.
Benjamin Hardin, Ky.   George R. Gilmer, Ga.
Henry R. Warfield, Md.   George Plumer, Penn.

PUBLIC BUILDINGS

Chairman: William S. Blackedge, N.C.

William W. Van Wyck, N.Y.   Joshua Cushman, Me.
George Cassedy, N.J.   Aaron Hobart, Mass.
John Brown, Penn.   Jared Williams, Va.

ON ROADS AND CANALS

Chairman: Joseph Hemphill, Penn.

Robert R. Reid, Ga.   William L. Ball, Va.
James Hawkes, N.Y.   Hutchins G. Burton, N.C.
Aaron Matson, N.H.   Joseph Vance, Ohio

ON INDIAN AFFAIRS

Chairman: Thomas Metcalfe, Ky.

James S. Mitchell, Penn.   Elijah Spencer, N.Y.
Thomas Bayly, Md.   Lewis Bigelow, Mass.
Thomas H. Hall, N.C.   Charles F. Mercer, Va.

MILITIA

Chairman: George R. Gilmer, Ga.

John J. Morgan, N.Y.   James Blair, S.C.
John Randolph, Va.   Samuel Swan, N.J.
Gideon Barstow, Mass.   James McSherry, Penn.

JOINT COMMITTEES

LIBRARY OF CONGRESS

House	Senate
Joel R. Poinsett, S.C.	Mahlon Dickerson, N.J.
Alexander Smyth, Va.	John W. Walker, Ala.
Thomas Whipple, Jr., N.H.	John Elliott, Ga.

ON ENROLLED BILLS

House	Senate
Joseph Dane, Me.	Nehemiah R. Knight, R.I.
Thomas Murray, Jr., Penn.	

STANDING COMMITTEES OF THE SENATE OF THE UNITED STATES

FOREIGN RELATIONS

Chairman: Rufus King, N.Y.

Nathaniel Macon, N.C.	Ethan Allen Brown, Ohio
James Barbour, Va.	John Elliott, Ga.

FINANCES

Chairman: John Holmes, Me.

John H. Eaton, Tenn.	Nathaniel Macon, N.C.
Martin Van Buren, N.Y.	Walter Lowrie, Penn.

COMMERCE AND MANUFACTURES

Chairman: Mahlon Dickerson, N.J.

Benjamin Ruggles, Ohio	James De Wolf, R.I.
James Lanman, Conn.	William Findlay, Penn.

MILITARY AFFAIRS

Chairman: John Williams, Tenn.

Waller Taylor, Ind.	Richard M. Johnson, Ky.
John Elliott, Ga.	John Chandler, Me.

MILITIA

Chairman: James S. Noble, Ind.

Montfort Stokes, N.C.	James Lanman, Conn.
John Chandler, Me.	Horatio Seymour, Vt.

NAVAL AFFAIRS

Chairman: James Pleasants, Va.

John F. Parrott, N.H.
Freeman Walker, Ga.

Thomas H. Williams, Miss.
Nicholas Ware, Ga.

PUBLIC LANDS

Chairman: Jesse B. Thomas, Ill.

Nicholas Van Dyke, Del.
John H. Eaton, Tenn.

Walter Lowrie, Penn.
Thomas H. Benton, Mo.

INDIAN AFFAIRS

Chairman: Henry Johnson, La.

William R. King, Ala.
Thomas H. Benton, Mo.

Richard M. Johnson, Ky.
David Holmes, Miss.

CLAIMS

Chairman: Benjamin Ruggles, Ohio

John F. Parrott, N.H.[23]
David Barton, Mo.

Nicholas Van Dyke, Del.
Elijah Boardman, Conn.

JUDICIARY

Chairman: William Smith, S.C.

John Holmes, Me.
Samuel L. Southard, N.J.

Harrison Gray Otis, Mass.
Martin Van Buren, N.Y.

POST OFFICE AND POST ROADS

Chairman: Montfort Stokes, N.C.

William A. Palmer, Vt.
David Barton, Mo.

John Chandler, Me.
William R. King, Ala.

PENSIONS

Chairman: James Noble, Ind.

John H. Eaton, Tenn.
John Elliott, Ga.

Horatio Seymour, Vt.
Nicholas Ware, Ga.

DISTRICT OF COLUMBIA

Chairman: James Barbour, Va.

James Lanman, Conn.
Samuel L. Southard, N.J.

Edward Lloyd, Md.
James De Wolf, R.I.

---

[23] The *Journal of the House of Representatives* lists David L. Morril (N.H.) in place of John F. Parrott (N.H.).

ROADS AND CANALS

Chairman: Richard M. Johnson, Ky.

Rufus King, N.Y.   Walter Lowrie, Penn.
Nathaniel Macon, N.C.   Elijah H. Mills, Mass.

CONTINGENT EXPENSES

Chairman: James Lanman, Conn.

Nathaniel Macon, N.C.   Walter Lowrie, Penn.

CONGRESSIONAL DIRECTORY

SEVENTEENTH CONGRESS, SECOND SESSION
(December 2, 1822–March 3, 1823)

Mr. Burch, Capitol Hill
Joel Abbot, Ga.
Robert Allen, Tenn.
Henry W. Connor, N.C.
George R. Gilmer, Ga.
Benjamin Hardin, Ky.
William Smith, Va.
William Smith (S), S.C.
Wiley Thompson, Ga.

Brown's Hotel, Penn. Ave.
Philip P. Barbour, Va.
James Barbour (S), Va.
William L. Ball, Va.
Thomas Bayly, Md.
Elisha Litchfield, N.Y.
Richard McCarty, N.Y.
Nathaniel Pitcher, N.Y.
Andrew Stevenson, Va.
James Stephenson, Va.
John Scott, Mo.
Arthur Smith, Va.
David Trimble, Ky.
Waller Taylor (S), Ind.
Reuben H. Walworth, N.Y.

Mrs. Blake, Tenth St., West
George Holcombe, N.J.
Joseph Kent, Md.
Raphael Neale, Md.
Samuel L. Southard (S),[1] N.J.
Montfort Stokes (S), N.C.
Samuel H. Woodson, Ky.

Rev. Brown, near General Post Office
John T. Johnson, Ky.
Richard M. Johnson (S), Ky.

Mrs. Claxton, Capitol Hill
Burwell Bassett, Va.
David Barton (S), Mo.
John Cocke, Tenn.
Matthew Harvey, N.H.
Aaron Hobart, Mass.
Francis Jones, Tenn.
Jabez Leftwich, Va.
Anthony New, Ky.
William Plumer, Jr., N.H.
Thomas Whipple, Jr., N.H.

Mr. Coyle, Capitol Hill
Francis Baylies, Mass.
Joseph Hemphill, Penn.
David Holmes (S), Miss.
John S. Parrott (S), N.H.
Christopher Rankin, Miss.
Thomas H. Williams (S), Miss.

Mrs. Clark, F St., North
Hutchins G. Burton, N.C.
Joseph Kirkland, N.Y.
John J. Morgan, N.Y.
Nicholas Van Dyke (S), Del.

Mr. Dowson, No. 1, Capitol Hill
James De Wolf (S), R.I.
William Eustis, Mass.
John Holmes (S), Me.
Jonathan Russell, Mass.
Samuel Smith (S),[2] Md.

Mr. Dowson, No. 2, Capitol Hill
Mark Alexander, Va.
William S. Archer, Va.

[1] Resigned Mar. 3, 1823.
[2] Took his seat Dec. 17, 1822, resigning his House seat the same day. Isaac McKim was elected to fill the House vacancy, and took his seat Jan. 8, 1823.

Thomas H. Benton (S), Mo.
Weldon H. Edwards, N.C.
John Elliott (S), Ga.
Thomas H. Hall, Va.
James Jones, Va.
Nathaniel Macon (S), N.C.
John Randolph, Va.
Romulus M. Saunders, N.C.
Edward F. Tattnall, Ga.

Mr. Davis, E St., North
Francis Johnson, Ky.
Thomas Metcalfe, Ky.

Mr. Dunn, Capitol Hill
Josiah Crudup, N.C.

Mr. Emack, Capitol Hill
David L. Morril (S), N.H.
Thomas Murray, Jr., Penn.
Aaron Matson, N.H.
Starling Tucker, S.C.
Silas Wood, N.Y.

Mr. Fletcher, near General Post Office
Samuel C. Allen, Mass.
Lewis Bigelow, Mass.
Charles Borland, Jr., N.Y.
Joshua Cushman, Me.
Samuel Lathrop, Mass.
Micah Sterling N.Y.
Phineas White, Vt.
William D. Williamson, Me.

Mr. Frost, Capitol Hill
Elijah Boardman (S), Conn.
John Chandler (S), Me.
Mark Harris, Me.
Nehemiah R. Knight (S), R.I.
Jeremiah H. Pierson, N.Y.
Benjamin Ruggles (S), Ohio
John Sloane, Ohio
Gideon Tomlinson, Conn.

Franklin House, Penn. Ave.
John D. Dickinson, N.Y.
John H. Eaton (S), Tenn.
Edward Lloyd (S), Md.
Elijah H. Mills (S), Mass.
Walter Patterson, N.Y.

Mrs. Gaither, Penn. Ave.
Ephraim Bateman, N.J.
William McCoy, Va.
James Matlack, N.J.
Jared Williams, Va.

Mr. Gardiner, Penn. Ave.
Levi Barber, Ohio
John W. Campbell, Ohio
Thomas R. Mitchell, S.C.

Mrs. Hickey, Capitol Hill
Josiah Butler, N.H.
William S. Blackledge, N.C.
Mark L. Hill, Me.
David Woodcock, N.Y.

Mrs. Hamilton, Capitol Hill
Samuel C. Crafts, Vt.
Elias Keyes, Vt.
John Mattocks, Vt.
William A. Palmer (S), Vt.
Horatio Seymour (S), Vt.

Miss Heyer, Capitol Hill
Gideon Barstow, Mass.
James McSherry, Penn.

Mr. Hyatt, Penn. Ave.
Joseph Dane, Me.
Jeremiah Nelson, Mass.
John Russ, Conn.
John Reed, Mass.

Mr. Handy, Penn. Ave.
James W. Bates, Deleg., Ark. Terr.
James D. Breckinridge, Ky.
John S. Smith, Ky.

Mr. Kervand, Seven Buildings
Churchill C. Cambreleng, N.Y.
Henry W. Dwight, Mass.
Joel R. Poinsett, S.C.

Mr. McLeod, Capitol Hill
Alfred Conkling, N.Y.
Cadwallader D. Colden, N.Y.
Lewis Condict, N.J.
Job Durfee, R.I.
Samuel Eddy, R.I.
John Gebhard, N.Y.
Charles H. Ruggles, N.Y.

Mrs. McCardle, Penn. Ave.
Newton Cannon, Tenn.
Edward B. Jackson, Va.
Thomas Montgomery, Ky.
Alexander Smyth, Va.

Mrs. Meyer, opposite Centre Market
John Brown, Penn.
William Darlington, Penn.
Timothy Fuller, Mass.
John Findlay, Penn.
James S. Mitchell, Penn.
Thomas Patterson, Penn.
John Phillips, Penn.
Daniel Udree,[3] Penn.

Mr. McGowan, Penn. Ave.
Robert S. Garnett, Va.
Thomas Newton, Jr., Va.
Hugh Nelson,[4] Va.

Miss Polk, C St., North
Ethan Allen Brown (S), Ohio
Jonathan Jennings, Ind.
James Noble (S), Ind.
George Plumer, Penn.
Thomas R. Ross, Ohio
John Tod, Penn.
John Vance,[5] Ohio

Mrs. Peyton, C St., North
John Carter,[6] S.C.
Alfred Cuthbert, Ga.
John Floyd, Va.
Andrew R. Govan,[7] S.C.
James Lanman (S), Conn.
Robert R. Reid, Ga.
Isham Talbot (S), Ky.
Nicholas Ware (S), Ga.
John Williams (S), Tenn.

Mrs. Pratt, Penn. Ave.
John W. Taylor, N.Y.

Peck's Hotel, Georgetown
Samuel Edwards, Penn.

Benjamin Gorham, Mass.
Rufus King (S), N.Y.
Charles F. Mercer, Va.
Lewis McLane, Del.
John Nelson, Md.
Stephen Van Rensselaer, N.Y.
Martin Van Buren (S), N.Y.
Henry R. Warfield, Md.

Queen's Hotel, Capitol Hill
Noyes Barber, Conn.
George Cassedy, N.J.
Charles Hooks, N.C.
Ebenezer Herrick, Me.
Thomas H. Hubbard, N.Y.
Rollin C. Mallary, Vt.
Philip Reed, Md.
Thomas J. Rogers, Penn.
William B. Rochester, N.Y.
Samuel Swan, N.J.
Ebenezer Stoddard, Conn.
Ansel Sterling, Conn.
William W. Van Wyck, N.Y.
Nathaniel Upham, N.H.
Robert Wright, Md.

Mrs. Queen, the Elder, Penn. Ave.
Samuel Campbell, N.Y.
James Hawkes, N.Y.
Elijah Spencer, N.Y.

Mrs. Queen, the Younger, Penn. Ave.
Samuel D. Ingham, Penn.
Ninian Edwards (S), Ill.
William Findlay (S), Penn.
John Long, N.C.
Archibald McNeill, N.C.

Mr. Rapine, Capitol Hill
Joseph Gist, S.C.
John Wilson, S.C.

Mr. Scott, Capitol Hill
Daniel Rodney, Del.

[3] Took his seat Dec. 23, 1822.
[4] Resigned Jan. 14, 1823.
[5] Listed as Joseph Vance in the *Biographical Directory of the American Congress, 1774-1961*. See note 15 on p. 128.
[6] Took his seat Dec. 11, 1822.
[7] Took his seat Dec. 4, 1822.

Mr. Sawyer, Penn. Ave.
George Denison, Penn.
Walter Forward, Penn.
Samuel Gross, Penn.
Walter Lowrie (S), Penn.
Jesse B. Thomas (S), Ill
Lewis Williams, N.C.

Mr. Sardo, Penn. Ave.
Patrick Farrelly, Penn.
Gabriel Moore, Ala.

Sandford's Hotel, Penn. Ave.
John Rhea, Tenn.

Mr. Tims, Capitol Hill
Mahlon Dickerson (S), N.J.
John Gaillard (S), S.C.
Caesar A. Rodney (S),[8] Del.

Mrs. Tucker, opposite Centre Market
David Chambers, Ohio
Thomas Forrest, Penn.
Enoch Lincoln, Me.

Solomon Sibley, Deleg., Mich. Terr.
Albert H. Tracy, N.Y.

Mrs. Wilson, F St., North
Josiah S. Johnston, La.
Henry Johnson (S), La.
George Tucker, Va.

Mr. Woodside, Six Buildings
James Lloyd (S), Mass.

Mr. Young, Capitol Hill
Daniel P. Cook, Ill.
Henry W. Edwards, Conn.
Andrew Stewart, Penn.

Private Residences
Mr. Friend, near the Navy Yard
Daniel Burrows, Mass.
Mr. Little, near the Navy Yard
Peter Little, Md.
Col. Henderson, Marine Garrison
Thomas L. Moore, Va.
Corner of Fourteenth and E St.
James Brown (S), La.

APPENDIX

William R. King (S), Ala.
John W. Walker (S),[9] Ala.
Lemuel Sawyer, N.C.
Felix Walker, N.C.
James Buchanan, Penn.
John Sergeant, Penn.
James Hamilton, Jr.,[10] S.C.

George McDuffie, S.C.
Henry H. Bryan,[11] Tenn.
Charles Rich, Vt.
James Pleasants,[12] Va.
Joseph M. Hernandez,[13] Deleg., Terr. of
Fla.

[8] Resigned Jan. 29, 1823, having been appointed minister to Buenos Aires.
[9] Resigned Dec. 12, 1822. William Kelly was elected to fill the vacancy, and took his seat Jan. 21, 1823.
[10] Took his seat Jan. 6, 1823.
[11] The Committee on Elections reported on Feb. 17, 1823, that he had been duly elected, but he appears never to have taken his seat.
[12] Resigned Dec. 15, 1822. John Taylor was elected to fill the vacancy, and took his seat Dec. 30, 1822.
[13] Took his seat as a Delegate on Jan. 3, 1823.

STANDING COMMITTEES OF THE
HOUSE OF REPRESENTATIVES

ELECTIONS
Chairman: John Sloane, Ohio
Weldon N. Edwards, N.C.   Thomas J. Rogers, Penn.
Joseph Kirkland, N.Y.   Rollin C. Mallary, Vt.
Thomas L. Moore, Va.   Starling Tucker, S.C.

WAYS AND MEANS
Chairman: Samuel Smith, Md.
Louis McLane, Del.   Wiley Thompson, Ga.
Thomas R. Mitchell, S.C.   Andrew Stevenson, Va.
Francis Jones, Tenn.   Churchill C. Cambreling, N.Y.

CLAIMS
Chairman: Lewis Williams, N.C.
William McCoy, Va.   Thomas Forrest, Penn.
Henry W. Edwards, Conn.   Aaron Matson, N.H.
Elisha Litchfield, N.Y.   Philip Reed, Md.

COMMERCE
Chairman: Thomas Newton, Jr., Va.
Gideon Tomlinson, Conn.   John J. Morgan, N.Y.
Mark L. Hill, Me.   Benjamin Hardin, Ky.
Joel Abbot, Ga.   Job Durfee, R.I.

PUBLIC LANDS
Chairman: Christopher Rankin, Miss.
John Scott, Mo.   Micah Sterling, N.Y.
Daniel P. Cook, Ill.   Burwell Bassett, Va.
Newton Cannon, Tenn.   Jonathan Jennings, Ind.

POST OFFICE AND POST ROADS
Chairman: Francis Johnson, Ky.
Charles Hooks, N.C.   Samuel Campbell, N.Y.
Samuel Gross, Penn.   Ephraim Bateman, N.J.
Ebenezer Stoddard, Conn.   John Wilson, S.C.

DISTRICT OF COLUMBIA
Chairman: Joseph Kent, Md.
Charles F. Mercer, Va.   Thomas Patterson, Penn.
Raphael Neale, Md.   William B. Rochester, N.Y.
James Stephenson, Va.   James Matlack, N.J.

JUDICIARY

Chairman: Hugh Nelson, Va.

William Plumer, Jr., N.H.
John D. Dickinson, N.Y.
Hutchins G. Burton, N.C.

Romulus M. Saunders, N.C.
Josiah S. Johnston, La.
Joseph Hemphill, Penn.

PENSIONS AND REVOLUTIONARY CLAIMS

Chairman: John Rhea, Tenn.

Peter Little, Md.
Samuel Eddy, R.I.
Robert Allen, Tenn.

William Smith, Va.
Thomas H. Hubbard, N.Y.
Levi Barber, Ohio

PUBLIC EXPENDITURES

Chairman: Thomas Montgomery, Ky.

Henry W. Dwight, Mass.
Samuel C. Crafts, Vt.
John Gebhard, N.Y.

Joseph Gist, S.C.
Edward F. Tattnall, Ga.
Mark Harris, Me.

PRIVATE LAND CLAIMS

Chairman: John W. Campbell, Ohio

Alfred Conkling, N.Y.
Gabriel Moore, Ala.
Nathaniel Upham, N.H.

Ansel Sterling, Conn.
Josiah Crudup, N.C.
Stephen Van Rensselaer, N.Y.

MANUFACTURES

Chairman: John Tod, Penn.

Samuel H. Woodson, Ky.
John Floyd, Va.
Henry W. Connor, N.C.

John Nelson, Md.
Lewis Condict, N.J.
Walter Forward, Penn.

AGRICULTURE

Chairman: Josiah Butler, N.H.

Francis Baylies, N.H.
Robert S. Garnett, Va.
Archibald McNeill, N.C.

Joseph Vance, Ohio
John Findlay, Penn.
Anthony New, Ky.

REVISAL AND UNFINISHED BUSINESS

Chairman: Thomas R. Ross, Ohio

James Hawkes, N.Y.

John Brown, Penn.

ACCOUNTS

Chairman: Samuel C. Allen, Mass.

Samuel Swan, N.J.

Charles H. Ruggles, N.Y.

MILITARY AFFAIRS
Chairman: William Eustis, Mass.

John Cocke, Tenn.	John S. Smith, Ky.
Reuben H. Walworth, N.Y.	William McCoy, Va.
William Darlington, Penn.	John Mattocks, Vt.

NAVAL AFFAIRS
Chairman: Timothy Fuller, Mass.

John Randolph, Va.	Henry R. Warfield, Md.
George R. Gilmer, Ga.	George Plumer, Penn.
Cadwallader D. Colden, N.Y.	Matthew Harvey, N.H.

FOREIGN AFFAIRS
Chairman: Jonathan Russell, Mass.

Robert Wright, Md.	William S. Archer, Va.
David Trimble, Ky.	Patrick Farrelly, Penn.
John W. Taylor, N.Y.	Daniel Rodney, Del.

INDIAN AFFAIRS
Chairman: Thomas Metcalfe, Ky.

Lewis Bigelow, Mass.	Richard McCarty, N.Y.
James S. Mitchell, Penn.	William D. Williamson, Me.
Charles F. Mercer, Va.	Jared Williams, Va.

On Expenditures in the Department of State

Chairman: Silas Wood, N.Y.

Mark Alexander, Va.	Noyes Barber, Conn.

On Expenditures in the Treasury Department

Chairman: Albert H. Tracy, N.Y.

Elias Keyes, Vt.	George Holcombe, N.J.

On Expenditures in the War Department

Chairman: George Tucker, Va.

David Chambers, Ohio	Enoch Lincoln, Me.

On Expenditures in the Navy Department

Chairman: Samuel Edwards, Penn.[14]

Walter Patterson, N.Y.	Phineas White, Vt.

[14] The committees on expenditures in the various departments appear to be carry-overs from the first session of the Seventeenth Congress. Therefore, I am assuming that the *Congressional Directory's* listing of Edwards refers to Samuel Edwards of Penn. rather than Henry W. Edwards of Conn. or Weldon N. Edwards of N.C.

On Expenditures on the Public Buildings

Chairman: Jeremiah Nelson, Mass.
Jeremiah H. Pierson, N.Y.   Jabez Leftwich, Va.

SELECT COMMITTEES

MILITIA

Chairman: Newton Cannon, Tenn.
Richard McCarty, N.Y.   John T. Johnson, Ky.
John Findlay, Penn.   Romulus M. Saunders, N.C.
Arthur Smith, Va.   John Reed, Mass.

SLAVE TRADE

Chairman: Benjamin Gorham, Mass.
John Phillips, Penn.   James Jones, Va.
Andrew R. Govan, S.C.   Thomas H. Hall, N.C.
Charles Borland, Jr., N.Y.   Ebenezer Herrick, Me.

CUMBERLAND ROAD

Chairman: Joseph Hemphill, Penn.
Nathaniel Pitcher, N.Y.   John Long, N.C.
John Russ, Conn.   Joshua Cushman, Me.
Edward B. Jackson, Va.   Andrew Stewart, Penn.

BEAUMARCHIS' CLAIM

Chairman: Andrew Stevenson, Va.
Churchill C. Cambreleng, N.Y.   Henry W. Dwight, Mass.
Francis Johnson, Ky.   George Holcombe, N.J.

REVOLUTIONARY PENSIONS

Chairman: John Cocke, Tenn.
Aaron Hobart, N.J.   William H. Van Wyck, N.Y.
George Cassedy, N.J.   James McSherry, Penn.
Daniel Burrows, Conn.   Felix Walker, N.C.

OWNERS OF BASTROP'S GRANT

Chairman: Louis McLane, Del.
Samuel D. Ingham, Penn.   Francis Jones, Tenn.
Edward F. Tattnall, Ga.   William S. Blackledge, N.C.

PUBLIC BUILDINGS

Chairman: William S. Blackledge, N.C.
Joshua Cushman, Me.   William H. Van Wyck, N.Y.
George Cassedy, N.J.   John Brown, Penn.
Aaron Hobart, Mass.   Jabez Leftwich, Va.

ROADS AND CANALS

Chairman: Andrew Stewart, Penn.

Robert R. Reid, Ga.   James Hawkes, N.Y.
Aaron Matson, N.H.   William L. Ball, Va.
Hutchins G. Burton, N.C.   Joseph Vance, Ohio

JOINT COMMITTEE

LIBRARY OF CONGRESS

House

Alexander Smyth, Va.
Thomas Whipple, Jr., N.H.
Alfred Cuthbert, Ga.

Senate

Mahlon Dickerson, N.J.
John Elliott, Ga.
Elijah H. Mills, Mass.

STANDING COMMITTEES OF THE SENATE OF THE UNITED STATES

FOREIGN AFFAIRS

Chairman: James Barbour, Va.

James Brown, La.   Nathaniel Macon, N.C.
Rufus King, N.Y.   John Elliott, Ga.

FINANCES

Chairman: Walter Lowrie, Penn.

John Holmes, Me.   Martin Van Buren, N.Y.
John H. Eaton, Tenn.   Nathaniel Macon, N.C.

COMMERCE AND MANUFACTURES

Chairman: Mahlon Dickerson, N.J.

Benjamin Ruggles, Ohio   James De Wolf, R.I.
William Findlay, Penn.   James Lanman, Conn.

MILITARY AFFAIRS

Chairman: John Williams, Tenn.

John Chandler, Me.   Waller Taylor, Ind.
Richard M. Johnson, Ky.   John Elliott, Ga.

MILITIA

Chairman: James Noble, Ind.

Horatio Seymour, Vt.   Montfort Stokes, N.C.
James Lanman, Conn.   John Chandler, Me.

NAVAL AFFAIRS

Chairman: James Pleasants, Va.

Thomas H. Williams, Miss.   John F. Parrott, N.H.
Nicholas Ware, Ga.   James Lloyd, Mass.

PUBLIC LANDS

Chairman: Nicholas Van Dyke, Del.

Jesse B. Thomas, Ill.   Walter Lowrie, Penn.
John H. Eaton, Tenn.   Thomas H. Benton, Mo.

INDIAN AFFAIRS

Chairman: Henry Johnson, La.

Richard M. Johnson, Ky.   David Holmes, Miss.
William R. King, Ala.   Thomas H. Benton, Mo.

CLAIMS

Chairman: Benjamin Ruggles, Ohio

Nicholas Van Dyke, Del.   Elijah Boardman, Conn.
David Barton, Mo.   David L. Morril, N.H.

JUDICIARY

Chairman: William Smith, S.C.

Samuel L. Southard, N.J.   Martin Van Buren, N.Y.
John Holmes, Me.   Ethan Allen Brown, Ohio

POST OFFICE AND POST ROADS

Chairman: Montfort Stokes, N.C.

William A. Palmer, Vt.   David Barton, Mo.
John Chandler, Me.   William R. King, Ala.

PENSIONS

Chairman: James Noble, Ind.

John H. Eaton, Tenn.   Horatio Seymour, Vt.
Nicholas Ware, Ga.   John Elliott, Ga.

DISTRICT OF COLUMBIA

Chairman: James Barbour, Va.

Edward Lloyd, Md.   James De Wolf, R.I.
James Lanman, Conn.   Samuel L. Southard, N.J.

CONTINGENT EXPENSES

Chairman: Nathaniel Macon, N.C.

Walter Lowrie, Penn.   James Lanman, Conn.

ENGROSSED BILLS

Chairman: James Lanman, Conn.

Thomas H. Benton, Mo.   John Holmes, Me.

CONGRESSIONAL DIRECTORY

EIGHTEENTH CONGRESS, FIRST SESSION
(December 1, 1823 – May 27, 1824)

Mrs. Arguelles, Penn. Ave.
Henry W. Dwight, Mass.
Henry W. Edwards (S), Conn.
Timothy Fuller, Mass.
Philip S. Markley, Penn.
George Tucker, Va.
William C. Rives, Va.
Henry Wilson, Penn.

Mr. Burch, Capitol Hill
Robert Allen, Tenn.
Joel Abbot, Ga.
Philemon Beecher, Ohio
Henry W. Connor, N.C.
George Cary, Ga.
Robert P. Henry, Ky.
John Long, N.C.
William Smith, Va.
Wiley Thompson, Ga.
Starling Tucker, S.C.

Brown's Hotel, Penn. Ave.
William L. Ball,[1] Va.
Philip P. Barbour, Va.
James Barbour (S), Va.
Henry W. Conway, Deleg. Ark. Terr.
Rowland Day, N.Y.
Justin Dwinell, N.Y.
Lewis Eaton, N.Y.
Charles A. Foote, N.Y.
Elisha Litchfield, N.Y.
William Prince, Ind.
John Scott, Mo.
Andrew Stevenson, Va.

James Stephenson, Va.
Egbert Ten Eyck, N.Y.
David Trimble, Ky.
Waller Taylor (S), Ind.
Samuel F. Vinton, Ohio
John C. Wright, Ohio
Isaac Wilson,[2] N.Y.

Mrs. Blake, Penn. Ave.
James Buchanan, Penn.
Samuel Edwards, Penn.
George Holcombe, N.J.
Joseph Kent, Md.
George E. Mitchell, Md.
Raphael Neale, Md.

Mr. Bestor, Capitol Hill
John Culpepper, N.C.
John Herkimer, N.Y.
Issac Williams, Jr., N.Y.

Mr. Brown, E St., North
John T. Johnson, Ky.
Richard M. Johnson (S), Ky.

Mrs. Ball, near General Post Office
David White, Ky.

Mrs. Claxton, Capitol Hill
Adam R. Alexander, Tenn.
John Blair, Tenn.
David Barton (S), Mo.
John Cocke, Tenn.
Samuel Houston, Tenn.

[1] Died Feb. 28, 1824. John Taliaferro was elected to fill the vacancy, and took his seat Apr. 8, 1824.
[2] Served until Jan 7, 1824. He was succeeded by Parmenio Adams who successfully contested the election.

Jacob C. Isacks, Tenn.
Jabez Leftwich, Va.
James B. Reynolds, Tenn.
James T. Sandford, Tenn.
James Standifer, Tenn.

Mr. Coyle, Capitol Hill
Joseph Hemphill, Penn.
David Holmes (S), Miss.
John McKee, Ala.
John F. Parrott (S), Mass.
Christopher Rankin, Miss.
Isaac Wayne, Penn.
Daniel Webster, Mass.
Thomas H. Williams (S), Miss.

Mrs. Cochran, F St., North
Robert S. Garnett, Va.
Thomas Newton, Jr., Va.

Mrs. Clark, F St., North
Thomas H. Benton (S), Mo.
John Elliott (S), Ga.
Romulus M. Saunders, N.C.

Mr. Dowson, No. 1, Capitol Hill
William L. Brent, La.
Henry H. Gurley, La.
Edward Livingston, La.
Isaac McKim, Md.
George W. Owen, Ala.
Samuel Smith (S), Md.

Mr. Dowson, No. 2, Capitol Hill
Mark Alexander, Va.
Hutchins G. Burton,[3] N.C.
John Branch (S), N.C.
Thomas W. Cobb,[4] Ga.
Weldon N. Edwards, N.C.
Thomas H. Hall, N.C.
Willie P. Mangum, N.C.
Nathaniel Macon (S), N.C.
John Randolph, Va.
Richard D. Spaight, Jr., N.C.

Mr. Charles Davis, E St., North
Francis Johnson, Ky.
Thomas Metcalfe, Ky.

Mr. John Davis, Ninth St., West
Henry Clay, Ky.
Robert P. Letcher, Ky.

Mr. Fletcher, near General Post Office
Samuel C. Allen, Mass.
Daniel P. Cook, Ill.
Joshua Cushman, Me.
John Findlay, Penn.
Samuel D. Ingham, Penn.
Samuel Lathrop, Mass.
Samuel McKean, Penn.
Thomas J. Rogers,[5] Penn.
James Strong, N.Y.
John Tod, Penn.
James Wilson, Penn.

Mr. Frost, Capitol Hill
Nehemiah R. Knight (S), R.I.
John Patterson, Ohio
Benjamin Ruggles (S), Ohio
John Sloane, Ohio
Gideon Tomlinson, Conn.
Jesse B. Thomas, Ill.
Elisha Whittlesey, Ohio

Mrs. Galvin, Capitol Hill
Ethan Allen Brown (S), Ohio
Arthur Livermore, N.H.
Walter Lowrie (S), Penn.
Thomas R. Ross, Ohio
Andrew Stewart, Penn.
John W. Taylor, N.Y.

Mrs. Gaither, Penn. Ave.
Daniel Garrison, N.J.
James Matlack, N.J.
William McCoy, Va.
Jared Williams, Va.

Mr. Gardiner, Penn. Ave.
John W. Campbell, Ohio
Robert Harris, Penn.
George Plumer, Penn.
Alexander Smyth, Va.

Gadsby's Hotel, near West Market
Robert B. Campbell, S.C.

---

[3] Resigned Mar. 23, 1824.
[4] Resigned Dec. 6, 1824, having been elected Senator.
[5] Resigned Apr. 20, 1824.

William Heyward, Jr., Md.
Edward Lloyd (S), Md.
Elijah H. Mills (S), Mass.

Mr. Hyatt, Penn. Ave.
Richard A. Buckner, Ky.
Duncan McArthur, Ohio
Thomas P. Moore, Ky.
James Noble (S), Ind.
Philip Thompson, Ky.
John Test, Ind.
Charles A. Wickliffe, Ky.
Joseph Vance, Ohio

Mrs. Hamilton, Capitol Hill
Samuel C. Crafts, Vt.
William Kelly (S), Ala.
Aaron Matson, N.H.
William A. Palmer (S), Vt.
Charles Rich, Vt.
Horatio Seymour (S), Vt.

Mrs. Hickey, Capitol Hill
Samuel Breck, Penn.
James Lloyd (S), Mass.

Miss Heyer
James De Wolf (S), R.I.
John J. Morgan,[6] N.Y.

Mr. Hall, near City Hall
William C. Bradley, Vt.

Mr. Handy, Penn. Ave.
John S. Spence, Md.

Mr. McLeod, Capitol Hill
Lewis Condict, N.J.
Job Durfee, R.I.
Samuel Eddy, R.I.
Matthew Harvey, N.H.
Lemuel Jenkins, N.Y.
Stephen Longfellow, Me.
William Plumer, Jr., N.H.
Peter Sharpe, N.Y.
John J. Morgan,[7] N.Y.

Mrs. Meyer, near Centre Market
Lot Clark, N.Y.

James L. Hogeboom, N.Y.
George Kremer, Penn.
James S. Mitchell, Penn.
Thomas Patterson, Penn.
John Richards, N.Y.
Daniel Udree, Penn.

Mrs. O'Neale, near West Market
Richard K. Call, Deleg., Terr. of Fla.
John H. Eaton (S), Tenn.
Andrew Jackson (S), Tenn.

Miss Polk, Capitol Hill
James W. Gazlay, Ohio

Mrs. Peyton, C St., North
John W. Cady, N.Y.
John Carter, S.C.
Ela Collins, N.Y.
Andrew R. Govan, S.C.
Samuel Lawrence, N.Y.
George McDuffie, S.C.
Robert R. Rose, N.Y.
Henry R. Storrs, N.Y.

Peck's Hotel, Georgetown
William S. Archer, Va.
Martin Van Buren (S), N.Y.
Alfred Cuthbert, Ga.
Rufus King (S), N.Y.
John Lee, Md.
Louis McLane, Del.
Charles F. Mercer, Va.
Stephen Van Rensselaer, N.Y.
Henry R. Warfield, Md.

Queen's Hotel, Capitol Hill
Daniel A. A. Buck, Vt.
Noyes Barber, Conn.
George Cassedy, N.J.
Samuel A. Foote, Conn.
Joel Frost, N.Y.
Walter Foward, Penn.
Alfred M. Gatlin, N.C.
Ebenezer Herrick, Me.
Moses Hayden, N.Y.
Charles Hooks, N.C.
Jonathan Jennings, Ind.
Dudley Marvin, N.Y.

---

[6] Also listed at McLeod's.
[7] Also listed at Miss Heyer's.

Rollin C. Mallary, Vt.
Henry C. Martindale, N.Y.
Arthur Smith, Va.
Samuel Swan, N.J.
Ebenezer Stoddard, Conn.
Ansel Sterling, Conn.
Jacob Tyson, N.Y.
Robert B. Vance, N.C.
William Van Wyck, N.Y.
Lewis Williams, N.C.
Silas Wood, N.Y.
Lemuel Whitman, Conn.

Mrs. Queen, the Elder, Capitol Hill
Francis Baylies, Mass.
Hector Craig, N.Y.
William Cox Ellis, Penn.
Aaron Hobart, Mass.
Thomas Whipple, Jr., N.H.
William Woods, N.Y.

Mrs. Queen, the Younger, Capitol Hill
Ninian Edwards (S),[8] Ill.
John Locke, Mass.
Gabriel Moore, Ala.
Jeremiah Nelson, Mass.
John Reed, Mass.
Jonas Sibley, Mass.

Mr. Rapine, Capitol Hill
Burwell Bassett, Va.
Joseph Gist, S.C.
John Wilson, S.C.

Mr. Sardo, Penn. Ave.
James Allison, Jr., Penn.
Mordecai Bartley, Ohio
John Brown, Penn.
Patrick Farrelly, Penn.
William Findlay (S), Penn.
Joseph Johnson, Va.
William Wilson, Ohio

Strother's Hotel, Penn. Ave.
John S. Barbour, Va.
James Hamilton, Jr., S.C.
Robert Y. Hayne (S), S.C.

Mr. Tims, Capitol Hill
Samuel Bell (S), N.H.
John Chandler (S), Me.
Mahlon Dickerson (S), N.J.
John Gaillard (S), S.C.
John Holmes (S), Me.

Mrs. Tucker, near Centre Market
Ichabod Bartlett, N.H.
William Burleight, Me.
James Lanman (S), Conn.
Enoch Lincoln, Me.
Albert H. Tracy, N.Y.

Tennison's Hotel, Penn. Ave.
Henry Johnson (S), La.

Mr. Wurtz, near Tyber Creek
David Kidder, Me.
Jeremiah O'Brien, Me.

Mrs. Wilson, F St., North
Benjamin W. Crowinshield, Mass.

Private Residences
  Mrs. Young, Near City Hall
John Bailey,[9] Mass.
  No. 5, Seven Buildings
Churchill C. Cambreleng, N.Y.
  No. 5, Seven Buildings
Joel R. Poinsett, S.C.
  Georgetown
John Forsyth, Ga.
  Col. Fowler, Georgetown
Peter Little, Md.
  Mr. McLane, Post Master General,
  Georgetown
William McLane, Ohio
  Rev. McIlvaine, Georgetown
James McIlvaine (S), N.J.
  Rev. Lucas, Capitol Hill
Gabriel Richard, Deleg., Mich Terr.
  Dr. William Thornton, F St., North
Isham Talbot (S), Ky.

---

[8] Resigned Mar. 4, 1824, having been appointed minister to France.
[9] By resolution of Mar. 18, 1824, was declared not entitled to seat; he was subsequently elected, and took his seat Dec. 13, 1824.

APPENDIX

William R. King (S), Ala.
Thomas Clayton (S),[10] Del.
Nicholas Van Dyke (S), Del.
Edward F. Tattnall, Ga.
Nicholas Ware (S), Ga.

James Brown (S),[11] La.
Daniel H. Miller, Penn.
John Floyd, Va.
John Taylor (S), Va.

STANDING COMMITTEES OF THE
HOUSE OF REPRESENTATIVES

ELECTIONS

Chairman: John Sloane, Ohio

Rollin C. Mallary, Vt.
William L. Ball, Va.
Starling Tucker, S.C.

Thomas H. Hall, N.C.
James Standifer, Tenn.
Philip Thompson, Ky.

WAYS AND MEANS

Chairman: Louis McLane, Del.

Samuel D. Ingham, Penn.
Wiley Thompson, Ga.
Andrew Stevenson, Va.

Churchill C. Cambreleng, N.Y.
George McDuffie, S.C.
Isaac McKim, Md.

CLAIMS

Chairman: Lewis Williams, N.C.

William McCoy, Va.
Charles Rich, Vt.
Elisha Litchfield, N.Y.

Aaron Matson, N.H.
Elisha Whittlesey, Ohio
Jacob C. Isacks, Tenn.

COMMERCE

Chairman: Thomas Newton, Jr.,Va.

Gideon Tomlinson, Conn.
Joel Abbot, Ga.
Job Durfee, R.I.

Henry W. Dwight, Mass.
Willie P. Mangum, N.C.
John J. Morgan, N.Y.

PUBLIC LANDS

Chairman: Christopher Rankin, Miss.

John Scott, Mo.
Daniel P. Cook, Ill.
Jonathan Jennings, Ind.

James Strong, N.Y.
Samuel F. Vinton, Ohio
William C. Bradley, Vt.

[10] Elected to fill the vacancy caused by the resignation of Caesar A. Rodney in the preceding Congress, and took his seat Jan. 15, 1824. Vacancy in this class from Jan. 29, 1823, to Jan. 8, 1824.
[11] Resigned Dec. 10, 1823, having been appointed minister to France. Josiah S. Johnston was elected to fill the vacancy, and took his seat Mar. 12, 1824.

POST OFFICE AND POST ROADS

Chairman: Francis Johnson, Ky.

Charles Hooks, N.C.
Ebenezer Stoddard, Conn.
John Wilson, S.C.

Samuel McKean, Penn.
Adam R. Alexander, Tenn.
Mordecai Bartley, Ohio

DISTRICT OF COLUMBIA

Chairman: Joseph Kent, Md.

Raphael Neale, Md.
James Matlack, N.J.
John Findlay, Penn.

Mark Alexander, Va.
John W. Gazlay, Ohio
John Blair, Tenn.

JUDICIARY

Chairman: Daniel Webster, Mass.

Philip P. Barbour Va.
William Plumer, Jr., N.H.
Hutchins G. Burton, N.C.

James Buchanan, Penn.
Romulus M. Saunders, N.C.
William L. Brent, La.

PENSIONS AND REVOLUTIONARY CLAIMS

Chairman: Peter Little Md.

Samuel Eddy, R.I.
Robert Allen, Tenn.
William Smith, Va.

John Culpepper, N.C.
George Plumer, Penn.
Daniel Udree, Penn.

PUBLIC EXPENDITURES

Chairman: Thomas W. Cobb, Ga.

Lot Clark, N.Y.
Samuel C. Crafts, Vt.
Philip S. Markley, Penn.

Joseph Gist, S.C.
James T. Sandford, Tenn.
John S. Barbour, Va.

PRIVATE LAND CLAIMS

Chairman: John W. Campbell, Ohio

Gabriel Moore, Ala.
Ansel Sterling, Conn.
William Prince, Ind.

Daniel Garrison, N.J.
John Locke, Mass.
Isaac Williams, Jr., N.Y.

MANUFACTURES

Chairman: John Tod, Penn.

Walter Forward, Penn.
Lewis Condict, N.J.
Henry W. Connor, N.C.

John C. Wright, Ohio
Hector Craig, N.Y.
Dudley Marvin, N.Y.

AGRICULTURE

Chairman: Stephen Van Rensselaer, N.Y.

Francis Baylies, Mass.
Robert S. Garnett, Va.
Robert Harris, Penn.

Robert S. Rose, N.Y.
Lemuel Whitmen, Conn.
Thomas Patterson, Penn.

INDIAN AFFAIRS

Chairman: John Cocke, Tenn.

James S. Mitchell, Penn.
Jared Williams, Va.
John McKee, Ala.

William McLean, Ohio
Egbert Ten Eyck, N.Y.
Alfred M. Gatlin, N.C.

MILITARY AFFAIRS

Chairman: James Hamilton, Jr., S.C.

Thomas J. Rogers, Penn.
George E. Mitchell, Md.
Duncan McArthur, Ohio

Samuel Houston, Tenn.
Joseph Vance, Ohio
Robert B. Campbell, S.C.

NAVAL AFFAIRS

Chairman: Benjamin W. Crowninshield, Mass.

Timothy Fuller, Mass.
John Randolph, Va.
Henry R. Warfield, Md.

John W. Cady, N.Y.
George Holcombe, N.J.
Matthew Harvey, N.H.

FOREIGN AFFAIRS

Chairman: John Forsyth, Ga.

John W. Taylor, N.Y.
Henry R. Storrs, N.Y.
David Trimble, Ky.

William S. Archer, Va.
Patrick Farrelly, Penn.
Joel R. Poinsett, S.C.

REVISAL AND UNFINISHED BUSINESS

Chairman: Thomas R. Ross, Ohio

Samuel Lathrop, Mass.

John Brown, Penn.

ACCOUNTS

Chairman: Samuel C. Allen, Mass.

Samuel Swan, N.J.

Robert P. Letcher, Ky.

EXPENDITURES IN THE DEPARTMENT OF STATE

Chairman: Silas Wood, N.Y.

Noyes Barber, Conn.

John Bailey, Mass.

EXPENDITURES IN THE DEPARTMENT OF THE TREASURY

Chairman: Weldon N. Edwards, N.C.

William Heyward, Jr., Md.

William Burleigh, Me.

EXPENDITURES IN THE DEPARTMENT OF WAR

Chairman: George Tucker, Va.

Enoch Lincoln, Me.

David White, Ky.

EXPENDITURES IN THE DEPARTMENT OF THE NAVY

Chairman: Samuel Edwards, Penn.

Aaron Hobart, Mass.   Jeremiah O'Brien, Me.

EXPENDITURES IN THE POST OFFICE

Chairman: William Van Wyck, N.Y.

William Wilson, Ohio   Samuel Lawrence, N.Y.

EXPENDITURES ON THE PUBLIC BUILDINGS

Chairman: Jeremiah Nelson, Mass.

William Cox Ellis, Penn.   Thomas P. Moore, Ky.

CUMBERLAND ROAD

Chairman: Joseph Hemphill, Penn.

Andrew Stewart, Penn.   John T. Johnson, Ky.
Philemon Beecher, Ohio   James B. Reynolds, Tenn.
Joseph Johnson, Va.   George W. Owen, Ala.

CHESAPEAKE AND OHIO CANAL

Chairman: Charles F. Mercer, Va.

John Lee, Md.   William Woods, N.Y.
Samuel Breck, Penn.   James Stephenson, Va.
Richard A. Buckner, Ky.   John Patterson, Ohio

REVOLUTIONARY PENSIONS

Chairman: Weldon N. Edwards, N.C.

George Cassedy, N.J.   David Kidder, Me.
George Kremer, Penn.   Arthur Smith, Va.
James L. Hogeboom, N.Y.   Robert B. Vance, N.C.

ROADS AND CANALS

Chairman: Joseph Hemphill, Penn.

Andrew Stewart, Penn.   Robert P. Henry, Ky.
Alfred Cuthbert, Ga.   John Herkimer, N.Y.
Peter Sharpe, N.Y.   William C. Rives, Va.

LIBRARY

House   Senate
Alexander Smyth, Va.   Mahlon Dickerson, N.J.
William C. Bradley, Vt.   John Elliot, Ga.
John W. Taylor, N.Y.   Thomas H. Williams, Miss.

ENROLLED BILLS

House   Senate
Samuel A. Foote   Nehemiah R. Knight, R.I.
Jabez Leftwich, Va.

STANDING COMMITTEES OF THE SENATE

FOREIGN RELATIONS

Chairman: James Barbour, Va.

Nathaniel Macon, N.C.

Andrew Jackson, Tenn.

John Elliot, Ga.

Elijah H. Mills, Mass.[12]

FINANCE

Chairman: Samuel Smith, Md.

Nathaniel Macon, N.C.

Rufus King, N.Y.

John Holmes, Me.

Walter Lowrie, Penn.

COMMERCE AND MANUFACTURES

Chairman: Mahlon Dickerson, N.J.

Benjamin Ruggles, Ohio

James De Wolf, R.I.

William Findlay, Penn.

James Lloyd, Mass.

MILITIA

Chairman: John Chandler, Me.

William Findlay, Penn.

Nehemiah R. Knight, R.I.

John Branch, N.C.

Samuel Bell, N.H.

MILITARY AFFAIRS

Chairman: Andrew Jackson, Tenn.

Thomas H. Benton, Mo.

John Chandler, Me.

Waller Taylor, Ind.

Richard M. Johnson, Ky.

NAVAL AFFAIRS

Chairman: James Lloyd, Mass.

Thomas H. Williams, Miss.

John F. Parrott, N.H.

Edward Lloyd, Md.

Robert Y. Hayne, S.C.

PUBLIC LANDS

Chairman: David Barton, Mo.

Jesse B. Thomas, Ill.

Thomas H. Williams, Miss.

John H. Eaton, Tenn.

Walter Lowrie, Penn.

INDIAN AFFAIRS

Chairman: Thomas H. Benton, Mo.

Ninian Edwards, Ill.

Henry Johnson, La.

John Elliot, Ga.

Henry W. Edwards, Conn.

[12]The *House Journal* lists Rufus King (N.Y.) in place of Mills.

CLAIMS

Chairman: Benjamin Ruggles, Ohio

David Holmes, Miss.
William A. Palmer, Vt.

Samuel Bell, N.H.
Joseph McIlvaine, N.J.

JUDICIARY

Chairman: Martin Van Buren, N.Y.

John Holmes, Me.
Isham Talbot, Ky.

James Brown, La.[13]
Horatio Seymour, Vt.

POST OFFICE AND POST ROADS

Chairman: James Lanman, Conn.

Richard M. Johnson, Ky.
David Holmes, Miss.

Nehemiah R. Knight, R.I.
Joseph McIlvaine, N.J.

PENSIONS

Chairman: James Noble, Ind.

Isham Talbot, Ky.
Henry Johnson, La.

James Lanman, Conn.
John Branch, N.C.

DISTRICT OF COLUMBIA

Chairman: Edward Lloyd, Md.

James Barbour, Va.
James Noble, Ind.

John H. Eaton, Tenn.
John F. Parrott, N.H.

ROADS AND CANALS

Chairman: James Brown, La.

Ninian Edwards, Ill.
William A. Palmer, Vt.

Samuel Smith, Md.
Joseph McIlvaine, N.J.

[13]The *House Journal* lists Ethan Allen Brown (Ohio) in place of James Brown.

CONGRESSIONAL DIRECTORY

EIGHTEENTH CONGRESS, SECOND SESSION
(December 6, 1824–March 3, 1825)

Mrs. Arguelles, Penn. Ave.
Ichabod Bartlett, N.H.
Robert B. Campbell, S.C.
John Carter, S.C.
Timothy Fuller, Mass.
Philip S. Markley, Penn.
William C. Rives, Va.
George Tucker, Va.
Henry Wilson, Penn.

Mr. Burch, Capitol Hill
Robert Allen, Tenn.
Joel Abbot, Ga.
Henry W. Connor, N.C.
George Cary, Ga.
Robert P. Henry, Ky.
Samuel Houston, Tenn.
John Long, N.C.
William Smith, Va.

Brown's Hotel, Penn. Ave.
Philip P. Barbour, Va.
Ela Collins, N.Y.
John W. Cady, N.Y.
Henry W. Conway, Deleg., Ark. Terr.
Justin Dwinell, N.Y.
Lewis Eaton, N.Y.
John Floyd, Va.
Elisha Litchfield, N.Y.
Thomas P. Moore, Ky.
John Scott, Mo.
James Stephenson, Va.
Andrew Stevenson, Va.
Waller Taylor (S), Ind.
David Trimble, Ky.
Egbert Ten Eyck, N.Y.
Robert B. Vance, N.C.
Charles A. Wickliffe, Ky.

Mrs. Ball, Penn. Ave.
Gabriel Moore, Ala.
David White, Ky.

Mr. Bestor, near City Hall
John Culpepper, N.C.
Isaac Williams, Jr., N.Y.

Mrs. Blake, Penn. Ave.
David Barton (S), Mo.
James Buchanan, Penn.
George Holcombe, N.J.
David Holmes (S), Miss.
Joseph Kent, Md.
George E. Mitchell, Md.
John McKee, Ala.
Raphael Neale, Md.
James B. Reynolds, Tenn.
Thomas H. Williams (S), Miss.

Mrs. Claxton, Capitol Hill
Adam R. Alexander, Tenn.
John Blair, Tenn.
John S. Barbour, Va.
John Cocke, Tenn.
George Kremer, Penn.
Jabez Leftwich, Va.
James T. Sandford, Tenn.
James Standifer, Tenn.

Mr. Coyle, Capitol Hill
Francis Baylies, Mass.
Henry W. Dwight, Mass.
Samuel Edwards, Penn.
Joseph Hemphill, Penn.
John F. Parrott (S), N.H.
Henry R. Storrs, N.Y.
Daniel Webster, Mass.

Mrs. Clark, F St., North
John Elliott (S), Ga.
John J. Morgan, N.Y.
Christopher Rankin, Miss.
Jesse B. Thomas (S), Ill.
Thomas H. Benton (S), Mo.

Mrs. Cochran, F St., North
Thomas Newton, Jr., Va.

Mr. Dowson, No. 1, Capitol Hill
William Heyward, Jr., Md.
Edward Lloyd (S), Md.
Isaac McKim, Md.
George W. Owen, Ala.
Samuel Smith (S), Md.
Henry R. Warfield, Md.

Mr. Dowson, No. 2, Capitol Hill
Mark Alexander, Va.
Thomas W. Cobb (S), Ga.
Weldon N. Edwards, N.C.
Thomas H. Hall, N.C.
William R. King (S), Ala.
Willie P. Mangum, N.C.
Nathaniel Macon (S), N.C.
John Randolph, Va.
Richard D. Spaight, Jr., N.C.
Edward F. Tattnall, Ga.
John Branch (S),[1] N.C.

Mrs. Dunn, Capitol Hill
John Branch (S),[2] N.C.

Mr. Charles Davis, E St., North
Francis Johnson, Ky.
Thomas Metcalfe, Ky.

Mr. John Davis, Ninth St., West
Henry Clay, Ky.
Robert P. Letcher, Ky.

Mr. Frost, Capitol Hill
Samuel Bell (S), N.H.
Benjamin Ruggles (S), Ohio
John Sloane, Ohio
Gideon Tomlinson, Conn.
Elisha Whittlesey, Ohio

Mr. Fletcher, near General Post Office
Samuel C. Allen, Mass.
Joshua Cushman, Me.
Daniel P. Cook, Ill.
John Findlay, Penn.
Samuel D. Ingham, Penn.
Jacob C. Isacks, Tenn.
Samuel Lathrop, Mass.
Samuel McKean, Penn.
Daniel H. Miller, Penn.

Mrs. Galvin, Capitol Hill
Ethan Allen Brown (S), Ohio
Walter Lowrie (S), Penn.
Arthur Livermore, N.H.
Thomas R. Ross, Ohio
Andrew Stewart, Penn.

Mrs. Gaither, Penn. Ave.
Daniel Garrison, N.J.
William McCoy, Va.
James Matlack, N.J.
Jared Williams, Va.

Gadsby's Hotel, Penn. Ave.
Richard K. Call, Deleg., Terr. of Fla.
John H. Eaton (S), Tenn.
Andrew Jackson (S), Tenn.

Mrs. Hamilton, Capitol Hill
Samuel C. Crafts, Vt.
Aaron Matson, N.H.
William Kelly (S), Ala.
William A. Palmer (S), Vt.
Horatio Seymour (S), Vt.
Henry Olin,[3] Vt.

Mrs. Hickey, Capitol Hill
Samuel Breck, Penn.
James Lloyd (S), Mass.

Mr. Hough, Capitol Hill
Daniel A. A. Buck, Conn.
George Cassedy, N.J.
Henry C. Martindale, N.Y.
Ansel Sterling, Conn.
Jacob Tyson, N.Y.
Lemuel Whitman, Conn.

[1] Also listed at Mrs. Dunn's.
[2] Also listed at Mr. Dowson's, No. 2.
[3] Elected to fill the vacancy caused by the death of Charles Rich, and took his seat Dec. 13, 1824. Also listed at Queen's Hotel.

Mr. Hyatt, Penn. Ave.
Walter Forward, Penn.
John Locke, Mass.
Duncan McArthur, Ohio
Jeremiah Nelson, Mass.
William Plumer, Jr., N.H.
John Reed, Mass.

Mr. Handy, Penn. Ave.
Nicholas Van Dyke (S), Del.
John S. Spence, Md.

Mr. McLeod, Capitol Hill
Lewis Condict, N.J.
Job Durfee, R.I.
Samuel Eddy, R.I.
Matthew Harvey, N.H.
Lemuel Jenkins, N.Y.
Nehemiah R. Knight (S), R.I.
Stephen Longfellow, Me.
Peter Sharpe, N.Y.

Mrs. Meyer, near Centre Market
Lot Clark, N.Y.
Rowland Day, N.Y.
Charles A. Foote, N.Y.
James L. Hogeboom, N.Y.
James S. Mitchell, Penn.
Thomas Patterson, Penn.
John Patterson, Ohio
John Richards, N.Y.
Daniel Udree, Penn.
George Wolfe,[4] Penn.

Mrs. McCardle, Capitol Hill
Hector Craig, N.Y.
Joel Frost, N.Y.
Silas Wood, N.Y.

Mr. Mechlin, near West Market
Churchill C. Cambreleng, N.Y.
Joel R. Poinsett, S.C.

Mrs. Peyton, C St., North
Andrew R. Govan, S.C.
George McDuffie, S.C.
Robert R. Rose, N.Y.

Miss Polk, Capitol Hill
Joseph Gist, S.C.
Starling Tucker, S.C.
John Wilson, S.C.

Queen's Hotel, Capitol Hill
Noyes Barber, Conn.
William C. Bradley, Vt.
Ebenezer Herrick, Me.
Charles Hooks, N.C.
Jonathan Jennings, Ind.
Rollin C. Mallary, Vt.
Henry Olin,[5] Vt.
Samuel Swan, N.J.
Ebenezer Stoddard, Conn.
Jonas Sibley, Mass.
Wiley Thompson, Ga.
William W. Van Wyck, N.Y.

Mrs. Queen, the Elder, Penn. Ave.
Parmenio Adams, N.Y.
William Cox Ellis, Penn.
William Findlay (S), Penn.
Samuel Lawrence, N.Y.
Alexander Smyth, Va.
Alexander Thomson, Penn.
Samuel F. Vinton, Ohio
William Woods, N.Y.
John C. Wright, Ohio

Mrs. Queen, the Younger, Penn. Ave.
John W. Campbell, Ohio
Robert Harris, Penn.
George Plumer Penn.
Joseph Vance, Ohio

Mr. Rapine, Capitol Hill
Patrick Farrelly, Penn.
Aaron Hobart, Mass.
Isaac Wayne, Penn.
Thomas Whipple, Jr., N.H.

Mr. Scott, near Centre Market
James Barbour (S), Va.
Burwell Bassett, Va.
Alfred M. Gatlin, N.C.
Dudley Marvin, N.Y.
Romulus M. Saunders, N.C.
Lewis Williams, N.C.

[4] Elected to fill the vacancy caused by the resignation of Thomas J. Rogers, and took his seat Dec. 9, 1824.
[5] Also listed at Mrs. Hamilton's.

Mr. Sawyer, La. Ave.
James W. Gazlay, Ohio
John W. Taylor, N.Y.
Albert H. Tracy, N.Y.

Mr. Sardo, Penn. Ave.
John Allison, Jr., Penn.
Mordecai Bartley, Ohio
John Brown, Penn.
Joseph Johnson, Va.
Arthur Smith, Va.
John Test, Ind.

Mr. Tims, Capitol Hill
John Chandler (S), Me.
John Holmes (S), Me.
Mahlon Dickerson (S), N.J.
John Gaillard (S), S.C.

Mr. Tucker, Capitol Hill
William Burleigh, Me.
Enoch Lincoln, Me.

Tennison's Hotel, Penn. Ave.
James Strong, N.Y.

Mr. Wurtz, near Tyber Creek
David Kidder, Me.
Jeremiah O'Brien, Me.
William Wilson, Ohio
James Wilson, Penn.

Miss Warner, Penn. Ave.
Richard A. Buckner, Ky.
James Noble (S), Ind.
Philip Thompson, Ky.

Williamson's Hotel, Penn. Ave.
William S. Archer, Va.
Philemon Beecher, Ohio
Henry H. Gurley, La.
Robert S. Garnett, Va.
Robert Y. Hayne (S), S.C.
James Hamilton, Jr., S.C.
Rufus King (S), N.Y.
Edward Livingston, La.

John Lee, Md.
Charles F. Mercer, Va.

Mr. Wilson, Seven Buildings
Benjamin Crowninshield, Mass.

Mr. Young, Capitol Hill
Thomas Clayton (S), Del.
Henry W. Edwards (S), Conn.
Samuel A. Foote, Conn.
James Lanman (S), Conn.

Private Residences
Georgetown
William L. Brent, La.
Mrs. Young, near City Hall
John Bailey,[6] Mass.
Corner of F and Twelfth St., North
Martin Van Buren, N.Y.
Georgetown
John Forsyth, Ga.
Rev. Brown, near General Post Office
John T. Johnson, Ky.
Richard M. Johnson (S), Ky.
Mr. Robert Brown, F St., North[7]
Josiah S. Johnston (S), La.
Major Hook, Fourteenth St., West
Peter Little, Md.
Rev. McIlvaine, Georgetown
James McIlvaine, N.J.
Mr. McLean, Post Master General, Georgetown
William McLean, Ohio
Mr. Lee, Seven Buildings
Elijah H. Mills (S), Mass.
Rev. Mathews, Western Chapple
Gabriel Richard, Deleg., Mich. Terr.
Mr. Southard, Sec. of the Navy
John Taliaferro, Va.
Dr. William Thornton, F St., North
Isham Talbot (S), Ky.
Corner of F and Twelfth St., North
Stephen Van Rensselaer, N.Y.
Corner of F and Twelfth St., North
Louis McLane, Del.

---

[6] By resolution of Mar. 18, 1824 was declared not entitled to his seat; subsequently elected, and took his seat Dec. 13, 1824.
[7] Also listed as Mr. Robert Miller, F St.

APPENDIX

Thomas W. Cobb,[8] Ga.
Alfred Cuthbert, Ga.
John McLean, (S),[9] Ill.
John Call,[10] Ind.
Dominique Bouligny, (S),[11] La.

Moses Hayden, N.Y.
John Herkimer, N.Y.
George Outlaw,[12] N.C.
James De Wolf (S), R.I.
Littleton W. Tazewell, (S)[13] Va.

STANDING COMMITTEES OF THE
HOUSE OF REPRESENTATIVES

ELECTIONS

Chairman: John Sloane, Ohio

John Taliaferro, Va.
Starling Tucker, S.C.
James Standifer, Tenn.

Thomas H. Hall, N.C.
Philip Thompson, Ky.
Daniel H. Miller, Penn.

WAYS AND MEANS

Chairman: Louis McLane, Del.

Samuel D. Ingham, Penn.
Wiley Thompson, Ga.
Andrew Stevenson, Va.

Churchill C. Cambreleng, N.Y.
George McDuffie, S.C.
Isaac McKim, Md.

CLAIMS

Chairman: Lewis Williams, N.C.

William McCoy, Va.
Elisha Litchfield, N.Y.
Elisha Whittlesey, Ohio

Aaron Matson, N.H.
Jacob C. Isacks, Tenn.
James Wilson, Penn.

PUBLIC LANDS

Chairman: Christopher Rankin, Miss.

John Scott, Mo.
Henry H. Gurley, La.
Jonathan Jennings, Ind.

James Strong, N.Y.
Samuel F. Vinton, Ohio
Thomas Whipple, Jr., N.H.

[8] Resigned Dec. 6, 1824, having been elected Senator. Richard H. Wilde was elected to fill the vacancy, and took his seat Feb. 7, 1825.
[9] Elected to fill the vacancy caused by the resignation of Ninian Edwards, and took his seat Dec. 20, 1824.
[10] Elected to fill the vacancy caused by the death of William Prince, and took his seat Dec. 23, 1824.
[11] Elected to fill the vacancy caused by the resignation of Henry Johnson, and took his seat Dec. 21, 1824.
[12] Elected to fill the vacancy caused by the resignation of Hutchins G. Burton, and took his seat Jan. 19, 1825.
[13] Elected to fill the vacancy caused by the death of John Taylor, and took his seat Dec. 29, 1824.

COMMERCE

Chairman: Thomas Newton, Jr., Va.

Gideon Tomlinson, Conn.
Joel Abbot, Ga.
Job Durfee, R.I.

Henry W. Dwight, Mass.
Willie P. Mangum, N.C.
John J. Morgan, N.Y.

POST OFFICE AND POST ROADS

Chairman: John T. Johnson, Ky.

Charles Hooks, N.C.
Ebenezer Stoddard, Conn.
Samuel McKean, Penn.

Adam R. Alexander, Tenn.
Mordecai Bartley, Ohio
Parmenio Adams, N.Y.

DISTRICT OF COLUMBIA

Chairman: Joseph Kent, Md.

James Matlack, N.J.
John Findlay, Penn.
Mark Alexander, Va.

James W. Gazlay, Ohio
John Blair, Tenn.
Alexander Thomson, Penn.

JUDICIARY

Chairman: Daniel Webster, Mass.

Philip P. Barbour, Va.
William Plumer, Jr., N.H.
James Buchanan, Penn.

William L. Brent, La.
Richard A. Buckner, Ky.
Thomas R. Ross, Ohio

PENSIONS AND REVOLUTIONARY CLAIMS

Chairman: Peter Little, Md.

Samuel Eddy, R.I.
Robert Allen, Tenn.
William Smith, Va.

John Culpepper, N.C.
George Plumer, Penn.
Daniel Udree, Penn.

PUBLIC EXPENDITURES

Chairman: Duncan McArthur, Ohio

Lot Clark, N.Y.
Joseph Gist, S.C.
James T. Sandford, Tenn.

John S. Barbour, Va.
James Allison, Jr., Penn.
William W. Van Wyck, N.Y.

PRIVATE LAND CLAIMS

Chairman: John W. Campbell, Ohio

Gabriel Moore, Ala.
Ansel Sterling, Conn.
Daniel Garrison, N.J.

John Locke, Mass.
Isaac Williams, Jr., N.Y.
Philip S. Markley, Penn.

MANUFACTURES

Chairman: Walter Forward, Penn.

Lewis Condict, N.J.
Henry W. Connor, N.C.
John C. Wright, Ohio

Hector Craig, N.Y.
Dudley Marvin, N.Y.
Rollin C. Mallary, Vt.

AGRICULTURE

Chairman: Stephen Van Rensselaer, N.Y.

Francis Baylies, Mass.   Robert S. Rose, N.Y.
Robert S. Garnett, Va.   Lemuel Whitman, Conn.
Robert Harris, Penn.   Thomas Patterson, Penn.

INDIAN AFFAIRS

Chairman: John Cocke, Tenn.

James S. Mitchell, Penn.   William McLean, Ohio
Jared Williams, Va.   Egbert Ten Eyck, N.Y.
John McKee, Ala.   Alfred M. Gatlin, N.C.

FOREIGN AFFAIRS

Chairman: John Forsyth, Ga.

John W. Taylor, N.Y.   William S. Archer, Va.
Henry R. Storrs, N.Y.   Patrick Farrelly, Penn.
David Trimble, Ky.   Joel R. Poinsett, S.C.

MILITARY AFFAIRS

Chairman: James Hamilton, Jr., S.C.

George E. Mitchell, Md.   Joseph Vance, Ohio
Duncan McArthur, Ohio   Robert B. Campbell, S.C.
Samuel Houston, Tenn.   Edward F. Tattnall, Ga.

NAVAL AFFAIRS

Chairman: Benjamin W. Crowninshield, Mass.

Timothy Fuller, Mass.   George Holcombe, N.J.
Henry R. Warfield, Md.   Matthew Harvey, N.H.
John W. Cady, N.Y.   Burwell Bassett, Va.

REVISAL AND UNFINISHED BUSINESS

Chairman: Samuel Lathrop, Mass.

Samuel A. Foote, Conn.   Albert H. Tracy, N.Y.

ACCOUNTS

Chairman: Samuel C. Allen, Mass.

Samuel Swan, N.J.   Jabez Leftwich, Va.

SUPPRESSION OF THE AFRICAN SLAVE TRADE

Chairman: Andrew R. Govan, S.C.

Ebenezer Herrick, Me.   Richard P. Spaight, Jr., N.C.
John Test, Ind.   Lewis Eaton, N.Y.
Isaac Wayne, Penn.   John Herkimer, N.Y.

ROADS AND CANALS

Chairman: Joseph Hemphill, Penn.

Peter Sharpe, N.Y.
Andrew Stewart, Penn.
Robert P. Henry, Ky.

Charles F. Mercer, Va.
William C. Rives, Va.
Philemon Beecher, Ohio

SERVICES AND SACRIFICES OF GENERAL LAFAYETTE

Chairman: John Randolph, Va.

Andrew Stevenson, Va.
Edward Livingston, La.
Henry R. Storrs, N.Y.
Louis McLane, Del.
George E. Mitchell, Md.
Rollin C. Mallary, Vt.

David Trimble, Ky.
Samuel P. Ingham, Penn.
John Forsyth, Ga.
George McDuffie, S.C.
Willie P. Mangum, N.C.
Samuel Eddy, R.I.

ESTABLISHMENT OF A MILITARY POST AT THE MOUTH OF THE COLUMBIA RIVER

Chairman: Alexander Smyth, Va.

John Scott, Mo.
Thomas Metcalfe, Ky.
Francis Baylies, Mass.

William McLean, Ohio
Jonathan Jennings, Ind.
Samuel Houston, Tenn.

JOINT COMMITTEES

ENROLLED BILLS

House
Matthew Harvey, N.H.
Lemuel Jenkins, N.Y.

Senate
Nehemiah R. Knight, R.I.

LIBRARY OF CONGRESS

House
William C. Rives, Va.
William C. Bradley, Vt.
Joel R. Poinsett, S.C.

Senate
Mahlon Dickerson, N.J.
John Elliott, Ga.
Thomas H. Williams, Miss.

REVOLUTIONARY PENSIONS

Chairman: Weldon N. Edwards, N.C.

George Kremer, Penn.
David Kidder, Me.
Robert B. Vance, N.C.

George Cassedy, N.J.
James L. Hogeboom, N.Y.
Arthur Smith, Va.

EXPENDITURES IN THE DEPARTMENT OF STATE

Chairman: Silas Wood, N.Y.

Noyes Barber, Conn.

one vacancy

EXPENDITURES IN THE TREASURY DEPARTMENT
Chairman: Weldon N. Edwards, N.C.
William Heyward, Jr., Md.   William Burleigh, Me.

EXPENDITURES IN THE DEPARTMENT OF WAR
Chairman: George Tucker, Va.
Enoch Lincoln, Me.   David White, Ky.

EXPENDITURES IN THE NAVY DEPARTMENT
Chairman: Samuel Edwards, Penn.
Aaron Hobart, Mass.   Jeremiah O'Brien, Me.

EXPENDITURES IN THE POST OFFICE DEPARTMENT
Chairman: William W. Van Wyck, N.Y.
William Wilson, Ohio   Samuel Lawrence, N.Y.

EXPENDITURES ON THE PUBLIC BUILDINGS
Chairman: Jeremiah Nelson, Mass.
William Cox Ellis, Penn.   Thomas P. Moore, Ky.

STANDING COMMITTEES OF THE SENATE

FOREIGN RELATIONS
Chairman: James Barbour, Va.
Andrew Jackson, Tenn.   John Elliott, Ga.
Nathaniel Macon, N.C.   Elijah H. Mills, Mass.

FINANCE
Chairman: Samuel Smith, Md.
Rufus King, N.Y.   John Holmes, Me.
Nathaniel Macon, N.C.   Walter Lowrie, Penn.

COMMERCE AND MANUFACTURES
Chairman: Mahlon Dickerson, N.J.
Benjamin Ruggles, Ohio   James Lloyd, Mass.
William Findlay, Penn.   Thomas Clayton, Del.

MILITARY AFFAIRS
Chairman: Andrew Jackson, Tenn.
Thomas H. Benton, Mo.   Waller Taylor, Ind.
John Chandler, Me.   Richard M. Johnson, Ky.

NAVAL AFFAIRS

Chairman: James Lloyd, Mass.

Thomas H. Williams, Miss.   Edward Lloyd, Md.
John F. Parrott, N.H.   Robert Y. Hayne, S.C.

PUBLIC LANDS

Chairman: David Barton, Mo.

Jesse B. Thomas, Ill.   William R. King, Ala.
John H. Eaton, Tenn.   Nicholas Van Dyke, Del.

INDIAN AFFAIRS

Chairman: Thomas H. Benton, Mo.

Henry W. Edwards, Conn.   John Elliott, Ga.
Josiah S. Johnston, La.   William Kelly, Ala.

CLAIMS

Chairman: Benjamin Ruggles, Ohio

David Holmes, Miss.   Samuel Bell, N.H.
William A. Palmer, Vt.   Joseph McIlvaine, N.J.

JUDICIARY

Chairman: Martin Van Buren, N.Y.

John Holmes, Me.   Ethan Allen Brown, Ohio
Isham Talbot, Ky.   Horatio Seymour, Vt.

POST OFFICE AND POST ROADS

Chairman: James Lanman, Conn.

Richard M. Johnson, Ky.   Joseph McIlvaine, N.J.
Nehemiah R. Knight, R.I.   Waller Taylor, Ind.

PENSIONS

Chairman: James Noble, Ind.

Isham Talbot, Ky.   John Branch, N.C.
James Lanman, Conn.   Thomas W. Cobb, Ga.

DISTRICT OF COLUMBIA

Chairman: Edward Lloyd, Md.

James Barbour, Va.   John H. Eaton, Tenn.
James Noble, Ind.   John F. Parrott, N.H.

ACCOUNTS

Chairman: Horatio Seymour, Vt.

Robert Y. Hayne, S.C.   Henry W. Edwards, Conn.

MILITIA

Chairman: John Chandler, Me.

William Findlay, Penn.   John Branch, N.C.
Nehemiah R. Knight, R.I.   Samuel Bell, N.H.

ENGROSSED BILLS

Chairman: James Lanman, Conn.

Joseph McIlvaine, N.J.   Thomas W. Cobb, Ga.

ROADS AND CANALS

Chairman: Ethan Allen Brown, Ohio

Jesse B. Thomas, Ill.   Walter Lowrie, Penn.
Samuel Bell, N.H.   Thomas Clayton, Del.

CONGRESSIONAL DIRECTORY

NINETEENTH CONGRESS-FIRST SESSION
(December 5, 1825–May 22, 1826)

Mrs. Arguelles, Penn. Ave.
Henry W. Dwight, Mass.
Henry Wilson, Penn.
Benjamin Estil, Va.
Henry H. Gurley, La.

Capt. Benjamin Burch, Capitol Hill
Robert Allen, Tenn.
John H. Marable, Tenn.
James K. Polk, Tenn.
James C. Mitchell, Tenn.
Samuel Houston, Tenn.
Samuel P. Carson, N.C.
Charles E. Haynes, Ga.
George Gary, Ga.
Joseph Gist, S.C.
William Smith, Va.

Mrs. Blake, Penn. Ave.
David Barton (S), Mo.
Daniel P. Cook, Ill.
Joseph Kent,[1] Md.
George E. Mitchell, Md.
Thomas C. Worthington, Md.
John Wurts, Penn.
George Holcombe, Md.

Mrs. Bradford, F St.
James Strong, N.Y.

Rev. O. B. Brown, near General
  Post Office
Richard M. Johnson (S), Ky.
James Johnson, Ky.

Brown's Hotel, Penn. Ave.
Thomas H. Benton (S), Mo.
John Rowan (S), Ky.
Richard A. Buckner, Ky.
Thomas Davenport, Va.
David Jennings, Ind.
Thomas P. Moore,[2] Ky.
John Scott, Mo.
Charles A. Wickliffe, Ky.

Mrs. Ball, Penn. Ave.
Philemon Beecher, Ohio
Nathaniel H. Claiborne, Va.
Gabriel Moore, Ala.

Capt. John Coyle, Capitol Hill
Thomas H. Williams (S), Miss.
Francis Baylies, Mass.
Daniel Webster, Mass.
John McKee, Ala.
Henry R. Storrs, N.Y.
Gulian C. Verplanck, N.Y.
Jeromus Johnson, N.Y.

Mrs. Clarke, F St.
William Henry Harrison (S), Ohio
Benjamin W. Crowninshield, Mass.
Clement Dorsey, Md.
John Barney, Md.

Mrs. Cochrane, F St.
Romulus M. Saunders, N.C.
John Carter, S.C.
Thomas Newton, Jr., Va.

---

[1] Resigned Jan. 6, 1826, having been elected Governor. John C. Weems was elected to fill the vacancy, and took his seat Feb. 7, 1826.
[2] Also listed at Mrs. Kean's.

168

Mrs. Carlisle, Penn. Ave.
Henry W. Edwards (S), Conn.
John Davis, Mass.
Abraham H. Hasbrouck, N.Y.
Ralph J. Ingersoll, Conn.
Henry H. Ross, N.Y.

Mrs. Claxton, Capitol Hill
John Alexander, Tenn.
John Cocke, Tenn.
John Blair, Tenn.
Willis Alston, N.C.
George Kremer,[3] Penn.

Mr. Alfred R. Dowson, No. 1,
  Capitol Hill
Powhatan Ellis (S),[4] Miss.
William R. King (S), Ala.
Samuel Smith (S), Md.
George W. Owen, Ala.
John L. Kerr, Md.
Robert N. Martin, Md.
Richard Hines, N.C.
Christopher Rankin,[5] Miss.

Mr. Alfred R. Dowson, No. 2,
  Capitol Hill
Thomas W. Cobb (S), Ga.
Nathaniel Macon (S), N.C.
John Randolph (S),[6] Va.
Mark Alexander, Va.
John H. Bryan, N.C.
Willie P. Mangum,[7] N.C.
Weldon N. Edwards, N.C.
James Meriwether, Ga.
James Trezvant, Va.
John Macpherson Berrien (S),[8] Ga.
Edward Tattnall,[9] Ga.

Mr. William Deming, near *Natl.*
  Intelligencer Office
Benjamin Ruggles (S), Ohio

Mr. Dunn, Capitol Hill
John Branch (S), N.C.
Gabriel Holmes, N.C.

Mr. John Davis, C St.
David Trimble, Ky.
James Clark, N.Y.
William S. Young, Ky.
William Armstrong, Va.
Charles Miner, Penn.
Joseph Vance, Ohio
Henry W. Connor, N.C.
Lewis Williams, N.C.
Thomas Metcalfe, Ky.
Robert P. Letcher, Ky.
Dudley Marvin, N.Y.

Mr. Noah Fletcher, East of General
  Post Office
Samuel C. Allen, Mass.
Samuel Lathrop, Mass.
John Findlay, Penn.
Samuel McKean, Penn.
George Wolf, Penn.
Robert Taylor, Va.
Jacob C. Isacks, Tenn.
Daniel H. Miller, Penn.
Samuel D. Ingham, Penn.
Espy Van Horne, Penn.

John T. Frost, Capitol Hill
George Cassedy, N.J.
Nicoll Fosdick, N.Y.
Henry C. Martindale, N.Y.
John Sloane, Ohio
Gideon Tomlinson, Conn.
Elisha Whittlesey, Ohio

Mrs. Galvin, Capitol Hill
William Hendricks (S), Ind.
William Marks (S), Penn.
James Noble (S), Ind.
Robert Orr, Jr., Penn.

[3] Also listed at Mrs. Meyer's.
[4] Appointed to fill the vacancy caused by the resignation of David Holmes, and took his seat Dec. 12, 1825.
[5] Died Mar. 14, 1826.
[6] Took his seat Dec. 26, 1825. Vacancy in this class from Mar. 28, 1825, to Dec. 8, 1825. He resigned from the House effective Dec. 26, 1825, without qualifying, having been elected Senator.
[7] Resigned Mar. 18, 1826.
[8] Also listed at Mrs. Homans'.
[9] Also listed at Mrs. Homans'.

Gadsby's Hotel, West end of the City
Andrew Stevenson, Va.

Mr. Seth Hyatt, Penn. Ave.
Noyes Barber, Conn.
William C. Bradley, Vt.
Daniel G. Garnsey, N.Y.
Samuel F. Vinton, Ohio
John Woods, Ohio
John C. Wright, Ohio
Austin E. Wing, Deleg., Mich. Terr.

Mrs. Hickey, Capitol Hill
Edward Everett, Mass.

Mrs. Homans, opposite Tennison's Hotel
John Macpherson Berrien (S),[10] Ga.
Edward Tattnall,[11] Ga.

Mr. A. E. Hough, Capitol Hill
George E. Wales, Vt.
Rollin C. Mallary, Vt.
Ezra Meech, Vt.

Mrs. Hamilton, Capitol Hill
Horatio Seymour (S), Vt.
Starling Tucker, S.C.
John Wilson, S.C.
John Matlocks, Vt.

Mr. Handy, Penn. Ave.
Philip S. Markley, Penn.
Samuel Edwards, Penn.
James S. Stevenson, Penn.
James Buchanan, Penn.

Major Hook, near and East of
  Treas. Dept.
Peter Little, Md.

Mrs. Kean, Penn. Ave.
Henry W. Conway, Deleg., Ark. Terr.
Thomas P. Moore, Ky.

Mrs. Lanphier, Penn. Ave.
Peleg Sprague, Me.
Ichabod Bartlett, N.H.

John Locke, Mass.
John Reed, Mass.
John Varnum, Mass.

Mr. John McLeod, Capitol Hill
Nehemiah Eastman, N.H.
Thomas Whipple, Jr., N.H.
Aaron Hobart, Mass.
Lewis Condict, N.J.

Mrs. Meyer, opposite the East end
  of Centre Market
William Adams, Penn.
James S. Mitchell, Penn.
John Mitchell, Penn.
George Kremer,[12] Penn.

Mrs. McCardle, Capitol Hill
Joshua Sands, N.Y.
Silas Wood, N.Y.
John Miller, N.Y.
Robert P. Henry, Ky.
Dutee J. Pearce, R.I.
Luther Badger, N.Y.

Mr. Miller, F St.
William Drayton, S.C.
William S. Archer, Va.
George McDuffie, S.C.
Andrew R. Govan, S.C.

Mrs. O'Neale, near Gadsby's Hotel
John H. Eaton (S), Tenn.

Mr. Hiel Peck, Penn. Ave.
Nehemiah R. Knight (S), R.I.
Levi Woodbury (S), N.H.
Tristam Burges, R.I.

Mrs. Peyton, Penn. Ave.
Robert Y. Hayne (S), S.C.
Hugh L. White (S),[13] Tenn.
Littleton W. Tazewell (S), Va.
James Hamilton, Jr., S.C.

[10] Also listed at Dowson's No. 2.
[11] Also listed at Dowson's No. 2.
[12] Also listed at Mrs. Claxton's.
[13] Took his seat Dec. 12, 1825.

Queen's Hotel, Carroll's Row,
  Capitol Hill
William Findlay (S), Penn.
Ebenezer Herrick, Me.
David Kidder, Me.
Titus Brown, N.H.
Jonathan Harvey, N.H.
Joseph Healy, N.H.
Wiley Thompson, Ga.
Ratliff Boon, Ind.
Jonathan Jennings, Ind.
James Findlay, Ohio
Elisha Phelps, Conn.
Alexander Thomson,[14] Penn.
Moses Hayden, N.Y.
Bartow White, N.Y.
William McManus, N.Y.
Aaron Ward, N.Y.
Samuel Swan, N.J.
Henry Markell, N.Y.
William Wilcox, Ohio
Asher Robbins (S),[15] R.I.

Mrs. Queen, the Elder, Penn. Ave.
Charles Kellogg, N.Y.
John Hallock, Jr., N.Y.
Charles Humphreys, N.Y.
Henry Ashley, N.Y.
Michael Hoffman, N.Y.
William G. Angel, N.Y.
Joseph Johnson, Va.
James Wilson, Penn.
Jeremiah O'Brien, Me.

Mrs. Queen, the Younger, Penn. Ave.
John W. Campbell, Ohio
George Plumer, Penn.
Joseph Lawrence, Penn.
Archibald McNeill, N.C.
Daniel Garrison, N.J.
Robert Harris, Penn.

Mrs. Ronckendorff, Penn. Ave.
William Deitz, N.Y.
John S. Barbour, Va.

Mrs. Raphine, near and South of
  the Capitol
Orange Merwin, Conn.
Ebenezer Tucker, N.J.

Mr. Sardo, Penn. Ave.
Parmenio Adams, N.Y.
Timothy H. Porter, N.Y.
Mordecai Bartley, Ohio
John Test, Ind.
Daniel Hugunin, Jr.,[16] N.Y.

Mr. Cary Selden, near and South of
  City Hall
Robert S. Rose, N.Y.

Mr. Skinner, East of the General
  Post Office
Calvin Willey (S), Conn.
Joseph Lecompte, Ky.
John Baldwin, Conn.
John Thomson, Ohio
Samuel Bell (S), N.H.

Mrs. Turner, above Mauro's
  auction rooms
Burwell Bassett, Va.
William McCoy, Va.
William L. Brent, La.
Charles F. Mercer, Va.
Robert S. Garnett, Va.
Joseph M. White, Deleg., Terr. of Fla.

Mr. Tims, near and Southeast of
  the Capitol
John Chandler (S), Me.
John Holmes (S), Me.
Mahlon Dickerson (S), N.J.
John Gaillard (S),[17] Me.
John Anderson, Me.

Mr. B. O. Tyler, near and Northeast
  of the Capitol
Dudley Chase (S), Vt.
John W. Taylor, N.Y.

[14] Resigned May 1, 1826.
[15] Also listed at Mrs. Tucker's.
[16] Successfully contested the election of Egbert Ten Eyck, and took his seat Dec. 15, 1825.
[17] Died Feb. 26, 1826. William Harper was appointed to fill the vacancy, and took his seat Mar. 28, 1826.

Joseph Hemphill, Penn.
Andrew Stewart, Penn.

Mrs. Tucker, Northeast of the Capitol
Jesse B. Thomas (S), Ill.
Elias K. Kane (S), Ill.
Asher Robbins (S),[18] R.I.
William Burleigh, Me.
Enoch Lincoln,[19] Me.

Williamson's Hotel, Penn. Ave.
Martin Van Buren (S), N.Y.
Edward Livingston, La.
Stephen Van Renssalaer, N.Y.
Alfred H. Powell, Va.
Thomas R. Mitchell, S.C.
John Forsyth, Ga.
Churchill C. Cambreleng, N.Y.
Louis McLane, Del.

Mrs. Wertz, Penn. Ave.
Lemuel Sawyer, N.C.

Mrs. Young, near and East of City Hall
John Bailey, Mass.

Mr. James Young, near and South
  of the Capitol
Thomas Clayton (S),[20] Del.
James McIlvaine (S), N.J.
Nicholas Van Dyke (S), Del.
Samuel Bell (S),[21] N.H.

Private Residences
  Mr. Kervand, Seven Buildings
James Lloyd (S), Mass.
  Mr. William Lee, Seven Buildings
Elijah H. Mills (S), Mass.
  Major Peter, Georgetown
George Peter, Md.
  At C. Davis, North of Post Office
Francis Johnson, Ky.
  Mr. McLean, Postmaster General
William McLean, Ohio
  Union Tavern, Georgetown
Dominique Bouligny (S), La.
  Mr. Adams, F St.
Josiah S. Johnston (S), La.
  Mr. Southard, Sec. of the Navy
John Taliaferro, Va.

APPENDIX

Henry Chambers (S),[22] Ala.
Alfred Cuthbert, Ga.
Edward Lloyd (S),[23] Md.
Nathan Sanford (S),[24] N.Y.
Elisha Whitmore, N.Y.

John Long, N.C.
Patrick Farrelly,[25] Penn.
George W. Crump,[26] Va.
John Floyd, Va.
William C. Rives, Va.

[18] Also listed at Queen's Hotel.
[19] Resigned in Jan. 1826, having been elected Governor.
[20] Died May 21, 1826.
[21] Also listed at Mr. Skinner's.
[22] Died Jan. 24, 1826. Israel Pickens was appointed to fill the vacancy, and took his seat Apr. 10, 1826.
[23] Resigned in Jan. 1826. Ezekiel F. Chambers was elected to fill the vacancy, and took his seat Feb. 22, 1826.
[24] Elected to fill the vacancy in the term commencing Mar. 4, 1825, and took his seat Jan. 31, 1826. Vacancy in this class from Mar. 4, 1825 to Jan. 14, 1826.
[25] Died Jan. 12, 1826. Thomas H. Sill was elected to fill the vacancy, and took his seat Apr. 3, 1826.
[26] Elected to fill the vacancy caused by the resignation of John Randolph, and took his seat Feb. 6, 1826.

STANDING COMMITTEES OF THE
HOUSE OF REPRESENTATIVES

ELECTIONS

Chairman: John Sloane, Ohio

Moses Hayden, N.Y.	Michael Hoffman, N.Y.
Starling Tucker, N.C.	Alfred H. Powell, Va.
Elisha Phelps, Conn.	John H. Bryan, N.C.

WAYS AND MEANS

Chairman: Louis McLane, Del.

Daniel P. Cook, Ill.	Henry W. Dwight, Mass.
Andrew Stevenson, Va.	Dudley Marvin, N.Y.
George McDuffie, S.C.	William L. Brent, La.

CLAIMS

Chairman: Lewis Williams, N.C.

William McCoy, Va.	Noyes Barber, Conn.
Elisha Whittlesey, Ohio	Henry C. Martindale, N.Y.
James Wilson, Penn.	George W. Owen, Ala.

PUBLIC LANDS

Chairman: Christopher Rankin, Miss.

John Scott, Mo.	Samuel F. Vinton, Ohio
Jonathan Jennings, Ind.	Thomas Whipple, Jr., N.H.
James Strong, N.Y.	Benjamin Estil, Va.

COMMERCE

Chairman: Thomas Newton, Jr., Va.

Gideon Tonlinson, Conn.	Wiley Thompson, Ga.
Churchill C. Cambreleng, N.Y.	Willie P. Mangum, N.C.
John Reed, Mass.	John Wurts, Penn.

POST OFFICE AND POST ROADS

Chairman: Samuel D. Ingham, Penn.

Mordecai Bartley, Ohio	James Meriwether, Ga.
Adam R. Alexander, Tenn.	Timothy H. Porter, N.Y.
Samuel McKean, Penn.	John Baldwin, Conn.

DISTRICT OF COLUMBIA

Chairman: Joseph Kent, Md.

Mark Alexander, Va.	Samuel Lathrop, Mass.
John Blair, Tenn.	Robert N. Martin, Md.
Alexander Thomson, Penn.	Charles Humphrey, N.Y.

JUDICIARY

Chairman: Daniel Webster, Mass.

Edward Livingston, La.
James Buchanan, Penn.
John C. Wright, Ohio

James Clark, Ky.
William Drayton, S.C.
Clement Dorsey, Md.

PENSIONS AND REVOLUTIONARY CLAIMS

Chairman: Peter Little, Md.

Robert Allen, Tenn.
William Smith, Va.
George Plumer, Penn.

Abraham B. Hasbrouck, N.Y.
Ebenezer Tucker, N.J.
Peleg Sprague, Me.

MILITARY PENSIONS

Chairman: Tristam Burges, R.I.

Silas Wood, N.Y.
Robert S. Garnett, Va.
George Cary, Ga.

John Varnum, Mass.
John Thompson, Ohio
Jonathan Harvey, N.H.

PUBLIC EXPENDITURES

Chairman: Weldon N. Edwards, N.C.

Joseph Gist, S.C.
Aaron Hobart, Mass.
David Kidder, Me.

Henry Markell, N.Y.
George E. Wales, Vt.
Espy Van Horne, Penn.

PRIVATE LAND CLAIMS

Chairman: John W. Campbell, Ohio

Gabriel Moore, Ala.
Daniel Garrison, N.J.
John Locke, Mass.

John Test, Ind.
Nicoll Fosdick, N.Y.
William Armstrong, Va.

MANUFACTURES

Chairman: Rollin C. Mallary, Vt.

Lewis Condict, N.J.
Henry W. Connor, N.C.
Charles A. Wickliffe, Ky.

John Davis, Mass.
Bartow White, N.Y.
Tristam Burges, R.I.

AGRICULTURE

Chairman: Stephen Van Rensselaer, N.Y.

Robert Harris, Penn.
John Hallock, Jr., N.Y.
Ezra Meech, Vt.

Ornage Merwin, Conn.
John Wilson, S.C.
Robert Taylor, Va.

INDIAN AFFAIRS

Chairman: John Cocke, Tenn.

John McKee, Ala.
William McLean, Ohio
Richard A. Buckner, Ky.

John Taliaferro, Va.
William McManus, N.Y.
Charles Miner, Penn.

FOREIGN AFFAIRS

Chairman: John Forsyth, Ga.

Benjamin W. Crowninshield, Mass. Thomas C. Worthington, Md
David Trimble, Ky. Edward Everett, Mass.
William S. Archer, Va. James S. Stevenson, Penn.

MILITARY AFFAIRS

Chairman: James Hamilton, Jr., S.C.

George E. Mitchell, Md. Joseph Vance, Ohio
Samuel Houston, Tenn. Enoch Lincoln, Me.
Edward F. Tattnall, Ga. Aaron Ward, N.Y.

NAVAL AFFAIRS

Chairman: Henry R. Storrs, N.Y.

George Holcombe, N.J. Philip S. Markley, Penn.
Ichabod Bartlett, N.H. Francis Johnson, Ky.
Romulus M. Saunders, N.C. Joshua Sands, N.Y.

TERRITORIES

Chairman: James Strong, N.Y.

Charles F. Mercer, Va. Joseph Vance, Ohio
Gideon Tomlinson, Conn. William Drayton, S.C.
Daniel P. Cook, Ill. John McKee, Ala.

REVISAL AND UNFINISHED BUSINESS

Chairman: Thomas P. Moore, Ky

James S. Mitchell, Penn. Ebenezer Herrick, Me.

ACCOUNTS

Chairman: Samuel C. Allen, Mass.

George Peter, Md. Archibald McNeill, N.C.

EXPENDITURES IN THE DEPARTMENT OF STATE

Chairman: John Bailey, Mass.

George Cassedy, N.J. Henry Ashley, N.Y.

EXPENDITURES IN THE TREASURY DEPARTMENT

Chairman: William Burleigh, Me.

Henry H. Ross, N.Y. Thomas Davenport, Va.

EXPENDITURES IN THE DEPARTMENT OF WAR

Chairman: John Mattocks, Vt.

George Kremer, Penn. Luther Badger, N.Y.

EXPENDITURES IN THE NAVY DEPARTMENT

Chairman: Jeremiah O'Brien, Me.

Thomas R. Mitchell, S.C.   John Miller, N.Y.

EXPENDITURES IN THE POST OFFICE DEPARTMENT

Chairman: William Wilson, Ohio

John Findlay, Penn.   William Deitz, N.Y.

EXPENDITURES OF THE PUBLIC BUILDINGS

Chairman: Joseph Johnson, Va.

Samuel Swan, N.J.   Robert Orr, Jr., Penn.

SELECT COMMITTEES

ON THE MILITIA

Chairman: Thomas Metcalfe, Ky.

Gabriel Holmes, N.C.   Andrew R. Govan, N.C.
John Barney, Md.   Egbert Ten Eyck, N.Y.
James Findlay, Ohio   James C. Mitchell, Tenn.

ON ROAD AND CANALS

Chairman: Joseph Hemphill, Penn.

Philemon Beecher, Ohio   Robert P. Henry, Ky.
Andrew Stewart, Penn.   Charles E. Haynes, Ga.
Parmenio Adams, N.Y.   Robert I. Ingersoll, Conn.

ON POST AT COLUMBIA RIVER AND SURVEY OF NORTHWEST COAST

Chairman: Francis Baylies, Mass.

John S. Barbour, Va.   Joseph Lawrence, Penn.
William G. Angel, N.Y.   James K. Polk, Tenn.
Samuel P. Carson, N.C.   John Thomson, Ohio

ON A NATIONAL UNIVERISTY AND OBSERVATORY

Chairman: Charles F. Mercer, Va.

John Carter, S.C.   Robert P. Letcher, Ky.
Gulian C. Verplanck, N.Y.   Lemuel Sawyer, N.C.
Samuel Edwards, Penn.   John Woods, Ohio

ON WEIGHTS AND MEASURES

Chairman: William C. Bradley, Vt.

Jeromus Johnson, N.Y.   James Trezvant, Va.
Daniel H. Miller, Penn.   Charles Kellogg, N.Y.
James Johnson, Ky.   Titus Brown, N.H.

ON THE EXECUTIVE DEPARTMENTS

Chairman: Daniel Webster, Mass.

Louis McLane, Del.
George Forsyth, Ga.
Joseph Hemphill, Penn.

Benjamin W. Crowninshield, Mass.
Edward Livingston, La.
Francis Johnson, Penn.

ON THE WASHINGTON MONUMENT

Chairman: Burwell Bassett, Va.

Willis Alston, N.C.
Robert S. Rose, N.Y.
Henry Wilson, Penn.

John L. Keer, Md.
Ratliff Boon, Ind.
George Wolf, Penn.

ON THE PETITIONS OF REVOLUTIONARY OFFICERS

Chairman: Joseph Hemphill, Penn.

Lewis Condict, N.J.
John Anderson, Me.
Joseph Lecompte, Ky.

John Mitchell, Penn.
John H. Marable, Tenn.
Nathaniel H. Claiborne, Va.

ON THE MEMORIAL OF THE KENTUCKY INSTITUTION
FOR THE TUITION OF DEAF AND DUMB

Chairman: Thomas P. Moore, Ky.

Dutee J. Pearce, R.I.
Richard Hines, N.C.
William S. Young, Ky.

William Addams, Penn.
Nehemiah Eastman, N.H.
David Jennings, Ohio

ON BOSTROP'S AND MAISON ROGUE'S LAND CLAIMS

Chairman: William L. Brent, La.

Philemon Beecher, Ohio
Thomas Whipple, Jr., N.H.

Jacob C. Isacks, Tenn.
Daniel G. Garnsey, N.Y.

ON THE MEMORIAL OF DOCTORS NANCREDE AND SMITH
RESPECTING THE ESTABLISHMENT OF A VACCINE INSTITUTION

Chairman: John Wurts, Penn.

Lewis Condict, N.J.
John Miller, N.Y.

Samuel P. Carson, N.C.
Joseph Healey, N.H.

ON ALTERATIONS IN THE HALL OF REPRESENTATIVES

Chairman: George McDuffie, S.C.

Charles F. Mercer, Va.
Silas Wood, N.Y.
John Reed, Mass.

Lewis Williams, N.C.
Samuel P. Ingham, Penn.
Henry H. Gurley, La.

ON ALTERATIONS IN THE ELECTION LAWS OF THE STATES

Chairman: Willis Alston, N.C.

John Sloane, Ohio
George W. Owen, Ala.
John Carter, S.C.

Ebenezer Herrick, Me.
Dutee J. Pearce, R.I.
Dudley Marvin, N.Y.

JOINT COMMITTEES

ON ENROLLED BILLS

House
Jacob C. Isacks, Tenn.
Daniel G. Garnsey, N.Y.

Senate
Nehemiah R. Knight, R.I.

ON THE LIBRARY OF CONGRESS

House
Edward Everett, Mass.
William C. Bradley, Vt.
Silas Wood, N.Y.

Senate
Mahlon Dickerson, N.J.
John Gaillard, S.C.
Asher Robbins, R.I.

CARE AND PRESERVATION OF THE CAPITOL AND PUBLIC GROUNDS WITHIN THE CITY

House
Stephen Van Rensselaer, N.Y.
Samuel Lathrop, Mass.
James Wilson, Penn.
John Test, Ind.
Willis Alston, N.C.

Senate
Samuel Bell, N.H.
Powhatan Ellis, Miss.
William Hendricks, Ind.

STANDING COMMITTEES OF THE SENATE

FOREIGN RELATIONS

Chairman: Nathaniel Macon, N.C.
Littleton W. Tazewell, Va.
John Gaillard, S.C.

Elijah H. Mills, Mass.
Hugh Lawson White, Tenn.

FINANCE

Chairman: Samuel Smith, Md.
John Macpherson Berrien, Ga.
John Holmes, Me.

Robert Y. Hayne, S.C.
Levi Woodbury, N.H.

COMMERCE

Chairman: James Lloyd, Mass.
Nicholas Van Dyke, Del.
Josiah S. Johnston, La.

Thomas H. Williams, Miss.
Henry W. Edwards, Conn.

MANUFACTURES

Chairman: Mahlon Dickerson, N.J.
Benjamin Ruggles, Ohio
William Findlay, Penn.

James Lloyd, Mass.
Thomas Clayton, Del.

AGRICULTURE

Chairman: William Findlay, Penn.

Edward Lloyd, Md.   Levi Woodbury, N.H.
John Branch, N.C.   Dominique Bouligny, La.

MILITARY AFFAIRS

Chairman: William Henry Harrison, Ohio

Thomas H. Benton, Mo.   William Hendricks, Ind.
John Chandler, Me.   Richard M. Johnson, Ky.

MILITIA

Chairman: John Chandler, Me.

John Branch, N.C.   William Henry Harrison, Ohio
Nehemiah R. Knight, R.I.   Samuel Bell, N.H.

NAVAL AFFAIRS

Chairman: Robert Y. Hayne, S.C.

Thomas H. Williams, Miss.   Asher Robbins, R.I.
Horatio Seymour, Vt.   Elias K. Kane, Ill.

PUBLIC LANDS

Chairman: David Barton, Mo.

Jesse B. Thomas, Ill.   William R. King, Ala.
John H. Eaton, Tenn.   Nicholas Van Dyke, Del.

INDIAN AFFAIRS

Chairman: Thomas H. Benton, Mo.

Hugh Lawson White, Tenn.   Henry W. Edwards, Conn.
William R. King, Ala.   Thomas W. Cobb, Ga.

CLAIMS

Chairman: Benjamin Ruggles, Ohio

Samuel Bell, N.H.   Joseph McIlvaine, N.J.
Dudley Chase, Vt.   Thomas Clayton, Del.

JUDICIARY

Chairman: Martin Van Buren, N.Y.

John Holmes, Me.   John Macpherson Berrien, Ga.
John Rowan, Ky.   Elijah H. Mills, Mass.

POST OFFICE AND POST ROADS

Chairman: Richard M. Johnson, Ky.

Josiah S. Johnston, La.   Joseph McIlvaine, N.J.
Jesse B. Thomas, Ill.   Calvin Willey, Conn.

PENSIONS

Chairman: James Noble, Ind.

Dudley Chase, Vt.   Thomas W. Cobb, Ga.
William Marks, Penn.   Powhatan Ellis, Miss.

DISTRICT OF COLUMBIA

Chairman: Edward Lloyd, Md.

John Rowan, Ky.   John H. Eaton, Tenn.
James Noble, Ind.   Dominique Bouligny, La.

CONTINGENT EXPENSES OF THE SENATE

Chairman: Horatio Seymour, Vt.

Elias K. Kane, Ill.   William Hendricks, Ind.

ENGROSSED BILLS

Chairman: William Marks, Penn.

Calvin Willey, Conn.   Powhatan Ellis, Miss.

SELECT COMMITTEES

ON IMPRISONMENT FOR DEBT AND BANKRUPTCY

Chairman: Richard M. Johnson, Ky.

Robert Y. Hayne, S.C.   Elijah H. Mills, Mass.
James Lloyd, Mass.   Thomas H. Benton, Mo.
Nicholas Van Dyke, Del.   John Macpherson Berrien, Ga.

ON ROADS AND CANALS

Chairman: William Hendricks, Ind.

Dudley Chase, Vt.   Jesse B. Thomas, Ill.
William Marks, Penn.   William R. King, Ala.

ON MONUMENT OF GENERAL WASHINGTON

Chairman: Elias K. Kane, Ill.

John Gaillard, S.C.   Henry W. Edwards, Conn.
Josiah S. Johnston, La.   Calvin Willey, Conn.

ON AMENDMENTS TO THE CONSTITUTION

Chairman: Thomas H. Benton, Mo.

Nathaniel Macon, N.C.   Mahlon Dickerson, N.J.
Martin Van Buren, N.Y.   John Holmes, Me.
Hugh Lawson White, Tenn.   Robert Y. Hayne, S.C.
William Findlay, Penn.   Richard M. Johnson, Ky

ON THE ORGANIZATION OF EXECUTIVE DEPARTMENTS

Chairman: Horatio Seymour, Vt.

Samuel Bell, N.H.	John Branch, N.C.
John Rowan, Ky.	Thomas W. Cobb, Ga.

ON CLAIMS OF SURVIVING OFFICERS OF THE REVOLUTION

Chairman: Elijah H. Mills, Mass.

Robert Y. Hayne, S.C.	Nathaniel Macon, N.C.
Samuel Smith, Md.	William Henry Harrison, Ohio

CONGRESSIONAL DIRECTORY

NINETEENTH CONGRESS, SECOND SESSION
(December 4, 1825–March 3, 1827)

Mrs. Arguelles, Penn. Ave.
Henry H. Gurley, La.
Peleg Sprague, Me.
John Reed, Mass.
Henry H. Ross, N.Y.
John Locke, Mass.
Abraham B. Hasbrouck, N.Y.
John Davis, Mass.

Capt. Benjamin Burch, Capitol Hill
Robert Allen, Tenn.
John Cocke, Tenn.
John Blair, Tenn.
William Smith, Va.
Thomas R. Mitchell, S.C.
Archibald McNeill, N.C.
John Carter, S.C.

Mrs. Blake, near Penn. Ave.
James K. Polk, Tenn.
Thomas C. Worthington, Md.
William L. Brent, La.
George Holcombe, N.J.
John Wurts, Penn.
Daniel P. Cook, Ill.
Levi Woodbury (S), N.H.
Ezekiel F. Chambers (S), Md.
Thomas B. Reed (S), Miss.

Mrs. Ball, Penn. Ave.
Nathaniel H. Claiborne, Va.
Willis Alston, N.C.
Joseph Lecompte, Ky.
Gabriel Moore, Ala.
Elisha Phelps, Conn.

Henry Ashley, N.Y.
William G. Angel, N.Y.
Michael Hoffman, N.Y.
Robert McHatton,[1] Ky.
Philemon Beecher, Ohio

Mrs. Bradford, F St.
James Strong, N.Y.

Mr. Bayne
Daniel Garrison, N.J.
John Long, N.C.
David L. Barringer, N.C.
Robert Harris, Penn.
George Plumer, Penn.
Joseph Lawrence, Penn.

Brown's Hotel, Penn. Ave.
John Scott, Mo.
John C. Weems, Md.
George Cassedy, N.J.

Mrs. Clark, F St.
Benjamin W. Crowninshield, Mass.
Henry W. Conway, Deleg., Ark. Terr.
Alfred H. Powell, Va.
John Barney, Md.
Andrew Stewart, Penn.
Joseph M. White, Deleg., Terr. of Fla.
Nathaniel Silsbee (S), Mass.
William Henry Harrison (S), Ohio
Burwell Bassett,[2] Va.

Mrs. Cochrane, F St.
James Findlay, Ohio
Burwell Bassett,[3] Va.

[1] Took his seat Dec. 7, 1826.
[2] Also listed at Mrs. Cochrane's.
[3] Also listed at Mrs. Clark's.

Romulus M. Saunders, N.C.
Thomas Newton, Jr., Va.

Mr. Coyle, Capitol Hill
Henry R. Storrs, N.Y.
Francis Baylies, Mass.
John McKee, Ala.
William C. Rives, Va.
Thomas H. Williams (S), Miss.
Elijah Hunt Mills (S), Mass.
William Smith (S),[4] S.C.

Mrs. Carlisle, Penn. Ave.
Ralph I. Ingersoll, Conn.
Aaron Hobart, Mass.
Nicoll Fosdick, N.Y.
Nehemiah R. Knight (S), R.I.
Henry W. Edwards (S), Conn.

Mrs. Cottringer, Thirteenth St.
Stephen Van Rensselaer, N.Y.
Louis McLane, Del.
Martin Van Buren (S), N.Y.

Dowson's No. 1, Capitol Hill
William Haile, Miss.
Robert N. Martin, Md.
George W. Owen, Ala.
Richard Hines, N.C.
John L. Kerr, Md.
Samuel Smith (S), Md.
William R. King (S), Ala.

Dowson's No. 2, Capitol Hill
James Trezvant, Va.
Weldon N. Edwards, N.C.
Mark Alexander, Va.
George Cary, Ga.
James Meriwether, Ga.
Charles E. Haynes, Ga.
William S. Archer, Va.
John Randolph (S), Va.
Nathaniel Macon (S), N.C.
Thomas W. Cobb (S), Ga.
John McKinley (S),[5] Ala.

Mrs. Dunn, Capitol Hill
Gabriel Holmes, N.C.
John Branch (S), N.C.

John Davis, near City Hall
Joseph Vance, Ohio
Lewis Williams, N.C.
Charles Miner, Penn.
William Armstrong, Va.
William S. Young, Ky.
James Clark, Ky.
William McCoy, Va.
Dudley Marvin, N.Y.
John Bailey, Mass.
Henry W. Connor, N.C.
Thomas Metcalfe, Ky.
Robert P. Letcher, Ky.

Charles B. Davis, near Mr. Gale's
Mordecai Bartley, Ohio
Francis Johnson, Ky.
John F. Henry,[6] Ky.

Noah Fletcher, near Post Office
Samuel C. Allen, Mass.
Samuel D. Ingham, Penn.
Jacob C. Isacks, Tenn.
John Findlay, Penn.
Samuel Lathrop, Mass.
Daniel H. Miller, Penn.
Samuel McKean, Penn.
Robert Taylor, Va.
Espy Van Horne, Penn.
George Wolf, Penn.

Mrs. Galvin, Capitol Hill
Robert Orr, Jr., Penn.
Thomas Shannon, Ohio
William Marks (S), Penn.
Benjamin Ruggles (S), Ohio
William Hendricks (S), Ind.
James Noble (S), Ind.

Mr. Greer, near and South of the Capitol
Chauncey Forward, Penn.
John W. Campbell, Ohio

Mr. Hyatt, Penn. Ave.
Noyes Barber, Conn.
George E. Wales, Vt.
Rollin C. Mallary, Vt.

[4] Took his seat Dec. 7, 1826. Also listed at Mr. Hughes'.
[5] Took his seat Dec. 21, 1826.
[6] Took his seat Dec. 11, 1826.

Samuel Houston, Tenn.
John H. Marable, Tenn.
Orange Merwin, Conn.

Mrs. Hickey, Capitol Hill
Edward Everett, Mass.

Mr. Handy, Penn. Ave.
James Buchanan, Penn.
James S. Stevenson, Penn.
Philip S. Markley, Penn.
Samuel Edwards, Penn.
Thomas Kittera, Penn.

Mr. Hughes, nearly opposite Brown's
  Hotel
Andrew Stevenson, Va.
Samuel P. Carson, N.C.
John Floyd, Va.
George W. Crump,[7] Va.
Thomas P. Moore,[8] Ky.
John Rowan (S), Ky.
Thomas H. Benton (S), Mo.
William Smith (S),[9] S.C.

Mrs. Hamilton, Capitol Hill
John Baldwin, Conn.
John Wilson, S.C.
Joseph Gist, S.C.
Starling Tucker, S.C.
John Mattocks, Vt.
Calvin Willey (S), Conn.
Horatio Seymour (S), Vt.

Mrs. Heyer, N.J. Ave.
Jeromus Johnson, N.Y.
Gulian C. Verplanck, N.Y.

Mr. Kervand, Penn. Ave.
William Drayton, S.C.
Churchill C. Cambreleng, N.Y.
James Hamilton, Jr., S.C.

Mrs. Lanphier, Penn. Ave.
John C. Wright, Ohio
John Woods, Ohio
Samuel F. Vinton, Ohio
Austin E. Wing, Deleg., Mich. Terr.

Thomas H. Sill, Penn.
Ichabod Bartlett, N.H.

Mrs. McCubbin, opposite Brown's Hotel
Richard A. Buckner, Ky.

Mr. McIntyre, Penn. Ave.
Daniel Webster, Mass.

Mr. McLeod, Capitol Hill
Nehemiah Eastman, N.H.
John Sloane, Ohio
Elisha Whittlesey, Ohio
Tristam Burges, R.I.
Lewis Condict, N.J.
Gideon Tomlinson, Conn.

Mrs. Meyer, opposite and East of Centre
  Market
William Addams, Penn.
Jacob Krebs, Penn.
James S. Mitchell, Penn.
Daniel Hugunin, Jr., N.Y.
John Mitchell, Penn.

Mrs. McCardle, Northeast of the Capitol
Silas Wood, N.Y.
Joshua Sands, N.Y.
Elias Whitmore, N.Y.
John Miller, N.Y.
Dutee J. Pearce, R.I.
Luther Badger, N.Y.

Mrs. Miller, F St.
Andrew R. Govan, S.C.
John H. Bryan, N.C.
George McDuffie, S.C.

Mr. O'Neale, near West Market
John H. Eaton (S), Ky.

Miss Polk, nearly opposite Williamson's
Nathan Sanford (S), N.Y.

Mrs. Peyton, Penn. Ave.
John Thomson, Ohio
Charles A. Wickliffe, Ky.
Mahlon Dickerson (S), N.J.

---

[7] Also listed at Kean's.
[8] Also listed at Kean's.
[9] Took his seat Dec. 7, 1826. Also listed at Mr. Coyle's.

Littleton W. Tazewell (S), Va.
Robert Y. Hayne (S), S.C.
Hugh Lawson White (S), Tenn.

Mr. Peck, near Treasury Dept.
Peter Little, Md.

Mrs. Queen, nearly opposite Brown's
    Hotel
Titus Brown, N.H.
Jonathan Harvey, N.H.
Thomas Whipple, Jr., N.H.
Parmenio Adams, N.Y.
John Hallock, Jr., N.Y.
Timothy H. Porter, N.Y.
Charles Kellogg, N.Y.
Jeremiah O'Brien, Me.
William Findlay (S), Penn.

Mr. N. L. Queen, Capitol Hill
Ratliff Boon, Ind.
Wiley Thompson, Ga.
Jonathan Jennings, Ind.
David Kidder, Me.
William Burleigh, Me.

Mrs. Rockendorff, nearly opposite
    Brown's Hotel
James C. Mitchell, Tenn.
Robert S. Garnett, Va.
George Kremer, Penn.

Mr. Sawkins, Penn. Ave.
John Test, Ind.

Mr. Tims, Southeast of the Capitol
John Anderson, Me.
John Chandler (S), Me.
John Holmes (S), Me.
David Barton (S), Mo.

Mrs. Turner, over Mauro's Auction
    Room
Charles F. Mercer, Va.
Daniel G. Garnsey, N.Y.
James Wilson, Penn.
Bartow White, N.Y.
Ezra Meech, Vt.
Charles Humphrey, N.Y.

Joseph Johnson, Va.
Henry Markell, N.Y.

Mr. Tennison, Tenth St. West
Henry W. Dwight, Mass.
Edward Livingston, La.
Moses Hayden, N.Y.
Aaron Ward, N.Y.

Mr. Tyler, Capitol Hill
John W. Taylor, N.Y.
William C. Bradley, Vt.
Samuel Swan, N.J.
Clement Dorsey, Md.
Dudley Chase (S), Vt.
Henry C. Martindale, N.Y.

Mrs. Tucker, Northeast of the Capitol
Ebenezer Tucker, N.J.
Asher Robbins (S), R.I.
Ephraim Bateman (S),[10] N.J.
Jesse B. Thomas (S), Ill.

Mr. Tilley, Union Hotel, Georgetown
Benjamin Estil, Va.
John Forsyth, Ga.

Mrs. Wertz, Penn. Ave.
Lemuel Sawyer, N.C.
Joseph Healy, N.H.
William Dietz, N.Y.
William McManus, N.Y.
William Wilson, Ohio
Ebenezer Herrick, Me.

Capt. Wright's, opposite Williamson's
John S. Barbour, Va.

Mr. Young, near and South of the
    Capitol
George E. Mitchell, Md.
Samuel Bell (S), N.H.
Thomas Clayton (S), Del.
Daniel Rodney (S), Del.
Elias K. Kane (S), Ill.

Private Residences
Opposite Centre Market
John Varnum, Mass.

[10]Elected to fill the vacancy caused by the death of Joseph McIlvaine, and
took his seat Dec. 7, 1826.

Mr. Selden, Capitol Hill
Robert S. Rose, N.Y.

Mr. Dick, Georgetown
George Peter, Md.

Kean's, Penn. Ave.
Thomas Davenport, Va.
George Crump,[11] Va.

Sec. of Navy, Southard
John Taliaferro, Va.

Near Branch Bank
John Macpherson Berrien (S), Ga.
Rev. Brown's, near Post Office
Richard M. Johnson (S), Ky.
Blair's, near Post Office
William McLean, Ohio
Cox's Row, Georgetown
Dominique Bouligny (S), La.
F St.
Josiah S. Johnston (S), La.

APPENDIX

Alfred Cuthbert, Ga.
Edward F. Tattnall, Ga.
David Trimble, Ky.

James W. Ripley, Me.
Adam R. Alexander, Tenn.

STANDING COMMITTEES OF THE
HOUSE OF REPRESENTATIVES

ELECTIONS

Chairman: John Sloane, Ohio

Moses Hayden, N.Y.
Starling Tucker, S.C.
Elisha Phelps, Conn.

Michael Hoffman, N.Y.
Willis Alston, N.C.
Nathaniel H. Claiborne, Va.

WAYS AND MEANS

Chairman: Louis McLane, Del.

Daniel P. Cook, Ill.
Peleg Sprague, Me.
Andrew Stevenson, Va.

Henry W. Dwight, Mass.
Dudley Marvin, N.Y.
William L. Brent, La.

CLAIMS

Chairman: Lewis Williams, N.C.

William McCoy, Va.
Elisha Whittlesey, Ohio
James Wilson, Penn.

Noyes Barber, Conn.
Henry C. Martindale, N.Y.
William Haile, Miss.

PUBLIC LANDS

Chairman: John Scott, Mo.

Samuel F. Vinton, Ohio
Jonathan Jennings, Ind.
James Strong, N.Y.

Thomas Whipple, Jr., N.H.
Henry H. Gurley, La.
George E. Wales, Vt.

[11] Also listed at Mr. Hughes'.

COMMERCE

Chairman: Gideon Tomlinson, Conn.

Churchill C. Cambreleng, N.Y.   Wiley Thompson, Ga.
John Reed, Mass.   Peter Little, Md.
John Wurts, Penn.   Dutee J. Pearce, R.I.

POST OFFICE AND POST ROADS

Chairman: Samuel D. Ingham, Penn.

Mordecai Bartley, Ohio   James Meriwether, Ga.
John Barney, Md.   Timothy H. Porter, N.Y.
Samuel McKean, Penn.   John Baldwin, Conn.

DISTRICT OF COLUMBIA

Chairman: Mark Alexander, Va.

John Blair, Tenn.   James Buchanan, Penn.
Alfred H. Powell, Va.   Robert N. Martin, Md.
Ralph I. Ingersoll, Conn.   Gulian C. Verplanck, N.Y.

JUDICIARY

Chairman: Daniel Webster, Mass.

John C. Wright, Ohio   Charles Humphrey, N.Y.
William C. Rives, Va.   George W. Owen, Ala.
Robert P. Letcher, Ky.   John L. Kerr, Md.

REVOLUTIONARY CLAIMS

Chairman: Robert Allen, Tenn.

William Smith, Va.   Ebenezer Tucker, N.J.
George Plumer, Penn.   Elias Whitmore, N.Y.
Abraham B. Hasbrouck, N.Y.   Joseph Healy, N.H.

MILITARY PENSIONS

Chairman: Tristam Burges, R.I.

John Anderson, Me.   John Thomson, Ohio
George Cary, Ga.   Jonathan Harvey, N.H.
John Varnum, Mass.   John C. Weems, Md.

PUBLIC EXPENDITURES

Chairman: Weldon N. Edwards, N.C.

Joseph Gist, S.C.   Espy Van Horne, Penn.
Aaron Hobart, Mass.   Nehemiah Eastman, N.H.
David Kidder, Me.   James K. Polk, Tenn.

PRIVATE LAND CLAIMS

Chairman: Richard A. Buckner, Ky.

Gabriel Moore, Ala.   John Test, Ind.
Daniel Garrison, N.J.   Henry Markell, N.Y.
John Locke, Mass.   William Armstrong, Va.

MANUFACTURES

Chairman: Rollin C. Mallary, Vt.

Lewis Condict, N.J.
Henry W. Connor, N.C.
Charles A. Wickliffe, Ky.

John Davis, Mass.
Bartow White, N.Y.
James S. Stevenson, Penn.

AGRICULTURE

Chairman: Stephen Van Rensselaer, N.Y.

Robert Harris, Penn.
John Hallock, Jr., N.Y.
Ezra Meech, Vt.

Orange Merwin, Conn.
John Wilson, S.C.
Robert Taylor, Va.

INDIAN AFFAIRS

Chairman: John Cocke, Tenn.

John McKee, Ala.
William McLean, Ohio
Charles Miner, Penn.

Daniel G. Garnsey, N.Y.
William S. Young, Ky.
Samuel Swan, N.J.

FOREIGN AFFAIRS

Chairman: John Forsyth, Ga.

Benjamin W. Crowninshield, Mass.
William S. Archer, Va.
Edward Everett, Mass.

James Clark, Ky.
Thomas C. Worthington, Md.
Joseph Lawrence, Penn.

MILITARY AFFAIRS

Chairman: Joseph Vance, Ohio

William Drayton, S.C.
Samuel Houston, Tenn.
Aaron Ward, N.Y.

John Taliaferro, Va.
Thomas Kittera, Penn.
John Long, N.C.

NAVAL AFFAIRS

Chairman: Henry R. Storrs, N.Y.

George Holcombe, N.J.
Ichabod Bartlett, N.H.
Clement Dorsey, Md.

Philip S. Markley, Penn.
Francis Johnson, Ky.
Joshua Sands, N.Y.

TERRITORIES

Chairman: James Strong, N.Y.

Francis Baylies, Mass.
Lemuel Sawyer, N.C.
Jeromus Johnson, N.Y.

Samuel Edwards, Penn.
Daniel L. Barringer, N.C.
Thomas Shannon, Ohio

REVISAL AND UNFINISHED BUSINESS

Chairman: Thomas P. Moore, Ky.

James S. Mitchell, Penn.

Ebenezer Herrick, Me.

ACCOUNTS

Chairman: Samuel C. Allen, Mass.
George Peter, Md.   Archibald McNeill, N.C.

EXPENDITURES IN THE DEPARTMENT OF STATE

Chairman: John Bailey, Mass.
George Cassedy, N.J.   Henry Ashley, N.Y.

EXPENDITURES IN THE TREASURY DEPARTMENT

Chairman: William Burleigh, Me.
Henry H. Ross, N.Y.   Thomas Davenport, Va.

EXPENDITURES IN THE DEPARTMENT OF WAR

Chairman: John Mattocks, Vt.
George Kremer, Penn.   Luther Badger, N.Y.

EXPENDITURES IN THE NAVY DEPARTMENT

Chairman: Jeremiah O'Brien, Me.
Thomas R. Mitchell, S.C.   John Miller, N.Y.

EXPENDITURES IN THE POST OFFICE DEPARTMENT

Chairman: William Wilson, Ohio
John Findlay, Penn.   William Dietz, N.Y.

EXPENDITURES ON THE PUBLIC BUILDINGS

Chairman: Joseph Johnson, Va.
Samuel Swan, N.J.   Robert Orr, Jr., Penn.

SELECT COMMITTEES

ON THE MILITIA

Chairman: Thomas Metcalfe, Ky.
Gabriel Holmes, N.C.   Andrew R. Govan, S.C.
John Barney, Md.   Daniel Hugunin, Jr., N.Y.
James Findlay, Ohio   James C. Mitchell, Tenn.

ON ROADS AND CANALS

Chairman: Charles F. Mercer, Va.
Andrew Stewart, Penn.   John Woods, Ohio
Parmenio Adams, N.Y.   George E. Mitchell, Md.
Samuel Lathrop, Mass.   Jacob C. Isacks, Tenn.

JOINT COMMITTEES

ON ENROLLED BILLS

House	Senate
Jacob C. Isacks, Tenn.	Nehemiah R. Knight, R.I.
Daniel G. Garnsey, N.Y.	

ON THE LIBRARY OF CONGRESS

House	Senate
Edward Everett, Mass.	Mahlon Dickerson, N.J.
William C. Bradley, Vt.	Asher Robbins, R.I.
Silas Wood, N.Y.	Nathan Sanford, N.Y.

STANDING COMMITTEES OF THE SENATE

FOREIGN RELATIONS

Chairman: Nathan Sanford, N.Y.

Littleton W. Tazewell, Va.	Samuel Bell, N.H.
Nathaniel Macon, N.C.	Ezekiel F. Chambers, Md.

FINANCE

Chairman: Samuel Smith, Md.

John Holmes, Me.	William Smith, S.C.
Hugh Lawson White, Tenn.	Dudley Chase, Vt.

COMMERCE

Chairman: Josiah S. Johnston, La.

Nathaniel Silsbee, Mass.	Levi Woodbury, N.H.
Henry W. Edwards, Conn.	John Rowan, Ky.

MANUFACTURES

Chairman: Mahlon Dickerson, N.J.

Benjamin Ruggles, Ohio	Thomas B. Reed, Miss.
Thomas Clayton, Del.	Nehemiah R. Knight, R.I.

AGRICULTURE

Chairman: Calvin Willey, Conn.

John Branch, N.C.	Ephraim Bateman, N.J.
Dominique Bouligny, La.	Daniel Rodney, Del.

MILITARY AFFAIRS

Chairman: William Henry Harrison, Ohio

John Chandler, Me.	Richard M. Johnson, Ky.
Thomas H. Benton, Mo.	William Marks, Penn.

MILITIA

Chairman: John Chandler, Me.

John Branch, N.C.
Nehemiah R. Knight, R.I.

William Henry Harrison, Ohio
William Findlay, Penn.

NAVAL AFFAIRS

Chairman: Robert Y. Hayne, S.C.

Thomas H. Williams, Miss.
Elias K. Kane, Ill.

Asher Robbins, R.I.
Horatio Seymour, Vt.

PUBLIC LANDS

Chairman: David Barton, Mo.

William R. King, Ala.
John H. Eaton, Tenn.

Jesse B. Thomas, Ill.
Thomas B. Reed, Miss.

INDIAN AFFAIRS

Chairman: Thomas H. Benton, Mo.

William R. King, Ala.
Henry W. Edwards, Conn.

William Hendricks, Ind.
Josiah S. Johnston, La.

CLAIMS

Chairman: Benjamin Ruggles, Ohio

Samuel Bell, N.H.
Thomas Clayton, Del.

Ephraim Bateman, N.J.
Thomas W. Cobb, Ga.

JUDICIARY

Chairman: Martin Van Buren, N.Y.

James Macpherson Berrien, Ga.
John Holmes, Me.

Asher Robbins, R.I.
Horatio Seymour, Vt.

POST OFFICE AND POST ROADS

Chairman: Richard M. Johnson, Ky.

Jesse B. Thomas, Ill.
John Branch, N.C.

Nathaniel Silsbee, Mass.
William Findlay, Penn.

PENSIONS

Chairman: James Noble, Ind.

William Marks, Penn.
Thomas W. Cobb, Ga.

Dudley Chase, Vt.
Calvin Willey, Conn.

DISTRICT OF COLUMBIA

Chairman: Ezekiel F. Chambers, Md.

John H. Eaton, Tenn.
James Noble, Ind.

John Rowan, Ky.
Dominique Bouligny, La.

CONTINGENT EXPENSES OF THE SENATE

Chairman: Elias K. Kane, Ill.

Thomas H. Williams, Miss.   William Hendricks, Ind.

ENGROSSED BILLS

Chairman: William Marks, Penn.

Ephraim Bateman, N.J.   Daniel Rodney, Del.

SELECT COMMITTEES

ON THE BANKRUPT BILL

Chairman: Robert Y. Hayne, S.C.

John Macpherson Berrien, Ga.   Martin Van Buren, N.Y.
Nathaniel Silsbee, Mass.   Richard M. Johnson, Ky.
Samuel Smith, Md.   Nathan Sanford, N.Y.

ON THE BILL TO ABOLISH IMPRISONMENT FOR DEBT

Chairman: Richard M. Johnson, Ky.

Nathaniel Macon, N.C.   William Henry Harrison, Ohio
James Macpherson Berrien, Ga.   Ezekiel F. Chambers, Md.

ON ROADS AND CANALS

Chairman: William Hendricks, Ind.

William Marks, Penn.   Dudley Chase, Vt.
Jesse B. Thomas, Ill.   William R. King, Ala.

CONGRESSIONAL DIRECTORY

TWENTIETH CONGRESS, FIRST SESSION
(December 3, 1827–May 26, 1828)

Mrs. Arguelles, Penn. Ave.
David Woodcock, N.Y.
Henry R. Storrs, N.Y.
Peleg Sprague, Me.
Ichabod Bartlett, N.H.
John Reed, Mass.
John Locke, Mass.
James L. Hodges, Mass.
Henry H. Gurley, La.

Brown's Hotel
John Macpherson Berrien (S), Ga.
John Rowan (S), Ky.
Joseph M. White, Deleg., Terr. of Fla.
Samuel P. Carson, N.C.
William Stanbery, Ohio
Chittenden Lyon, Ky.
Thomas P. Moore, Ky.
Thomas Davenport, Ky.
Joseph Duncan, Ill.
William R. Davis, S.C.

Capt. Burch, Capitol Hill
David Barton (S), Mo.
John Blair, Tenn.
John Roane, Va.
George Kremer, Penn.
Starling Tucker, S.C.

Mrs. Blake, Corner Eighth St. West,
  near Centre Market
Ezekiel F. Chambers (S), Md.
Thomas H. Blake, Ind.
William L. Brent, La.
Henry W. Dwight, Mass.
John Sergeant, Penn.
Ebenezer Tucker, N.J.
Benjamin Gorham, Mass.
Isaac C. Bates, Mass.

Rev. O. B. Brown, F St., near General
  Post Office
Richard M. Johnson (S), Ky.
Wilson Lumkin, Ga.

Mrs. Ball, nearly opposite Brown's Hotel
Robert McHatton, Ky.
David Crockett, Tenn.
John C. Clark, N.Y.
John G. Stower, N.Y.
Nathaniel H. Claiborne, Va.
Joseph Lecompte, Ky.
Elisha Phelps, Conn.
Gabriel Moore, Ala.
Willis Alston, N.C.
Joel Yancey, Ky.

Mr. Bayne, Penn. Ave.
Joseph Lawrence, Penn.
James Wilson, Penn.
Richard Coulter, Penn.
Philemon Beecher, Ohio
John Long, N.C.
Daniel L. Barringer, N.C.
Hedge Thompson, N.J.

Mr. Burdick, Penn. Ave.
Charles A. Wickliffe, Ky.
James C. Mitchell, Tenn.
Robert Desha, Tenn.
Henry Daniel, Ky.
John H. Marable, Tenn.

Mrs. Cottringer, Thirteenth St.
Stephen Van Rensselaer, N.Y.

Mrs. Clark, F St.
William Henry Harrison (S),[1] Ohio
Nathaniel Silsbee (S), Mass.
John Barney, Md.
Daniel D. Barnard, N.Y.
Benjamin W. Crowninchield, Mass.
John D. Dickinson, N.Y.

Capt. Coyle, near and Southeast of the
  Capitol
William Smith (S), S.C.
Thomas H. Williams (S), Miss.
John McKee, Ala.
William C. Rives, Va.
George R. Gilmer, Ga.
William S. Archer, Va.
William T. Nuckolls, S.C.

Mr. Coburn, near Metropolis Bank
Edward Everett, Mass.

Mrs. Cochrane, F St.
James Findlay, Ohio
Burwell Bassett, Va.
Thomas Newton, Jr., Va.
Stephen Barlow, Penn.

Mrs. Carlisle, nearly opposite the
  National Hotel
Daniel A. A. Buck, Vt.
Richard Keese, N.Y.

John Davis, C St.
Joseph Vance, Ohio
William Creighton, Jr., Ohio
James Clark, Ky.
Thomas Metcalfe, Ky.
William Armstrong, Va.
Isaac Leffler, Va.
William Russell, Ohio
John W. Taylor, N.Y.
Charles Miner, Penn.
Richard A. Buckner, Ky.
Samuel Anderson, Penn.
Lewis Williams, N.C.
Dudley Marvin, N.Y.
Phineas L. Tracy, N.Y.

Mrs. Dunn, near and Northeast of
  the Capitol
John Branch (S), N.C.
Gabriel Holmes, N.C.

Mr. Dowson, No. 1, Capitol Hill
William R. King (S), Ala.
John McKinley (S), Ala.
Henry M. Ridgely (S), Del.
Samuel Smith (S), Md.

Mr. Dowson, No. 2, Capitol Hill
Thomas W. Cobb (S), Ga.
Nathaniel Macon (S), N.C.
Thomas H. Hall, N.C.
James Trezvant, Va.
Charles E. Haynes, Ga.
Daniel Turner, N.C.
John Floyd, Ga.
John Randolph, Va.
Mark Alexander, Va.

Mr. C. B. Davis, E St., near Tenth St.
Mordecai Bartley, Ohio
Robert P. Letcher, Ky.
John Davenport, Ohio

Mrs. Fleury, near Williamson's Hotel
George McDuffie, S.C.
William D. Martin, S.C.

Mr. Fletcher, E St., near the Post Office
Samuel McKean, Penn.
John Richardson, Mass.
Jacob C. Isacks, Tenn.
William Ramsey, Penn.
Samuel D. Ingham, Penn.
Innis Green, Penn.
George Wolf, Penn.
Daniel H. Miller, Penn.
Samuel C. Allen, Mass.
Joel B. Sutherland, Penn.

Mr. William Greer, E St., near the Post
  Office
Chauncey Forward, Penn.

[1] Resigned May 20, 1828.

Mr. Gardiner, F St., near the Catholic
   Church
John L. Kerr, Md.
Levin Gale, Md.
John Carter, S.C.

Mrs. Galvin, Carroll's Row, Capitol Hill
Isaac D. Barnard (S), Penn.
William Hendricks (S), Ind.
William Marks (S), Penn.
Benjamin Ruggles (S), Ohio
Robert Orr, Jr., Penn.

Mr. Hyatt, nearly opposite Brown's
   Hotel
George E. Wales, Vt.
Samuel F. Vinton, Ohio
Noyes Barber, Conn.
Orange Merwin, Conn.
John Woods, Ohio
Austin E. Wing, Deleg., Mich Terr.
Rollin C. Mallary, Vt.
John C. Wright, Ohio
Benjamin Swift, Vt.

Mr. Hebb, near the Capitol
Clement Dorsey, Md.
Tomlinson Fort, Ga.
Edward Bates, Mo.

Mrs. Hamilton, Carroll's Row, Capitol
   Hill
Horatio Seymour (S), Vt.
Calvin Willey (S), Conn.
Wiley Thompson, Ga.
John Baldwin, Conn.
Jonathan Jennings, Ind.

Miss Heyer, N.J. Ave.
Thomas H. Benton (S),[2] Mo.
Jesse B. Thomas (S),[3] Ill.
Jeromus Johnson, N.Y.
Thomas J. Oakley,[4] N.Y.

Mr. Thomas Hughes, nearly opposite
   Brown's Hotel
John Tyler (S), Va.

John Floyd, Va.
Robert Allen, Va.

Mr. Handy, Penn. Ave. between Twelfth
   and Thirteenth St.
James S. Stevenson, Penn.
John B. Sterigere, Penn.
James Buchanan, Penn.

Mrs. King, G St., near Wirt's
George W. Owen, Ala.

Mr. Kervand, Seven Buildings, Penn. Ave.
James Hamilton, Jr., S.C.

Mrs. Lanphier, nearly opposite Gunton's
   Apothecary Store
Nathan Sanford (S), N.Y.
Henry W. Connor, N.C.
Selah R. Hobbie, N.Y.
George C. Belden, N.Y.
John Magee, N.Y.

Legg's Hotel, near the Centre Market
Espy Van Horne, Penn.

Mrs. Myer, near the Centre Market
Alexander Smyth, Va.
Adam King, Penn.
Joseph Fry, Jr., Penn.
John Mitchell, Penn.
William Addams, Penn.
William McCoy, Va.
Philip P. Barbour, Va.
Peter Little Md.

Mrs. McCardle, near and Northeast of
   the Capitol
Silas Wood, N.Y.
David Plant, Conn.
Dutee J. Pearce, R.I.
Jeremiah O'Brien, Me.
Samuel Butman, Me.

Mrs. McIntire, nearly opposite the
   National Hotel
Daniel Webster (S),[5] Mass.

---

[2] Also listed at Miss Polk's.
[3] Also listed at Miss Polk's and Mrs. Tucker's.
[4] Resigned May 9, 1828.
[5] Took his seat Dec. 17, 1827.

Mr. McLeod, N.J. Ave.
Nehemiah R. Knight (S), R.I.
Lewis Condict, N.J.
Isaac Pierson, N.J.
Elisha Whittlesey, Ohio
John Sloane, Ohio
Tristam Burges, R.I.

Mr. Miller, F St. North at Dr.
  Thornton's.
Louis McLane (S), Del.
Martin Van Buren (S), N.Y.
Churchill C. Cambreleng, N.Y.
William Drayton, S.C.

Mrs. O'Neal, Back of the West Market
John H. Eaton (S), Tenn.

Mrs. Peyton, No. 1, Penn. Ave., nearly
  opposite the National Hotel
Mahlon Dickerson (S), N.J.
Powhatan Ellis (S), Miss.
Littleton W. Tazewell (S), Va.
Levi Woodbury (S), N.H.
Hugh Lawson White (S), Tenn.
Pryor Lea, Tenn.
William Haile, Miss.
Gulian C. Verplanck, N.Y.
Ralph Bunner, N.Y.
James K. Polk, Tenn.
John Bell, Tenn.

Mrs. Peyton, No. 2, Penn. Ave., near
  Gunton's Apothecary Store
Robert Y. Hayne (S), S.C.

Miss Polk, N.J. Ave.
Thomas H. Benton (S),[6] Mo.
Jesse B. Thomas (S),[7] Ill.

Mrs. Queen, Nearly Opposite Brown's
  Hotel
Silas Wright, Jr. (S), N.Y.
Nathaniel Garrow, N.Y.
Jonas Earll, Jr., N.Y.
Michael Hoffman, N.Y.
Lewis Maxwell, Va.
John Hallock, Jr., N.Y.

John Maynard, N.Y.
Titus Brown, N.H.
Jonathan Harvey, N.H.
John J. Wood,[8] N.Y.

Mrs. Stelle, near Four and One-Half St.
  Bridge
John S. Barbour, Va.
Michael C. Sprigg, Md.

Dr. Smether, Penn. Ave., nearly
  opposite Brown's Hotel
John C. Weems, Md.

Mr. William Sawyer, near the
  Unitarian Church
Daniel G. Garnsey, N.Y.

Mrs. Turner, over Mauro's Rooms
Charles F. Mercer, Va.
Aaron Ward, N.Y.
John H. Bryan, N.C.
Henry Markell, N.Y.
Augustine H. Shepperd, N.C.

Mrs. Taylor, Ninth St., near E St.
Andrew Stevenson, Va.

Mr. Henry Tims, near and Southeast
  of the Capitol
John Chandler (S), Me.
James Noble (S), Ind.
Albion K. Parris (S), Me.
Oliver H. Smith, Ind.
James W. Ripley, Me.
John Anderson, Me.
Rufus McIntire, Me.

Mr. B. O. Tyler, near the Capitol
Ephraim Bateman (S), N.J.
Dudley Chase (S), Vt.
Joseph Healy, N.H.
Andrew Stewart, Penn.
Samuel Swann, N.J.
Thomas Whipple, Jr., N.H.
Jonathan Hunt, Vt.
John Culpepper, N.C.

---

[6] Also listed at Miss Heyer's.
[7] Also listed at Miss Heyer's and Mrs. Tucker's.
[8] Also listed at J. Wood's, near Gunton's Apothecary Store.

Mr. Widmer, Penn. Ave.
Lemuel Sawyer, N.C.

Williamson's Hotel, Penn. Ave.
Edward Livingston, La.

Williamson's Boarding House
Ralph I. Ingersoll, Conn.
Samuel Chase, N.Y.
John I. De Graff, N.Y.
James Strong, N.Y.

Mr. James Young, N.J. Ave.
Samuel Bell (S), N.H.
Samuel A. Foote (S), Conn.
Elias K. Kane (S), Ill.
Asher Robbins (S), R.I.
David Barker, Jr., N.H.
Kensey Johns, Jr., Del.

Adams' House, F St. North
Dominique Bouligny (S), La.
Josiah S. Johnston (S), La.

Private Residences
    Corner of Sixth St. and La. Ave.
John Bailey, Mass.
    Postmaster General, C St.
William McLean, Ohio
    Dr. Ewell, East of the Capitol
Henry C. Martindale, N.Y.
    Sec. of the Navy, Samuel L. Southard
John Taliaferro, Va.
    Mrs. Tucker, Corner Tenth St. West
Jesse B. Thomas (S),[9] Ill.
    Corner of Eighth St. and La. Ave.
John Varnum, Mass.
    Georgetown
George C. Washington, Md.
    Mrs. Handy, I St.
Ephraim K. Wilson, Md.
    Commodore Tingey, Navy Yard
Joseph F. Wingate, Me.
    J. Wood, near Gunton's Apothecary Store
John J. Wood,[10] N.Y.

APPENDIX

Ambrose H. Sevier,[11] Deleg. Ark. Terr.
Richard H. Wilde,[12] Ga.
Vacancy,[13] Ky.

John Davis, Mass.
George Holcombe,[14] N.J.
Thomas R. Mitchell, S.C.

STANDING COMMITTEES OF THE
HOUSE OF REPRESENTATIVES

ELECTIONS

Chairman: John Sloane, Ohio

John Anderson, Me.
Willis Alston, N.C.
Starling Tucker, S.C.

Nathaniel H. Claiborne, Va.
Elisha Phelps, Conn.
John G. Stower, N.Y.

[9] Also listed at Miss Heyer's and Miss Polk's.
[10] Also listed at Mrs. Queen's.
[11] Took his seat Feb. 13, 1828.
[12] Took his seat Feb. 13, 1828.
[13] John Calhoon and Thomas Chilton were candidates to fill the vacancy caused by the death of William S. Young; with the vote of one county being thrown out, the certificate of election was given to Mr. Calhoon. By mutual agreement Calhoon resigned and both contestants then petitioned the Governor for a new election. Calhoon was subsequently elected, and took his seat Jan. 11, 1828.
[14] Took his seat Jan. 14, 1828.

WAYS AND MEANS

Chairman: George McDuffie,[15] S.C.

Peleg Sprague, Me.	William L. Brent, La.
Gulian C. Verplanck, N.Y.	George R. Gilmer, Ga.
Henry W. Dwight, Mass.	Alexander Smyth, Va.

CLAIMS

Chairman: Lewis Williams, N.C.

William McCoy, Va.	John C. Clark, N.Y.
Elisha Whittlesey, Ohio	Rufus McIntire, Me.
Noyes Barber, Conn.	William Ramsey, Penn.

COMMERCE

Chairman: Churchill C. Cambreleng, N.Y.

Thomas Newton, Jr., Va.	John Barney, Md.
Wiley Thompson, Ga.	Jonathan Harvey, N.H.
Benjamin Gorham, Mass.	Joel B. Sutherland, Penn.

PUBLIC LANDS

Chairman: Jacob C. Isacks, Tenn.

Samuel F. Vinton, Ohio	William Haile, Miss.
Thomas Whipple, Jr., N.H.	Joseph Duncan, Ill.
Jonathan Jennings, Ind.	Warren R. Davis, S.C.

POST OFFICE AND POST ROADS

Chairman: Samuel D. Ingham, Penn.

Samuel McKean, Penn.	John Magee, N.Y.
Joel Yancey, Ky.	James L. Hodges, Mass.
Henry W. Connor, N.C.	William Russell, Ohio

DISTRICT OF COLUMBIA

Chairman: Mark Alexander, Va.

Ralph I. Ingersoll, Conn.	George Kremer, Penn.
John H. Bryan, N.C.	John Varnum, Mass.
John C. Weems, Md.	Robert Allen, Va.

JUDICIARY

Chairman: Philip P. Barbour, Va.

Edward Livingston, La.	Charles A. Wickliffe, Ky.
James Buchanan, Penn.	John L. Kerr, Md.
William C. Rives, Va.	Henry R. Storrs, N.Y.

[15]The *Journal of the House of Representatives* lists John Randolph (Va.) as Chairman, George McDuffie (S.C.) as a committee member, and does not include Alexander Smyth (Va.) as a committee member.

REVOLUTIONARY CLAIMS
Chairman: George Wolf, Penn.

Jonathan Hunt, Vt.

Ebenezer Tucker, N.J.

William Creighton, Jr., Ohio

Joseph Fry, Jr. Penn.

John D. Dickinson, N.Y.

Joseph Healy, N.H.

PUBLIC EXPENDITURES
Chairman: Jeromus Johnson, N.Y.

John S. Barbour, Va.

Daniel A. A. Buck, Vt.

John Bailey, Mass.

Levin Gale, Md.

Henry C. Martindale, N.Y.

William T. Nuckolls, S.C.

PRIVATE LAND CLAIMS
Chairman: Richard A. Buckner, Ky.

Gabriel Moore, Ala.

Augustine H. Shepperd, N.C.

William Armstrong, Va.

Edward Bates, Mo.

Jonas Earll, Jr., N.Y.

John B. Sterigere, Penn.

MANUFACTURES
Chairman: Rollin C. Mallary, Vt.

James S. Stevenson, Penn.

Silas Wright, Jr., N.Y.

Lewis Condict, N.J.

William Stanbery, Ohio

Thomas P. Moore, Ky.

William D. Martin, S.C.

INDIAN AFFAIRS
Chairman: William McLean, Ohio

John McKee, Ala.

Samuel Swan, N.J.

Samuel P. Carson, N.C.

Wilson Lumpkin, Ga.

Henry Daniel, Ky.

Oliver H. Smith

FOREIGN AFFAIRS
Chairman: Edward Everett, Mass.

John W. Taylor, N.Y.

William Drayton, S.C.

William S. Archer, Va.

George W. Owen, Ala.

John Sergeant, Penn.

James K. Polk, Tenn.

MILITARY AFFAIRS
Chairman: James Hamilton, Jr., S.C.

Joseph Vance, Ohio

John Floyd, Ga.

Alexander Smyth, Va.

Selah R. Hobbie, N.Y.

Robert Desha, Tenn.

Robert Orr, Jr., Penn.

NAVAL AFFAIRS
Chairman: Michael Hoffman, N.Y.

Ichabod Bartlett, N.H.

Daniel H. Miller, Penn.

Benjamin W. Crowninshield, Mass.

Clement Dorsey, Md.

John Carter, S.C.

James W. Ripley, Me.

200

TWENTIETH CONGRESS, FIRST SESSION

AGRICULTURE

Chairman: Stephen Van Rensselaer, N.Y.

John Roane, Va.
Ephraim K. Wilson, Md.
Stephen Barlow, Penn.

John Hallock, Jr., N.Y.
Orange Merwin, Conn.
John Culpepper, N.C.

TERRITORIES

Chairman: James Strong, N.Y.

James Clark, N.Y.
Lemuel Sawyer, N.C.
John C. Wright, Ohio

Rudolph Bunner, N.Y.
Pryor Lea, Tenn.
Richard Coulter, Penn.

MILITARY PENSIONS

Chairman: Tristam Burges, R.I.

James C. Mitchell, Tenn.
Isaac C. Bates, Mass.
Joseph Lawrence, N.Y.

John Long, N.C.
Joseph Lecompte, Ky.
Chauncey Forward, Penn.

REVISAL AND UNFINISHED BUSINESS

Chairman: Dutee J. Pearce, R.I.

John Reed, Mass.

James Wilson, Penn.

ACCOUNTS

Chairman: Samuel C. Allen, Mass.

George O. Belden, N.Y.

David Plant, Conn.

EXPENDITURES IN THE DEPARTMENT OF STATE

Chairman: John Blair, Tenn.

Robert P. Letcher, Ky.

James Trezvant, Va.

EXPENDITURES IN THE DEPARTMENT OF THE TREASURY

Chairman: Thomas H. Hall, N.C.

John Mitchell, Penn.

Daniel L. Barringer, N.C.

EXPENDITURES IN THE DEPARTMENT OF WAR

Chairman: Charles E. Haynes, Ga.

David Woodcock, N.Y.

Daniel Turner, N.C.

EXPENDITURES IN THE DEPARTMENT OF THE NAVY

Chairman: Peter Little, Md.

Chittenden Lyon, Ky.

Richard Keese, N.Y.

EXPENDITURES IN THE POST OFFICE DEPARTMENT

Chairman: Gabriel Holmes, N.C.

Isaac Leffler, Va.

Jeremiah O'Brien, Me.

EXPENDITURES ON THE PUBLIC BUILDINGS

Chairman: Michael C. Sprigg, Md.

John J. Wood, N.Y.   Benjamin Swift, Vt.

SELECT COMMITTEES

ON ROADS AND CANALS

Chairman: Charles F. Mercer, Va.

Andrew Stewart, Penn.   John Davis, Mass.
John Woods, Ohio   Henry H. Gurley, La.
Dudley Marvin, N.Y.   John Bell, Tenn.

ON THE MILITIA

Chairman: Thomas Metcalfe, Ky.

John Floyd, Va.   Philemon Beecher, Ohio
James Findlay, Ohio   Robert McHatton, Ky.
Aaron Ward, N.Y.   Kensey Johns, Jr., Del.

JOINT COMMITTEE

ON THE LIBRARY OF CONGRESS

House   Senate
Edward Everett, Mass.   Mahlon Dickerson, N.J.
Silas Wood, Jr., N.Y.   Nathan Sanford, N.Y.
Charles Miner, Penn.   Asher Robbins, R.I.

STANDING COMMITTEES OF THE SENATE

FOREIGN RELATIONS

Chairman: Nathaniel Macon, N.C.

Nathan Sanford, N.Y.   Samuel Bell, N.H.
Littleton W. Tazewell, Va.   Hugh Lawson White, Tenn.

FINANCE

Chairman: Samuel Smith, Md.

Louis McLane, Del.   William Smith, S.C.
Albion K. Parris, Me.   John Branch, N.C.

COMMERCE

Chairman: Levi Woodbury, N.H.

Nathaniel Silsbee, Mass.   Louis McLane, Del.
Josiah S. Johnston, La.   Thomas H. Williams, Miss.

MANUFACTURES

Chairman: Mahlon Dickerson, N.J.

Nehemiah R. Knight, R.I.   Henry M. Ridgely, Del.
Benjamin Ruggles, Ohio   Isaac D. Barnard, Penn.

AGRICULTURE

Chairman: John Branch, N.C.

Ephraim Bateman, N.J.   Calvin Willey, Conn.
Dominique Bouligny, La.   Isaac D. Barnard, Penn.

MILITARY AFFAIRS

Chairman: William Henry Harrison, Ohio

Richard M. Johnson, Ky.   John Chandler, Me.
Thomas H. Benton, Mo.   William Hendricks, Ind.

MILITIA

Chairman: John Chandler, Me.

William Henry Harrison, Ohio   John McKinley, Ala.
William Marks, Penn.   John Tyler, Va.

NAVAL AFFAIRS

Chairman: Robert Y. Hayne, S.C.

Asher Robbins, R.I.   Littleton W. Tazewell, Va.
Horatio Seymour, Vt.   Levi Woodbury, N.H.

PUBLIC LANDS

Chairman: David Barton, Mo.

William R. King, Ala.   Powhatan Ellis, Miss.
John H. Eaton, Tenn.   Elias K. Kane, Ill.

PRIVATE LAND CLAIMS

Chairman: William Smith, S.C.

John Macpherson Berrier, Ga.   Elias K. Kane, Ill.
John McKinley, Ala.   Jesse B. Thomas, Ill.

INDIAN AFFAIRS

Chairman: Thomas H. Benton, Mo.

Samuel A. Foote, Conn.   Thomas W. Cobb, Ga.
William R. King, Ala.   Hugh Lawson White, Tenn.

CLAIMS

Chairman: Benjamin Ruggles, Ohio

Samuel Bell, N.H.   Dudley Chase, Vt.
Thomas W. Cobb, Ga.   John Rowan, Ky.

JUDICIARY

Chairman: Martin Van Buren, N.Y.

Horatio Seymour, Vt.	John Rowan, Ky.
John Macpherson Berrien, Ga.	Robert Y. Hayne, S.C.

POST OFFICE AND POST ROADS

Chairman: Richard M. Johnson, Ky.

Nathaniel Silsbee, Mass.	Josiah S. Johnston, La.
Powhatan Ellis, Miss.	John Tyler, Va.

PENSIONS

Chairman: James Noble, Ind.

Dudley Chase, Vt.	Thomas W. Cobb, Ga.
William Marks, Penn.	Samuel A. Foote, Conn.

DISTRICT OF COLUMBIA

Chairman: John H. Eaton, Tenn.

Dominique Bouligny, La.	James Noble, Ind.
Ezekiel F. Chambers, Md.	Henry M. Ridgely, Del.

CONTINGENT EXPENSES OF THE SENATE

Chairman: Elias K. Kane, Ill.

William Hendricks, Ind.	Ezekiel F. Chambers, Md.

ENGROSSED BILLS

Chairman: William Marks, Penn.

Albion K. Parris, Me.	Calvin Willey, Conn.

SELECT COMMITTEES

ON ROADS AND CANALS

Chairman: William Hendricks, Ind.

William Marks, Penn.	Jesse B. Thomas, Ill.
Dudley Chase, Vt.	William R. King, Ala.

ON THE BILL TO ABOLISH IMPRISONMENT FOR DEBT

Chairman: Richard M. Johnson, Ky.

John Macpherson Berrien, Ga.	John Tyler, Va.
Nathaniel Macon, N.C.	Isaac D. Barnard, Penn.
Ezekiel F. Chambers, Md.	Louis McLane, Del.

ON MEMORIALS ON ACCOUNTS OF FRENCH SPOLIATIONS, PRIOR TO 1800

Chairman: Ezekiel F. Chambers, Md.

Daniel Webster, Mass.   William R. King, Ala.
John Macpherson Berrien, Ga.   Albion K. Parris, Me.
Littleton W. Tazewell, Va.   Josiah S. Johnston, La.

ON THE BILL FOR DISTRIBUTION OF PART OF THE REVENUE OF THE UNITED STATES AMONG THE STATES

Chairman: Mahlon Dickerson, N.J.

John Branch, N.C.   Samuel Smith, Md.
John Rowan, Ky.   Littleton W. Tazewell, Va.
Hugh Lawson White, Tenn.   Daniel Webster, Mass.

ON MEMORIAL OF SURVIVING OFFICERS OF THE REVOLUTION

Chairman: Levi Woodbury, N.H.

William Henry Harrison, Ohio   Martin Van Buren, N.Y.
John Macpherson Berrien, Ga.   Daniel Webster, Mass.

CONGRESSIONAL DIRECTORY

TWENTIETH CONGRESS, SECOND SESSION
(December 1, 1828–March 3, 1829)

Arguelles, Penn. Ave.
Peleg Sprague, Me.
James L. Hodges, Mass.
John Locke, Mass.
John Reed, Mass.
Henry H. Gurley, La.
Ichabod Bartlett, N.H.

Mrs. Ball, opposite Brown's
John Baldwin, Conn.
David Plant, Conn.
John C. Clark, N.Y.
Nathaniel H. Claiborne, Va.
Thomas Chilton, Ky.
Joseph Lecompte, Ky.
Chittenden Lyon, Ky.
Ambrose H. Sevier, Deleg., Ark. Terr.
Robert McHatton, Ken.
John G. Stower, N.Y.
David Crockett, Tenn.

Ballard's, opposite Centre Market
Nathaniel Garrow, N.Y.
John Hallock, Jr., N.Y.
Thomas Taber, 2d, N.Y.

Blake's, opposite Centre Market
Nathaniel Silsbee (S), Mass.
Ezekiel F. Chambers (S), Md.
Isaac C. Bates, Mass.
Benjamin W. Crowninshield, Mass.
John Sergeant, Penn.
Thomas H. Blake, Ind.

Burke's, E St.
George McDuffie, S.C.
William D. Martin, S.C.

Mr. Bernard, Penn. Ave.
Josiah S. Johnston (S), La.
Ralph I. Ingersoll, Conn.
John D. Dickinson, N.Y.
James Strong, N.Y.

Brown's Hotel, Penn. Ave.
John Varnum, Mass.
Willis Alston, N.C.
John H. Marable, Tenn.
John C. Weems, Md.
Henry Markell, N.Y.

O. B. Brown, E St.
Richard M. Johnson (S), Ky.
Wilson Lumkin, Ga.

Burch, Capitol Hill
Gabriel Moore, Ala.
John Roane, Va.
James C. Mitchell, Tenn.
William T. Nuckolls, S.C.
Joel Yancey, Ky.
John Blair, Tenn.
Starling Tucker, S.C.

Mrs. Carlisle, Penn. Ave.
Daniel A. A. Buck, Vt.
Richard Keese, N.Y.

Clement's, Corner E and Twelfth St.
Louis McLane (S), Del.

Coburn's, F St.
John Barney, Md.

Cochran's, F St.
Thomas Newton, Jr., Va.
Stephen Barlow, Penn.

James Findlay, Ohio
Burwell Bassett, Va.

Cottringers, Thirteenth St.
Levin Gale, Md.
James Buchanan, Penn.
James S. Stevenson, Penn.
John B. Sterigere, Penn.

Coyle's, Capitol Hill
William Smith (S), S.C.

Mr. J. Davis, C St.
Charles F. Mercer, Va.
Isaac Leffler, Va.
William Armstrong, Va.
Phineas L. Tracy, N.Y.
Samuel Anderson, Penn.
Joseph Vance, Ohio
William Russell, Ohio
Richard A. Buckner, Ky.
John W. Taylor, N.Y.
Charles Miner, Penn.
Lewis Williams, N.C.
John Chambers, Ky.

Dowson's, No. 1, Capitol Hill
Samuel Smith (S), Md.
William R. King (S), Ala.
John McKinley (S), Ala.
Oliver H. Prince (S),[1] Ga.
John S. Barbour, Va.
Philip P. Barbour, Va.

Dowson's, No. 2, Capitol Hill
Mark Alexander, Va.
George R. Gilmer, Ga.
John Randolph, Va.
James Trezvant, Va.
Thomas H. Hall, N.C.
Daniel Turner, N.C.
John Floyd, Ga.
Thomas H. Benton (S), Mo.
Oliver H. Prince (S),[2] Ga.

Mrs. Dunn, opposite the Capitol
Robert Allen, Va.
John Rowan (S), Ky.
Thomas H. Williams (S), Miss.

John Branch (S), N.C.
John Bell, Tenn.
Thomas P. Moore, Ky.
John McKee, Ala.
Gabriel Holmes, N.C.

Fleury's, Penn. Ave.
William S. Archer, Va.
Andrew Stevenson, Va.

Mrs. Eliot's, Penn. Ave.
Andrew Stewart, Penn.

Fletcher's, North of the Post Office
Samuel C. Allen, Mass.
Joseph Richardson, Mass.
Daniel A. Miller, Penn.
Samuel McKean, Penn.
Robert Orr, Jr., Penn.
William Ramsey, Penn.
Joel B. Sutherland, Penn.
George Wolf, Penn.
Jacob C. Isacks, Tenn.
Innis Green, Penn.
Richard Coulter, Penn.

French's, F St., North of the Post
 Office
Richard H. Wilde, Ga.
Joseph M. White, Deleg., Terr. of Fla.

Gibson's, Penn. Ave.
George O. Belden, N.Y.
Henry W. Dwight, Mass.
John I. De Graff, N.Y.
Jeromus Johnson, N.Y.
Aaron Ward, N.Y.
Austin E. Wing, Deleg., Mich. Terr.

Gardner's, F St.
John L. Kerr, Md.

Mrs. Galvin, Capitol Hill
William Marks (S), Penn.
Benjamin Ruggles (S), Ohio
William Hendricks (S), Ind.
James Noble (S), Ind.
Oliver H. Smith, Ind.

[1] Also listed at Dowson's No. 2.
[2] Also listed at Dowson's No. 1.

Greer's, near Post Office
Dudley Chase (S), Vt.
John Long, N.C.
Joseph Healy, N.H.
John J. Wood, N.Y.
Chauncey Forward, Penn.
Joseph Lawrence, Penn.
James Wilson, Penn.
David L. Barringer, N.C.
Lewis Maxwell, Va.

Handy's, I St., opposite Williamson's
Ephraim K. Wilson, Md.
Elias K. Kane (S),[3] Ill.

Hamilton's, Capitol Hill
Calvin Willey (S), Conn.
Samuel Butman, Me.
Wiley Thompson, Ga.

Hobb's, F St.
Henry R. Storrs, N.Y.
Clement Dorsey, Md.
John Taliaferro, Va.
Edward Bates, Mo.

Hyatt's, opposite Brown's
Noyes Barber, Conn.
Orange Merwin, Conn.
Elisha Phelps, Conn.
Rollin C. Mallary, Vt.
Benjamin Swift, Vt.
George E. Wales, Vt.
David Woodcock, N.Y.
Samuel F. Vinton, Ohio
John Woods, Ohio
John C. Wright, Ohio

Holtzman's, Georgetown
George Kremer, Penn.

Harbaugh's, Seventh St.
Michael C. Sprigg, Md.
William Stanbery, Ohio

Ironside's, Corner F and Twelfth St.
John H. Bryan, N.C.
John Carter, S.C.

Robert P. Letcher, Ky.
Augustine H. Shepperd, N.C.

Judson's, Penn. Ave.
John Baily, Mass.

Latourno's, Penn. Ave.
John Macpherson Berrien (S), Ga.

Lanphier's, Penn. Ave.
Nathan Sanford (S), N.Y.

McCardle's, Capitol Hill
Dutee J. Pearce, R.I.
Silas Wood, N.Y.
James F. Randolph, N.J.
Isaac Pierson, N.J.
Thomas Sinnickson, N.J.
Samuel Swann, N.J.

McDonald's, Penn. Ave.
Samuel Chase, N.Y.
Jonathan Jennings,[4] Ind.

Mrs. McDaniel, Ninth St.
Rufus McIntire, Me.
Jeremiah O'Brien, Me.
Jonathan Jennings,[5] Ind.

McLeod's, Four and One-Half St.
Levi Woodbury (S), N.H.

McIntyre's, Penn. Ave.
Jonathan Hunt, Vt.

Miller's, F St.
William Drayton, S.C.
Churchill C. Cambreleng, N.Y.
William C. Rives, Va.

O'Neal's, West Market
John H. Eaton (S), Tenn.

Myer's, opposite Gadsby's
Selah R. Hobbie, N.Y.
Joseph Fry, Jr., Penn.
Adam King, Penn.
Peter Little, Md.

[3] Also listed at Young's.
[4] Also listed at Mrs. McDaniel's.
[5] Also listed at McDonald's.

William McCoy, Va.
Alexander Smyth, Va.
John Magee, N.Y.
Henry W. Connor, N.C.

Queen's, Penn. Ave.
Titus Brown, N.H.
Jonathan Harvey, N.H.
Jonas Earll, Jr., N.Y.
Silas Wright, Jr.,[6] N.Y.

Peyton's, opposite Gadsby's
Mahlon Dickerson (S),[7] N.J.
Robert Y. Hayne (S), S.C.
Hugh Lawson White (S), Tenn.
Powhatan Ellis (S), Miss.
Littleton W. Tazewell (S), Va.
Gulian C. Verplanck, N.Y.
Robert Desha, Tenn.
Pryor Lea, Tenn.
James K. Polk, Tenn.

Mr. Timm, Capitol Hill
John Chandler (S), Me.
David Barton (S), Mo.
John Anderson, Me.
James W. Ripley, Me.

Turner's, opposite Centre Market
Nehemiah R. Knight (S), R.I.
Horatio Seymour (S), Vt.
Tristam Burges, R.I.
Lewis Condict, N.J.
Kensey Johns, Jr., Del.

Ustick's, Penn. Ave.
John Culpepper, N.C.

Washington's, Penn. Ave.
Samuel P. Carson, N.C.
Charles E. Haynes, Ga.
Charles A. Wickliffe, Ky.
Henry Daniel, Ky.

Wagoman's, Twelfth St.
John Tyler (S), Va.

Wright's, Penn. Ave.
Daniel G. Garnsey, N.Y.
Dudley Marvin, N.Y.
John Maynard, N.Y.

Williamson's, Penn. Ave.
Edward Everett, Mass.
Benjamin Gorham, Mass.
Stephen Van Rensselaer, N.Y.

Young's, Capitol Hill
Samuel Bell (S), N.H.
Asher Robbins (S), R.I.
Samuel A. Foote (S), Conn.
David Barker, Jr., N.H.
John Sloane, Ohio
Elisha Whittlesey, Ohio
Elias K. Kane (S),[8] Ill.
Jesse B. Thomas (S), Ill.

Private Residences
Opposite Old Branch Bank
Dominique Bouligny (S), La.
Cox's Row, Georgetown
William L. Brent, La.
Mr. Clarke, E St.
Joseph Duncan, Ill.
John McLean, C St.
William McLean, Ohio
Dr. Ewell, opposite the Capitol
Henry C. Martindale, N.Y.
F St.
George W. Owen, Ala.
Georgetown
George C. Washington, Md.
Dean's, Penn. Ave.
Thomas Whipple, Jr., N.H.
Commodore Tingey, Navy Yard
John F. Wingate, Me.

APPENDIX

Henry M. Ridgely (S), Del.
Tomlinson Fort, Ga.

James Clark, Ky.
Edward Livingston, La.

[6] Resigned Feb. 16, 1829.
[7] Resigned Jan. 30, 1829. He was elected to fill the vacancy caused by the resignation of Ephraim Bateman, and took his seat Feb. 9, 1829.
[8] Also listed at Handy's.

John Davis, Mass.
Daniel Webster, Mass.
John Holmes (S),[9] Me.
Thomas Hinds,[10] Miss.
Ephraim Bateman (S), N.J.
Ebenezer Tucker, N.J.
Rudolph Bunner, N.Y.
Michael Hoffman, N.Y.
Martin Van Buren (S),[11] N.Y.
James Iredell,[12] N.C.
Lemuel Sawyer, N.C.
Philemon Beecher, Ohio

Jacob Burnet (S),[13] Ohio
Francis S. Muhlenberg,[14] Ohio
William Addams, Penn.
Isaac D. Barnard (S),[15] Penn.
Samuel D. Ingham, Penn.
John Mitchell, Penn.
Espy Van Horne, Penn.
Warren R. Davis, S.C.
James Hamilton, Jr., S.C.
Thomas R. Mitchell, S.C.
Thomas Davenport, Va.
John Floyd, Va.

STANDING COMMITTEES OF THE HOUSE OF REPRESENTATIVES

ELECTIONS

Chairman: John Anderson, Me.

Willis Alston, N.C.
Nathaniel H. Claiborne, Va.
Elisha Phelps, Conn.

John G. Stower, N.Y.
John Davenport, Ohio
James F. Randolph, N.J.

WAYS AND MEANS

Chairman: George McDuffie, S.C.

Peleg Sprague, Me.
Gulian C. Verplanck, N.Y.
Henry W. Dwight, Mass.

William L. Brent, La.
George R. Gilmer, Ga.
Alexander Smyth, Va.

CLAIMS

Chairman: William McCoy, Va.

Elisha Whittlesey, Ohio
Noyes Barber, Conn.
John C. Clark, N.Y.

Rufus McIntire, Me.
William Ramsey, Penn.
Pryor Lea, Tenn.

[9] Elected to fill the vacancy caused by the resignation of Albion K. Parris, and took his seat Jan. 26, 1829.

[10] Elected to fill the vacancy caused by the resignation of William Haile, and took his seat Dec. 8, 1828.

[11] Resigned Dec. 20, 1828. Charles E. Dudley was elected to fill the vacancy, and took his seat Jan. 29, 1829.

[12] Elected to fill the vacancy caused by the resignation of Nathaniel Macon, and took his seat Dec. 23, 1828.

[13] Elected to fill the vacancy caused by the resignation of William Henry Harrison, and took his seat Dec. 29, 1828.

[14] Elected to fill the vacancy caused by the resignation of William Creighton, Jr., and took his seat Dec. 19, 1828.

[15] Resigned Jan. 12, 1829.

COMMERCE

Chairman: Churchill C. Cambreleng, N.Y.

Thomas Newton, Jr., Va.	Jonathan Harvey, N.H.
Benjamin Gorham, Mass.	Joel B. Sutherland, Penn.
John Barney, Md.	John I. De Graff, N.Y.

PUBLIC LANDS

Chairman: Jacob C. Isacks, Tenn.

Samuel F. Vinton, Ohio	Augustine H. Shepherd, N.C.
Jonathan Jennings, Ind.	Jonathan Hunt, Vt.
Joseph Duncan, Ill.	Henry H. Gurley, La.

POST OFFICE AND POST ROADS

Chairman: Samuel McKean, Penn.

Joel Yancey, Ky.	John Magee, N.Y.
John H. Marable, Tenn.	James L. Hodges, Mass.
Henry W. Connor, N.C.	William Russell, Ohio

DISTRICT OF COLUMBIA

Chairman: Mark Alexander, Va.

Ralph I. Ingersoll, Conn.	John Varnum, Mass.
John C. Weems, Md.	Robert Allen, Va.
George Kremer, Penn.	George C. Washington, Md.

JUDICIARY

Chairman: Philip P. Barbour, Va.

James Buchanan, Penn.	John L. Kerr, Md.
William C. Rives, Va.	Henry R. Storrs, N.Y.
Charles A. Wickliffe, Ky.	John Bell, Tenn.

REVOLUTIONARY CLAIMS

Chairman: George Wolf, Penn.

John D. Dickinson, N.Y.	Joseph Healy, N.H.
Ebenezer Tucker, N.J.	Joseph F. Wingate, Me.
Joseph Fry, Jr., Penn.	John Sloane, Ohio

PUBLIC EXPENDITURES

Chairman: Jeromus Johnson, N.Y.

John S. Barbour, Va.	Daniel D. Barnard, N.Y.
Levin Gale, Md.	Mordecai Bartley, Ohio
John Maynard, N.Y.	John Chambers, Ky.

PRIVATE LAND CLAIMS

Chairman: Richard A. Buckner, Ky.

Gabriel Moore, Ala.	Edward Bates, Mo.
Jonas Earll, Jr., N.Y.	William T. Nuckolls, S.C.
John B. Sterigere, Penn.	Thomas H. Blake, Ind.

MANUFACTURES

Chairman: Rollin C. Mallary, Vt.

James B. Stevenson, Penn.
Lewis Condict, N.J.
Thomas P. Moore, Ky.

Silas Wright, Jr., N.Y.
William Stanbery, Ohio
William D. Martin, S.C.

INDIAN AFFAIRS

Chairman: William McLean, Ohio

John McKee, Ala.
Samuel P. Carson, N.C.
Henry Daniel, Ky.

Samuel Swan, N.J.
Wilson Lumpkin, Ga.
Oliver H. Smith, Ind.

FOREIGN AFFAIRS

Chairman: Edward Everett, Mass.

John W. Taylor, N.Y.
William S. Archer, Va.
John Sergeant, Penn.

George W. Owen, Ala.
James K. Polk, Tenn.
Richard H. Wilde, Ga.

MILITARY AFFAIRS

Chairman: William Drayton, S.C.

Joseph Vance, Ohio
Robert Desha, Tenn.
John Floyd, Ga.

Selah R. Hobbie, N.Y.
Robert Orr, Jr., Penn.
Daniel A. A. Buck, Vt.

NAVAL AFFAIRS

Chairman: Michael Hoffman, N.Y.

Ichabod Bartlett, N.H.
Banjamin W. Crowninshield, Mass.
John Carter, S.C.

Daniel H. Miller, Penn.
Clement Dorsey, Md.
James W. Ripley, Me.

AGRICULTURE

Chairman: Stephen Van Rensselaer, N.Y.

John Roane, Va.
Ephraim K. Wilson, Md.
Stephen Barlow, Penn.

Henry C. Martindale, N.Y.
Orange Merwin, Conn.
John Culpepper, N.C.

TERRITORIES

Chairman: James Strong, N.Y.

James Clark, Ky.
John C. Wright, Ohio
Innis Green, Penn.

Nathaniel Garrow, N.Y.
William Armstrong, Va.
Tomlinson Fort, Ga.

MILITARY PENSIONS

Chairman: James C. Mitchell, Tenn.

Isaac C. Bates, Mass.
Joseph Lawrence, Penn.
John Long, N.C.

Joseph Lecompte, Ky.
Chauncey Forward, Penn.
Henry Markell, N.Y.

REMOVAL AND UNFINISHED BUSINESS

Chairman: Dutee J. Pearce, R.I.

John Reed, Mass.   Isaac Pierson, N.J.

ACCOUNTS

Chairman: Samuel C. Allen, Mass.

David Plant, Conn.   Samuel Anderson, Penn.

SELECT COMMITTEES

ON ROADS AND CANALS

Chairman: Charles F. Mercer, Va.

Andrew Stewart, Penn.   Dudley Marvin, N.Y.
John H. Bryan, N.C.   David Barker, Jr., N.H.
John Woods, Ohio   Samuel Butman, Me.

ON THE FIFTH CENSUS

Chairman: Henry R. Storrs, N.Y.

James Buchanan, Penn.   Henry Daniel, Ky.
Gabriel Holmes, N.C.   Kensey Johns, Jr., Del.
Peter Little, Md.   Joseph Duncan, Ill.

ON THE MILITIA

Chairman: Wiley Thompson, Ga.

James Findlay, Ohio   Starling Tucker, S.C.
Aaron Ward, N.Y.   John Taliaferro, Va.
Robert McHatton, Ky.   Adam King, Penn.

ON EXPENDITURES IN THE DEPARTMENT OF STATE

Chairman: John Blair, Tenn.

Robert P. Letcher, Ky.   James Trezvant, Va.

ON EXPENDITURES IN THE DEPARTMENT OF THE TREASURY

Chairman: Thomas H. Hall, N.C.

John Mitchell, Penn.   David L. Barringer, N.C.

ON EXPENDITURES IN THE DEPARTMENT OF WAR

Chairman: Charles E. Haynes, Ga.

David Woodcock, N.Y.   Daniel Turner, N.C.

ON EXPENDITURES IN THE DEPARTMENT OF THE NAVY

Chairman: Peter Little, Md.

Chittenden Lyon, Ky.   Richard Keese, N.Y.

ON THE POST OFFICE DEPARTMENT
Chairman: Gabriel Holmes, N.C.
Isaac Leffler, Va.   Jeremiah O'Brien, Me.

ON THE PUBLIC BUILDINGS
Chairman: Michael C. Sprigg, Md.
John J. Wood, N.Y.   Benjamin Swift, Vt.

STANDING COMMITTEES OF THE SENATE

FOREIGN RELATIONS
Chairman: Littleton W. Tazewell, Va.
Nathan Sanford, N.Y.   John Macpherson Berrien, Ga.
Hugh Lawson White, Tenn.   Samuel Bell, N.H.

FINANCE
Chairman: Samuel Smith, Md.
Louis McLane, Del.   John Branch, N.C.
William Smith, S.C.   Nathaniel Silsbee, Mass.

COMMERCE
Chairman: Levi Woodbury, N.H.
Nathaniel Silsbee, Mass.   Thomas H. Williams, Miss.
Josiah S. Johnston, La.   Louis McLane, Del.

MANUFACTURES
Chairman: Mahlon Dickerson, N.J.
Benjamin Ruggles, Ohio   Isaac D. Barnard, Penn.
Nehemiah R. Knight, R.I.   Henry M. Ridgely, Del.

AGRICULTURE
Chairman: Ephraim Bateman, N.J.
Dominique Bouligny, La.   William Marks, Penn.
Calvin Willey, Conn.   Ezekiel F. Chambers, Md.

MILITARY AFFAIRS
Chairman: Thomas H. Benton, Mo.
Richard M. Johnson, Ky.   John Chandler, Me.
Isaac D. Barnard, Penn.   William Hendricks, Ind.

MILITIA
Chairman: John Chandler, Me.
William Marks, Penn.   John McKinley, Ala.
John Tyler, Va.   John Branch, N.C.

NAVAL AFFAIRS

Chairman: Robert Y. Hayne, S.C.

Asher Robbins, R.I.   Levi Woodbury, N.H.
Horatio Seymour, Vt.   Littleton W. Tazewell, Va.

PUBLIC LANDS

Chairman: David Barton, Mo.

William R. King, Ala.   Powhatan Ellis, Miss.
John H. Eaton, Tenn.   Elias K. Kane, Ill.

PRIVATE LAND CLAIMS

Chairman: John McKinley,[16] Ala.

Jesse B. Thomas, Ill.
Elias K. Kane, Ill.
David Barton, Mo.

INDIAN AFFAIRS[17]

Chairman: Hugh Lawson White, Tenn.

William R. King, Ala.
Oliver H. Prince, Ga.
Thomas H. Benton, Mo.

JUDICIARY

Chairman: John Macpherson Berrien, Ga.

Horatio Seymour, Vt.   John Rowan, Ky.
Daniel Webster, Mass.   Robert Y. Hayne, S.C.

CLAIMS

Chairman: Benjamin Ruggles, Ohio

Samuel Bell, N.H.   John Rowan, Ky.
Dudley Chase, Vt.   Daniel Webster, Mass.

PENSIONS

Chairman: James Noble, Ind.

William Marks, Penn.   Samuel A. Foot, Conn.
Dudley Chase, Vt.   Oliver H. Prince, Ga.

DISTRICT OF COLUMBIA

Chairman: John H. Eaton, Tenn.

Dominique Bouligny, La.   James Noble, Ind.
Ezekiel F. Chambers, Md.   Henry M. Ridgely, Del.

---

[16] According to the *Journal of the Senate*, William Smith (S.C.) is listed as Chairman and John McKinley (Ala.) is listed as a committee member.
[17] According to the *Journal of the Senate*, Samuel A. Foote (Conn.) is listed as a committee member.

CONTINGENT EXPENSES OF THE SENATE
Chairman: Elias K. Kane, Ill.

William Hendricks, Ind.   Ezekiel F. Chambers, Md.

POST OFFICE AND POST ROADS
Chairman: Richard M. Johnson, Ky.

Powhatan Ellis, Miss.   Josiah S. Johnston, La.
John Tyler, Va.   Nathaniel Silsbee, Mass.

ENGROSSED BILLS[18]

Calvin Willey, Conn.   Ephraim Bateman, N.J.

SELECT COMMITTEE
On the Petition of George Taylor Praying Indemnification for French Spoliations

Chairman: John Tyler, Va.

Ezekiel F. Chambers, Md.   Samuel Bell, N.H.
Josiah S. Johnston, La.   Nathan Sanford, N.Y.

[18] According to the *Journal of the Senate*, William Marks (Penn.) is listed as Chairman of this committee.

CONGRESSIONAL DIRECTORY

TWENTY-FIRST CONGRESS, FIRST SESSION
(December 7, 1829–May 31, 1830)

Mrs. Ball, nearly opposite
Brown's Hotel
Charles G. De Witt, N.Y.
Nathaniel H. Claiborne, Va.
Thomas Chilton, Ky.
Chittenden Lyon, Ky.
Joseph Lecompte, Ky.
David Crockett, Tenn.
Robert E.B. Baylor, Ala.
Robert Craig, Va.
Ambrose H. Sevier, Deleg., Ark. Terr.

Mr. Ballard, opposite Centre Market
Henry R. Storrs, N.Y.
Jonathan Hunt, Vt.
Horace Everett, Vt.

Mr. Bayne, Penn. Ave.
Edmund Deberry, N.C.
Willis Alston, N.C.

Barnard's, Mansion Hotel, Penn. Ave.
Josiah S. Johnston (S), La.
Edward Everett, Mass.
Ralph I. Ingersoll, Conn.
Ebenezer F. Norton, N.Y.
Clement Dorsey, Md.
Isaac C. Bates, Mass.
Benjamin C. Howard, Md.

Mrs. Blake, near and North of
Centre Market
Ezekiel F. Chambers (S), Md.
Dutee J. Pearce, R.I.
Benjamin W. Crowninshield, Mass.
Benedict J. Semmes, Md.

Mrs. Brannan, nearly North of
Centre Market
Benjamin Gorham, Mass.

Mr. Buckner, opposite King's Gallery,
Twelfth St.
James Clark, Ky.

Mrs. Burke, opposite Late
Dr. Thornton's, F St.
Thomas Maxwell, N.Y.
Jonas Earll, Jr., N.Y.
Gershom Powers, N.Y.
John Magee, N.Y.
Michael Hoffman, N.Y.
William G. Angel, N.Y.

Brown's Hotel, Penn. Ave.
Thomas Hinds, Miss.
Edward B. Dudley,[1] N.C.

Rev. O. B. Brown, near General
Post Office
Richard M. Johnson, Ky.
Wilson Lumpkin, Ga.

Mr. Brodhead (?), N.J. Ave.,
near the Capitol
John Brodhead, N.H.
Thomas Chandler, N.H.
John W. Weeks, N.H.

Mrs. Carlisle, Penn. Ave.
Peter Ihrie, Jr., Penn.
George C. Leiper, Penn.
Thomas Irwin, Penn.

[1] Elected to fill the vacancy caused by the death of Gabriel Holmes, and took his seat Dec. 14, 1829.

216

Mrs. Clements, Penn. Ave.
Nathaniel Silsbee (S), Mass.

Mrs. Cochrane, F St., near
  Late Dr. Thornton's
Nathan Sanford (S), N.Y.
Thomas Newton, Jr.,[2] Va.
Richard Coke, Jr., Va.

Mrs. Cottringer, F St., near
  Twelfth St.
John Bell, Tenn.
Henry W. Dwight, Mass.

Mr. Coyle, near and Southeast of
  the Capitol
William Smith (S), S.C.
William R. King (S), Ala.
John McKinley (S), Ala.
James M. Wayne, Ga.

Mr. Davis, F St., near Treasury Dept.
Joseph Vance, Ohio
Joseph H. Crane, Ohio

Mr. A. R. Dowson, No. 1, near and
  Northeast of the Capitol
Samuel Smith (S), Md.
Elias Brown, Md.
Rufus McIntire, Me.
Richard Spencer, Md.
James W. Ripley,[3] Me.
George E. Mitchell, Md.
John Biddle, Deleg., Mich. Terr.

Mr. A. R. Dowson, No. 2,
  Adjoining the Above
Thomas H. Benton (S), Mo.
Thomas H. Hall, N.C.
Joel Yancey, Ky.

Mrs. R. Dunn, Northeast of the Capitol
Samuel P. Carson, N.C.
Dixon H. Lewis, Ala.
Warren R. Davis, S.C.
Jesse Speight, N.C.

Mrs. Eliot, Penn. Ave.
John Blair, Tenn.
James Standifer, Tenn.
Starling Tucker, S.C.
James Blair, S.C.
Henry W. Connor, N.C.
William T. Nuckolls, S.C.

Mrs. Flectcher, E St., near
  General Post Office
Felix Grundy (S), Tenn.
John McLean (S), Ill.
Thomas H. Crawford, Penn.
Jacob C. Isacks, Tenn.
William Russell, Ohio
Cave Johnson, Tenn.
James Findlay, Ohio
Richard Coulter, Penn.

Mr. French, Corner F and
  Thirteenth St.
Joseph M. White, Deleg., Terr. of Fla.
Joseph Hemphill, Penn.
Richard H. Wilde, Ga.

Mrs. Galvin, C St., near Four
  and one-half St.
William Marks (S), Penn.
Benjamin Ruggles (S), Ohio
William Hendricks (S), Ind.
James Noble (S), Ind.
William Armstrong, Va.
William Creighton, Jr., Ohio
William Kennon, Ohio

Gadsby's Hotel, Penn. Ave.
Levi Woodbury (S), N.H.
Charles E. Dudley (S), N.Y.
Henry Hubbard, N.H.
Campbell P. White, N.Y.
Spencer D. Pettis, Mo.
George McDuffie, S.C.
John Campbell, S.C.
Daniel H. Miller, Penn.
Joel B. Sutherland, Penn.
Alem Marr, Penn.
Andrew Stevenson, Va.
James Strong, N.Y.
Augustine H. Shepperd, N.C.

[2] Served until Mar. 9, 1830, when he was succeeded by George Loyall who had contested his election.
[3] Resigned Mar. 12, 1830.

Mr. Gibson, North and opposite
  Centre Market
Peleg Sprague (S), Me.
Robert Potter, N.C.
Thomas T. Bouldin, Va.
John Taliaferro, Va.
Tristam Burges, R.I.
William B. Shepard, N.C.
Joseph F. Wingate, Me.
George Evans, Me.
John Reed, Mass.

Mr. Greer, E St., near
  the Post Office
John Gilmore, Penn.
John Scott, Penn.
Lewis Maxwell, Va.
Chauncey Forward, Penn.
Daniel L. Barringer, N.C.
Mordecai Bartley, Ohio

Mrs. Hamilton, Carroll's Row,
  Capitol Hill
Calvin Willey (S), Conn.
Wiley Thompson, Ga.

Mrs. Handy, near and West of the
  War Office
Ephraim K. Wilson, Md.

Mrs. Hesselius, opposite Bank of
  the Metropolis
William S. Archer, Va.

Mr. Tayloe, West of the Navy Office
John D. Dickinson, N.Y.

Mr. Heeb, near and Southeast of
  the Capitol
David Barton (S), Mo.

Mrs. Hungerford, Penn. Ave.
Robert S. Rose, N.Y.
Lewis Williams, N.C.

Mr. Harbaugh, Seventh near E St.
James Ford, Penn.
William Ramsey, Penn.
William Stanbery, Ohio
William W. Irvin, Ohio

Michael C. Sprigg, Md.
Philander Stephens, Penn.

M. St. Clair Clarke, E St., near
  the Post Office
Joseph Duncan, Ill.

Mr. Hyatt, nearly opposite
  Brown's Hotel
Noyes Barber, Conn.
William L. Storrs, Conn.
William W. Ellsworth, Conn.
Jabez W. Huntington, Conn.
Benjamin Swift, Vt.
Joseph G. Kendall, Mass.
George Grenell, Jr., Mass.
Rollin C. Mallary, Vt.
William Cahoon, Vt.
Samuel Butman, Me.
John Davis, Mass.
Ebenezer Young, Conn.
James L. Hodges, Mass.

Mr. Hughes, Penn. Ave.
John Rowan (S), Ky.
Nathaniel Gaither, Ky.
Robert Allen, Va.
Nicholas D. Coleman, Ky.
John Kincaid, Ky.
Thomas Davenport, Va.

Mrs. Judson, C St., near Four
  and one-half St.
John Bailey, Mass.

Mr. Kervand, Seven Buildings,
  Penn. Ave.
Edward Livingston (S), La.
William Drayton, S.C.
Churchill C. Cambreleng, N.Y.

Mr. Latourno, Penn. Ave.
George M. Troup (S), Ga.

Mrs. Lanphier, Lenox's Row,
  Penn. Ave.
Hector Craig, N.Y.
James Lent, N.Y.
Jacob Crocheron, N.Y.
George Fisher,[4] N.Y.
Joseph Hawkins, N.Y.

---

[4] Served until Feb. 5, 1830; the election was successfully contested by Silas Wright, Jr., who resigned Mar. 9, 1830. Wright, never having qualified, preferred to continue as comptroller of the state.

Mrs. McCardle, near and Northeast
   of the Capitol
Samuel Swan, N.J.
Thomas H. Hughes, N.J.
Richard M. Cooper, N.J.

Mr. John McLeod, Penn. Ave.
Nehemiah R. Knight (S), R.I.
Theodore Frelinghuysen (S), N.J.
Lewis Condict, N.J.
James F. Randolph, N.J.
Isaac Pierson, N.J.

Mrs. Meyer, Penn. Ave.
John Thomson, Ohio
William McCreery, Penn.
Joseph Fry, Jr., Penn.
Henry A.P. Muhlenberg, Penn.
Robert Monell, N.Y.
Peter I. Borst, N.Y.
Isaac Finch, N.Y.
Jehiel H. Halsey, N.Y.
Samuel A. Smith, Penn.
Adam King, Penn.
Thomas H. Sill, Penn.

Mrs. McDaniel, Penn. Ave.
Ratliff Boon, Ind.
Jonathan Jennings, Ind.
Alexander Smyth,[5] Va.
Innis Green, Penn.
Jonathan Harvey, N.H.

Mrs. Miller, F St., near Late
   Dr. Thornton's
James Buchanan, Penn.
John B. Sterigere, Penn.

Mrs. A. Peyton, Penn. Ave.
Mahlon Dickerson (S), N.J.
Hugh Lawson White (S), Tenn.
Powhatan Ellis (S), Miss.
Elias K. Kane (S), Ill.
James Iredell (S), N.C.
James K. Polk, Tenn.
John M. Goodenow, Ohio
Clement C. Clay, Ala.
Robert W. Barnwell, S.C.
Gulian C. Verplanck, N.Y.
Henry G. Lamar, Ga.
Pryor Lea, Tenn.
William D. Martin, S.C.

Mrs. E. Peyton, Penn. Ave.
Robert Y. Hayne (S), S.C.
Walter H. Overton, La.
Edward D. White, La.
Charles F. Mercer, Va.

Mr. M. Poor, E St., near the
   City Hall
Joseph Richardson, Mass.

Mrs. Queen, Ninth near E St.
Joseph Hammons, N.H.
Ambrose Spencer, N.Y.
Benedict Arnold, N.Y.
Perkins King, N.Y.
Abraham Bockee, N.Y.
Thomas Beekman, N.Y.
Henry B. Cowles, N.Y.

Mrs. Sawyer, Seventh St., near
   General Post Office
Dudley Chase (S), Vt.
Horatio Seymour (S), Vt.
Isaac D. Barnard (S), Penn.
Joshua Evans, Jr., Penn.

Dr. Smether, nearly opposite
   Brown's Hotel
Henry H. Gurley, La.

Mr. Sawkins, Penn. Ave.
John Test, Ind.
Robert P. Letcher, Ky.

Mr. Tayloe, near the Navy Yard
John D. Dickinson, N.Y.

Mrs. J. Taylor, Corner of Seventh
   and E St.
Phineas L. Tracy, N.Y.
Henry C. Martindale, N.Y.
John W. Taylor, N.Y.

Mrs. Wilson, F St., near Twelfth St.
James Shields, Ohio

Mrs. Washington, C St.,
   opposite the Circus
George M. Bibb (S), Ky.
Charles E. Haynes, Ga.
Henry Daniel, Ky.

[5] Died Apr. 17, 1830.

Robert Desha, Tenn.
Thomas F. Foster, Ga.
Charles A. Wickliffe, Ky.

Elisha Whittlesey, Ohio
Samuel F. Vinton, Ohio
Kensey Johns, Jr., Del.

Mr. James Young, N.J. Ave.
Samuel Bell (S), N.H.
John Holmes (S), Me.
Asher Robbins (S), R.I.
Samuel A. Foote (S), Conn.
John M. Clayton (S), Del.
Jacob Burnet (S), Ohio

Private Residences
Shoff's, Georgetown
John Forsyth (S),[6] Ga.
Eighth St., near R. Jones
John Varnum, Mass.
Georgetown, near Tilley's
George C. Washington, Md.

APPENDIX

Arnold Naudain (S),[7] Del.
John Anderson, Me.
Leonard Jarvis, Me.
Daniel Webster, Mass.
Robert H. Adams (S),[8] Miss.
Timothy Childs, N.Y.
Bedford Brown (S),[9] N.C.
Abraham Rencher, N.C.
Harman Denny,[10] Penn.
Mark Alexander, Va.

John S. Barbour, Va.
Philip P. Barbour, Va.
Philip Doddridge, Va.
William F. Gordon,[11] Va.
William McCoy, Va.
John Roane, Va.
Littleton W. Tazewell, Va.
James Trezvant, Va.
John Tyler (S), Va.

STANDING COMMITTEES OF THE
HOUSE OF REPRESENTATIVES

ELECTIONS

Chairman: Willis Alston, N.C.

Starling Tucker, S.C.
Nathaniel H. Claiborne, Va.
James F. Randolph, N.J.

Cave Johnson, Tenn.
Thomas Beekman, N.Y.
Nicholas D. Coleman, Ky.

---

[6] Elected to fill the vacancy caused by the resignation of John Macpherson Berrien, and took his seat Dec. 8, 1829.

[7] Elected to fill the vacancy caused by the resignation of Louis McLane, and took his seat Jan. 13, 1830.

[8] Elected to fill the vacancy caused by the death of Thomas B. Reed, and took his seat Feb. 8, 1830.

[9] Elected to fill the vacancy caused by the resignation of John Branch, and took his seat Dec. 28, 1929.

[10] Elected to fill the vacancy caused by the resignation of William Wilkins, and took his seat Dec. 30, 1829.

[11] Elected to fill the vacancy caused by the resignation of William C. Rives, and took his seat Jan. 25, 1830.

WAYS AND MEANS

Chairman: George McDuffie, S.C.

Gulian C. Verplanck, N.Y.	Ralph I. Ingersoll, Conn.
Henry W. Dwight, Mass.	John Gilmore, Penn.
Alexander Smyth, Va.	Walter H. Overton, La.

CLAIMS[12]

Chairman: Elisha Whittlesey, Ohio

Noyes Barber, Conn.	Pryor Lea, Tenn.
Rufus McIntire, Me.	James Lent, N.Y.
William Ramsey, Penn.	Joseph H. Crane, Ohio

COMMERCE

Chairman: Churchill C. Cambreleng, N.Y.

Thomas Newton, Jr., Va.	Joel B. Sutherland, Penn.
Benjamin Gorham, Mass.	Benjamin C. Howard, Md.
Jonathan Harvey, N.H.	James M. Wayne, Ga.

PUBLIC LANDS

Chairman: Jacob C. Isacks, Tenn.

Jonathan Jennings, Ind.	Robert Potter, N.C.
Joseph Duncan, Ill.	William W. Irvin, Ohio
Jonathan Hunt, Vt.	Clement C. Clay, Ala.

POST OFFICE AND POST ROADS

Chairman: Richard M. Johnson, Ky.

Henry W. Connor, N.C.	William Russell, Ohio
John Magee, N.Y.	William McCreery, Penn.
James L. Hodges, Mass.	John Campbell, S.C.

DISTRICT OF COLUMBIA

Chairman: Gershom Powers, N.Y.

Robert Allen, Va.	John Taliaferro, Va.
George C. Washington, Md.	Peter Ihrie, Jr., Penn.
John Varnum, Mass.	Benedict J. Semmes, Md.

JUDICIARY

Chairman: James Buchanan, Penn.

Charles A. Wickliffe, Ky.	Thomas T. Bouldin, Va.
Henry R. Storrs, N.Y.	William W. Ellsworth, Conn.
Warren R. Davis, S.C.	Edward D. White, La.

---

[12] According to the *Journal of the House of Representatives*, Lewis Williams (N.C.) is listed as chairman, Elisha Whittlesey (Ohio) as a committee member, and Joseph H. Crane (Ohio) is not listed as a committee member.

REVOLUTIONARY CLAIMS

Chairman: Tristam Burges, R.I.

John D. Dickinson, N.Y.
Joseph Fry, Jr., Penn.
Joseph F. Wingate, Me.

John M. Goodenow, Ohio
Ebenezer Young, Conn.
Elias Brown, Md.

PUBLIC EXPENDITURES

Chairman: Thomas H. Hall, N.C.

Thomas Davenport, Va.
Chittenden Lyon, Ky.
Thomas Maxwell, N.Y.

Richard Spencer, Md.
John Thomson, Ohio
Ebenezer F. Norton, N.Y.

PRIVATE LAND CLAIMS

Chairman: Henry H. Gurley, La.

John B. Sterigere, Penn.
William T. Nuckolls, S.C.
Spencer D. Pettis, Mo.

John Test, Ind.
Thomas F. Foster, Ga.
Robert E. B. Baylor, Ala.

MANUFACTURES

Chairman: Rollin C. Mallary, Vt.

William Stanbery, Ohio
Lewis Condict, N.J.
William D. Martin, S.C.

Henry Daniel, Ky.
Thomas Irwin, Penn.
Robert Monell, N.Y.

INDIAN AFFAIRS

Chairman: John Bell, Tenn.

Wilson Lumpkin, Ga.
Thomas Hinds, Miss.
William L. Storrs, Conn.

Henry Hubbard, N.H.
Nathan Gaither, Ky.
Dixon H. Lewis, Ala.

FOREIGN AFFAIRS

Chairman: William S. Archer, Va.

Edward Everett, Mass.
John W. Taylor, N.Y.
James K. Polk, Tenn.

Richard H. Wilde, Ga.
Thomas H. Crawford, Penn.
Robert W. Barnwell, S.C.

MILITARY AFFAIRS

Chairman: William Drayton, S.C.

Joseph Vance, Ohio
Robert Desha, Tenn.
James Findlay, Ohio

James Blair, S.C.
George E. Mitchell, Md.
Jesse Speight, N.C.

NAVAL AFFAIRS

Chairman: Michael Hoffman, N.Y.

Benjamin W. Drowninshield, Mass.
Daniel H. Miller, Penn.
James W. Ripley, Me.

Samuel P. Carson, N.C.
Clement Dorsey, Md.
Campbell P. White, N.Y.

AGRICULTURE

Chairman: Ambrose Spencer, N.Y.

Ephraim K. Wilson, Md.   James Standifer, Tenn.
Robert S. Rose, N.Y.   Edmund Deberry N.C.
Samuel A. Smith, Penn.   Thomas Chandler, N.H.

TERRITORIES

Chairman: James Clark, Ky.

Innis Green, Penn.   William G. Angel, N.Y.
William Creighton, Jr., Ohio   Henry B. Cowles, N.Y.
William Armstrong, Va.   William B. Shepard, N.C.

MILITARY PENSIONS

Chairman: Isaac C. Bates, Mass.

Joseph Lecompte, Ky.   Joseph Hammons, N.H.
Chauncey Forward, Penn.   Abraham Bockee, N.Y.
Thomas Chilton, Ky.   James Ford, Penn.

REVISAL AND UNFINISHED BUSINESS

Chairman: Dutee J. Pearce, R.I.

John Reed, Mass.   Isaac Pierson, N.J.

ACCOUNTS

Chairman: Jehiel H. Halsey, N.Y.

Samuel Swan, N.J.   John Brodhead, N.H.

ON EXPENDITURES IN THE DEPARTMENT OF STATE

Chairman: Jonas Earll, Jr., N.Y.

Thomas H. Sill, Penn.   Perkins King, N.Y.

ON EXPENDITURES IN THE TREASURY DEPARTMENT

Chairman: George C. Leiper, Penn.

Jacob Crocheron, N.Y.   Joseph G. Kendall, Mass.

ON EXPENDITURES IN THE DEPARTMENT OF WAR

Chairman: Lewis Maxwell, Va.

Henry A.P. Muhlenberg, Penn.   David Crockett, Tenn.

ON EXPENDITURES IN THE NAVY DEPARTMENT

Chairman: Augustine H. Shepperd, N.C.

Mordecai Bartley, Ohio   Joshua Evans, Jr., Penn.

ON EXPENDITURES IN THE POST OFFICE DEPARTMENT

Chairman: Joel Yancey, Ky.

Peter I. Borst, N.Y.   John Scott, Penn.

ON EXPENDITURES IN THE PUBLIC BUILDINGS

Chairman: Michael C. Sprigg, Md.

John Bailey, Mass.   Benjamin Swift, Vt.

SELECT COMMITTEES

ON INTERNAL IMPROVEMENTS

Chairman: Joseph Hemphill, Penn.

John Blair, Tenn.   Samuel F. Vinton, Ohio
Charles E. Haynes, Ga.   Robert Craig, Va.
Robert P. Letcher, Ky   Samuel Butman, Me.

ON THE MILITIA

Chairman: Wiley Thompson, Ga.

Adam King, Penn.   Hector Craig, N.Y.
Daniel L. Barringer, N.C.   John Kincaid, Ky.
John W. Weeks, N.H.   William Cahoon, Vt.

ON RETRENCHMENT

Chairman: Charles A. Wickliffe, Ky.

Richard Coulter, Penn.   Richard Coke, Jr., Vt.
John Davis, Mass.   Jabez W. Huntington, Conn.
Henry G. Lamar, Ga.   Charles G. De Witt, N.Y.

ON THE FIFTH CENSUS

Chairman: Henry R. Storrs, N.Y.

Joseph H. Crane, Ohio   Joseph Richardson, Mass.
Kensey Johns, Jr., Del.   Ratliff Boon, Ind.
Horace Everett, Vt.   Richard M. Cooper, N.J.

ON THE PRESIDENTIAL ELECTION

Chairman: George McDuffie, S.C.

Charles E. Haynes, Ga.   Henry C. Martindale, N.Y.
Samuel P. Carson, N.C.   Philander Stephens, Penn.
Pryor Lea, Tenn.   Thomas H. Hughes, N.J.

ON PUBLIC LANDS IN TENNESSEE

Chairman: David Crockett, Tenn.

George Evans, Me.   James K. Polk, Tenn.
Phineas L. Tracy, N.Y.   Joseph Hawkins, N.Y.
William Kennon, Ohio   George Grennell, Jr., Mass.

JOINT COMMITTEE

LIBRARY OF CONGRESS

House	Senate
Edward Everett, Mass.	Asher Robbins, R.I.
Gulian C. Verplanck, N.Y.	Levi Woodbury, N.H.
James M. Wayne, Ga.	Felix Grundy, Tenn.

STANDING COMMITTEES OF THE SENATE

FOREIGN RELATIONS
Chairman: Littleton W. Tazewell, Va.

Nathan Sanford, N.Y.	Samuel Bell, N.H.
Hugh Lawson White, Tenn.	William R. King, Ala.

FINANCE
Chairman: Samuel Smith, Md.

William Smith, S.C.	William R. King, Ala.
Nathaniel Silsbee, Mass.	Josiah S. Johnston, La.

COMMERCE
Chairman: Levi Woodbury, N.H.

Josiah S. Johnston, La.	Nathan Sanford, N.Y.
Nathaniel Silsbee, Mass.	John Forsyth, Ga.

MANUFACTURES
Chairman: Mahlon Dickerson, N.J.

Benjamin Ruggles, Ohio	Horatio Seymour, Vt.
Nehemiah R. Knight, R.I.	George M. Bibb, Ky.

AGRICULTURE
Chairman: William Marks, Penn.

Calvin Willey, Conn.	Louis McLane, Del.
James Noble, Ind.	Horatio Seymour, Vt.

MILITARY AFFAIRS
Chairman: Thomas H. Benton, Mo.

Isaac D. Barnard, Penn.	William Hendricks, Ind.
George M. Troup, Ga.	Edward Livingston, La.

MILITIA

Chairman: Isaac D. Barnard, Penn.

John Tyler, Va.   Charles E. Dudley, N.Y.
John M. Clayton, Del.   James Noble, Ind.

NAVAL AFFAIRS

Chairman: Robert Y. Hayne, S.C.

Littleton W. Tazewell, Va.   Levi Woodbury, N.H.
Asher Robbins, R.I.   Daniel Webster, Mass.

PUBLIC LANDS

Chairman: David Barton, Mo.

Edward Livingston, La.   Powhatan Ellis, Miss.
Elias K. Kane, Ill.   John McKinley, Ala.

PRIVATE LAND CLAIMS

Chairman: Jacob Burnet, Ohio

David Barton, Mo.   Elias K. Kane, Ill.
Peleg Sprague, Me.   Felix Grundy, Tenn.

INDIAN AFFAIRS

Chairman: Hugh Lawson White, Tenn.

George M. Troup, Ga.   Charles E. Dudley, N.Y.
William Hendricks, Ind.   Thomas H. Benton, Mo.

CLAIMS

Chairman: Benjamin Ruggles, Ohio

Samuel Bell, N.H.   Samuel A. Foote, Conn.
Dudley Chase, Vt.   Louis McLane, Del.

JUDICIARY

Chairman: John Rowan, Ky.

John McKinley, Ala.   Robert Y. Hayne, S.C.
Daniel Webster, Mass.   Theodore Frelinghuysen, N.J.

POST OFFICE AND POST ROADS

Chairman: George M. Bibb, Ky.

Jacob Burnet, Ohio   Powhatan Ellis, Miss.
John Forsyth, Ga.   Horatio Seymour, Vt.

PENSIONS

Chairman: John Holmes, Me.

William Marks, Penn.   Dudley Chase, Vt.
Samuel A. Foote, Conn.   Ezekiel F. Chambers, Md.

DISTRICT OF COLUMBIA

Chairman: Ezekiel F. Chambers, Md.

John Tyler, Va.   John M. Clayton, Del.
John Holmes, Me.   Peleg Sprague, Me.

AUDIT AND CONTROL THE CONTINGENT FUND

Chairman: Elias K. Kane, Ill.

James Iredell, N.C.   Nehemiah R. Knight, R.I.

ENGROSSED BILLS

Chairman: William Marks, Penn.

Calvin Willey, Conn.   Felix Grundy, Tenn.

SELECT COMMITTEES

ROADS AND CANALS

Chairman: William Hendricks, Ind.

John Tyler, Va.   Charles E. Dudley, N.Y.
Daniel Webster, Mass.   Benjamin Ruggles, Ohio

THE STATE OF THE CURRENT COINS

Chairman: Nathan Sanford, N.Y.

Mahlon Dickerson, N.J.   James Iredell, N.C.
Edward Livingston, La.   Littleton W. Tazewell, Va.

CONGRESSIONAL DIRECTORY

TWENTY-FIRST CONGRESS, SECOND SESSION
(December 6, 1830–March 3, 1831)

Mrs. Arguelles, Penn. Ave.
John McKinley (S), Ala.
William R. King (S), Ala.
Henry H. Gurley, La.

Mrs. Ball, Penn. Ave.
Robert E. B. Baylor, Ala.
Thomas Chilton, Ky.
Nathaniel H. Claiborne, Va.
David Crockett, Tenn.
Robert Craig, Va.
Charles G. De Witt, N.Y.
Joseph Draper, Va.
John Roane, Va.
John Test, Ind.

Barnard's, Mansion Hotel, Penn. Ave.
Charles E. Dudley (S), N.Y.
Josiah S. Johnston (S), La.
Daniel Webster (S), Mass.
Isaac C. Bates, Mass.
Timothy Childs, N.Y.
Richard Coulter, Penn.
Henry W. Dwight, Mass.
Edward Everett, Mass.
Ralph I. Ingersoll, Conn.
John Magee, N.Y.
Dutee J. Pearce, R.I.
William Stanbery, Ohio

Brown's Hotel, N.J. Ave., Capitol Hill
James Noble,[1] Ind.
Edward B. Dudley, N.C.
Thomas Hinds, Miss.
Andrew Stevenson, Va.
Ambrose H. Sevier, Deleg., Ark. Terr.

Barnes' Hotel, Corner Penn. Ave. and
    Four and One-Half St.
Ratliff Boon, Ind.
John Blair, Tenn.
Joseph Lecompte, Ky.
Chittenden Lyon, Ky.
James Standifer, Tenn.
Wiley Thompson, Ga.
Joel Yancey, Ky.

Mr. Brodhead (?), N.J. Ave., Capitol Hill
John Brodhead, N.H.
Thomas Chandler, N.H.
Charles E. Haynes, Ga.

Mrs. Brannan, Penn. Ave.
George M. Bibb (S), Ky.
John Bell, Tenn.
Robert Desha, Tenn.
Abraham Rencher, N.C.
Joseph Duncan, Ill.
Cave Johnson, Tenn.

Mr. Ballard, opposite Centre Market
Isaac D. Barnard (S), Penn.
John B. Sterigere, Penn.
William Ramsey, Penn.

Mrs. Blake, Corner Eighth St, near
    Centre Market
Ezekiel F. Chambers (S), Md.
Peleg Sprague (S), Me.
Henry B. Cowles, N.Y.
William B. Shepard, N.C.
Benedict J. Semmes, Md.

[1] Died Feb. 26, 1831.

Mrs. Burke, F St., near Late Dr. Thornton's
Edward Livingston (S), La.
Churchill C. Cambreleng, N.Y.
William Drayton, S.C.
Thomas Maxwell, N.Y.

Capt. Beard, near the Navy Yard
Joseph Hawkins, N.Y.

Rev. O. B. Brown, E St., near General Post Office
Richard M. Johnson, Ky.
Wilson Lumpkin, Ga.

Mrs. Clements, nearly opposite Barnard's Mansion Hotel
Benjamin W. Crowninshield, Mass.

Mrs. Cochran, F near Fourteenth St.
Nathan Sanford (S), N.Y.
Richard Coke, Jr., Va.

Mrs. Cottringer, Ninth between D and E St.
Joshua Evans, Jr., Penn.
John Kincaid, Ky.

Mrs. Cummings, N.J. Ave., Capitol Hill
Willis Alston, N.C.
William G. Angel, N.Y.

John Davis, near the Circus
Jacob Burnet (S), Ohio
William Armstrong, Va.
James Clark, Ky.
William Creighton, Jr., Ohio
William Russell, Ohio
Thomas H. Sill, Penn.
John W. Taylor, N.Y.
Joseph Vance, Ohio
Samuel F. Vinton, Ohio
Lewis Williams, N.C.
Joseph H. Crane, Ohio

Dowson's No. 1, near and North of the Capitol
Samuel Smith (S), Md.
John S. Barbour, Va.

Elias Brown, Md.
John Biddle,[2] Deleg., Mich. Terr.

Dowson's No. 2, near and North of the Capitol
Thomas H. Benton (S), Mo.
Mark Alexander, Va.
Thomas H. Hall, N.C.
Robert Potter, N.C.
James Trezvant, Va.
James Blair, S.C.

Capt. Dove, Navy Yard
Starling Tucker, S.C.

Mr. Denny, Four and One-Half St., near City Hall
Jonathan Hunt, Vt.

Mrs. R. Dunn, near and North of the Capitol
George Poindexter (S), Miss.
Samuel P. Carson, N.C.
Warren R. Davis, S.C.
Dixon H. Lewis, Ala.
Jesse Speight, N.C.

Mr. Fletcher, E St., near General Post Office
Felix Grundy (S), Tenn.
William W. Ellsworth, Conn.
George Evans, Me.
George Grennell, Jr., Mass.
John Reed, Mass.
Joseph Richardson, Mass.

Mr. French, Corner F and Thirteenth St.
Benjamin C. Howard, Md.

Gadsby's, National Hotel, Penn. Ave.
Benjamin Gorham, Mass.
Joseph Hemphill, Penn.
Ephraim K. Wilson, Md.
Campbell P. White, N.Y.

Mrs. Galvin, C St., near Third
William Marks (S), Penn.
Benjamin Ruggles (S), Ohio
William Hendricks (S), Ind.
David Barton (S), Mo.

[2] Resigned Feb. 21, 1831.

Philip Doddridge, Va.
William Kennon, Ohio

Mr. Gibson, over Gowen and Jacobs,
  Seventh St.
Benedict Arnold, N.Y.
Thomas Beekman, N.Y.
Tristam Burges, R.I.
Henry R. Storrs, N.Y.
John Taliaferro, Va.
Lewis Condict, N.J.

Mr. Greer, Corner E and Ninth St.
Daniel Barringer, N.C.
Mordecai Bartley, Ohio
Chauncey Forward, Penn.
Alem Marr, Penn.
Lewis Maxwell, Va.

Mrs. Hamilton, Thirteenth St, between
  E and F St.
Calvin Willey (S), Conn.

Mr. Hamilton, C St., between Third and
  Four and One-Half St.
John Campbell, S.C.
Spencer Pettis, Mo.

Mr. Harbaugh, Seventh St. West, near E.
James Buchanan, Penn.
James Ford, Penn.
William W. Irvin, Ohio
Thomas Irwin, Penn.
George C. Leiper, Penn.
Philander Stephens, Penn.

Mr. Hill, Penn. Ave.
Henry Daniel, Ky.
Michael C. Sprigg, Md.
Charles A. Wickliffe, Ky.

Mr. Hyatt, opposite Brown's Hotel
Noyes Barber, Conn.
Samuel Butman, Me.
William Cahoon, Vt.
Jabez W. Huntington, Conn.
James L. Hodges, Mass.

Joseph G. Kendall, Mass.
Rollin C. Mallary, Vt.
William L. Storrs, Conn.
Benjamin Swift, Vt.
Ebenezer Young, Conn.
John Davis, Mass.

Mrs. Hungerford, Penn. Ave.
Charles F. Mercer, Va.
Ebenezer F. Norton, N.Y.
Robert S. Rose, N.Y.
Joseph F. Wingate, Me.

Mr. Hughes, Penn. Ave.
John Tyler (S), Va.
Robert Allen, Va.
Nicholas D. Coleman, Ky.
Henry W. Connor, N.C.
Thomas Davenport, Va.
Nathan Gaither, Ky.

Mrs. Judson, C St., near Third
John Bailey, Mass.

Mrs. James, F between Twelfth and
  Thirteenth St.
James Strong, N.Y.

Mr. Letourno, nearly opposite National
  Hotel
Clement Dorsey, Md.
Jonathan Jennings, Ind.
William D. Martin, S.C.
Richard H. Wilde, Ga.
Joseph M. White, Deleg., Terr. of Fla.

Mr. Lindsley, nearly opposite National
  Hotel
Robert W. Barnwell, S.C.

Mrs. Lanphier, Lenox's Row, Penn. Ave.
David J. Baker (S),[3] Ill.
Elias K. Kane (S), Ill.

Mrs. McCardle, near and Northeast of
  the Capitol
Richard M. Cooper, N.J.

---

[3] Appointed to fill the vacancy caused by the death of John McLean, and took his seat Dec. 6, 1830; subsequently replaced by John M. Robinson, who was elected to fill the vacancy caused by the death of John McLean and who took his seat Jan. 4, 1831.

Thomas H. Hughes, N.J.
Peter Ihrie, Jr., Penn.
Isaac Pierson, N.J.
Samuel Swan, N.J.

Mr. McLeod, nearly opposite Gadsby's
 Hotel
Nehemiah R. Knight (S), R.I.
Theodore Frelinghuysen (S), N.J.
James F. Randolph, N.J.
Phineas L. Tracy, N.Y.

Mrs. McDaniel, Penn. Ave.
Joseph Hammons, N.H.
Jonathan Harvey, N.H.
Innis Green, Penn.
John W. Weeks, N.H.

Mrs. McPherson, Thirteenth, between E
 and F St.
Thomas F. Foster, Ga.

Mrs. Miller, F St., between Thirteenth
 and Fourteenth
William Smith (S), S.C.
William S. Archer, Va.
James M. Wayne, Ga.

Mrs. Myer, Penn. Ave.
Isaac Finch, N.Y.
Joseph Fry, Jr., Penn.
John Gilmore, Penn.
Adam King, Penn.
Humphrey H. Leavitt, Ohio
William McCoy, Va.
William McCreery, Penn.
Henry A. Muhlenberg, Penn.
Samuel A. Smith, Penn.
John Thomson, Ohio

Mrs. Ann Peyton, Penn. Ave.
Mahlon Dickerson (S), N.J.
Littleton W. Tazewell (S), Va.
Bedford Brown (S), N.C.
James Iredell (S), N.C.
Hugh Lawson White (S), Tenn.
Powhatan Ellis (S), Miss.
Clement C. Clay, Ala.
James Findlay, Ohio

William F. Gordon, Va.
Pryor Lea, Tenn.
James K. Polk, Tenn.
John M. Patton, Va.
Gulian C. Verplanck, N.Y.

Mrs. Eliza Peyton, Penn. Ave.
Robert Y. Hayne (S), S.C.
George McDuffie, S.C.
William T. Nuckolls, S.C.
Walter H. Overton, La.
Edward D. White, La.

Mr. Poor, E St., above Unitarian Church
Levi Woodbury (S), N.H.
Henry Hubbard, N.H.

Mrs. Queen, Penn. Ave.
Abraham Bockee, N.Y.
Peter I. Borst, N.Y.
Jacob Crocheron, N.Y.
Jonas Earll, Jr., N.Y.
Jehiel H. Halsey, N.Y.
Michael Hoffman, N.Y.
Perkins King, N.Y.
James Lent, N.Y.
Robert Monell,[4] N.Y.
Gershom Powers, N.Y.
Jonah Sanford, N.Y.

Mrs. Runnell, Lenox Row, Penn. Ave.
George M. Troup (S), Ga.
Henry G. Lamar, Ga.

Mr. Sawkins, Penn. Ave.
Robert P. Letcher, Ky.

Mrs. Sawyer, Seventh St., near General
 Post Office
Dudley Chase (S), Vt.
Horatio Seymour (S), Vt.
Samuel W. Eager, N.Y.
Horace Everett, Vt.
Kensey Johns, Jr., Del.
Henry C. Martindale, N.Y.

Mr. Selden, N.J. Ave., Capitol Hill
George Loyall, Va.

[4] Resigned Feb. 21, 1831.

Mrs. Smith, Seventh near General Post
   Office
Daniel H. Miller, Penn.
John Scott, Penn.
Joel B. Sutherland, Penn.

Mr. Tims, near and South of the Capitol
John Anderson, Me.
Cornelius Holland, Me.
Leonard Jarvis, Me.
Rufus McIntire, Me.
George E. Mitchell, Md.

Mrs. Turner, Georgetown Heights
Augustine H. Shepperd, N.C.

Mrs. Wilson, F, near Twelfth St.
James Shields, Ohio

Mrs. Walker, Corner Ninth and E St.
Nathaniel Silsbee (S), Mass.
Thomas H. Crawford, Penn.

Harmar Denny, Penn.
Ambrose Spencer, N.Y.
Richard Spencer, Del.

Mr. Young, N.J. Ave., Capitol Hill
John Holmes (S), Me.
Samuel Bell (S), N.H.
Asher Robbins (S), R.I.
Samuel A. Foote (S), Conn.
John M. Clayton (S), N.J.
Arnold Naudain (S), N.J.
Elisha Whittlesey, Ohio

Private Residences
   Corner Eighth St., near Centre Market
John Varnum, Mass.
   Mr. Tayloe, near Executive Offices
John D. Dickinson, N.Y.
   Georgetown
George C. Washington, Md.
   Schoff's, Georgetown
John Forsyth (S), Ga.

APPENDIX

John Rowan, Ky.
Edmund Deberry, N.C.

Jacob C. Isacks, Tenn.
Thomas T. Bouldin, Va.

STANDING COMMITTEES OF THE HOUSE OF REPRESENTATIVES

ELECTIONS

Chairman: Willis Alston, N.C.
Starling Tucker, S.C.
Nathaniel H. Claiborne, Va.
James F. Randolph, N.J.

Cave Johnson, Tenn.
Thomas Beekman, N.Y.
Nicholas D. Coleman, Ky.

WAYS AND MEANS

Chairman: George McDuffie, S.C.
Gulian C. Verplanck, N.Y.
Henry W. Dwight, Mass.
Ralph I. Ingersoll, Conn.

John Gilmore, Penn.
Walter H. Overton, La.
Mark Alexander, Va.

CLAIMS

Chairman: Elisha Whittlesey, Ohio
Lewis Williams, N.C.
William McCoy, Va.
Noyes Barber, Conn.

Rufus McIntire, Me.
William Ramsey, Penn.
Pryor Lea, Tenn.

COMMERCE

Chairman: Churchill C. Cambreleng, N.Y.

Benjamin Gorham, Mass.
Jonathan Harvey, N.H.
Joel B. Sutherland, Penn.

Benjamin C. Howard, Md.
George Loyall, Va.
Henry G. Lamar, Ga.

PUBLIC LANDS

Chairman: Charles A. Wickliffe, Ky.

Jonathan Jennings, Ind.
Joseph Duncan, Ill.
Jonathan Hunt, Vt.

Robert Potter, N.C.
William W. Irvin, Ohio
Clement C. Clay, Ala.

POST OFFICE AND POST ROADS

Chairman: Richard M. Johnson, Ky.

Henry W. Connor, N.C.
John Magee, N.Y.
James L. Hodges, Mass.

William Russell, Ohio
William McCreery, Penn.
James Lent, N.Y.

DISTRICT OF COLUMBIA

Chairman: Gershom Powers, N.Y.

Robert Allen, Va.
George C. Washington, Md.
John Varnum, Mass.

John Taliaferro, Va.
Peter Ihrie, Jr., Penn.
Benedict J. Semmes, Md.

JUDICIARY

Chairman: James Buchanan, Penn.

Warren R. Davis, S.C.
William W. Ellsworth, Conn.
Henry Daniel, Ky.

Edward D. White, La.
Thomas F. Foster, Ga.
William F. Gordon, Va.

REVOLUTIONARY CLAIMS

Chairman: Tristam Burges, R.I.

John D. Dickinson, N.Y.
Joseph F. Wingate, Me.
Joel Yancey, Ky.[5]

Charles G. De Witt, N.Y.
Elias Brown, Md.
Joseph H. Crane, Ohio

PUBLIC EXPENDITURES

Chairman: Thomas H. Hall, N.C.

Thomas Davenport, Va.
Chittenden Lyon, Ky.
Jehiel H. Halsey, N.Y.

Richard Spencer, Md.
John Thomson, Ohio
Ebenezer F. Norton, N.Y.

---

[5] The *Journal of the House of Representatives* lists Ebenezer Young (Conn.) in lieu of Joel Yancey (Ky.).

PRIVATE LAND CLAIMS

Chairman: John B. Sterigere, Penn.

William T. Nuckolls, S.C.   Harmar Denny, Penn.
Spencer D. Pettis, Mo.   Edward B. Dudley, N.C.
Robert E. B. Baylor, Ala.   Joseph Draper, Va.

MANUFACTURES

Chairman: Rollin C. Mallary, Vt.

William Stanbery, Ohio   Robert Monell, N.Y.
Lewis Condict, N.J.   John S. Barbour, Va.
Thomas Irwin, Penn.   Jabez W. Huntington, Conn.

INDIAN AFFAIRS

Chairman: John Bell, Tenn.

Wilson Lumpkin, Ga.   Henry Hubbard, N.H.
Thomas Hinds, Miss.   Nathan Gaither, Ky.
William L. Storrs, Conn.   Dixon H. Lewis, Ala.

FOREIGN AFFAIRS

Chairman: William S. Archer, Va.

Edward Everett, Mass.   Thomas H. Crawford, Penn.
John W. Taylor, N.Y.   Robert W. Barnwell, S.C.
James K. Polk, Tenn.   James M. Wayne, Ga.

MILITARY AFFAIRS

Chairman: William Drayton, S.C.

Joseph Vance, Ohio   James Blair, S.C.
Robert Desha, Tenn.   George E. Mitchell, Md.
James Findlay, Ohio   Jesse Speight, N.C.

NAVAL AFFAIRS

Chairman: Michael Hoffman, N.Y.

Benjamin W. Crowninshield, Mass.   Clement Dorsey, Md.
Daniel H. Miller, Penn.   Campbell P. White, N.Y.
Samuel P. Carson, N.C.   John Anderson, Me.

AGRICULTURE

Chairman: Ambrose Spencer, N.Y.

John Roane, Va.   Samuel A. Smith, Penn.
Ephraim K. Wilson, Md.   James Standifer, Tenn.
Robert S. Rose, N.Y.   Thomas Chandler, N.H.

TERRITORIES

Chairman: James Clark, Ky.

James Strong, N.Y.   William G. Angel, N.Y.
William Creighton, Jr., Ohio   Henry B. Cowles, N.Y.
William Armstrong, Va.   William B. Shepard, N.C.

MILITARY PENSIONS

Chairman: James Trezvant, Va.

Joseph Lecompte, Ky.   Abraham Bockee, N.Y.
Thomas Chilton, Ky.   James Ford, Penn.
Joseph Hammons, N.H.   Samuel Butman, Me.

REVISAL AND UNFINISHED BUSINESS

Chairman: Dutee J. Pearce, R.I.

John Reed, Mass.   Isaac Pierson, N.J.

ACCOUNTS

Chairman: Thomas Maxwell, N.Y.

Samuel Swan, N.J.   John Brodhead, N.H.

ON EXPENDITURES IN THE DEPARTMENT OF STATE

Chairman: Jonas Earll, Jr., N.Y.

Thomas H. Sill, Penn.   Perkins King, N.Y.

ON EXPENDITURES IN THE DEPARTMENT OF THE TREASURY

Chairman: George C. Leiper, Penn.

Jacob Crocheron, N.Y.   Joseph G. Kendall, Mass.

ON EXPENDITURES IN THE DEPARTMENT OF WAR

Chairman: Lewis Maxwell, Va.

Henry A. P. Muhlenberg, Penn.   David Crockett, Tenn.

ON EXPENDITURES IN THE DEPARTMENT OF THE NAVY

Chairman: Augustine H. Shepperd, N.C.

Mordecai Bartley, Ohio   Joshua Evans, Jr., Penn.

ON EXPENDITURES IN THE POST OFFICE DEPARTMENT

Chairman: Joel Yancey, Ky.

Peter I. Borst, N.Y.   John Scott, Penn.

ON EXPENDITURES ON THE PUBLIC BUILDINGS

Chairman: Michael C. Sprigg, Md.

John Bailey, Mass.   Benjamin Swift, Vt.

SELECT COMMITTEES

ON INTERNAL IMPROVEMENTS

Chairman: Joseph Hemphill, Penn.

Charles F. Mercer, Va.	Robert P. Letcher, Ky.
John Blair, Tenn.	Samuel F. Vinton, Ohio
Charles E. Haynes, Ga.	Robert Craig, Va.

ON DISTRIBUTION OF SURPLUS REVENUE

Chairman: James K. Polk, Tenn.

John M. Patton, Va.	Leonard Jarvis, Me.
Joseph Fry, Jr., Penn.	Humphrey H. Leavitt, Ohio
Jonas Earll, Jr., N.Y.	George Evans, Me.

AMENDMENTS OF CONSTITUTION

Chairman: George McDuffie, S.C.

Richard Coke, Jr., Va.	Thomas H. Hughes, N.J.
Jonah Sanford, N.Y.	Innis Green, Penn.
Philander Stephens, Penn.	Abraham Rencher, N.C.

ON ENROLLED BILLS

Joseph Richardson, Mass.	James Shields, Ohio

JOINT COMMITTEE

LIBRARY OF CONGRESS

House	Senate
Edward Everett, Mass.	Asher Robbins, R.I.
Gulian C. Verplanck, N.Y.	Levi Woodbury, N.H.
James M. Wayne, Ga.	Theodore Frelinghuysen, N.J.

STANDING COMMITTEES OF THE SENATE

FOREIGN AFFAIRS

Chairman: Littleton W. Tazewell, Va.

Nathan Sanford, N.Y.	Samuel Bell, N.H.
Hugh Lawson White, Tenn.	William R. King, Ala.

FINANCE

Chairman: Samuel Smith, Md.

William Smith, S.C.	William R. King, Ala.
Nathaniel Silsbee, Mass.	Josiah S. Johnston, La.

COMMERCE
Chairman: Levi Woodbury, N.H.
Josiah S. Johnston, La.   Nathan Sanford, N.Y.
Nathaniel Silsbee, Mass.   John Forsyth, Ga.

MANUFACTURES
Chairman: Mahlon Dickerson, N.J.
Benjamin Ruggles, Ohio   Horatio Seymour, Vt.
Nehemiah R. Knight, R.I.   .   George M. Bibb, Ky.

AGRICULTURE
Chairman: William Marks, Penn.
Calvin Willey, Conn.   Bedford Brown, N.C.
James Noble, Ind.   Horatio Seymour, Vt.

MILITARY AFFAIRS
Chairman: Thomas H. Benton, Mo.
Isaac D. Barnard, Penn.   Arnold Naudain, Del.
George M. Troup, Ga.   James Iredell, N.C.

MILITIA
Chairman: Isaac D. Barnard, Penn.
Theodore Frelinghuysen, N.J.   James Noble, Ind.
John M. Clayton, Del.   George M. Bibb, Ky.

NAVAL AFFAIRS
Chairman: Robert Y. Hayne, S.C.
Littleton W. Tazewell, Va.   Edward Livingston, La.
Asher Robbins, R.I.   Daniel Webster, Mass.

PUBLIC LANDS
Chairman: David Barton, Mo.
John McKinley, Ala.   Powhatan Ellis, Miss.
Elias K. Kane, Ill.   Peleg Sprague, Me.

PRIVATE LAND CLAIMS
Chairman: Elias K. Kane, Ill.
Jacob Burnet, Ohio   Felix Grundy, Tenn.
George Poindexter, Miss.   Arnold Naudain, Del.

INDIAN AFFAIRS
Chairman: Hugh Lawson White, Tenn.
George M. Troup, Ga.   Charles E. Dudley, N.Y.
Williams Hendricks, Ind.   Thomas H. Benton, Mo.

CLAIMS

Chairman: Benjamin Ruggles, Ohio

Samuel Bell, N.H.
Dudley Chase, Vt.

Samuel A. Foote, Conn.
Bedford Brown, N.C.

JUDICIARY

Chairman: John Rowan, Ky.

John McKinley, Ala.
Daniel Webster, Mass.

Robert Y. Hayne, S.C.
Theodore Frelinghuysen, N.J.

POST OFFICE AND POST ROADS

Chairman: Felix Grundy, Tenn.

Jacob Burnet, Ohio
John Forsyth, Ga.

Powhatan Ellis, Miss.
Horatio Seymour, Vt.

ROADS AND CANALS

Chairman: William Hendricks, Ind.

John Tyler, Va.
Benjamin Ruggles, Ohio

Charles E. Dudley, N.Y.
George Poindexter, Miss.

PENSIONS

Chairman: Samuel A. Foote, Conn.

John Holmes, Me.
William Marks, Penn.

Dudley Chase, Vt.
Ezekiel F. Chambers, Md.

DISTRICT OF COLUMBIA

Chairman: Ezekiel F. Chambers, Md.

John Tyler, Va.
John Holmes, Me.

John M. Clayton, Del.
Peleg Sprague, Me.

AUDIT AND CONTROL THE CONTINGENT FUND

Chairman: James Iredell, N.C.

David J. Baker, Ill.

Nehemiah R. Knight, R.I.

ENGROSSED BILLS

Chairman: William Marks, Penn.

Calvin Willey, Conn.

David J. Baker, Ill.

SELECT COMMITTEES

ON THE STATE OF CURRENT COINS

Chairman: Nathan Sanford, N.Y.

Mahlon Dickerson, N.J.
James Iredell, N.C.

Levi Woodbury, N.H.
John M. Clayton, Del.

ON THE FRENCH SPOLIATIONS PRIOR TO SEPTEMBER, 1800

Chairman: Edward Livingston, La.

Ezekiel F. Chambers, Md.　　　　Nathan Sanford, N.Y.
Nathaniel Silsbee, Mass.　　　　John Holmes, Me.

ON SURPLUS REVENUES OF THE UNITED STATES

Chairman: Mahlon Dickerson, N.J.

Nathan Sanford, N.Y.　　　　Horatio Seymour, Vt.
Levi Woodbury, N.H.　　　　Felix Grundy, Tenn.

ON THE PRESENT CONDITION OF THE POST OFFICE

Chairman: John M. Clayton, Del.

Felix Grundy, Tenn.　　　　Levi Woodbury, N.H.
John Holmes, Me.　　　　William Hendricks, Ind.

CONGRESSIONAL DIRECTORY

TWENTY-SECOND CONGRESS, FIRST SESSION
(December 5, 1831–July 16, 1832)

Mr. J. Adams, near St John's Church
John Quincy Adams, Mass.

Mrs. Arguelles, Penn. Ave.
Thomas F. Foster, Ga.
Thomas T. Bouldin, Va.
Charles C. Johnston,[1] Va.
Henry G. Lamar, Ga.
Abraham Rencher, N.C.
Ambrose H. Sevier, Deleg., Ark. Terr.
William T. Nuckolls, S.C.

Mrs. Ball, nearly opposite Brown's Hotel
Nathaniel H. Claiborne, Va.
James Blair, S.C.
Robert Craig, Va.
Lewis Dewart, Penn.
James Ford, Penn.
Joseph Lecompte, Ky.
John J. Roane, Va.
Thomas R. Mitchell, S.C.
Joseph W. Chinn, Va.

Mrs. Blake, opposite Centre Market
Ezekiel F. Chambers (S), Md.
William B. Shepard, N.C.
Thomas H. Crawford, Penn.
Harmar Denny, Penn.
John G. Watmough, Penn.

Mrs. Barnes, Penn. Ave.
Alexander Buckner (S), Mo.
Felix Grundy (S), Tenn.
Chittenden Lyon, Ky.
John Blair, Tenn.
James Standifer, Tenn.
Ratliff Boon, Ind.

John Carr, Ind.
William Hall, Tenn.
Jacob C. Isacks, Tenn.
Cave Johnson, Tenn.
Johnathan McCarty, Ind.
Wiley Thompson, Ga.

Barnard's Hotel, Penn. Ave.
Charles E. Dudley (S), N.Y.
Josiah S. Johnston (S), La.
Edward Everett, Mass.
Edmund H. Pendleton, N.Y.
Campbell P. White, N.Y.

Mr. Ballard, Penn. Ave.
Jonathan Hunt,[2] Vt.

Mr. Brodhead, Capitol Hill
John Brodhead, N.H.
Thomas Chandler, N.H.

Mrs. Brannan, Penn. Ave.
Grattan H. Wheeler, N.Y.
Daniel Wardwell, N.Y.
Freeborn G. Jewett, N.Y.
John King, N.Y.
Samuel Beardsley, N.Y.
Charles Dayan, N.Y.
Job Pierson, N.Y.
Gerrit Y. Lansing, N.Y.

Brown's Hotel, Penn. Ave.
Andrew Stevenson, Va.
Nathaniel Pitcher, N.Y.
Philander Stephens, Penn.
William H. Ashley, Mo.

[1] Died June 17, 1832.
[2] Died May 14, 1832.

240

Rev. O. B. Brown, near the General Post Office
John M. Robinson (S), Ill.
Richard M. Johnson, Ky.
William Fitzgerald, Tenn.
Albert G. Hawes, Ky.

Mrs. Cochrane, F St.
Thomas Newton, Jr., Va.
Richard Coke, Jr., Va.

Mr. Coburn, F St.
William S. Archer, Va.

Mrs. Clement, opposite Mansion Hotel
George M. Dallas (S),[3] Penn.

Mrs. Burke, F St.
William G. Angel, N.Y.
John T. Bergen, N.Y.
James Bates, Me.
Joseph Bouck, N.Y.
John C. Brodhead, N.Y.
Michael Hoffman, N.Y.
James Lent, N.Y.
Edward C. Reed, N.Y.
Nathan Soule, N.Y.

Mrs. Coyle, Capitol Hill
Henry A. Bullard, La.
John J. Milligan, Del.

Mr. J. Davis, C St., opposite the Circus
Thomas Ewing (S), Ohio
William Armstrong, Va.
Chilton Allan, Ky.
Robert Allison, Penn.
Joseph H. Crane, Ohio
Thomas Corwin, Ohio
Lewis Williams, N.C.
Samuel F. Vinton, Ohio
William Russell, Ohio
Joseph Vance, Ohio
William Creighton, Jr., Ohio
George Burd, Penn.
Christopher Tompkins, Ky.

Mr. Denny, Four and One-Half St., near the City Hall
James M. Wayne, Ga.

Mr. Dowson's, No. 1, near the Capitol
Samuel Smith (S), Md.
Willie P. Mangum (S), N.C.
William R. King (S), Ala.
Thomas H. Benton (S), Mo.
John S. Barbour, Va.
Cornelius Holland, Me.
George E. Mitchell,[4] Md.
Rufus McIntire, Me.

Mr. Dowson's, No. 2, near the Capitol
Thomas H. Hall, N.C.
Mark Alexander, Va.

Mr. Ditty, C St.
George M. Troup (S), Ga.

Mrs. Dunn, near the Capitol
George Poindexter (S), Miss.
Samuel P. Carson, N.C.
Warren R. Davis, S.C.
Dixon H. Lewis, Ala.

Mr. Fletcher, E St., near General Post Office
Samuel Prentiss (S), Vt.
Horace Everett, Vt.
Joseph G. Kendall, Mass.
George Grennell, Jr., Mass.
George Evans, Me.
George N. Briggs, Mass.
John Reed, Mass.
Samuel J. Wilkin, N.Y.

Mrs. French, Corner F and Fourteenth St.
Benjamin C. Howard, Md.
Francis Thomas, Md.
John T. H. Worthington, Md.

Gadsby's Hotel, Penn. Ave.
Nathaniel Silsbee (S), Mass.
Bedford Brown (S), N.C.

---

[3] Elected to fill the vacancy caused by the resignation of Isaac D. Barnard, and took his seat Dec. 21, 1831.
[4] Died June 28, 1832.

Daniel Webster (S), Mass.
Nathan Appleton, Mass.

Mrs. Galvin, C St.
William Hendricks (S), Ind.
Robert Hanna (S),[5] Ind.
Benjamin Ruggles (S), Ohio
Philip Doddridge, Va.
William Kennon, Sr., Ohio

Mr. Greer, near General Post Office
Daniel L. Barringer, N.C.
Lauchlin Bethune, N.C.

Mr. Handy, Penn. Ave.
John S. Spence, Md.

Mrs. Handy, Thirteenth St., near F.
Aaron Ward, N.Y.
Austin E. Wing, Deleg., Mich. Terr.

Mr. Hobbie, C St.
Erastus Root, N.Y.

Mr. Harbaugh, Seventh St., near General
  Post Office
William W. Irvin, Ohio
Richard Coulter, Penn.
John Banks, Penn.
Andrew Stewart, Penn.
Robert McCoy, Penn.
Thomas M. T. McKennan, Penn.

Mr. S. S. Hamilton, C St. North
Joel B. Sutherland, Penn.
Henry King, Penn.
David Potts, Jr., Penn.

Mr. Hughes, opposite Brown's Hotel
John Tyler (S), Va.
Robert Allen, Va.
Henry W. Connor, N.C.
William McCoy, Va.
Thomas Davenport, Va.

Mrs. Hungerford, Penn. Ave., near the
  Tiber Bridge
Charles F. Mercer, Va.
Daniel Newnan, Ga.

Mr. Hyatt, Penn. Ave.
Jabez W. Huntington, Conn.
Noyes Barber, Conn.
William L. Storrs, Conn.
William Cahoon, Vt.
John Davis, Mass.
Ebenezer Young, Conn.
Eleutheros Cooke, Ohio
Dutee J. Pearce, R.I.

Mrs. Ironside, Seventh St.
John Branch, N.C.

Mrs. Judson, C St., near the City Hall
Robert W. Barnwell S.C.

Mrs. Kennedy, Third St.
Isaac Hill (S), N.H.
William L. Marcy (S), N.Y.
Ulysses F. Doubleday, N.Y.
Joseph M. Harper, N.H.

Mr. Kane, Eleventh St., North of F
Elias K. Kane (S), Ill.

Mrs. King, Penn. Ave.
George M. Bibb (S), Ky.
Henry Daniel, Ky.
Charles A. Wickliffe, Ky.

Mr. Keyworth, Penn. Ave.
Isaac C. Bates, Mass.

Mr. Letourno, nearly opposite Gadsby's
  Hotel
Franklin E. Plummer, Miss.

Mr. Lindsley, Penn. Ave.
Lewis Condict, N.J.
Silas Condit, N.J.

Mrs. Meyer, Penn. Ave.
Adam King, Penn.
John Gilmore, Penn.
Henry A. P. Muhlenberg, Penn.
John Thomson, Ohio
William Hiester, Penn.
Philemon Thomas, La.
Humphrey H. Leavitt, Ohio

[5] Appointed to fill the vacancy caused by the death of James Noble, and took his seat Dec. 5, 1831. Subsequently John Tipton was elected to fill the vacancy caused by the death of James Noble, and took his seat Jan. 3, 1832.

Samuel A. Smith, Penn.
John C. Bucher, Penn.
Henry Horn, Penn.

Mr. McLeod, opposite Centre Market
Nehemiah R. Knight (S), R.I.
Gideon Tomlinson (S), Conn.
Theodore Frelinghuysen, N.J.
James F. Randolph, N.J.
Isaac Southard, N.J.
Phineas L. Tracy, N.Y.
Tristam Burges, R.I.

Mrs. Miller, F St.
Churchill C. Cambreleng, N.Y.
William Drayton, S.C.

Mrs. McCardle, Capitol Hill
Gabriel Moore (S), Ala.
John Anderson, Me.
Peter Ihrie, Jr., Penn.
Richard M. Cooper, N.J.
Joel K. Mann, Penn.
Thomas H. Hughes, N.J.
Edward Kavanagh, Me.

Mrs. McDaniel, Penn. Ave.
Clement C. Clay, Ala.
Samuel W. Mardis, Ala.
John Y. Mason, Va.
Jesse Speight, N.C.

Mrs. Purcell, opposite Brown's Hotel
Nathan Gaither, Ky.

Poor's, E St., near the City Hall
John W. Weeks, N.H.
Henry Hubbard, N.H.
Joseph Hammons, N.H.

Mrs. Ann Peyton, Penn. Ave.
Hugh Lawson White (S), Tenn.
Mahlon Dickerson (S), N.J.
Littleton W. Tazewell (S), Va.
James Findlay, Ohio
Gulian C. Verplanck, N.Y.
John Bell, Tenn.
James K. Polk, Tenn.
William F. Gordon, Va.
Joseph Duncan, Ill.
John M. Patton, Va.
Leonard Jarvis, Me.

Mrs. Eliza Peyton, Penn. Ave.
Robert Y. Hayne (S), S.C.
Stephen D. Miller (S), S.C.
John K. Griffin, S.C.
George McDuffie, S.C.
John M. Felder, S.C.
Edward D. White, La.

Mrs. Polk, Thirteenth St.
William Wilkins (S), Penn.

Mrs. Queen, Penn. Ave.
John Dickson, N.Y.
Bates Cooke, N.Y.
Frederick Whittlesey, N.Y.
Thomas D. Arnold, Tenn.
William Stanbery, Ohio
William Slade, Vt.
John W. Taylor, N.Y.
Lewis Maxwell, Va.

Mrs. Read, Corner of C and Third St.
John A. Collier, N.Y.
Gamaliel H. Barstow, N.Y.
William Babcock, N.Y.
Ralph I. Ingersoll, Conn.

Mrs. Sawyer, Seventh St., near General Post Office
Horatio Seymour (S), Vt.
Peleg Sprague (S), Me.
Joshua Evans, Jr., Penn.

Sawkin's, Penn. Ave.
Robert P. Letcher, Ky.

Dr. Sewall, Penn. Ave.
Rufus Choate, Mass.

Mr. N. Smith, Seventh St., near General Post Office
Henry Clay (S), Ky.
Thomas A. Marshall, Ky.
Daniel Jenifer, Md.

R. Semmes, Georgetown
Benedict J. Semmes, Md.

A. Shaaff, Georgetown
John Forsyth (S), Ga.

Mrs. Turner, Georgetown
Augustine H. Shepperd, Va.

Mrs. Walker, Corner of E and Ninth St.
Henry A. S. Dearborn, Mass.
William W. Ellsworth, Conn.

Washington House, Capitol Hill
John Adair, Ky.
Joseph M. White, Deleg., Terr. of Fla.
Richard H. Wilde, Ga.

Mr. Winn's, Navy Yard
Powhatan Ellis (S), Miss.

Young's, N.J. Ave., Capitol Hill
Samuel Bell (S), N.H.

John Holmes (S), Me.
Samuel A. Foote (S), Conn.
Arnold Naudain (S), Del.
Asher Robbins (S), R.I.
Elisha Whittlesey, Ohio

Private Residences
 F St., near the Catholic Church
William Hogan, N.Y.
 C St., between Third and Four and
 One-Half
John L. Kerr, Md.
 Georgetown
George C. Washington, Md.

APPENDIX

John M. Clayton (S), Del.
Augustin S. Clayton,[6] Ga.
George A. Waggaman (S),[7] La.
James L. Hodges, Mass.

Jeremiah Nelson, Mass.
Micajah T. Hawkins,[8] N.C.
James I. McKay, N.C.
Heman Allen, Vt.

STANDING COMMITTEES OF THE
HOUSE OF REPRESENTATIVES

ELECTIONS

Chairman: Nathaniel H. Claiborne, Va.

James F. Randolph, N.J.
John K. Griffin, S.C.
John A. Collier, N.Y.

Cornelius Holland, Me.
Lauchlin Bethune, Me.
Thomas D. Arnold, Tenn.

WAYS AND MEANS

Chairman: George McDuffie, S.C.

Gulian C. Verplanck, N.Y.
John Gilmore, Penn.
Richard H. Wilde, Ga.

Ralph I. Ingersoll
Mark Alexander, Va.
Nathan Gaither, Ky.

CLAIMS

Chairman: Elisha Whittlesey, Ohio

Noyes Barber, Conn.
John M. Patton, Va.
William Hogan, N.Y.

Rufus McIntire, Me.
Peter Ihrie, Jr., Penn.
Abraham Rencher, N.C.

---

[6] Elected to fill the vacancy caused by the resignation of Wilson Lumpkin, and took his seat Jan. 21, 1832.

[7] Elected to fill the vacancy caused by the resignation of Edward Livingston, and took his seat Jan. 3, 1832.

[8] Elected to fill the vacancy caused by the resignation of Robert Potter, and took his seat Jan. 6, 1832.

COMMERCE

Chairman: Churchill C. Cambreleng, N.Y.

Benjamin C. Howard, Md.   Leonard Jarvis, Me.
Joel B. Sutherland, Penn.   Henry G. Lamar, Ga.
Thomas Newton, Jr., Va.   John Davis, Mass.

PUBLIC LANDS

Chairman: Charles A. Wickliffe, Ky.

Joseph Duncan, Ill.   Jonathan Hunt, Vt.
William W. Irvin, Ohio   Clement C. Clay, Ala.
Ratliff Boon, Ind.   Franklin E. Plummer, Miss.

POST OFFICE AND POST ROADS

Chairman: Richard M. Johnson, Ky.

Henry W. Connor, N.C.   William Russell, Ohio
Dutee J. Pearce, R.I.   Freeborn G. Jewett, N.Y.
Charles C. Johnston, Va.   Daniel Newnan, Ga.

DISTRICT OF COLUMBIA

Chairman: Philip Doddridge, Va.

George C. Washington, Md.   Benedict J. Semmes, Md.
William Armstrong, Va.   Francis Thomas, Md.
Robert McCoy, Penn.   Joseph W. Chinn, Va.

JUDICIARY

Chairman: Warren R. Davis, S.C.

William W. Ellsworth, Conn.   Henry Daniel, Ky.
Edward D. White, La.   Thomas F. Foster, Ga.
William F. Gordon, Va.   Samuel Beardsley, N.Y.

REVOLUTIONARY CLAIMS

Chairman: Henry A. P. Muhlenberg, Penn.

William T. Nuckolls, S.C.   Thomas T. Bouldin, Va.
Joseph H. Carne, Ohio   Isaac C. Bates, Mass.
Joseph Hammons, N.H.   James Standifer, Tenn.

PUBLIC EXPENDITURES

Chairman: Thomas H. Hall, N.C.

Thomas Davenport, Va.   Chittenden Lyon, Ky.
John Thomson, Ohio   Richard Coulter, Penn.
Job Pierson, N.Y.   Henry King, Penn.

PRIVATE LAND CLAIMS

Chairman: Cave Johnson, Tenn.

Richard Coke, Jr., Va.   William Stanbery, Ohio
Samuel W. Mardis, Ala.   Thomas A. Marshall, Ky.
John Carr, Ind.   Henry A. Bullard, La.

MANUFACTURES

Chairman: John Quincy Adams, Mass.

Lewis Condict, N.J.
Henry Horn, Penn.
John T. H. Worthington, Md.

James Findlay, Ohio
Charles Dayan, N.Y.
John S. Barbour, Va.

AGRICULTURE

Chairman: Erastus Root, N.Y.

William McCoy, Va.
Thomas Chandler, N.H.
Grattan H. Wheeler, N.Y.

Samuel A. Smith, Penn.
Daniel Jenifer, Md.
Christopher Tompkins, Ky.

INDIAN AFFAIRS

Chairman: John Bell, Tenn.

Dixon H. Lewis, Ala.
William G. Angel, N.Y.
John Y. Mason, Va.

Wiley Thompson, Ga.
William L. Storrs, Conn.
Joseph Lecompte, Ky.

MILITARY AFFAIRS

Chairman: William Drayton, S.C.

Joseph Vance, Ohio
George E. Mitchell, Md.
John Adair, Ky.

James Blair, S.C.
Jesse Speight, N.C.
Aaron Ward, N.Y.

NAVAL AFFAIRS

Chairman: Michael Hoffman, N.Y.

Samuel P. Carson, N.C.
John Anderson, Me.
John J. Milligan, Del.

Campbell, P. White, N.Y.
John Branch, N.C.
John G. Watmough, Penn.

FOREIGN AFFAIRS

Chairman: William S. Archer, Va.

Edward Everett, Mass.
James K. Polk, Tenn.
Robert W. Barnwell, S.C.

John W. Taylor, N.Y.
Thomas H. Crawford, Penn.
James M. Wayne, Ga.

TERRITORIES

Chairman: John L. Kerr, Md.

William Creighton, Jr., Ohio
Lewis Williams, N.C.
Chilton Allan, Ky.

William B. Shepard, N.C.
Jabez W. Huntington, Conn.
John J. Roane, Va.

REVOLUTIONARY PENSIONS
Chairman: Henry Hubbard, N.H.

Thomas R. Mitchell, S.C.   Harmar Denny, Penn.
Edmund H. Pendleton, N.Y.   Ulysses F. Doubleday, N.Y.
Edward Kavanagh, Me.   Jacob C. Isacks, Tenn.[9]

INVALID CLAIMS
Chairman: Tristam Burgess, R.I.

James Ford, Penn.   George Evans, Me.
Edward C. Reed, N.Y.   Nathan Appleton, Mass.
Gerrit Y. Lansing, N.Y.   Isaac Southard, N.J.

REVISAL AND UNFINISHED BUSINESS
Chairman: John Reed, Mass.

William Kennon, Ohio   Nathan Soule, N.Y.

ACCOUNTS
Chairman: Robert Allen, Va.

George Burd, Penn.   John T. Bergen, N.Y.

ON EXPENDITURES IN THE DEPARTMENT OF STATE
Chairman: James Lent, N.Y.

Joshua Evans, Jr., Penn.   James I. McKay, N.C.

ON EXPENDITURES IN THE TREASURY DEPARTMENT
Chairman: Philander Stephens, Penn.

Daniel Wardwell, N.Y.   William Fitzgerald, Tenn.

ON EXPENDITURES IN THE WAR DEPARTMENT
Chairman: Augustine H. Sheppard, N.C.

Joel K. Mann, Penn.   John M. Felder, S.C.

ON EXPENDITURES IN THE NAVY DEPARTMENT
Chairman: Lewis Maxwell, Va.

William Hall, Tenn.   Joseph M. Harper, N.H.

ON EXPENDITURES IN THE POST OFFICE DEPARTMENT
Chairman: Albert G. Hawes, Ky.

James Bates, Me.   John C. Brodhead, N.Y.

[9] Omitted in the *Congressional Directory* but listed in the *Journal of the House of Representatives*.

ON EXPENDITURES ON THE PUBLIC BUILDINGS
Chairman: Ebenezer Young, Conn.

John S. Spence, Md.   Phineas L. Tracy, N.Y.

SELECT COMMITTEES

RATIO OF REPRESENTATION UNDER THE FIFTH CENSUS
Chairman: James K. Polk, Tenn.

Cornelius Holland, Me.   John Thomson, Ohio
John King, N.Y.   Philemon Thomas, La.
Gamaliel H. Barstow, N.Y.   John C. Bucher, Penn.

ON INTERNAL IMPROVEMENTS
Chairman: Charles F. Mercer, Va.

John Blair, Tenn.   Robert P. Letcher, Ky.
Samuel F. Vinton, Ohio   Robert Craig, Va.
Humphrey H. Leavitt, Ohio   Johnathan McCarty, Ind.

ON THE SUBJECT OF PATENTS
Chairman: John W. Taylor, N.Y.

Rufus Choate, Mass.   Thomas Corwin, Ohio
David Potts, Jr., Penn.   Samuel J. Wilkin, N.Y.
Silas Condit, N.J.   John Banks, Penn.

IMPRISONMENT FOR DEBT
Chairman: Cave Johnson, Tenn.

Richard M. Cooper, N.J.   Thomas M. T. McKennan, Penn.
Joseph Bouck, N.Y.   Eleutheros Cooke, Ohio
Lewis Dewart, Penn.   Frederick Whittlesey, N.Y.

ON THE MILITIA
Chairman: Daniel L. Barringer, N.C.

Adam King, Penn.   John W. Weeks, N.H.
Nathaniel Pitcher, N.Y.   Henry A. S. Dearborn, Mass.
William Cahoon, Vt.   Andrew Stewart, Penn.

ON THE MEMORIAL OF THE NEW ENGLAND ASYLUM FOR THE BLIND
Chairman: Edward Everett, Mass.

Joseph G. Kendall, Mass.   John Dickson, N.Y.
Horace Everett, Vt.   George N. Briggs, Mass.
Bates Cooke, N.Y.   William Hiester, Penn.

ON THE SYSTEM OF KEEPING PUBLIC ACCOUNTS
Chairman: James M. Wayne, Ga.

Campbell P. White, N.Y.
George Grennell, Jr., Mass.
William Babcock, N.Y.

Thomas Davenport, Va.
William B. Shepard, N.C.
William Slade, Vt.

ON THE SUBJECT OF PRESIDENT, VICE PRESIDENT, ETC.
Chairman: George McDuffie, S.C.

Erastus Root, N.Y.
John Adair, Ky.
Wiley Thompson, Ga.

William McCoy, Va.
Thomas H. Hughes, N.J.
Francis Thomas, Md.

MEMORIAL OF THE STATE OF VIRGINIA FOR AN ADJUSTMENT OF THE CLAIMS OF HER CITIZENS FOR CERTAIN REVOLUTIONARY SERVICES
Chairman: John S. Barbour, Va.

William T. Nuckolls, S.C.
George Burd, Penn.
John King, N.Y.

Joseph Kendall, Mass.
Augustine H. Shepperd, N.C.
Thomas A. Marshall, Ky.

ON THE MEMORIAL OF TRANSYLVANIA UNIVERSITY
Chairman: Chilton Allan, Ky.

Richard M. Johnson, Ky.
William W. Ellsworth, Conn.

Tristam Burgess, R.I.
Rufus Choate, Mass.

JOINT COMMITTEE

LIBRARY OF CONGRESS

House
Edward Everett, Mass.
Gulian C. Verplanck, N.Y.
James M. Wayne, Ga.

Senate
Asher Robbins, R.I.
Theodore Frelinghuysen, N.J.
George Poindexter, Miss.

STANDING COMMITTEES OF THE SENATE

FOREIGN RELATIONS
Chairman: Littleton W. Tazewell, Va.

Hugh Lawson White, Tenn.
John Forsyth, Ga.

William R. King, Ala.
Samuel Bell, N.H.

FINANCE

Chairman: Samuel Smith, Md.

John Tyler, Va.
Nathaniel Silsbee, Mass.

William L. Marcy, N.Y.
Josiah S. Johnston, La.

COMMERCE

Chairman: John Forsyth, Ga.

Charles E. Dudley, N.Y.
Josiah S. Johnston, La.

Nathaniel Silsbee, Mass.
William Wilkins, Penn.

MANUFACTURES

Chairman: Mahlon Dickerson, N.J.

Henry Clay, Ky.
Stephen D. Miller, S.C.

Nehemiah R. Knight, R.I.
Horatio Seymour, Vt.

AGRICULTURE

Chairman: Horatio Seymour, Vt.

Bedford Brown, N.C.
Robert Hanna, Ind.

Gabriel Moore, Ala.
George A. Waggaman, La.

MILITARY AFFAIRS

Chairman: Thomas H. Benton, Mo.

Isaac D. Barnard, Penn.[10]
Henry Clay, Ky.

George M. Troup, Ga.
Elias K. Kane, Ill.

MILITIA

Chairman: Isaac D. Barnard, Penn.

Theodore Frelinghuysen, N.J.
Samuel Prentiss, Vt.

John M. Clayton, Del.
George A. Waggaman, La.

NAVAL AFFAIRS

Chairman: Robert Y. Hayne, S.C.

Littleton W. Tazewell, Va.
Daniel Webster, Mass.

Asher Robbins, R.I.
George M. Bibb, Ky.

PUBLIC LANDS

Chairman: William R. King, Ala.

Powhatan Ellis, Miss.
John M. Robinson, Ill.

John Holmes, Me.
Robert Hanna, Ind.

[10] Omitted in the *Congressional Directory* but listed in the *Journal of the Senate of the United States*.

PRIVATE LAND CLAIMS
Chairman: Elias K. Kane, Ill.
Arnold Naudian, Del.   Samuel Prentiss, Vt.
Benjamin Ruggles, Ohio   William Hendricks, Ind.

INDIAN AFFAIRS
Chairman: Hugh Lawson White, Tenn.
George M. Troup, Ga.   George Poindexter, Miss.
William Wilkins, Penn.   Thomas H. Benton, Mo.

CLAIMS
Chairman: Benjamin Ruggles, Ohio
Samuel Bell, N.H.   Arnold Naudain, Del.
Bedford Brown, N.C.   Gabriel Moore, Ala.

JUDICIARY
Chairman: William L. Marcy, N.Y.
Robert Y. Hayne, S.C.   Daniel Webster, Mass.
Theodore Frelinghuysen, N.J.   Felix Grundy, Tenn.

POST OFFICE AND POST ROADS
Chairman: Felix Grundy, Tenn.
Powhatan Ellis, Miss.   Thomas Ewing, Ohio
Isaac Hill, N.H.   Gideon Tomlinson, Conn.

ROADS AND CANALS
Chairman: William Hendricks, Ind.
George Poindexter, Miss.   Willie P. Mangum, N.C.
Isaac Hill, N.H.   Peleg Sprague, Me.

PENSIONS
Chairman: Samuel A. Foote, Conn.
Ezekiel F. Chambers, Md.   Willie P. Mangum, N.C.
Alexander Buckner, Mo.   Peleg Sprague, Me.

DISTRICT OF COLUMBIA
Chairman: Ezekiel F. Chambers, Md.
John Tyler, Va.   John Holmes, Me.
John M. Clayton, Del.   Stephen D. Miller, S.C.

AUDIT AND CONTROL THE CONTINGENT FUND
Chairman: Nehemiah R. Knight, R.I.
Charles E. Dudley, N.Y.   Gideon Tomlinson, Conn.

ENGROSSED BILLS

Chairman: John M. Robinson, Ill.

Thomas Ewing, Ohio   Alexander Buckner, Mo.

SELECT COMMITTEES

ON THE MEMORIAL OF THE LEGISLATURE OF OHIO FOR SETTLING THE BOUNDARY DISPUTE BETWEEN THAT STATE AND THE MICHIGAN TERRITORY

Chairman: Thomas Ewing, Ohio

William Wilkins, Penn.   William Hendricks, Ind.
Felix Grundy, Tenn.   Arnold Naudain, Del.

ON THE BILL CONCERNING MARTHA RANDOLPH, ONLY SURVIVING CHILD OF THOMAS JEFFERSON

Chairman: George Poindexter, Miss.

Henry Clay, Ky.   Robert Y. Hayne, S.C.
John Tyler, Va.   Daniel Webster, Mass.

ON THE BILL TO SETTLE CLAIMS FOR FRENCH SPOLIATIONS PRIOR TO 1800

Chairman: William Wilkins, Penn.

Daniel Webster, Mass.   Bedford Brown, N.C.
Ezekiel F. Chambers, Md.   Charles E. Dudley, N.Y.

CONGRESSIONAL DIRECTORY

TWENTY-SECOND CONGRESS, SECOND SESSION
(December 3, 1832 – March 2, 1833)

American Hotel, Col. McCarty's,
  Penn. Ave.
Josiah S. Johnston (S), La.
Edward Everett, Mass.
Robert P. Letcher, Ky.

Mrs. Arguelles, Penn. Ave.
John M. Robinson (S), Ill.
Willie P. Mangum (S), N.C.
William R. King (S), Ala.
Thomas T. Bouldin, Va.
Augustine S. Clayton, Ga.
Micajah T. Hawkins, N.C.
Rufus McIntire, Me.

Alexander's nearly opposite Gadsby's
John J. Milligan, Del.
Thomas A. Marshall, Ky.
Thomas Newton, Jr., Va.

Mr. J. Adams, near St. John's Church
John Quincy Adams, Mass.

Col. Ashton, Penn. Ave.
George M. Bibb (S), Ky.

Bernay's Penn. Ave.
William S. Archer, Va.
James M. Wayne, Ga.

Rev. O. B. Brown, near the General
  Post Office
Richard M. Johnson, Ky.
Ambrose H. Sevier, Deleg., Ark. Terr.

Mrs. Blake, Penn. Ave.
Ezekiel F. Chambers (S), Md.

John Banks, Penn.
Harmar Denny, Penn.
Benedict J. Semmes, Md.
William B. Shepard, N.C.

Brown's Hotel, Penn. Ave.
Andrew Stevenson, Va.
John S. Barbour, Va.
Ratliff Boon, Ind.
Daniel Pitcher, N.Y.
William T. Nuckolls, S.C.
John S. Spence, Md.
Philander Stephens, Penn.
Augustine H. Shepperd, N.C.
Jesse Speight, N.C.
Johnathan McCarty, Ind.
George A. Waggaman, La.
Daniel L. Barringer, N.C.

Blackwell's Congress Hall, Penn. Ave.
Albert G. Hawes, Ky.
Franklin E. Plummer, Miss.
William Fitzgerald, Tenn.
Thomas F. Foster, Ga.
Henry G. Lamar, Ga.

Brodhead's, Capitol Hill
John C. Brodhead, N.Y.
John Brodhead, N.H.
Thomas Chandler, N.H.

Mrs. Ball's, opposite Brown's Hotel
Nathaniel H. Claiborne, Va.
Richard Coulter, Penn.
Robert Craig, Va.
Joseph Draper,[1] Va.
James Ford, Penn.

[1] Elected to fill the vacancy caused by the death of Charles C. Johnston, and took his seat Dec. 12, 1832.

Joseph Lecompte, Ky.
John J. Roane, Va.
Chittenden Lyon, Ky.
Lewis Dewart, Penn.

Col. Brearley, B St.
Thomas H. Hughes, N.J.

Mrs. Cochrane, F St.
Richard Coke, Jr., Va.
James Findlay, Ohio
William Hogan, N.Y.

Mrs. Coyle, Capitol Hill
William Babcock, N.Y.
Gamaliel H. Barstow, N.Y.
Bates Cooke, N.Y.
John Dickson, N.Y.
Frederick Whittlesey, N.Y.

Mrs. Cummings, F St.
William G. Angel, N.Y.
Nathan Soule, N.Y.

Mrs. Clement, Third St.
Henry Daniel, Ky.
Freeborn G. Jewett, N.Y.
John King, N.Y.
Job Pierson, N.Y.
Austin E. Wing, Deleg., Mich. Terr.
Gerrit Y. Lansing, N.Y.

Mr. M. St. C. Clarke, E St., near General
  Post Office
Joseph Duncan, Ill.

Mrs. Cottringer, F St., between Twelfth
  and Thirteenth St.
Peter Ihrie, Jr., Penn.

M. Davis, C St.
Thomas Ewing (S), Ohio
Chilton Allan, Ky.
William Armstrong, Va.
Robert Allison, Penn.
Thomas Corwin, Ohio
Joseph H. Crane, Ohio
William Creighton, Jr., Ohio
Charles F. Mercer, Va.

William Stanbery, Ohio
William Russell, Ohio
Christopher Tompkins, Ky.
Joseph Vance, Ohio
Samuel F. Vinton, Ohio
Lewis Williams, N.C.

Dowson's No. 1, Capitol Hill
Thomas H. Benton (S), Mo.
John Black (S),[2] Miss.
Samuel Smith (S), Md.

Dowson's No. 2, Capitol Hill
Thomas H. Hall, N.C.
James I. McKay, N.C.

Mrs. Dunn, Capitol Hill
Warren R. Davis, S.C.
Dixon H. Lewis, Ala.

Mr. Ditty, C St.
John Bell, Tenn.
Abraham Rencher, N.C.

Mr. Denny, Four and One-Half St.
Benjamin C. Howard, Md.

Davis, Franklin Row, K St.
Joseph Hammons, N.H.

Fletcher's, E St., East of General Post
  Office
Samuel Prentiss (S), Vt.
Heman Allen, Vt.
George N. Briggs, Mass.
Joseph G. Kendall, Mass.
Lewis Maxwell, Va.
Samuel J. Wilkin, N.Y.

French's, Penn. Ave.
William Wilkins (S), Penn.
George M. Dallas (S), Penn.
Samuel Beardsley, N.Y.

Gadsby's National Hotel, Penn. Ave.
Bedford Brown (S), N.C.
Charles E. Dudley (S), N.Y.
Daniel Webster (S), Mass.
Nathan Appleton, Mass.

[2] Appointed to fill the vacancy caused by the resignation of Powhatan Ellis, and took his seat Dec. 12, 1832; subsequently elected.

John M. Felder, S.C.
Aaron Ward, N.Y.
Campbell P. White, N.Y.
George M. Troup (S), Ga.

Mrs. Galvin, C St.
Alexander Buckner (S), Mo.
William Hendricks (S), Ind.
Benjamin S. Ruggles (S), Ohio
William Kennon Sr., Ohio

Mr. Greer, Ninth St.
Launchlin Bethune, N.C.
George Burd, Penn.

Mrs. Hills, Penn. Ave.[3]
Mahlon Dickerson (S), N.J.
John Forsyth (S), Ga.
John Tyler (S), Va.
Henry W. Connor, N.C.
John M. Patton, Va.
Thomas Davenport, Va.
William F. Gordon, Va.
William McCoy, Va.

Lindsley's Rooms, adjoining Mrs. Hills,
    nearly opposite Gadsby's
Hugh Lawson White (S), Tenn.
Joseph W. Chinn, Va.
James K. Polk, Tenn.

Mrs. Hamilton, Corner of E and
    Fifth St.
David Potts, Jr., Penn.
Thomas D. Arnold, Tenn.
Joel B. Sutherland, Penn.
John W. Taylor, N.Y.

Miss Hamilton, C St.
Horatio Seymour (S), Vt.
William W. Irvin, Ohio
Dutee J. Pearce, R.I.

Mr. Hyatt, Penn. Ave., opposite Brown's
    Hotel
Noyes Barber, Conn.
William Cahoon, Vt.
Eleutheros Cooke, Ohio
John Davis, Mass.

Jabez W. Huntington, Conn.
William Slade, Vt.
William L. Storrs, Conn.
Ebenezer Young, Conn.
Andrew Stewart, Penn.

Harbaugh's, Seventh St.
Robert McCoy, Penn.
Thomas M. Y. McKennan, Penn.

Mrs. Hungerford, Eleventh St.
Daniel Newnan, Ga.

Henry V. Hill, Penn. Ave.
Jacob C. Isacks, Tenn.
Charles A. Wickliffe, Ky.
Cave Johnson, Tenn.

Mrs. Ironside, Seventh St.
John Branch, N.C.

Mrs. Keyworth, Penn. Ave.
Isaac C. Bates, Mass.
John A. Collier, N.Y.
Ralph I. Ingersoll, Conn.

Mr. Kane, near West Market
Elias K. Kane (S), Ill.

Mrs. Kennedy, Four and One-Half St.
Isaac Hill, N.H.
Joseph M. Harper, N.H.
Henry Hubbard, N.H.
Henry King, Penn.

Dr. Lindsey, near Brown's Hotel
Lewis Condict, N.J.
Silas Condit, N.J.

Mr. McLeod, opposite Centre Market
Nehemiah R. Knight (S), R.I.
Gideon Tomlinson (S), Conn.
Theodore Freylinghuysen (S), N.J.
Tristam Burges, R.I.
James F. Randolph, N.J.
Phineas L. Tracy, N.Y.

McCardle's, Capitol Hill
James Blair, S.C.

---

[3] Formerly Mrs. Ann Peyton's. For a continuation of this mess see Lindsley's Rooms.

Richard M. Cooper, N.J.
Edward Kavanagh, Me.
Joel K. Mann, Penn.
Thomas R. Mitchell, S.C.
Isaac Southard, N.J.

Mrs. Myer, Penn. Ave.
John C. Bucher, Penn.
Joshua Evans, Jr., Penn.
John Gilmore, Penn.
William Hiester, Penn.
Henry Horn, Penn.
Adam King, Penn.
Humphrey H. Leavitt, Ohio
Henry A. P. Muhlenberg, Penn.
Samuel A. Smith, Penn.
Philemon Thomas, La.
John Thomson, Ohio

Mrs. McDaniel, Mo. Ave.
Mark Alexander, Va.
Francis Thomas, Md.
Clement C. Clay, Ala.
Samuel W. Mardis, Ala.
John Y. Mason, Va.

Mrs. Miller, F St.
Churchill C. Cambreleng, N.Y.

Mrs. Peyton, Penn. Ave.
Stephen D. Miller (S), S.C.
Robert W. Barnwell, S.C.
John K. Griffin, S.C.
George McDuffie, S.C.
Edward D. White, La.

Mrs. Owner, Penn. Ave.
Felix Grundy (S), Tenn.
John Tipton (S), Ind.
John Blair, Tenn.
John Carr, Ind.
William Hall, Tenn.
James Standifer, Tenn.
Wiley Thompson, Ga.
John T. H. Worthington, Md.
Gabriel Moore (S), Ala.

Poor's near City Hall
George Evans, Me.
Horace Everett, Vt.

George Grennell, Jr., Mass.
James L. Hodges, Mass.
Jeremiah Nelson, Mass.
John Reed, Mass.

Miss Polk, Thirteenth St.
William H. Ashley, Mo.

Mr. Pleasanton, near Glass House
John G. Watmough, Penn.

Mr. Purcell, opposite Brown's Hotel
Nathan Gaither, Ky.
Robert Allen, Va.

Mrs. Queen, Penn. Ave.
John T. Bergen, N.Y.
James Bates, Me.
Joseph Bouck, N.Y.
Ulysses F. Doubleday, N.Y.
Michael Hoffman, N.Y.
James Lent,[4] N.Y.
Edward C. Reed, N.Y.
John W. Weeks, N.H.

Mrs. Read, Corner C and Third St.
John Anderson, Me.
Leonard Jarvis, Me.
John L. Kerr, Md.

Mr. N. Smith, Seventh St., near General
   Post Office
Henry Clay (S), Ky.
Peleg Sprague (S), Me.
Daniel Jenifer, Md.

Sawkins', Penn. Ave.
William Drayton, S.C.

Dr. Sewal, Penn. Ave.
Rufus Choate, Mass.

Mrs. Tims, Capitol Hill
Charles Dayan, N.Y.
Cornelius Holland, Me.
Erastus Root, N.Y.
Grattan H. Wheeler, N.Y.
Daniel Wardwell, N.Y.

[4] Died Feb. 22, 1833.

Mrs. Thompson, opposite Centre Market
George Poindexter (S), Miss.
Edmund Pendleton, N.Y.

Mrs. Walker, Corner Ninth and E St.
Nathaniel Silsbee (S), Mass.
Henry A. Bullard, La.
Henry A. S. Dearborn, Mass.
Gulian C. Verplanck, N.Y.
Thomas H. Crawford, Penn.
William W. Ellsworth, Conn.

Washington House, Capitol Hill
John Adair, Ky.
Joseph M. White, Deleg., Terr. of Fla.
Richard H. Wilde, Ga.

Mr. James Young, N.J. Ave.,
    Capitol Hill
Samuel Bell (S), N.H.
John Holmes (S), Me.
Samuel A. Foote (S), Conn.
Arnold Naudain (S), Del.
John M. Clayton (S), Del.
Asher Robbins (S), R.I.
Elisha Whittlesey, Ohio

Private Residence
    Georgetown
George C. Washington, Md.

APPENDIX

Charles S. Sewall, Md.
William L. Marcy (S),[5] N.Y.
Samuel P. Carson, N.C.
Robert Y. Hayne (S),[6] S.C.

Hiland Hall,[7] Vt.
Joseph Johnson,[8] Va.
William C. Rives,[9] Va.

STANDING COMMITTEES OF THE
HOUSE OF REPRESENTATIVES

ELECTIONS

Chairman: Nathaniel H. Claiborne, Va.
James F. Randolph, N.J.
John K. Griffin, S.C.
John A. Collier, N.Y.

Cornelius Holland, Me.
Launchlin Bethune, N.C.
Thomas D. Arnold, Tenn.

WAYS AND MEANS

Chairman: Gulian C. Verplanck, N.Y.
Ralph I. Ingersoll, Conn.
Mark Alexander, Va.
Nathan Gaither, Ky.

John Gilmore, Penn.
Richard H. Wilde, Ga.
James K. Polk, Tenn.

[5] Resigned Jan. 1, 1833, having been elected Governor. Silas Wright, Jr., was elected to fill the vacancy, and took his seat Jan. 14, 1833.
[6] Resigned Dec. 13, 1822, having been elected Governor. John C. Calhoun was elected to fill the vacancy, and took his seat Jan. 4, 1833.
[7] Elected to fill the vacancy caused by the death of Jonathan Hunt, and took his seat Jan. 21, 1833.
[8] Elected to fill the vacancy caused by the death of Philip Doddridge, and took his seat Jan. 21, 1833.
[9] Elected to fill the vacancy caused by the resignation of Littleton W. Tazewell, and took his seat Jan. 4, 1833.

CANALS

Chairman: Elisha Whittlesey, Ohio

Noyes Barber, Conn.
Peter Ihrie, Jr., Penn.
Charles Dayan, N.Y.

Rufus McIntire, Me.
Abraham Rencher, N.C.
George Grennell, Jr., Mass.

COMMERCE

Chairman: Churchill C. Cambreleng, N.Y.

Benjamin C. Howard, Md.
Thomas Newton, Jr., Va.
Leonard Jarvis, Me.

Joel B. Sutherland, Penn.
John Davis, Mass.
Joseph M. Harper, N.H.

PUBLIC LANDS

Chairman: Charles A. Wickliffe, Ky.

Joseph Duncan, Ill.
William W. Irvin, Ohio
Franklin E. Plummer, Miss.

Clement C. Clay, Ala.
Ratliff Boon, Ind.
John Y. Mason, Va.

POST OFFICE AND POST ROADS

Chairman: Henry W. Connor, N.C.

William Russell, Ohio
Joseph Hammons, N.H.
Ulysses F. Doubleday, N.Y.

Dutee J. Pearce, R.I.
Edward Kavanagh, Me.
John J. Roane, Va.

DISTRICT OF COLUMBIA

Chairman: George C. Washington, Md.

Benedict J. Semmes, Md.
Joseph W. Chinn, Va.
William B. Shepard, N.C.

William Armstrong, Va.
Daniel Jenifer, Md.
Thomas M. T. McKennan, Penn.

JUDICIARY

Chairman: John Bell, Tenn.

William W. Ellsworth, Conn.
Thomas F. Foster, Ga.
Samuel Beardsley, N.Y.

Henry Daniel, Ky.
William F. Gordon, Va.
Richard Coulter, Penn.

REVOLUTIONARY CLAIMS

Chairman: Henry A. P. Muhlenberg, Penn.

William T. Nuckolls, S.C.
Isaac C. Bates, Mass.
Thomas A. Marshall, Ky.

Joseph H. Crane, Ohio
James Standifer, Tenn.
Daniel Newnan, Ga.

PUBLIC EXPENDITURES

Chairman: Thomas H. Hall, N.C.

Thomas Davenport, N.C.
John Thomson, Ohio
Henry King, Penn.

Chittenden Lyon, Ky.
Job Pierson, N.Y.
George N. Briggs, Mass.

PRIVATE LAND CLAIMS

Chairman: Cave Johnson, Tenn.

Richard Coke, Jr. Va.
Samuel W. Mardis, Ala.
Henry A. Bullard, La.

William Stanbery, Penn.
John Carr, Ind.
William H. Ashley, Mo.

MANUFACTURES

Chairman: John Quincy Adams, Mass.

Michael Hoffman, N.Y.
Henry Horn, Penn.
John S. Barbour, Va.

Lewis Condict, N.J.
James Findlay, Ohio
John T. H. Worthington, Md.

AGRICULTURE

Chairman: Erastus Root, N.Y.

William McCoy, Va.
Thomas Chandler, N.H.
Robert McCoy, Penn.

Samuel A. Smith, Penn.
Grattan H. Wheeler, N.Y.
Christopher Tompkins, Ky.

INDIAN AFFAIRS

Chairman: Dixon H. Lewis, Ala.

Wiley Thompson, Ga.
William L. Storrs, Conn.
William Kennon, Sr., Ohio

William G. Angel, N.Y.
Joseph Lecompte, Ky.
Micajah T. Hawkins, N.C.

MILITARY AFFAIRS

Chairman: Richard M. Johnson, Ky.

Joseph Vance, Ohio
James Blair S.C.,[10]
Jesse Speight, N.C.

Aaron Ward, N.Y.
John Adair, Ky.
Philemon Thomas, La.

NAVAL AFFAIRS

Chairman: John Anderson, Me.

Campbell P. White, N.Y.
John G. Watmough, Penn.
Henry A. S. Dearborn, Mass.

John J. Milligan, Del.
John M. Patton, Va.
Gerrit Y. Lansing, N.Y.

FOREIGN AFFAIRS

Chairman: William S. Archer, Va.

Edward Everett, Mass.
Thomas H. Crawford, Penn.
James M. Wayne, Ga.

John W. Taylor, N.Y.
Robert W. Barnwell, S.C.
Francis Thomas, Md.

[10] Omitted in the *Congressional Directory* but listed in the *Journal of the House of Representatives.*

TERRITORIES

Chairman: John L. Kerr, Md.

William Creighton, Jr., Ohio
Jabez W. Huntington, Conn.
David Potts, Jr., Penn.

Lewis Williams, N.C.
Chilton Allan, Ky.
John King, N.Y.

REVOLUTIONARY PENSIONS

Chairman: Henry Hubbard, N.H.

Jacob C. Isacks, Tenn.
Edward H. Pendleton, N.Y.
Nathan Soule, N.Y.

Harmar Denny, Penn.
John C. Bucher, Penn.
Rufus Choate, Mass.

INVALID PENSIONS

Chairman: Tristam Burges, R.I.

James Ford, Penn.
Edward C. Reed, N.Y.
William Slade, Vt.

George Evans, Me.
Lewis Dewart, Penn.
Isaac Southard, N.J.

ROADS AND CANALS

Chairman: Charles F. Mercer, Va.

John Blair, Tenn.
Samuel F. Vinton, Ohio
Humphrey H. Leavitt, Ohio

Robert P. Letcher, Ky.
Robert Craig, Va.
Freeborn G. Jewett, N.Y.

REVISAL AND UNFINISHED BUSINESS

Chairman: John Reed, Mass.

Joseph Bouck, N.Y.

Silas Condit, N.J.

ACCOUNTS

Chairman: John T. Berger, N.Y.

George Burd, Penn.

James L. Hodges, Mass.

ON EXPENDITURES IN THE DEPARTMENT OF STATE

Chairman: James Lent, N.Y.

Joshua Evans, Jr., Penn.

James I. McKay, N.C.

ON EXPENDITURES IN THE DEPARTMENT OF THE TREASURY

Chairman: Philander Stephens, Penn.

Daniel Wardwell, N.Y.

William Fitzgerald, Tenn.

ON EXPENDITURES IN THE DEPARTMENT OF WAR

Chairman: Augustine H. Shepperd, N.C.

Joel K. Mann, Penn.

John M. Felder, S.C.

ON EXPENDITURES IN THE DEPARTMENT OF THE NAVY

Chairman: Lewis Maxwell Va.

William Hall, Tenn.   Joseph M. Harper, N.H.

ON EXPENDITURES IN THE POST OFFICE DEPARTMENT

Chairman: Albert G. Hawes, Ky.

James Bates, Me.   John C. Brodhead, N.Y.

ON EXPENDITURES ON THE PUBLIC BUILDINGS

Chairman: Ebenezer Young, Conn.

John S. Spence, Md.   Phineas L. Tracy, N.Y.

SELECT COMMITTEES

PUBLIC BUILDINGS

Chairman: Leonard Jarvis, Me.

Augustin S. Clayton, Ga.   Robert Allen, Va.
William Hogan, N.Y.   Nathan Appleton, Mass.
John Banks, Penn.   Eleutheros Cooke, Ohio

ON THE MILITIA

Chairman: Daniel L. Barringer, N.C.

Adam King, Penn.   John W. Weeks, N.H.
Nathaniel Pitcher, N.Y.   William Cahoon, Vt.
Andrew Stewart, Penn.   Johnathan McCarty, Ind.

INTERNAL IMPROVEMENTS AND THE EXERCISE OF DOUBTFUL POWERS BY CONGRESS

Chairman: Henry Daniel, Ky.

Jesse Speight, N.C.   James K. Polk, Tenn.
Edward Everett, Mass.   William S. Archer, Va.
Joseph Vance, Ohio   Samuel Beardsley, N.Y.

STANDING COMMITTEES OF THE SENATE

FOREIGN RELATIONS

Chairman: John Forsyth, Ga.

William R. King, Ala.   Samuel Bell, N.H.[11]
Willie P. Mangum, S.C.   Gideon Tomlinson, Conn.

[11] The *Journal of the Senate of the United States* lists George M. Bibb (Ky.) in lieu of Samuel Bell (N.H.).

FINANCE

Chairman: Samuel Smith, Md.

John Tyler, Va.
Josiah S. Johnston, La.

Nathaniel Silsbee, Mass.
John Forsyth, Ga.

COMMERCE

Chairman: William R. King, Ala.

Charles E. Dudley, N.Y.
Josiah S. Johnston, La.

Nathaniel Silsbee, Mass.
George M. Bibb, Ky.

MANUFACTURES

Chairman: Mahlon Dickerson, N.J.

Henry Clay, Ky.
Stephen D. Miller, S.C.

Nehemiah R. Knight, R.I.
Horatio Seymour, Vt.

AGRICULTURE

Chairman: Horatio Seymour, Vt.

Bedford Brown, N.C.
George A. Waggaman, La.

John M. Robinson, Ill.
Samuel A. Foote, Conn.

MILITARY AFFAIRS

Chairman: Thomas H. Benton, Mo.

George M. Troup, Ga.
John M. Clayton, Del.

Elias K. Kane, Ill.
John Tipton, Ind.

MILITIA

Chairman: John M. Robinson, Ill.

John M. Clayton, Del.
Henry Clay, Ky.

George A. Waggaman, La.
William Hendricks, Ind.

NAVAL AFFAIRS

Chairman: George M. Dallas, Penn.

Samuel Smith, Md.
Daniel Webster, Mass.

Asher Robbins, R.I.
George M. Bibb, Ky.

PUBLIC LANDS

Chairman: Elias K. Kane, Ill.

John Tipton, Ind.
John Holmes, Me.

Gabriel Moore, Ala.
Samuel Prentiss, Vt.

PRIVATE LAND CLAIMS

Chairman: George Poindexter, Miss.

Arnold Naudain, Del.
Benjamin Ruggles, Ohio

Samuel Prentiss, Vt.
Nehemiah R. Knight, R.I.

INDIAN AFFAIRS

Chairman: George M. Troup, Ga.

Thomas H. Benton, Mo.   George Poindexter, Miss.
William Wilkins, Penn.   Theodore, Frelinghuysen, N.J.

CLAIMS

Chairman: Benjamin Ruggles, Ohio

Samuel Bell, N.H.   Arnold Naudian Del.
Bedford, Brown, N.C.   Gabriel Moore, Ala.

JUDICIARY

Chairman: William Wilkins, Penn.

Daniel Webster, Mass.   Theodore Frelinghuysen, N.J.
Felix Grundy, Tenn.   Willie P. Mangum, N.C.

POST OFFICE AND POST ROADS

Chairman: Felix Grundy, Tenn.

Isaac Hill, N.H.   Thomas Ewing, Ohio
Gideon Tomlinson, Conn.   Alexander Buckner, Mo.

ROADS AND CANALS

Chairman: William Hendricks, Ind.

Peleg Sprague, Me.   George M. Dallas, Penn.
Isaac Hill, N.H.   Alexander Buckner, Mo.

PENSIONS

Chairman: Samuel A. Foote, Conn.

Ezekiel F. Chambers, Md.   Mahlon Dickerson, N.J.
Peleg Sprague, Me.   George Poindexter, Miss.

DISTRICT OF COLUMBIA

Chairman: Ezekiel F. Chambers, Md.

John Tyler, Va.   John Holmes, Me.
John M. Clayton, Del.   Stephen D. Miller, S.C.

AUDIT AND CONTROL THE CONTINGENT FUND

Chairman: Nehemiah R. Knight, R.I.

Charles E. Dudley, N.Y.   Gideon Tomlinson, Conn.

ENGROSSED BILLS

Chairman: Asher Robbins, R.I.

John M. Robinson, Ill.   Thomas Ewing, Ohio

SELECT COMMITTEE

ON THE BILL TO SETTLE CLAIMS FOR THE FRENCH SPOLIATIONS, PRIOR TO 1800

Chairman: Daniel Webster, Mass.

Ezekiel F. Chambers, Md.	Charles E. Dudley, N.Y.
Bedford Brown, N.C.	John Tyler, Va.

CONGRESSIONAL DIRECTORY

TWENTY-THIRD CONGRESS, FIRST SESSION
(December 2, 1833–June 30, 1834)

J. Adams', near the President's
John Quincy Adams, Mass.

Alexander's, Penn. Ave.
James M. Bell, Ohio
David Spangler, Ohio

Ashton's, Penn. Ave.
George M. Bibb (S), Ky.

Mrs. Ball, nearly opposite Brown's Hotel
Thomas Chilton, Ky.
David Crockett, Tenn.
Nathaniel H. Claiborne, Va.
Edmund Deberry, N.C.
William McComas, Va.

Mrs. Ballard, Penn. Ave.
Thomas T. Bouldin,[1] Va.
Benjamin Jones, Ohio
Thomas F. Foster, Ga.
Henry L. Pinckney, S.C.
Augustine S. Clayton, Ga.
Roger L. Gamble, Ga.

Chester Bailey, Seventh Ave., near
  General Post Office
Joseph Hall, Me.
Edward Kavanagh, Me.
Gorham Parks, Me.

Mrs. Burgh, near and East of the
  Capitol
Benjamin Hardin, Ky.

Christopher Tompkins, Ky.
John Bull, Mo.
Martin Beaty, Ky.

Mrs. Blake, Penn. Ave.
Ezekiel F. Chambers (S), Md.
Joseph Kent (S), Md.
Harmar Denny, Penn.
Horace Binney, Penn.
William B. Shepard, N.C.
John G. Watmough, Penn.

Rev. O. B. Brown, E St., near General
  Post Office
Richard M. Johnson, Ky.
Ambrose H. Sevier, Deleg., Ark. Terr.

Brown's Hotel, Penn. Ave.
Chilton Allan, Ky.
Daniel L. Barringer, N.C.
Ratliff Boon, Ind.
Richard Coulter, Penn.
James Graham, N.C.
Lewis F. Linn (S),[2] Mo.
Edward Lucas, Va.
Thomas L. Hamer, Ohio
Jesse Speight, N.C.
Andrew Stevenson,[3] Va.
Albert G. Hawes, Ky.
Patrick H. Pope, Ky.
Taylor Webster, Ohio

[1] Died Feb. 11, 1834. James W. Bouldin was elected to fill the vacancy, and took his seat Mar. 28, 1834.
[2] Appointed to fill the vacancy caused by the death of Alexander Buckner, and took his seat Dec. 16, 1833; subsequently elected.
[3] Resigned June 2, 1834.

Mrs. Carlisle, Corner of C and Four and One-Half St.
Nathan Smith (S), Conn.
Gideon Tomlinson (S), Conn.
George Chambers, Penn.

Miss Corcoran, Four and One-Half St.
George Loyall, Va.

Clement's, Third St., near Penn. Ave.
Samuel W. Mardis, Ala.
Clement C. Clay, Ala.
Joseph W. Chinn, Va.
James K. Polk, Tenn.
Henry Hubbard, N.H.
Leonard Jarvis, Me.
Henry King, Penn.
Robert T. Lytle,[4] Ohio

Mrs. Coyle, B St. South, near the Capitol
William K. Clowney, S.C.
John Dickson, N.Y.
George R. Gilmer, Ga.
Abner Hazeltine, N.Y.
Seaborn Jones, Ga.
Frederick Whittlesey, N.Y.

Mrs. Cochrane, F between Thirteenth and Fourteenth St.
William S. Archer, Va.

Mrs. Denny, Four and One-Half St.
John Y. Mason, Va.
William P. Taylor, Va.

Ditty's, C St.
Henry Clay (S), Ky.
Thomas A. Marshall, Ky.

Dowson's No. 1, Capitol Hill
Thomas H. Benton (S), Mo.
Willie P. Mangum (S), N.C.
William Allen, Ohio

Dowson's No. 2, Capitol Hill
John C. Calhoun (S), S.C.
William C. Preston (S),[5] S.C.

John H. Fulton, Va.
Thomas H. Hall, N.C.
James J. McKay, N.C.

Carroll's Row, East of the Capitol
Warren R. Davis, S.C.
Dixon H. Lewis, Ala.

Mrs. Emmon, Penn. Ave.
Peleg Sprague (S), Me.
George Poindexter (S), Miss.

Fuller's, Penn. Ave.
George A. Waggaman (S), La.
Charles A. Barnitz, Penn.
William Baylies, Mass.
Edward Everett, Mass.
Benjamin Gorham, Mass.
William H. Ashley, Mo.

Fletcher's, E St., near General Post Office
Samuel Prentiss (S), Vt.
Samuel McKean (S), Penn.
Heman Allen, Vt.
John Banks, Penn.
George N. Briggs, Mass.
William Clark, Penn.
Philo C. Fuller, N.Y.
Millard Fillmore, N.Y.
James Harper, Penn.
Hilland Hall, Vt.

Gadsby's, Penn. Ave.
Henry Cage, Miss.
Cornelius W. Lawrence,[6] N.Y.
Isaac McKim, Va.
Gayton P. Osgood, Mass.
Dudley Selden, N.Y.
William Cost Johnson, Va.
Aaron Ward, N.Y.
Campbell P. White, N.Y.

Mrs. Galvin, C between Three and Four and One-Half St.
William Hendricks (S), Ind.
Samuel Clark, N.Y.
John Ewing, Ind.

[4] Resigned Mar. 10, 1834.
[5] Elected to fill the vacancy caused by the resignation of Stephen D. Miller in the preceding Congress, and took his seat Dec. 9, 1833.
[6] Resigned May 14, 1834, having been elected Mayor of New York City.

Ransom H. Gillet, N.Y.
Edward Howell, N.Y.
Gideon Hard, N.Y.
Edgar C. Wilson, Va.

Gooch's, B St., Capitol Hill
Nathaniel P. Tallmadge (S), N.Y.
Silas Wright, Jr. (S), N.Y.
Franklin E. Plummer, Miss.

Mrs. Hamilton, nearly opposite
  Gadsby's
Abraham Bockee, N.Y.
Rowland Day, N.Y.
William K. Fuller, N.Y.
Gerrit Y. Lansing, N.Y.
Job Pierson, N.Y.
William Taylor, N.Y.
Reuben Wahllon, N.Y.

Mrs. Hamilton, C St., near Public Baths
John Coffee, Ga.
Amos Davis, Ky.
James Love, Ky.
Horace Everett, Vt.
William Schley, Ga.

Judge Hayward, F St.
Jeremiah McLene, Ohio

Harbaugh's, Seventh St., near E.
Joseph B. Anthony, Penn.
Samuel S. Harrison, Penn.
Joseph Henderson, Penn.
John Laporte, Penn.
Thomas M. T. McKennan, Penn.
Jesse Miller, Penn.
Andrew Stewart, Penn.

Hebb's, near and South of the Capitol
James P. Heath, Va.
James Turner, Va.

Henry Hills, Penn. Ave.
Henry W. Connor, N.C.
Cave Johnson, Tenn.
Abraham Rencher, S.C.

Mrs. S. A. Hill, nearly opposite Gadsby's
Isaac Hill (S), N.H.
Ether Shepley (S), Me.
William Wilkins (S), Penn.

Hugh L. White (S), Tenn.
Samuel Beardsley, N.Y.
Philemon Dickerson, N.J.
Noadiah Johnson, N.Y.
Rufus McIntire, Me.
Franklin Pierce, N.H.
Sherman Page, N.Y.
Francis O. J. Smith, Me.
Aaron Vanderpoel, N.Y.

Hyatt's, opposite Brown's Hotel
Benjamin Swift (S), Vt.
Noyes Barber, Conn.
Isaac C. Bates, Mass.
Benjamin F. Deming, Vt.
William W. Ellsworth, Conn.
Jabez W. Huntington, Conn.
Henry C. Martindale, N.Y.
William Slade, Vt.
Jonathan Sloane, Ohio
Samuel Tweedy, Conn.
Ebenezer Young, Conn.

Mrs. Hungerford, E St., Bayle's Row
Gabriel Moore, Ala.
John Blair, Tenn.
John B. Forester, Tenn.
George L. Kinnard, Ind.

Mrs. Kane
Elias K. Kane (S), Ill.

Kennedy's, Four and One-Half St.
Thomas Ewing (S), Ohio
Charles F. Mercer, Va.
Joseph Vance, Ohio
Thomas Corwin, Ohio
Lewis Williams, N.C.
Samuel F. Vinton, Ohio
Joseph H. Crane, Ohio

Mrs. A. Johnson, Twelfth St.
George Burd, Penn.

Langdon's, Sixth between E and F St.
David Potts, Jr., Penn.
Joel B. Sutherland, Penn.

McLeod's, opposite Centre Market
Theodore Frelinghuysen (S), N.J.
Nehemiah R. Knight (S), R.I.
Arnold Naudain (S), Del.

Tristam Burges, R.I.
George W. Lay, N.Y.

Mrs. Myer, nearly opposite Gadsby's
John Chaney, Ohio
Edward Darlington, Penn.
William Hiester, Penn.
John Galbraith, Penn.
Humphrey H. Leavitt, Ohio
Robert Mitchell, Ohio
William Patterson, Ohio
Philemon Thomas, La.
Henry A. Muhlenberg, Penn.
Isaac B. Van Houten, N.Y.
Abel Huntington, N.Y.
John Thomson, Ohio

Mount Hope, Georgetown
Augustine H. Shepperd, N.C.

Mrs. Miller, F St., between Thirteenth
and Fourteenth
Churchill C. Cambreleng, N.Y.
James M. Wayne, Ga.

Mrs. McDaniel, Penn. Ave.
Thomas Morris (S), Ohio
John Tyler (S), Va.
John Tipton (S), Ind.
Thomas Davenport, Va.
Samuel Fowler, N.J.
William F. Gordon, Va.
Thomas Lee, N.J.
Samuel McDowell Moore, Va.
John M. Patton, Va.
William N. Shinn, N.J.
Ferdinand S. Schenck, N.J.

McCardle's, Capitol Hill
Robert Ramsey, Penn.
David D. Wagener, Penn.
Joel K. Mann, Penn.
Duttee J. Pearce, R.I.
Andrew Beaumont, Penn.

Rev. J. M. McVean, Georgetown
Charles McVean, N.Y.

M. St. Clair Clark, E St.
Joseph Duncan, Ill.

Mrs. Owner, Penn. Ave.
John M. Robinson (S), Ill.
Felix Grundy (S), Tenn.
Samuel Bunch, Tenn.
Zadoc Casey, Ill.
John Carr, Ind.
William C. Dunlap, Tenn.
Edward A. Hannegan, Ind.
Luke Lea, Tenn.
Chittenden Lyon, Ky.
Charles Slade, Ill.
James Standifer, Tenn.

Mrs. Peyton, Corner Penn. Ave. and
Four and One-Half St.
John J. Allen, Va.
John M. Felder, S.C.
James H. Gholson, Va.
William J. Grayson, S.C.
John K. Griffin, S.C.
George McDuffie, S.C.
Edward D. White, La.

Mr. Pleasant, Thirteenth St.
Richard H. Wilde, Ga.

Miss Polk's No. 1, Penn Ave.
Littleton P. Dennis,[7] Md.
John T. Stoddert, Md.
Richard B. Carmichael, Md.
Jesse A. Bynum, N.C.
Francis Thomas, Va.
Henry A. Wise, Va.

Miss Polk's No. 2, Penn. Ave.
Bedford Brown (S), N.C.
William R. King (S), Ala.
John Bell, Tenn.
Balie Peyton, Tenn.
David W. Dickinson, Tenn.
Micajah T. Hawkins, N.C.
William M. Inge, Tenn.

Miss Polk's No. 3, Penn. Ave.
Lucius Lyon, Deleg., Mich. Terr.

Poor's, near the City Hall
Samuel Southard (S), N.J.
George Evans, Me.

[7] Died Apr. 14, 1834. John N. Steele was elected to fill the vacancy, and took his seat June 9, 1834.

George Grennell, Jr., Mass.
John Reed, Mass.

Mrs. Pittman, F St.
Amos Lane, Ind.
Daniel Wardwell, N.Y.

Pursell's, opposite Brown's
James M. H. Beale, Va.

Mrs. Queen's, Penn. Ave.
John Adams, N.Y.
John W. Brown, N.Y.
Benning M. Bean, N.H.
Charles Bodle, N.Y.
Robert Burns, N.H.
John Cramer, N.Y.
Samuel G. Hathaway, N.Y.
Nicoll Halsey, N.Y.
Joseph M. Harper, N.H.
Henry Mitchell, N.Y.

Rush's House, H St.
William C. Rives,[8] Va.

Dr. Sewall, opposite Brown's
Rufus Choate, Mass.

Shaff's, Georgetown
John Forsyth (S),[9] Ga.

Mrs. Stettinus, Penn. Ave.
Johnathan McCarty, Ind.

Mrs. Thompson, opposite Centre Market
Nathaniel Silsbee (S), Mass.
Daniel Webster (S), Mass.

Timm's, near the Capitol
James Blair,[10] S.C.
John Murphy, Ala.

Mrs. Varnum, Eighth St.
John Davis,[11] Mass.

S.P. Walker's, C St., near the Public
  Baths
John McKinley, Ala.
James Parker, N.J.
Abijah Mann, Jr., N.Y.
Joel Turrill, N.Y.

Young's, N.J. Ave., Capitol Hill
Samuel Bell (S), N.H.
Asher Robbins (S), R.I.
Samuel A. Foote (S),[12] Conn.
Elisha Whittlesey, Ohio

Mrs. Zantzinger, near the Cith Hall
Henry A. Bullard (S),[13] Conn.
John J. Milligan, Del.

APPENDIX

John M. Clayton (S), Del.   John P. King (S),[14] Ga.
Joseph M. White, Deleg., Terr. of Fla.   Ky.[15]

[8] Resigned Feb. 22, 1834. Benjamin W. Leigh was elected to fill the vacancy, and took his seat Mar. 5, 1834.
[9] Resigned June 27, 1834, having been appointed Secretary of State.
[10] Died Apr. 1, 1834.
[11] Resigned Jan. 14, 1834, having been elected Governor. Levi Lincoln was elected to fill the vacancy, and took his seat Mar. 5, 1834.
[12] Resigned May 9, 1834, having been elected Governor.
[13] Resigned Jan. 4, 1834, having been appointed judge of the Supreme Court of La.
[14] Elected to fill the vacancy caused by the resignation of George M. Troup, and took his seat Dec. 31, 1833.
[15] The seat for the fifth district was claimed by Thomas P. Moore, who presented his credentials on Dec. 2, 1833, but was not sworn pending a contest by Robert P. Letcher. On June 2, 1834, the House ordered a new election, "it being impracticable for this House to determine with any certainty who is the rightful Representative of this district." Letcher was subsequently elected, and took his seat Dec. 1, 1834.

Alexander Porter (S),[16] La.
William Jackson, Mass.
Moses Mason, Jr., Me.

John Black (S),[17] Miss.
Robert B. Campbell,[18] S.C.

STANDING COMMITTEES OF THE
HOUSE OF REPRESENTATIVES

ELECTIONS

Chairman: Nathaniel H. Claiborne, Va.

John K. Griffin, S.C.
Micajah T. Hawkins, N.C.
John Banks, Penn.
Aaron Vanderpoel, N.Y.

Seaborn Jones, Ga.
Balie Peyton, Tenn.
Thomas L. Hamer, Ohio
Edward A. Hannegan, Ind.

WAYS AND MEANS

Chairman: James K. Polk, Tenn.

Richard H. Wilde, Ga.
Churchill C. Cambreleng, N.Y.
Benjamin Gorham, Mass.
Isaac McKim, Md.

Horace Binney, Penn.
George Loyall, Va.
John McKinley, Ala.
Henry Hubbard, N.H.

CLAIMS

Chairman: Elisha Whittlesey, Ohio

Noyes Barber, Conn.
Rufus McIntire, Me.
George Grennell, Jr., Mass.
Henry King, Penn.

James H. Gholson, Va.
John Cramer, N.Y.
John B. Forester, Tenn.
Jesse A. Bynum, N.C.

COMMERCE

Chairman: Joel B. Sutherland, Penn.

John Davis, Mass.
Joseph M. Harper, N.H.
Samuel A. Foote, Conn.
James I. McKay, N.C.

Cornelius W. Lawrence, Penn.
Henry L. Pinckney, S.C.
James P. Heath, Md.
Dudley Selden, Penn.

PUBLIC LANDS

Chairman: Clement C. Clay, Ala.

Joseph Duncan, Ill.
Ratliff Boon, Ind.
Moses Mason, Jr., Me.
John M. Clayton, Del.

William Slade, Vt.
Humphrey H. Leavitt, Ohio
William H. Ashley, Mo.
William M. Inge, Tenn.

[16] Elected to fill the vacancy caused by the death of Josiah S. Johnston, and took his seat Jan. 6, 1834.

[17] Elected to fill the vacancy in the term commencing Mar. 4, 1833, and took his seat Dec. 23, 1833; vacancy in this class from Mar. 4–Nov. 21, 1833, because of recess of the legislature.

[18] Elected to fill the vacancy caused by the death of Thomas D. Singleton, and took his seat Feb. 27, 1834.

POST OFFICE AND POST ROADS

Chairman: Henry W. Connor, N.C.

Edward Kavanagh, Me.
Dutee J. Pearce, R.I.
Philemon Thomas, La.
George N. Briggs, Mass.

John Murphy, Ala.
Amos Lane, Ind.
Robert T. Lytle, Ohio
John Laporte, Penn.

DISTRICT OF COLUMBIA

Chairman: Joseph W. Chinn, Va.

William B. Shepard, N.C.
Thomas M. T. McKennan, Penn.
John T. Stoddert, Md.
John J. Allen, Va.

Littleton P. Dennis, Md.
William Hiester, Penn.
Millard Fillmore, N.Y.
William Taylor, N.Y.

JUDICIARY

Chairman: John Bell, Tenn.

William W. Ellsworth, Conn.
Thomas F. Foster, Del.
William F. Gordon, Va.
Samuel Beardsley, N.Y.

Francis Thomas, Md.
Benjamin Hardin, Ky.
Gorham Parks, Me.
Franklin Pierce, N.H.

REVOLUTIONARY CLAIMS

Chairman: Henry A. P. Muhlenberg, Penn.

Joseph H. Crane, Ohio
Isaac C. Bates, Mass.
James Standifer, Tenn.
Thomas T. Bouldin, Va.

Thomas A. Marshall, Ky.
Ebenezer Young, Conn.
William Baylies, Mass.
Joel Turrill, N.Y.

PUBLIC EXPENDITURES

Chairman: Thomas Davenport, Va.

Chittenden Lyon, Ky.
Sherman Page, N.Y.
William Clark, Penn.
Samuel Tweedy, Conn.

Ransom H. Gillet, Penn.
Hiland Hall, Vt.
Jeremiah McLene, Ohio
George L. Kinnard, Ind.

PRIVATE LAND CLAIMS

Chairman: Cave Johnson, Tenn.

Samuel W. Mardis, Ala.
John Carr, Ind.
John Galbraith, Penn.
Abijah Mann, Jr., N.Y.

Henry Cage, Miss.
John M. Felder, S.C.
Zadoc Casey, Ill.
John Bull, Mo.

MANUFACTURES

Chairman: John Quincy Adams, Mass.

Jabez W. Huntington, Conn.
Harmar Denny, Penn.
Warren R. Davis, S.C.
Thomas Corwin, Ohio

Philemon Dickerson, N.J.
Henry C. Martindale, N.Y.
William McComas, Va.
Gayton P. Osgood, Mass.

AGRICULTURE

Chairman: Abraham Bockee, N.Y.

William P. Taylor, Va.
Samuel G. Hathaway, N.Y.
Charles A. Barnitz, Penn.
Benning M. Bean, N.H.

William C. Dunlap, Tenn.
William K. Clowney, S.C.
James Turner, Md.
Amos Davis, Ky.

INDIAN AFFAIRS

Chairman: Dixon H. Lewis, Ala.

George R. Gilmer, Ga.
Johnathan McCarty, Ind.
Horace Everett, Vt.
James Graham, N.C.

William Allen, Ohio
David W. Dickinson, Tenn.
Edward Howell, N.Y.
James Love, Ky.

MILITARY AFFAIRS

Chairman: Richard M. Johnson, Ky.

Joseph Vance, Ohio
Jesse Speight, N.C.
Aaron Ward, N.Y.
James Blair, S.C.

John Thomson, Ohio
George Burd, Penn.
John Coffee, Ga.
Samuel Bunch, Tenn.

NAVAL AFFAIRS

Chairman: Campbell P. White, N.Y.

John J. Milligan, Del.
John G. Watmough, Penn.
John M. Patton, Va.
Gerrit Y. Lansing, N.Y.

John Reed, Mass.
William J. Grayson, S.C.
James Parker, N.J.
Francis O. J. Smith, Me.

FOREIGN RELATIONS

Chairman: William S. Archer, Va.

Edward Everett, Mass.
James M. Wayne, Ga.
George McDuffie, S.C.
Thomas H. Hall, N.C.

Richard Coulter, Penn.
Leonard Jarvis, Me.
Job Pierson, N.Y.
Richard B. Carmichael, Md.

TERRITORIES

Chairman: Lewis Williams, N.C.

Chilton Allan, Ky.
David Potts, Jr., Penn.
Noadiah Jonson, N.Y.
Joseph B. Anthony, Penn.

Edgar C. Wilson, Va.
Benjamin Jones, Ohio
John Ewing, Ind.
Roger L. Gamble, Ga.

REVOLUTIONARY PENSIONS

Chairman: David Wardwell, N.Y.

Daniel L. Barringer, N.C.
Christopher Tompkins, Ky.
Samuel McDowell Moore, Va.
Luke Lea, Tenn.

Benjamin F. Deming, Vt.
William K. Fuller, N.Y.
Samuel Fowler, N.J.
James M. Bell, Ohio

INVALID PENSIONS

Chairman: Tristam Burges, R.I.

George Evans, Me.   Ferdinand S. Schenck, N.J.
James M. H. Beale, Va.   Thomas Chilton, Ky.
William Schley, Ga.   John Chaney, Ohio
John Adams, N.Y.   Robert Mitchell, Ohio

ROADS AND CANALS

Chairman: Charles F. Mercer, Va.

John Blair, Tenn.   William Cost Johnson, Md.
Samuel F. Vinton, Ohio   Edward Lucas, Va.
Andrew Stewart, Penn.   Patrick H. Pope, Ky.
Abraham Rencher, N.C.   Charles Slade, Ill.

REVISAL AND UNFINISHED BUSINESS

Chairman: John Dickson, N.Y.

Samuel S. Harrison, Penn.   William N. Shinn, N.J.
Charles McVean, N.Y.   Martin Beaty, Ky.

ACCOUNTS

Chairman: Joel K. Mann, Penn.

Thomas Lee, N.J.   David Crockett, Tenn.
Henry Mitchell, N.Y.   Jesse Miller, Penn.

EXPENDITURES IN THE DEPARTMENT OF STATE

Chairman: Augustine H. Shepperd, N.C.

Rowland Day, N.Y.   Charles Bodle, N.Y.
Andrew Beaumont, Penn.   William Patterson, Ohio

EXPENDITURES IN THE DEPARTMENT OF THE TREASURY

Chairman: Heman Allen, Vt.

Philo C. Fuller, N.Y.   David Spangler, Ohio
James Harper, Penn.[19]   Samuel Clark, N.Y.

EXPENDITURES IN THE DEPARTMENT OF WAR

Chairman: Frederick Whittlesey, N.Y.

Edmund Deberry, N.C.   Taylor Webster, Ohio
George Chambers, Penn.   Nicoll Halsey, N.Y.

EXPENDITURES IN THE DEPARTMENT OF THE NAVY

Chairman: Joseph Hall, Me.

Abel Huntington, N.Y.   Jonathan Sloane, Ohio
Robert Ramsey, Penn.   Isaac B. Van Houten, N.Y.

[19] Omitted in the *Congressional Directory* but listed in the *Journal of the House of Representatives.*

EXPENDITURES IN THE POST OFFICE DEPARTMENT
Chairman: Albert G. Hawes, Ky.

John H. Fulton, Va.   David D. Wagener, Penn.
Robert Burns, N.H.   George W. Lay, N.Y.

EXPENDITURES ON THE PUBLIC BUILDINGS
Chairman: Reuben Whallon, N.Y.

Edward Darlington, Penn.   Joseph Henderson, Penn.
John W. Brown, N.Y.   Gideon Hard, N.Y.

JOINT COMMITTEE

LIBRARY OF CONGRESS

House   Senate
Edward Everett, Mass.   Asher Robbins, R.I.
James M. Wayne, Ga.   George Poindexter, Miss.
George Loyall, Va.   George M. Bibb, Ky.

STANDING COMMITTEES OF THE SENATE

FOREIGN RELATIONS
Chairman: William Wilkins, Penn.

William C. Rives, Va.   Peleg Sprague, Me.
John Forsyth, Ga.   Willie P. Mangum, N.C.

FINANCE
Chairman: Daniel Webster, Mass.

John Tyler, Va.   Willie P. Mangum, N.C.
Thomas Ewing, Ohio   William Wilkins, Penn.

COMMERCE
Chairman: Nathaniel Silsbee, Mass.

William R. King, Ala.   George A. Waggaman, La.
Silas Wright, Jr., N.Y.   Peleg Sprague, Me.

MANUFACTURES
Chairman: Theodore Frelinghuysen, N.J.

Nehemiah R. Knight, R.I.   Lewis F. Linn, Mo.
Thomas Morris, Ohio   Samuel Prentiss, Vt.

AGRICULTURE

Chairman: Bedford Brown, N.C.

John M. Robinson, Ill.
Joseph Kent, Md.

Silas Wright, Jr., N.Y.
Benjamin Swift, Vt.

MILITARY AFFAIRS

Chairman: Thomas H. Benton, Mo.

John Tipton, Ind.
William C. Preston, S.C.

John M. Clayton, Del.
William R. King, Ala.

MILITIA

Chairman: John M. Robinson, Ill.

William Hendricks, Ind.
George A. Waggaman, La.

Samuel McKean, Penn.
John M. Clayton, Del.

NAVAL AFFAIRS

Chairman: Samuel L. Southard, N.J.

George M. Bibb, Ky.
Asher Robbins, R.I.

Nathaniel P. Tallmadge, N.Y.
Ezekiel F. Chambers, Md.

PUBLIC LANDS

Chairman: George Poindexter, Miss.

Gabriel Moore, Ala.
Samuel Prentiss, Vt.

Samuel McKean, Penn.
Henry Clay, Ky.

PRIVATE LAND CLAIMS

Chairman: Elias K. Kane, Ill.

Louis F. Linn, Mo.
Arnold Naudain, Del.

George Poindexter, Miss.
Nathaniel Silsbee, Mass.

INDIAN AFFAIRS

Chairman: Hugh Lawson White, Tenn.

Theodore Frelinghuysen, N.J.
John Tipton, Ind.

Benjamin Swift, Vt.
Nathan Smith, Conn.

CLAIMS

Chairman: Samuel Bell, N.H.

Bedford Brown, N.C.
Arnold Naudain, Del.

Silas Wright, Jr., N.Y.
John Tipton, Ind.

JUDICIARY

Chairman: John M. Clayton, Del.

George M. Bibb, Ky.
William C. Preston, S.C.

Nathan Smith, Conn.
Samuel Bell, N.H.

POST OFFICE AND POST ROADS

Chairman: Felix Grundy, Tenn.

Thomas Ewing, Ohio   Nehemiah R. Knight, R.I.
William C. Rives, Va.   John M. Clayton, Del.

ROADS AND CANALS

Chairman: William Hendricks, Ind.

Isaac Hill, N.H.   Ether Shepley, Me.
Samuel L. Southard, N.J.   Joseph Kent, Md.

PENSIONS

Chairman: Gideon Tomlinson, Conn.

Samuel Prentiss, Vt.   Nathaniel P. Tallmadge, N.Y.
Samuel McKean, Penn.   Elias K. Kane, Ill.

DISTRICT OF COLUMBIA

Chairman: Ezekiel F. Chambers, Md.

John Tyler, Va.   George M. Bibb, Ky.
Samuel L. Southard, N.J.   Gideon Tomlinson, Conn.

REVOLUTIONARY CLAIMS

Chairman: Gabriel Moore, Ala.

Nathan Smith, Conn.   Hugh Lawson White, Tenn.
Isaac Hill, N.H.   Ether Shepley, Me.

TO AUDIT AND CONTROL THE CONTINGENT FUND

Chairman: Nehemiah R. Knight, R.I.

Gideon Tomlinson, Conn.   Nathaniel P. Tallmadge, N.Y.

ENGROSSED BILLS

Chairman: Ether Shepley, Me.

Thomas Morris, Ohio   John M. Robinson, Ill.

SELECT COMMITTEES

ON CONTESTED ELECTIONS (MR. POTTER VS. MR. ROBBINS)

Chairman: George Poindexter, Miss.

William C. Rives, Va.   Silas Wright, Jr., N.Y.
Theodore Frelinghuysen, N.J.   Peleg Sprague, Me.

ON FRENCH SPOLIATIONS PRIOR TO THE YEAR 1800

Chairman: Daniel Webster, Mass.

William C. Preston, S.C.   Felix Grundy, Tenn.
Ezekiel F. Chambers, Md.   Samuel Prentiss, Vt.

CONGRESSIONAL DIRECTORY

TWENTY-THIRD CONGRESS, SECOND SESSION
(December 1, 1834–March 3, 1835)

Mrs. Arguelle, Corner Penn. Ave.
  and Ninth St.
John M. Robinson (S), Ill.
Albert G. Hawes, Ky.
Jesse Speight, N.C.
Patrick H. Page, Ky.
James W. Bouldin, Va.

Mrs. Ball, Penn. Ave.
Thomas Chilton, Ky.
Nathaniel H. Claiborne, Va.
Edmund Deberry, N.C.
William McComas, Va.
William Clark, Penn.

Mrs. Ballard, Penn. Ave.
Edward Darlington, Penn.
Henry L. Pinckney S.C.
William Hiester, Penn.
David Spangler, Ohio
William Patterson, Ohio

Mr. Birth, Third St., near Penn.
Samuel Beardsley, N.Y.
James Parker, N.J.
Franklin Pierce, N.H.
Philemon Dickerson, N.J.

Chester Bailey's, Seventh St, near
  General Post Office
Moses Mason, Jr., Me.

Bayliss', opposite Centre Market
Daniel Webster (S), Mass.

Brown's Hotel, Penn. Ave.
Jesse A. Bynum, N.C.
William H. Ashley, Mo.

George Loyall, Va.
James Graham, N.C.
Richard Coulter, Penn.
David Crockett, Tenn.
George Burd, Penn.
Taylor Webster, Ohio
Benjamin Hardin, Ky.

Rev. O. B. Brown, E St., near
  General Post Office
Richard M. Johnson, Ky.
Ambrose H. Sevier, Deleg., Ark. Terr.

Clement's, Third St., near Penn. Ave.
Joseph W. Chinn, Va.
James K. Polk, Tenn.
Henry King, Penn.
John McKinley, Ala.

Mrs. Connor, Penn. Ave.
James P. Heath, Md.
James Turner, Md.

Miss Corcoran, Penn. Ave.
Nathaniel Silsbee (S), Mass.
John Reed, Mass.
George Grennell, Jr., Mass.
Levi Lincoln, Mass.
Harmar Denny, Penn.

Mrs. Coyle, B St. South, near
  the Capitol
William K. Clowney, S.C.
John Dickson, N.Y.
George R. Gilmer, Ga.
Abner Hazeltine, N.Y.
Frederick Whittlesey, N.Y.
Seaborn Jones, Ga.

Mr. Davis, E St.
Christopher Tompkins, Ky.
John Bull, Mo.
Martin Beaty, Ky.

Mrs. Denny, Four and One-Half St.
William Cost Johnson, Md.
Richard I. Manning,[1] S.C.
Robert B. Campbell, S.C.
John Black (S), Miss.

Dowson's No. 1, Capitol Hill
Thomas Benton (S), Mo.
Louis F. Linn (S), Mo.
William Allen, Ohio
Thomas L. Hamer, Ohio
Francis Thomas, Md.
Daniel Kilgore, Ohio
James I. McKay, N.C.
Richard B. Carmichael, Md.
Franklin E. Plummer, Miss.

Dowson's No. 2, Capitol Hill
John C. Calhoun (S), S.C.
Willie P. Mangum (S), N.C.
William C. Preston (S), S.C.
Benjamin W. Leigh (S), Va.
John M. Felder, S.C.
Thomas H. Hall, N.C.
Francis W. Pickens,[2] S.C.
William S. Archer, Va.

Fletcher's, E St., near General
   Post Office
John M. Robinson (S), Ill.
Samuel Prentiss (S), Vt.
Henry F. Janes,[3] Vt.
Heman Allen, Vt.
George N. Briggs, Mass.
Millard Fillmore, N.Y.
James Harper, Penn.
Hiland Hall, Vt.
William Jackson, Mass.
John Banks, Penn.

Fuller's Hotel, Penn. Ave.
William Baylies, Mass.
Benjamin Gorham, Mass.

Gadsby's, Penn. Ave.
Henry Cage, Miss.
Gayton P. Osgood, Mass.
Aaron Ward, N.Y.
Campbell P. White, N.Y.
Isaac McKim, Md.

Mrs. Galvin, C St., between Third
   and Four and One-Half St.
William Hendricks (S), Ind.
Samuel Clark, N.Y.
Edward Howell, N.Y.
Gideon Hard, N.Y.
John W. Brown, N.Y.
Henry Mitchell, N.Y.
Nicoll Halsey, N.Y.
Reuben Whallon, N.Y.

Miss Gardner, Penn. Ave.
John N. Steele, Md.
Thomas F. Foster, Ga.
Augustine H. Shepperd, N.C.

Mrs. Hamilton, nearly opposite Gadsby's
Abraham Bockee, N.Y.
Rowland Day, N.Y.
William K. Fuller, N.Y.
Gerrit Y. Lansing N.Y.
Job Pierson, N.Y.
William Taylor, N.Y.

Miss Hamilton, C St., near the
   Public Baths
Henry A. Wise, Va.
John Coffee, Ga.
James Love, Ky.
William Schley, Ga.
Edgar C. Wilson, Va.

[1] Elected to fill the vacancy caused by the death of James Blair, and took his seat Dec. 8, 1834.
[2] Elected to fill the vacancy caused by the resignation of George McDuffie, and took his seat Dec. 8, 1834.
[3] Elected to fill the vacancy caused by the death of Benjamin F. Deming, and took his seat Dec. 2, 1834.

Harbaugh's, Seventh St., near
   General Post Office
Joseph B. Anthony, Penn.
John Laporte, Penn.
Thomas M.T. McKennan, Penn.
Jesse Miller, Penn.
Andrew Stewart, Penn.

Mrs. S. A. Hill, nearly opposite Gadsby's
Isaac Hill (S), N.H.
John J. Morgan, N.Y.
John Adams, N.Y.
Robert Burns, N.H.
Thomas Lee, N.J.
Henry Hubbard, N.H.
Joseph M. Harper, N.H.
Joseph Hall, Me.
Noadiah Johnson, N.Y.
Francis O.J. Smith, Me.
Aaron Vanderpoel, N.Y.

Henry V. Hill, Penn. Ave.
Hugh Lawson White (S), Tenn.
Henry W. Connor, N.C.
James Standifer, Tenn.
Luke Lea, Tenn.
Cave Johnson, Tenn.
Samuel Bunch, Tenn.

Miss Handy, Thirteenth St.
James H. Gholson, Va.

Mrs. Hungerford, Corner E and
   Fifth St.
John H. Fulton, Va.
John B. Forester, Tenn.
John Blair, Tenn.

Hyatt's, opposite Brown's Hotel
Arnold Naudain (S), Del.
Nathan Smith (S), Conn.
Benjamin Swift (S), Vt.
Noyes Barber, Conn.
Henry C. Martindale, N.Y.
William Slade, Vt.
Jonathan Sloane, Ohio
Samuel Tweedy, Conn.
Ebenezer Young, Conn.
Joseph Trumbull, Conn.
Phineas Miner, Conn.

Hutton's, Thirteenth St. Between E
   and F St.
Horace Binney, Penn.
Richard M. Wilde, Ga.
Joseph M. White, Deleg., Terr. of Fla.

Mrs. Johnson, Ninth St. near E.
Joseph Vance, Ohio
Amos Davis, Ky.
Chilton Allan, Ky.

Kennedy's, Four and One-Half St.
Thomas Ewing (S), Ohio
Charles F. Mercer, Va.
Thomas Corwin, Ohio
Joseph H. Crane, Ohio
Lewis Williams, N.C.
Samuel F. Vinton, Ohio
George Chambers, Penn.
James M. Bell, Ohio

Keyworth's, Penn. Ave.
Edward Everett, Mass.

Langdon's, Sixth St., between E
   and F St.
David Potts, Jr., Penn.
Joel B. Sutherland, Penn.

Mrs. Latimer, President's Square
John T. Stoddert, Md.
Leonard Jarvis, Me.

Lindsley's, Penn. Ave.
William M. Inge, Tenn.
David W. Dickinson, Tenn.
Balie Peyton, Tenn.
Micajah T. Hawkins, N.C.

McCardle's, Capitol Hill
Robert Ramsey, Penn.
David D. Wagener, Penn.
Joel K. Mann, Penn.
Dutee J. Pearce, Penn.
Andrew Beaumont, Penn.
Samuel Fowler, N.J.

Mrs. McDaniel, Penn. Ave.
John Tyler (S), Va.
John Tipton (S), Ind.
Abraham Rencher, N.C.

Rice Garland, La.
Roger L. Gamble, Ga.
Thomas Davenport, Va.
William F. Gordon, Va.
Augustin S. Clayton, Ga.
John Robertson,[4] Va.
Dixon H. Lewis, Ala.

McLeod's, opposite Centre Market
Theodore Frelinghuysen (S), N.J.
Nehemiah R. Knight (S), R.I.
Gideon Tomlinson (S), Conn.
John G. Watmough, Penn.
George W. Lay, N.Y.
Tristam Burges, R.I.

Mrs. McPherson, F St.
Isaac C. Bates, Me.

Mrs. McKnight, Four and One-Half St.
Samuel W. Mardis, Ala.
Clement C. Clay, Ala.
John Murphy, Ala.

Mrs. Miller, F St., between Thirteenth and Fourteenth
Churchill C. Cambreleng, N.Y.
James M. Wayne,[5] Ga.

Mrs. Myer, nearly opposite Gadsby's
John Chaney, Ohio
John Galbraith, Penn.
Robert Mitchell, Ohio
Philemon Thomas, Ohio
Henry A.P. Muhlenberg, Penn.
Isaac B. Van Houten, N.Y.
Abel Huntington, N.Y.
John Thomson, Ohio
Charles G. Ferris, N.Y.
Jeremiah McLene, Ohio

Mrs. Mountz, Penn. Ave.
John Reynolds, Ill.

Mrs. Owner, Penn. Ave.
Samuel McKean (S), Penn.

Felix Grundy (S), Tenn.
Thomas Morris (S), Ohio
John P. King (S), Ga.
Zadoc Casey, Ill.
John Carr, Ind.
Edward A. Hannegan, Ind.
George L. Kinnard, Ind.
Chittenden Lyon, Ky.
Ratliff Boon, Ind.
William L. May, Ill.
William N. Shinn, N.J.
Benjamin Jones, Ohio

Mrs. Peyton, Corner Penn. Ave. and Four and One-Half St.
Peleg Sprague (S),[6] Me.
John J. Allen, Va.
William J. Grayson, S.C.
John K. Griffin, S.C.
Stephen C. Phillips, Mass.

Miss Polk, Penn. Ave.
Ether Shepley (S), Me.
Nathaniel P. Tallmadge (S), N.Y.
Silas Wright, Jr. (S), N.Y.
John Cramer, N.Y.
Gorham Parks, Me.
Rufus McIntire, Me.
Ransom H. Gillet, N.Y.
Charles McVean, N.Y.
Abijah Mann, Jr., N.Y.
Edward Kavanagh, Me.
Lucius Lyon, Deleg., Mich. Terr.

Mrs. Pitman, F St., near Twelfth St.
Amos Lane, Ind.
Daniel Wardwell, N.Y.
Sherman Page, N.Y.

Pursell's, opposite Brown's
James M.H. Beale, Va.
Wiliam C. Dunlap, Tenn.

Private Residences
Mr. Tasteff (?), Penn. Ave.
John Bell, Tenn.

[4] Elected to fill the vacancy caused by the resignation of Andrew Stevenson, and took his seat Dec. 4, 1834.
[5] Resigned Jan. 13, 1835.
[6] Resigned Jan. 1, 1835. John Ruggles was elected to fill the vacancy, and took his seat Feb. 6, 1835.

First North of President's House
John Quincy Adams, Mass.
*Two doors from corner of Tenth and
E St.*
Samuel S. Harrison, Penn.
Four and One-Half St.
George Poindexter (S), Miss.
Near the West Market
Elias K. Kane (S), Ill.
*Mr. Niles, Twelfth St., between Penn.
Ave. and E St.*
George M. Bibb (S), Ky.
Sawkin's, corner of Twelfth and F St.
Robert P. Letcher, Ky.
Col. Henderson, near the Navy Yard
William B. Shepard, N.C.
Mrs. Glover, Tenth St.
Daniel L. Barringer, N.C.
Georgetown, Cox's Row
Henry Johnson, La.

Mrs. Queen, Penn. Ave.
John M. Patton, Va.
Benning M. Bean, N.H.
Samuel McDowell Moore, Va.
William P. Taylor, Va.
Ferdinand S. Schenck, N.J.
Samuel G. Hathaway, N.Y.
John Y. Mason, Va.

Mrs. Renner, Mo. Ave.
Gabriel Moore (S), Ala.
John Ewing, Ind.
Johnathan McCarty, Ind.

Saunder's, E St., near the General
   Post Office
Bedford Brown (S), N.C.

James Buchanan (S),[7] Penn.
William R. King (S), Ala.
Edward Lucas, Va.

Mr. Nathan Smith, near the General
   Post Office
Henry Clay (S), Ky.
Samuel L. Southard (S), N.J.
Joseph Kent (S), Md.
Alexander Porter (S), La.
Thomas A. Marshall, Ky.
John J. Milligan, Del.

Mrs. Sprigg, Capitol Hill
Joseph Henderson, Penn.

Mr. Stettinius, Penn. Ave.
Ebenezer Jackson, Jr., Conn.

Vivan's, Penn. Ave.
George A. Waggaman (S), La.

Mrs. Walker, E. St.
Charles A. Barnitz, Penn.
Joel Turrill, N.Y.

Whittlesey's, Capitol Hill
George Evans, Me.

Young's, N.J. Ave., Capitol Hill
John Clayton (S), Del.
Samuel Bell (S), N.H.
Asher Robbins (S), R.I.
Philo C. Fuller, N.Y.
Elisha Whittlesey, Ohio
Horace Everett, Vt.

APPENDIX

Alfred Cuthbert (S),[8] Ga.
Robert H. Goldsborough (S),[9] Md.
Charles Bodle, N.Y.

Robert T. Lytle,[10] Ohio
Warren R. Davis,[11] S.C.

[7] Elected to fill the vacancy caused by the resignation of William Wilkins, and took his seat Dec. 15, 1834.
[8] Elected to fill the vacancy caused by the resignation of John Forsyth, and took his seat Jan. 12, 1835.
[9] Elected to fill the vacancy caused by the resignation of Ezekiel F. Chambers, and took his seat Jan. 23, 1835.
[10] Resigned Mar. 10, 1834; elected to fill the vacancy caused by his own resignation, and took his seat Dec. 27, 1834.
[11] Died Jan. 29, 1835.

STANDING COMMITTEES OF THE
HOUSE OF REPRESENTATIVES

ELECTIONS

Chairman: Nathaniel H. Claiborne, Va.

John K. Griffin, S.C.
Micajah T. Hawkins, N.C.
Aaron Vanderpoel, N.Y.
Edward A. Hannagean, Ind.

Gideon Hard, N.Y.
Robert Burns, N.H.
James W. Bouldin, Va.
Daniel Kilgore, Ohio

WAYS AND MEANS

Chairman: James K. Polk, Tenn.

Richard H. Wilde, Ga.[12]
Churchill C. Cambreleng, N.Y.
Isaac McKim, Md.
Horace Binney, Penn.

George Loyall, Va.
John McKinley, Ala.
Henry Hubbard, N.H.
Thomas Corwin, Ohio

CLAIMS

Chairman: Elisha Whittlesey, Ohio

Noyes Barber, Conn.
Rufus McIntire, Me.
James H. Gholson, Va.
John B. Forester, Tenn.

John T. Stoddert Md.
John Banks, Penn.
John H. Fulton, Va.
Phineas Miner, Conn.

COMMERCE

Chairman: Joel B. Sutherland, Penn.

Joseph M. Harper, N.H.
Henry L. Pinckney, S.C.
James P. Heath, Md.
Dutee J. Pearce, R.I.

Ransom H. Gillet, N.Y.
Stephen C. Phillips, Mass.
Henry Johnson, La.
John J. Morgan, N.Y.

PUBLIC LANDS

Chairman: Clement C. Clay, Ala.

Ratliff Boon, Ind.
Augustin S. Clayton, Ga.
William Slade, Vt.
William H. Ashley, Mo.

William M. Inge, Tenn.
Lewis Williams, N.C.
Levi Lincoln, Mass.
Zadoc Casey, Ill.

POST OFFICE AND POST ROADS

Chairman: Henry W. Connor, N.C.

Edward Kavanagh, Me.
Phineas Thomas, La.
George M. Briggs, Mass.
John Murphy, Ala.

Amos Lane, Ind.
John Laporte, Penn.
Hiland Hall, Vt.
William Schley, Ga.

---

[12] Omitted in the *Congressional Directory* but listed in the *Journal of the House of Representatives*.

DISTRICT OF COLUMBIA

Chairman: Joseph W. Chinn, Va.

William B. Shepard, N.C.
Thomas M.T. McKennan, Penn.
John J. Allen, Va.
William Hiester, Penn.

Henry King, Penn.
Aaron Vanderpoel, N.Y.
John N. Steele, Md.

JUDICIARY

Chairman: Thomas F. Foster, Ga.

William F. Gordon, Va.
Samuel Beardsley, N.Y.
Francis Thomas, Md.
Benjamin Hardin, Ky.

Gorham Parks, Me.
Franklin Pierce, N.H.
John Robertson, Va.
Thomas L. Hamer, Ohio

REVOLUTIONARY CLAIMS

Chairman: Henry A.P. Muhlenberg, Penn.

Joseph H. Crane, Ohio
Isaac C. Bates, Mass.
James Standifer, Tenn.
Thomas A. Marshall, Ky.

Ebenezer Young, Conn.
William Baylies, Mass.
Joel Turrill, N.Y.
George L. Kinnard, Ind.

PUBLIC EXPENDITURES

Chairman: Thomas Davenport, Va.

Chittenden Lyon, Ky.
Samuel Page, N.Y.
William Clark, Penn.
Samuel Tweedy, Conn.

Jeremiah McLene, Ohio
William Jackson, Mass.
Abner Hazeltine, N.Y.
Charles G. Ferris N.Y.

PRIVATE LAND CLAIMS

Chairman: Cave Johnson, Tenn.

Samuel W. Mardis, Ala.
John Carr, Ind.
John Galbraith, Penn.
Abijah Mann, Jr., N.Y.

John Bull, Mo.
George Chambers, Penn.
Amos Davis, Ky.
William L. May, Ill.

MANUFACTURES

Chairman: John Quincy Adams, Mass.

Harmar Denny, Penn.
Philemon Dickerson, N.J.
Henry C. Martindale, N.Y.
William McComas, Va.

Gayton P. Osgood, Mass.
William K. Clowney, S.C.
John Cramer, N.Y.
Ebenezer Jackson, Jr., Conn.

AGRICULTURE

Chairman: Abraham Bockee, N.Y.

William P. Taylor, Va.
Samuel G. Hathaway, N.Y.
Charles A. Barnitz, Penn.
Benning M. Bean, N.H.

William C. Dunlap, Tenn.
William K. Clowney, S.C.
James Turner, Md.
Martin Beaty, Ky.

INDIAN AFFAIRS

Chairman: George R. Gilmer, Ga.

Johnathan McCarty, Ind.
Horace Everett, Vt.
James Graham, N.C.
William Allen, Ohio

David W. Dickinson, Tenn.
Edward Howell, N.Y.
James Love, Ky.
George Grennell, Jr., Mass.

MILITARY AFFAIRS

Chairman: Richard M. Johnson, Ky.

Joseph Vance, Ohio
Jesse Speight, N.C.
Aaron Ward, N.Y.
John Thomson, Ohio

John Coffee, Ga.
Samuel Bunch, Tenn.
James I. McKay, N.C.
Joseph B. Anthony, Penn.

NAVAL AFFAIRS

Chairman: Campbell P. White, N.Y.

John J. Milligan, Del.
John G. Watmough, Penn.
Gerrit Y. Lansing N.Y.
John Reed, Mass.

William J. Grayson, S.C.
James Parker, N.J.
Francis O.J. Smith, Me.
Henry A. White, Va.

FOREIGN AFFAIRS

Chairman: James M. Wayne, Ga.

Edward Everett, Mass.
Thomas H. Hall, N.C.
Richard Coulter, Penn.
Leonard Jarvis, Me.

Job Pierson, N.Y.
John M. Patton, Va.
Robert P. Letcher, Ky.
Balie Peyton, Tenn.

TERRITORIES

Chairman: Chilton Allan, Ky.

David Potts, Jr., Penn.
Noadiah Johnson, N.Y.
Edgar C. Wilson, Va.
Benjamin Jones, Ohio

John Ewing, Ind.
Roger L. Gamble, Ga.
Henry Cage, Miss.
Joseph Trumbull, Conn.

REVOLUTIONARY PENSIONS

Chairman: Daniel Wardwell, N.Y.

Daniel L. Barringer, N.C.
Christopher Tompkins, Ky.
Samuel McDowell Moore, Va.
Luke Lea, Tenn.

William K. Fuller, N.Y.
Samuel Fowler, N.J.
James M. Bell, Ohio
George W. Lay, N.Y.

INVALID PENSIONS

Chairman: Jesse Miller, Penn.

James M.H. Beale, Va.
John Adams, N.Y.
Ferdinand S. Schenck, N.J.
Thomas Chilton, Ky.

Robert Mitchell, Ohio
John W. Brown, N.Y.
Henry F. Janes, Vt.
John Chaney, Ohio

ROADS AND CANALS
Chairman: Charles F. Mercer, Va.

John Blair, Tenn.
Samuel F. Vinton, Ohio
Andrew Stewart, Penn.
Abraham Rencher, N.C.

William Cost Johnson, Md.
Edward Lucas, Va.
Patrick H. Pope, Ky.
John Reynolds, Ill.

REVISAL AND UNFINISHED BUSINESS
Chairman: John Dickson, N.Y.

Samuel S. Harrison, Penn.
Charles McVean, N.Y.

William N. Shinn, N.J.
William Taylor, N.Y.

ACCOUNTS
Chairman: Joel K. Mann, Penn.

Thomas Lee, N.J.
Henry Mitchell, N.Y.

David Crockett, Tenn.
Gayton P. Osgood, Mass.

EXPENDITURES IN THE DEPARTMENT OF STATE
Chairman: Augustine H. Shepperd, N.C.

Rowland Day, N.Y.
Andrew Beaumont, Penn.

Charles Bodle, N.Y.
William Patterson, Ohio

EXPENDITURES IN THE DEPARTMENT OF THE TREASURY
Chairman: Heman Allen, Vt.

Philo C. Fuller, N.Y.
James Harper, Penn.

David Spangler, Ohio
Samuel Clark, N.Y.

EXPENDITURES IN THE DEPARTMENT OF WAR
Chairman: Frederick Whittlesey, N.Y.

Edmund Deberry, N.C.
George Chambers, Penn.

Taylor Webster, Ohio
Nicoll Halsey, N.Y.

EXPENDITURES IN THE DEPARTMENT OF THE NAVY
Chairman: Joseph Hall, Me.

Abel Huntington, N.Y.
Robert Ramsey, Penn.

Jonathan Sloane, Ohio
Isaac B. Van Houten, N.Y.

EXPENDITURES IN THE POST OFFICE DEPARTMENT
Chairman: Albert G. Hawes, Ky.

John H. Fulton, Va.
Robert Burns, N.H.

David D. Wagener, Penn.
George W. Lay, N.Y.

EXPENDITURES ON THE PUBLIC BUILDINGS
Chairman: Reuben Whallon, N.Y.

Edward Darlington, Penn.
John W. Brown, N.Y.

Joseph Henderson, Penn.
Gideon Hard, N.Y.

SELECT COMMITTEES

PUBLIC GROUNDS AND BUILDINGS
Chairman: Leonard Jarvis, Me.

Aaron Ward, N.Y.

John G. Watmough, Penn

Levi Lincoln, Mass.

William B. Shepard, N.C.

MILITARY ACADEMY
Chairman: Albert G. Hawes, Ky.

Francis O.J. Smith, Me.

Franklin Pierce, N.H.

George N. Briggs, Mass.

Dutee J. Pearce, R.I.

Ebenezer Young, Conn.

Hiland Hall, Vt.

Abijah Mann, Jr., N.Y.

Philemon Dickerson, N.J.

John Laporte, Penn.

John J. Milligan, Del.

Richard B. Carmichael, Md.

James H. Gholson, Va.

Augustine H. Shepperd, N.C.

Robert B. Campbell, S.C.

Roger L. Gamble, Ga.

John B. Forester, Tenn.

William Allen, Ohio

Rice Garland, La.

Edward A. Hannegan, Ind.

Henry Cage, Miss.

Zadoc Casey, Ill.

Dixon H. Lewis, Ala.

William H. Ashley, Mo.

REORGANIZATION OF THE TREASURY DEPARTMENT
Chairman: James M. Wayne, Ga.

John Y. Mason, Va.

Thomas M.T. McKennan, Penn.

Churchill C. Cambreleng, N.Y.

Abraham Rencher, N.C.

George Evans, Me.

Patrick H. Pope, Ky.

Leonard Jarvis, Me.

Jarvis I. McKay, N.C.

ON THE ELECTION OF PRESIDENT AND VICE PRESIDENT
Chairman: George R. Gilmer, Ga.

William S. Archer, Va.

Horace Binney, Penn.

Samuel Beardsley, N.Y.

Benjamin Gorham, Mass.

Richard M. Johnson, Ky.

Jesse Speight, N.C.

Henry Hubbard, N.H.

John Carr, Ind.

ON THE MEMORIAL OF THE RHODE ISLAND BRIGADE
Chairman: Tristam Burges, R.I.

Augustine H. Shepperd, N.C.

Thomas A. Marshall, Ky.

William Cost Johnson, Md.

Henry A. Wise, Va.

Abner Hazeltine, N.Y.

Samuel Tweedy, Conn.

ON THE HEIRS OF ROBERT FULTON
Chairman: Campbell P. White, N.Y.

Edward Kavanagh, Me.

George Loyall, Va.

James Love, Ky.

Richard I. Manning, S.C.

William Cost Johnson, Md.

Joseph Trumbull, Conn.

JOINT COMMITTEES

LIBRARY OF CONGRESS

House	Senate
Edward Everett, Mass.	Asher Robbins, R.I.
George Loyall, Va.	George Poindexter, Miss.
	George M. Bibb, Ky.

ON THE DEATH OF LAFAYETTE

House	Senate
Henry Hubbard, N.H.	Henry Clay, Ky.
Levi Lincoln, Mass.	Hugh Lawson White, Tenn.
Campbell P. White, N.Y.	John C. Calhoun, S.C.
John J. Allen, Va.	Daniel Webster, Mass.
Thomas A. Marshall, Ky.	James Buchanan, Penn.

COMMITTEES OF THE SENATE

FOREIGN RELATIONS

Chairman: Henry Clay, Ky.

John P. King, Ga.	Peleg Sprague, Me.
Willie P. Mangum, N.C.	Nathaniel P. Tallmadge, N.Y.

FINANCE

Chairman: Daniel Webster, Mass.

Silas Wright, Jr., N.Y.	Willie P. Mangum, N.C.
John Tyler, Va.	Thomas Ewing, Ohio

COMMERCE

Chairman: Nathaniel Silsbee, Mass.

William R. King, Ala.	Peleg Sprague, Me.
George A. Waggaman, La.	Silas Wright, Jr., N.Y.

MANUFACTURES

Chairman: Theodore Frelinghuysen, N.J.

Thomas Morris, Ohio	Samuel Prentiss, Vt.
Nehemiah R. Knight, R.I.	John Tyler, Va.

AGRICULTURE

Chairman: Bedford Brown, N.C.

Joseph Kent, Md.	John M. Robinson, Ill.
Benjamin Swift, Vt.	Thomas Morris, Ohio

MILITARY AFFAIRS

Chairman: Thomas H. Benton, Mo.

John Tipton, Ind.
William C. Preston, S.C.

William R. King, Ala.
John M. Clayton, Del.

MILITIA

Chairman: John M. Robinson, Ill.

William Hendricks, Ind.
Samuel McKean, Penn.

George A. Waggaman, La.
Benjamin Swift, Vt.

NAVAL AFFAIRS

Chairman: Samuel L. Southard, N.J.

Asher Robbins, R.I.
Nathaniel P. Tallmadge, N.Y.

George M. Bibb, Ky.
John Black, Miss.

PUBLIC LANDS

Chairman: George Poindexter, Miss.

Gabriel Moore, Ala.
Samuel Prentiss, Vt.

Samuel McKean, Penn.
Henry Clay, Ky.

PRIVATE LAND CLAIMS

Chairman: John Black, Miss.

Elias K. Kane, Ill.
Arnold Naudian, Del.

Alexander Porter, La.
Ether Shepley, Me.

INDIAN AFFAIRS

Chairman: Hugh Lawson White, Tenn.

John Tipton, Ind.
Nathan Smith, Conn.

Benjamin Swift, Vt.
Theordore Frelinghuysen, N.J.

CLAIMS

Chairman: Samuel Bell, N.H.

John Tipton, Ind.
Arnold Naudian, Del.

Bedford Brown, N.C.
Ether Shepley, Me.

JUDICIARY

Chairman: John M. Clayton, Del.

William C. Preston, S.C.
Samuel Bell, N.H.

Nathan Smith, Conn.
Benjamin W. Leigh, Va.

POST OFFICE AND POST ROADS

Chairman: Felix Grundy, Tenn.

Thomas Ewing, Ohio
John M. Robinson, Ill.

Nehemiah R. Knight, R.I.
Samuel L. Southard, N.J.

PENSIONS

Chairman: Gideon Tomlinson, Conn.

Nathaniel P. Tallmadge, N.Y.　　　Samuel Prentiss, Vt.
Samuel McKean, Penn.　　　　　　William C. Preston, S.C.

ROADS AND CANALS

Chairman: William Hendricks, Ind.

Joseph Kent, Md.　　　　　　Asher Robbins, R.I.
John M. Robinson, Ill.　　　Samuel McKean, Penn.

DISTRICT OF COLUMBIA

Chairman: John Tyler, Va.

Joseph Kent, Md.　　　　　Samuel L. Southard, N.J.
George M. Bibb, Ky.　　　 Gideon Tomlinson, Conn.

REVOLUTIONARY CLAIMS

Chairman: Gabriel Moore, Ala.

Nathan Smith, Conn.　　　　　　　Benjamin W. Leigh, Va.
Hugh Lawson White, Tenn.　　　　Theodore Frelinghuysen, N.J.

TO AUDIT AND CONTROL THE CONTINGENT FUND

Chairman: Nehemiah R. Knight, R.I.

Gideon Tomlinson, Conn.　　　　Thomas Morris, Ohio

ENGROSSED BILLS

Chairman: Ether Shepley, Ohio

Thomas Morris, Ohio　　　　　John M. Robinson, Ill.

SELECT COMMITTEES

ON FRENCH SPOLIATIONS PRIOR TO SEPT. 30, 1800

Chairman: Daniel Webster, Mass.

Felix Grundy, Tenn.　　　　　William C. Preston, S.C.
Samuel Prentiss, Vt.　　　　 Ether Shepley, Me.

TO PURCHASE THE RIGHT OF USING THE VAPOR BATH OF BOYD REILLY

Chairman: Arnold Naudain, Del.

Asher Robbins, R.I.　　　　　Samuel Prentiss, Vt.
Joseph Kent, Md.　　　　　　 Peleg Sprague, Me.

CONGRESSIONAL DIRECTORY

TWENTY-FOURTH CONGRESS, FIRST SESSION
(December 7, 1835 – July 4, 1836)

G. Anderson's, Four and One-Half St.
Chilton Allan, Ky.
James Harlan, Ky.
John Chambers, Ky.

Mrs. Bacon, Penn. Ave.
William L. May, Ill.
Eli Moore, N.Y.

Mrs. Ball, opposite Brown's
Robert Craig, Va.
George W. Hopkins, Va.
William S. Morgan, Va.
William Clark, Penn.
Edmund Deberry, N.C.
John Roane, Va.
Nathaniel H. Claiborne, Va.

Mrs. Ballard, Penn. Ave.
Henry L. Pinckney, S.C.
William Hiester, Penn.
Edward Darlington, Penn.
David Spangler, Ohio

Chester Bailey's, Seventh St.
John Bell, Tenn.

Mr. Bayliss, opposite Centre Market
Daniel Webster (S), Mass.

Mr. Birth, Third St.
Bedford Brown (S), N.C.
Garret D. Wall (S), N.J.
Samuel Beardsley,[1] N.Y.
James Parker, N.J.

Brown's Hotel
George W. Jones,[2] Deleg., Mich. Terr.
William H. Ashley, Mo.
John B. Forester, Tenn.
Jesse Speight, N.C.
Ratliff Boon, Ind.
James M. H. Beale, Va.
Reuben Chapman, Ala.
Taylor Webster, Ohio
Micajah T. Hawkins, N.C.
James Graham,[3] N.C.
John Robertson, Va.
James Rogers, S.C.

Rev. O. B. Brown, nearly Opposite the
  General Post Office
Richard M. Johnson, Ky.
Ambrose H. Sevier,[4] Deleg., Ark. Terr.
Moses Mason, Jr., Me.

Mrs. Brown, Penn. Ave.
Gabriel Moore (S), Ala.
Benjamin Hardin, Ky.
Johnathan McCarty, Ind.

---

[1] Resigned Mar. 29, 1836.
[2] Served as a delegate from the Michigan Territory until Dec. 5, 1836, when he became the delegate from the new Territory of Wisconsin.
[3] Presented credentials as a member-elect and took his seat on Dec. 7, 1835; David Newlands contested the election, and on Mar. 29, 1836, the seat was declared vacant; Graham won the subsequent election, and took his seat Dec. 5, 1836.
[4] Served as Delegate until June 15, 1836, when the Arkansas Territory was granted statehood; subsequently elected Senator.

Dr. Brodhead, Capitol Hill
Isaac Hill (S),[5] N.H.
Charles E. Haynes, Ga.
Benning M. Bean, N.H.
Robert Burns, N.H.
Samuel Cushman, N.H.

Mrs. Child, Georgetown
James W. Bouldin, Va.
William McComas, Va.

Mr. Clements, C St.
Henry Clay (S), Ky.
John J. Crittenden (S), Ky.
Alexander Porter (S), La.

Mrs. Connor, Penn. Ave.
William J. Graves, Ky.
William Montgomery, N.C.

Mrs. Cochran, F St.
Timothy Childs, N.Y.

Miss Corcoran, Penn. Ave.
Levi Lincoln, Mass.
Harmar Denny, Penn.
David Potts, Jr., Penn.
Joel B. Sutherland, Penn.

Mrs. Coyle, Capitol Hill
John Davis (S), Mass.
John P. King (S), Ga.
Abner Hazeltine, N.Y.
David A. Russell, N.Y.
Seaton Grantland, Ga.
Jabez Y. Jackson, Ga.
George W. Owens, Ga.

Mr. Dashiel, Capitol Hill
Jesse A. Bynum, N.C.

Mrs. Denny, Four and One-Half St.
Rice Garland, La.

Dowson's No. 1, Capitol Hill
Thomas H. Benton (S), Mo.

Thomas L. Hamer, Ohio
Francis Thomas, Md.
James I. McKay, N.C.
Franklin Pierce, N.H.
William B. Carter, Tenn.
Adam Huntsman, Tenn.
Edward A. Hannegan, Ind.

Dowson's No. 2, Capitol Hill
Ebenezer J. Shields, Tenn.
Cave Johnson, Tenn.
William C. Dunlap, Tenn.

Mrs. Dyer, near the Old Theatre
John Black (S), Miss.
Benjamin W. Leigh (S), Va.
Willie P. Mangum (S), N.C.

Mr. Fletcher, E St. near the General
    Post Office
Samuel Prentiss (S), Vt.
Henry F. Janes, Vt.
George N. Briggs, Mass.
Heman Allen, Vt.
Hiland Hall, Vt.
William B. Calhoun, Mass.
Caleb Cushing, Mass.
John Banks, Penn.
Philo C. Fuller, N.Y.
John Laporte, Penn.

Mrs. Fletcher, F St.
Dutee J. Pearce, R.I.
William Sprague, R.I.
Nathaniel B. Borden, Mass.

Fuller's Hotel
Louis F. Linn (S), Mo.
Nathaniel P. Tallmadge (S), N.Y.
Silas Wright, Jr. (S), N.Y.
Stephen C. Phillips, Mass.

Gadsby's Hotel
Aaron Ward, N.Y.
Isaac McKim, Md.
Abbott Lawrence, Mass.
Francis Granger, N.Y.
Robert B. Campbell, S.C.

[5] Resigned May 30, 1836, having been elected Governor. John Pope was elected
to fill the vacancy, and took his seat June 13, 1836.

Mrs. Galvin, C St.
William Hendricks (S), Ind.
Samuel McKean (S), Penn.
William Kennon, Sr., Ohio
Daniel Kilgore, Ohio
William Patterson, Ohio
Joseph Johnson, Va.

Mrs. Gardner, opposite Centre Market
Joseph Henderson, Penn.
Job Mann, Penn.
Eleazer W. Ripley, La.

Mrs. Hamilton, nearly opposite Gadsby's
Ransom H. Gillet, N.Y.
Samuel Barton, N.Y.
Abraham Bockee, N.Y.
William K. Fuller, N.Y.
Gerrit Y. Lansing, N.Y.
William Mason, N.Y.
Nicholas Sickles, N.Y.
William Taylor, N.Y.

Miss Hamilton, C St.
John Coffee, Ga.
Thomas Glascock, Ga.
Jesse F. Cleveland, Ga.
Hopkins Holsey, Ga.
George W. B. Towns, Ga.

Mr. Harbaugh, Seventh St.
Felix Grundy (S), Tenn.
John M. Robinson (S), Ill.
Abijah Mann, Jr., N.Y.
Joseph B. Anthony, Penn.
Richard French, Ky.
Albert G. Hawes, Ky.
Henry W. Connor, N.C.
John W. Davis, Ind.

Mr. Havenner, C St.
John White, Ky.
John Calhoon, Ky.

H. V. Hill's, Corner of C and
  Third St.
Thomas Ewing (S), Ohio
George Chambers, Penn.
Bellamy Storer, Ohio
Samuel F. Vinton, Ohio
George Evans, Ohio
William K. Bond, Ohio
Gideon Hard, N.Y.
Elias Howell, Ohio

Mrs. S. A. Hill,[6] nearly opposite
  Gadsby's
John Ruggles (S), Me.
Ether Shepley (S), Me.
John M. Niles (S),[7] Conn.
Isaac Toucey, Conn.
Lancelot Phelps, Conn.
Hiram P. Hunt, N.Y.
Ulysses F. Doubleday, N.Y.
Stephen B. Leonard, N.Y.
Joshua Lee, N.Y.
Joseph Hall, Me.
John Fairfield, Me.

John Hutton's Thirteenth St.
Joseph M. White, Deleg., Terr. of Fla.

Mr. Hyatt's, opposite Brown's
Arnold Naudain (S),[8] Del.
Benjamin Swift (S), Vt.
Gideon Tomlinson (S), Conn.
William Slade, Vt.
Jonathan Sloane, Ohio
George Grennell, Jr., Mass.
John Reed, Mass.
John Taliaferro, Va.
Samuel Hoar, Mass.
William Jackson, Mass.

Mrs. Ironside, Seventh Street
John J. Milligan, Del.
Joseph R. Ingersoll, Penn.

---

[6] John Norvell and Isaac E. Crary, of Michigan, claiming seats as Senator and Representative respectively, resided in this mess. Michigan was granted statehood on Jan. 26, 1837, and Norvell took his seat the same day, while Crary took his seat on Jan. 27, 1837.
[7] Appointed to fill the vacancy caused by the death of Nathan Smith, and took his seat Dec. 21, 1835; he was subsequently elected.
[8] Resigned June 16, 1836. Richard H. Bayard was elected to fill the vacancy, and took his seat June 20, 1836.

Mrs. Kennedy, Four and One-Half St.
Thomas Corwin, Ohio
Lewis Williams, N.C.
Joseph H. Crane, Ohio
Samson Mason, Ohio
Joseph R. Underwood, Ky.
Charles F. Mercer, Va.
Mathias Morris, Penn.
Abraham Rencher, N.C.
Thomas M. T. Mckennan, Penn.

Mr. Keyworth, Penn. Ave.
Samuel L. Southard (S), N.J.

Mrs. Latimer, President's Square
Leonard Jarvis, Me.
Aaron Vanderpoel, N.Y.
Walter Coles, Va.
John Cramer, N.Y.
Gorham Parks, Me.

Mr. Lindsley, nearly opposite Gadsby's
James K. Polk, Tenn.

Mrs. Lindenberger, Capitol Hill
John C. Calhoun (S), S.C.
William C. Preston (S), S.C.
James H. Hammond,[9] S.C.
Francis W. Pickens, S.C.
Waddy Thompson, Jr.,[10] S.C.

Mr. McLeod, opposite City Hall
George W. Lay, N.Y.
Thomas C. Love, N.Y.
Jeremiah Bailey, Me.

Mrs. McDaniel, Mo. Ave.
John Tipton (S), Ind.
John Tyler (S),[11] Va.
Ferdinand S. Schenck, N.J.
Samuel Fowler, N.J.

Mr. Masi, Penn. Ave.
Henry Hubbard (S), N.H.
Francis O. J. Smith, Me.

Mrs. McCardle, Penn. Ave.
David D. Wagener, Penn.
Jacob Fry, Jr., Penn.
John Klingensmith, Jr., Penn.
Henry Logan, Penn.
Andrew Beaumont, Penn.
Michael W. Ash, Penn.

Mrs. McKnight, F St.
Amos Lane, Ind.

Mrs. Miller, F St.
Churchill C. Cambreleng, N.Y.

Mrs. Meyer, nearly opposite Gadsby's
Henry A. P. Muhlenberg, Penn.
Edward B. Hubley, Penn.
Joseph Reynolds, N.Y.
Dudley Farlin, N.Y.
William Seymour, N.Y.
Matthias J. Bovee, N.Y.
Valentine Efner, N.Y.
Jeremiah McLene, Ohio
Abel Huntington, N.Y.
John Chaney, Ohio
John Galbraith, Penn.
John Thomson, Ohio

Mrs. Owner, Penn. Ave.
Thomas Morris (S), Ohio
Benjamin Jones, Ohio
William N. Shinn, N.J.
Thomas Lee, N.J.
Linn Boyd, Ky.
Albert G. Harrison, Mo.
John Reynolds, Ill.
Zadoc Casey, Ill.
Joseph Weeks, N.H.
John Carr, Ind.
George L. Kinnard, Ind.

Mrs. Peyton, Penn. Ave.
William J. Grayson, S.C.
John K. Griffin, S.C.
James Harper, Penn.

[9] Resigned Feb. 26, 1836.
[10] Elected to fill the vacancy caused by the death of Representative-elect Warren R. Davis in the preceding Congress, and took his seat Dec. 16, 1835.
[11] Resigned Feb. 29, 1836. William C. Rives was elected to fill the vacancy, and took his seat Mar. 14, 1836.

Mrs. Pittman, Third St.[12]
Andrew T. Judson, Conn.
Daniel Wardwell, N.Y.
Andrew Buchanan, Penn.
Sherman Page, N.Y.
John W. Brown, N.Y.
Graham H. Chapin, N.Y.
Samuel Ingham, Conn.
Elisha Haley, Conn.
Gideon Lee, N.Y.

Miss Polk, Penn. Ave.
Robert H. Goldsborough (S), Md.
Joseph Kent (S), Md.
John N. Steele, Md.
James A. Pearce, Md.
James Turner, Md.
Ebenezer Pettigrew, N.C.
William B. Shepard, N.C.

Private Residence
First St. North of the President's House
John Quincy Adams, Mass.
Major Garland, West of President's Square
James Garland, Va.
Mount Hope, Georgetown
Augustine H. Shepperd, N.C.
Corner of Tenth and E St.
Samuel S. Harrison, Penn.
Georgetown
George C. Washington, Md.
Six Buildings
Henry Johnson, La.
Mr. Guest, Tenth, near F St.
James Buchanan (S), Penn.

Mrs. Queen, Penn. Ave.
John Y. Mason, Va.
Joshua L. Martin, Ala.

Francis S. Lyon, Ala.
John M. Patton, Va.
George Loyall, Va.
George C. Dromgoole, Va.
John W. Jones, Va.

Mrs. Ronckendorff, Penn. Ave.
Hugh Lawson White (S), Tenn.
Balie Peyton, Tenn.
Henry A. Wise, Va.
James Standifer, Tenn.
Luke Lea, Tenn.
Samuel Bunch, Tenn.
Joab Lawler, Ala.
Abram P. Maury, Tenn.

Mr. Saunders, Seventh St.
William R. King (S), Ala.
Edward Lucas, Va.

Mr. Stettinius, opposite Brown's
Sherrod Williams, Ky.

Mrs. Ulrick, H St., between Seventeenth and Eighteenth St.
Philemon Dickerson, N.J.
John McKeon, N.Y.

Mr. Vivan, West of President's Square
Benjamin C. Howard, Md.

Mrs. Walker, E St., near the General Post Office
Joel Turrill, N.Y.
Jesse Miller, N.Y.

Mr. Young, Capitol Hill
John M. Clayton (S), Del.
Nehemiah R. Knight (S), R.I.
Asher Robbins (S), R.I.
Elisha Whittlesey, Ohio
Horace Everett, Vt.

APPENDIX

Dixon H. Lewis, Ala.
Zalmon Wildman,[13] Conn.

Alfred Cuthbert (S), Ga.
Elias K. Kane (S),[14] Ill.

[12] Lucius Lyon, claiming a seat as a Senator from Michigan, also lived at this mess. Michigan was granted statehood on Jan. 26, 1837, and Lyon took his seat the same day.
[13] Died Dec. 10, 1835. Thomas T. Whittlesey was elected to fill the vacancy, and took his seat Apr. 29, 1836.
[14] Died Dec. 12, 1835. William L. D. Ewing was elected to fill the vacancy, and took his seat Jan. 25, 1836.

Robert C. Nicholas (S),[15] La.   David Dickson, Miss.
Daniel Jenifer, Md.   Robert J. Walker (S), Miss.
John F. H. Claiborne, Miss.   Richard I. Manning,[16] S.C.

STANDING COMMITTEES OF THE
HOUSE OF REPRESENTATIVES

ELECTIONS

Chairman: Nathaniel H. Claiborne, Va.

John K. Griffin, S.C.   Daniel Kilgore, Ohio
Micajah T. Hawkins, N.C.   Andrew Buchanan, Penn.
Gideon Hard, N.Y.   Abram P. Maury, Tenn.
Robert Burns, N.H.   Linn Boyd, Ky.

WAYS AND MEANS

Chairman: Churchill C. Cambreleng, N.Y.

Isaac McKim, Md.   Francis O. J. Smith, Me.
George Loyall, Va.   Abbott Lawrence, Mass.
Thomas Corwin, Ohio   Joseph R. Ingersoll, Penn.
Cave Johnson, Tenn.   George W. Owens, Ga.

CLAIMS

Chairman: Elisha Whittlesey, Ohio

John B. Forester, Tenn.   John W. Davis, Ind.
John Banks, Penn.   John Taliaferro, Va.
Jesse A. Bynum, N.C.   Philo C. Fuller, N.Y.
George Grenell, Jr., Mass.   John Chambers, Ky.

COMMERCE

Chairman: Joel B. Sutherland, Penn.

Henry L. Pinckney, S.C.   Henry Johnson, La.
Dutee J. Pearce, R.I.   Samuel Ingham, Conn.
Ransom H. Gillet, N.Y.   Samuel Cushman, N.H.
Stephen C. Phillips, Mass.   John McKeon, N.Y.

PUBLIC LANDS

Chairman: Ratliff Boon, Ind.

William Slade, Vt.   William Kennon, Sr., Ohio
Lewis Williams, N.C.   William C. Dunlap, Tenn.
Levi Lincoln, Mass.   Reuben Chapman, Ala.
Zadoc Casey, Ill.   Albert G. Harrison, Mo.

---

[15] Was elected to the term beginning Mar. 4, 1835, and took his seat Nov. 4, 1836. Charles E. A. Gayarre was elected but resigned on account of ill health without qualifying; vacancy in this class from Mar. 4, 1835 to Jan. 13, 1836.
[16] Died May 1, 1836.

POST OFFICE AND POST ROADS

Chairman: Henry W. Connor, N.C.

George N. Briggs, Mass.
John Laporte, Penn.
Hiland Hall, Vt.
Abijah Mann, Jr., N.Y.

Jesse F. Cleveland, Ga.
Richard French, Ky.
Ebenezer J. Shields, Tenn.
George W. Hopkins, Va.

DISTRICT OF COLUMBIA

Chairman: William B. Shepard, N.C.

William Hiester, Penn.
Aaron Vanderpoel, N.Y.
James W. Bouldin, Va.
George C. Washington, Md.

Amos Lane, Ind.
James Rogers, S.C.
John Fairfield, Me.
George W. B. Townes, Ga.

JUDICIARY

Chairman: Samuel Beardsley, N.Y.

Francis Thomas, Md.
James Hardin, Ky.
Franklin Pierce, N.H.
John Robertson, Va.

Balie Peyton, Tenn.
Isaac Toucey, Conn.
John W. Jones, Va.
Joshua L. Martin, Ala.

REVOLUTIONARY CLAIMS

Chairman: Henry A. P. Muhlenberg, Penn.

Joseph H. Crane, Ohio
James Standifer, Tenn.
Joel Turrill, N.Y.
George L. Kinnard, Ind.

Andrew Beaumont, Penn.
Robert Craig, Va.
Graham H. Chapin, N.Y.
Joseph R. Underwood, Ky.

PUBLIC EXPENDITURES

Chairman: Sherman Page, N.Y.

William Clark, Penn.
Jeremiah McLene, Ohio
Moses Mason, Jr., Me.
Edmund Deberry, N.C.

Stephen B. Leonard, N.Y.
Elisha Haley, Conn.
John White, Ky.
Joseph Weeks, N.H.

PRIVATE LAND CLAIMS

Chairman: John Carr, Ind.

John Galbraith, Penn.
William Patterson, Ohio
George Chambers, Penn.
William L. May, Ill.

James Garland, Va.
James H. Hammond, S.C.
Adam Huntsman, Tenn.
Joab Lawler, Ala.

MANUFACTURES

Chairman: John Quincy Adams, Mass.

Harmar Denny, Penn.
Philemon Dickerson, N.J.
William McComas, Va.
Taylor Webster, Ohio

Gideon Lee, N.Y.
Andrew T. Judson, Conn.
Hopkins Holsey, Ga.
Francis Granger, N.Y.

AGRICULTURE

Chairman: Abraham Bockee, N.Y.

Benning M. Bean, N.H.
John Roane, Va.
William N. Shinn, N.J.
Edmund Deberry, N.C.

Jeremiah Bailey, Me.
Henry Logan, Penn.
Lancelot Phelps, Conn.
Valentine Efner, N.Y.

INDIAN AFFAIRS

Chairman: John Bell, Tenn.

Johnathan McCarty, Ind.
Horace Everett, Vt.
James Graham, N.C.
William H. Ashley, Mo.

Charles E. Haynes, Ga.
Francis S. Lyon, Ala.
Albert G. Hawes, Ky.
John Chaney, Ohio

MILITARY AFFAIRS

Chairman: Richard M. Johnson, Ky.

Jesse Speight, N.C.
Aaron Ward, N.Y.
John Thomson, Ohio
John Coffee, Ga.

Samuel Burch, Tenn.
James I. McKay, N.C.
Joseph B. Anthony, Penn.
George C. Dromgoole, Va.

MILITIA

Chairman: Thomas Glascock, Ga.

Joseph Henderson, Penn.
William K. Fuller, N.Y.
David D. Wagener, Penn.
William B. Calhoun, Mass.

Joshua Lee, N.Y.
William B. Carter, Tenn.
Walter Coles, Va.
Sherrod Williams, Ky.

NAVAL AFFAIRS

Chairman: Leonard Jarvis, Me.

John J. Milligan, Del.
Gerrit Y. Lansing, N.Y.
John Reed, Mass.
William J. Grayson, S.C.

James Parker, N.J.
Henry A. Wise, Va.
Michael W. Ash, Penn.
Seaton Grantland, Ga.

FOREIGN AFFAIRS

Chairman: John Y. Mason, Va.

Benjamin C. Howard, Md.
Robert B. Campbell, S.C.
John Cramer, N.Y.
Thomas L. Hamer, Ohio

Chilton Allan, Ky.
Gorham Parks, Me.
Caleb Cushing, Mass.
Jabez Y. Jackson, Ga.

TERRITORIES

Chairman: John M. Patton, Va.

David Potts, Jr., Penn.
John W. Brown, N.Y.
Samuel Fowler, N.J.
Francis W. Pickens, S.C.

William Sprague, R.I.
James A. Pearce, Md.
Nathaniel B. Borden, Mass.
William Montgomery, N.C.

REVOLUTIONARY PENSIONS

Chairman: Daniel Wardwell, N.Y.

Luke Lea, Tenn.
George W. Lay, N.Y.
Henry F. Janes, Vt.
Bellamy Storer, Ohio

William S. Morgan, Va.
John Klingensmith, Jr., Penn.
William K. Bond, Ohio
Jacob Fry, Jr., Penn.

INVALID PENSIONS

Chairman: Jesse Miller, Penn.

James M.H. Beale, Va.
George Evans, Me.
Ferdinand S. Schenck, N.J.
William Taylor, N.Y.

Samuel S. Harrison, Penn.
Ulysses F. Doubleday, N.Y.
Samuel Hoar, Mass.
Elias Howell, Ohio

ROADS AND CANALS

Chairman: Charles F. Mercer, Va.

Samuel F. Vinton, Ohio
Abraham Rencher, N.C.
Edward Lucas, Va.
John Reynolds, Ill.

Edward A. Hannegan, Ind.
John N. Steele, Md.
William Jackson, Mass.
John Calhoon, Ky.

REVISAL AND UNFINISHED BUSINESS

Chairman: Abel Huntington, N.Y.

Job Mann, Penn.
Samson Mason, Ohio

James Harlan, Ky.
Dudley Farlin, N.Y.

ACCOUNTS

Chairman: Thomas Lee, N.J.

Edward Darlington, Penn.
Joseph Hall, Me.

Joseph Johnson, Va.
James Turner, Md.

EXPENDITURES IN THE DEPARTMENT OF STATE

Chairman: Augustine H. Shepperd, N.C.

William B. Calhoun, Mass.
Hiram P. Hunt, N.Y.

Mathias Morris, Penn.
Nicholas Sickles, N.Y.

EXPENDITURES IN THE DEPARTMENT OF THE TREASURY

Chairman: Heman Allen, Vt.

James Harper, Penn.
David Spangler, Ohio

David A. Russell, N.Y.
Samuel Barton, N.Y.

EXPENDITURES IN THE DEPARTMENT OF WAR

Chairman: Benjamin Jones, Ohio

Matthias J. Bovee, N.Y.
Joseph Johnson, Va.

Thomas C. Love, N.Y.
Edward B. Hubley, Penn.

EXPENDITURES IN THE DEPARTMENT OF THE NAVY

Chairman: Joseph Hall, Me.

Jonathan Sloane, Ohio   Ebenezer Pettigrew, N.C.
William Seymour, N.Y.   William Mason, N.Y.

EXPENDITURES IN THE POST OFFICE DEPARTMENT

Chairman: Albert G. Hawes, Ky.

Robert Burns, N.H.   Jeremiah Bailey, Me.
Timothy Childs, N.Y.   Joseph Reynolds, N.Y.

EXPENDITURES ON THE PUBLIC BUILDINGS

Chairman: Edward Darlington, Penn.

Abner Hazeltine, N.Y.   John Galbraith, Penn.
Dutee J. Pearce, R.I.   James M. H. Beale, Va.

SELECT COMMITTEES

ON THE RULES

Chairman: Abijah Mann, Jr., N.Y.

John Quincy Adams, Mass.   Horace Everett, Vt.
Francis Thomas, Md.   Gorham Parks, Me.
Lewis Williams, N.C.   James Parker, N.J.
Churchill C. Cambreleng, N.Y.   George Chambers, Penn.

ON THE OHIO AND MICHIGAN BOUNDARY

Chairman: John Quincy Adams, Mass.

Benjamin Hardin, Ky.   Philemon Dickerson, N.J.
John M. Patton, Va.   James I. McKay, N.C.
Franklin Pierce, N.H.   William J. Grayson, S.C.
Charles E. Haynes, Ga.   Andrew T. Judson, Conn.

PETITION OF MORGAN NEVILLE

Chairman: Bellamy Storer, Ohio

John Roane, Va.   Hiram P. Hunt, N.Y.
Richard M. Johnson, Ky.   William B. Calhoun, Mass.

TO AMEND THE CONSTITUTION

Chairman: George C. Dromgoole, Va.

Aaron Vanderpoel, N.Y.   Eleazer W. Ripley, La.
Luke Lea, Tenn.   George W. B. Towns, Ga.
William L. May, Ill.   Waddy Thompson, Jr., S.C.
George N. Briggs, Mass.   Jesse Miller, Penn.

JOINT COMMITTEE

LIBRARY OF CONGRESS

House	Senate
George Loyall, Ga.	William C. Preston, S.C.
John McKeon, N.Y.	Alexander Porter, La.
Waddy Thompson, Jr., S.C.	Asher Robbins, R.I.

STANDING COMMITTEES OF THE SENATE

FOREIGN RELATIONS

Chairman: Henry Clay, Ky.

John P. King, Ga.	Nathaniel P. Tallmadge, N.Y.
Willie P. Mangum, N.C.	Alexander Porter, La.

FINANCE

Chairman: Daniel Webster, Mass.

Alfred Cuthbert, Ga.	John Tyler, Va.
Silas Wright, Jr., N.Y.	Willie P. Mangum, N.C.

COMMERCE

Chairman: John Davis, Mass.

Robert H. Goldsborough, Md.	Samuel McKean, Penn.
Gideon Tomlinson, Conn.	Louis F. Linn, Mo.

MANUFACTURES

Chairman: Nehemiah R. Knight, R.I.

John Ruggles, Me.	William Hendricks, Ind.
Thomas Morris, Ohio	Samuel Prentiss, Vt.

AGRICULTURE

Chairman: Bedford Brown, N.C.

Joseph Kent, Md.	Thomas Morris, Ohio
William R. King, Ala.	Silas Wright, Jr., N.Y.

MILITARY AFFAIRS

Chairman: Thomas H. Benton, Mo.

Garret D. Wall, N.J.	William C. Preston, S.C.
Robert H. Goldsborough, Md.	John Tipton, Ind.

MILITIA

Chairman: John M. Robinson, Ill.

William Hendricks, Ind.	Garret D. Wall, N.J.
Samuel McKean, Penn.	Benjamin Swift, Vt.

NAVAL AFFAIRS

Chairman: Samuel L. Southard, N.J.

Nathaniel P. Tallmadge, N.Y.
John Black, Miss.

Asher Robbins, R.I.
Alfred Cuthbert, Ga.

PUBLIC LANDS

Chairman: Thomas Ewing, Ohio

Gabriel Moore, Ala.
Samuel Prentiss, Vt.

John J. Crittenden, Ky.
Samuel McKean, Penn.

PRIVATE LAND CLAIMS

Chairman: John Black, Miss.

Louis F. Linn, Mo.
John Ruggles, Me.

Alexander Porter, La.
John P. King, Ga.

INDIAN AFFAIRS

Chairman: Hugh Lawson White, Tenn.

John Tipton, Ind.
Robert H. Goldsborough, Md.

Benjamin Swift, Vt.
Bedford Brown, N.C.

CLAIMS

Chairman: Arnold Naudian, Del.

John Tipton, Ind.
Ether Shepley, Me.

Benjamin Swift, Vt.
Bedford Brown, N.C.

JUDICIARY

Chairman: John M. Clayton, Del.

James Buchanan, Penn.
William C. Preston, S.C.

Benjamin W. Leigh, Va.
John J. Crittenden, Ky.

POST OFFICE AND POST ROADS

Chairman: Felix Grundy, Tenn.

John M. Robinson, Ill.
Thomas Ewing, Ohio

Nehemiah R. Knight, R.I.
John Davis, Mass.

ROADS AND CANALS

Chairman: William Hendricks, Ind.

Samuel McKean, Penn.
John M. Robinson, Ill.

Joseph Kent, Md.
Asher Robbins, R.I.

PENSIONS

Chairman: Gideon Tomlinson, Conn.

Nathaniel P. Tallmadge, N.Y.
Louis F. Linn, Mo.

Samuel Prentiss, Vt.
Samuel McKean, Penn.

DISTRICT OF COLUMBIA

Chairman: John Tyler, Va.

Joseph Kent, Md.   Samuel L. Southard, N.J.
Arnold Naudian, Del.   William R. King, Ala.

REVOLUTIONARY CLAIMS

Chairman: Gabriel Moore, Ala.

Hugh Lawson White, Tenn.   Benjamin W. Leigh, Va.
Henry Hubbard, N.H.   Ether Shepley, Me.

TO AUDIT AND CONTROL THE CONTINGENT FUND

Chairman: Samuel McKean, Penn.

Gideon Tomlinson, Conn.   Bedford Brown, N.C.

ENGROSSED BILLS

Chairman: Ether Shepley, Me.

Isaac Hill, N.H.   Thomas Morris, Ohio

SELECT COMMITTEES

On so much of the President's Message as relates to the Circulation of Incendiary Publications by the Abolitionists

Chairman: John C. Calhoun, S.C.

John P. King, Ga.   John Davis, Mass.
Willie P. Mangum, N.C.   Louis F. Linn, Mo.

*On Admission of Michigan into the Union
And
The Northern Boundary of Ohio*

Chairman: Thomas H. Benton, Mo.

Silas Wright, Jr., N.Y.   John J. Crittenden, Ky.
John M. Clayton, Del.   Samuel Prentiss, Vt.

CONGRESSIONAL DIRECTORY

TWENTY-FOURTH CONGRESS, SECOND SESSION
(December 5, 1836–March 3, 1837)

Mrs. Auld, Penn. Ave.
John Reed, Mass.
George Grennell, Jr., Mass.
Samuel Hoar, Mass.

Mrs. Ball, opposite Brown's
William Clark, Penn.
John Reynolds, Ill.
Leonard Jarvis,[1] Me.

Mrs. Ballard, Penn. Ave.
Henry L. Pinckney, S.C.
Edward Darlington, Penn.
William Hiester, Penn.
Taylor Webster, Ohio
David Spangler, Ohio
James Graham, N.C.

Mrs. Belt, Penn. Ave.
James Black, Penn.

Mr. Birth, Third St.
Garret D. Wall (S), N.J.
George W. Owens, Ga.
James Parker, N.J.

Brown's Hotel
Robert J. Walker (S), Miss.
Daniel Webster (S), Mass.
Ratliff Boon, Ind.
Micajah T. Hawkins, N.C.
James M. H. Beale, Va.
Johnathan McCarty, Ind.
William H. Ashley, Mo.

William L. May, Ill.
John B. Forester, Tenn.
Thomas L. Hamer, Ohio
Hopkins Holsey, Ga.

O. B. Brown's, nearly opposite the
    General Post Office
Moses Mason, Jr., Me.

Dr. Brodhead, Capitol Hill
Charles E. Haynes, Ga.
Samuel Cushman, N.H.
Robert Burns, N.H.
Benning M. Bean, N.H.

Mrs. Carlisle, opposite Centre Market
John Ruggles (S), Me.
John Norvell (S),[2] Mich.
Joshua Lee, N.Y.
Isaac E. Crary,[3] Mich.

Mr. Clubb, Capitol Hill
John Davis (S), Mass.
George Evans, Me.
Caleb Cushing, Mass.

Mr. Clement, Penn. Ave.
Henry Clay (S), Ky.
John J. Crittenden (S), Ky.
Samuel L. Southard (S), N.J.
John Calhoon, Ky.

Mrs. Connor, Penn. Ave.
Leonard Jarvis,[4] Me.

---

[1] Also listed at Mrs. Connor's.
[2] Took his seat Jan. 26, 1837 when Michigan was admitted as a state.
[3] Took his seat Jan. 27, 1837.
[4] Also listed at Mrs. Ball's.

Miss Corcoran, Corner Penn. Ave. and
   Four and One-Half St.
John C. Calhoun (S), S.C.
Levi Lincoln, Mass.
David Potts, Jr., Penn.
Joel B. Sutherland, Penn.
Francis W. Pickens, S.C.
Harmar Denny, Penn.
John J. Pearson, Penn.

Mrs. Coyle, Capitol Hill
John P. King (S), Ga.
Jabez Y. Jackson, Ga.
Abner Hazeltine, N.Y.
David A. Russell, N.Y.
Bellamy Storer, Ohio
Seaton Grantland, Ga.

Mr. Cudlipp, Penn. Ave.
George C. Dromgoole, Va.

Mrs. Cumming, Penn. Ave.
Ely Moore, N.Y.

Mrs. Denny, Third St.
John Black (S), Miss.
Rice Garland, La.

Dowson's No. 1, Capitol Hill
Thomas H. Benton (S), Mo.
Adam Huntsman, Tenn.
Francis Thomas, Md.

Dowson's No. 2, Capitol Hill
Lewis F. Linn (S), Mo.
Cave Johnson, Tenn.
Ebenezer J. Shields, Tenn.
William C. Dunlap, Tenn.
George W. Jones, Deleg., Terr. of Wis.
James I. McKay, N.C.
Edward A. Hannegan, Ind.

Mr. Elliot, Penn. Ave.
William S. Fulton (S), Ark.
Silas Wright, Jr. (S), N.Y.
James K. Polk, Tenn.
Gorham Parks, Me.
John Cramer, N.Y.
John F. H. Claiborne, Miss.

Walter Coles, Va.
Archibald Yell, Ark.

Mrs. Fletcher, F St.
Dutee J. Pearce, R.I.
Nathaniel B. Borden, Mass.

Mr. Fletcher, E St., near the General
   Post Office
Samuel Prentiss (S), Vt.
Heman Allen, Vt.
William B. Calhoun, Mass.
George N. Briggs, Mass.
Henry F. Janes, Vt.
Hiland Hall, Vt.
William Slade, Vt.
John Laporte, Penn.
Thomas C. Love, N.Y.
William Jackson, Mass.

Mr. Follansbee, Capitol Hill
Chilton Allan, Ky.

Gadsby's Hotel
Francis Granger, N.Y.
Aaron Ward, N.Y.
Stephen C. Phillips, Mass.
Abbott Lawrence, Mass.
Rutger B. Miller, N.Y.
Robert B. Campbell, N.C.
Isaac McKim, Md.
Franklin H. Elmore,[5] S.C.

Mrs. Galvin, No. 1, C St.
William Hendricks (S), Ind.
Samuel McKean (S), Penn.
William Kennon, Sr., Ohio
Daniel Kilgore, Ohio
Joseph Johnson, Va.
William Patterson, Ohio

Mrs. Galvin, No. 2, C St.
James Buchanan (S), Penn.
William R. King (S), Ala.
Robert C. Nicholas (S), La.
Edward Lucas, Va.

Mrs. Hamilton, Penn. Ave.
Abraham Bockee, N.Y.

[5] Elected to fill the vacancy caused by the resignation of James H. Hammond, and took his seat Dec. 19, 1836.

Gerrit Y. Lansing, N.Y.
William Taylor, N.Y.
William Mason, N.Y.
Samuel Barton, N.Y.
William K. Fuller, N.Y.
Nicholas Sickles, N.Y.
Ransom H. Gillet, N.Y.

Mrs. Handy, Corner of La. Ave. and
  Sixth St.
Sherrod Williams, Ky.
John White, Ky.

Mr. Harbaugh, Seventh St.
Joseph B. Anthony, Penn.
Matthias J. Bovee, N.Y.
John W. Davis, Ind.
Samuel Ingham, Conn.
Orin Holt, Conn.
Lancelot Phelps, Conn.
Elisha Haley, Conn.

H. V. Hill's, Corner of C and Third St.
Thomas Ewing (S), Ohio
George Chambers, Penn.
Timothy Childs, N.Y.
Gideon Hard, N.Y.
Samuel F. Vinton, Ohio
Elias Howell, Ohio
Abraham Rencher, N.C.

Mrs. S. A. Hill, nearly opposite Gadsby's
Francis O. J. Smith, Me.
Joseph Hall, Me.
James W. Bouldin, Va.
Henry W. Connor, N.C.
John M. Patton, Va.
David D. Wagener, Penn.
George Loyall, Va.
Joshua L. Martin, Ala.
Andrew Beaumont, Penn.
Reuben Chapman, Ala.
John W. Jones, Va.
Francis S. Lyon, Ala.

Mr. Hyatt, opposite Brown's
Richard H. Bayard (S), Del.
Nehemiah R. Knight (S), R.I.
Benjamin Swift (S), Vt.
Gideon Tomlinson (S), Conn.
Elisha Whittlesey, Ohio
Jeremiah Bailey, Me.
Jonathan Sloane, Ohio

Mr. Ironside, Seventh St.
John J. Milligan, Del.
Joseph R. Ingersoll, Penn.

Mrs. Kennedy, Four and One-Half St.
Bedford Brown (S), N.C.
William C. Rives (S), Va.
Nathaniel P. Tallmadge (S), N.Y.

Mr. McLeod, opposite City Hall
George W. Lay, N.Y.

Mrs. McDaniel, Mo. St.
Thomas Morris (S), Ohio
John M. Niles (S), Conn.
John Tipton (S), Ind.
John Page (S), N.H.
Ulysses F. Doubleday, N.Y.
Samuel Fowler, N.J.
Stephen B. Leonard, N.Y.
Ferdinand S. Schenck, N.J.

Mrs. Miller, F St.
Churchill C. Cambreleng, N.Y.
Aaron Vanderpoel, N.Y.

Mrs. Meyer, nearly opposite Gadsby's
Job Mann, Penn.
William Seymour, N.Y.
Valentine Efner, N.Y.
Dudley Farlin, N.Y.
Abel Huntington, N.Y.
John Thomson, Ohio
John Chaney, Ohio
Henry A. P. Muhlenberg, Penn.
Edward B. Hubley, Penn.
John Galbraith, Penn.
Joseph Reynolds, N.Y.
Jeremiah McLene, Ohio

Mrs. Mount, Penn. Ave.
John M. Robinson (S), Ill.
Zadoc Casey, Ill.
William S. Morgan, Va.
George W. Hopkins, Va.
William Montgomery, N.C.

Mrs. Owner, Penn. Ave.
William L. D. Ewing (S), Ill.
Felix Grundy (S), Tenn.
Linn Boyd, Ky.
Benjamin Jones, Ohio

Joseph Weeks, N.H.
William N. Shinn, N.J.
John Young,[6] N.Y.
John Carr, Ind.
Thomas Lee, N.J.
Albert G. Harrison, Mo.

Mrs. Page, opposite Centre Market
Benjamin C. Howard, Md.
John Bell, Tenn.

Mrs. Peyton, Corner of Penn. Ave. and
Four and One-Half St.
James Harper, Penn.
William J. Grayson, S.C.
William J. Graves, Ky.
John K. Griffin, S.C.
John Robertson, Va.
Waddy Thompson, Jr., S.C.

Mr. Pierce, Penn. Ave.
Richard E. Parker (S),[7] Va.
Robert Strange (S),[8] N.C.

Mrs. Pitman, Third St.
Henry Hubbard (S), N.H.
Lucius Lyon (S),[9] Mich.
Graham H. Chapin, N.Y.
Thomas T. Whittlesey, Conn.
Gideon Lee, N.Y.
Andrew Buchanan, Penn.
Amos Lane, Ind.
John Fairfield, Me.
John W. Brown, N.Y.
Daniel Wardwell, N.Y.
Franklin Pierce, N.H.
Sherman Page, N.Y.
Isaac Toucey, Conn.

Miss Polk, Penn. Ave.
Joseph Kent (S), Md.
Richard H. Bayard (S), Del.
Ebenezer Pettigrew, N.C.
William B. Shepard, N.C.

John N. Steele, Md.
James A. Pearce, Md.
Abijah Mann, Jr., N.Y.

Private Residences:
Md. Ave., Capitol Hill
Ambrose H. Sevier (S), Ark.
Md. Ave., Capitol Hill
Richard M. Johnson, Ky.
Mrs. Taliaferro, Capitol Hill
John Taliaferro, Va.
Dr. Jones, Seventh St.
Daniel Jenifer, Md.
Corner Tenth and E St.
Samuel S. Harrison, Penn.
William Wood, Twelfth St.
William K. Bond, Ohio
Major Garland, West of President's Square
James Garland, Va.
I St., North of the President's House
John Quincy Adams, Mass.
Six Buildings
Henry Johnson, La.
Georgetown
George C. Washington, Md.
Mount Hope, Georgetown
Augustine H. Shepperd, N.C.
Seventh St.
Eleazer W. Ripley, La.

Mrs. Queen, Penn. Ave.
Hugh Lawson White (S), Tenn.
Joab Lawler, Ala.
Balie Peyton, Tenn.
Henry A. Wise, Va.
Samuel Bunch, Tenn.
James Standifer, Tenn.
Abram P. Maury, Tenn.
Luke Lea, Tenn.
William B. Carter, Tenn.

Mrs. Ronckendorff, Penn. Ave.
Charles F. Mercer, Va.

[6] Elected to fill the vacancy caused by the resignation of Philo C. Fuller, and took his seat Dec. 6, 1836.
[7] Elected to fill the vacancy caused by the resignation of Benjamin W. Leigh, and took his seat Dec. 15, 1836.
[8] Elected to fill the vacancy caused by the resignation of Willie P. Mangum, and took his seat Dec. 15, 1836.
[9] Took his seat Jan. 26, 1837, when Michigan was admitted as a state.

Lewis Williams, N.C.
John Chambers, Ky.
Samson Mason, Ohio
Joseph H. Crane, Ohio
James Harlan, Ky.
Joseph R. Underwood, Ky.
Thomas Corwin, Ohio
William Chetwood, N.J.

Mrs. Smith, Capitol Hill
Asher Robbins (S), R.I.
Hiram P. Hunt, N.Y.
William McComas, Va.
Albert G. Hawes, Ky.
Richard French, Ky.

Mrs. Sprigg, Capitol Hill
Gabriel Moore (S), Ala.
Horace Everett, Vt.
Dixon H. Lewis, Ala.

Mrs. Ulrick, H St., between Seventeenth
and Eighteenth
John McKeon, N.Y.

Mr. Vivan, West of President's Square
Joseph M. White, Deleg., Terr. of Fla.

Mr. Wailes, Four and One-Half St.
Thomas M. T. McKennan, Penn.
Joseph Henderson, Penn.

Mrs. Walker, E St., near the General Post
Office
Joel Turrill, N.Y.

Mr. Wallace, Capitol Hill
Michael W. Ash, Penn.
Henry Logan, Penn.
James Turner, Md.
Jacob Fry, Jr., Penn.
John Klingensmith, Jr., Penn.

Walker's, Sixth St., near Penn. Ave.
Thomas Glascock, Ga.
Jesse A. Bynum, N.C.
Jesse F. Cleveland, Ga.
James Rogers, S.C.

Mrs. Wolfenden, opposite Brown's
Nathaniel H. Claiborne, Va.
Edmund Deberry, N.C.
Robert Craig, Va.

APPENDIX

John M. Clayton (S),[10] Del.
Julius C. Alford,[11] Ga.
Alfred Cuthbert (S), Ga.
William C. Dawson,[12] Ga.
William Herod,[13] Ind.
Benjamin Hardin, Ky.

Alexander Porter (S),[14] La.
John S. Spence (S),[15] Md.
Judah Dana (S),[16] Me.
Samuel J. Gholson,[17] Miss.
Jesse Speight, N.C.
Matthias Morris, Penn.

[10] Resigned Dec. 29, 1836. Thomas Clayton was elected to fill the vacancy, and took his seat Jan. 19, 1837.
[11] Elected to fill the vacancy caused by the resignation of George W. B. Towns, and took his seat Jan. 31, 1837.
[12] Elected to fill the vacancy caused by the death of John Coffee, and took his seat Dec. 26, 1836.
[13] Elected to fill the vacancy caused by the death of George L. Kinnard, and took his seat Jan. 25, 1837.
[14] Resigned Jan. 5, 1837. Alexander Mouton was elected to fill the vacancy, and took his seat Feb. 2, 1837.
[15] Elected to fill the vacancy caused by the death of Robert H. Goldsborough, and took his seat Jan. 11, 1837.
[16] Appointed to fill the vacancy caused by the resignation of Ether Shepley, and took his seat Dec. 21, 1836.
[17] Elected to fill the vacancy caused by the death of Daniel Dickson, and took his seat Jan. 7, 1837.

William Sprague, R.I.
William C. Preston (S), S.C.
John P. Richardson,[18] S.C.

John Y. Mason,[19] Va.
John Roane, Va.

STANDING COMMITTEES OF THE
HOUSE OF REPRESENTATIVES

ELECTIONS

Chairman: Nathaniel H. Claiborne, Va.

John K. Griffin, S.C.
Micajah T. Hawkins, N.C.
Robert Burns, N.H.
Daniel Kilgore, Ohio

Andrew Buchanan, Penn.
Abram P. Maury, Tenn.
Linn Boyd, Ky.
John Young, N.Y.

WAYS AND MEANS

Chairman: Churchill C. Cambreleng, N.Y.

Isaac McKim, Md.
George Loyall, Va.
Thomas Corwin, Ohio
Cave Johnson, Tenn.

Francis O. J. Smith, Me.
Abbott Lawrence, Mass.
Joseph R. Ingersoll, Penn.
George W. Owens, Ga.

CLAIMS

Chairman: Elisha Whittlesey, Ohio

John B. Forester, Tenn.
George Grenell, Jr., Mass.
John W. Davis, Ind.
John Taliaferro, Va.

John Chambers, Ky.
Edward Darlington, Penn.
James Graham, N.C.
David A. Russell, N.Y.

COMMERCE

Chairman: Joel B. Sutherland, Penn.

Henry L. Pinckney, S.C.
Dutee J. Pearce, R.I.
Ransom H. Gillet, N.Y.
Stephen C. Phillips, Mass.

Henry Johnson, La.
Samuel Ingham, Conn.
Samuel Cushman, N.H.
John McKeon, N.Y.

PUBLIC LANDS

Chairman: Ratliff Bonn, Ind.

Lewis Williams, N.C.
Levi Lincoln, Mass.
Zadoc Casey, Ill.
William Kennon, Sr., Ohio

William C. Dunlap, Tenn.
Reuben Chapman, Ala.
Albert G. Harrison, Mo.
Archibald Yell, Ark.

---

[18] Elected to fill the vacancy caused by the death of Richard I. Manning, and took his seat Dec. 19, 1836.
[19] Resigned Jan. 11, 1837.

POST OFFICE AND POST ROADS

Chairman: Henry W. Connor, N.C.

George N. Briggs, Mass.
John Laporte, Penn.
Hiland Hall, Vt.
Jesse F. Cleveland, Ga.

Richard French, Ky.
Ebenezer J. Shields, Tenn.
George W. Hopkins, Va.
Daniel Kilgore, Ohio

DISTRICT OF COLUMBIA

Chairman: William B. Sheperd, N.C.

William Hiester, Penn.
James W. Bouldin, Va.
George C. Washington, Md.
Amos Lane, Ind.

James Rogers, S.C.
John Fairfield, Me.
Ely Moore, N.Y.
John F. H. Claiborne, Miss.

JUDICIARY

Chairman: Francis Thomas, Md.

Benjamin Hardin, Ky.
Franklin Pierce, N.H.
John Robertson, Va.
Balie Peyton, Tenn.

Isaac Toucey, Conn.
Joshua L. Martin, Ala.
Aaron Vanderpoel, N.Y.
Eleazer W. Ripley, La.

REVOLUTIONARY CLAIMS

Chairman: Henry A. P. Muhlenberg, Penn.

Joseph H. Crane, Ohio
James Standifer, Tenn.
Joel Turrill, N.Y.
Andrew Beaumont, Penn.

Robert Craig, Va.
Graham H. Chapin, N.Y.
Joseph R. Underwood, Ky.
Joseph Weeks, N.H.

PUBLIC EXPENDITURES

Chairman: Sherman Page, N.Y.

William Clark, Penn.
Jeremiah McLene, Ohio
Moses Mason, Jr., Me.
Stephen B. Leonard, N.Y.

Elisha Haley, Conn.
John White, Ky.
John J. Pierson, Penn.
William Chetwood, N.J.

PRIVATE LAND CLAIMS

Chairman: John Carr, Ind.

John Galbraith, Penn.
William Patterson, Ohio
George Chambers, Penn.
William L. May, Ill.

Adam Huntsman, Tenn.
Joab Lawler, Ala.
William Slade, Vt.
Rice Garland, La.

MANUFACTURES

Chairman: John Quincy Adams, Mass.

Harmar Denny, Penn.
William McComas, Va.
Taylor Webster, Ohio
Gideon Lee, N.Y.

Francis Granger, N.Y.
Jesse A. Bynum, N.C.
Samuel Fowler, N.J.
Thomas T. Whittlesey, Conn.

AGRICULTURE

Chairman: Abraham Bockee, N.Y.

Benning M. Bean, N.H.
William N. Shinn, N.J.
Edmund Deberry, N.C.
Jeremiah Bailey, Me.

Henry Logan, Penn.
Lancelot Phelps, Conn.
Valentine Efner, N.Y.
James Black, Penn.

INDIAN AFFAIRS

Chairman: John Bell, Tenn.

Johnathan McCarty, Ind.
Horace Everett, Vt.
William H. Ashley, Mo.
Charles E. Haynes, Ga.

Albert G. Hawes, Ky.
John Chaney, Ohio
William Montgomery, N.C.
James Garland, Va.

MILITARY AFFAIRS

Chairman: Richard M. Johnson, Ky.

Aaron Ward, N.Y.
John Thomson, Ohio
Samuel Bunch, Tenn.
James I. McKay, N.C.

Joseph B. Anthony, Penn.
Abijah Mann, Jr., N.Y.
Walter Coles, Va.
Thomas Glascock, Ga.

MILITIA

Chairman: Thomas Glascock, Ga.

Joseph Henderson, Penn.
William K. Fuller, N.Y.
David D. Wagener, Penn.
William B. Calhoun, Mass.

Joshua Lee, N.Y.
William B. Carter, Tenn.
William J. Graves, Ky.
Orrin Holt, Conn.

NAVAL AFFAIRS

Chairman: Leonard Jarvis, Me.

John J. Milligan, Del.
Gerrit Y. Lansing, N.Y.
John Reed, Mass.
William J. Grayson, S.C.

James Parker, N.J.
Henry A. Wise, Va.
Michael W. Ash, Penn.
Seaton Grantland, Ga.

FOREIGN AFFAIRS

Chairman: Benjamin C. Howard, Md.

John Cramer, N.Y.
Thomas L. Hamer, Ohio
Chilton Allan, Ky.
Gorham Parks, Me.

Caleb Cushing, Mass.
Jabez Y. Jackson, Ga.
George C. Dromgoole, Va.
Abraham Rencher, N.C.

TERRITORIES

Chairman: John M. Patton, Va.

David Potts, Jr., Penn.
John W. Brown, N.Y.
Francis W. Pickens, S.C.
James A. Pearce, Md.

Joseph Hall, Me.
Joseph Johnson, Va.
Linn Boyd, Ky.
Rutger B. Miller, N.Y.

REVOLUTIONARY PENSIONS

Chairman: Daniel Wardwell, N.Y.

Luke Lea, Tenn.
George W. Lay, N.Y.
Henry F. Janes, Vt.
Bellamy Storer, Ohio

William S. Morgan, Va.
John Klingensmith, Jr., Penn.
William K. Bond, Ohio
Jacob Fry, Jr., Penn.

INVALID PENSIONS

Chairman: James M. H. Beale, Va.

Ferdinand S. Schenck, N.J.
William Taylor, N.Y.
Samuel S. Harrison, Penn.
Ulysses F. Doubleday, N.Y.

Samuel Hoar, Mass.
Elias Howell, Ohio
Daniel Jenifer, Md.
Sherrod Williams, Ky.

ROADS AND CANALS

Chairman: Charles F. Mercer, Va.

Samuel F. Vinton, Ohio
Edward Lucas, Va.
John Reynolds, Ill.
John N. Steele, Md.

John Calhoon, Ky.
George Evans, Me.
Thomas M. T. McKennan, Penn.
Gideon Hard, N.Y.

REVISAL AND UNFINISHED BUSINESS

Chairman: Abel Huntington, N.Y.

Job Mann, Penn.
Samson Mason, Ohio

James Harlin, Ky.
Dudley Farlin, N.Y.

ACCOUNTS

Chairman: Thomas Lee, N.J.

Joseph Hall, Me.
Joseph Johnson, Va.

James Turner, Md.
Thomas M. T. McKennan, Penn.

EXPENDITURES IN THE DEPARTMENT OF STATE

Chairman: Augustine H. Shepperd, N.C.

William B. Calhoun, Mass.
Hiram P. Hunt, N.Y.

Mathias Morris, Penn.
Nicholas Sickles, N.Y.

EXPENDITURES IN THE DEPARTMENT OF THE TREASURY

Chairman: Heman Allen, Vt.

James Harper, Penn.
David Spangler, Ohio

David A. Russell, N.Y.
Samuel Barton, N.Y.

EXPENDITURES IN THE DEPARTMENT OF WAR

Chairman: Benjamin Jones, Ohio

Matthias J. Bovee, N.Y.
Joseph Johnson, Va.

Thomas C. Love, N.Y.
Edward B. Hubley, Penn.

EXPENDITURES IN THE DEPARTMENT OF THE NAVY

Chairman: Joseph Hall, Me.

Jonathan Sloane, Ohio   Ebenezer Pettigrew, N.C.
William Seymour, N.Y.   William Mason, N.Y.

EXPENDITURES IN THE POST OFFICE DEPARTMENT

Chairman: Albert G. Hawes, Ky.

Robert Burns, N.H.   Jeremiah Bailey, Me.
Timothy Childs, N.Y.   Joseph Reynolds, N.Y.

EXPENDITURES ON THE PUBLIC BUILDINGS

Chairman: Edward Darlington, Penn.

Abner Hazeltine, N.Y.   John Galbraith, Penn.
Dutee J. Pearce, R.I.   James M. H. Beale, Va.

SELECT COMMITTEES

WEST POINT ACADEMY

Albert G. Hawes, Ky.   Francis O. J. Smith, Me.
Edward A. Hannegan, Ind.   John W. Jones, Va.
Dixon H. Lewis, Ala.   Robert B. Campbell, S.C.
Franklin Pierce, N.H.   John W. Brown, N.Y.
George N. Briggs, Mass.

STEAMBOAT NAVIGATION

Edward A. Hannegan, Ind.   Nathaniel B. Borden, Mass.
Benjamin Hardin, Ky.   Cave Johnson, Tenn.
Hopkins Holsey, Ga.   Rice Garland, La.
Waddy Thompson, Jr., S.C.   David Spangler, Ohio
Ransom H. Gillet, N.Y.

AMENDMENTS TO THE CONSTITUTION

George C. Dromgoole, Va.   Joseph R. Underwood, Ky.
Aaron Vanderpoel, N.Y.   Henry Logan, Ky.
Luke Lea, Tenn.   Edward B. Hubley, Penn.
William L. May, Ill.   William McComas, Va.
Eleazer W. Ripley, La.

THE PATENT OFFICE

James Harper, Penn.   William Jackson, Mass.
Gorham Parks, Me.   John P. Richardson, S.C.
William Taylor, N.Y.

JOINT COMMITTEE

LIBRARY OF CONGRESS

House	Senate
John M. Patton, Va.	Asher Robbins, R.I.
John McKeon, N.Y.	William C. Preston, S.C.
Henry L. Pinckney, S.C.	Garret D. Wall, N.J.

STANDING COMMITTEES OF THE SENATE

FOREIGN RELATIONS

Chairman: James Buchanan, Penn.

Nathaniel P. Tallmadge, N.Y.	Henry Clay, Ky.
John P. King, Ga.	William C. Rives, Va.

FINANCE

Chairman: Silas Wright, Jr., N.Y.

Daniel Webster, Mass.	Robert C. Nicholas, La.
Alfred Cuthbert, Ga.	Thomas H. Benton, Mo.

COMMERCE

Chairman: William R. King, Ala.

John Davis, Mass.	Bedford Brown, N.C.
Lewis F. Linn, Mo.	John Ruggles, Me.

MANUFACTURES

Chairman: John M. Niles, Conn.

Thomas Morris, Ohio	Henry Hubbard, N.H.
John Black, Miss.	William C. Preston, S.C.

AGRICULTURE

Chairman: John Page, N.H.

Thomas Morris, Ohio	Samuel McKean, Penn.
Joseph Kent, Md.	Henry Clay, Ky.

MILITARY AFFAIRS

Chairman: Thomas H. Benton, Mo.

William C. Preston, S.C.	Garret D. Wall, N.J.
John Tipton, Ind.	William L. D. Ewing, Ill.

MILITIA

Chairman: Garret D. Wall, N.J.

William Hendricks, Ind.   William L. D. Ewing, Ill.
Benjamin Swift, Vt.   Gabriel Moore, Ala.

NAVAL AFFAIRS

Chairman: William C. Rives, Va.

Samuel L. Southard, N.J.   Alfred Cuthbert, Ga.
Nathaniel P. Tallmadge, N.Y.   Robert C. Nicholas, La.

PUBLIC LANDS

Chairman: Robert J. Walker, Miss.

Thomas Ewing, Ohio   John Ruggles, Me.
William R. King, Ala.   William S. Fulton, Ark.

PRIVATE LAND CLAIMS

Chairman: Lewis F. Linn, Mo.

Alexander Porter, La.   William C. Preston, S.C.
Richard H. Bayard, Del.   Ambrose H. Sevier, Ark.

INDIAN AFFAIRS

Chairman: Hugh Lawson White, Tenn.

Benjamin Swift, Vt.   Lewis F. Linn, Mo.
John Tipton, Ind.   Ambrose H. Sevier, Ark.

CLAIMS

Chairman: Henry Hubbard, N.H.

John Tipton, Ind.   John J. Crittenden, Ky.
Samuel Prentiss, Vt.   Thomas Ewing, Ill.

JUDICIARY

Chairman: Felix Grundy, Tenn.

John J. Crittenden, Ky.   John P. King, Ga.
Thomas Morris, Ohio   Garret D. Wall, N.J.

POST OFFICE AND POST ROADS

Chairman: John M. Robinson, Ill.

Nehemiah R. Knight, R.I.   Bedford Brown, N.C.
Felix Grundy, Tenn.   John M. Niles, Conn.

ROADS AND CANALS

Chairman: William Hendricks, Ind.

Samuel McKean, Penn.   Robert C. Nicholas, La.
John M. Robinson, Ill.   John Page, N.H.

PENSIONS

Chairman: Gideon Tomlinson, Conn.

Samuel Prentiss, Vt.   Thomas Morris, Ohio
Henry Hubbard, N.H.   Ambrose H. Sevier, Ark.

REVOLUTIONARY CLAIMS

Chairman: Bedford Brown, N.C.

Hugh Lawson White, Tenn.   John J. Crittenden, Ky.
Henry Hubbard, N.H.   John M. Niles, Conn.

DISTRICT OF COLUMBIA

Chairman: Joseph Kent, Md.

William R. King, Ala.   James Buchanan, Penn.
John P. King, Ga.   Robert C. Nicholas, La.

TO AUDIT AND CONTROL THE CONTINGENT FUND

Chairman: Samuel McKean, Penn.

William Hendricks, Ind.   Gideon Tomlinson, Conn.

ENGROSSED BILLS

Chairman: Thomas Morris, Ohio

John Page, N.H.   William S. Fulton, Ark.

SELECT COMMITTEE

ON THE PATENT OFFICE

Chairman: John Ruggles, Me.

Samuel Prentiss, Vt.   Richard E. Parker, Va.
Robert Strange, N.C.   Richard H. Bayard, Del.

CONGRESSIONAL DIRECTORY

TWENTY-FIFTH CONGRESS, FIRST SESSION
(September 4, 1837–October 16, 1837)

Mrs. Auld, Penn. Ave.
Edward Darlington, Penn.
Samson Mason, Ohio
Timothy Childs, N.Y.
William J. Graves, Ky.

Mrs. Ballard, Capitol Hill
William S. Morgan, Va.
Seaton Grantland, Ga.
George W. Hopkins, Va.
Archibald Stuart, Va.
Thomas T. Whittlesey, Conn.
Orrin Holt, Conn.
Isaac Toucey, Conn.
Hiram Gray, N.Y.
Andrew D. W. Bruyn, N.Y.
Robert Barnwell Rhett, S.C.

Mrs. Ball, opposite Brown's
Luther Reily, Penn.
Arnold Plumer, Penn.
William Beatty, Penn.
John Klingensmith, Jr., Penn.
William W. Potter, Penn.
Jacob Fry, Jr., Penn.

Mr. Bannerman, Penn. Ave.
James Harlan, Ky.
Richard H. Menifee, Ky.

Beer's Native American Hotel
Alexander Duncan, Ohio
Isaac E. Crary, Mich.

Mrs. Beale, Capitol Hill
Dixon H. Lewis, Ala.

Mr. Birth, Third St.
Franklin Pierce (S), N.H.

Garret D. Wall (S), N.J.
Reuel Williams (S), Me.
Jonathan Cilley, Me.

Mrs. Bladen, Penn. Ave.
Robert Strange (S), N.C.
Edward Stanly, N.C.

Brown's Hotel
Daniel Webster (S), Mass.
Jesse A. Bynum, N.C.
William Montgomery, N.C.
Ratliff Boon, Ind.
Micajah T. Hawkins, N.C.

Mrs. Carlisle, opposite Centre Market
Benjamin C. Howard, Md.
John T. H. Worthington, Md.
Francis Thomas, Md.
George W. Jones, Deleg., Terr. of Wis.

Mr. Clement, Penn. Ave.
Joseph Kent (S), Md.
John Calhoon, Ky.
Richard Hawes, Ky.
John Pope, Ky.

Mr. Clubb, Capitol Hill
Isaac Fletcher, N.Y.

Mrs. Coddington, B St.
John Bell, Tenn.

Mrs. Connor, Penn. Ave.
Millard Fillmore, N.Y.
Luther C. Peck, N.Y.
Charles F. Mitchell, N.Y.
Richard P. Marvin, N.Y.
William Patterson, N.Y.

Miss Corcoran, Corner of Penn. Ave.
and Four and One-Half St.
John C. Calhoun (S), S.C.
Levi Lincoln, Mass.
Charles Naylor, Penn.
John Sergeant, Penn.
David Potts, Jr., Penn.
Joseph L. Tillinghast, R.I.
George W. Toland, Penn.
Francis W. Pickens, S.C.
Edward Davies, Penn.
Robert B. Cranston, R.I.
Abraham Rencher, N.C.

Mr. Cudlipp, Penn. Ave.
George C. Dromgoole, Va.

Mr. Cumming, Penn. Ave.
Daniel Kilgore, Ohio
John Chaney, Ohio
Joseph Johnson, Va.

Mrs. Denny, Third Street
John Black (S), Miss.
Alexander Mouton (S), La.
Rice Garland, La.

Dowson's, No. 1, Capitol Hill
William Allen (S), Ohio
Thomas H. Benton (S), Mo.
Ely Moore, N.Y.
James I. McKay, N.C.

Mrs. Dyer, Seventh St.
Richard H. Bayard (S), Del.
James A. Pearce, Md.
Stephen C. Phillips, Mass.
John J. Milligan, Del.

Mr. Elliot, Penn. Ave.
Felix Grundy (S), Tenn.
Lewis F. Linn (S), Mo.
John M. Robinson (S), Ill.
Bedford Brown (S), N.C.
Hopkins L. Turney, Tenn.
Abraham McClellan, Tenn.
John L. Murray, Ky.
James K. Polk, Tenn.

Mr. Fletcher, E St.
John Davis (S), Mass.
Richard Fletcher, Mass.

Caleb Cushing, Mass.
William B. Calhoun, Mass.

Fuller's Hotel
William Cost Johnson, Md.

Gadsby's Hotel
J. Ogden Hoffman, N.Y.
Edward Curtis, N.Y.
Mark H. Sibley, N.Y.
Isaac McKim, Md.
Charles Downing, Deleg., Terr. of Fla.

Mrs. Galvin, C St.
Samuel McKean (S), Penn.
Oliver H. Smith (S), Ind.
Patrick G. Goode, Ohio
Calvary Morris, Ohio
James Rariden, Ind.
James Alexander, Jr., Ohio
William Graham, Ind.
Joseph Ridgway, Ohio
Albert S. White, Ind.

Mrs. Hamilton, nearly opposite
Gadsby's
William Taylor, N.Y.
William H. Noble, N.Y.
Albert Gallup, N.Y.
John Palmer, N.Y.
James B. Spencer, N.Y.
Obadiah Titus, N.Y.
Bennet Bicknell, N.Y.
John T. Andrews, N.Y.

Mrs. Handy's, Corner Sixth and La. Ave.
Samuel L. Southard (S), N.J.
Henry Clay (S), Ky.
John J. Crittenden (S), Ky.

Mr. Harbaugh, Seventh St.
Arphaxed Loomis, N.Y.
Nathaniel Jones, N.Y.
Abraham Vanderveer, N.Y.
Thomas B. Jackson, N.Y.
John C. Brodhead, N.Y.
John Edwards, N.Y.

H. V. Hill's, Corner Third and C St.
Clement C. Clay (S), Ala.
William H. Roane (S), Va.
James W. Bouldin, Va.

Reuben Chapman, Ala.
Joshua L. Martin, Ala.
Francis S. Lyon, Ala.

Mrs. S. A. Hill, nearly Opposite
   Gadsby's
Henry W. Connor, N.C.
George W. B. Towns, Ga.
Francis E. Rives, Va.
William L. May, Ill.
Francis O. J. Smith, Me.
John W. Jones, Va.
Charles G. Atherton, N.H.

Mr. Hyatt, opposite Brown's
Benjamin Swift (S), Vt.
William Slade, Vt.
John P. B. Maxwell, N.J.
John B. Aycrigg, N.J.
Joseph F. Randolph, N.J.
Charles C. Stratton, N.J.
Thomas Jones Yorke, N.J.
Thomas Henry, Penn.
John Taliaferro, Va.
Elisha Whittlesey, Ohio

Mr. Ironside, Seventh St.
James Buchanan (S), Penn.
William R. King (S), Ala.
John P. King (S), Ga.
Robert C. Nicholas (S), La.

Mrs. Kennedy, Four and One-Half St.
William S. Fulton (S), Ark.
Henry Hubbard (S), N.H.
Lucius Lyon (S), Mich.
John Norvell (S), Mich.
Silas Wright, Jr. (S), N.Y.
Walter Coles, Va.
Isaac S. Pennybacker, Va.
Andrew Beirne, Va.

Mrs. King, nearly Opposite Gadsby's
David D. Wagener, Penn.
Samuel W. Morris, Penn.
David Petrikin, Penn.
Daniel P. Leadbetter, Ohio
Matthias Shepler, Ohio
Daniel Sheffer, Penn.
Henry Logan, Penn.
Charles McClure, Penn.
Robert H. Hammond, Penn.

Edward B. Hubley, Penn.
Henry A. P. Muhlenberg, Penn.

Mrs. Lindenberger, Capitol Hill
William C. Preston (S), S.C.
William K. Clowney, S.C.
Franklin H. Elmore, S.C.
John Campbell, S.C.
Waddy Thompson, Jr., S.C.
William C. Dawson, Ga.
John P. Richardson, S.C.
Charles B. Shepard, S.C.
Samuel T. Sawyer, N.C.

Mrs. McDaniel, Mo. Ave.
John M. Niles (S), Conn.
Perry Smith (S), Conn.
John Tipton (S), Ind.

Mr. McLeod, opposite City Hall
Nehemiah R. Knight (S), R.I.
William Halstead, N.J.

Mrs. McCubbins, West of the City Post
   Office
Thomas L. Hamer, Ohio

Mr. McKelden, Seventh St.
James Graham, N.C.

Mrs. Milligan, Corner Fifteenth St. and
   N.Y. Ave.
Henry Vail, N.Y.

Mrs. Miller, F St.
Churchill C. Cambreleng, N.Y.
John I. De Graff, N.Y.

Mrs. Mountz, Penn. Ave.
Nathaniel B. Borden, Mass.

Mrs. Owner, Penn. Ave.
Thomas Morris (S), Ohio
Richard M. Young (S), Ill.
Albert G. Harrison, Mo.
John Miller, Mo.
Hopkins Holsey, Ga.
William Parmenter, Mass.
Taylor Webster, Ohio
Zadoc Casey, Ill.
Jesse F. Cleveland, Ga.
Thomas Davee, Me.

Archibald Yell, Ark.
John F. H. Claiborne, Miss.
Samuel J. Gholson, Miss.

Mrs. Peyton, Corner Penn. Ave. and
Four and One-Half St.
John K. Griffin, S.C.
John Robertson, Va.
Charles Ogle, Penn.
Francis Mallory, Va.
Robert M. T. Hunter, Va.

Mr. Pierce, Penn. Ave.
Hiland Hall, Vt.
George N. Briggs, Mass.
George Grennell, Jr., Mass.
John Reed, Mass.
William S. Hastings, Mass.
David A. Russell, N.Y.
Joseph C. Noyes, Me.

Mrs. Pitman, Third St.
John Ruggles (S), Me.
John Fairfield, Me.
Samuel Birdsall, N.Y.
Isaac H. Bronson, N.Y.
Henry A. Foster, N.Y.
Amasa J. Parker, N.Y.
Robert McClellan, N.Y.
John H. Prentiss, N.Y.
John C. Clark, N.Y.
Andrew Buchanan, Penn.
Zadock Pratt, N.Y.
Hugh J. Anderson, Me.
Abraham P. Grant, N.Y.
Timothy J. Carter, Me.
John W. Allen, Ohio

Miss Polk, Penn. Ave.
Heman Allen, Vt.

Private Residences:
Mr. Young, Capitol Hill
Thomas Clayton (S), Del.
Col. Johnson, Capitol Hill
Ambrose H. Sevier (S), Ark.
Seven Buildings
Robert J. Walker (S), Miss.
Dr. Jones, Seventh St.
Daniel Jenifer, Md.
Mr. Woods, Twelfth St.
William K. Bond, Ohio

Mr. William Hunter, Thirteenth St.
William H. Hunter, Ohio
I St., North of the President's House
John Quincy Adams, Mass.
Mr. Wolf, I St.
James Garland, Va.
Six Buildings
Henry Johnson, La.
Mount Hope, Georgetown
Augustine H. Shepperd, N.C.

Mrs. Queen, Penn. Ave.
Hugh Lawson White (S), Tenn.
Christopher H. Williams, Tenn.
John W. Crockett, Tenn.
William B. Campbell, Tenn.
Abram P. Maury, Tenn.
Henry A. Wise, Va.
John Dennis, Md.
William B. Carter, Tenn.
Richard Cheatam, Tenn.

Mrs. Ronckendorf, Penn. Ave.
Lewis Williams, N.C.
Alexander Harper, Ohio
John Chambers, Ky.
Edward Rumsey, Ky.
Joseph R. Underwood, Ky.
Charles F. Mercer, Va.
Andrew W. Loomis, Ohio
William W. Southgate, Ky.
Thomas Corwin, Ohio

Mrs. Smith, Capitol Hill
Asher Robbins (S), R.I.
Mathias Morris, Penn.
George W. Owens, Ga.
Jabez Y. Jackson, Ga.
George Evans, Me.

Mrs. Sprigg, Capitol Hill
Horace Everett, Vt.
William Herod, Ind.
George H. Dunn, Ind.
John Ewing, Ind.

Mrs. Turner, opposite Brown's
Sherrod Williams, Ky.
John White, Ky.
Adam W. Snyder, Ill.

Mrs. Ulrich, Corner of Fifteenth and G St.
William C. Rives (S), Va.
Nathaniel P. Tallmadge (S), N.Y.
Hugh S. Legare, S.C.
James M. Mason, Va.

Mr. Vivan, West of President's Square
Gouverneur Kemble, N.Y.

Mr. Wallace, Capitol Hill
Samuel Cushman, N.H.
Charles E. Haynes, Ga.
Lemuel Paynter, Penn.
Jared W. Williams, N.H.
James Farrington, N.H.
Joseph Weeks, N.H.

Mrs. Walker, E St.
Richard Biddle, Penn.

Mr. William, Four and One-Half St.
Thomas M. T. McKennan, Penn.

Mrs. Wilson, Capitol Hill
Samuel Ingham, Conn.
Lancelot Phelps, Conn.
Elisha Haley, Conn.

Mrs. Wolfenden, opposite Brown's
Robert Craig, Va.
Edmund Deberry, N.C.

APPENDIX

Joab Lawler, Ala.
Alfred Cuthbert (S), Ga.
Thomas Glascock, Ga.
Eleazer W. Ripley,[1] La.
John S. Spence (S), Md.

Ebenezer J. Shields, Tenn.
William Stone,[2] Tenn.
Joseph L. Williams, Tenn.
Samuel Prentiss, Vt.

STANDING COMMITTEES OF THE HOUSE OF REPRESENTATIVES

ELECTIONS

Chairman: Andrew Buchanan, Penn.

John K. Griffin, S.C.
Micajah T. Hawkins, N.C.
Daniel Kilgore, Ohio
Abram P. Maury, Tenn.

George W. B. Towns, Ga.
Isaac H. Bronson, N.Y.
Isaac S. Pennybacker, Va.
William S. Hastings, Mass.

WAYS AND MEANS

Chairman: Churchill C. Cambreleng, N.Y.

Isaac McKim, Md.
George W. Owens, Ga.
John Sergeant, Penn.
Thomas L. Hamer, Ohio

John W. Jones, Va.
Richard Fletcher, Mass.
Charles G. Atherton, N.H.
Robert Barnwell Rhett, S.C.

---

[1] Never qualified owing to prolonged illness.
[2] Elected to fill the vacancy caused by the death of James Standifer, and took his seat Oct. 6, 1837.

CLAIMS

Chairman: Elisha Whittlesey, Ohio

George Grennell, Jr., Mass.
John Chambers, Ky.
Edward Darlington, Penn.
James Graham, N.C.

David A. Russell, N.Y.
William B. Campbell, Tenn.
John C. Clark, N.Y.
Timothy J. Carter, Me.

COMMERCE

Chairman: Francis O. J. Smith, Me.

Stephen C. Phillips, Mass.
Henry Johnson, La.
Samuel Cushman, N.H.
John I. De Graff, N.Y.

Hugh S. Legare, S.C.
George W. Toland, Penn.
Edward Curtis, N.Y.
James M. Mason, Va.

PUBLIC LANDS

Chairman: Ratliff Boon, Ind.

Lewis Williams, N.C.
Levi Lincoln, Mass.
Zadoc Casey, Ill.
Reuben Chapman, Ala.

Albert H. Harrison, Mo.
Hugh J. Anderson, Me.
Alexander Duncan, Ohio
Hopkins L. Turney, Tenn.

POST OFFICE AND POST ROADS

Chairman: Henry W. Connor, S.C.

George N. Briggs, Mass.
Hiland Hall, Vt.
Jesse F. Cleveland, Ga.
George W. Hopkins, Va.

Edward B. Hubley, Penn.
John Calhoon, Ky.
John Palmer, N.Y.
John T. H. Worthington, Md.

DISTRICT OF COLUMBIA

Chairman: James W. Bouldin, Va.

Augustine H. Shepperd, N.C.
Daniel Jenifer, Md.
William C. Dawson, Ga.
Jonathan Cilley, Me.

John H. Prentiss, N.Y.
Andrew Beirne, Va.
Christopher H. Williams, Tenn.
William H. Hunter, Ohio

JUDICIARY

Chairman: Francis Thomas, Md.

John Robertson, Va.
Isaac Toucey, Conn.
Joshua L. Martin, Ala.
Thomas Corwin, Ohio

Jesse A. Bynum, N.C.
James Garland, Va.
Josiah Ogden Hoffman, N.Y.
William W. Potter, Penn.

REVOLUTIONARY CLAIMS

Chairman: Henry A. P. Muhlenberg, Penn.

Robert Craig, Va.
Joseph R. Underwood, Ky.
John Taliaferro, Va.
Franklin H. Elmore, S.C.

Henry A. Foster, N.Y.
William Parmenter, Mass.
Alexander Harper, Ohio
Samuel Birdsall, N.Y.

PUBLIC EXPENDITURES

Chairman: Elisha Haley, Conn.

Charles Ogle, Penn.
James Alexander, Jr., Ohio
Obadiah Titus, N.Y.
Charles C. Stratton, N.J.

Edward Rumsey, Ky.
Isaac Fletcher, Vt.
John W. Crockett, Tenn.
William Patterson, N.Y.

PRIVATE LAND CLAIMS

Chairman: William L. May, Ill.

Rice Garland, La.
William B. Calhoun, Mass.
James Harlan, Ky.
Andrew D. W. Bruyn, N.Y.

Francis Mallory, Va.
William Beatty, Penn.
James Rariden, Ind.
Daniel P. Leadbetter, Ohio

MANUFACTURES

Chairman: John Quincy Adams, Mass.

Taylor Webster, Ohio
Thomas T. Whittlesey, Conn.
Hopkins Holsey, Ga.
William Slade, Vt.

Richard Biddle, Penn.
Joseph L. Tillinghast, R.I.
Henry Vail, N.Y.
Charles Naylor, Penn.

AGRICULTURE

Chairman: Edmund Deberry, N.C.

Henry Logan, Penn.
Lancelot Phelps, Conn.
Joseph Weeks, N.H.
James B. Spencer, N.Y.

Joseph C. Noyes, Me.
Edward Davies, Penn.
Joseph F. Randolph, N.J.
Charles F. Mitchell, N.Y.

INDIAN AFFAIRS

Chairman: John Bell, Tenn.

Horace Everett, Vt.
Charles E. Haynes, Ga.
John Chaney, Ohio
William Montgomery, N.C.

Amasa J. Parker, N.Y.
John Campbell, S.C.
John L. Murray, Ky.
Samuel W. Morris, Penn.

MILITARY AFFAIRS

Chairman: James I. McKay, N.C.

Walter Coles, Va.
Thomas Glascock, Ga.
Waddy Thompson, Jr., S.C.
Samuel J. Gholson, Miss.

John Miller, Mo.
Francis E. Rives, Va.
Gouverneur Kemble, N.Y.
Abraham McClellan, Tenn.

MILITIA

Chairman: Thomas Glascock, Ga.

David D. Wagener, Penn.
William B. Carter, Tenn.
Orrin Holt, Conn.
Robert H. Hammond, Penn.

Zadock Pratt, N.Y.
Robert M. T. Hunter, Va.
William Halstead, N.J.
John W. Allen, Ohio

NAVAL AFFAIRS

Chairman: Samuel Ingham, Conn.

John J. Milligan, Del.
John Reed, Mass.
Henry A. Wise, Va.
Seaton Grantland, Ga.

Ely Moore, N.Y.
John P. Richardson, S.C.
Lemuel Paynter, Penn.
Jared W. Williams, N.H.

FOREIGN AFFAIRS

Chairman: Benjamin C. Howard, Md.

Thomas L. Hamer, Ohio
Caleb Cushing, Mass.
Jabez Jackson, Ga.
George C. Dromgoole, Va.

Abraham Rencher, N.C.
John Pope, Ky.
John F. H. Claiborne, Miss.
John Fairfield, Me.

TERRITORIES

Chairman: John M. Patton, Va.

David Potts, Jr., Penn.
Francis W. Pickens, S.C.
James A. Pearce, Md.
Nathaniel B. Borden, Mass.

William J. Graves, Ky.
Thomas Davee, Me.
Nathaniel Jones, N.Y.
James Farrington, N.H.

REVOLUTIONARY PENSIONS

Chairman: William S. Morgan, Va.

John Klingensmith, Jr., Penn.
William K. Bond, Ohio
Jacob Fry, Jr., Penn.
Joseph Johnson, Va.

Mark H. Sibley, N.Y.
John Ewing, Ind.
Hiram Gray, N.Y.
Andrew W. Loomis, Ohio

INVALID PENSIONS

Chairman: William Taylor, N.Y.

Sherrod Williams, Ky.
Heman Allen, Vt.
Robert McClellan, N.Y.
David Petrikin, Penn.

Archibald Stuart, Va.
William Herod, Ind.
Luther Reily, Penn.
Edward Stanly, N.C.

ROADS AND CANALS

Chairman: Charles F. Mercer, Va.

George Evans, Me.
Thomas M. T. McKennan, Penn.
Adam W. Snyder, Ill.
John White, Ky.

Millard Fillmore, N.Y.
William Cost Johnson, Md.
Bennet Bicknell, N.Y.
Albert S. White, Ind.

REVISAL AND UNFINISHED BUSINESS

Chairman: Samson Mason, Ohio

William H. Noble, N.Y.
William W. Southgate, Ky.

Thomas Henry, Penn.
Luther C. Peck, N.Y.

ACCOUNTS

Chairman: Joseph Johnson, Va.

Abraham P. Grant, N.Y.	Charles B. Shepard, N.C.
Charles McClure, Penn.	William Cost Johnson, Md.

EXPENDITURES IN THE DEPARTMENT OF STATE

Chairman: Mathias Morris, Penn.

Thomas B. Jackson, N.Y.	Thomas Jones Yorke, N.J.
Matthias Shepler, Ohio	John T. Andrews, N.Y.

EXPENDITURES IN THE DEPARTMENT OF THE TREASURY

Chairman: Heman Allen, Vt.

Daniel Sheffer, Penn.	Hiram Gray, N.Y.
John B. Aycrigg, N.J.	Hopkins Holsey, Ga.

EXPENDITURES IN THE DEPARTMENT OF WAR

Chairman: William K. Clowney, S.C.

Abraham Vanderveer, N.Y.	Calvary Morris, Ohio
Orrin Holt, Conn.	Richard P. Marvin, N.Y.

EXPENDITURES IN THE DEPARTMENT OF THE NAVY

Chairman: John C. Brodhead, N.Y.

John P. B. Maxwell, N.J.	John Edwards, N.Y.
Patrick G. Goode, Ohio	William Graham, Ind.

EXPENDITURES IN THE POST OFFICE DEPARTMENT

Chairman: Timothy Childs, N.Y.

John Dennis, Md.	Albert Gallup, N.Y.
Richard Hawes, Ky.	Arnold Plumer, Penn.

EXPENDITURES ON THE PUBLIC BUILDINGS

Chairman: Samuel T. Sawyer, N.C.

Robert B. Cranston, R.I.	George H. Dunn, Ind.
Richard H. Menifee, Ky.	Joseph Ridgway, Ohio

JOINT COMMITTEES

LIBRARY OF CONGRESS

House	Senate
John M. Patton, Va.	Asher Robbins, R.I.
Isaac E. Crary, Mich.	William C. Preston, S.C.
Levi Lincoln, Mass.	Garret D. Wall, N.J.

ENROLLED BILLS

House	Senate
George N. Briggs, Mass.	Perry Smith, Conn.
Archibald Yell, Ark.	Lucius Lyon, Mich.
Samuel W. Morris, Penn.	William Allen, Ohio

STANDING COMMITTEES OF THE SENATE

FOREIGN RELATIONS

Chairman: James Buchanan, Penn.

Nathaniel P. Tallmadge, N.Y.	Henry Clay, Ky.
John P. King, Ga.	William C. Rives, Va.

FINANCE

Chairman: Silas Wright, Jr., N.Y.

Daniel Webster, Mass.	Thomas H. Benton, Mo.
Robert C. Nicholas, La.	Henry Hubbard, N.H.

COMMERCE

Chairman: William R. King, Ala.

John Davis, Mass.	John Ruggles, Me.
Bedford Brown, N.C.	John Norvell, Mich.

MANUFACTURES

Chairman: John M. Niles, Conn.

James Buchanan, Penn.	Robert Strange, N.C.
William C. Preston, S.C.	Franklin Pierce, N.H.

AGRICULTURE

Chairman: Perry Smith, Conn.

John S. Spence, Md.	Samuel McKean, Penn.
Lewis F. Linn, Mo.	John Black, Miss.

MILITARY AFFAIRS

Chairman: Thomas H. Benton, Mo.

William C. Preston, S.C.	Garret D. Wall, N.J.
John Tipton, Ind.	William Allen, Ohio

MILITIA

Chairman: Garret D. Wall, N.J.

Benjamin Swift, Vt.	Alexander Mouton, La.
Clement C. Clay, Ala.	Oliver H. Smith, Ind.

NAVAL AFFAIRS

Chairman: William C. Rives, Va.

Samuel L. Southard, N.J.   Alfred Cuthbert, Ga.
Nathaniel P. Tallmadge, N.Y.   Reuel Williams, Me.

PUBLIC LANDS

Chairman: Robert J. Walker, Miss.

William S. Fulton, Ark.   William H. Roane, Va.
Clement C. Clay, Ala.   Samuel Prentiss, Vt.

PRIVATE LAND CLAIMS

Chairman: Lewis F. Linn, Mo.

Ambrose H. Sevier, Ark.   Alexander Mouton, La.
Richard H. Bayard, Del.   Lucius Lyon, Mich.

INDIAN AFFAIRS

Chairman: Hugh Lawson White, Tenn.

Ambrose H. Sevier, Ark.   Lewis F. Linn, Mo.
John Tipton, Ind.   Benjamin Swift, Vt.

CLAIMS

Chairman: Henry Hubbard, N.H.

John Tipton, Ind.   Robert Strange, N.C.
John J. Crittenden, Ky.   Robert M. Young, Ill.

JUDICIARY

Chairman: Felix Grundy, Tenn.

Thomas Morris, Ohio   Garret D. Wall, N.J.
John P. King, Ga.   Thomas Clayton, Del.

POST OFFICE AND POST ROADS

Chairman: John M. Robinson, Ill.

Felix Grundy, Tenn.   Bedford Brown, N.C.
Nehemiah R. Knight, R.I.   John M. Niles, Conn.

ROADS AND CANALS

Chairman: John Tipton, Ind.

Samuel McKean, Penn.   Richard M. Young, Ill.
Robert C. Nicholas, La.   Reuel Williams, Me.

PENSIONS

Chairman: Thomas Morris, Ohio

Ambrose H. Sevier, Ark.   Franklin Pierce, N.H.
Samuel Prentiss, Vt.   William H. Roane, Va.

REVOLUTIONARY CLAIMS

Chairman: Bedford Brown, N.C.

Hugh Lawson White, Tenn.   John Norvell, Mich.
John J. Crittenden, Ky.   Perry Smith, Conn.

DISTRICT OF COLUMBIA

Chairman: Joseph Kent, Md.

William R. King, Ala.   William H. Roane, Va.
Robert C. Nicholas, La.   William Allen, Ohio

ON PATENTS AND THE PATENT OFFICE

Chairman: John Ruggles, Me.

Robert Strange, N.C.   Samuel Prentiss, Vt.
Richard H. Bayard, Del.   John M. Robinson, Ill.

TO AUDIT AND CONTROL THE CONTINGENT FUND

Chairman: Samuel McKean, Penn.

William S. Fulton, Ark.   John Black, Miss.

ENGROSSED BILLS

Chairman: Clement C. Clay, Ala.

Oliver H. Smith, Ind.   John Norvell, Mich.

CONGRESSIONAL DIRECTORY

TWENTY-FIFTH CONGRESS, SECOND SESSION
(December 4, 1837–July 9, 1838)

Mrs. Auld, Penn. Ave.
Mark H. Sibley, N.Y.
Abraham P. Grant, N.Y.
Henry A. Foster, N.Y.

Mrs. Ballard, Capitol Hill
Nathaniel P. Tallmadge (S), N.Y.
William S. Morgan, Va.
Jabez Y. Jackson, Ga.
Thomas T. Whittlesey, Conn.
Archibald Stuart, Va.
George W. Hopkins, Va.
Seaton Grantland, Ga.
Sherrod Williams, Ky.
Andrew D. W. Bruyn, N.Y.
Hiram Gray, N.Y.

Mrs. Ball, opposite Brown's
William Beatty, Penn.
Arnold Plumer, Penn.
John C. Brodhead, N.Y.
William W. Potter, Penn.
Luther Reily, Penn.

Mr. Bannerman, Penn. Ave.
John Pope, Ky.

Mrs. Beale, Capitol Hill
Oliver H. Smith (S), Ind.
James Rariden, Ind.

Beer's Native American Hotel
Jesse F. Cleveland, Ga.

Mrs. Bihler, Corner Fourteenth and F
St.
William Cost Johnson, Md.

Mr. Birth, Third St.
Reuel Williams (S), Me.
Franklin Pierce (S), N.H.
Garret D. Wall (S), N.J.
Jonathan Cilley,[1] Me.
Timothy J. Carter,[2] Me.

Mrs. Bladen, Penn. Ave.
William Stone, Tenn.
Edward Stanly, N.C.
Timothy Childs, N.Y.
Joseph L. Williams, Tenn.

Brown's Hotel
Ratliff Boon, Ind.
William Montgomery, N.C.
Micajah T. Hawkins, N.C.

Mrs. Clement, Penn. Ave.
Daniel Webster (S), Mass.
Edward Curtis, N.Y.

Mr. Clubb, Capitol Hill
Alfred Cuthbert (S), Ga.
Isaac Fletcher, Vt.

Mrs. Connor, Penn. Ave.
Luther C. Peck, N.Y.
Richard P. Marvin, N.Y.
William Patterson, N.Y.

[1] Killed in a duel with William J. Graves (Ky.) on Feb. 24, 1838. Edward Robinson was elected to fill the vacancy, and took his seat Apr. 28, 1838.
[2] Died Mar. 14, 1838. Virgil D. Parris was elected to fill the vacancy, and took his seat May 29, 1838.

Mrs. Corcoran, Corner Penn. Ave. and
Four and One-Half St.
Bedford Brown (S), N.C.
Levi Lincoln, Mass.
David Potts, Jr., Penn.
Robert B. Cranston, R.I.
Joseph L. Tillinghast, R.I.
Charles Naylor, Penn.
John Sergeant, Penn.
Edward Davies, Penn.
George W. Toland, Penn.

Mr. Cudlipp, Penn. Ave.
George C. Dromgoole, Va.

Mrs. Denny, Third St.
John Black (S),[3] Miss.
Alexander Mouton (S), La.

Dowson's No. 1, Capitol Hill
William Allen (S), Ohio
Thomas H. Benton (S), Mo.
John Palmer, N.Y.
James I. McKay, N.C.

Mrs. Dyer, Seventh St.
Richard H. Bayard (S), Del.
James A. Pearce, Md.
John J. Milligan, Del.
Stephen C. Phillips, Mass.

Mr. Elliot, Penn. Ave.
Clement C. Clay (S), Ala.
Lewis F. Linn (S), Mo.
James K. Polk, Tenn.
John L. Murray, Ky.
George W. Jones, Deleg., Terr. of Wis.
Isaac S. Pennybacker, Va.
Walter Coles, Va.
John W. Jones, Va.
Francis E. Rives, Va.
George W. B. Towns, Ga.

Mr. Fletcher, E St.
Richard Fletcher, Mass.
William B. Calhoun, Mass.

Edward Darlington, Penn.
Samuel Mason, Ohio
Caleb Cushing, Mass.

Mr. Follansbee, Capitol Hill
Lancelot Phelps, Conn.

Fuller's Hotel
Orrin Holt, Conn.
Henry Vail, N.Y.

Gadsby's Hotel
Isaac McKim,[4] Md.
Samuel T. Sawyer, N.C.

Mrs. Galvin, No. 1, C St.
Samuel McKean (S), Penn.
Joseph Ridgway, Ohio
William Graham, Ind.
Calvary Morris, Ohio
James Alexander, Jr., Ohio
Patrick G. Goode, Ohio

Mrs. Galvin, No. 2, C St.
Robert Barnwell Rhett, S.C.

Mrs. Hamilton, nearly opposite Gadsby's
Bennet Bicknell, N.Y.
John T. Andrews, N.Y.
William Taylor, N.Y.
James B. Spencer, N.Y.
William H. Noble, N.Y.
Thomas B. Jackson, N.Y.
Albert Gallup, N.Y.
Obadiah Titus, N.Y.
Arphaxed Loomis, N.Y.

Mr. Harbaugh, Seventh St.
Joseph Johnson, Va.
Daniel Kilgore,[5] Ohio
John Edwards, N.Y.
John Chaney, Ohio
Robert H. Hammond, Penn.
Thomas L. Hamer, Ohio

[3] Resigned Jan. 22, 1838. James F. Trotter was elected to fill the vacancy, and took his seat Feb. 19, 1838.
[4] Died Apr. 1, 1838. John P. Kennedy was elected to fill the vacancy, and took his seat Apr. 30, 1838.
[5] Resigned July 4, 1838.

H. V. Hill, Corner Third and C St.
William S. Fulton (S), Ark.
William H. Roane (S), Va.
Reuben Chapman, Ala.
John M. Patton,[6] Va.
Joshua L. Martin, Ala.
Francis S. Lyon, Ala.

Mrs. S. A. Hill, nearly opposite Gadsby's
Henry Clay (S), Ky.
John J. Crittenden (S), Ky.
Samuel L. Southard (S), N.J.
Richard Hawes, Ky.
Richard H. Menifee, Ky.
William L. May, Ill.
William J. Graves, Ky.
Thomas Corwin, Ohio

Mr. Hyatt, opposite Brown's
Benjamin Swift (S), Vt.
John Taliaferro, Va.
John B. Aycrigg, N.J.
William Halstead, N.J.
John P. B. Maxwell, N.J.
Joseph F. Randolph, N.J.
Charles C. Stratton, N.J.
Thomas Jones Yorke, N.J.
Elisha Whittlesey, Ohio
Abraham Rencher, N.C.

Mrs. Ironside, Seventh St.
James Buchanan (S), Penn.
William R. King (S), Ala.
Robert C. Nicholas (S), La.

Mrs. Keen, Capitol Hill
John Davis (S), Mass.
Abraham Vanderveer, N.Y.
Nathaniel Jones, N.Y.
James W. Bouldin, Va.
Charles F. Mercer, Va.
John Bell, Tenn.
Lewis Williams, N.C.
Charles B. Shepard, N.C.

Mrs. Kennedy, Four and One-Half St.
Henry Hubbard (S), N.H.

Lucius Lyon (S), Mich.
John Norvell (S), Mich.
Silas Wright, Jr. (S), N.Y.
Isaac E. Crary, Mich.
Charles G. Atherton, N.H.
Isaac Toucey, Conn.

Mrs. King, nearly opposite Gadsby's
Matthias Shepler, Ohio
David D. Wagener, Penn.
Daniel Sheffer, Penn.
Henry A. P. Muhlenberg,[7] Penn.
Samuel W. Morris, Penn.
David Petrikin, Penn.
Edward B. Hubley, Penn.
Daniel P. Leadbetter, Ohio
Henry Logan, Penn.
Charles McClure, Penn.

Mrs. Lindenberger, Capitol Hill
William C. Preston (S), S.C.
William C. Dawson, Ga.
William K. Clowney, S.C.
Waddy Thompson, Jr., S.C.

Mrs. McDaniel, Mo. Ave.
George N. Briggs, Mass.
George Grennell, Jr., Mass.
Joseph C. Noyes, Me.
Hiland Hall, Vt.
John Reed, Mass.
William S. Hastings, Mass.
Nathaniel B. Borden, Mass.

Mr. Masi, C St.
Francis O. J. Smith, Me.

Mrs. McCubbin, West of City Post Office
John White, Ky.

Mrs. McCardle, Penn. Ave.
John W. Allen, Ohio
John C. Clark, N.Y.

Mr. McKelden, Seventh St.
Richard Biddle, Penn.
Josiah Ogden Hoffman, N.Y.

[6] Resigned in 1838. Linn Banks was elected to fill the vacancy, and took his seat May 19, 1838.
[7] Resigned Feb. 9, 1838. George M. Keim was elected to fill the vacancy, and took his seat Mar. 17, 1838.

Mrs. Miller, F St.
Churchill C. Cambreleng, N.Y.
John I. De Graff, N.Y.

Mr. Mountz, Penn. Ave.
Joab Lawler,[8] Ala.

Mrs. Owner, Penn. Ave.
Felix Grundy (S),[9] Tenn.
John M. Robinson (S), Ill.
Richard M. Young (S), Ill.
John Miller, Mo.
Hopkins L. Turney, Tenn.
Adam W. Snyder, Ill.
William Parmenter, Mass.
Zadoc Casey, Ill.
Samuel J. Gholson,[10] Miss.
Abraham McClellan, Tenn.
Taylor Webster, Ohio
Albert G. Harrison, Mo.

Mrs. Page, opposite Centre Market
John C. Calhoun (S), S.C.
John Campbell, S.C.

Mr. Pettibone, Ninth St.
Jacob Fry, Jr., Penn.
John Klingensmith, Jr., Penn.

Mrs. Peyton, Corner Penn. Ave. and
Four and One-Half St.
John K. Griffin, S.C.
John Robertson, Va.
Francis Mallory, Va.
Robert M. T. Hunter, Va.
Charles Ogle, Penn.
James M. Mason, Va.

Mr. Pierce, Penn. Ave.
John M. Niles (S), Conn.
John Ruggles (S), Me.
Perry Smith (S), Conn.
Robert Strange (S), N.C.
Archibald Yell, Ark.
Andrew Beirne, Va.

Mrs. Pitman, Third St.
Nehemiah R. Knight (S), R.I.
Samuel Prentiss (S), Vt.
Heman Allen, Vt.
Millard Fillmore, N.Y.
Hugh J. Anderson, Me.
John Fairfield, Me.
Samuel Birdsall, N.Y.
Amasa J. Parker, N.Y.
Robert McClellan, N.Y.
John H. Prentiss, N.Y.
Zadock Pratt, N.Y.
Andrew Buchanan, Penn.
Albert S. White, Ind.
Hopkins Holsey, Ga.

Miss Polk, Penn. Ave.
Joseph S. Spence (S), Md.
Isaac H. Bronson, N.Y.

Private Residences
At the Vice President's, Md. Ave., Capitol Hill
Ely Moore, N.Y.
Wilson Lumpkin (S), Ga.
Ambrose H. Sevier (S), Ark.
John Tipton (S), Ohio
Dr. Jones, Seventh St.
Daniel Jenifer, Md.

---

[8] Died May 8, 1838.
[9] Resigned July 4, 1838.
[10] Mississippi elected its representatives in November of odd-numbered years (after the beginning of the Congressional term). As Congress had been called to meet in September, the Governor issued writs for a special election to fill vacancies until the regular election. John F. H. Claiborne and Samuel J. Gholson presented credentials and were seated Sept. 4, 1837, when, at their request, the question of the validity of their election was referred to the Committee on Elections. On October 3, 1837, the House decided that they had been elected for the full term. Sergeant S. Prentiss and Thomas J. Word presented credentials on December 27, 1837, and on Feb. 5, 1838, the House rescinded its former decision and declared the seats vacant. Prentiss and Word were subsequently elected, and took their seats May 10, 1838.

Dr. Reily, F St.
Alexander Duncan, Ohio
Mr. Woods, Twelfth St.
William K. Bond, Ohio
Mr. William Hunter, Thirteenth St.
William H. Hunter, Ohio
I St., North of President's Square
John Quincy Adams, Mass.
G St., West of the War Dept.
John F. H. Claiborne,[11] Miss.
Mount Hope, Georgetown
Augustine H. Shepperd, N.C.
Third St.
William C. Rives (S), Va.
Seven Buildings
Robert J. Walker (S), Miss.
Mr. Young, Capitol Hill
Thomas Clayton (S), Del.
Mr. Wailes, Capitol Hill
Thomas Morris (S), Ohio
*South Side Penn. Ave. between Third
and Four and One-Half St.*
Charles Downing, Deleg., Terr. of Fla.
Six Buildings
Henry Johnson, La.

Mrs. Queen, Penn. Ave.
Hugh Lawson White (S), Tenn.
Abraham P. Maury, Tenn.
William B. Carter, Tenn.
John W. Crockett, Tenn.
William B. Campbell, Tenn.
John Dennis, Md.
Christopher H. Williams, Tenn.
Richard Cheatham, Tenn.
Henry A. Wise, Va.

Mrs. Ronckendorf, Penn. Ave.
William W. Southgate, Ky.
James Harlan, Ky.
John Chambers, Ky.
Edward Rumsey, Ky.
Alexander Harper, Ohio
John Calhoon, Ky.
Charles D. Coffin,[12] Ohio

Mr. Sawkins, Corner of Twelfth and
F St.
Francis Thomas, Md.

Mrs. Smith, Capitol Hill
Asher Robbins (S), R.I.
Mathias Morris, Penn.
David A. Russell, N.Y.
Horace Everett, Vt.
Thomas Henry, Penn.
William Slade, Vt.
George Evans, Me.

Mrs. W. Smith, Penn. Ave. between
Ninth and Tenth St.
John T. H. Worthington, Md.

Mrs. Sprigg, Capitol Hill
John Ewing, Ind.
George H. Dunn, Ind.
William Herod, Ind.

Union Hotel, Georgetown
Joseph R. Underwood, Ky.

Mrs. Ulrick, Fifteenth St.
Hugh S. Legare, S.C.

Mr. Vivan, West of President's Square
Benjamin C. Howard, Md.
Gouverneur Kemble, N.Y.

Mr. Wallace, Capitol Hill
James Farrington, N.H.
Samuel Cushman, N.H.
Lemuel Paynter, Penn.
Jared W. Williams, N.H.
Thomas Davee, Me.
Charles E. Haynes, Ga.
Joseph Weeks, N.H.

Mr. Williams, Four and One-Half St.
Thomas M. T. McKennan, Penn.
Ebenezer J. Shields, Tenn.

Mrs. Wilson, Capitol Hill
James Garland, Va.
Elisha Haley, Conn.

Mrs. Wolfenden, opposite Brown's
Edmund Deberry, N.C.
Robert Crary, Va.
Samuel Ingham, Conn.

[11] See note 10.
[12] Elected to fill the vacancy caused by the resignation of Andrew W. Loomis, and took his seat Dec. 20, 1837.

APPENDIX

Dixon H. Lewis, Ala.
Thomas Glascock, Ga.
George W. Owens, Ga.
Rice Garland, La.
Eleazer W. Ripley,[13] La.
William D. Merrick (S),[14] Md.
Charles F. Mitchell, N.Y.

Jesse A. Bynum, N.C.
Henry W. Connor, N.C.
James Graham, N.C.
Franklin H. Elmore, S.C.
Francis W. Pickens, S.C.
John P. Richardson, S.C.

STANDING COMMITTEES OF THE
HOUSE OF REPRESENTATIVES

ELECTIONS

Chairman: Andrew Buchanan, Penn.

John K. Griffin, S.C.
Micajah T. Hawkins, N.C.
Daniel Kilgore, Ohio
Abram P. Maury, Tenn.

George W. B. Towns, Ga.
Isaac H. Bronson, N.Y.
Isaac S. Pennybacker, Va.
William S. Hastings, Mass.

WAYS AND MEANS

Chairman: Churchill C. Cambreleng, N.Y.

Isaac McKim, Md.
Thomas L. Hamer, Ohio
John Sergeant, Penn.
John W. Jones, Va.

John Pope, Ky.[15]
Charles G. Atherton, N.H.
Charles E. Haynes, Ga.
Abraham Rencher, N.C.

CLAIMS

Chairman: Elisha Whittlesey, Ohio

John Chambers, Ky.
Edward Darlington, Penn.
David A. Russell, N.Y.
William B. Campbell, Tenn.

John C. Clark, N.Y.
Timothy J. Carter, Me.
Archibald Stuart, Va.
Jared W. Williams, N.H.

COMMERCE

Chairman: Francis O. J. Smith, Me.

Stephen C. Phillips, Mass.
Samuel Cushman, N.H.
John I. De Graff, N.Y.
George W. Toland, Penn.

Edward Curtis, N.Y.
James M. Mason, Va.
John T. H. Worthington, Md.
William H. Hunter, Ohio

---

[13] Never qualified owing to prolonged illness.
[14] Elected to fill the vacancy caused by the death of Joseph Kent, and took his seat Jan. 5, 1838.
[15] The *Journal of the House of Representatives* lists Richard Fletcher (Mass.) in place of John Pope (Ky.).

PUBLIC LANDS

Chairman: Ratliff Boon, Ind.

Lewis Williams, N.C.
Levi Lincoln, Mass.
Zadoc Casey, Ill.
Reuben Chapman, Ala.

Albert G. Harrison, Mo.
Archibald Yell, Ark.
Ebenezer J. Shields, Tenn.
Samuel J. Gholson, Miss.

POST OFFICE AND POST ROADS

Chairman: William Montgomery, N.C.

George N. Briggs, Mass.
Hiland Hall, Vt.
George W. Hopkins, Va.
Edward B. Hubley, Penn.

John Calhoon, Ky.
George W. B. Towns, Ga.
Alexander Duncan, Ohio
John Palmer, N.Y.

DISTRICT OF COLUMBIA

Chairman: James W. Bouldin, Va.

Daniel Jenifer, Md.
William C. Dawson, Ga.
John H. Prentiss, N.Y.
Micajah T. Hawkins, N.C.

Andrew Beirne, Va.
Christopher H. Williams, Tenn.
Thomas Davee, Me.
David Petrikin, Penn.

JUDICIARY

Chairman: Francis Thomas, Md.

John Robertson, Va.
Isaac Toucey, Conn.
Thomas Corwin, Ohio
James Garland, Va.

Andrew D. W. Bruyn, N.Y.
Samuel W. Morris, Penn.
Hopkins L. Turney, Tenn.
Jonathan Cilley, Me.

REVOLUTIONARY CLAIMS

Chairman: Henry A. P. Muhlenberg, Penn.

Robert Craig, Va.
Joseph R. Underwood, Ky.
John Taliaferro, Va.
William Parmenter, Mass.

Alexander Harper, Ohio
Samuel Birdsall, N.Y.
Augustine H. Shepperd, N.C.
Joseph L. Williams, Tenn.

PUBLIC EXPENDITURES

Chairman: Elisha Haley, Conn.

James Alexander, Jr., Ohio
Obadiah Titus, N.Y.
Charles C. Stratton, N.J.
Edward Rumsey, Ky.

Isaac Fletcher, Vt.
John W. Crockett, Tenn.
William Patterson, N.Y.
Daniel Sheffer, Penn.

PRIVATE LAND CLAIMS

Chairman: William L. May, Ill.

William B. Calhoun, Mass.
Joab Lawler, Ala.
James Harlan, Ky.
William Beatty, Penn.

James Rariden, Ind.
Daniel P. Leadbetter, Ohio
Arphaxed Loomis, N.Y.
Richard Cheatam, Tenn.

MANUFACTURES

Chairman: John Quincy Adams, Mass.

Taylor Webster, Ohio	Henry Vail, N.Y.
William Slade, Vt.	Charles Naylor, Penn.
Richard Biddle, Penn.	Henry A. Foster, N.Y.
Joseph L. Tillinghast, R.I.	Robert M. T. Hunter, Va.

AGRICULTURE

Chairman: Edmund Deberry, N.C.

Henry Logan, Penn.	Joseph C. Noyes, Me.
Lancelot Phelps, Conn.	Edward Davies, Penn.
Joseph Weeks, N.H.	Joseph F. Randolph, N.J.
James B. Spencer, N.Y.	William Stone, Tenn.

INDIAN AFFAIRS

Chairman: John Bell, Tenn.

Horace Everett, Vt.	John L. Murray, Ky.
John Chaney, Ohio	James Graham, N.C.
Amasa J. Parker, N.Y.	Isaac E. Crary, Mich.
John Campbell, S.C.	Isaac S. Pennybacker, Va.

MILITARY AFFAIRS

Chairman: James I. McKay, N.C.

Walter Coles, Va.	Gouverneur Kemble, N.Y.
George Grennell, Jr., Mass.	Samson Mason, Ohio
John Miller, Mo.	Abraham McClellan, Tenn.
Francis E. Rives, Va.	William Halstead, N.J.

MILITIA

Chairman: David D. Wagener, Penn.

William B. Carter, Tenn.	Albert Gallup, N.Y.
Orrin Holt, Conn.	George H. Dunn, Ind.
John W. Allen, Ohio	William W. Southgate, Ky.
John K. Griffin, S.C.	John Dennis, Md.

NAVAL AFFAIRS

Chairman: Samuel Ingham, Conn.

John J. Milligan, Del.	Ely Moore, N.Y.
John Reed, Mass.	Daniel Kilgore, Ohio
Henry A. Wise, Va.	Lemuel Paynter, Penn.
Seaton Grantland, Ga.	Hugh J. Anderson, Me.

FOREIGN AFFAIRS

Chairman: Benjamin C. Howard, Md.

Caleb Cushing, Mass.	John Fairfield, Me.
Jabez Y. Jackson, Ga.	John M. Patton, Va.
George C. Dromgoole, Va.	Hugh S. Legare, S.C.
John F. H. Claiborne, Miss.	Josiah Ogden Hoffman, N.Y.

TERRITORIES

Chairman: Isaac H. Bronson, N.Y.

David Potts, Jr., Penn.
James A. Pearce, Md.
Nathaniel B. Borden, Mass.
Nathaniel Jones, N.Y.

James Farrington, N.H.
John White, Ky.
Robert H. Hammond, Penn.
Charles B. Shepard, N.C.

REVOLUTIONARY PENSIONS

Chairman: William S. Morgan, Va.

John Klingensmith, Jr., Penn.
William K. Bond, Ohio
Jacob Fry, Jr., Penn.
Joseph Johnson, Va.

Mark H. Sibley, N.Y.
John Ewing, Ind.
Thomas T. Whittlesey, Conn.
Timothy Childs, N.Y.

INVALID PENSIONS

Chairman: William Taylor, N.Y.

Sherrod Williams, Ky.
Heman Allen, Vt.
Robert McClellan, N.Y.
William Herod, Ind.

Edward Stanly, N.C.
Francis Mallory, Va.
John B. Aycrigg, N.J.
Arnold Plumer, Penn.

ROADS AND CANALS

Chairman: Charles F. Mercer, Va.

George Evans, Me.
Thomas M. T. McKennan, Penn.
Adam W. Snyder, Ill.
Millard Fillmore, N.Y.

William Cost Johnson, Md.
Albert S. White, Ind.
William J. Graves, Ky.
Abraham P. Grant, N.Y.

PATENTS

Chairman: Isaac Fletcher, Vt.

Lancelot Phelps, Conn.
Richard H. Menifee, Ky.

Bennet Bicknell, N.Y.
Mathias Morris, Penn.

PUBLIC BUILDINGS AND GROUNDS

Chairman: Levi Lincoln, Mass.

Hugh S. Legare, S.C.
Zadock Pratt, N.Y.

Charles F. Mercer, Va.
Jabez Y. Jackson, Ga.

REVISAL AND UNFINISHED BUSINESS

Chairman: Matthias Shepler, Ohio

William H. Noble, N.Y.
William W. Southgate, Ky.

Thomas Henry, Penn.
Luther C. Peck, N.Y.

ACCOUNTS

Chairman: Joseph Johnson, Va.

William Cost Johnson, Md.   Bennet Bicknell, N.Y.
Samuel W. Morris, Penn.   Richard Hawes, Ky.

MILEAGE

Chairman: William C. Dawson, Ga.

Benjamin C. Howard, Md.   John Miller, Mo.
George N. Briggs, Mass.   John F. H. Claiborne, Miss.

THE FOLLOWING COMMITTEES, APPOINTED LAST SESSION, STAND THROUGH THE CONGRESS

EXPENDITURES IN THE DEPARTMENT OF STATE

Chairman: Mathias Morris, Penn.

Thomas B. Jackson, N.Y.   Thomas Jones Yorke, N.J.
Matthias Shepler, Ohio   John T. Andrews, N.Y.

EXPENDITURES IN THE DEPARTMENT OF THE TREASURY

Chairman: Heman Allen, Vt.

Daniel Sheffer, Penn.   Hiram Gray, N.Y.
John B. Aycrigg, N.J.   Hopkins Holsey, Ga.

EXPENDITURES IN THE DEPARTMENT OF WAR

Chairman: William K. Clowney, S.C.

Abraham Vanderveer, N.Y.   Calvary Morris, Ohio
Orrin Holt, Conn.   Richard P. Marvin, N.Y.

EXPENDITURES IN THE DEPARTMENT OF THE NAVY

Chairman: John C. Brodhead, N.Y.

John P. B. Maxwell, N.J.   John Edwards, N.Y.
Patrick G. Goode, Ohio   William Graham, Ind.

EXPENDITURES IN THE POST OFFICE DEPARTMENT

Chairman: Timothy Childs, N.Y.

John Dennis, Md.   Albert Gallup, N.Y.
Richard Hawes, Ky.   Arnold Plumer, Penn.

EXPENDITURES ON THE PUBLIC BUILDINGS

Chairman: Samuel T. Sawyer, N.C.

Robert B. Cranston, R.I.   George H. Dunn, Ind.
Richard H. Menifee, Ky.   Joseph Ridgway, Ohio

SELECT COMMITTEES

INDIAN FIGHTERS

Chairman: William B. Carter, Tenn.

Jesse F. Cleveland, Ga.

Joshua L. Martin, Ala.

Richard H. Menifee, Ky.

Charles Ogle, Penn.

ON THE MEMORIAL OF DANIEL BOONE'S HEIRS

Chairman: Albert G. Harrison, Mo.

George W. Hopkins, Va.

Samuel T. Sawyer, N.C.

William W. Southgate, Ky.

George H. Dunn, Ind.

ON THE MEMORIAL OF DUFF GREEN

Chairman: John Taliaferro, Va.

John Pope, Ky.

William W. Potter, Penn.

Jesse F. Cleveland, Ga.

Robert Barnwell Rhett, S.C.

ON THE MEMORIAL OF THE HEIRS AND REPRESENTATIVES OF JAMES RUMSEY

Chairman: Joseph R. Underwood, Ky.

Hiram Gray, N.Y.

Francis S. Lyon, Ala.

Luther Reily, Penn.

Hopkins Holsey, Ga.

JOINT COMMITTEE

LIBRARY OF CONGRESS

House

Senate

John M. Patton, Va.

Asher Robbins, R.I.

John Pope, Ky.

William Allen, Ohio

Charles McClure, Penn.

Garret D. Wall, N.J.

STANDING COMMITTEES OF THE SENATE

FOREIGN RELATIONS

Chairman: James Buchanan, Penn.

Nathaniel P. Tallmadge, N.Y.

William C. Rives, Va.

Henry Clay, Ky.

William R. King, Ala.

FINANCE

Chairman: Silas Wright, Jr., N.Y.

Daniel Webster, Mass.

Thomas H. Benton, Mo.

Robert C. Nicholas, La.

Henry Hubbard, N.H.

COMMERCE

Chairman: William R. King, Ala.

John Davis, Mass.
Bedford Brown, N.C.

John Ruggles, Me.
John Norvell, Mich.

MANUFACTURES

Chairman: John M. Niles, Conn.

James Buchanan, Penn.
William C. Preston, S.C.

Robert Strange, N.C.
Franklin Pierce, N.H.

AGRICULTURE

Chairman: Perry Smith, Conn.

John S. Spence, Md.
Lewis F. Linn, Mo.

Samuel McKean, Penn.
John Black, Miss.

MILITARY AFFAIRS

Chairman: Thomas H. Benton, Mo.

William C. Preston, S.C.
John Tipton, Ind.

Garret D. Wall, N.J.
William Allen, Ohio

MILITIA

Chairman: Garret D. Wall, N.J.

Benjamin Swift, Vt.
Clement C. Clay, Ala.

Alexander Mouton, La.
Oliver H. Smith, Ind.

NAVAL AFFAIRS

Chairman: William C. Rives, Va.

Samuel L. Southard, N.J.
Nathaniel P. Tallmadge, N.Y.

Alfred Cuthbert, Ga.
Reuel Williams, Me.

PUBLIC LANDS

Chairman: Robert J. Walker, Miss.

William S. Fulton, Ark.
Clement C. Clay, Ala.

William Allen, Ohio
Samuel Prentiss, Vt.

PRIVATE LAND CLAIMS

Chairman: Lewis F. Linn, Mo.

Ambrose H. Sevier, Ark.
Richard H. Bayard, Del.

Alexander Mouton, La.
Lucius Lyon, Mich.

INDIAN AFFAIRS

Chairman: Hugh Lawson White, Tenn.

Ambrose H. Sevier, Ark.
John Tipton, Ind.

Lewis F. Linn, Mo.
Benjamin Swift, Vt.

CLAIMS

Chairman: Henry Hubbard, N.H.

John Tipton, Ind.
John J. Crittenden, Ky.

John S. Spence, Md.
Richard M. Young, Ill.

JUDICIARY

Chairman: Felix Grundy, Tenn.

Thomas Morris, Ohio
Garret D. Wall, N.J.

Thomas Clayton, Del.
Robert Strange, N.C.

POST OFFICE AND POST ROADS

Chairman: John M. Robinson, Ill.

Felix Grundy, Tenn.
Nehemiah R. Knight, R.I.

Bedford Brown, N.C.
John M. Niles, Conn.

ROADS AND CANALS

Chairman: John Tipton, Ind.

Samuel McKean, Penn.
Robert C. Nicholas, La.

Richard M. Young, Ill.
Lucius Lyon, Mich.

PENSIONS

Chairman: Thomas Morris, Ohio

Samuel Prentiss, Vt.
Franklin Pierce, N.H.

William H. Roane, Va.
Reuel Williams, Me.

REVOLUTIONARY CLAIMS

Chairman: Bedford Brown, N.C.

Hugh Lawson White, Tenn.
John J. Crittenden, Ky.

John Norvell, Mich.
Perry Smith, Conn.

DISTRICT OF COLUMBIA

Chairman: William H. Roane, Va.

Reuel Williams, Me.
Robert C. Nicholas, La.

John S. Spence, Md.
Richard H. Bayard, Del.

PATENTS AND THE PATENT OFFICE

Chairman: John Ruggles, Me.

Robert Strange, N.C.
John Davis, Mass.

Samuel Prentiss, Vt.
John M. Robinson, Ill.

TO AUDIT AND CONTROL THE CONTINGENT FUND

Chairman: Samuel McKean, Penn.

William S. Fulton, Ark.

John Black, Miss.

ENGROSSED BILLS

Chairman: Clement C. Clay, Ala.

Oliver H. Smith, Ind.   John Norvell, Mich.

SELECT COMMITTEES

ON THE EXPLOSIONS OF STEAMBOILERS

Felix Grundy, Tenn.   John C. Calhoun, S.C.
Garret D. Wall, N.J.   Daniel Webster, Mass.
Thomas Clayton, Del.   Robert J. Walker, Miss.
Thomas H. Benton, Mo.

ON THE MEMORIAL OF DUFF GREEN

Lewis F. Linn, Mo.   Wilson Lumpkin, Ga.
Ambrose H. Sevier, Ark.   John Davis, Mass.
Asher Robbins, R.I.

CONGRESSIONAL DIRECTORY

TWENTY-FIFTH CONGRESS, THIRD SESSION
(December 3, 1838–March 3, 1839)

Mrs. Arguelle, nearly opposite Gadsby's
Levi Lincoln, Mass.
William K. Bond, Ohio
Edward Stanly, N.C.

Mrs. Auld, Penn. Ave. between Four
and One-Half and Sixth St.
John Davis (S), Mass.
George Evans, Me.
Mark H. Sibley, N.Y.
Leverett Saltonstall,[1] Mass.

Mrs. Ballard, Capitol Hill
Robert Strange (S), N.C.
Jabez Y. Jackson, Ga.
Christopher H. Williams, Tenn.
Lancelot Phelps, Conn.
George W. Hopkins, Va.
Isaac Toucey, Conn.
Thomas T. Whittlesey, Conn.
Seaton Grantland, Ga.
Archibald Stuart, Va.
Hiram Gray, N.Y.
William K. Clowney, S.C.

Mrs. Ball, opposite Brown's
Luther Reily, Penn.
William Beatty, Penn.
Samuel W. Morris, Penn.
Jacob Fry, Jr., Penn.
Arnold Plumer, Penn.
William W. Potter, Penn.

Mrs. Beale, Capitol Hill
Dixon H. Lewis, Ala.
Joshua L. Martin, Ala.

Beer's Native American Hotel,
Penn. Ave.
Thomas Glascock, Ga.

Mr. Birth, Third St.
Ephraim H. Foster (S), Tenn.
William B. Campbell, Tenn.
Richard Cheatham, Tenn.
John Bell, Tenn.

Brown's
William C. Preston (S), S.C.
William C. Dawson, Ga.
Waddy Thompson, Jr., S.C.
James W. Bouldin,[2] Va.

Mrs. Burch, Capitol Hill
James Farrington, N.H.
Joseph Weeks, N.H.

Mr. Clement, Penn. Ave.
Nathaniel P. Tallmadge (S), N.Y.
Henry A. Foster, N.Y.
Abraham P. Grant, N.Y.
John C. Clark, N.Y.

Miss Corcoran, Corner Penn. Ave. and
Four and One-Half St.
Joseph L. Tillinghast, R.I.
Timothy Childs, N.Y.
George W. Toland, Penn.
Edward Davies, Penn.
Charles Naylor, Penn.
David Potts, Jr., Penn.
Robert B. Cranston, R.I.
R. Barnwell Rhett, S.C.

[1] Elected to fill the vacancy caused by the resignation of Stephen C. Phillips, and took his seat Dec. 5, 1838.
[2] Also listed at Mr. Wallace's.

Mrs. Denny, Third St.
Rice Garland, La.
Sergeant S. Prentiss, Miss.

Dowson's No. 1, Capitol Hill
William Allen (S), Ohio
Thomas H. Benton (S), Mo.
Clement C. Clay (S), Ala.
Thomas H. Williams (S), [3] Miss.
John Miller, Mo.

Dowson's No. 2, Capitol Hill
Franklin H. Elmore, S.C.
John P. Richardson, S.C.

Mrs. Dyson, Capitol Hill
Henry A. Wise, Va.
Thomas J. Word, Miss.

Mr. Elliot, Penn. Ave.
James K. Polk, Tenn.
Isaac H. Bronson, N.Y.

Mr. Fletcher, E between Sixth and
  Seventh St.
Joshua R. Giddings, Ohio
Luther C Peck, N.Y.
Millard Fillmore, N.Y.
Charles F. Mitchell, N.Y.
Harvey Putnam, N.Y.
Richard Fletcher, Mass.
Richard P. Marvin, N.Y.

Gadsby's
Charles Downing, Deleg., Terr. of Fla.
John I. De Graff, N.Y.
John T. H. Worthington, Md.
William Cost Johnson, Md.

Mrs. Galvin, No. 1, C between Third
  and Four and One-Half St.
Samuel McKean (S), Penn.
Patrick G. Goode, Ohio
Joseph Ridgway, Ohio
James Alexander, Jr., Ohio
John W. Crockett, Tenn.
Calvary Morris, Ohio

Mrs. Galvin, No. 2, C between Third
  and Four and One-Half St.
John Dennis, Md.

John J. Milligan, Del.
James A. Pearce, Md.

Mrs. Hamilton, nearly opposite Gadsby's
James B. Spencer, N.Y.
Bennet Bicknell, N.Y.
William H. Noble, N.Y.
Cyrus Beers, N.Y.
William Taylor, N.Y.
John T. Andrews, N.Y.
Virgil D. Parris, Me.

Mr. Harbaugh, Seventh, between D and
  E St.
Robert H. Hammond, Penn.
John Edwards, N.Y.
Thomas L. Hamer, Ohio

Mrs. S. A. Hill, nearly opposite Gadsby's
Charles G. Atherton, N.H.
Henry W. Connor, N.C.
Francis E. Rives, Va.
Linn Banks, Va.
Reuben Chapman, Ala.
Francis S. Lyon, Ala.
George W. B. Towns, Ga.
Micajah T. Hawkins, N.C.
George W. Crabb, Ala.
John W. Jones, Va.
Andrew Beirne, Va.

H. V. Hill's, Capitol Hill
John C. Calhoun (S), S.C.
Francis W. Pickens, S.C.
Robert M. T. Hunter, Va.
Francis Mallory, Va.
James M. Mason, Va.
Samuel T. Sawyer, N.C.

Mrs. Hughes, nearly opposite Brown's
Henry Hubbard (S), N.H.
John M. Niles (S), Conn.
Perry Smith (S), Conn.
Silas Wright, Jr., (S), N.Y.

Mr. Hyatt, opposite Brown's
Benjamin Swift (S), Vt.
Joseph F. Randolph, N.J.
Samson Mason, Ohio
John Taliaferro, Va.

[3] Appointed to fill the vacancy caused by the resignation of James F. Trotter, and took his seat Dec. 13, 1838; subsequently elected.

John B. Aycrigg, N.J.
John P. B. Maxwell, N.J.
William Halstead, N.J.
Charles C. Stratton, N.J.
Thomas Jones Yorke, N.J.
Abraham Rencher, N.C.

Mrs. Ironside, E between Ninth
   and Tenth St.
James Buchanan (S), Penn.
Robert C. Nicholas (S), La.
William R. King (S), Ala.

Mrs. Kennedy, Four and One-
   Half St.
Reuel Williams (S), Me.
Lucius Lyon (S), Mich.
John Norvell (S), Mich.
Franklin Pierce (S), N.H.
Garret D. Wall (S), N.J.
Isaac E. Crary, Mich.

Mrs. King, nearly opposite Gadsby's
David D. Wagener, Penn.
Henry Logan, Penn.
Edward B. Hubley, Penn.
John Chaney, Ohio
Matthias Shepler, Ohio
Henry Swearingen, Ohio
Daniel Sheffer, Penn.
Thomas B. Jackson, N.Y.
Daniel P. Leadbetter, Ohio
Obadiah Titus, N.Y.

Mr. Knowles, D between Second
   and Third St.
Thomas Morris (S), Ohio
Orrin Holt, Conn.

Mrs. McDaniel, Mo. Ave.
Hiland Hall, Vt.
Nathaniel B. Borden, Mass.
George N. Briggs, Mass.
Edward Robinson, Me.
William S. Hastings, Mass.
George Grennell, Jr., Mass.
John Reed, Mass.

Dr. Mayo, B between Second
   and Third St.
John J. Crittenden (S), Ky.
John Calhoon, Ky.
Richard Hawes, Ky.

Mrs. McCubbins, near Central
   Post Office
Richard H. Menifee, Ky.
John White, Ky.

Mrs. McGunnigle, Tenth St.,
   between D and E.
David Petrikin, Penn.
John L. Murray, Ky.
William Montgomery, N.C.
Hopkins L. Turney, Tenn.
James I. McKay, N.C.
Jesse A. Bynum, N.C.
John C. Brodhead, N.Y.
Abraham McClellan, Tenn.

Mr. McKelden, Seventh St., between
   D and E.
Samuel L. Southard (S), N.J.
Josiah Ogden Hoffman, N.Y.

Mrs. Owner, Penn. Ave.
Alexander Mouton (S), La.
Lewis F. Linn (S), Mo.
John M. Robinson (S), Ill.
Richard M. Young (S), Ill.
Adam W. Snyder, Ill.
Zadoc Casey, Ill.
William W. Chapman, Deleg., Terr.
   of Iowa
William Parmenter, Mass.
Archibald Yell, Ark.
George W. Jones,[4] Deleg., Terr. of Wis.
Albert G. Harrison, Mo.

Mrs. Page, opposite Centre Market
John Campbell, S.C.

Mr. Pettibone, Ninth St.
Sherrod Williams, Ky.
Joseph L. Williams, Tenn.

---

[4] Served until Jan. 14, 1839; succeeded by James D. Doty, who successfully
contested the election.

Mrs. Peyton, Penn. Ave., Corner
Four and One-Half St.
John K. Griffin, S.C.
John Robertson, Va.
Abram P. Maury, Tenn.
Charles Ogle, Penn.

Mrs. Pitman, Third St.
Nehemiah R. Knight (S), R.I.
Samuel Prentiss (S), Vt.
Andrew Buchanan, Penn.
Heman Allen, Vt.
Samuel Birdsall, N.Y.
John Fairfield,[5] Conn.
Hugh J. Anderson, Me.
Nathaniel Jones, N.Y.
Samuel Cushman, N.H.
Amasa J. Parker, N.Y.
Robert McClellan, N.Y.
Albert Gallup, N.Y.
Zadock Pratt, N.Y.
John H. Prentiss, N.Y.
Arphaxed Loomis, N.Y.
John Palmer, N.Y.

Miss Polk, Penn. Ave., Corner
Third St.
Bedford Brown (S), N.C.
Richard H. Bayard (S), Del.
Edward Curtis, N.Y.

Private Residences:
Dr. Thomas D. Jones, Seventh be-
tween D and E St.
Daniel Jenifer, Md.
Mrs. Hellen, D between Ninth and
Tenth St.
John Pope, Ky.
Mrs. Dashiell, C between Four and
One-Half and Sixth St.
Charles B. Shepard, N.C.
Over Johnson's Snuff Store, Penn.
Ave., between Eleventh and Twelfth
Benjamin C. Howard, Md.
Mrs. Denham, Penn. Ave., between
Ninth and Tenth St.
Taylor Webster, Ohio
Mrs. Mount, near Gadsby's
Edward Darlington, Penn.

Mr. Murphey, Corner Penn. Ave. and
Four and One-Half St.
Richard Biddle, Penn.
A. B. Waller, near Bradley's Wharf
Joseph C. Noyes, Me.
Mrs. Reily, Penn. Ave. between
Third and Four and One-Half St.
Ely Moore, N.Y.
Mrs. Holdsworth, Capitol Hill
Abraham Vanderveer, N.Y.
Mr. Follanbee, Capitol Hill
Caleb Cushing, Mass.
Mr. Waile, Capitol Hill
Thomas Davee, Me.
Over Mr. Lamb's, Penn. Ave.
opposite Fuller's
Alexander Duncan, Ohio
Mr. Hunter, Thirteenth St.
William H. Hunter, Ohio
Mrs. Miner, West of President's
Square
John Sergeant, Penn.
Penn. Ave. near Corner Twentieth St.
Francis Thomas, Md.
F between Thirteenth and
Fourteenth St.
John Quincy Adams, Mass.
Six Buildings
Henry Johnson, La.
Mr. Aaron Vail, H between
Fifteenth and Sixteenth St.
Henry Vail, N.Y.
Mr. Boulanger, nearly opposite
Gadsby's
Henry Clay (S), Ky.
Mr. Young, Capitol Hill
Thomas Clayton (S), Del.
Georgetown
William S. Fulton (S), Ark.
Rev. Matthew, Corner F and Tenth St.
William D. Merrick (S), Md.
Seven Buildings
Robert J. Walker (S), Miss.
Mr. Brereton, Corner of Seventh
and F St.
John S. Spence, Md.

Mr. Purcell, opposite Brown's
Thomas Corwin, Ohio
James Graham, N.C.

[5] Resigned Dec. 24, 1838, after having been elected governor.

Mrs. Ronckendorf, Penn. Ave. near Corner Third St.
Thomas M. T. McKennan, Penn.
James Harlan, Ky.
John Chambers, Ky.
Charles D. Coffin, Ohio
John W. Allen, Ohio
William W. Southgate, Ky.
Alexander Harper, Ohio
William L. May, Ill.

Mrs. Scott, Penn. Ave. between Third and Four and One-Half St.
Wilson Lumpkin (S), Ga.
Oliver H. Smith (S), Ind.
John Tipton (S), Ind.
James Rariden, Ind.
Albert S. White, Ind.

Mrs. Smith, Capitol Hill
Asher Robbins (S), R.I.
Horace Everett, Vt.
David A. Russell, N.Y.
William B. Calhoun, Mass.
Lewis Williams, N.C.
Charles F. Mercer, Va.

Mrs. Sprigg, Capitol Hill
Mathias Morris, Penn.
William Herod, Ind.
William Slade, Vt.
John Ewing, Ind.
Thomas Henry, Penn.
William Graham, Ind.
George H. Dunn, Ind.
William Stone, Tenn.

Mrs. Thompson, Capitol Hill
William S. Morgan, Va.
Joseph Johnson, Va.
George C. Dromgoole, Va.
Jesse F. Cleveland, Ga.

Mrs. Turner, opposite Brown's
William H. Roane (S), Va.
Walter Coles, Va.

Mrs. Ulrick, opposite the State Dept.
William C. Rives (S), Va.
Hugh S. Legare, S.C.

Union Hotel, Georgetown
Joseph R. Underwood, Ky.

Mr. Upperman, Penn. Ave. near Corner Third St.
John P. Kennedy, Md.
William J. Graves, Ky.
Edward Rumsey, Ky.

Mr. Vivan, West of President's Square
Churchill C. Cambreleng, N.Y.
Gouverneur Kemble, N.Y.

Mr. Wallace, Capitol Hill
Lemuel Paynter, Penn.
Isaac Fletcher, Vt.
Charles McClure, Penn.
Charles E. Haynes, Ga.
George M. Keim, Penn.
James Garland, Va.
John Klingensmith, Jr., Penn.
Jared W. Williams, N.H.
Ratliff Boon, Ind.
James W. Bouldin,[6] Va.

Mr. Williams, Four and One-Half St.
Ebenezer J. Shields, Tenn.
William B. Carter, Tenn.

Mr. Wimsatt, Penn. Ave. between Third and Four and One-Half St.
John Ruggles (S), Me.
Samuel Ingham, Conn.
Edmund Deberry, N.C.
Robert Craig, Va.
Elisha Haley, Conn.
Augustine H. Shepperd, N.C.

APPENDIX

Ambrose H. Sevier (S), Ark.
Francis O. J. Smith, Conn.

Alfred Cuthbert (S), Ga.
Hopkins Holsey, Ga.

[6] Also listed at Brown's.

George W. Owens, Ga.
Eleazer W. Ripley,[7] La.
Daniel Webster (S), Mass.

Hugh Lawson White (S), Tenn.
Isaac Pennybacker, Va.

STANDING COMMITTEES OF THE
HOUSE OF REPRESENTATIVES

ELECTIONS

Chairman: Andrew Buchanan, Penn.

John K. Griffin, S.C.
Micajah T. Hawkins, N.C.
Abram P. Maury, Tenn.
George W. B. Towns, Ga.

Isaac H. Bronson, N.Y.
William S. Hastings, Mass.
Francis E. Rives, Va.
Henry Swearingen, Ohio

WAYS AND MEANS

Chairman: Churchill C. Cambreleng, N.Y.

John Sergeant, Penn.
John W. Jones, Va.
Charles G. Atherton, N.H.
Charles E. Haynes, Ga.

Abraham Rencher, N.C.
John Pope, Ky.
Robert Barnwell Rhett, S.C.
Taylor Webster, Ohio

CLAIMS

Chairman: John Chambers, Ky.

Edward Darlington, Penn.
David A. Russell, N.Y.
William B. Campbell, Tenn.
Archibald Stuart, Va.

Jared W. Williams, N.H.
Hiram Gray, N.Y.
Leverett Saltonstall, Mass.
Joshua R. Giddings, Ohio

COMMERCE

Chairman: Samuel Cushman, N.H.

John I. De Graff, N.Y.
George W. Toland, Penn.
Edward Curtis, N.Y.
James M. Mason, Va.

John T. H. Worthington, Md.
Henry Johnson, La.
William Montgomery, N.C.
Luther Reily, Penn.

PUBLIC LANDS

Chairman: Zadoc Casey, Ill.

Lewis Williams, N.C.
Levi Lincoln, Mass.
Reuben Chapman, Ala.
Ebenezer J. Shields, Tenn.

Arphaxed Loomis, N.Y.
John L. Murray, Ky.
Alexander Duncan, Ohio
Thomas J. Word, Miss.

[7] Never qualified owing to prolonged illness.

POST OFFICE AND POST ROADS

Chairman: Henry W. Connor, N.C.

George N. Briggs, Mass.
Hiland Hall, Vt.
George W. Hopkins, Va.
Edward B. Hubley, Penn.

John Calhoon, Ky.
George W. B. Towns, Ga.
John Palmer, N.Y.
Daniel P. Leadbetter, Ohio

DISTRICT OF COLUMBIA

Chairman: James W. Bouldin, Va.

Daniel Jenifer, Md.
William C. Dawson, Ga.
John H. Prentiss, N.Y.
Micajah T. Hawkins, N.C.

Andrew Beirne, Va.
Christopher H. Williams, Tenn.
Thomas Davee, Me.
Francis S. Lyon, Ala.

JUDICIARY

Chairman: Francis Thomas, Md.

John Robertson, Va.
Isaac Toucey, Conn.
Thomas Corwin, Ohio
James Garland, Va.

Samuel W. Morris, Penn.
Hopkins L. Turney, Tenn.
Joshua L. Martin, Ala.
Henry A. Foster, N.Y.

REVOLUTIONARY CLAIMS

Chairman: Robert Craig, Va.

Joseph R. Underwood, Ky.
John Taliaferro, Va.
William Parmenter, Mass.
Alexander Harper, Ohio

Samuel Birdsall, N.Y.
Augustine H. Shepperd, N.C.
Joseph L. Williams, Tenn.
George M. Keim, Penn.

PUBLIC EXPENDITURES

Chairman: Elisha Haley, Conn.

James Alexander, Jr., Ohio
Obadiah Titus, N.Y.
Charles C. Stratton, N.J.
Edward Rumsey, Ky.

Isaac Fletcher, Vt.
John W. Crockett, Tenn.
Daniel Sheffer, Penn.
Harvey Putnam, N.Y.

PRIVATE LAND CLAIMS

Chairman: William L. May, Ill.

William B. Calhoun, Mass.
James Harlan, Ky.
William Beatty, Penn.
James Rariden, Ind.

Richard Cheatham, Tenn.
Rice Garland, La.
Richard Fletcher, Mass.
George W. Crabb, Ala.

MANUFACTURES

Chairman: John Quincy Adams, Mass.

William Slade, Vt.
Richard Biddle, Penn.
Joseph L. Tillinghast, R.I.
Henry Vail, N.Y.

Charles Naylor, Penn.
Robert M. T. Hunter, Va.
Franklin H. Elmore, S.C.
John P. Kennedy, Md.

AGRICULTURE
Chairman: Edmund Deberry, N.C.

Henry Logan, Penn.
Lancelot Phelps, Conn.
Joseph Weeks, N.H.
James B. Spencer, N.Y.

Joseph C. Noyes, Me.
Edward Davies, Penn.
Joseph F. Randolph, N.J.
William Stone, Tenn.

INDIAN AFFAIRS
Chairman: John Bell, Tenn.

Horace Everett, Vt.
John Chaney, Ohio
Amasa J. Parker, N.Y.
James Graham, N.C.

Dixon H. Lewis, Ala.
David Petrikin, Penn.
Linn Banks, Va.
Virgil D. Parris, Me.

MILITARY AFFAIRS
Chairman: James I. McKay, N.C.

Walter Coles, Va.
George Grennell, Jr., Mass.
Francis E. Rives, Va.
Gouverneur Kemble, N.Y.

Samson Mason, Ohio
Abraham McClellan, Tenn.
William Halstead, N.J.
Thomas Glascock, Ga.

MILITIA
Chairman: David D. Wagener, Penn.

William B. Carter, Tenn.
Orrin Holt, Conn.
John W. Allen, Ohio
John K. Griffin, S.C.

Albert Gallup, N.Y.
George H. Dunn, Ind.
William W. Southgate, Ky.
John Dennis, Md.

NAVAL AFFAIRS
Chairman: Samuel Ingham, Conn.

John J. Milligan, Del.
John Reed, Mass.
Henry A. Wise, Va.
Seaton Grantland, Ga.

Ely Moore, N.Y.
Lemuel Paynter, Penn.
Hugh J. Anderson, Me.
Francis W. Pickens, S.C.

FOREIGN AFFAIRS
Chairman: Benjamin C. Howard, Md.

Caleb Cushing, Mass.
Jabez Y. Jackson, Ga.
George C. Dromgoole, Va.
John Fairfield, Me.

Hugh S. Legare, S.C.
Josiah Ogden Hoffman, N.Y.
Jesse A. Bynum, N.C.
Isaac E. Crary, Mich.

TERRITORIES
Chairman: Isaac H. Bronson, N.Y.

David Potts, Jr., Penn.
James A. Pearce, Md.
Nathaniel B. Borden, Mass.
Nathaniel Jones, N.Y.

James Farrington, N.H.
John White, Ky.
Robert H. Hammond, Penn.
Charles B. Shepard, N.C.

REVOLUTIONARY CLAIMS

Chairman: William S. Morgan, Va.

John Klingensmith, Jr., Penn.
William K. Bond, Ohio
Jacob Fry, Jr., Penn.
Joseph Johnson, Va.

Mark H. Sibley, N.Y.
John Ewing, Ind.
Thomas T. Whittlesey, Conn.
Timothy Childs, N.Y.

INVALID CLAIMS

Chairman: William Taylor, N.Y.

Sherrod Williams, Ky.
Heman Allen, Vt.
Robert McClellan, N.Y.
William Herod, Ind.

Edward Stanly, N.C.
Fancis Mallory, Va.
Arnold Plumer, Penn.
Charles F. Mitchell, N.Y.

ROADS AND CANALS

Chairman: Charles F. Mercer, Va.

George Evans, Me.
Thomas M. T. McKennan, Penn.
Adam W. Snyder, Ill.
Millard Fillmore, N.Y.

William Cost Johnson, Md.
Albert S. White, Ind.
William J. Graves, Ky.
Abraham P. Grant, N.Y.

PATENTS

Chairman: Isaac Fletcher, Vt.

Lancelot Phelps, Conn.
Richard H. Menifee, Ky.

Cyrus Beers, N.Y.
Edward Robinson, Me.

PUBLIC BUILDINGS AND GROUNDS

Chairman: Levi Lincoln, Mass.

Zadock Pratt, N.Y.
Charles F. Mercer, Va.

Charles McClure, Penn.
Jabez Y. Jackson, Ga.

REVISAL AND UNFINISHED BUSINESS

Chairman: Matthias Shepler, Ohio

William H. Noble, N.Y.
William W. Southgate, Ky.

Thomas Henry, Penn.
Luther C. Peck, N.Y.

ACCOUNTS

Chairman: Joseph Johnson, Va.

William Cost Johnson, Md.
Samuel W. Morris, Penn.

Bennet Bicknell, N.Y.
Richard Hawes, Ky.

MILEAGE

Chairman: William C. Dawson, Ga.

Benjamin C. Howard, Md.
George N. Briggs, Mass.

Charles D. Coffin, Ohio
Bennet Bicknell, N.Y.

The following committees were appointed at the first session of the Congress, and, by the rules, remain during the Congress:

EXPENDITURES IN THE DEPARTMENT OF STATE

Chairman: Mathias Morris, Penn.

Thomas B. Jackson, N.Y.   Thomas Jones Yorke, N.J.
Matthias Shepler, Ohio   John T. Andrews, N.Y.

EXPENDITURES IN THE DEPARTMENT OF THE TREASURY

Chairman: Heman Allen, Vt.

Daniel Sheffer, Penn.   Hiram Gray, N.Y.
John B. Aycrigg, N.J.   Hopkins Holsey, Ga.

EXPENDITURES IN THE DEPARTMENT OF WAR

Chairman: William K. Clowney, S.C.

Abraham Vanderveer, N.Y.   Calvary Morris, Ohio
Orrin Holt, Conn.   Richard P. Marvin, N.Y.

EXPENDITURES IN THE DEPARTMENT OF THE NAVY

Chairman: John C. Brodhead, N.Y.

John P. B. Maxwell, N.J.   John Edwards, N.Y.
Patrick G. Goode, Ohio   William Graham, Ind.

EXPENDITURES IN THE POST OFFICE DEPARTMENT

Chairman: Timothy Childs, N.Y.

John Dennis, Md.   Albert Gallup, N.Y.
Richard Hawes, Ky.   Arnold Plumer, Penn.

EXPENDITURES ON THE PUBLIC BUILDINGS

Chairman: Samuel T. Sawyer, N.C.

Robert B. Cranston, R.I.   George H. Dunn, Ind.
Richard H. Menifee, Ky.   Joseph Ridgway, Ohio

ENROLLED BILLS

Archibald Yell, Ark.   Joseph C. Noyes, Me.

SELECT COMMITTEES

DUELLING WITHIN THE DISTRICT OF COLUMBIA

John Quincy Adams, Mass.   Seaton Grantland, Ga.
Isaac Toucey, Conn.   John C. Clark, N.Y.
Franklin H. Elmore, S.C.   Thomas Henry, Penn.
James Rariden, Ind.   Charles D. Coffin, Ohio
George Grennell, Jr., Mass.

PRESIDENT'S TWO MESSAGES, SMITHSONIAN BEQUEST

John Quincy Adams, Mass.	Waddy Thompson, Jr., S.C.
Francis O. J. Smith, Me.	William H. Hunter, Ohio
Charles Ogle, Penn.	John P. Kennedy, Md.
Charles B. Shepard, N.C.	James Garland, Va.
Orrin Holt, Conn.	

SECRETARY OF THE TREASURY'S REPORT ON STEAM ENGINES

John Sergeant, Penn.	Richard H. Menifee, Ky.
Thomas L. Hamer, Ohio	Archibald Yell, Ark.
John Campbell, S.C.	Nathaniel B. Borden, Mass.
Lancelot Phelps, Conn.	

ON THE MEMORIAL OF THE HEIRS OF J. RUMSEY

Joseph R. Underwood, Ky.	Orrin Holt, Conn.
Richard Hawes, Ky.	John Miller, Mo.
Dixon H. Lewis, Ala.	Ratliff Boon, Ind.
Daniel Jenifer, Md.	

ON THE TOBACCO TRADE

Daniel Jenifer, Md.	John Sergeant, Penn.
Walter Coles, Va.	Daniel P. Leadbetter, Ohio
Ebenezer J. Shields, Tenn.	Joseph R. Underwood, Ky.
Benjamin C. Howard, Md.	Henry Johnson, La.
Albert G. Harrison, Mo.	

ON THE MEMORIAL OF THE STATE OF GEORGIA FOR THE PAYMENT OF A CERTIFICATE OF REVOLUTIONARY DEBT

William C. Dawson, Ga.	Robert M. T. Hunter, Va.
William W. Potter, Penn.	William W. Southgate, Ky.
John B. Aycrigg, N.J.	

JOINT COMMITTEE

LIBRARY OF CONGRESS

House	Senate
John Pope, Ky.	Asher Robbins, R.I.
Charles McClure, Penn.	Garret D. Wall, N.J.
Jesse F. Cleveland Ga.	William Allen, Ohio

STANDING COMMITTEES OF THE SENATE

FOREIGN RELATIONS

Chairman: James Buchanan, Penn.

Nathaniel P. Tallmadge, N.Y.	William C. Rives, Va.
Henry Clay, Ky.	John M. Niles, Conn.

FINANCE

Chairman: Silas Wright, Jr., N.Y.

Daniel Webster, Mass.　　　　　　Thomas H. Benton, Mo.
Robert C. Nicholas, La.　　　　　　Henry Hubbard, N.H.

COMMERCE

Chairman: William R. King, Ala.

John Daivs, Mass.　　　　　　　　John Norvell, Mich.
Bedford Brown, N.C.　　　　　　　John Ruggles, Me.

MANUFACTURES

Chairman: John M. Niles, Conn.

Wilson Lumpkin, Ga.　　　　　　　Robert Strange, N.C.
William C. Preston, S.C.　　　　　John Ruggles, Me.

AGRICULTURE

Chairman: Perry Smith, Conn.

John S. Spence, Md.　　　　　　　Samuel McKean, Penn.
Lewis F. Linn, Mo.　　　　　　　　Alexander Mouton, La.

MILITARY AFFAIRS

Chairman: Thomas H. Benton, Mo.

William C. Preston, S.C.　　　　　Garret D. Wall, N.J.
John Tipton, Ind.　　　　　　　　William Allen, Ohio

MILITIA

Chairman: Clement C. Clay, Ala.

Benjamin Swift, Vt.　　　　　　　Oliver H. Smith, Ind.
Alexander Mouton, La.　　　　　　Ephraim H. Foster, Tenn.

NAVAL AFFAIRS

Chairman: William C. Rives, Va.

Samuel L. Southard, N.J.　　　　　Alfred Cuthbert, Ga.
Nathaniel P. Tallmadge, N.Y.　　　Reuel Williams, Me.

PUBLIC LANDS

Chairman: Robert J. Walker, Miss.

William S. Fulton, Ark.　　　　　　William Allen, Ohio
Clement C. Clay, Ala.　　　　　　　Samuel Prentiss, Vt.

PRIVATE LAND CLAIMS

Chairman: Lewis F. Linn, Mo.

Ambrose H. Sevier, Ark.　　　　　Alexander Mouton, La.
Richard H. Bayard, Del.　　　　　Lucius Lyon, Mich.

INDIAN AFFAIRS

Chairman: Hugh Lawson White, Tenn.

Ambrose H. Sevier, Ark.	Lewis F. Linn, Mo.
John Tipton, Ind.	Benjamin Swift, Vt.

CLAIMS

Chairman: Henry Hubbard, N.H.

John Tipton, Ind.	Richard M. Young, Ill.
John J. Crittenden, Ky.	William D. Merrick, Md.

JUDICIARY

Chairman: Garret D. Wall, N.J.

Thomas Morris, Ohio	Robert Strange, N.C.
Thomas Clayton, Del.	Franklin Pierce, N.H.

POST OFFICE AND POST ROADS

Chairman: John M. Robinson, Ill.

Wilson Lumpkin, Ga.	Bedford Brown, N.C.
Nehemiah R. Knight, R.I.	William D. Merrick, Md.

ROADS AND CANALS

Chairman: John Tipton, Ind.

Samuel McKean, Penn.	Lucius Lyon, Mich.
Richard M. Young, Ill.	Ephraim H. Foster, Tenn.

PENSIONS

Chairman: Thomas Morris, Ohio

Samuel Prentiss, Vt.	William H. Roane, Va.
Franklin Pierce, N.H.	Reuel Williams, Me.

REVOLUTIONARY CLAIMS

Chairman: Bedford Brown, N.C.

Hugh Lawson White, Tenn.	John Norvell, Mich.
John J. Crittenden, Ky.	Perry Smith, Conn.

DISTRICT OF COLUMBIA

Chairman: William H. Roane, Va.

Robert C. Nicholas, La.	Richard H. Bayard, Del.
John S. Spence, Md.	Samuel McKean, Penn.

PATENTS AND THE PATENT OFFICE

Chairman: Robert Strange, N.C.

John Davis, Mass.	John M. Robinson, Ill.
Samuel Prentiss, Vt.	Lucius Lyon, Mich.

TO AUDIT AND CONTROL THE CONTINGENT FUND

Chairman: Samuel McKean, Penn.

William S. Fulton, Ark.   Nehemiah R. Knight, R.I.

PUBLIC BUILDINGS

Chairman: William S. Fulton, Ark.

Richard H. Bayard, Del.   William C. Rives, Va.

ENGROSSED BILLS

Chairman: John Norvell, Mich.

Oliver H. Smith, Ind.   William D. Merrick, Md.

SELECT COMMITTEE

ON THE "BILL TO PROVIDE FOR THE PROTECTION OF THE CITIZENS OF THE UNITED STATES, RESIDING IN THE OREGON TERRITORY, OR TRADING ON THE COLUMBIA RIVER OR ITS TRIBUTARIES"

Lewis F. Linn, Mo.   Franklin Pierce, N.H.
John C. Calhoun, S.C.   Henry Clay, Ky.
Robert J. Walker, Miss.

CONGRESSIONAL DIRECTORY

TWENTY-SIXTH CONGRESS, FIRST SESSION
(December 2, 1839–July 21, 1840)

Mrs. Auld, nearly opposite Gadsby's
Benjamin Randall, Me.
George Evans, Me.
Leverett Saltonstall, Mass.
Edward Custis, N.Y.

Mrs. Ballard, Capitol Hill
Walter T. Colquitt, Ga.
Edward J. Black, Ga.
Richard W. Habersham, Ga.
Eugenius A. Nisbet, Ga.
Lott Warren, Ga.
Mark A. Cooper, Ga.
George W. Hopkins, Va.
Robert Barnwell Rhett, S.C.

Mrs. Ball, opposite Brown's
Tilghman A. Howard, Ind.
Thomas Smith, Ind.
Julius W. Blackwell, Tenn.
William Beatty, Penn.
John Davis, Penn.
Hopkins L. Turney, Tenn.
George McCulloch, Penn.
David A. Starkweather, Ohio

Mrs. Bannerman, Penn. Ave. between
  Third and Four and One-Half St.
Robert Strange (S), N.C.
Reuel Williams (S), Me.
Clement C. Clay (S), Ala.
William S. Fulton (S), Ark.
Ambrose H. Sevier (S), Ark.

Mr. Bassett, East Capitol St., Capitol Hill
Oliver H. Smith (S), Ind.
James Rariden, Ind.

Mrs. Brawner, Penn. Ave., between
  Second and Third St.
Isaac Fletcher, Vt.
James Rogers, S.C.

Mr. Bronaugh, Capitol Hill
John Campbell, S.C.
Thomas D. Sumter, S.C.
Francis W. Pickens, S.C.
Robert M. T. Hunter, Va.

Miss Corcoran, Corner Penn. Ave. and
  Four and One-Half St.
Joseph L. Tillinghast, Mass.
Charles Naylor, Penn.
Edward Davies, Penn.
John Sergeant, Penn.
William B. Calhoun, Mass.
James Cooper, Penn.
Robert B. Cranston, Mass.
Levi Lincoln, Mass.
Landaff W. Andrews, Ky.

Mrs. Coyle, C St., between Four and
  One-Half and Sixth St.
David Petrikin, Penn.
James Gerry, Penn.
Thomas Davee, Me.

Mrs. Cummings, Penn. Ave., between
  First and Second St.
Christopher H. Williams, Tenn.
John W. Crockett, Tenn.
John Hill, N.C.

Mr. Dashiell, C St., between Four and
  One-Half and Sixth St.
Nehemiah R. Knight (S), R.I.
Samuel S. Phelps (S),[1] Vt.

---

[1] Also listed at Mrs. Pitman's.

John Henderson (S), Miss.
Nathan F. Dixon (S), R.I.

Mrs. Denny, Third St.
Henry Clay (S), Ky.
Rice Garland, La.
Thomas W. Chinn, La.

Mr. Fletcher, E, between Sixth and
    Seventh St.
Luther C. Peck, N.Y.
Anson Brown, N.Y.
Seth M. Gates, N.Y.
Thomas C. Chittenden, N.Y.
Rufus Palen, N.Y.
Thomas Kempshall, N.Y.

Gadsby's Hotel
Francis Granger, N.Y.
Abbott Lawrence, Mass.

Mrs. Galvin, No. 1, C St., between Third
    and Four and One-Half St.
John White, Ky.
William J. Graves, Ky.
Willis Green, Ky.
Garrett Davis, Ky.

Mrs. Galvin, No. 2, C St., between Third
    and Four and One-Half St.
Thomas H. Benton (S), Mo.

Mrs. Hamilton, nearly opposite Gadsby's
Nehemiah H. Earl, N.Y.
Edward Rogers, N.Y.
James De la Montanya, N.Y.
James Garland, Va.
Amasa Dana, N.Y.
James D. Doty, Deleg., Terr. of Wis.
Virgil D. Parris, Me.
Jared W. Williams, N.H.

Mr. Harbaugh, Seventh St., between D
    and E St.
John W. Davis, Ind.
Samuel W. Morris, Penn.
Joseph Johnson, Va.
Robert H. Hammond, Penn.

H. V. Hill's, Capitol Hill
John C. Calhoun (S), S.C.
Cave Johnson, Tenn.
Harvey M. Watterson, Tenn.
David Hubbard, Ala.
Aaron V. Brown, Tenn.
Jacob Thompson, Miss.
Philip F. Thomas, Md.

Mr. Houston, Capitol Hill
Dixon H. Lewis, Ala.
George M. Keim, Penn.
Enos Hook, Penn.
Linn Banks, Va.

Mrs. Hughes, nearly opposite Brown's
William L. Goggin, Va.
John Hill, Va.
William B. Campbell, Tenn.
Meredith P. Gentry, Tenn.

Mr. Hyatt, opposite Brown's
John Davis (S), Mass.
Thaddeus Betts (S),[2] Conn.
John H. Brockway, Conn.
Thomas W. Williams, Conn.
Thomas B. Osborne, Conn.
Truman Smith, Conn.
Christopher Morgan, N.Y.
John B. Aycrigg,[3] N.J.
William Halstead,[3] N.J.
John Taliaferro, Va.
John P. B. Maxwell,[3] N.J.
Thomas Jones Yorke,[3] N.J.
John Reed, Mass.

[2] Died Apr. 7, 1840. Jabez W. Huntington was elected to fill the vacancy, and took his seat June 2, 1840.
[3] Messrs. John B. Aycrigg, John P. B. Maxwell, William Halstead, Charles C. Stratton, and Thomas Jones Yorke contested the election of Messrs. Peter D. Vroom, Philemon Dickerson, Joseph Kille, William R. Cooper, and Daniel B. Ryall. The House at the first declined to seat either set of candidates, but by resolution of Mar. 10, 1840, the five last named were admitted "without prejudice to the final rights of the claimants," and, on July 17, 1840, were adjudged entitled to their seats.

Mrs. Ironside, E St., between Ninth
and Tenth St.
James Buchanan (S), Penn.
Willaim R. King (S), Ala.
Robert C. Nicholas (S), La.
William S. Ramsey, Penn.

Mrs. Janney, nearly opposite Brown's
Francis James, Penn.
John Edwards, Penn.

Dr. Jones, Penn. Ave., between Third
and Four and One-Half St.
Waddy Thompson, Jr., S.C.
William C. Dawson, Ga.
Daniel Jenifer, Md.
Thomas Butler King, Ga.

Mrs. Kennedy, nearly opposite
Gadsby's
Henry W. Connor, N.C.
Francis E. Rives, Va.
Hugh J. Anderson, Me.
Nathan Clifford, Me.
Joel Holleman, Va.
Micajah T. Hawkins, N.C.
Green B. Samuels, Va.
Reuben Chapman, Ala.
Walter Coles, Va.
John W. Jones, Va.
Andrew Beirne, Va.
William Lucas, Va.

Mrs. King, nearly opposite Gadsby's
Jonathan Taylor, Ohio
Joshua A. Lowell, Me.
Peter Newhard, Penn.
John Galbraith, Penn.
Albert G. Marchand, Penn.
David D. Wagener, Penn.
John Hastings, Ohio
Thomas B. Jackson, N.Y.
John Ely, N.Y.
Henry Swearingen, Ohio
Daniel P. Leadbetter, Ohio

Mrs. McDaniel, Four and One-Half St.
Hiland Hall, Vt.
Millard Fillmore, N.Y.
Charles F. Mitchell, N.Y.
Peter J. Wagner, N.Y.
William S. Hastings, Mass.
Charles Johnston, N.Y.
George Briggs, Mass.
Joseph Ridgway, Ohio

Dr. Mayo, B St., between Second and
Third
John J. Crittenden (S), Ky.
Philip Triplett, Ky.
Thomas Corwin,[4] Ohio

Mr. McKelden, Seventh St., between
D and E
Samuel L. Southard (S), N.J.
Josiah Ogden Hoffman, N.Y.

Mrs. McKnight, opposite Centre
Market
Perry Smith (S), Conn.
William Allen (S), Ohio
Benjamin Tappan (S), Ohio
William Doan, Ohio
William Medill, Ohio
John B. Weller, Ohio
Isaac Leet, Penn.
Joseph Fornance, Penn.
Lewis Steenrod, Va.

Mrs. Owner, Penn. Ave., between
Second and Third St.
Felix Grundy, (S)[5] Tenn.
Alexander Mouton (S), La.
John M. Robinson (S), Ill.
Richard M. Young (S), Ill.
Lewis F. Linn (S), Mo.
William Parmenter, Mass.
Henry Williams, Mass.
John Jameson,[6] Mo.
Linn Boyd, Ky.
John Carr, Ind.

[4] Resigned May 30, 1840.
[5] Elected to fill the vacancy (Mar. 4 to Dec. 14, 1839) caused by the resignation of Ephraim H. Foster, and took his seat Jan. 3, 1840.
[6] Elected to fill the vacancy caused by the death of Albert G. Harrison, and took his seat Dec. 12, 1839.

Mrs. Page, opposite Centre Market
William C. Preston (S), S.C.
John Bell, Tenn.

Mr. Pettibone, Penn. Ave., between
    Ninth and Tenth
Sherrod Williams, Ky.
Joseph L. Williams, Tenn.
Julius C. Alford, Ga.

Mrs. Peyton, Corner Penn. Ave. and
    Four and One-Half St.
Hugh Lawson White (S),[7] Tenn.
John K. Griffin, S.C.
Sampson H. Butler, S.C.
Charles Ogle, Penn.
George W. Crabb, Ala.
William B. Carter, Tenn.

Mrs. Pitman, Third St.
Samuel Prentiss (S), Vt.
Samuel S. Phelps (S),[8] Vt.
William L. Storrs,[9] Conn.
Joseph Trumbull, Conn.
Albert Smith, Me.
Nathaniel Jones, N.Y.
Andrew W. Doig, N.Y.
John H. Prentiss, N.Y.
Augustus C. Hand, N.Y.
Theron R. Strong, N.Y.
Judson Allen, N.Y.
John W. Allen, Ohio
Richard P. Marvin, N.Y.
John C. Clark, N.Y.

Miss Polk, Penn. Ave., between Third
    and Four and One-Half St.
Garret D. Wall (S), N.J.
Bedford Brown (S), N.C.
Daniel B. Ryall,[10] N.J.
Peter D. Vroom,[10] N.J.
William R. Cooper,[10] N.J.
Joseph Killie,[10] N.J.
Charles Shepard, N.C.

Private Residence:
    At the Vice President's, Md. Ave.,
    Capitol Hill
Wilson Lumpkin (S), Ga.
John Norvell (S), Mich.
Alexander Duncan, Ohio
    Mrs. Tims, Capitol Hill
Alfred Cuthbert (S), Ga.
    Mrs. Child, Tenth St. near
    Catholic Church
Franklin Pierce (S), N.H.
    Seven Buildings
Robert J. Walker (S), Miss.
    Sixth St., between D and E
William D. Merrick (S), Md.
John S. Spence (S), Md.
    Mrs. Turner, opposite Brown's
William H. Roane (S), Va.
    Mr. Young, Capitol Hill
Thomas Clayton (S), Del.
    Mr. Rooker, Capitol Hill
John Miller, Mo.
Edward Cross, Ark.
    Mr. Humphrey, Penn. Ave., between
    Third and Four and One-Half St.
Richard Biddle, Penn.
    Sixth St., between E and F
Charles Downing, Deleg. Terr. of Fla.
    Mr. Hart, Corner F and Twelfth St.
Caleb Cushing, Mass.
    Mrs. Hellen, D St., between Ninth
    and Tenth
John Pope, Ky.
    F St., between Thirteenth and
    Fourteenth
John Quincy Adams, Mass.
    Mrs. Belt, Tenth St.
George Sweeny, Ohio
    Mrs. Miller, F St., between Thir-
    teenth and Fourteenth
Daniel D. Barnard, N.Y.
    Vivan's, G St.
Gouverneur Kemble, N.Y.
    Mr. Cudlipp, Penn. Ave., between
    Third and Four and One-Half St.
Zadoc Casey, Ill.

[7] Resigned Jan. 13, 1840. Alexander Anderson was elected to fill the vacancy, and took his seat Feb. 26, 1840.
[8] Also listed at Mr. Dashiell's.
[9] Resigned in June 1840 to become associate judge of the court of errors.
[10] See note 3.

William W. Chapman, Deleg., Terr.
of Iowa
Mr. Pettibone, Corner Penn. Ave.,
between Third and Four and One-
Half St.
Isaac E. Crary, Mich.
Mrs. Mount, Penn. Ave., between
Third and Four and One-Half St.
Richard Hawes, Ky.
Mr. Wallace, Capitol Hill
Lemuel Paynter, Penn.
Mr. Upperman, Penn. Ave., between
Third and Four and One-Half St.
George H. Proffit, Ind.
Mr. Birth, Third St.
James Carroll, Md.
Col. Cox, Georgetown
Joseph R. Underwood, Ky.
Mrs. Mechlin, Corner I and
Twenty-first St.
Francis Thomas, Md.
N.Y. Ave., between Thirteenth
and Fourteenth St.
Edward D. White, La.
Mr. Greer, Tenth St.
Abraham McClellan, Tenn.
Mrs. Bihler, Penn. Ave., between
Ninth and Tenth
James Monroe, N.Y.
Mrs. Parker, Penn. Ave., between
Ninth and Tenth
James Dellet, Ala.
Mr. V. King, Penn. Ave., between
Tenth and Eleventh
Isaac Parrish, Ohio
Mrs. Taylor, Corner E and Fifth St.
Charles Fisher, N.C.
Mr. Ennis (Cummings?), Penn Ave.,
between First and Second St.
William Montgomery, N.C.

Mrs. Ronckendorf, Penn. Ave.,
between Third and Four and One-
Half St.
Lewis Williams, N.C.
Samson Mason, Ohio
William K. Bond, Ohio
Simeon H. Anderson, Ky.
John M. Botts, Va.
John T. Stuart, Ill.

Henry A. Wise, Va.
Edward Stanly, N.C.
Kenneth Rayner, N.C.

Mrs. Scott, Penn Ave., between
Third and Four and One-Half St.
Henry Hubbard (S), N.H.
Silas Wright, Jr., N.Y.
John Smith, Vt.
Charles G. Atherton, N.H.
John G. Floyd, N.Y.
Ira A. Eastman, N.H.
John Fine, N.Y.
Edmund Burke, N.H.
Tristam Shaw, N.H.

Mrs. Smith, Capitol Hill
Albert S. White (S), Ind.
Horace Everett, Vt.
George W. Toland, Penn.
Joseph F. Randolph, N.J.
Hiram P. Hunt, N.Y.
Charles C. Stratton,[11] N.J.
David A. Russell, N.Y.

Mrs. Sprigg, Capitol Hill
Thomas Henry, Penn.
William Slade, Vt.
Joshua R. Giddings, Ohio
William Simonton, Penn.

Mrs. Thompson, Mo. Ave.
William W. Wick, Ind.
William O. Butler, Ky.

Mrs. Thompson, Capitol Hill
George C. Dromgoole, Va.
James I. McKay

Todd's Rooms, near Brown's
Solomon Hillen, Jr., Md.
John T. H. Worthington, Md.
Thomas Robinson, Jr., Del.
Albert G. Brown, Miss.

Mrs. Ulrick, opposite the State Dept.
Philemon Dickerson,[12] N.J.
Moses H. Grinnell, N.Y.
Aaron Vanderpoel, N.Y.

[11] See note 3.
[12] See note 3.

Mrs. Van Coble, Four and One-
　Half St.
Patrick G. Goode, Ohio
Calvary Morris, Ohio

Mrs. Whitwell, Capitol Hill
Isaac E. Holmes, S.C.

Mr. Williams, Four and One-Half St.
Jesse A. Bynum, N.C.
William Cost Johnson, Md.

Mrs. Wimsatt, Penn. Ave., between
　Third and Four and One-Half St.
John Ruggles (S), Me.
Robert Craig, Va.
David P. Brewster, N.Y.
Edmund Deberry, N.C.
Stephen B. Leonard, N.Y.
Meredith Mallory, N.Y.
John Reynolds, Ill.

APPENDIX

Vacancy (S) Sept. 19, 1839–Jan. 11,
　1841, Del.
John Dennis, Md.
Osmyn Baker,[13] Mass.
Daniel Webster (S), Mass.
Augustus S. Porter (S),[14] Mich.

James Graham, N.C.
Nathaniel P. Tallmadge (S), N.Y.
Daniel Sturgeon (S),[15] Penn.
Vacancy (S) Mar. 4, 1839–Jan. 18,
　1841 Va.
Charles F. Mercer,[16] Va.

STANDING COMMITTEES OF THE
HOUSE OF REPRESENTATIVES

ELECTIONS

Chairman: John Campbell, S.C.

Francis E. Rives, Va.
Millard Fillmore, N.Y.
William Medill, Ohio
George W. Crabb, Ala.

Aaron V. Brown, Tenn.
Charles Fisher, N.C.
Truman Smith, Conn.
John M. Botts, Va.

WAYS AND MEANS

Chairman: John W. Jones, Va.

Richard Biddle, Penn.
Charles G. Atherton, N.H.
Abbott Lawrence, Mass.
Robert Barnwell Rhett, S.C.

Aaron Vanderpoel, N.Y.
George Evans, Me.
Henry W. Connor, N.C.
Mark A. Cooper, Ga.

[13] Elected to fill the vacancy caused by the death of James C. Alvord, and took his seat Jan. 14, 1840.
[14] Took his seat Feb. 7, 1840. Vacancy in this class from Mar. 4, 1839–Jan. 19, 1840 caused by the failure of the legislature to elect.
[15] Elected Jan. 14, 1840, to fill the vacancy in the term commencing Mar. 4, 1839, caused by the failure of the legislature to elect, and took his seat Jan. 24, 1840.
[16] Resigned Dec. 26, 1839. William M. McCarty was elected to fill the vacancy, and took his seat Jan. 25, 1840.

CLAIMS

Chairman: David A. Russell, N.Y.

William C. Dawson, Ga.
Linn Banks, Va.
Joshua R. Giddings, Ohio
Jared W. Williams, N.H.

Meredith P. Gentry, Tenn.
John Hill, N.C.
John Galbraith, Penn.
Meredith Mallory, N.Y.

COMMERCE

Chairman: Edward Curtis, N.Y.

Solomon Hillen, Jr., Md.
Edward White, La.
Edmund Burke, N.H.
George W. Toland, Penn.

Richard W. Habersham, Ga.
Virgil D. Parris, Me.
John M. Botts, Va.
John B. Weller, Ohio

PUBLIC LANDS

Chairman: Thomas Corwin, Ohio

John Reynolds, Ill.
Levi Lincoln, Mass.
Isaac E. Crary, Mich.
John White, Ky.

Charles Fisher, N.C.
James Garland, Va.
David Hubbard, Ala.
Jacob Thompson, Miss.

POST OFFICE AND POST ROADS

Chairman: James I. McKay, N.C.

George W. Hopkins, Va.
Reuben Chapman, Ala.
Richard P. Marvin, N.Y.
Daniel P. Leadbetter, Ohio

Joseph L. Williams, Tenn.
Simeon H. Anderson, Ky.
Sampson H. Butler, S.C.
Albert G. Brown, Miss.

DISTRICT OF COLUMBIA

Chairman: William Cost Johnson, Md.

Christopher H. Williams, Tenn.
Andrew Beirne, Va.
John C. Clark, N.Y.
Thomas Davee, Me.

James Graham, N.C.
Robert B. Cranston, R.I.
Edward J. Black, Ga.
Micajah T. Hawkins, N.C.

JUDICIARY

Chairman: John Sergeant, Penn.

Isaac E. Crary, Mich.
Josiah Ogden Hoffman, N.Y.
Hopkins L. Turney, Tenn.
Samson Mason, Ohio

Green B. Samuels, Va.
Walter T. Colquitt, Ga.
William L. Storrs, Conn.
Daniel D. Barnard, N.Y.

REVOLUTIONARY CLAIMS

Chairman: Robert Craig, Va.

Joseph F. Randolph, N.J.
Hiland Hall, Vt.
John Taliaferro, Va.
William Parmenter, Mass.

William Montgomery, N.C.
James Rogers, S.C.
John Ely, N.Y.
Henry Swearingen, Ohio

PUBLIC EXPENDITURES

Chairman: George N. Briggs, Mass.

Albert Smith, Me.
William K. Bond, Ohio
James Rariden, Ind.
Alexander Duncan, Ohio

John W. Crockett, Tenn.
Hiland Hall, Vt.
Harvey M. Watterson, Tenn.
George McCulloch, Penn.

PRIVATE LAND CLAIMS

Chairman: Zadoc Casey, Ill.

Rice Garland, La.
William B. Calhoun, Mass.
James Dellet, Ala.
William W. Wick, Ind.

William O. Butler, Ky.
William S. Hastings, Mass.
John Jameson, Mo.
Edward D. White, La.

MANUFACTURES

Chairman: John Quincy Adams, Mass.

Eugenius A. Nisbet, Ga.
William Slade, Vt.
Joseph L. Tillinghast, R.I.
John T. H. Worthington, Md.

George C. Dromgoole, Va.
Charles F. Mitchell, N.Y.
Ira A. Eastman, N.H.
John Davis, Penn.

AGRICULTURE

Chairman: Edmund Deberry, N.C.

John Dennis, Md.
Abraham McClellan, Tenn.
John Smith, Vt.
Robert H. Hammond, Penn.

Tristam Shaw, N.H.
George Sweeny, Ohio
Andrew W. Doig, N.Y.
Enos Hook, Penn.

INDIAN AFFAIRS

Chairman: John Bell, Tenn.

Lewis Williams, N.C.
Julius C. Alford, Ga.
Edward Cross, Ark.
Thomas W. Chinn, La.

Charles B. Shepard, N.C.
William Lucas, Va.
Hiram P. Hunt, N.Y.
John W. Davis, Ind.

MILITARY AFFAIRS

Chairman: Cave Johnson, Tenn.

Waddy Thompson, Jr., S.C.
John Miller, Mo.
Walter Coles, Va.
Gouverneur Kemble, N.Y.

John W. Allen, Ohio
James Monroe, N.Y.
Thomas D. Sumter, S.C.
William L. Goggin, Va.

MILITIA

Chairman: George M. Keim, Penn.

William B. Carter, Tenn.
John K. Griffin, S.C.
David D. Wagener, Penn.
Philip F. Thomas, Md.

Patrick G. Goode, Ohio
Edward Rogers, N.Y.
Philip Triplett, Ky.
Joseph Ridgway, Ohio

NAVAL AFFAIRS

Chairman: Francis Thomas, Md.

John Reed, Mass.
Isaac E. Holmes, S.C.
Thomas Butler King, Ga.
Moses H. Grinnell, N.Y.

Hugh J. Anderson, Me.
Thomas Robinson, Jr., Del.
Joel Holleman, Va.
George H. Proffit, Ind.

FOREIGN AFFAIRS

Chairman: Francis W. Pickens, S.C.

Caleb Cushing, Mass.
George C. Dromgoole, Va.
Francis Granger, N.Y.
Jesse A. Bynum, N.C.

Richard Hawes, Ky.
Tilghman A. Howard, Ind.
Horace Everett, Vt.
Nathan Clifford, Me.

TERRITORIES

Chairman: John Pope, Ky.

Daniel Jenifer, Md.
William S. Ramsey, Penn.
William B. Campbell, Tenn.
John T. Stuart, Ill.

David P. Brewster, N.Y.
Garrett Davis, Ky.
James De la Montanya, N.Y.
John Fine, N.Y.

REVOLUTIONARY PENSIONS

Chairman: John Taliaferro, Va.

John Carr, Ind.
Landaff W. Andrews, Ky.
Lewis Steenrod, Va.
Kenneth Rayner, N.C.

Edward Davies, Penn.
John H. Brockway, Conn.
Jonathan Taylor, Ohio
Augustus C. Hand, N.Y.

INVALID PENSIONS

Chairman: Sherrod Williams, Ky.

Calvary Morris, Ohio
Thomas C. Chittenden, N.Y.
William Doan, Ohio
Theron R. Strong, N.Y.

Benjamin Randall, Me.
Samuel W. Morris, Penn.
Rufus Palen, N.Y.
John Edwards, Penn.

ROADS AND CANALS

Chairman: Charles Ogle, Penn.

William J. Graves, Ky.
James Carroll, Md.
John Hill, Va.
Thomas Smith, Ind.

David A. Starkweather, Ohio
Kenneth Rayner, N.C.
Walter T. Colquitt, Ga.
Julius W. Blackwell, Tenn.

PATENTS

Chairman: Isaac Fletcher, Vt.

William Beatty, Penn.
John H. Prentiss, N.Y.

Peter Newhard, Penn.
Lemuel Paynter, Penn.

PUBLIC BUILDINGS AND GROUNDS
Chairman: Levi Lincoln, Mass.

David Petrikin, Penn.   George M. Keim, Penn.
Stephen B. Leonard, N.Y.   John Hastings, Ohio

REVISAL AND UNFINISHED BUSINESS
Chairman: Luther C. Peck, N.Y.

Isaac Parrish, Ohio   Francis James, Penn.
Thomas B. Jackson, N.Y.   Amasa Dana, N.Y.

ACCOUNTS
Chairman: Joseph Johnson, Va.

Abbot Lawrence, Mass.   Albert G. Marchand, Penn.
Charles Johnston, N.Y.   John G. Floyd, N.Y.

MILEAGE
Chairman: Thomas W. Williams, Conn.

Henry Williams, Mass.   Isaac Leet, Penn.
Christopher Morgan, N.Y.   Judson Allen, N.Y.

THE FOLLOWING COMMITTEES, BY THE RULES, REMAIN DURING THE CONGRESS

EXPENDITURES IN THE DEPARTMENT OF STATE
Chairman: Joseph R. Underwood, Ky.

Jesse A. Bynum, N.C.   Joshua A. Lowell, Me.
George W. Crabb, Ala.   Joseph Trumbull, Conn.

EXPENDITURES IN THE DEPARTMENT OF THE TREASURY
Chairman: George Evans, Me.

Charles G. Atherton, N.H.   Lot Warren, Ga.
Thomas B. Osborne, Conn.   Nathaniel Jones, N.Y.

EXPENDITURES IN THE DEPARTMENT OF WAR
Chairman: Rice Garland, La.

Tilghman A. Howard, Ind.   Isaac E. Holmes, S.C.
Peter J. Wagner, N.Y.   James Cooper, Penn.

EXPENDITURES IN THE DEPARTMENT OF THE NAVY
Chairman: Leverett Saltonstall, Mass.

Aaron Vanderpoel, N.Y.   Willis Green, Ky.
William Simonton, Penn.   James Gerry, Penn.

EXPENDITURES IN THE POST OFFICE DEPARTMENT
Chairman: Richard P. Marvin, N.Y.

Linn Boyd, Ky.
Joshua A. Lowell, Me.

Garrett Davis, Ky.
Anson Brown, N.Y.

EXPENDITURES ON THE PUBLIC BUILDINGS
Chairman: Edward Stanly, N.C.

Joseph Fornance, Penn.
Seth M. Gates, N.Y.

Thomas Henry, Penn.
Nehemiah H. Earll, N.Y.

SELECT COMMITTEES

RULES AND ORDERS

Josiah Ogden Hoffman, N.Y.
John Bell, Tenn.
Linn Banks, Va.
John Sergeant, Penn.
George N. Briggs, Mass.

Francis W. Pickens, S.C.
Charles G. Atherton, N.H.
Aaron Vanderpoel, N.Y.
George M. Keim, Penn.

ON THE BILL, INTRODUCED BY MR. ADAMS, TO PROVIDE FOR THE DISPOSAL AND MANAGEMENT OF THE FUNDS BEQUEATHED BY JAMES SMITHSON

John Quincy Adams, Mass.
Charles Ogle, Penn.
Charles B. Shepard, N.C.
James Garland, Va.
Dixon H. Lewis, Ala.

Albert Smith, Me.
Daniel D. Barnard, N.Y.
Thomas Corwin, Ohio
John Campbell, S.C.

JOINT COMMITTEES

LIBRARY OF CONGRESS

House
Dixon H. Lewis, Ala.
Joseph L. Tillinghast, R.I.
Charles Naylor, Penn.

Senate
Benjamin Tappan, Ohio
William C. Preston, S.C.
Garret D. Wall, N.J.

ENROLLED BILLS

House
Edmund Burke, N.H.
Charles Naylor, Penn.

Senate
Benjamin Tappan, Ohio
Nathan F. Dixon, R.I.

STANDING COMMITTEES OF THE SENATE

FOREIGN AFFAIRS
Chairman: James Buchanan, Penn.

Henry Clay, Ky.

Bedford Brown, N.C.

William H. Roane, Va.

William Allen, Ohio

FINANCE
Chairman: Silas Wright, Jr., N.Y.

Daniel Webster, Mass.

Robert C. Nicholas, La.

Thomas H. Benton, Mo.

Henry Hubbard, N.H.

COMMERCE
Chairman: William R. King, Ala.

John Davis, Mass.

John Norvell, Mich.

John Ruggles, Me.

Alexander Mouton, La.

MANUFACTURES
Chairman: Wilson Lumpkin, Ga.

William C. Preston, S.C.

Nehemiah R. Knight, R.I.

James Buchanan, Penn.

William Allen, Ohio

AGRICULTURE
Chairman: Alexander Mouton, La.

John Spence, Md.

Lewis F. Linn, Mo.

Bedford Brown, N.C.

Perry Smith, Conn.

MILITARY AFFAIRS
Chairman: Thomas H. Benton, Mo.

William C. Preston, S.C.

Garret D. Wall, N.J.

Franklin Pierce, N.H.

Robert C. Nicholas, La.

MILITIA
Chairman: Clement C. Clay, Ala.

Oliver H. Smith, Ind.

Samuel S. Phelps, Vt.

William S. Fulton, Ark.

Benjamin Tappan, Ohio

NAVAL AFFAIRS
Chairman: Reuel Williams, Me.

Samuel L. Southard, N.J.

Alfred Cuthbert, Ga.

Robert Strange, N.C.

Benjamin Tappan, Ohio

PUBLIC LANDS

Chairman: Robert J. Walker, Miss.

William S. Fulton, Ark.
Clement C. Clay, Ala.

Samuel Prentiss, Vt.
John Norvell, Mich.

PRIVATE LAND CLAIMS

Chairman: Lewis Linn, Mo.

Ambrose H. Sevier, Ark.
Thomas Clayton, Del.

Alexander Mouton, La.
Thaddeus Betts, Conn.

INDIAN AFFAIRS

Chairman: Hugh Lawson White, Tenn.

Ambrose H. Sevier, Ark.
Lewis F. Linn, Mo.

Albert S. White, Ind.
Samuel S. Phelps, Vt.

CLAIMS

Chairman: Henry Hubbard, N.H.

Richard M. Young, Ill.
William D. Merrick, Md.

Reuel Williams, Me.
Thaddeus Betts, Conn.

REVOLUTIONARY CLAIMS

Chairman: Perry Smith, Conn.

Hugh Lawson White, Tenn.
Nehemiah R. Knight, R.I.

John J. Crittenden, Ky.
John M. Robinson, Ill.

JUDICIARY

Chairman: Garret D. Wall, N.J.

Thomas Clayton, Del.
Robert Strange, N.C.

John J. Crittenden, Ky.
Oliver H. Smith, Ind.

POST OFFICE AND POST ROADS

Chairman: John M. Robinson, Ill.

Wilson Lumpkin, Ga.
Nehemiah R. Knight, R.I.

William S. Fulton, Ark.
John Henderson, Miss.

ROADS AND CANALS

Chairman: Richard M. Young, Ill.

Samuel S. Phelps, Vt.
John Henderson, Miss.

John S. Spence, Md.
Oliver H. Smith, Ind.

PENSIONS

Chairman: Franklin Pierce, N.H.

Samuel Prentiss, Vt.
Albert S. White, Ind.

William H. Roane, Va.
Thaddeus Betts, Conn.

DISTRICT OF COLUMBIA
Chairman: William D. Merrick, Md.

John J. Crittenden, Ky.   Samuel L. Southard, N.J.
Wilson Lumpkin, Ga.   Thomas Clayton, Del.

PATENTS AND THE PATENT OFFICE
Chairman: Robert Strange, N.C.

John Davis, Mass.   John M. Robinson, Ill.
Samuel Prentiss, Vt.   John S. Spence, Md.

TO AUDIT AND CONTROL THE CONTINGENT FUND
Chairman: Nehemiah R. Knight, R.I.

William S. Fulton, Ark.   Wilson Lumpkin, Ga.

PUBLIC BUILDINGS
Chairman: William S. Fulton, Ark.

William D. Merrick, Md.   Perry Smith, Conn.

ENGROSSED BILLS
Chairman: Oliver H. Smith, Ind.

John Henderson, Miss.   Samuel S. Phelps, Vt.

ON THE MEMORIAL OF SAMUEL FORREY

John C. Calhoun, S.C.   John S. Spence, Md.
Lewis F. Linn, Mo.

ON THE OREGON TERRITORY

Lewis F. Linn, Mo.   Franklin Pierce, N.H.
William C. Preston, S.C.   Robert J. Walker, Miss.
Garret D. Wall, N.J.

ON THE LEGISLATIVE POWER OF THE UNION TO ASSUME THE DEBTS OF THE SEVERAL STATES

Felix Grundy, Tenn.   Henry Hubbard, N.H.
Wilson Lumpkin, Ga.   William Allen, Ohio
Oliver H. Smith, Ind.   William D. Merrick, Md.
Richard M. Young, Ill.

CONGRESSIONAL DIRECTORY

TWENTY-SIXTH CONGRESS, SECOND SESSION
(December 7, 1840 – March 3, 1841)

American Hotel
Jared W. Williams, N.H.

Mrs. Arguelles, nearly opposite Gadsby's
Henry Clay (S), Ky.
James D. Doty, Deleg., Terr. of Wiscon.
Willis Green, Ky.
Edward Stanly, N.C.
John M. Botts, Va.
George W. Crabb, Ala.

Mrs. Auld, nearly opposite Gadsby's
Nathan F. Dixon (S), R.I.
Albert S. White (S), Ind.
George Evans, Me.
Benjamin Randall, Me.
William S. Hastings, Mass.
Samson Mason, Ohio

Mrs. Ballard, Capitol Hill
George W. Hopkins, Va.
Cave Johnson, Tenn.
Joseph L. Williams, Tenn.
James Garland, Va.
John Pope,[1] Ky.

Mrs. Ball, opposite Brown's
Daniel Sturgeon (S), Penn.
Julius W. Blackwell, Tenn.
William Beatty, Penn.
George McCulloch, Penn.
John Davis, Penn.
Daniel P. Leadbetter, Ohio
Edward Rogers, N.Y.

Mrs. Brawner, Penn. Ave., between Second and Third
John M. Robinson (S), Ill.
Garret D. Wall (S), N.J.
Reuel Williams (S), Penn.
Richard M. Young (S), Ill.
Harvey M. Watterson,[2] Tenn.
William Parmenter, Mass.
Peter D. Vroom, N.J.
Isaac Fletcher, Vt.
Daniel B. Ryall, N.J.
Aaron V. Brown, Tenn.
James Rogers, S.C.

Brown's Hotel
William C. Preston (S),[3] S.C.
Micajah T. Hawkins, N.C.
William B. Carter, Tenn.

O. B. Brown's, E St., between Eighth and Ninth
Thomas Smith,[4] Ind.
John Carr, Ind.

Miss Corcoran, Corner Penn Ave. and Four and One-Half St.
Joseph L. Tillinghast, R.I.
Robert B. Cranston, R.I.
Edward Davies, Penn.
Levi Lincoln, Mass.
Osmyn Baker, Mass.
John Sergeant,[5] Penn.
Landaff W. Andrews, Ky.
Charles Naylor, Penn.
Henry Wise, Va.

[1] Moved to McCubbins'.
[2] Moved to Mrs. Bronaugh's Capitol Hill.
[3] Moved to Turner's, opposite Centre Market.
[4] Moved to Mrs. Houston's.
[5] Moved to Mrs. Brauner's.

Mr. Crabb, Capitol Hill
Robert M. T. Hunter, Va.
Thomas D. Sumter, S.C.
Francis Mallory,[6] Va.

Mr. Cudlipp, Penn. Ave., between
Third and Four and One-Half St.
John Norvell (S), Mich.
Isaac E. Crary, Mich.

Mrs. Dashiell, C between Four and
One-Half and Sixth St.
William J. Graves, Ky.
Henry S. Lane, Ind.
Garrett Davis, Ky.
John B. Thompson, Ky.

Dowson's No. 1, Capitol Hill
William W. Wick,[7] Ind.
Hopkins L. Turney, Tenn.
Joseph Kille, N.J.
John Jameson, Mo.
William R. Cooper, N.J.
Linn Boyd, Ky.
Charles Fisher, N.C.

Dowson's No. 2, Capitol Hill
Francis Thomas, Md.

Mr. Fletcher, E between Sixth
and Seventh
Luther C. Peck, N.Y.
Thomas C. Chittenden, N.Y.
Seth M. Gates, N.Y.
Rufus Palen, N.Y.
Thomas Kempshall, N.Y.

Mr. Follansbee, Capitol Hill
John W. Crockett, Tenn.
John Hill, Va.

Gadsby's Hotel
Charles Downing, Deleg., Terr. of Fla.
Francis Granger N.Y.
John Dennis,[8] Md.

Mrs. Hamilton, nearly opposite Gadsby's
Ira A. Eastman, N.H.
Charles G. Atherton, N.H.
Nehemiah H. Earll, N.Y.
Amasa Dana, N.Y.
John Ely, N.Y.
William O. Butler, Ky.

Mrs. Hewitt, Penn. Ave. near
Third St.
Daniel Webster,[9] Mass.
Edward Curtis, N.Y.

H. V. Hill's, Capitol Hill
John C. Calhoun (S), S.C.
Francis W. Pickens, S.C.
David Hubbard, Ala.
Charles B. Shepard, N.C.
Philip F. Thomas, Md.
Dixon H. Lewis, Ala.
David A. Starkweather,[10] Ohio
Alexander Anderson (S), Tenn.
John Campbell, S.C.
Robert Barnwell Rheet, S.C.

Mr. Harbaugh, Seventh St.
Thomas Davee, Me.
Robert H. Hammond, Penn.
Joshua A. Lowell, Me.
Henry Williams, Mass.
John W. Davis, Ind.
Charles McClure, Penn.

Mrs. Holmead, Penn. Ave., between
Third and Four and One-Half St.
Zadoc Casey,[11] Ill.
James Rariden,[12] Ind.

[6] Elected to fill the vacancy caused by the resignation of Joel Holleman, and took his seat Jan. 7, 1841.
[7] Moved to Mrs. Bronaugh's, Capitol Hill.
[8] Moved to Mrs. Peyton's.
[9] Resigned Feb. 22, 1841. Rufus Choate was elected to fill the vacancy, and took his seat Mar. 1, 1841.
[10] Moved to Mrs. Galvin, C between Third and Four and One-Half St.
[11] Moved to Mrs. Galvin, C between Third and Four and One-Half St.
[12] Moved to Mrs. King's.

Mr. Houston, Capitol Hill
Enos Hook, Penn.
George C. Dromgoole, Va.
James I. McKay, N.C.
Henry W. Connor, N.C.
Reuben Chapman, Ala.

Mr. Hyatt, opposite Brown's
John Davies (S),[13] Mass.
Jabez W. Huntington (S), Conn.
Nehemiah R. Knight (S), R.I.
John Raliaferro, Va.
Joseph Trumbull, Conn.
William W. Boardman, Conn.
Truman Smith, Conn.
Thomas W. Williams, Conn.
John H. Brockway, Conn.
John Reed, Mass.
Christopher Morgan, N.Y.

Mrs. Ironside, E between Ninth and
Tenth
James Buchanan (S), Penn.
William R. King (S), Ala.
Robert C. Nicholas (S), Lou.
William H. Roane (S), Va.

Mrs. Janney, nearly opposite
Brown's
Francis James, Penn.
John Edwards, Penn.

Dr. T. D. Jones, Penn. Ave. be-
tween Third and Four and One-
Half St.
Daniel Jenifer, Md.
William C. Dawson, Ga.
Eugenius A. Nisbet, Ga.
Richard W. Habersham, Ga.
Kenneth Rayner, N.C.
James Cooper, Penn.
Richard H. Bayard (S),[14] Del.
Thomas Butler King, Ga.

Mrs. Kennedy, nearly opposite Gadsby's
Gadsby's
Green B. Samuels, Va.
William Lucas, Va.
Andrew Beirne, Va.
Linn Banks, Va.
Augustus C. Hand, N.Y.
Theron R. Strong, N.Y.
Jacob Thompson, Miss.
Nathan Clifford, Me.
Hugh J. Anderson, Me.
John W. Jones, Va.
Francis E. Rives, Va.
Virgil D. Parris, Me.
Walter Coles, Va.

Mrs. King, Penn. Ave., nearly opposite
Gadsby's
David D. Wagener, Penn.
Thomas B. Jackson, N.Y.
John Hastings, Ohio
John Galbraith, Penn.
Peter Newhard, Penn.
Albert G. Marchand, Penn.
Jonathan Taylor, Ohio
James De la Montanya, N.Y.
Henry Swearingen, Ohio

Mrs. Laurie, Capitol Hill
William Allen (S), Ohio
Benjamin Tappan (S), Ohio
John B. Weller, Ohio
John Miller,[15] Mo.
William Medill, Ohio
Lewis Steenrod, Va.
William Doan, Ohio

Mrs. McDaniel, Four and One-Half
St.
Henry Hubbard (S), N.H.
Silas Wright, Jr., (S), N.Y.
Nathaniel Jones, N.Y.
John Smith, Vt.
John Fine, N.Y.

[13] Resigned Jan. 5, 1841. Isaac C. Bates was elected to fill the vacancy, and took his seat Jan. 21, 1841. Bates resided at Brown's Hotel.
[14] Resigned Sept. 19, 1839, to become chief justice of Delaware; reelected to fill the vacancy caused by his own resignation, and took his seat Jan. 19, 1941. Vacancy in this class from Sept. 19, 1939 to Jan. 19, 1841.
[15] Moved to Mrs. Howard, opposite the General Post Office.

John G. Floyd, N.Y.
Edmund Burke, N.H.

Dr. Mayo, B, between Second and
  Third St.
John J. Crittenden (S), Ky.
Richard Hawes, Ky.
Philip Triplett, Ky.

Mrs. McCubbins, nearly opposite
  City Hall
John White,[16] Ky.
Sherrod Williams, Ky.

Mrs. McKnight, Penn. Ave. between
  Second and Third St.
Clement C. Clay (S), Ala.
William S. Fulton (S), Ark.
Lewis F. Linn (S), Mo.
Ambrose H. Sevier (S), Ark.
Edward Cross, Ark.
Augustus C. Dodge,[17] Deleg., Terr.
  of Iowa
Perry Snith (S), Conn.

Mrs. Mount, Penn. Ave., between
  Third and Four and One-Half St.
John Henderson (S), Miss.
Robert C. Winthrop, Mass.
Leverett Saltonstall, Mass.

Mrs. Owner, Penn Ave., between
  Third and Four and One-Half St.
John Bell, Tenn.
Christopher H. Williams, Tenn.
William B. Campbell, Tenn.
Meredith P. Gentry, Tenn.

Thomas W. Chinn, La.
John Moore,[18] La.

Mr. Pettibone, Corner Penn Ave.
  and Ninth St.
John Hill,[19] N.C.
William Montgomery,[20] N.C.
Joseph Johnson,[21] Va.

Mrs. Peyton, Corner Penn. Ave. and
  Four and One-Half St.
Augustus S. Porter (S), Mich.
Joseph F. Randolph, N.J.
Sampson H. Butler, S.C.
John K. Griffin, S.C.
John W. Allen, Ohio
Charles Ogle, Penn.
John L. Kerr (S),[22] Md.

Mrs. Pitman, Third St.
Samuel Prentiss (S), Vt.
Albert Smith, Me.
Thomas B. Osborne, Conn.
Charles Johnston, N.Y.
Nicholas B. Doe, N.Y.
Peter J. Wagner, N.Y.
John H. Prentiss, N.Y.
Isaac Leet, Penn.
Joseph Ridgway, Ohio
John C. Clark, N.Y.
Millard Fillmore, N.Y.
Richard P. Marvin, N.Y.
Charles F. Mitchell, N.Y.
James Gerry, Penn.

Mrs. Preuss, Mo. Ave.
Willie P. Mangum (S),[23] N.C.
William A. Graham (S),[24] N.C.
James Graham, N.C.

[16] Moved to Dr. Mayo's, B St.
[17] Elected in compliance with the act of Mar. 3, 1839, and took his seat Dec. 8, 1840.
[18] Elected to fill the vacancy caused by the resignation of Rice Garland, and took his seat Dec. 17, 1840.
[19] Moved to Mrs. Hall, Penn. Ave., opposite Brown's.
[20] Moved to Mrs. Hall, Penn. Ave., opposite Brown's.
[21] Moved to Mrs. Hall, Penn. Ave., opposite Brown's.
[22] Elected to fill the vacancy caused by the death of John S. Spence, and took his seat Jan. 13, 1841.
[23] Elected to fill the vacancy caused by the resignation of Bedford Brown, and took his seat Dec. 9, 1840.
[24] Elected to fill the vacancy caused by the resignation of Robert Strange, and took his seat Dec. 10, 1840.

Private Residences:
Seven Buildings
Robert J. Walker (S), Miss.
Mrs. Galvin, C St., between Third and Four and One-Half St.
Thomas H. Benton (S), Mo.
Mr. Young, Capitol Hill
Thomas Clayton (S), Del.
Fifth St. near D
William D. Merrick (S), Md.
E. L. Child's Tenth St.
Franklin Pierce (S), N.H.
Mr. McGrath, Corner Ninth St. and Penn. Ave.
Oliver H. Smith (S),[25] Ind.
Mr. Wallace, Capitol Hill
Lemuel Paynter, Penn.
Mr. Murphey, Penn. Ave. between Third and Four and One-Half
Caleb Cushing, Mass.
Mr. Furgerson, Tenth St.
Isaac Parrish, Ohio
Mr. Birth, Third St.
James Carroll, Md.
Miss Handy, Corner La. Ave. and Sixth St.
William M. McCarty,[26] Va.
Mrs. Coyle, C St., between Four and One-Half and Sixth
David Petrikin, Penn.
Mrs. Walker, E, between Sixth and Seventh St.
Samuel W. Morris,[27] Penn.
Mr. McKelden, Seventh St.
James Monroe, N.Y.
Mrs. Belt, Tenth St.
George Sweeny, Ohio
Mr. Greer, Tenth St. near F
Abraham McClellan, Tenn.
Mrs. Miller, F Between Thirteenth and Fourteenth St.
Daniel D. Barnard, N.Y.
F, between Thirteenth and Fourteenth St.
John Quincy Adams, Mass.

N.Y. Ave., between Thirteenth and Fourteenth St.
Edward D. White, La.
Mr. Vivan, West of President's Square
Gouverneur Kemble, N.Y.
Col. Cox, Georgetown
Joseph R. Underwood, Ky.
Mrs. Leidberg, opposite Brown's
Joseph Fornance, Penn.
Mr. Sawkin (s?), F, between Thirteenth and Fourteenth St.
Julius C. Alford, Ga.
Mrs. McGunnegal, Tenth St.
Edward J. Black, Ga.
Mrs. Daws, Penn. Ave. between First and Second
Alexander Mouton (S), La.
Mrs. Thomas, Tenth St.
Jesse A. Bynum, N.C.
Clement's, Capitol Hill
Isaac E. Holmes, S.C.

Mrs. Ronckendorf, near Gadsby's
John T. Stuart, Ill.
Jeremiah Morrow, Ohio
William K. Bond,[28] Ohio
Lewis Williams, N.C.

Mrs. Scott, Penn. Ave., between Third and Four and One-Half St.
Wilson Lumpkin (S), Ga.
Lott Warren, Ga.
Mark A. Cooper, Ga.

Mrs. Smith, Capitol Hill
Samuel S. Phelps (S), Vt.
Nathaniel P. Tallmadge (S), N.Y.
Horace Everett, Vt.
David A. Russell, N.Y.
George W. Toland, Penn.
Hiram P. Hunt, N.Y.

Mrs. Sprigg, Capitol Hill
Thomas Henry, Penn.
William Slade, Vt.

[25] Moved to Galvin's, C between Third and Four and One-Half St.
[26] Elected to fill the vacancy caused by the resignation of Charles F. Mercer, and took his seat Jan. 25, 1840.
[27] Moved to Mrs. Hall's, Penn. Ave., opposite Brown's.
[28] Moved to Miss Corcoran's.

William Simonton, Penn.
William B. Calhoun, Mass.
Joshua R. Giddings, Ohio
Henry M. Brackenridge,[29] Penn.

Todd's Rooms, near Brown's
Solomon Hillen, Jr., Md.
Albert G. Brown,[30] Miss.
John T. H. Worthington, Md.
George H. Proffit, Ind.

Mrs. Townley, opposite the General
Post Office
George M. Keim, Penn.
Alexander Duncan, Ohio

Mrs. Ulrick, opposite the State
Department
Philemon Dickerson, N.J.
Aaron Vanderpoel, N.Y.
William C. Rives,[31] Va.

Mrs. Van Coble, Four and One-
Half St.
Calvary Morris, Ohio
Patrick G. Goode, Ohio

Mrs. Whitwell, Capitol Hill
Samuel L. Southard (S), N.J.
Moses H. Grinnell, N.Y.
Josiah Ogden Hoffman, N.Y.

Mr. Williams, Four and One-Half St.
Hiland Hall, Vt.
George N. Briggs, Mass.
Tristam Shaw, N.H.
Waddy Thompson, Jr., S.C.
James Dellet, Ala.
William Cost Johnson, Md.

Mrs. Wimsatt, Penn. Ave., between
Third and Four and One-Half St.
John Ruggles (S), Me.
Robert Craig, Va.
David P. Brewster, N.Y.
Meredith Mallory, N.Y.
Edmund Deberry, N.C.
Stephen B. Leonard, N.Y.
Andrew W. Doig, N.Y.
Judson Allen, N.Y.
William L. Goggin, Va.
John Ruggles, Ill.

APPENDIX

Thomas Robinson, Jr., Del.
Alfred Cuthbert (S), Ga.
Hines Holt,[32] Ga.

James Rogers, S.C.
Felix Grundy (S),[33] Tenn.

STANDING COMMITTEES OF THE
HOUSE OF REPRESENTATIVES

ELECTIONS

Chairman: Francis E. Rives, Va.

Millard Fillmore, N.Y.
William Medill, Ohio
Aaron V. Brown, Tenn.
Truman Smith, Conn.

John M. Botts, Va.
Benjamin Randall, Me.
Philip F. Thomas, Md.
James Rariden, Ind.

[29] Elected to fill the vacancy caused by the resignation of Richard Biddle, and took his seat Dec. 10, 1840.
[30] Moved to Brown's Hotel.
[31] Elected to fill the vacancy in the term commencing Mar. 4, 1839, caused by the failure of the legislature to elect, and took his seat Jan. 30, 1841. Vacancy in this class from Mar. 4, 1839, to Jan. 18, 1841.
[32] Elected to fill the vacancy caused by the resignation of Walter T. Colquitt, and took his seat Feb. 1, 1841.
[33] Died Dec. 19, 1840. Alfred O. P. Nicholson was appointed to fill the vacancy, and took his seat Jan. 11, 1841. Nicholson resided at Mrs. Brawner's.

WAYS AND MEANS

Chairman: John W. Jones, Va.

George Evans, Me.
Charles G. Atherton, N.H.
Aaron Vanderpoel, N.Y.
Henry W. Connor, N.C.

Mark A. Cooper, Ga.
Samson Mason, Ohio
Leverett Saltonstall, Mass.
David Hubbard, Ala.

CLAIMS

Chairman: David A. Russell, N.Y.

William C. Dawson, Ga.
Linn Banks, Va.
Joshua R. Giddings, Ohio
Jared W. Williams, N.H.

Meredith P. Gentry, Tenn.
John Hill, N.C.
John Galbraith, Penn.
Meredith Mallory, N.Y.

COMMERCE

Chairman: Edward Curtis, N.Y.

Solomon Hillen, Jr., Md.
Edmund Burke, N.H.
George W. Toland, Penn.
Richard W. Habersham, Ga.

Virgil D. Parris, Me.
John M. Botts, Va.
John B. Weller, Ohio
Robert C. Winthrop, Mass.

PUBLIC LANDS

Chairman: Jeremiah Morrow, Ohio

Levi Lincoln, Mass.
Isaac E. Crary, Mich.
John White, Ky.
Charles Fisher, N.C.

James Garland, Va.
Jacob Thompson, Miss.
Zadoc Casey, Ill.
Reuben Chapman, Ala.

POST OFFICE AND POST ROADS

Chairman: James I. McKay, N.C.

George W. Hopkins, Va.
George N. Briggs, Mass.
Richard P. Marvin, N.Y.
Daniel P. Leadbetter, Ohio

Joseph L. Williams, Tenn.
Albert G. Brown, Miss.
John Reynolds, Ill.
John B. Thompson, Ky.

DISTRICT OF COLUMBIA

Chairman: William Cost Johnson, Md.

Christopher H. Williams, Tenn.
Andrew Beirne, Va.
John C. Clark, N.Y.
Thomas Davee, Me.

James Graham, N.C.
Robert B. Cranston, R.I.
Micajah T. Hawkins, N.C.
William M. McCarty, Va.

JUDICIARY

Chairman: John Sergeant, Penn.

Josiah Ogden Hoffman, N.Y.
Hopkins L. Turney, Tenn.
Green B. Samuels, Va.
Daniel D. Barnard, N.Y.

Edward Stanly, N.C.
Sampson H. Butler, S.C.
Joseph Trumbull, Conn.
David Starkweather, Ohio

REVOLUTIONARY CLAIMS

Chairman: Joseph F. Randolph, N.J.

Hiland Hall, Vt.
John Taliaferro, Va.
William Parmenter, Mass.
William Montgomery, N.C.

John Ely, N.Y.
Henry Swearingen, Ohio
Francis James, Penn.
Nathaniel Jones, N.Y.

PUBLIC EXPENDITURES

Chairman: William K. Bond, Ohio

Alexander Duncan, Ohio
John W. Crockett, Tenn.
Harvey M. Watterson, Tenn.
George McCulloch, Penn.

Willis Green, Ky.
Charles McClure, Penn.
Osmyn Baker, Mass.
Henry M. Brackenridge, Penn.

PRIVATE LAND CLAIMS

Chairman: William B. Calhoun, Mass.

James Dellet, Ala.
William W. Wick, Ind.
William S. Hastings, Mass.
John Jameson, Mo.

Edward Cross, Ark.
Lott Warren, Ga.
Peter D. Vroom, N.J.
William W. Boardman, Conn.

MANUFACTURES

Chairman: John Quincy Adams, Mass.

Eugenius A. Nisbet, Ga.
William Slade, Vt.
Joseph L. Tillinghast, R.I.
John T. H. Worthington, Md.

George C. Dromgoole, Va.
Charles F. Mitchell, N.Y.
Ira A. Eastman, N.H.
John Davis, Penn.

AGRICULTURE

Chairman: Edmund Deberry, N.C.

John Dennis, Md.
Abraham McClellan, Tenn.
John Smith, Vt.
Robert H. Hammond, Penn.

Tristam Shaw, N.H.
Andrew W. Doig, N.Y.
Enos Hook, Penn.
Joseph Ridgway, Ohio

INDIAN AFFAIRS

Chairman: John Bell, Tenn.

Lewis Williams, N.C.
Julius C. Alford, Ga.
Thomas W. Chinn, La.
William Lucas, Va.

Hiram P. Hunt, N.Y.
John W. Davis, Ind.
Isaac Parrish, Ohio
Daniel B. Ryall, N.J.

MILITARY AFFAIRS

Chairman: Waddy Thompson, Jr. S.C.

John Miller, Mo.
Walter Coles, Va.
Gouverneur Kemble, N.Y.
John W. Allen, Ohio

James Monroe, N.Y.
Thomas D. Sumter, S.C.
William L. Goggin, Va.
William O. Butler, Ky.

MILITIA

Chairman: George M. Keim, Penn.

William B. Carter, Tenn.
John K. Griffin, S.C.
David D. Wagener, Penn.
Patrick G. Goode, Ohio

Edward Rogers, N.Y.
Philip Triplett, Ky.
Peter J. Wagner, N.Y.
Thomas B. Jackson, N.Y.

NAVAL AFFAIRS

Chairman: Francis Thomas, Md.

John Reed, Mass.
Moses H. Grinnell, N.Y.
Hugh J. Anderson, Me.
George H. Proffit, Ind.

Charles B. Shepard, N.C.
Charles Naylor, Penn.
Philemon Dickerson, N.J.
James De la Montanya, N.Y.

FOREIGN AFFAIRS

Chairman: Francis W. Pickens, S.C.

Caleb Cushing, Mass.
George C. Dromgoole, Va.
Francis Granger, N.Y.
Richard Hawes, Ky.

Horace Everett, Vt.
Nathan Clifford, Me.
Isaac Leet, Penn.
John Fine, N.Y.

TERRITORIES

Chairman: John Pope, Ky.

Daniel Jenifer, Md.
William B. Campbell, Tenn.
John T. Stuart, Ill.
David P. Brewster, N.Y.

Garrett Davis, Ky.
James Cooper, Penn.
Christopher Morgan, N.Y.
Amasa Dana, N.Y.

REVOLUTIONARY CLAIMS

Chairman: John Taliaferro, Va.

John Carr, Ind.
Landaff W. Andrews, Ky.
Lewis Steenrod, Va.
Edward Davies, Penn.

John H. Brockway, Conn.
Jonathan Taylor, Ohio
Augustus C. Hand, N.Y.
Luther C. Peck, N.Y.

INVALID PENSIONS

Chairman: Sherrod Williams, Ky.

Calvary Morris, Ohio
Thomas C. Crittenden, N.Y.
William Doan, Ohio
Theron R. Strong, N.Y.

Samuel W. Morris, Penn.
Rufus Palen, N.Y.
George Sweeny, Ohio
John Edwards, Penn.

ROADS AND CANALS

Chairman: Charles Ogle, Penn.

James Carroll, Md.
John Hill, Va.
Thomas Smith, Ind.
Kenneth Rayner, N.C.

Julius W. Blackwell, Tenn.
Joseph R. Underwood, Ky.
Albert Smith, Me.
George W. Crabb, Ala.

PATENTS

Chairman: Isaac Fletcher, Vt.

William Beatty, Penn.   Peter Newhard, Penn.
John H. Prentiss, N.Y.   Lemuel Paynter, Penn.

PUBLIC BUILDINGS AND GROUNDS[34]

Chairman: Stephen B. Leonard, N.Y.

George M. Keim, Penn.   Thomas B. Osborne, Conn.
John Hastings, Ohio   John H. Prentiss, N.Y.

REVISAL AND UNFINISHED BUSINESS

Chairman: Luther C. Peck, N.Y.

Isaac Parrish, Ohio   Joseph Kille, N.J.
Francis James, Penn.   William R. Cooper, N.J.

ACCOUNTS

Chairman: Joseph Johnson, Va.

Charles Johnson, N.Y.   John G. Floyd, N.Y.
Albert G. Marchand, Penn.   Landaff W. Andrews, Ky.

MILEAGE

Chairman: Thomas W. Williams, Conn.

Henry Williams, Mass.   Thomas Henry, Penn.
Judson Allen, N.Y.   Thomas Kempshall, N.Y.

THE FOLLOWING STANDING COMMITTEES WERE APPOINTED
AT THE FIRST SESSION,
AND STAND THROUGH THE CONGRESS:

EXPENDITURES IN THE DEPARTMENT OF STATE

Chairman: Joseph R. Underwood, Ky.

Jesse A. Bynum, N.C.   Joshua A. Lowell, Me.
George W. Crabb, Ala.   Joseph Trumbull, Conn.

EXPENDITURES IN THE DEPARTMENT OF THE TREASURY

Chairman: George Evans, Me.

Charles G. Atherton, N.H.   Lott Warren, Ga.
Thomas B. Osborne, Conn.   Nathaniel Jones, N.Y.

[34] The *Journal of the House of Representatives* lists David Petrikin (Penn.) as Chairman, and Leonard, Keim, Hastings, and Osborne as members. Prentiss is not listed as a committee member.

EXPENDITURES IN THE DEPARTMENT OF WAR

Chairman: Peter J. Wagner, N.Y.

Isaac E. Holmes, S.C.
James Cooper, Penn.

Reuben Chapman, Ala.
Nicholas B. Doe, N.Y.

EXPENDITURES IN THE DEPARTMENT OF THE NAVY

Chairman: Leverett Saltonstall, Mass.

Aaron Vanderpoel, N.Y.
William Simonton, Penn.

Willis Green, Ky.
James Gerry, Penn.

EXPENDITURES IN THE POST OFFICE DEPARTMENT

Chairman: Richard P. Marvin, N.Y.

Linn Boyd, Ky.
Joshua A. Lowell, Me.

Garrett Davis, Ky.
Henry S. Lane, Ind.

EXPENDITURES ON THE PUBLIC BUILDINGS

Chairman: Edward Stanly, N.C.

Joseph Fornance, Penn.
Seth M. Gates, N.Y.

Thomas Henry, Penn.
Nehemiah H. Earll, N.Y.

SELECT COMMITTEES

COMMITTEE TO INVESTIGATE A DISCREPANCY BETWEEN THE TRANS-LATED AND PRINTED COPY OF A DOCUMENT ACCOMPANYING THE PRESIDENT'S MESSAGE OF THE LAST SESSION, IN RELATION TO THE SCHOONER *AMISTAD*

Chairman: John Quincy Adams, Mass.

James I. McKay, N.C.
Daniel D. Barnard, N.Y.

William Medill, Ohio
John Dennis, Md.

COMMITTEE ON THE TOBACCO TRADE

Chairman: Daniel Jenifer, Md.

Walter Coles, Va.
John Sergeant, Penn.
William C. Dawson, Ga.
James Carroll, Md.

Moses H. Grinnell, N.Y.
Philip Triplett, Ky.
Isaac Parrish, Ohio
John Miller, Mo.

JOINT COMMITTEES

LIBRARY OF CONGRESS

House

Joseph Tillinghast, R.I.
Caleb Cushing, Mass.
George M. Keim, Penn.

Senate

Garret D. Wall, N.J.
William C. Preston, S.C.
Benjamin Tappan, Ohio

ENROLLED BILLS

House	Senate
Edmund Burke, N.H.	Benjamin Tappan, Ohio
Charles Naylor, Penn.	Nathan F. Dixon, R.I.

STANDING COMMITTEES OF THE SENATE

FOREIGN AFFAIRS

Chairman: James Buchanan, Penn.

Henry Clay, Ky.	William H. Roane, Va.
John C. Calhoun, S.C.	William Allen, Ohio

FINANCE

Chairman: Silas Wright, Jr., N.Y.

Daniel Webster, Mass.	Thomas H. Benton, Mo.
Robert C. Nicholas, La.	Henry Hubbard, N.H.

COMMERCE

Chairman: William R. King, Ala.

John Davis, Mass.	John Ruggles, Me.
John Norvell, Mich.	Alexander Mouton, La.

MANUFACTURES

Chairman: Wilson Lumpkin, Ga.

William C. Preston, S.C.	James Buchanan, Penn.
Nehemiah R. Knight, R.I.	William Allen, Ohio

AGRICULTURE

Chairman: Alexander Mouton, La.

Nathan F. Dixon, R.I.	Daniel Sturgeon, Penn.
Lewis F. Linn, Mo.	Perry Smith, Conn.

MILITARY AFFAIRS

Chairman: Thomas H. Benton, Mo.

William C. Preston, S.C.	Franklin Pierce, N.H.
Garret D. Wall, N.J.	Robert C. Nicholas, La.

MILITIA

Chairman: Clement C. Clay, Ala.

Oliver H. Smith, Ind.	William S. Fulton, Ark.
Alexander Anderson, Tenn.	Willie P. Mangum, N.C.

NAVAL AFFAIRS

Chairman: Reuel Williams, Me.

Samuel L. Southard, N.J.
Alfred Cuthbert, Ga.

Nathaniel P. Tallmadge, N.Y.
Benjamin Tappan, Ohio

PUBLIC LANDS

Chairman: Robert J. Walker, Miss.

William S. Fulton, Ark.
Clement C. Clay, Ala.

Samuel Prentiss, Vt.
John Norvell, Mich.

PRIVATE LAND CLAIMS

Chairman: Lewis F. Linn, Mo.

Ambrose H. Sevier, Ark.
Thomas Clayton, Del.

Alexander Mouton, La.
Jabez W. Huntington, Conn.

INDIAN AFFAIRS

Chairman: Ambrose H. Sevier, Ark.

Lewis F. Linn, Mo.
Albert S. White, Ind.

Samuel S. Phelps, Vt.
Wilson Lumpkin, Ga.

CLAIMS

Chairman: Henry Hubbard, N.H.

Richard M. Young, Ill.
William D. Merrick, Md.

Reuel Williams, Me.
Jabez W. Huntington, Conn.

REVOLUTIONARY CLAIMS

Chairman: Perry Smith, Conn.

Daniel Sturgeon, Penn.
William A. Graham, N.C.

John J. Crittenden, Ky.
John M. Robinson, Ill.

JUDICIARY

Chairman: Garret D. Wall, N.J.

Thomas Clayton, Del.
Alexander Anderson, Tenn.

John J. Crittenden, Ky.
Oliver H. Smith, Ind.

POST OFFICE AND POST ROADS

Chairman: John M. Robinson, Ill.

Wilson Lumpkin, Ga.
Nehemiah R. Knight, R.I.

William S. Fulton, Ark.
John Henderson, Miss.

ROADS AND CANALS

Chairman: Richard M. Young, Ill.

Samuel S. Phelps, Vt.
John Henderson, Miss.

Willie P. Mangum, N.C.
Oliver H. Smith, Ind.

PENSIONS

Chairman: Franklin Pierce, N.H.

Samuel Prentiss, Vt.   William H. Roane, Va.
Albert S. White, Ind.   Jabez W. Huntington, Conn.

DISTRICT OF COLUMBIA

Chairman: William D. Merrick, Md.

John J. Crittenden, Ky.   Samuel L. Southard, N.J.
Willie P. Mangum, N.C.   Thomas Clayton, Del.

PATENTS AND THE PATENT OFFICE

Chairman: Daniel Sturgeon, Penn.

John Davis, Mass.   John M. Robinson, Ill.
Samuel Prentiss, Vt.   Augustus S. Porter, Mich.

TO AUDIT AND CONTROL THE CONTINGENT FUND

Chairman: Nehemiah R. Knight, R.I.

William S. Fulton, Ark.   Augustus S. Porter, Mich.

PUBLIC BUILDINGS

Chairman: William S. Fulton, Ark.

William D. Merrick, Md.   Perry Smith, Conn.

ENGROSSED BILLS

Chairman: John Henderson, Miss.

Augustus S. Porter, Mich.   Samuel S. Phelps, Vt.

APPENDIX

STANDING COMMITTEES OF THE HOUSE OF REPRESENTATIVES

FIRST CONGRESS, FIRST SESSION
(March 4, 1789–September 29, 1789)

ELECTIONS

George Clymer, Pa.
Fisher Ames, Mass.
Egbert Benson, N.Y.
Daniel Carroll, Md.

Alexander White, Va.
Benjamin Huntington, Conn.
Nicholas Gilman, N.H.

JOINT COMMITTEE ON ENROLLED BILLS

House
George Partridge, Mass.
Alexander White, Va.

Senate
Paine Wingate, N.H.

STANDING COMMITTEES OF THE HOUSE OF REPRESENTATIVES

FIRST CONGRESS, SECOND SESSION
(January 4, 1790–August 12, 1790)

ELECTIONS

Fisher Ames, Mass.
Roger Sherman, Conn.
Egbert Benson, N.Y.
Thomas Sinnickson, N.J.

Henry Wynkoop, Pa.
Alexander White, Va.
Michael Jenifer Stone, Md.

NOTE: Until 1816, the Senate of the United States had made provision for only four Standing Committees, and two of these were joint committees with the House of Representatives. The Senate Standing Committees were the Joint Standing Committee on Enrolled Bills (July 31, 1789), the Senate Committee on Engrossed Bills (March 26, 1806), the Joint Standing Committee for the Library (December 17, 1806), and the Senate Committee to Audit and Control the Contingent Expenses of the Senate (November 4, 1807). The historian of the United States Senate wrote that "the needless inconvenience of the frequent choice of select committees taxed the Senate's patience. At the opening of the second session of the Fourteenth Congress a motion, that the Senate raise thirteen select committees for the consideration of the various portions of President Madison's annual message, was laid over; and a few days later in its place there was passed a resolution, introduced by Senator Barbour of Virginia, that eleven additional standing committees should be appointed at each session; namely, Committees of Foreign Relations, Finance, Commerce and Manufactures, Military Affairs, the Militia, Naval Affairs, Public Lands, Claims, the Judiciary, the Post Office and Post Roads, and Pensions." See George H. Haynes, *The Senate of the United States* (Boston, Houghton Mifflin, 1938), 1:272.

JOINT COMMITTEE ON ENROLLED BILLS

House	Senate
Nicholas Gilman, N.H.	Paine Wingate, N.H.
Alexander White, Va.	

STANDING COMMITTEES OF THE HOUSE OF REPRESENTATIVES

FIRST CONGRESS, THIRD SESSION
(December 6, 1790–March 3, 1791)

ELECTIONS[1]

JOINT COMMITTEE ON ENROLLED BILLS

House	Senate
William Floyd, N.Y.	Theodore Foster, R.I.
John Peter G. Muhlenberg, Pa.	

STANDING COMMITTEES OF THE HOUSE OF REPRESENTATIVES

SECOND CONGRESS, FIRST SESSION
(October 24, 1791–May 8, 1792)

ELECTIONS

Samuel Livermore, N.H.	Benjamin Bourn, R.I.
Elias Boudinot, N.J.	James Hillhouse, Conn.
William B. Giles, Va.	John Steele, N.C.
Elbridge Gerry, Mass.	

JOINT COMMITTEE ON ENROLLED BILLS

House	Senate
Shearjashub Bourne, Mass.	John Rutherfurd, N.J.
Israel Smith, Vt.	

[1] Not listed in the *Journal of the House of Representatives* for the Third Session of the First Congress.

STANDING COMMITTEES OF THE HOUSE OF REPRESENTATIVES

SECOND CONGRESS, SECOND SESSION
(November 5, 1792–March 2, 1793)

ELECTIONS[2]

JOINT COMMITTEE ON ENROLLED BILLS

House	Senate
Daniel Hiester, Pa.	John Brown, Ky.
Andrew Moore, Va.	

STANDING COMMITTEES OF THE HOUSE OF REPRESENTATIVES

THIRD CONGRESS, FIRST SESSION
(December 2, 1793–June 9, 1794)

ELECTIONS

William L. Smith, S.C.	Richard Bland Lee, Va.
Shearjashub Bourne, Mass.	Jonathan Dayton, N.J.
William Irvine, Pa.	James Gordon, N.Y.
Nathaniel Macon, N.C.	

JOINT COMMITTEE ON ENROLLED BILLS

House	Senate
John Peter G. Muhlenberg, Pa.	John Vining, Del.
Anthony New, Va.	

STANDING COMMITTEES OF THE HOUSE OF REPRESENTATIVES

THIRD CONGRESS, SECOND SESSION
(November 3, 1794–March 3, 1795)

ELECTIONS

Jonathan Dayton, N.J.	Richard Bland Lee, Va.
James Hillhouse, Conn.	Nathaniel Macon, N.C.
John S. Sherburne, N.H.	John Hunter, S.C.
George Dent, Md.	

[2] Not listed in the *Journal of the House of Representatives* for the Second Session of the Second Congress.

CLAIMS

Uriah Tracy, Conn.
Dwight Foster, Mass.
Francis Malbone, R.I.
William Montgomery, Pa.

John Heath, Va.
Gabriel Christie, Md.
Alexander Mebane, N.C.

JOINT COMMITTEE ON ENROLLED BILLS

House
John Peter G. Muhlenberg, Pa.
Anthony New, Va.

Senate
James Ross, Pa.

STANDING COMMITTEES OF THE HOUSE OF REPRESENTATIVES

FOURTH CONGRESS, FIRST SESSION
(December 7, 1795–June 1, 1796)

ELECTIONS

Abraham B. Venable, Va.
George Dent, Md.
John Wilkes Kittera, Pa.
Zephaniah Swift, Conn.

Henry Dearborn, Mass.
Robert Goodloe Harper, S.C.
Thomas Blount, N.C.

CLAIMS

Uriah Tracy, Conn.
Dwight Foster, Mass.
Francis Malbone, R.I.
Gabriel Duvall, Md.

John Heath, Va.
Absalom Tatom, N.C.
Daniel Hiester, Pa.

COMMERCE AND MANUFACTURES

Benjamin Goodhue, Mass.
Benjamin Bourn, R.I.
Edward Livingston, N.Y.
John Swanick, Pa.

Samuel Smith, Md.
Josiah Parker, Va.
William L. Smith, S.C.

REVISAL AND UNFINISHED BUSINESS[3]

WAYS AND MEANS

William L. Smith, S.C.
Nicholas Gilman, N.H.
Benjamin Bourn, R.I.
Theodore Sedgwick, Mass.
Daniel Buck, Vt.
James Hillhouse, Conn.
Ezekiel Gilbert, N.Y.

Isaac Smith, N.J.
Albert Gallatin, Pa.
John Patten, Del.
William Vans Murray, Md.
James Madison, Va.
Thomas Blount, N.C.
Abraham Baldwin, Ga.

[3] The House of Representatives resolved on December 14, 1795, to appoint a Standing Committee on Revisal and Unfinished Business at the commencement of future sessions of Congress.

JOINT COMMITTEE ON ENROLLED BILLS

House	Senate
Anthony New, Va.	Elijah Paine, Vt.
Isaac Smith, N.J.	

STANDING COMMITTEES OF THE HOUSE OF REPRESENTATIVES

FOURTH CONGRESS, SECOND SESSION
(December 5, 1796–March 3, 1797)

ELECTIONS

Abraham B. Venable, Va.	William Blount, Tenn.
George Dent, Md.	Frederick A. C. Muhlenberg, Pa.
Zephaniah Swift, Conn.	Abiel Foster, N.H.
Henry Dearborn, Mass.	

CLAIMS

Dwight Foster, Conn.	Samuel Maclay, Pa.
Francis Malbone, R.I.	Nathaniel Macon, N.C.
John Heath, Va.	John Williams, N.Y.
Mark Thomson, N.J.	

COMMERCE AND MANUFACTURES

John Swanick, Pa.	Samuel Sewall, Mass.
William L. Smith, S.C.	Josiah Parker, Va.
Joshua Coit, Conn.	George Dent, Md.
Thomas Blount, N.C.	

REVISAL AND UNFINISHED BUSINESS

Nicholas Gilman, N.H.	Nathaniel Macon, N.C.
Richard Sprigg, Jr., Md.	

WAYS AND MEANS

William L. Smith, S.C.	Isaac Smith, N.J.
Nicholas Gilman, N.H.	Albert Gallatin, Pa.
Francis Malbone, R.I.	John Patten, Del.
Theophilus Bradbury, Mass.	William Hindman, Md.
Nathaniel Smith, Conn.	James Madison, Va.
Israel Smith, Vt.	Thomas Blount, N.C.
Christopher Greenup, Ky.	Abraham Baldwin, Ga.
Ezekiel Gilbert, N.Y.	Andrew Jackson, Tenn.

JOINT COMMITTEE ON ENROLLED BILLS

House	Senate
Abiel Foster, N.H.	Richard Stockton, N.J.
Theodorus Bailey, N.Y.	

STANDING COMMITTEES OF THE HOUSE OF REPRESENTATIVES

FIFTH CONGRESS, FIRST SESSION
(May 15, 1797–July 10, 1797)

ELECTIONS

Joshua Coit, Conn.	George Dent, Md.
Joseph Bradley Varnum, Mass.	Carter B. Harrison, Va.
John Williams, N.Y.	Abraham Baldwin, Ga.
Thomas Hartley, Pa.	

CLAIMS[4]

COMMERCE AND MANUFACTURES[4]

REVISAL AND UNFINISHED BUSINESS

Jeremiah Smith, N.H.	Nathaniel Macon, N.C.
Andrew Gregg, Pa.	

WAYS AND MEANS

William L. Smith, S.C.	Robert Williams, N.C.
Albert Gallatin, Pa.	Joshua Coit, Conn.
Harrison Gray Otis, Mass.	James Cochran, N.Y.
William B. Giles, Va.	

JOINT COMMITTEE ON ENROLLED BILLS

House	Senate
John Reed, Mass.	Isaac Tichenor, Vt.
Jonathan N. Havens, N.Y.	

[4] Not listed in the *Journal of the House of Representatives* for the First Session of the Fifth Congress.

STANDING COMMITTEES OF THE HOUSE OF
REPRESENTATIVES

FIFTH CONGRESS, SECOND SESSION
(November 13, 1797–July 16, 1798)

ELECTIONS

Joshua Coit, Conn.
Joseph Bradley Varnum, Mass.
John Williams, N.Y.
Thomas Hartley, Pa.

George Dent, Md.
Abraham Baldwin, Ga.
Thomas Evans, Va.

CLAIMS

Dwight Foster, Mass.
Joshua Coit, Conn.
Mark Thomson, N.J.
John A. Hanna, Pa.

George Baer, Jr., Md.
Walter Jones, Va.
Richard Stanford, N.C.

COMMERCE AND MANUFACTURES

Edward Livingston, N.Y.
Christopher G. Champlin, R.I.
Roger Griswold, Conn.
James Schureman, N.J.

John Swanick, Pa.
William Barry Grove, N.C.
George Dent, Md.

REVISAL AND UNFINISHED BUSINESS

Nathaniel Macon, N.C.
Samuel Lyman, Mass.

Jonathan N. Havens, N.Y.

WAYS AND MEANS

Robert Goodloe Harper, S.C.
Albert Gallatin, Pa.
Roger Griswold, Conn.
Thomas Blount, N.C.
Hezekiah L. Hosmer, N.Y.
William Craik, Md.
Richard Brent, Va.
Abiel Foster, N.H.

Samuel Sewall, Mass.
Lewis R. Morris, Vt.
Thomas T. Davis, Ky.
Thomas Sinnickson, N.J.
William C. C. Claiborne, Tenn.
James A. Bayard, Del.
Christopher G. Champlin, R.I.
Abraham Baldwin, Ga.

JOINT COMMITTEE ON ENROLLED BILLS

House
William Edmond, Conn.
John Clopton, Va.

Senate
Ray Greene, R.I.

STANDING COMMITTEES OF THE HOUSE OF REPRESENTATIVES

FIFTH CONGRESS, THIRD SESSION
(December 3, 1798–March 3, 1799)

ELECTIONS

Joseph Bradley Varnum, Mass.
Chauncey Goodrich, Conn.
John Williams, N.Y.
John Wilkes Kittera, Pa.

George Dent, Md.
Anthony New, Va.
Abraham Baldwin, Ga.

CLAIMS

Dwight Foster, Mass.
Nathaniel Macon, N.C.
John A. Hanna, Pa.
Jonathan Freeman, N.H.

James H. Imlay, N.J.
Richard Sprigg, Jr., Md.
John E. Van Alen, N.Y.

COMMERCE AND MANUFACTURES

Samuel Smith, Md.
Samuel Sewall, Mass.
Robert Waln, Pa.
John Rutledge, Jr., S.C.

James Schureman, N.J.
Thomas Tillinghast, R.I.
William Blount, Tenn.

REVISAL AND UNFINISHED BUSINESS

George Thacher, Mass.
Richard Thomas, Pa.

Anthony New, Va.

WAYS AND MEANS

Robert Goodloe Harper, S.C.
Albert Gallatin, Pa.
Nathaniel Smith, Conn.
James Cochran, N.Y.
Walter Jones, Va.

Isaac Parker, Mass.
William Hindman, Md.
Thomas Blount, N.C.
Thomas Sinnickson, N.J.

JOINT COMMITTEE ON ENROLLED BILLS

House
Peleg Wadsworth, Mass.
Thomas Evans, Va.

Senate
Joseph Anderson, Tenn.

STANDING COMMITTEES OF THE HOUSE OF
REPRESENTATIVES

SIXTH CONGRESS, FIRST SESSION
(December 2, 1799–May 14, 1800)

ELECTIONS

Samuel W. Dana, Conn.
Thomas Sumter, S.C.
John Wilkes Kittera, Pa.
Anthony New, Va.

Archibald Henderson, N.C.
William Gordon, N.H.
Theodorus Bailey, N.Y.

CLAIMS

Dwight Foster, Mass.
Nathaniel Macon, N.C.
Jonathan Brace, Conn.
Lewis R. Morris, Vt.

James H. Imlay, Pa.
John A. Hanna, Pa.
John C. Thomas, Md.

COMMERCE AND MANUFACTURES

Samuel Smith, Md.
Samuel Sewall, Mass.
Robert Waln, Pa.
John Rutledge, Jr., S.C.

John Brown, R.I.
Franklin Davenport, N.J.
Benjamin Taliaferro, Ga.

REVISAL AND UNFINISHED BUSINESS

Roger Griswold, Conn.
Thomas Evans, Va.

George Dent, Md.

WAYS AND MEANS

Robert Goodloe Harper, S.C.
Roger Griswold, Conn.
Harrison Gray Otis, Mass.
Albert Gallatin, Pa.
Levin Powell, Va.

John Brown, R.I.
David Stone, N.C.
Abraham Nott, S.C.
Jonas Platt, N.Y.

JOINT COMMITTEE ON ENROLLED BILLS

House
Peleg Wadsworth, Mass.
Edwin Gray, Va.

Senate
William H. Wells, Del.

STANDING COMMITTEES OF THE HOUSE OF
REPRESENTATIVES

SIXTH CONGRESS, SECOND SESSION
(November 17, 1800–March 3, 1801)

ELECTIONS

George Dent, Md.
Lemuel Williams, Mass.
William Edmond, Conn.
John Peter G. Muhlenberg, Pa.

Thomas Evans, Va.
Joseph Dickson, N.C.
William C. C. Claiborne, Tenn.

CLAIMS

Nathaniel Macon, N.C.
John C. Smith, Conn.
Gouverneur Morris, N.Y.
John C. Thomas, Md.

Andrew Gregg, Pa.
David Holmes, Va.
Bailey Bartlett, Mass.

COMMERCE AND MANUFACTURES

Samuel Smith, Md.
Robert Waln, Pa.
Franklin Davenport, N.J.
Benjamin Huger, S.C.

Josiah Parker, Va.
Elizur Goodrich, Conn.
Silas Lee, Mass.

REVISAL AND UNFINISHED BUSINESS

Jonas Platt, N.Y.
Thomas Evans, Va.

Willis Alston, N.C.

WAYS AND MEANS

Roger Griswold, Conn.
Levin Powell, Va.
Bailey Bartlett, Mass.
John Nicholas, Va.
James H. Imlay, N.J.

Joseph H. Nicholson, Md.
Benjamin Taliaferro, Ga.
Henry Woods, Pa.
John Smilie, Pa.

JOINT COMMITTEE ON ENROLLED BILLS

House
Benjamin Huger, S.C.
James H. Imlay, N.J.

Senate
Dwight Foster, Mass.

STANDING COMMITTEES OF THE HOUSE OF REPRESENTATIVES

SEVENTH CONGRESS, FIRST SESSION
(December 7, 1801–May 3, 1802)

ELECTIONS

John Milledge, Ga.
Samuel Tenney, N.H.
John Condit, N.J.
John Dennis, Md.

John A. Hanna, Pa.
John Stanly, N.C.
John Taliaferro, Va.

CLAIMS

John C. Smith, Conn.
Andrew Gregg, Pa.
David Holmes, Va.
Ebenezer Mattoon, Mass.

John Smith, N.Y.
Thomas Plater, Md.
Thomas Moore, S.C.

COMMERCE AND MANUFACTURES

Samuel Smith, Md.
William Eustis, Mass.
Samuel W. Dana, Conn.
Samuel L. Mitchill, N.Y.

William Jones, Pa.
Thomas Newton, Jr., Va.
Thomas Lowndes, S.C.

REVISAL AND UNFINISHED BUSINESS

John Davenport, Conn.
Matthew Clay, Va.

Willis Alston, N.C.

WAYS AND MEANS

John Randolph, Va.
Roger Griswold, Conn.
Israel Smith, Vt.
James A. Bayard, Del.
John Smilie, Pa.

Nathan Read, Mass.
Joseph H. Nicholson, Md.
Killian K. Van Rensselaer, N.Y.
William Dickson, Tenn.

JOINT COMMITTEE ON ENROLLED BILLS

House
Richard Cutts, Mass.
Abram Trigg, Va.

Senate
Robert Wright, Md.

STANDING COMMITTEES OF THE HOUSE OF REPRESENTATIVES

SEVENTH CONGRESS, SECOND SESSION
(December 6, 1802–March 3, 1803)

ELECTIONS

John Bacon, Mass.
Samuel Tenney, N.H.
John Condit, N.J.
John Dennis, Md.

Ebenezer Elmer, N.J.
John Stanly, N.C.
Anthony New, Va.

CLAIMS

John C. Smith, Conn.
Andrew Gregg, Pa.
David Holmes, Va.
Thomas Plater, Md.

John Smith, N.Y.
Thomas Moore, S.C.
Manasseh Cutler, Mass.

COMMERCE AND MANUFACTURES

Samuel Smith, Md.
Samuel W. Dana, Conn.
Samuel L. Mitchill, N.Y.
Thomas Newton, Jr., Va.

Thomas Wynns, N.C.
Samuel Hunt, N.H.
Michael Leib, Pa.

REVISAL AND UNFINISHED BUSINESS

John Davenport, Conn.
Willis Alston, N.C.

John Dawson, Va.

WAYS AND MEANS

John Randolph, Va.
Roger Griswold, Conn.
John Smilie, Pa.
Nathan Read, Mass.

Joseph H. Nicholson, Md.
Killian K. Van Rensselaer, N.Y.
James Holland, N.C.

JOINT COMMITTEE ON ENROLLED BILLS

House
Richard Cutts, Mass.
Abram Trigg, Va.

Senate
William Plumer, N.H.

STANDING COMMITTEES OF THE HOUSE OF REPRESENTATIVES

EIGHTH CONGRESS, FIRST SESSION
(October 7, 1803–March 27, 1804)

ELECTIONS

William Findley, Pa.
Calvin Goddard, Conn.
Matthew Clay, Va.
Samuel Hunt, N.H.

Joseph B. Varnum, Mass.
Henry W. Livingston, N.Y.
William Kennedy, N.C.

CLAIMS

John C. Smith, Conn.
Andrew Gregg, Pa.
Thomas Plater, Md.
David Holmes, Va.

Thomas Moore, S.C.
William Chamberlain, Vt.
George M. Bedinger, Ky.

COMMERCE AND MANUFACTURES

Samuel L. Mitchill, N.Y.
Samuel W. Dana, Conn.
Jacob Crowninshield, Mass.
William McCreery, Md.

Michael Leib, Pa.
Thomas Newton, Jr., Va.
Thomas Wynns, N.C.

REVISAL AND UNFINISHED BUSINESS

Samuel Tenney, N.H.
John Boyle, Ky.

William Dickson, Tenn.

WAYS AND MEANS

John Randolph, Va.
Joseph H. Nicholson, Md.
Roger Griswold, Conn.
Caesar A. Rodney, Del.

Seth Hastings, Mass.
Joseph Clay, Pa.
Joshua Sands, N.Y.

JOINT COMMITTEE ON ENROLLED BILLS

House
Jacob Richards, Pa.
John W. Eppes, Va.

Senate
Israel Smith, Vt.

STANDING COMMITTEES OF THE HOUSE OF REPRESENTATIVES

EIGHTH CONGRESS, SECOND SESSION
(November 5, 1804–March 3, 1805)

ELECTIONS

William Findley, Pa.
Joseph B. Varnum, Mass.
Henry W. Livingston, N.Y.
William Kennedy, N.C.

John W. Eppes, Va.
Clifton Clagett, N.H.
Ebenezer Elmer, N.J.

CLAIMS

John C. Smith, Conn.
David Holmes, Va.
Thomas Plater, Md.
William Chamberlain, Vt.

George M. Bedinger, Ky.
Richard Stanford, N.C.
Joseph Stanton, Jr., R.I.

COMMERCE AND MANUFACTURES

Samuel L. Mitchill, N.Y.
Jacob Crowninshield, Mass.
William McCreery, Md.
Michael Leib, Pa.

Thomas Newton, Jr., Va.
Peter Early, Ga.
Martin Chittenden, Vt.

REVISAL AND UNFINISHED BUSINESS

Samuel Tenney, N.H.
William Dickson, Tenn.

John B. Earle, S.C.

WAYS AND MEANS

John Randolph, Va.
Joseph Clay, Pa.
Gaylord Griswold, N.Y.
John Boyle, Ky.

John Davenport, Conn.
Nicholas R. Moore, Md.
David Meriwether, Ga.

ACCOUNTS

Peter Early, Ga.
William Blackledge, N.C.

Killian K. Van Rensselaer, N.Y.

JOINT COMMITTEE ON ENROLLED BILLS

House
Jacob Richards, Pa.
Thomas M. Randolph, Va.

Senate
Andrew Moore, Va.

STANDING COMMITTEES OF THE HOUSE OF REPRESENTATIVES

NINTH CONGRESS, FIRST SESSION
(December 2, 1805–April 21, 1806)

ELECTIONS

William Findley, Pa.
Ebenezer Elmer, N.J.
John W. Eppes, Va.
Martin Chittenden, Vt.

Martin G. Schuneman, N.Y.
Barnabus Bidwell, Mass.
Caleb Ellis, N.H.

CLAIMS

John C. Smith, Conn.
David Holmes, Va.
George M. Bedinger, Ky.
Richard Stanford, N.C.

Joseph Stanton, Jr., R.I.
Nicholas R. Moore, Md.
Thomas Moore, S.C.

COMMERCE AND MANUFACTURES

Jacob Crowninshield, Mass.
William McCreery, Md.
Michael Leib, Pa.
Peter Early, Ga.

Samuel W. Dana, Conn.
Thomas Newton, Jr., Va.
Gurdon S. Mumford, N.Y.

REVISAL AND UNFINISHED BUSINESS

Samuel Tenney, N.H.
Willis Alston, N.C.

John Claiborne, Va.

WAYS AND MEANS

John Randolph, Va.
Joseph H. Nicholson, Md.
Joseph Clay, Pa.
Josiah Quincy, Mass.

David Meriwether, Ga.
William Dickson, Tenn.
Jonathan O. Moseley, Conn.

ACCOUNTS

Frederick Conrad, Pa.
John Davenport, Conn.

Richard Cutts, Mass.

PUBLIC LANDS

Andrew Gregg, Pa.
Jeremiah Moore, Ohio
John Boyle, Ky.
George Clinton, Jr., N.Y.

William Helms, N.J.
Matthew Clay, Va.
Joseph Bryan, Ga.

JOINT COMMITTEE ON ENROLLED BILLS

House
Thomas M. Randolph, Va.
Richard Cutts, Mass.

Senate
Nicholas Gilman, N.H.

STANDING COMMITTEES OF THE
HOUSE OF REPRESENTATIVES

NINTH CONGRESS, SECOND SESSION
(December 1, 1806–March 3, 1807)

ELECTIONS

William Findley, Pa.
Ebenezer Elmer, N.J.
John W. Eppes, Va.
Martin Chittenden, Vt.

Martin G. Schuneman, N.Y.
Barnabus Bidwell, Mass.
Caleb Ellis, N.H.

CLAIMS

David Holmes, Va.
Nicholas R. Moore, Md.
Thomas Moore, S.C.
George M. Bedinger, Ky.

Richard Stanford, N.C.
Joseph Stanton, Jr., R.I.
Benjamin Tallmadge, Conn.

COMMERCE AND MANUFACTURES

Jacob Crowninshield, Mass.
William McCreery, Md.
Peter Early, Ga.
Samuel W. Dana, Conn.

Thomas Newton, Jr., Va.
Robert Marion, S.C.
Jacob Richards, Pa.

REVISAL AND UNFINISHED BUSINESS

Samuel Tenney, N.H.
Willis Alston, N.C.

John Claiborne, Va.

WAYS AND MEANS

Joseph Clay, Pa.
Roger Nelson, Md.
Josiah Quincy, Mass.
David R. Williams, S.C.

Jonathan O. Moseley, Conn.
James M. Garnett, Va.
David Meriwether, Ga.

ACCOUNTS

Frederick Conrad, Pa.
John Davenport, Conn.

Richard Cutts, Mass.

PUBLIC LANDS

John Boyle, Ky.
Jeremiah Morrow, Ohio
Ezra Darby, N.J.
Burwell Bassett, Va.

John Russell, N.Y.
George W. Campbell, Tenn.
Seth Hastings, Mass.

JOINT COMMITTEE ON ENROLLED BILLS

House
Thomas M. Randolph, Va.
John Porter, Pa.

Senate
James Turner, N.C.

STANDING COMMITTEES OF THE HOUSE OF REPRESENTATIVES

TENTH CONGRESS, FIRST SESSION

(October 26, 1807–April 25, 1808)

ELECTIONS

William Findley, Pa.
David R. Williams, S.C.
Matthew Clay, Va.
John Lambert, N.J.

John Blake, Jr., N.Y.
Lewis B. Sturges, Conn.
James Elliott, Vt.

CLAIMS

David Holmes, Va.
Thomas Moore, S.C.
Roger Nelson, Md.
Timothy Pitkin, Conn.

Ebenezer Seaver, Mass.
Richard M. Johnson, Ky.
Reuben Humphrey, N.Y.

COMMERCE AND MANUFACTURES

Thomas Newton, Jr., Va.
William McCreery, Md.
Richard Cutts, Mass.
Samuel W. Dana, Conn.

Robert Marion, S.C.
David Thomas, N.Y.
John Porter, Pa.

REVISAL AND UNFINISHED BUSINESS

John Clopton, Va.
Killian K. Van Rensselaer, N.Y.

Daniel M. Durell, N.H.

WAYS AND MEANS

George W. Campbell, Tenn.
Willis Alston, N.C.
John W. Eppes, Va.
John Smilie, Pa.

Benjamin Tallmadge, Conn.
James Fisk, Vt.
John Montgomery, Md.

ACCOUNTS

Nicholas R. Moore, Md.
William Stedman, Mass.

William Milnor, Pa.

PUBLIC LANDS

John Boyle, Ky.
Jeremiah Morrow, Ohio
Peterson Goodwyn, Va.
John Russell, N.Y.

Ezra Darby, N.J.
William Ely, Mass.
Dennis Smelt, Del.

DISTRICT OF COLUMBIA

Philip B. Key, Md.
Nicholas Van Dyke, Del.
John Love, Va.
James Holland, N.C.

Robert Brown, Pa.
Edward St. Loe Livermore, Mass.
John Taylor, S.C.

JOINT COMMITTEE ON ENROLLED BILLS

House
James M. Garnett, Va.
Ezekiel Bacon, Mass.

Senate
Jonathan Robinson, Vt.

STANDING COMMITTEES OF THE
HOUSE OF REPRESENTATIVES

TENTH CONGRESS, SECOND SESSION
(November 7, 1808–March 3, 1809)

ELECTIONS

William Findley, Pa.
David R. Williams, S.C.
Matthew Clay, Va.
John Lambert, N.J.

John Blake, Jr., N.Y.
Lewis B. Sturges, Conn.
James Elliott, Vt.

CLAIMS

David Holmes, Va.
Timothy Pitkin, Conn.
Ebenezer Seaver, Mass.
Richard M. Johnson, Ky.

Reuben Humphrey, N.Y.
Robert Brown, Pa.
William Butler, S.C.

COMMERCE AND MANUFACTURES

Thomas Newton, Jr., Va.
William McCreery, Md.
Richard Cutts, Mass.
Robert Marion, S.C.

Samuel W. Dana, Conn.
Gurdon S. Mumford, N.Y.
John Porter, Pa.

REVISAL AND UNFINISHED BUSINESS

John Clopton, Va.   Daniel M. Durell, N.H.
Killian K. Van Rensselaer, N.Y.

WAYS AND MEANS

George W. Campbell, Tenn.   Benjamin Tallmadge, Conn.
Willis Alston, N.C.   James Fisk, Vt.
John W. Eppes, Va.   John Montgomery, Md.
John Smilie, Pa.

ACCOUNTS

Nicholas R. Moore, Md.   William Milnor, Pa.
William Stedman, Mass.

PUBLIC LANDS

Jeremiah Morrow, Ohio   William Ely, Mass.
Peterson Goodwyn, Va.   William W. Bibb, Ga.
John Russell, N.Y.   Benjamin Howard, R.I.
Adam Boyd, N.J.

DISTRICT OF COLUMBIA

Joseph Lewis, Jr., Va.   John Rea, Pa.
Archibald Van Horne, Md.   Lemuel J. Alston, S.C.
Henry Southard, N.J.   Jesse Wharton, Tenn.
William Blackledge, N.C.

POST OFFICE AND POST ROADS

John Rhea, Tenn.   Thomas Newbold, N.J.
Isaac L. Green, Mass.   Daniel C. Verplanck, N.Y.
Martin Chittenden, Vt.   John Pugh, Pa.
John Davenport, Conn.   Clement Storer, N.H.
Richard Stanford, N.C.   Jeremiah Morrow, Ohio
John Calhoun, S.C.   Charles Goldsborough, Md.
George M. Troup, Ga.   Nathan Wilson, N.Y.
Joseph Desha, Ky.   Isaac Wilbour, R.I.
Robert Whitehill, Pa.

JOINT COMMITTEE ON ENROLLED BILLS

House   Senate
John G. Jackson, Va.   Buckner Thruston, Ky.
James I. Van Alen, N.Y.

STANDING COMMITTEES OF THE
HOUSE OF REPRESENTATIVES

ELEVENTH CONGRESS, FIRST SESSION
(May 22, 1809–June 28, 1809)

ELECTIONS

William Findley, Pa.
Matthew Clay, Va.
Lewis B. Sturges, Conn.
George M. Troup, Ga.

John Taylor, S.C.
Killian K. Van Rensselaer, N.Y.
Barzillai Gannett, Mass.

CLAIMS

Richard M. Johnson, Ky.
Ebenezer Seaver, Mass.
William Butler, S.C.
Timothy Pitkin, Conn.

Robert Brown, Pa.
Walter Jones, Va.
John Stanly, N.C.

COMMERCE AND MANUFACTURES

Thomas Newton, Jr., Va.
Samuel W. Dana, Conn.
Robert Marion, S.C.
Richard Cutts, Mass.

Gurdon S. Mumford, N.Y.
John Porter, Pa.
Alexander McKim, Md.

REVISAL AND UNFINISHED BUSINESS

Henry Southard, N.J.
Richard Jackson, Jr., R.I.

Samuel Shaw, Vt.

WAYS AND MEANS

John W. Eppes, Va.
Willis Alston, N.C.
Benjamin Tallmadge, Conn.
John Montgomery, Md.

Ezekiel Bacon, Mass.
John Rea, Pa.
Nathaniel A. Haven, N.H.

ACCOUNTS

Nicholas R. Moore, Md.
William Stedman, Mass.

William Milnor, Pa.

PUBLIC LANDS

Jeremiah Morrow, Ohio
Peterson Goodwyn, Va.
William W. Bibb, Ga.
William Ely, Mass.

Adam Boyd, N.J.
Benjamin Howard, Ky.
Thomas Sammons, N.Y.

DISTRICT OF COLUMBIA

John Love, Va.
James Holland, N.C.
Archibald Van Horne, Md.
Lemuel J. Alston, S.C.

Thomas Newbold, N.J.
Samuel Smith, Pa.
Barent Gardenier, N.Y.

POST OFFICE AND POST ROADS

John Rhea, Tenn.
William Helms, N.J.
John Thompson, N.Y.
Joseph Desha, Ky.
Thomas Kenan, N.C.
Joseph Calhoun, S.C.
Dennis Smelt, Ga.
Jeremiah Morrow, Ohio
John Davenport, Conn.

Martin Chittenden, Vt.
Charles Goldsborough, Md.
Robert Whitehill, Pa.
Elisha R. Potter, R.I.
John Smith, Va.
Jabez Upham, Mass.
James Wilson, N.H.
David Bard, Pa.

JOINT COMMITTEE ON ENROLLED BILLS

House
Thomas Gholson, Jr., Va.
Jonathan Fisk, N.Y.

Senate
Return J. Meigs, Jr., Ohio

STANDING COMMITTEES OF THE
HOUSE OF REPRESENTATIVES
ELEVENTH CONGRESS, SECOND SESSION
(November 27, 1809–May 1, 1810)

ELECTIONS

William Findley, Pa.
Matthew Clay, Va.
Lewis B. Sturges, Conn.
George M. Troup, Ga.

John Taylor, S.C.
Killian K. Van Rensselaer, N.Y.
Barzillai Gannett, Mass.

CLAIMS

Richard M. Johnson, Ky.
Timothy Pitkin, Conn.
William Butler, S.C.
Robert Brown, Pa.

John Stanly, N.C.
Thomas Gholson, Jr., Va.
Peter B. Porter, N.Y.

COMMERCE AND MANUFACTURES

Thomas Newton, Jr., Va.
Samuel W. Dana, Conn.
Robert Marion, S.C.
Richard Cutts, Mass.

Nicholas R. Moore, Md.
Ebenezer Sage, N.Y.
Adam Seybert, Pa.

REVISAL AND UNFINISHED BUSINESS

Henry Southard, N.J.
Samuel Shaw, Vt.

Richard Jackson, Jr., R.I.

WAYS AND MEANS

John W. Eppes, Va.
Willis Alston, N.C.
Benjamin Tallmadge, Conn.
John Montgomery, Md.

Ezekiel Bacon, Mass.
John Smilie, Pa.
Erastus Root, N.Y.

ACCOUNTS

William Milnor, Pa.
William Kennedy, N.C.

Charles Turner, Jr., Mass.

PUBLIC LANDS

Jeremiah Morrow, Ohio
Peterson Goodwyn, Va.
William Ely, Mass.
Adam Boyd, N.J.

Benjamin Howard, Ky.
Thomas R. Gold, N.Y.
Howell Cobb, Ga.

DISTRICT OF COLUMBIA

John Love, Va.
Archibald Van Horne, Md.
Lemuel J. Alston, S.C.
Thomas Newbold, N.J.

Samuel Smith, Pa.
Samuel Taggart, Mass.
Nathaniel A. Haven, N.H.

POST OFFICE AND POST ROADS

John Rhea, Tenn.
William Helms, N.J.
John Thompson, N.Y.
Joseph Desha, Ky.
Richard Stanford, N.C.
Joseph Calhoun, S.C.
George M. Troup, Ga.
Jeremiah Morrow, Ohio

John Davenport, Conn.
Martin Chittenden, Vt.
Charles Goldsborough, Md.
Robert Whitehill, Pa.
Elisha R. Potter, R.I.
John Smith, Va.
Jabez Upham, Mass.
James Wilson, N.H.

JOINT COMMITTEE ON ENROLLED BILLS

House
William Crawford, Pa.
John Roane, Va.

Senate
John Condit, N.J.

STANDING COMMITTEES OF THE
HOUSE OF REPRESENTATIVES

ELEVENTH CONGRESS, THIRD SESSION
(December 3, 1810–March 3, 1811)

ELECTIONS

William Findley, Pa.
Matthew Clay, Va.
Lewis B. Sturges, Conn.
George M. Troup, Ga.

John Taylor, S.C.
Killian K. Van Rensselaer, N.Y.
Samuel Taggart, Mass.

CLAIMS

Erastus Root, N.Y.
William Butler, S.C.
Robert Brown, Pa.
John Stanly, N.C.

Thomas Gholson, Jr., Va.
Charles Goldsborough, Md.
Samuel Shaw, Vt.

COMMERCE AND MANUFACTURES

Thomas Newton, Jr., Va.
Samuel L. Mitchill, N.Y.
Richard Cutts, Mass.
Timothy Pitkin, Conn.

Alexander McKim, Md.
Adam Seybert, Pa.
William W. Bibb, Ga.

REVISAL AND UNFINISHED BUSINESS

Henry Southard, N.J.
Richard Jackson, Jr., R.I.

Robert Witherspoon, S.C.

WAYS AND MEANS

John W. Eppes, Va.
Willis Alston, N.C.
Benjamin Tallmadge, Conn.
John Montgomery, Md.

Ezekiel Bacon, Mass.
John Smilie, Pa.
Richard M. Johnson, Ky.

ACCOUNTS

Nicholas R. Moore, Md.
Charles Turner, Jr., Mass.

Thomas Kenan, N.C.

PUBLIC LANDS

Jeremiah Morrow, Ohio
Peterson Goodwyn, Va.
William Ely, Mass.
Adam Boyd, N.J.

Thomas R. Gold, N.Y.
Howell Cobb, Ga.
Samuel McKee, Ky.

DISTRICT OF COLUMBIA

Archibald Van Horne, Md.
Lemuel J. Alston, S.C.
Robert Weakley, Tenn.
George Smith, Pa.

John C. Chamberlain, N.H.
Uri Tracy, N.Y.
James Breckinridge, Va.

POST OFFICE AND POST ROADS

John Rhea, Tenn.
John Thompson, N.Y.
Joseph Desha, Ky.
Richard Stanford, N.C.
George M. Troup, Ga.
Joseph Calhoun, S.C.
Jeremiah Morrow, Ohio
John Davenport, Conn.

Martin Chittenden, Vt.
Philip B. Key, Md.
Robert Whitehill, Pa.
John Smith, Va.
Elisha R. Potter, R.I.
James Wilson, N.H.
Ebenezer Seaver, Mass.
Jacob Hufty, N.J.

JOINT COMMITTEE ON ENROLLED BILLS

House
William Anderson, Pa.
David S. Garland, Va.

Senate
Charles Cutts, N.H.

STANDING COMMITTEES OF THE
HOUSE OF REPRESENTATIVES

TWELFTH CONGRESS, FIRST SESSION

(November 4, 1811–July 6, 1812)

ELECTIONS

William Findley, Pa.
Nathaniel Macon, N.C.
Lewis B. Sturges, Conn.
George M. Troup, Ga.

James Pleasants, Va.
James Emott, N.Y.
James Fisk, Vt.

CLAIMS

Burwell Bassett, Va.
William Butler, S.C.
Samuel Shaw, Vt.
Robert Brown, Pa.

Jonathan O. Moseley, Conn.
Richard Stanford, N.C.
Stevenson Archer, Md.

COMMERCE AND MANUFACTURES

Thomas Newton, Jr., Va.
William Lowndes, S.C.
Samuel L. Mitchill, N.Y.
Alexander McKim, Md.

Benjamin Tallmadge, Conn.
Adam Seybert, Pa.
Peleg Tallman, Mass.

REVISAL AND UNFINISHED BUSINESS

Adam Seybert, Pa.
Richard Jackson, Jr., R.I.

William Ely, Mass.

WAYS AND MEANS

Ezekiel Bacon, Mass.
Langdon Cheves, S.C.
John Smilie, Pa.
William W. Bibb, Ga.

William A. Burwell, Va.
Richard M. Johnson, Ky.
Timothy Pitkin, Conn.

ACCOUNTS

Charles Turner, Jr., Mass.
Thomas Blount, N.C.

Peter Little, Md.

PUBLIC LANDS

Jeremiah Morrow, Ohio
Samuel McKee, Ky.
Thomas R. Gold, N.Y.
James Breckinridge, Va.

William Blackledge, N.C.
Adam Boyd, N.J.
George Smith, Pa.

DISTRICT OF COLUMBIA

Joseph Lewis, Jr., Va.
Samuel Ringgold, Md.
William Piper, Pa.
Joseph Pearson, N.C.

John Baker, Va.
Silas Stow, N.Y.
Stephen Ormsby, Ky.

POST OFFICE AND POST ROADS

John Rhea, Tenn.
Peter B. Porter, N.Y.
Aaron Lyle, Pa.
Samuel Dinsmoor, N.H.
Samuel Taggart, Mass.
Elisha R. Potter, R.I.
Lyman Law, Conn.
Martin Chittenden, Vt.
Jacob Hufty, N.J.

Henry M. Ridgely, Del.
Joseph Kent, Md.
Daniel Sheffey, Va.
William R. King, N.C.
Elias Earle, S.C.
Bolling Hall, Ga.
Joseph Desha, Ky.
Jeremiah Morrow, Ohio

JOINT COMMITTEE ON ENROLLED BILLS

House
William Crawford, Pa.
Peterson Goodwyn, Va.

Senate
Joseph B. Varnum, Mass.

STANDING COMMITTEES OF THE
HOUSE OF REPRESENTATIVES

TWELFTH CONGRESS, SECOND SESSION
(November 12, 1812–March 3, 1813)

ELECTIONS

William Findley, Pa.
Nathaniel Macon, N.C.
John Davenport, Conn.
George M. Troup, Ga.

John Dawson, Va.
James Emott, N.Y.
Willis Alston, N.C.

CLAIMS

Thomas Gholson, Jr., Va.
Robert Brown, Pa.
Jonathan O. Moseley, Conn.
Samuel Shaw, Vt.

Ebenezer Sage, N.Y.
Stevenson Archer, Md.
Richard Stanford, N.C.

COMMERCE AND MANUFACTURES

Thomas Newton, Jr., Va.
William Lowndes, S.C.
Samuel L. Mitchill, N.Y.
Alexander McKim, Md.

Adam Seybert, Pa.
Epaphroditus Champion, Conn.
William Widgery, Mass.

REVISAL AND UNFINISHED BUSINESS

Burwell Bassett, Va.
William Ely, Mass.

Richard Jackson, Jr., R.I.

WAYS AND MEANS

Langdon Cheves, S.C.
William W. Bibb, Ga.
James Pleasants, Va.
Jonathan Roberts, Pa.

Richard M. Johnson, Ky.
Timothy Pitkin, Conn.
James Fisk, Vt.

ACCOUNTS

Charles Turner, Jr., Mass.
Peter Little, Md.

Israel Pickens, N.C.

PUBLIC LANDS

Jeremiah Morrow, Ohio
William Blackledge, N.C.
Abner Lacock, Pa.
Thomas Wilson, Va.

Stephen Ormsby, Ky.
Adam Boyd, N.J.
Abijah Bigelow, Mass.

DISTRICT OF COLUMBIA

Joseph Lewis, Jr., Va.   John Baker, Va.
Samuel Ringgold, Md.   Lewis Condit, N.J.
Joseph Pearson, N.C.   Joseph Kent, Md.
David Bard, Pa.

POST OFFICE AND POST ROADS

John Rhea, Tenn.   William R. King, N.C.
Aaron Lyle, Pa.   Bolling Hall, Ga.
Samuel Dinsmoor, N.H.   Lyman Law, Conn.
Martin Chittenden, Vt.

JOINT COMMITTEE ON ENROLLED BILLS

House   Senate
William Crawford, Pa.   Alexander Campbell, Ohio
Peterson Goodwyn, Va.

STANDING COMMITTEES OF THE
HOUSE OF REPRESENTATIVES

THIRTEENTH CONGRESS, FIRST SESSION
(May 24, 1813–August 2, 1813)

ELECTIONS

James Fisk, Vt.   Lewis Condit, N.J.
William A. Burwell, Va.   Daniel Avery, N.Y.
John Davenport, Conn.   Timothy Pickering, Mass.
William Anderson, Pa.

CLAIMS

Stevenson Archer, Md.   Richard Stanford, N.C.
Robert Brown, Pa.   Peterson Goodwyn, Va.
Jonathan O. Moseley, Conn.   James Caldwell, Ohio
Ebenezer Sage, N.Y.

COMMERCE AND MANUFACTURES

Thomas Newton, Jr., Va.   Adam Seybert, Pa.
Alexander McKim, Md.   James Parker, Mass.
William Reed, Mass.   Thomas Telfair, Ga.
Egbert Benson, N.Y.

REVISAL AND UNFINISHED BUSINESS

Willis Alston, N.C.   John Roane, Va.
William Ely, Mass.

WAYS AND MEANS

John W. Eppes, Va.
William W. Bibb, Ga.
James Pleasants, Va.
Jonathan Roberts, Pa.

Timothy Pitkin, Conn.
Theodore Gourdin, S.C.
Thomas Montgomery, Ky.

ACCOUNTS

Israel Pickens, N.C.
Nicholas R. Moore, Md.

Elisha J. Winter, N.Y.

PUBLIC LANDS

Samuel McKee, Ky.
Thomas B. Robertson, La.
James Breckinridge, Va.
Abijah Bigelow, Mass.

John McLean, Ohio
William R. King, N.C.
John Conrad, Pa.

DISTRICT OF COLUMBIA

John Dawson, Va.
Joseph Kent, Md.
Joseph Lewis, Jr., Va.
Joseph Pearson, N.C.

Samuel Ringgold, Md.
Thomas P. Grosvenor, N.Y.
John H. Bowen, Tenn.

POST OFFICE AND POST ROADS

John Rhea, Tenn.
Aaron Lyle, Pa.
Meshack Franklin, N.C.
Lyman Law, Conn.

Richard Jackson, Jr., R.I.
William C. Bradley, Vt.
Solomon P. Sharp, Ky.

JUDICIARY[5]

JOINT COMMITTEE ON ENROLLED BILLS

House
William Crawford, Pa.
Thomas M. Bayly, Va.

Senate
Joseph B. Varnum, Mass.

STANDING COMMITTEES OF THE
HOUSE OF REPRESENTATIVES

THIRTEENTH CONGRESS, SECOND SESSION
(December 6, 1813–April 18, 1814)

ELECTIONS

James Fisk, Vt.
Thomas Gholson, Jr., Va.
Cyrus King, Mass.
Israel Pickens, N.C.

Roger Vose, N.H.
Oliver C. Comstock, N.Y.
William Anderson, Pa.

[5] Resolutions to establish a Standing Committee on the Judiciary were read on June 1 and 3, 1813, but this committee was not constituted until the following session.

CLAIMS

Stevenson Archer, Md.
Bartlett Yancy, N.C.
Peterson Goodwyn, Va.
Lyman Law, Conn.

John Alexander, Ohio
David Bard, Pa.
John Davenport, Conn.

COMMERCE AND MANUFACTURES

Thomas Newton, Jr., Va.
William H. Murfree, N.C.
Adam Seybert, Pa.
Richard Jackson, Jr., R.I.

William Baylies, Mass.
Theodore Gourdin, S.C.
Thomas P. Grosvenor, N.Y.

REVISAL AND UNFINISHED BUSINESS

Lewis Condict, N.J.
Richard Stanford, N.C.

Laban Wheaton, Mass.

WAYS AND MEANS

John W. Eppes, Va.
John W. Taylor, N.Y.
Jonathan Roberts, Pa.
William Creighton, Jr., Ohio

Willis Alston, N.C.
Alexander McKim, Md.
William Coxe, N.J.

ACCOUNTS

Nicholas P. Moore, Md.
William Barnett, Ga.

John Reed, Mass.

PUBLIC LANDS

Samuel McKee, Ky.
Thomas B. Robertson, La.
Parry W. Humphreys, Tenn.
Jonathan O. Moseley, Conn.

Jared Irwin, Pa.
Timothy Pickering, Mass.
William McCoy, Va.

DISTRICT OF COLUMBIA

Joseph Kent, Md.
Joseph Lewis, Jr., Va.
Joseph Pearson, N.C.
William Crawford, Pa.

Solomon P. Sharp, Ky.
John H. Bowen, Tenn.
William C. Bradley, Vt.

POST OFFICE AND POST ROADS

John Rhea, Tenn.
Aaron Lyle, Pa.
Lewis B. Sturges, Conn.
Abijah Bigelow, Mass.

Elisha J. Winter, N.Y.
Meshack Franklin, N.C.
Bolling Hall, Ga.

JUDICIARY

Charles J. Ingersoll, Pa.
Hugh Nelson, Va.
Timothy Pitkin, Conn.
Richard Stockton, N.J.

Israel Pickens, N.C.
Thomas Montgomery, Ky.
Thomas J. Oakley, N.Y.

PENSIONS AND REVOLUTIONARY CLAIMS

Samuel D. Ingham, Pa.
John Clopton, Va.
John J. Chappell, S.C.
Philip Stuart, Md.

Ebenezer Sage, N.Y.
William Ely, Mass.
Reasin Beall, Ohio

PUBLIC EXPENDITURES

James Pleasants, Va.
Nathaniel Macon, N.C.
William Findley, Pa.

John Forsyth, Ga.
William Reed, Mass.
William Irving, N.Y.

JOINT COMMITTEE ON ENROLLED BILLS

House
Richard Skinner, Vt.
Hugh Caperton, Va.

Senate
Jesse Bledsoe, Ky.

STANDING COMMITTEES OF THE
HOUSE OF REPRESENTATIVES

THIRTEENTH CONGRESS, THIRD SESSION
(September 19, 1814–March 3, 1815)

ELECTIONS

James Fisk, Vt.
Charles Goldsborough, Md.
Roger Vose, N.H.
Oliver C. Comstock, N.Y.

William Anderson, Pa.
Willis Alston, N.C.
Thomas K. Harris, Tenn.

CLAIMS

Bartlett Yancy, N.C.
Solomon P. Sharp, Ky.
Peterson Goodwyn, Va.
John Davenport, Ky.

John Alexander, Ohio
David Bard, Pa.
Alexander Boyd, N.Y.

COMMERCE AND MANUFACTURES

Thomas Newton, Jr., Va.
Adam Seybert, Pa.
William H. Murfree, N.C.
Richard Jackson, Jr., R.I.

William Baylies, Mass.
Theodore Gourdin, S.C.
Nathaniel Ruggles, Mass.

REVISAL AND UNFINISHED BUSINESS

Richard Stanford, N.C.
Laban Wheaton, Mass.

George Bradbury, Mass.

WAYS AND MEANS

John W. Eppes, Va.
Jonathan Fisk, N.Y.
Stevenson Archer, Md.
Thomas J. Oakley, N.Y.

William Gaston, N.C.
William Creighton, Jr., Ohio
Samuel D. Ingham, Pa.

ACCOUNTS

John Kershaw, S.C.
William Barnett, Ga.

John Reed, Mass.

PUBLIC LANDS

Samuel McKee, Ky.
Parry W. Humphreys, Tenn.
Thomas Montgomery, Ky.
Jonathan O. Moseley, Conn.

James Geddes, N.Y.
Jared Irwin, Pa.
William McCoy, Va.

DISTRICT OF COLUMBIA

Joseph Kent, Md.
Joseph Lewis, Jr., Va.
William Crawford, Pa.
Joseph Pearson, N.C.

William C. Bradley, Vt.
Francis White, Va.
Peter Denoyelles, N.Y.

POST OFFICE AND POST ROADS

John Rhea, Tenn.
Aaron Lyle, Pa.
Elijah Brigham, Mass.
Thomas M. Bayly, Va.

Meshack Franklin, N.C.
Bolling Hall, Ga.
Charles Rich, Vt.

JUDICIARY

Charles J. Ingersoll, Pa.
James Pleasants, Va.
Thomas Telfair, Ga.
Lewis B. Sturges, Conn.

Thomas Cooper, Del.
James Fisk, Vt.
David R. Evans, S.C.

PENSIONS AND REVOLUTIONARY CLAIMS

John J. Chappell, S.C.
John H. Bowen, Tenn.
Thomas Wilson, Pa.
Ebenezer Sage, N.Y.

William Ely, Mass.
Jeduthun Wilcox, N.H.
John Conrad, Pa.

PUBLIC EXPENDITURES

Nathaniel Macon, N.C.
William Findley, Pa.
Epaphroditus Champion, Conn.
William R. King, N.C.

Moss Kent, N.Y.
Joseph H. Hawkins, Ky.
James Caldwell, Ohio

JOINT COMMITTEE ON ENROLLED BILLS

House
Richard Skinner, Vt.
Hugh Caperton, Va.

Senate
Jeremiah B. Howell, R.I.
Jonathan Roberts, Pa.
Joseph Kerr, Ohio

STANDING COMMITTEES OF THE
HOUSE OF REPRESENTATIVES

FOURTEENTH CONGRESS, FIRST SESSION
(December 4, 1815–April 30, 1816)

ELECTIONS

John W. Taylor, N.Y.
William Piper, Pa.
Solomon P. Sharp, Ky.
Timothy Pickering, Mass.

Roger Vose, N.H.
Philip P. Barbour, Va.
Lyman Law, Conn.

CLAIMS

Bartlett Yancy, N.C.
John Alexander, Ohio
Peterson Goodwyn, Va.
John Davenport, Conn.

Aaron Lyle, Pa.
Richard Stanford, N.C.
Daniel Chipman, Vt.

COMMERCE AND MANUFACTURES

Thomas Newton, Jr., Va.
William H. Murfree, N.C.
William Baylies, Mass.
Albion K. Parris, Mass.

John J. Chappell, S.C.
John L. Boss, Jr., R.I.
John Sergeant, Pa.

REVISAL AND UNFINISHED BUSINESS

Lewis Condict, N.J.
George Bradbury, Mass.

William Maclay, Pa.

WAYS AND MEANS

William Lowndes, S.C.
William A. Burwell, Va.
John W. Taylor, N.Y.
Jonathan O. Moseley, Conn.

Thomas B. Robertson, La.
Samuel D. Ingham, Pa.
William Gaston, N.C.

ACCOUNTS

John McLean, Ohio
John Reed, Mass.

Samuel R. Betts, N.Y.

PUBLIC LANDS

Thomas B. Robertson, La.
William Creighton, Jr., Ohio
James Clark, Ky.
Bolling Hall, Ga.

Cyrus King, Mass.
William McCoy, Va.
Lewis B. Sturges, Conn.

DISTRICT OF COLUMBIA

Henry St. George Tucker, Va.
Joseph Lewis, Jr., Va.
Jared Irwin, Pa.
John Savage, N.Y.

John C. Herbert, Md.
John Taylor, S.C.
Elijah Brigham, Mass.

POST OFFICE AND POST ROADS

Samuel D. Ingham, Pa.
Newton Cannon, Tenn.
James Breckinridge, Va.
Enos T. Throop, N.Y.

Samuel S. Connor, Mass.
James Caldwell, Ohio
Chauncey Langdon, Vt.

JUDICIARY

Thomas M. Nelson, Va.
Stephen Ormsby, Ky.
Thomas Cooper, Del.
Robert Wright, Md.

Richard Henry Wilde, Ga.
Thomas R. Gold, N.Y.
John Sergeant, Pa.

PENSIONS AND REVOLUTIONARY CLAIMS

John J. Chappell, S.C.
Oliver C. Comstock, N.Y.
Philip Stuart, Md.
William Milnor, Pa.

Henry Southard, N.J.
Bennett H. Henderson, Tenn.
Jeduthun Wilcox, N.H.

PUBLIC EXPENDITURES

William H. Murfree, N.C.
Thomas Gholson, Jr., Va.
Epaphroditus Champion, Conn.
Thomas Wilson, Pa.

Jabez D. Hammond, N.Y.
Jeremiah Nelson, Mass.
James M. Wallace, Pa.

PRIVATE LAND CLAIMS[6]

Expenditures in the Department of State[7]

John B. Yates, N.Y.   Weldon N. Edwards, N.C.
James B. Mason, R.I.

Expenditures in the Department of the Treasury

Samuel Smith, Md.   John Hahn, Pa.
John W. Hulbert, Mass.

Expenditures in the Department of War

Erastus Root, N.Y.   Daniel Sheffey, Va.
Daniel M. Forney, N.C.

Expenditures in the Department of the Navy

Stevenson Archer, Md.   Benjamin Huger, S.C.
Wilson Lumpkin, Ga.

Expenditures in the Post Office Department

Newton Cannon, Tenn.   William Milnor, Pa.
Albion K. Parris, Mass.

Expenditures in the Department of Public Buildings

Lewis Condict, N.J.   John Reed, Mass.
William Darlington, Pa.

JOINT COMMITTEE ON ENROLLED BILLS

House   Senate
William Crawford, Pa.   Jonathan Roberts, Pa.
Micah Taul, Ky.

[6] Resolutions to establish a Standing Committee on Public Expenditures were read on April 27 and 29, 1816, but this committee was not constituted until the following session.
[7] The committees on expenditures in the various departments were formally titled "Public Accounts and Expenditures in relation to . . ." the specific department referred to.